Communications in Computer and Information Science   **618**

Commenced Publication in 2007
Founding and Former Series Editors:
Alfredo Cuzzocrea, Dominik Ślęzak, and Xiaokang Yang

More information about this series at http://www.springer.com/series/7899

Constantine Stephanidis (Ed.)

HCI International 2016 –
Posters' Extended Abstracts

18th International Conference, HCI International 2016
Toronto, Canada, July 17–22, 2016
Proceedings, Part II

Springer

Editor
Constantine Stephanidis
University of Crete / Foundation
   for Research & Technology - Hellas
   (FORTH)
Heraklion, Crete
Greece

ISSN 1865-0929   ISSN 1865-0937 (electronic)
Communications in Computer and Information Science
ISBN 978-3-319-40541-4   ISBN 978-3-319-40542-1   (eBook)
DOI 10.1007/978-3-319-40542-1

Library of Congress Control Number: 2016941295

Printed on acid-free paper

This Springer imprint is published by Springer Nature
The registered company is Springer International Publishing AG Switzerland

Foreword

The 18th International Conference on Human-Computer Interaction, HCI International 2016, was held in Toronto, Canada, during July 17–22, 2016. The event incorporated the 15 conferences/thematic areas listed on the following page.

A total of 4,354 individuals from academia, research institutes, industry, and governmental agencies from 74 countries submitted contributions, and 1,287 papers and 186 posters have been included in the proceedings. These papers address the latest research and development efforts and highlight the human aspects of the design and use of computing systems. The papers thoroughly cover the entire field of human-computer interaction, addressing major advances in knowledge and effective use of computers in a variety of application areas. The volumes constituting the full 27-volume set of the conference proceedings are listed on pages IX and X.

I would like to thank the program board chairs and the members of the program boards of all thematic areas and affiliated conferences for their contribution to the highest scientific quality and the overall success of the HCI International 2016 conference.

This conference would not have been possible without the continuous and unwavering support and advice of the founder, Conference General Chair Emeritus and Conference Scientific Advisor Prof. Gavriel Salvendy. For his outstanding efforts, I would like to express my appreciation to the communications chair and editor of *HCI International News*, Dr. Abbas Moallem.

April 2016   Constantine Stephanidis

HCI International 2016 Thematic Areas
and Affiliated Conferences

Thematic areas:

- Human-Computer Interaction (HCI 2016)
- Human Interface and the Management of Information (HIMI 2016)

Affiliated conferences:

- 13th International Conference on Engineering Psychology and Cognitive Ergonomics (EPCE 2016)
- 10th International Conference on Universal Access in Human-Computer Interaction (UAHCI 2016)
- 8th International Conference on Virtual, Augmented and Mixed Reality (VAMR 2016)
- 8th International Conference on Cross-Cultural Design (CCD 2016)
- 8th International Conference on Social Computing and Social Media (SCSM 2016)
- 10th International Conference on Augmented Cognition (AC 2016)
- 7th International Conference on Digital Human Modeling and Applications in Health, Safety, Ergonomics and Risk Management (DHM 2016)
- 5th International Conference on Design, User Experience and Usability (DUXU 2016)
- 4th International Conference on Distributed, Ambient and Pervasive Interactions (DAPI 2016)
- 4th International Conference on Human Aspects of Information Security, Privacy and Trust (HAS 2016)
- Third International Conference on HCI in Business, Government, and Organizations (HCIBGO 2016)
- Third International Conference on Learning and Collaboration Technologies (LCT 2016)
- Second International Conference on Human Aspects of IT for the Aged Population (ITAP 2016)

Conference Proceedings Volumes Full List

1. LNCS 9731, Human-Computer Interaction: Theory, Design, Development and Practice (Part I), edited by Masaaki Kurosu
2. LNCS 9732, Human-Computer Interaction: Interaction Platforms and Techniques (Part II), edited by Masaaki Kurosu
3. LNCS 9733, Human-Computer Interaction: Novel User Experiences (Part III), edited by Masaaki Kurosu
4. LNCS 9734, Human Interface and the Management of Information: Information, Design and Interaction (Part I), edited by Sakae Yamamoto
5. LNCS 9735, Human Interface and the Management of Information: Applications and Services (Part II), edited by Sakae Yamamoto
6. LNAI 9736, Engineering Psychology and Cognitive Ergonomics, edited by Don Harris
7. LNCS 9737, Universal Access in Human-Computer Interaction: Methods, Techniques, and Best Practices (Part I), edited by Margherita Antona and Constantine Stephanidis
8. LNCS 9738, Universal Access in Human-Computer Interaction: Interaction Techniques and Environments (Part II), edited by Margherita Antona and Constantine Stephanidis
9. LNCS 9739, Universal Access in Human-Computer Interaction: Users and Context Diversity (Part III), edited by Margherita Antona and Constantine Stephanidis
10. LNCS 9740, Virtual, Augmented and Mixed Reality, edited by Stephanie Lackey and Randall Shumaker
11. LNCS 9741, Cross-Cultural Design, edited by Pei-Luen Patrick Rau
12. LNCS 9742, Social Computing and Social Media, edited by Gabriele Meiselwitz
13. LNAI 9743, Foundations of Augmented Cognition: Neuroergonomics and Operational Neuroscience (Part I), edited by Dylan D. Schmorrow and Cali M. Fidopiastis
14. LNAI 9744, Foundations of Augmented Cognition: Neuroergonomics and Operational Neuroscience (Part II), edited by Dylan D. Schmorrow and Cali M. Fidopiastis
15. LNCS 9745, Digital Human Modeling and Applications in Health, Safety, Ergonomics and Risk Management, edited by Vincent G. Duffy
16. LNCS 9746, Design, User Experience, and Usability: Design Thinking and Methods (Part I), edited by Aaron Marcus
17. LNCS 9747, Design, User Experience, and Usability: Novel User Experiences (Part II), edited by Aaron Marcus
18. LNCS 9748, Design, User Experience, and Usability: Technological Contexts (Part III), edited by Aaron Marcus
19. LNCS 9749, Distributed, Ambient and Pervasive Interactions, edited by Norbert Streitz and Panos Markopoulos
20. LNCS 9750, Human Aspects of Information Security, Privacy and Trust, edited by Theo Tryfonas

HCI International 2016 Conference

The full list with the program board chairs and the members of the program boards of all thematic areas and affiliated conferences is available online at:

http://www.hci.international/2016/

HCI International 2017

The 19th International Conference on Human-Computer Interaction, HCI International 2017, will be held jointly with the affiliated conferences in Vancouver, Canada, at the Vancouver Convention Centre, July 9–14, 2017. It will cover a broad spectrum of themes related to human-computer interaction, including theoretical issues, methods, tools, processes, and case studies in HCI design, as well as novel interaction techniques, interfaces, and applications. The proceedings will be published by Springer. More information will be available on the conference website: http://2017.hci.international/.

General Chair
Prof. Constantine Stephanidis
University of Crete and ICS-FORTH
Heraklion, Crete, Greece
E-mail: general_chair@hcii2017.org

http://2017.hci.international/

Contents – Part II

Gesture and Motion-Based Interaction

Technologies for Learning and Creativity

Location-based and Navigation Applications

Smart Environments and the Internet of Things

Design and Evaluation Case Studies

Contents – Part I

Design and Evaluation Methods, Techniques and Tools

Information Presentation and Visualization

Interaction Design

Design for Older Users

Human Modelling and Ergonomics

Web, Social Media and Communities

Standardizing the Human Interaction in Websites Using Web Application Frameworks

Fernando Arango Isaza and Danny Alvarez Eraso$^{(\boxtimes)}$

National University of Colombia, Medellín, Colombia
{farango,daalvareze}@unal.edu.co

Abstract. Web Application Frameworks (WAFs) are widely used nowadays to build quality web applications. However, developers have to code views one by one because WAFs offer little support for giving uniformity to the whole set of views. We propose the use of a View Code Generator (VCG) to automatize the process and assure views uniformity. Besides uniformity, our approach also reduces error sources, time to market and improves the resources allocation efficiency in the overall software life-cycle.

1 Introduction

Web Application Frameworks are widely used nowadays to build quality web applications [1–3]. WAFs offer developers, a pre-defined Model-View-Controller (MVC) architecture [4,5], improve code reuse [6], and several tools (or Helpers) to implement components. In particular, most WAFs fully support the construction of highly customizable views.

However, most current WAFs offer no means for standardizing the whole set of views. This means that developers must ensure that each application view follows the same data displaying and human interaction strategy; making more difficult the coding process.

This is inconvenient not only because the coding, per se, takes a great portion of the development effort –in a meting with start-up companies they estimated the coding task in 60 % of development effort–, but also because achieving the required view standardization is difficult, if not impossible, in an environment with multiple developers.

We propose the use of a View Code Generator (VCG) to assure views uniformity. In our approach the VCG divides the views specification in two steps. The first one, named *Object's Visible Data Specification* (or OVDS) specify the data to be displayed in a particular view. The second, named *Theme Specification* (TS) is common to all views and specify the data layout and view-user interaction strategy.

To test our approach we coded a VCG in the PISIS Framework, a proprietary WAF prototype. In our prototype the OVDSs were included as part of the classes definition. Meanwhile, the TS was hard coded as part of the VCG.

This paper is presented as follows: Sect. 1 covers the introduction, Sect. 2 presents antecedents to our work, Sect. 3 presents the VCG for displaying data,

C. Stephanidis (Ed.): HCII 2016 Posters, Part II, CCIS 618, pp. 3–7, 2016.
DOI: 10.1007/978-3-319-40542-1_1

Sect. 4 presents our proposal for human interaction standardization and in Sect. 5 we present the conclusions of our work and future work.

2   Antecedents

Rosales et al. in [7] present a recent systematic review on tools for automatic code generation. Computer-Aided Software Engineering (CASE) tools are among the most important tools. CASE tools are know for integrating methodologies and technologies for generating executable source code with the system model as input [7,8].

However CASE tools have disadvantages. Customization is limited in resulting applications, and those initial systems are harder to extend and maintain, and integration with other systems is hard. So, their usability in web applications that highly evolve is not easy.

On the other hand WAFs aid web development providing a flexible skeleton that serves as the base for any application. Every WAF offers a set of helpers for defining views: Sring Framework [9] aimed for java offers the JSP language RubyOnRails [10] uses .erb files, and [11] aimed for PHP offers simple PHP files as the template engine. Also, they offer pre-elaborated components for displaying data and designing forms.

However these tools are far from generating the application using the design diagrams as the only input. In particular, designing views with the available helpers is a manual process that must be done for every view; this is a lot of work. So, ensuring view uniformity is not easy.

As far as our knowledge reaches there is no WAF with automatic view generation are available.

3   View Code Generator and PISIS Framework

To reduce the work involved in designing views we propose the use of an automatic VCG that receives both the data to be displayed and the TS as input to generate all views following a set of conventions.

To test our approach we coded a VCG in the PISIS Framework, a proprietary WAF prototype written in the PHP language. In our prototype the OVDS was included as part of the classes definition. Meanwhile, the TS was hard coded as part of the VCG.

Defining Useful Class Models: We use the classes in the model layer of the MVC architecture as the core of our application. We added meta-data attributes to classes in order to make them useful not only to describe the business entities' data, but also to define what data will be displayed in the class views and the navigation paths; these two constitutes the OVDS.

The class views are, the main class view showing the attribute values for a class object, and the class "facets" that list the objects related to a class object trough the different class association links. By double clicking one of those objects, the display focus shift to the information of that object. This means that classes are the core of the navigation system, so, navigating from one object to one element in one of his facets also changes the displayed object.

Defining the View Code Generator: After extending classes with view and navigation information, we implemented an interpreter of that information to automatize how requests are managed to display all data contained in the database.

The PISIS Framework uses the Smarty template engine to implement the interpreter. After that, we extended Smarty functionality using plug-ins to code an interpreter of the object meta-data that constructs the corresponding HTML component: labels, tables, lists, urls, etc. This interpreter allocate both the object's primitive and the available facets data based on the OVDS. This plug-in is our VCG.

Even when our VCG is developed inside Smarty, it constitutes a new layer between the controller and views layer. Theoretically, replacing Smarty for other technology makes no difference.

About the Theme Support: Our VCG still needs a new interpreter for sporting multiple themes, which will be defined using a specialized language. However, as a first attempt, we hard-coded the theme inside the VCG.

4 Standardizing the Human Interaction Strategy

The views generated by our VCG cover CRUD (Create, Read, Update and Delete) operations. This is done by, standardizing how HTTP requests are managed by the controller layer and by including the same edition controls for table or data lists.

To do this we implemented a single class that works as a master controller capable of keeping track of the displayed object, managing transition to other object and serving the creation and edition of records. This mechanisms was automatically injected to all views.

This way we ensure that the human interaction strategy remains the same in all views making easier for the final user to learn how to use the application. This also reduces the need of developing multiple controllers and in consequence, this strategy reduces the total development effort and improves maintainability.

So, in Fig. 1 we show PISIS Framework MVC architecture for automatic view generation.

Reading and Displaying Records: The application has a default displayed object from where the user can navigate to all the objects in the system. The navigation elements displayed are the object facets and correspond to the object's visible data.

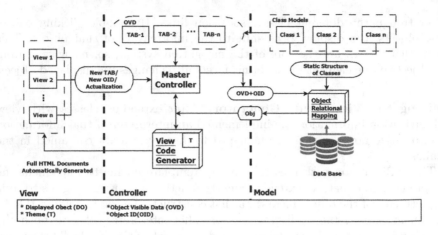

Fig. 1. PISIS Framework MVC architecture for automatic view generation.

We defined a *data manipulation layer* to read database records and transform them into objects. This layer is often referred as the WAF ORM (Object-Relational Mapping) implementation. The current version of PISIS deals with this by manually coding every interaction.

Inserting and Editing Records: Records can be inserted/edited in one of the displayed object facets by using the edition controls available in all views in edition mode, see Fig. 2. This allows the table lines to be used as edition forms, multiple changes can be applied to the list but they are not intermediately committed to database; data is written only after pushing the save button. The reader must note that this behavior is useful to support undo/redo operations, as well as convenient for reuse code for showing and editing records.

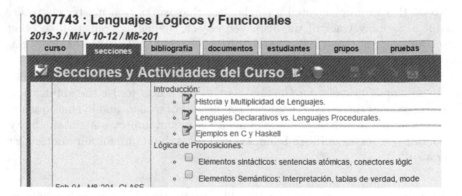

Fig. 2. PISIS Framework Edition controls.

5   Conclusions and Future Work

We proposed a VCG to automatize and standardize the view generation process in web applications using a Framework prototype. Also, we proposed a MCV architecture that eliminates the need of writing controllers using the class models as the core of the application definition. As a consequence, classes are the place where the developer should focus the development effort.

Our approach saves a lot of coding effort as well as it standardizes the whole set of views and the human interaction strategy. This is done by centralizing HTTP request regarding CRUD operations in a master controller that later passes the response to the VCG. Finally, the VCG generates the HTML document and inject standardized edition controls.

Our future research is focused on the definition of a TS interpreter that allows separating the Theme layout from the VCG. We will implement an interpreter for supporting different TSs so that developers can build their own layouts.

We will define an ORM to replace improve our *data manipulation layer* and reduce the need of writing SQL statements.

References

1. Chen, B., Hsu, H.-P., Huang, Y.: Bringing desktop applications to the web. IT Prof. **18**(1), 34–40 (2016)
2. Vuksanovic, I.P., Sudarevic, B.: Use of web application frameworks in the development of small applications. In: MIPRO, 2011 Proceedings of the 34th International Convention, pp. 458–462 (2011)
3. Shan, T.C., Bank, W., Hua, W.W.: Taxonomy of Java Web Application Frameworks, p. 07 (2006)
4. Krasner, G., Pope, S.: A description of the model-view-controller user interface paradigm in the smalltalk-80 system. J. Object Oriented Program. **1**, 26–49 (1988)
5. Leff, A., Rayfield, J.: Web-application development using the Model/View/Controller design pattern. In: Proceedings of the Fifth IEEE International Enterprise Distributed Object Computing Conference, pp. 118–127 (2001)
6. Schwabe, D., Rossi, G., Esmeraldo, L., Lyardet, F.: Web design frameworks: an approach to improve reuse in web applications. In: Murugesan, S., Desphande, Y. (eds.) Web Engineering. LNCS, vol. 2016, p. 335. Springer, Heidelberg (2001)
7. Rosales, V., Alor, G., García, J., Zatarain, R., Barrón, M.: An analysis of tools for automatic software development and automatic code generation, in Revista Facultad de Ingeniería Universidad de Antioquia, pp. 75–87 (2015)
8. Johns, M., Beyerlein, C., Giesecke, R., Posegga, J.: Secure code generation for web applications. In: Massacci, F., Wallach, D., Zannone, N. (eds.) ESSoS 2010. LNCS, vol. 5965, pp. 96–113. Springer, Heidelberg (2010)
9. Spring.io: Spring Framework (2002). https://projects.spring.io/spring-frame work/. Accessed 07 Apr 2016
10. Heinemeier, D.: Ruby on Rails (2005). http://rubyonrails.org/. Accessed 10 Mar 2016
11. EllisLab: CodeIgniter Web Framework (2006). https://www.codeigniter.com/. Accessed 07 Apr 2016

Analysis of Academic Research Networks to Find Collaboration Partners

Kavita Asiwal[✉], Bharath Kumar Suresh, and G. Ram Mohana Reddy

National Institute of Technology Karnataka, Surathkal, India
kavitaswl@gmail.com, bharath30may@gmail.com,
profgrmreddy@gmail.com

Abstract. Social network analysis has been used for decades to find behavioral patterns and relationships that exist between people in a network. Researchers have been collaborating for centuries with the aim of improving the quality of research, to broaden the scope of problems that they tackle, to speed up the output and to disseminate knowledge across authors. Sometimes it becomes difficult to find the right collaboration partner due to various reasons, the major one being the lack of data about individuals working in their chosen domain in geographically separated locations. In this paper, we explain how social network analysis can be used to help researchers in finding suitable collaboration partners with whom they have not worked in the past but can collaborate in the future. Further, we have considered two different analysis techniques – weighted and non-weighted graph and the results are compared based on the relevance of the outcomes.

Keywords: Academic research network · Social network analysis · Collaborative research

1 Introduction

It is observed that there has been an increase in the number of research topics that require interdisciplinary treatment, which makes it essential for departments or organizations belonging to different fields of knowledge to collaborate in the problem solving process [1–3]. To some extent, this rise can be attributed to the increasing specialization of individual academics and the broadening in scope of the problems that they tackle. Hence, it is possible to integrate scholarly communities and foster knowledge transfer between related fields through collaboration [4].

An academic research network is a network of researchers who are connected through relations like student-advisor, collaborations and citations. It can thus be used to analyze the collaboration relation among a group of authors. From the researcher's point of view, people who have worked together previously are much more likely to succeed in future collaborations, as they understand each other's areas of interest, approaches and methodologies [5]. In this paper, we propose an automated tool, which can be used by researchers to visualize their collaboration network, and thereby finding the prospective collaboration partners using a graph theory based approach.

© Springer International Publishing Switzerland 2016
C. Stephanidis (Ed.): HCII 2016 Posters, Part II, CCIS 618, pp. 8–14, 2016.
DOI: 10.1007/978-3-319-40542-1_2

As a case study, academic research network of National Institute of Technology Karnataka (NITK) Surathkal, Mangalore, India is considered, and the extracted results have been analyzed using social network analysis techniques. The remainder of this paper is presented as follows: Sect. 2 deals with the related work in the field of academic research network analysis. Section 3 describes thè proposed methodology. Section 4 describes the implementation details. Obtained results and discussion are presented in Sect. 5. Finally, the conclusion and future work are given in Sect. 6.

2   Related Work

Much of the previous research in this area has focused on co-authorship analysis to analyze the collaboration networks [6, 7]. The co-authorship networks exhibit characteristics similar to the much studied citation networks [8], but co-authorship implies a much stronger link than citation, which can occur without the authors knowing each other. Scientists who have authored a paper together are considered connected and a large number of such connections constitute the research network. Co-authorship analysis has been used to assess the collaboration among academic institutions in a certain geographical environment [1].

Scientific collaboration is accepted as a positive phenomenon and is found to have a significant influence on the performance of individual researchers and institutions, in terms of effectiveness, efficiency and productivity [9, 10]. The analysis of social networks has been widely used to understand the implications of the relationship patterns between researchers in various fields [11, 12]. Further, in [12] bibliometrics information for the period between 1999 and 2005 has been used.

3   Proposed Methodology for Development of Automated Tool

Figure 1 shows the proposed framework for creation of the automated tool using graph theory approach. In step 1, the data about researchers of NITK, Surathkal is collected and stored in the database. The data stored includes areas of interest and publications of each researcher. In step 2, the authors are divided into groups based on their research domain. Authors may belong to more than one group depending on how varied their research domain is. The grouping is done using natural language processing (NLP) as different researchers may use different terminology to specify the same area.

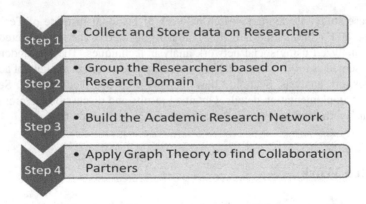

Fig. 1. Proposed framework

In step 3, the data stored is used to build the research network. From the data that is collected on papers authored by a researcher, his co-authors are found. The academic research network is represented in the form of an undirected Graph G= (V, E) where V denotes a finite set of nodes and E denotes a finite set of edges. Each node in V represents a researcher and each edge in E represents a co-authorship relation between a pair of researchers. In step 4, the network is analyzed using two different approaches, which are explained next.

3.1 Non-weighted Graph Approach

In this approach, the graph used for analysis has non-weighted edges i.e. all edges represent same type of association. A node is created for each researcher and an edge is added between a pair of nodes if the researchers representing those two nodes have co-authored a paper/journal. When researcher A tries to find his possible collaboration partners, a modification of breadth first search graph algorithm is applied which finds all nodes that can be reached indirectly starting from A i.e. D, E, F and G in Fig. 2. The nodes reached are sorted in ascending order of their distance from A i.e. F and D appear above G and E. The details of authors representing these nodes are then displayed to the researcher A followed by a list of authors from A's area of interest group which cannot be reached starting from A. This is done as there is always a slight probability for researchers with the same interests to collaborate irrespective of whether they have any association or not.

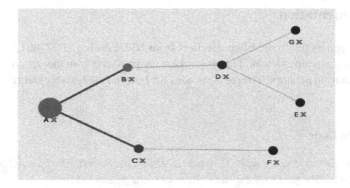

Fig. 2. Non-weighted graph

3.2 Weighted Graph Approach

In this approach, the graph used for analysis has weighted edges i.e. each edge is different in terms of strength of association. Just like non-weighted approach, here also a node is created for each researcher and an edge is added between a pair of nodes if the researchers representing those two nodes have co-authored a paper/journal. But unlike the previous approach here each edge is assigned a weight which is equal to the number of co-authored research papers/journals. When a researcher A tries to find out his possible collaboration partners, a modified depth first search graph algorithm is applied which finds all nodes that can be reached indirectly starting from A i.e. D, E, F and G in Fig. 3. The nodes reached are sorted in descending order of the weight of paths from A i.e. G, F, E and D in this case. The details of authors representing these nodes are then displayed to the user followed by a list of authors from A's area of interest group which cannot be reached starting from A (reason specified in Non-Weighted graph approach).

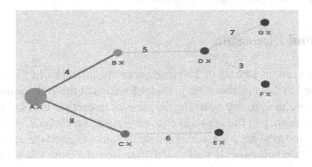

Fig. 3. Weighted graph

4   Implementation

The data on papers published by researchers from NITK during 2007–2012 are considered for co-authorship analysis. The researchers are provided with the option of viewing their collaboration network. The pseudo codes for both the analysis techniques are given next.

4.1   Pseudo Code

```
Input: A Network graph G and a vertex v of G for which
collaboration partners are to be suggested.
Output: A list of vertices which are the suggested col-
laboration partners for v.

procedure suggestCollaborationPartners(G,v,graphType):
1:  for all vertices v' in G do
2:     if there is an edge from v to v' then
3:        for all vertices v'' in G do
4:           if there is an edge from v' to v'' and no edge
              from v to v'' then
5:              if vertex v'' is not same as vertex v then
6:                 add v'' to the result_list
7:                 if graphType is Non-Weighted
8:                    update length of path for v'' in
                      path_length_list
9:                 else if graphType is Weighted
10:                   update weight of path for v'' in
                      path_length_list
11:    sort result_list based on path_length_list
12:    return sorted result_list
```

5   Results and Discussion

A study is conducted on a group of 200 researchers from NITK. In this study the tool developed is used to find collaboration partners for each of the 200 researchers and the results obtained are analyzed by matching the areas of research to find similarity or some kind of interdependency in the areas. In case of weighted technique, 94 % of the time the results are found to be accurate, while in case of Non-weighted the accuracy dropped down to 83 %. A comparison is performed based on the time taken to analyze the academic research network graph by varying the number of authors in the network. The results obtained are summarized in Fig. 4 and it is observed that the time taken is slightly higher in case of weighted technique.

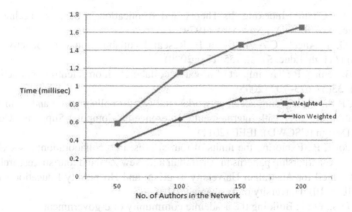

Fig. 4. Processing time versus No. of authors in the Network

6   Conclusion and Future Work

The tool developed helps the researchers in finding collaboration partners successfully. The time taken to analyze the network is comparatively less in case of non-weighted graph as the processing time spent for calculating the weights of edges is saved. The results obtained are more accurate in case of weighted approach as more importance is given to the strength of past successful collaborations. The limitation of this approach is that determining the accuracy of results obtained is a subjective process. Further research can be extended in this area by grouping authors based on factors other than area of research i.e. geographical location, work experience or affiliating institute etc.

References

1. Toral, S.L., et al.: An exploratory social network analysis of academic research networks. In: 2011 Third International Conference on Intelligent Networking and Collaborative Systems (INCoS). IEEE (2011)
2. Bessis, N., Bessis, N.: Grid Technology for Maximizing Collaborative Decision Management and Support: Advancing Effective Virtual Organizations. Information Science Reference (2009)
3. Bordons, M., et al.: Measuring interdisciplinary collaboration within a university: The effects of the multidisciplinary research programme. Scientometrics **46**(3), 383–398 (1999)
4. Nikhil, J., Ramage, D., Jurafsky, D.: A study of academic collaboration in computational linguistics with latent mixtures of authors. In: ACL HLT 2011, p. 124 (2011)
5. Cummings, J.N., Kiesler, S.: Who collaborates successfully?: prior experience reduces collaboration barriers in distributed interdisciplinary research. In: Proceedings of the 2008 ACM Conference on Computer Supported Cooperative Work. ACM (2008)
6. Rodriguez, M.A., Pepe, A.: On the relationship between the structural and socioacademic communities of a coauthorship network. J. Informetrics **2**(3), 195–201 (2008)
7. Farkas, I., et al.: Networks in life: Scaling properties and eigenvalue spectra. Physica A Stat. Mech. Appl. **314**(1), 25–34 (2002)

8. Garfield, E.: Citation Indexing: Its Theory and Application in Science, Technology, and Humanities, vol. 8. Wiley, New York (1979)
9. Abramo, G., D'Angelo, C.A., Di Costa, F.: Research collaboration and productivity: is there correlation? High. Educ. **57**(2), 155–171 (2009)
10. Lee, S., Bozeman, B.: The impact of research collaboration on scientific productivity. Soc. Stud. Sci. **35**(5), 673–702 (2005)
11. Monclar, R.S., et al.: Using social networks analysis for collaboration and team formation identification. In: 2011 15th International Conference on Computer Supported Cooperative Work in Design (CSCWD). IEEE (2011)
12. Benckendorff, P.: Exploring the limits of tourism research collaboration: a social network analysis of co-authorship patterns in Australian and New Zealand tourism research. In: 20th Annual Council for Australian University Tourism and Hospitality Education Conference (CAUTHE 2010). University of Tasmania (2010)
13. Sayogo, D.S., et al.: Building the academic community of e-government research on cross-boundary information integration and sharing. In: 2012 45th Hawaii International Conference on System Science (HICSS). IEEE (2012)

Promoting Engagement in Open Collaboration Communities by Means of Gamification

Ana Paula O. Bertholdo[✉] and Marco Aurélio Gerosa

Department of Computer Science, University of São Paulo, São Paulo, Brazil
{ana,gerosa}@ime.usp.br

Abstract. Open collaboration communities depend on contributors. To reduce users' engagement problems with collaborative systems, the use of gamification has been discussed. However, most gamification methods are generic and do not emphasize the collaborative aspects. This research aims to define a process to promote engagement in open collaboration communities by means of gamification. The process will be refined through action research cycles.

Keywords: Engagement · Gamification · 3C model · Voluntary participation · Online communities · Open collaboration communities

1 Introduction

A typical open collaboration system is an online environment that enables the collective production of artifacts by means of a technologically mediated collaboration platform, offering few barriers to entry and exit and supporting persistent social structures but malleable. Thus, it generates socio-technical systems that provide new opportunities for people to connect and create together [1].

Open collaboration communities depend on new contributors [1,2]. It is necessary to motivate, engage, and retain new participants to promote a sustainable community [3]. According to Bista et al. [4], it is essential to have active contributors for sustainability reasons of an online community and strengthening the engagement can be one of the ways to motivate members to contribute. In this context, an important concept for the operation of open collaboration communities emerges: engagement.

According to O'Brien and Toms, engagement is a category of user experience characterized by attributes of challenge, positive affect, aesthetic and sensory appeal, attention, feedback, variety/novelty, interactivity, and perceived control by the user. The engagement model contains four distinct phases - point of engagement, sustained engagement period, disengagement, and re-engagement [5].

To reduce users' engagement problems with collaborative systems, the use of gamification has been discussed [4]. Gamification is the use of elements and game design techniques in contexts that are not games. The practice and theory of gamification aims to encourage participation and engage people [6]. As stated

© Springer International Publishing Switzerland 2016
C. Stephanidis (Ed.): HCII 2016 Posters, Part II, CCIS 618, pp. 15–20, 2016.
DOI: 10.1007/978-3-319-40542-1_3

by Brito et al. [7], game design elements have been used in collaborative software to engage users to achieve the group's goal. However, most gamification methods are generic and do not emphasize the aspects of collaboration.

For these reasons, we defined the following research question (RQ): How to promote engagement in open collaboration communities by means of gamification? Thus, this research aims to define a process to insert gamification elements throughout the development of open collaboration communities to promote engagement.

2   Background

Creating and maintaining a system that motivate and engage participants is a challenge. Bista et al. [4] declare that the establishment of a new online community with a sustainable level of engagement of members is challenging because: (a) bootstrapping - how to bring members to the community and keep them engaged during the initial phase of the community; (b) monitoring - how to monitor community activities under different categories such as reading, rating, comments, making friends, among others; and (c) sustainability - how to sustain community engagement not only during the initial stage, but also throughout a period of time.

According Kraut and Resnick [8], to become an online community of success, it must meet a number of challenges: start a new community, attract and socialize new members, encourage commitment, encourage contribution, and regulate behavior. Online communities can have more difficulties in overcoming the challenges because of three characteristics that are unusual in groups and conventional organizations. The first is the anonymity in which veterans may be less able to analyze anonymous newcomers and newcomers can be less inhibited by social responsibility. The second is the ease of entry and exit, which leads to high turnover and inhibits building personal ties or commitment to the group. The third is the text communication, which is prone to misinterpretation because it lacks the fluidity and nonverbal cues of face-to-face interaction.

Motivation and engagement are different when participation is voluntary, which occurs in open collaboration communities. As Baran and Cagiltay [9] state, on voluntary participation, individuals often seek profissional development, and need to recognize the importance of socio-cultural environment, and how they benefit from the interaction with the system users.

The success of communities is dependent on the motivation related to participation of enough people, so that a critical mass of production can exist around a set of artifacts [10]. In the creation of online communities from scratch, designers face the critical mass problem in which the system has not yet enough content to attract users and also there are few users to create content that can attract other users [8]. Thus, the theory of critical mass highlights the tension between the individual's ability to derive benefits from the use of an interactive media and social or public benefits that may follow from individual use [11].

In seeking a solution to engagement issues, most gamification design guidelines are concerned to introduce reward elements like points, badges, and leaderboards (PBL). A reward-based project can result in putting collecting points as the main proposal instead of collaboration goal [7].

According to Deterding [12], game designers argue that the enjoyment of the game does not come from reward systems, but from significant choices in the execution of "difficult curiously goals". Most gamification implementations has put the least essential of games and represent as the core of experience [12]. Therefore, most gamification methods do not emphasize the aspects of collaboration [7], which represent the essence for creating and sustaining open collaboration communities.

3 Solution Proposal

Fuks et al. [13] define that "collaboration may be seen as the combination of communication, coordination and cooperation. Communication is related to the exchange of messages and information among people; coordination is related to the management of people, their activities and resources; and cooperation, which is the production taking place on a shared space". The 3C Collaboration Model is used in the literature for classification of collaborative systems. Collaborative systems are designed to facilitate group activities, even if users are in different places and times.

Taking into consideration that open collaboration communities are built from collaborative systems or groupware [13], it is possible to analyze them from the 3C collaboration model. The objective is to define a process to include gamification elements in development of open collaboration communities. This process includes a conceptual model, that supports the modeling in the analysis phase of the project; software components, engagement metrics, considerations abouts development and tests of gamification elements, and evaluation methods. The description of the process will be performed with formal notation, namely, Business Process Modeling Language (BPML).

The features of open collaboration communities arranged according to gamification elements, and the recommendations for association of engagement problems will be described using patterns, to put them under the same analysis component with a standard format - name, context, problem, solution and examples [14]. The aim is to facilitate the systematized mapping, where collaborative features patterns are associated with gamification patterns. For example, to the feature of comment that is classified as communication in the 3C model, which gamification elements improve the engagement in this type of feature, considering its context of use.

The gamification aims to engage users, but engagement, as O'Brien and Toms [5], has four distinct phases -point of engagement, sustained engagement period, disengagement and re-engagement. The collection of engagement data from the user interaction is a bridge between the disengagement and re-engagement, since it allows to understand what needs to be explored to bring the user to a new point of engagement.

The point of engagement relates to the bootstrapping, sustained engagement period relates to monitoring, because it is necessary to measure the engagement to sustain it and disengagement relates to sustainability, since it is necessary to perform actions to promote re-engagement. Therefore, the process will be described by means of the distinct phases of engagement.

4   Method

To achieve the objective of this research, an action research will be performed throughout the development of two open collaboration communities. The goal is the understanding of the real problem in a specific context and the application and refining of the process. The action research cycles are composed of the following steps: plan, act, observe, and reflect. The cycles developed before and after the definition of the process will be compared. The usability testing and the diary studies technique will be performed with system users to collect qualitative data on the user experience, especially related to the engagement. The data obtained in action research and in application of questionnaires and interviews with experts will be the basis to analysis with Grounded theory, and statistical analysis will be performed over the engagement data of systems where the action research has been applied. The process will be refined with experts through interviews using the methodological triangulation. The dependent variable of this research is the user engagement with the community, while the independent variables are the elements of gamification, the tools of collection and analysis of engagement and engagement metrics.

5   Performed Activities

The completed activities in the current state of research are the literature review to understand the areas involved in the research, a preliminary gamification element list based on the literature review, the preparation of one of the projects in which the action research is being carried out, and the development of the action research in this project.

For project preparation, the following activities were required: composition of a team with five members to work in software development; development of key collaborative features for user interaction; insertion of analytical tools for monitoring user interaction with the system, namely, Google Analytics and CrazzyEgg; and implementation of user actions logs for engagement data analysis.

In the cycle 0 of action research, the engagement data were collected prior to insertion of gamification, therefore, in subsequent cycles it will be possible to evaluate the evolution of engagement with the input of gamification elements according to specific collaboration features. A remote usability testing through SurveyGizmo and Loop11 tools was realized. The results are being analyzed in order to integrate the collected data in the logs of user actions, analytical tools and remote testing tools.

From the usability testing in earlier versions of the system it was defined a preliminary group of gamification elements to the cycle 1 of action research, which was implemented in parallel to the other activities of cycle 0, but not including the results in the system version in production. The cycle 1 of action research included gamification elements originated from an ad-hoc approach to compare the results with subsequent cycles where the proposed process will be instantiated.

6 Final Considerations

For reasons of sustainability of an online community, it presents itself as a need to have active contributors, and strengthening the engagement can be one way to motivate members to contribute. To reduce users' engagement problems with collaborative systems the use of Gamification has been discussed. However, most gamification methods are very generic and do not emphasize the aspects of collaboration [7].

This research proposes a process to promote engagement in open collaboration communities by means of gamification. The process will be defined by an action research in two collaborative systems in development and analysed with statistical methods, usability testing with users and diary studies, as well as validations of experts, through interviews and questionnaires, promoting methodological triangulation.

Acknowledgements. This research has been supported by FAPESP, Brazil, proc. 2015/06660-8.

References

1. Forte, A., Lampe, C.: Defining, understanding, and supporting open collaboration: lessons from the literature. Am. Behav. Sci. **57**(5), 535–547 (2013)
2. Steinmacher, I., Conte, T., Gerosa, M.A., Redmiles, D.: Social barriers faced by newcomers placing their first contribution in open source software projects. In: Proceedings of the 18th ACM Conference on Computer Supported Cooperative Work & Social Computing, pp. 1379–1392. ACM (2015)
3. Qureshi, I., Fang, Y.: Socialization in open source software projects: a growth mixture modeling approach. Organ. Res. Methods (2010)
4. Bista, S.K., Nepal, S., Colineau, N., Paris, C.: Using gamification in an online community. In: 2012 8th International Conference on Collaborative Computing: Networking, Applications and Worksharing (CollaborateCom), pp. 611–618. IEEE (2012)
5. O'Brien, H.L., Toms, E.G.: What is user engagement? A conceptual framework for defining user engagement with technology. J. Am. Soc. Inf. Sci. Technol. **59**(6), 938–955 (2008)
6. Deterding, S., Dixon, D., Khaled, R., Nacke, L.: From game design elements to gamefulness: defining gamification. In: Proceedings of the 15th International Academic MindTrek Conference: Envisioning Future Media Environments, pp. 9–15. ACM (2011)

7. Brito, J., Vieira, V., Duran, A.: Towards a framework for gamification design on crowdsourcing systems: the game approach. In: 2015 12th International Conference on Information Technology-New Generations (ITNG), pp. 445–450. IEEE (2015)
8. Kraut, R.E., Resnick, P.: Encouraging contribution to online communities. In: Evidence-Based Social Design, Building Successful Online Communities, pp. 21–76 (2011)
9. Baran, B., Cagiltay, K.: The dynamics of online communities in the activity theory framework. Edu. Technol. Soc. **13**(4), 155–166 (2010)
10. Burke, M., Marlow, C., Lento, T.: Feed me: motivating newcomer contribution in social network sites. In: Proceedings of the SIGCHI Conference on Human Factors in Computing Systems, pp. 945–954. ACM (2009)
11. Markus, M.L.: Toward a critical mass theory of interactive media universal access, interdependence and diffusion. Commun. Res. **14**(5), 491–511 (1987)
12. Deterding, S.: Gamification: designing for motivation. Interactions **19**(4), 14–17 (2012)
13. Fuks, H., Raposo, A.B., Gerosa, M.A., Lucena, C.J.: Applying the 3C model to groupware development. Int. J. Cooper. Inf. Syst. **14**(02n03), 299–328 (2005)
14. Alexander, C., Ishikawa, S., Silverstein, M., Jacobson, M., King, I.F., Angel, S.: A Pattern Language: Towns, Buildings, Construction. Center for Environmental Structure Series. Oxford University Press, USA (1977)

Usability and UX Evaluation of a Mobile Social Application to Increase Students-Faculty Interactions

Ticianne Darin[1(✉)], Rossana Andrade[2], José Macedo[2], David Araújo[2],
Lana Mesquita[2], and Jaime Sánchez[3]

[1] Virtual University Institute, Federal University of Ceará,
Humberto Monte, s/n, Fortaleza, Brazil
ticianne@virtual.ufc.br
[2] Department of Computer Science, Federal University of Ceará,
Humberto Monte, s/n, Fortaleza, Brazil
{rossana,lanabeatriz}@great.ufc.br, jose.macedo@lia.ufc.br,
david.brasillo@gmail.com
[3] Department of Computer Science, University of Chile, Blanco Encalada 2120, Santiago, Chile
jsanchez@dcc.uchile.cl

Abstract. The massive adoption of smart devices in the last years have
increased the use of mobile social applications, which can take advantage of
features like real-time location, to help people relate with their physical
communities and surroundings. The success of such applications depend on
achieving a critical mass of users, who share their personal information and
opinions. Thus, evaluating the usability and the user experience, according to
the context of use and to the community behavior is essential to deliver an
application that meets the user needs and expectations. This paper introduces
a mobile social application, called *Eai?*, developed to improve the interaction
between students and faculty in a Brazilian University, regarding the University Restaurant and news related to the campus. The main goal of this application is to empower the students, allowing them to expose their opinion on
the taste and quality of each meal, the staff service, and other relevant topics.
Moreover, we report an evaluation of usability and user experience of this
application, considering the challenges of deploying a mobile social system,
along to whether *Eai?* improves students-faculty interactions or not.

Keywords: Mobile social application · Usability · User experience · Student-
faculty interaction

1 Introduction

Student-faculty formal and informal interactions are positively related to student persis-
tence, satisfaction, and learning. Nevertheless, students who engage less with faculty
members and institutional agents are more likely to feel disconnected to the institution
and unsatisfied with the campus environment [1]. Students' social connections with
peers and faculty may also enhance students' sense of belonging to the institution, ultimately leading to greater classroom engagement in reasoning activities [2]. The students

© Springer International Publishing Switzerland 2016
C. Stephanidis (Ed.): HCII 2016 Posters, Part II, CCIS 618, pp. 21–29, 2016.
DOI: 10.1007/978-3-319-40542-1_4

consider that a high-quality student-faculty interaction occurs when faculty care and support them [3]. The Federal University of Ceará, in Brazil, supports low-income students with the University Restaurant (UR), a unit designed to provide balanced meals to students and staff. The UR has the capacity for 3,000 meals/day and serves breakfast, lunch and dinner. The students constantly discuss the taste and quality of each meal, the staff service, and the usually crowded lines. However, they are unable to expose their opinion for a massive group of students or give feedback to the institutional agents in a simple manner. As a result, the students may be uninspired to interact with faculty members and institutional agents, hence increasing the feeling of dissatisfaction with the campus environment.

To help to overcome this situation, the mobile social application *Eai?* (Brazilian Portuguese for "Hey, what´s up?") was developed. In this application, students can follow the weekly menu of the UR, qualify, and share opinions and reviews about the daily meals. The students can use the Android application *Eai?* to qualify the state of the UR lines and to know, in real time, what other users are saying about the lines, and to know when is the best time to go to the UR. Also, *Eai?* provides a news feed about the University, and other also miscellaneous news, where the students can also interact. This work presents the evaluation of usability and user experience (UX) of *Eai?*, which used a multi-method approach aiming to understand the system usage and to explore the quality of user's interaction and perceptions of the system. Our research hypotheses are: (1) *Eai?* can positively impact the students' behavior, increasing their social connections with peers; (2) *Eai?* is useful to assess the quality of the UR service, increasing the students-faculty interactions; (3) To provide tools like forum and news related to the University positively impacts student's sense of belonging to the institution. The results show that overall the students find *Eai?* useful, trustable, stimulating and easy to use, although they pointed some necessary improvements. We also discuss how the answers to hypotheses 2 and 3 vary according to the student's experience with the UR, and their use of the application.

2   *Eai?*, a Mobile Social Application

Eai? is a place-centric mobile social application, where college students can share a common interest and constantly interact, benefiting each other with the knowledge and experience related to their current location, the University Restaurant (UR). The application provides diverse facets of social interactions, such as social feedback mechanisms, personal identification, and identity expression [5]. Features such as rating, reviewing, discussion forum and customizable profiles support the possibilities of social interaction in *Eai?*. The application also allows students to share at any time, their opinions about each one's personal experience in the University Restaurant. In this manner, *Eai?* enables a real-time exchange of location-related experiences of locally dispersed participants, so the students became part of a mobile community [4]. Currently, the application has over 2600 downloads in the Google Play platform, counts 194 reviews (183 are 5 or 4 stars), and its rating is 4.7 in the Store. The main functionalities of the application are listing the weekly meal menu of the UR, sharing reviews about the meals, showing the states of UR lines, and providing news feed and a discussion forum (Fig. 1).

Fig. 1. (A) List of meals of the day, (B) Details of a selected meal, (C) Pop up for rating and commenting about a meal, (D) Home Screen showing the state of the restaurant lines and the News feed

The Fig. 1A illustrates the list of meals organized from Monday to Friday, according to the meal time. Figure 1B shows the details of a selected meal, as side dishes, and juice and desert options. Figure 1C demonstrates the reviewing process, where the user can rate and comment about a meal. At the Home Screen (Fig. 1D) the user can see the real-time state of the UR lines according to the interaction of users located at the UR. For this purpose, the application has a function where the users can classify the state of the line. The home screen also shows a short version of the news feed, which intends to increase the experience for a common user of the restaurant. The news is distributed into two categories: general news and news about the University campuses. This news is sorted by the user's interest, calculated in an algorithm focused on variables of continuous use. The students can 'like' or 'dislike' the articles in General News, while in each item about the University they can comment and interact with each other. These commentaries may become a bigger discussion about the subject. In this case, it can be discussed at the Forum named Boca no Trombone (Brazilian Portuguese for "Blow the whistle") where the students can expose their concerns and give feedback about the UR and other University services.

3   Evaluation Process

The assessment process of *Eai?* considered two of the challenges of deploying a mobile social application, utility and usability [6], while assessing the user experience as well. The evaluation planning was based on the DECIDE framework. To understand the system usage and to explore the quality of user's interaction and perceptions of the system, we applied quantitative and qualitative methods. First, we collected quantitative data in the form of a questionnaire, adapted by the authors from the Computer System Usability Questionnaire (CSUQ) [7], and from the Questionnaire for User Interface Satisfaction (QUIS) [8]. It was administered to 109 users, among students and university staff, in September 2015. Due to the context of the evaluation (in the restaurant, when users were coming for the lunch or leaving after it), its purpose was to obtain an overview of the user feedback on the application. The questionnaire consisted of 14 closed-ended questions, answered in 5-point Likert scales, plus three open-ended questions. The questions acquired information about the application's impact on the behavior of the users, the utility of the application to evaluate the UR service, and the user's expectations.

The second phase of the evaluation occurred from October to November in the same year, to refine the data and to expand the understanding of the user experience for new users. We gathered qualitative data with semi-structured contextual interviews, observation of usage and informal conversation with 34 participants, among users and potential users, allowing a depth research. We performed the evaluations in group sessions with students belonging to three categories: students who currently do not take meals at the University Restaurant; students who regularly have lunch or dinner at the UR, but are not *Eai?* users; and students who regularly have the same meals at the UR and currently are *Eai?* users. During this evaluation, users completed a pretest questionnaire about their experience with technology and with the University Restaurant. Then, each user performed eight tasks in the application, selected from possible usage scenarios. For each activity performed, we observed and took notes of the reactions and both correct and incorrect user interactions. After this, in a structured contextual interview, users gave their opinion about the clarity, the efficiency and the importance of the functionalities, in the context of use of the UR. Users were also asked about the mistakes, difficulties, and experience (regarding emotions and feelings) while performing the tasks. After finishing the activities, the users filled out a post-test questionnaire, adapted from the Final User Questionnaire for Usability Evaluation of websites [9] and QUIS. Each session lasted 30 min on average. After the individual evaluations, the users were divided into two focus groups, where they shared and discussed impressions, opinions, and suggestions on the application.

4   Results and Discussion

In the first evaluation, the average age of the 109 *Eai?* users (63 female) was 23.5 years for women and 23.7 years for men. Among these, 73 % were students of the university and 11 % were employees of the University or outsourced. Overall, the application was considered useful (95 %), trustworthy (90 %), easy to use (92 %), stimulating (67 %) and worthwhile (81 %). Regarding the organization of information and the sequence of screens during the interactions in the application, most users gave positive feedback, considering *Eai?* well-Organized (87 %), and with a clear sequence of screens (86 %).

The second phase of the evaluation consisted in a deeper investigation with 34 students (9 female), remaining the same age of the first evaluated group. We identified that 80 % of the participants used to interact with their smartphones while having meals at the UR. They mainly use applications of instant messaging (66.7 %), social networking

(47.6 %), music and games (28.6 %), and reading (19 %). It is important to point out that the functionalities of social networking and reading are also present in *Eai?*. It combines in a single application both the capabilities the students need for a better UR service and the ones they would like to have as pastime activities while at the UR. For this group of students, the overall evaluation presented slightly lower percentages, due to the number of students using *Eai?* for the first time (potential users). They considered the application useful (84 %), trustworthy (69 %), easy to use (66 %), and worthwhile (56 %).

The user experience assessment revealed some problems in the navigation, organization, and labeling which made the new users felt confuse and sometimes frustrated. It happened mainly in the activities of qualifying the lines, accessing the breakfast menu options, adding a meal as favorite and commenting on the news, and in the students' forum. These results evidenced that *Eai?* was not as easy to learn and efficient as it should be, although even the new users acknowledged the utility of its functionalities. The discussions on the focus groups showed that the students like the overall idea of the application. They were excited about the new possibilities and pleased with the initiative of the University to improve the UR service by creating a social application. They expressed the desire to use an improved version of the application. Moreover, they expect *Eai?* to become an essential application for any student of UFC. The students suggested that *Eai?* should integrate other features relevant to the UR, such as buying UR credits, as well as possibilities of direct interaction among people in the UR.

4.1   Research Hypothesis#1: *Eai?* Can Positively Impact the Students' Behavior

To find out if the current users were using application features according to the expected behavior, we evaluated how often they use the following functions: (1) to send information about the status of the line; (2) to access news; (3) to choose a dish based on application reviews, and (4) to send notes and reviews about the meals. The data collected from the questionnaires showed that *Eai?* can increase the students' perception of social connections with peers, through the rating and comments about the meals. As Table 1 summarizes, the users would like to consume the information *Eai?* provides, but so far they do not show the same eagerness to provide information and collaboratively feed the application.

Table 1. Summary of the answers about the impact of *Eai?* on the habits and behavior of the user

	Choose a meal based on comments	Send information about the lines	Access the news	Rates and comments about meals
Never	13 %	40 %	18 %	22 %
Almost never	19 %	23 %	19 %	20 %
Sometimes	31 %	18 %	27 %	24 %
Almost always	29 %	13 %	21 %	21 %
Always	9 %	6 %	15 %	12 %

According to the questionnaires, 69 % of the students choose their meals based on the other users' comments about the food quality on *Eai?*. Although for 31 % of them, it is not a daily practice yet. In the second phase of the evaluation, 77 % of the participants declared that most of the times they choose a meal just when they take a look at it, and not previously. It has been the predominant behavior pattern on the UR because there was no other trustful way to choose a good meal. The number of daily accesses to *Eai?* shows that this behavior is beginning to change. We believe that illustrating the menu with actual pictures of the meals available on the day, and allowing users to send their own pictures of the UR food will help to increase the number of students who choose their meals previously, based on the comments available on *Eai?*. These were suggestions the users gave to improve their sense of reliability on the application. However, to support sending pictures in this context is a very sensitive matter and must be planned carefully, to avoid problems of deceit, embarrassment, pranks, and violation of privacy.

The questionnaires' data showed that 63 % of the *Eai?* users access the News feature (Table 1). The second investigation explained that users access the News while waiting on the lines, or when they are having meals by themselves. However, among the new users, 26.5 % think that this feature is out of context in the application, and 52.9 % said they would not use it often. Sending information about the lines, and rating/commenting about the meals are crucial functionalities for the proper working of *Eai?*. While 57 % of the users send information about their meals, 63 % declare that they do not send information about the lines (Table 1). The observations and contextual interviews showed that 91,2 % of the users found such features useful. However, they do not have the commitment to feed the application frequently. For the success of the application, it is necessary that more users will feed it with both information about the lines and the food, on a daily basis. A gamification approach could be used to stimulate the behavior of feeding the application every time a user goes to the UR. This strategy associated with real prizes and UR credits.

4.2   Research Hypothesis #2: Eai? Is Useful to Assess the Quality of the UR Service, Increasing the Student-Faculty Interactions

To analyze the perception of the students about the impact that *Eai?* brings to the student-faculty interactions, we gathered their opinion about whether the application improved: (1) the way they use the UR; (2) the collaboration among students; and (3) the communication with the University. In general, the users feel that the application has benefited them in the context of interactions with the University. As shown in Table 2, all the results are positive, and the users found *Eai?* useful to analyze the quality of the service and the food of the UR. They considered that *Eai?* increases the student-faculty interactions by improving the way how they use the UR (76 %), their collaboration with one another (68 %), and their communication with the University (53 %). To promote a better communication with the University, the application can aggregate a feature for feedback from the UR staff about changes in the menu based on the students requests and opinions, showing how the University listens and support them.

Table 2. Summary of the answers related to the expectations and perceptions of the users

	The way you use the restaurant	Your collaboration with other students	Your communication with the University
Nothing changed	0 %	3 %	6 %
Changed a little	6 %	11 %	6 %
No opinion	19 %	18 %	36 %
Improved	47 %	45 %	39 %
Improved a lot	29 %	23 %	14 %

4.3 Research Hypothesis #3: To Provide Tools like Forum and News Related to the University Positively Impacts Student's Sense of Belonging to the Institution

Eai? provides a forum that intends to enhance students' social connections with peers, while the News feed is supposed to complement their connection with the faculty. A valuable and healthy social connection between student peers and with faculty may enhance students' sense of belonging to the institution [2]. During the focus groups, we discussed the quality of these tools from the students' point of view, and their perception of the benefits of using both the forum and the News. The answer varies according to the student's experience with the UR, and their use of the application. Overall, the forum and the News to enhance the students sense of belonging to the institution. However, the students declared that after fixing some interaction problems, the forum and the News would be able to help to reduce the feeling that the faculty board is far from the students. Also, they affirmed that whenever their discussion topics would become a subject of interest to the alumni and faculty staff, they would feel empowered, and an active part of the community. Some students suggested that the application should also provide an easy way for the students to get in touch with the ombudsman's office of the University.

The forum named *Boca no Trombone* is a virtual space where the students can expose their concerns and give feedback about the UR and other University services. However, during the evaluations, we realized that neither the users nor the new potential users were able to find this functionality in the application interface. It occurred because the forum was misplaced as if it was a category of News. This error explained the few comments existing until then in the forum. When introduced to the forum and explained about its purpose, the students were unanimous stating that is a feature they would certainly use, especially if they would receive any feedback from the faculty staff.

There are two categories of news available in the application: general and university-related. The users can comment and like the news using the same profile they use to comment and rate the meals. Although 76 % of the students classified it as easy to use, they suggested unifying the news, not to limit the number of characters of a comment, to offer options to edit and delete, and to provide clearer feedback that the comment was submitted. There were discrepancies about the News functionality, according to the user profiles. Among the current users, 63 % uses the News feature regularly. However, 52.9 % of the potential new users said they would not use this function often, despite they are very interested in using the other features of *Eai?*. We believe that the News tend to become more important to the users as they incorporate the use of *Eai?* to their daily routine.

5   Conclusion and Future Work

In this paper, we introduced *Eai?*, a mobile social application aiming to empower college students and to increase the student-faculty interaction. It allows the students to expose their opinion on the service provided by the University Restaurant, and to discuss other relevant topics. We also reported and discussed an evaluation of usability and user experience of this application. The results indicate that, although some improvements are necessary, *Eai?* is useful to assess the quality of the UR service, and can positively impact the students' behavior, and sense of belonging to the institution. The application can evolve according to the needs of users and to provide a pleasant and efficient use. A future work should include correcting the usability issues, improving the News and Forum features, incorporating a gamification strategy, and developing versions to other mobile operating systems.

The sense of belonging to a greater community can improve people's motivation, health, and happiness. In the case of students, a sense of belonging to the institution ultimately can lead to greater classroom engagement in reasoning activities [2]. However, to build a sense of belonging requires active effort and practice. There must exist a cooperation between the students and the University. While the institution provides and maintains an application carefully developed to enhance student's daily routine, the students have to commit to feeding the application frequently, instead of just expect to consume the information. In this sense, the success of the application depends on the interaction within the user community.

References

1. Stebletonand, M.J., Aleixo, M.B.: Examining undocumented latino/a student interactions with faculty and institutional agents. J. Hisp. High. Educ. **14**, 256–273 (2015). doi:10.1177/1538192715574097
2. Kim, Y.K., Lundberg, C.A.: A structural model of the relationship between student–Faculty interaction and cognitive skills development among college students. Res. High. Educ. **57**, 288–309 (2015). New York, NY, USA
3. Smith,M.A.: Who Cares? Student-Faculty Interaction at a Research University, Maryland, USA (2015). doi:10.13016/M2Q04P
4. Aschoff, F.R., Novak, J.: The mobile forum: real-time information exchange in mobile sms communities. In: Extended Abstracts on Human Factors in Computing Systems (CHI 2008), Florence, Italy, pp. 3489–3494. ACM (2008)
5. Jung,Y., Blom, J., Persson, P.: Scent field trial: understanding emerging social interaction. In: Proceedings of the 8th Conference on Human-Computer Interaction with Mobile Devices and Services (MobileHCI 2006), pp. 69–76. ACM, New York (2006)
6. Heyer, C., Brereton, M., Viller, S.: Cross-channel mobile social software: an empirical study. In: Proceedings of the SIGCHI Conference on Human Factors in Computing Systems, Florence, Italy, pp. 1525–1534. ACM (2008). doi:10.1145/1357054.1357294

7. Lewis, J.R.: Psychometric evaluation of the computer system usability questionnaire: The CSUQ (Technical report 54.723). International Business Machines Corporation, Boca Raton, FL (1992a)
8. Chin, J.P., Diehl, V.A., Norman, K.L.: Development of an instrument measuring user satisfaction of the human-computer interface. In: Proceedings of the SIGCHI Conference on Human Factors in Computing Systems, pp. 213–218. ACM, Washington (1988). EUA
9. Sánchez, J.: Final User Questionnaire for Usability Evaluation of Websites. Usability evaluation test. University of Chile (2004)

Automatic Adaptation Techniques to Increase the Web Accessibility for Blind Users

Mexhid Ferati[1](✉) and Lirim Sulejmani[2]

[1] Oslo and Akershus University College of Applied Sciences, Oslo, Norway
mexhid.ferati@hioa.no
[2] South East European University, Skopje, Macedonia
ls20522@seeu.edu.mk

Abstract. Despite the available guidelines and tools to build accessible websites, many still fail to be accessible and usable by the blind users. Web content adaptation has been used as an approach to enhance website accessibility by applying automatic transformation techniques. We describe here a system that automatically increases webpage accessibility by applying three different techniques: link enrichment, image enrichment, and navigation enrichment. Preliminary evaluation of these techniques reveals that the prototype successfully eliminates half of the accessibility errors identified by validating tools and it performs equally well regardless of the accessibility compliance level of the website.

Keywords: Web accessibility · Blind users · Content adaptation · Client-side

1 Introduction and Background

The Internet is becoming an increasingly important resource for education, employment, commerce, health care, and recreation. To ensure easy access and equal opportunity to disabled people, web content should be accessible by being compliant with the requirements of the Web Content Accessibility Guidelines (WCAG). Most websites, however, do not fulfill the WCAG requirements, which causes blind users to suffer when accessing and navigating digital content [4]. This often causes blind users to rely on help from others instead of having the ability to independently complete their tasks, which limits their active participation in the society [5].

Being aware of the difficulties blind users face when accessing the Web, inspired from this study [6], we have built a middleware solution that automatically increases website accessibility by implementing certain adaptation techniques. Previous studies have shown that webpage adaptation can be conducted on the server, intermediary or client-side level [2]. We adopt the later approach by developing an extension that will be installed on a web browser to automatically transform the webpages into more accessible version. The extension will initially check the website for accessibility errors, and then depending on the errors found, it applies one or more of the following techniques: link enrichment, image enrichment, and navigation enrichment technique.

© Springer International Publishing Switzerland 2016
C. Stephanidis (Ed.): HCII 2016 Posters, Part II, CCIS 618, pp. 30–36, 2016.
DOI: 10.1007/978-3-319-40542-1_5

Preliminary evaluation of these techniques reveals that the prototype successfully eliminates half of the accessibility errors identified by validating tools and it performs equally well regardless of the accessibility compliance level of the website.

2 Adaptation Approach

In order to increase the accessibility of websites, we implemented three techniques that automatically adapt the web content to improve navigation and access to information. These techniques provide adaptation of three entities: links, images, and skipping to the main content.

2.1 Link Enrichment

Very often links found on websites lack appropriate labelling that makes them invisible to screen readers and consequently inaccessible to blind users. For example, the webpage shown in Fig. 1 contains an image that is also a link. As identified by the accessibility validator, the link lacks a text that could be accessible to screen readers. On the left side, it is shown the webpage with one error listed related to the link, while on the right side the error is eliminated after the adaptation is applied.

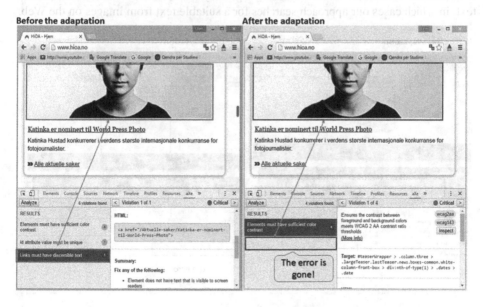

Fig. 1. A before and after depiction of a link enrichment adaptation

This technique begins by checking all hyperlinks on the page whether they lack any text or use a generic description such as 'read more', 'learn more' or 'click here'. If such hyperlink is found, then it checks whether it leads within that same page or to another page. In cases when the link leads within the page, the heading text of that part is included as an alternate text. If the link leads to another page, the text from the title or the heading of that page is used.

This approach provides an ARIA7 label to enable links to be visible by screen readers [1]. This will automatically add an *aria-labelledby* attribute inside an 'a' tag with brief content taken from the section where the link is pointing, as described above. This will help blind users get more information of the page or section and help them make a decision whether to visit before engaging the link. Moreover, this will display the same text in the links list, which is useful when screen reader users browse by links.

2.2   Image Enrichment

Providing an alternative text to images constitutes the first principles of web accessibility comprised in Guideline 1.1 Text Alternatives from WCAG 2.0 [8]. Despite this guideline requirement, only 39.6 % of images found on the homepages of the 500 most high-traffic websites, were assigned alternative text [3].

Our approach starts by identifying all images on a given page that lack an alternative text description. Once those images are identified, we initially check whether there is any text embedded in the image itself, similar to study [3]. The image is scanned using Optical Character Recognition (OCR) technique in Microsoft OneNote [9] to find any text, which is then added to the alternative tag. Very often, however, images contain no text, in which cases our approach searches for a suitable text from images on the Web.

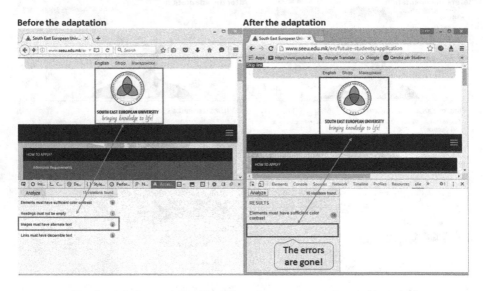

Fig. 2.   A before and after depiction of an image enrichment adaptation

To achieve this, we need to find similar images on Google and then use their description as a text for the alternative text. Since the Google Image Search API [10] is deprecated, we follow a work around by using the Imgur API [11]. The image lacking the alternative text is uploaded on imgur.com from where we obtain a unique URL. This

URL then is sent as a parameter to look for similar images on Google Images. Once such image is found, its description then is used as a text for the alternative tag of the image. Figure 2 on the left side shows two images found without an alternate text, while on the right side those two errors are eliminated after the adaptation is applied.

2.3 Navigation Enrichment

This technique enables blind users to easily skip to the main content of the page. This technique is created by automatically providing a link, usually invisible and only accessible by screen readers, called skip link. By engaging the skip link, blind users can bypass on listening to the navigation menu each time they load the page and just jump to the main content of the page [13]. Our approach will detect whether a webpage has the skip link implemented and if not, then it will be added at the top of the page. An example is depicted in Fig. 3, which shows that when the provided skip link is engaged, the two sections ('hioa-toolbar' and 'top') highlighted in red (box A) are skipped and focus moves into the main content highlighted in yellow (box B).

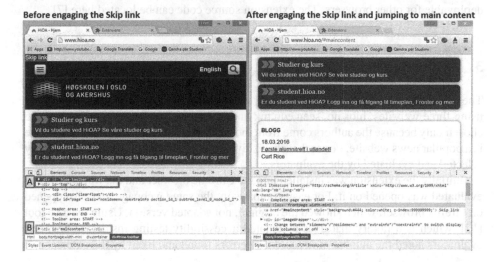

Fig. 3. A before and after engaging the skip link and jumping to the page's main content

2.4 Architecture and Implementation Details

The architecture and process of webpage adaptation starts by feeding the webpage into the Chrome extension (step 1), which calls the Web API (step 2). The webpage content then is gathered by the Web API and it triggers the Adaptation Plugin (step 3), which contains the adaptation knowledge base. Once the adaptation is finished, the result is sent back to the Chrome extension (step 4), which displays the webpage on the browser in an adapted, more accessible form (step 5). This process is depicted in Fig. 4.

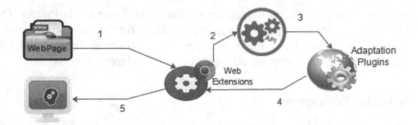

Fig. 4. The architecture and the process of webpage adaptation

The prototype extension for this study was developed using Visual C# along with Microsoft SQL Server 2012. Additionally, JavaScript and jQuery were used along with HTML5 and CSS3. The HTML Agility Pack was used for parsing html code from the webpages. The Chrome Extension was used to make the extension for the Chrome browser, although other browser's extensions can easily be used to make the prototype deployable for other browsers. The extension source code can be located here [7].

3   Evaluation

The evaluation of the adaptation techniques was conducted by two accessibility experts using three websites: hioa.no, seeu.edu.mk and bbc.com. The first two websites were chosen only because the authors come from those academic institutions and the last one is a popular news website. For each website, five random webpages were independently selected and evaluated by the evaluators.

Initially the extension was installed into the Chrome browser and the webpage being evaluated was opened on it. For easy comparison, the same webpage was also opened on Firefox browser, which showed the original, not adapted version. Using the aXe tool [12], which is a library that does automated accessibility testing inside the browser, evaluators noted the number of accessibility errors found and fixed by the extension.

3.1   Findings and Discussion

Preliminary findings of the evaluation reveal that the three adaptation techniques successfully identify and fix almost all link and image related errors found by the aXe accessibility validation tool. As shown on Fig. 5, the highest number of errors were found and fixed in the seeu.edu.mk website. Especially, the image enrichment technique had the highest impact by finding 51 errors and fixing 50 of those in ten random webpages. The lowest number of errors and fixes were found in the bbc.com website, which already scored high in accessibility. Similarly, the hioa.no website had minimal number of errors found and fixed.

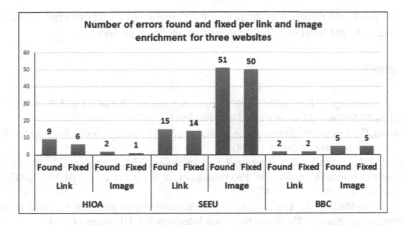

Fig. 5. The SEEU website with highest number of errors found and fixed

Our extension was successful in fixing 19 % (78 out of 421) of total errors found by the aXe tool. This tool, however, by default also identifies errors concerning the level of color contrast on the webpages (257 errors). Since color contrast affects only partially sighted and not the blind (our target users), disregarding this type of error, increases the percentage of fixed errors to 48 % (78 out of 164). In addition, considering that the lack of skip links is not identified as an error by the aXe tool, but our extension adds it when missing, the percentage of fixed errors raises to over 50 %. Hence, we could claim that our techniques successfully eliminate half of all the blind user related accessibility errors found on websites. Some of the errors not addressed by our extension include: *frames must have unique title attribute, documents must have title element to aid in navigation,* and *form elements must have labels.*

4   Conclusion, Limitations and Future Work

In this paper, we presented a browser extension that automatically increases website accessibility using three adaptive techniques: link enrichment, image enrichment, and navigation enrichment. The link enrichment technique fixes links found on a website that lack or provide only generic description. The image enrichment technique locates images that lack alternative text and adds a description. Navigation enrichment technique adds a skip to main content link to every page lacking such feature.

Preliminary evaluation of these techniques with three websites showed that the implemented adaptation techniques successfully eliminate half of all accessibility errors identified by validating tools that relate to blind users. The prototype works well for all types of websites, regardless of their compliance level of accessibility, although it performs significantly slower the more images the webpage contains. For the majority of webpages we tested, it usually took between 5 and 15 s.

In the future, we aim to improve our tool initially to identify reasons why some of the errors identified were not fixed. Additionally, we will work on optimizing the algorithm to decrease the time requires the webpage adaptation to be performed. Finally, a more thorough and rigorous evaluation will be conducted with both experts and blind users to measure the level of appropriateness of the fixes performed.

References

1. ARIA7 Techniques for WCAG 2.0. https://www.w3.org/WAI/GL/2015/WD-WCAG20-TECHS-20150106/ARIA7. Accessed 05 April 2016
2. Asakawa, C., Takagi, H.: Transcoding. In: Harper, S., Yesilada, Y. (eds.) Web Accessibility, pp. 231–260. Springer, London (2008)
3. Bigham, J.P., Kaminsky, R.S., Ladner, R.E., Danielsson, O.M., Hempton, G.L.: WebInSight: making web images accessible. In: Proceedings of the 8th International ACM SIGACCESS, pp. 181–188 (2006)
4. Di Blas, N., Paolini, P., Speroni, M.: Usable accessibility to the Web for blind users. In: Proceedings of 8th ERCIM Workshop: User Interfaces for All, Vienna (2004)
5. Hollier, S.E.: The disability divide: a study into the impact of computing and internet-related technologies on people who are blind or vision impaired. GLADNET Collection (2007)
6. Mbipom, G., Harper, S.: The transition from web content accessibility guidelines 1.0 to 2.0: what this means for evaluation and repair. In: Proceedings of the 27th ACM SIGDOC, pp. 37–44 (2009)
7. Extension source code. https://github.com/lirimsulejmani/adaptivetechnology
8. Text Alternatives, Understanding Guideline 1.1, WCAG 2.0. https://www.w3.org/TR/UNDERSTANDING-WCAG20/text-equiv.html. Accessed 05 April 2016
9. Extract text from pictures using OCR in OneNote. https://support.office.com/en-us/article/Extract-text-from-pictures-and-file-printouts-by-using-OCR-in-OneNote-93a70a2f-ebcd-42dc-9f0b-19b09fd775b4. Accessed 05 April 2016
10. Google Image Search API. http://developers.google.com/image-search. Accessed 05 April 2016
11. Imgur API. https://api.imgur.com/. Accessed 05 April 2016
12. aXe: the Accessibility Engine. http://www.deque.com/products/axe/. Accessed 05 April 2016
13. Techniques for WCAG 2.0, G1: Adding a link at the top of each page that goes directly to the main content area. https://www.w3.org/TR/WCAG20-TECHS/G1. Accessed 07 April 2016

Research the Role of Interactivity on ACG Website Usage Behavior Through Information Search Perspective: A Comparison of Experiential and Goal-Directed Behaviors

Juihsiang Lee[(⊠)]

Department of Digital Multimedia Design,
China University of Technology, Taipei, Taiwan
leockmail@gmail.com

Abstract. The purpose of this study is to examine the relationships between three dimensions of interactivity (user control, responsiveness and connectedness) and consumers' perceived value composed of utilitarian, hedonic and socialness on ACG resources searching, finally determining the level of overall satisfaction on using interactivity features in ACG portable site service. A pilot test to purify the items of questionnaire. And then confirmatory factor analysis will implicate on the second stage for model evaluation and modification.

Keywords: ACG · Perceived interactivity · Goal-directed · Experiential

1 Introduction

Along with the rapid growth of the Internet, online information search has become a prevalent Internet activity. The Internet is by definition an interactive medium (Rust and Varki 1996). Despite the potential for interactivity provided by the Internet, little attention has been paid to how interactivity might be more fully utilized (Johnson et al. 2006).

Drawing upon the affordances of digital representation of self in ACG website, participants assume the role of social actor in order to problem solve and achieve goals. The social dynamics in ACG website have led to the emergence of a broad range of sociocultural norms and artifacts, social structures and hierarchies, as well as social roles that impact users' behavior. However, little is known regarding how social behavior emerges within these environments and what factors contribute to such behavior.

ACG products and services are seldom routine purchases (Lee and You 2014). Choices of ACG products usually involve considerable emotional significance and perceived cost risk for the individual. Prior studies investigate factors that affect consumer preferences in online shopping websites. And, seldom distinguish between pre-purchase and post-purchase experiences and tend to focus on post-purchase assessment only. Therefore, this study aimed at the Internet users' searching behavior, and further probed into users' socialness of websites satisfaction.

© Springer International Publishing Switzerland 2016
C. Stephanidis (Ed.): HCII 2016 Posters, Part II, CCIS 618, pp. 37–43, 2016.
DOI: 10.1007/978-3-319-40542-1_6

2   Literature Review

2.1   Web Interactivity

Srinivasan et al. (2002, p. 42) operationalize interactivity as the availability and effectiveness of customer support tools on a website, and the degree to which two-way communication with customers is facilitated. Perceived interactivity is measured by user evaluations of the interactivity of the evaluated website using the Measures of Perceived Interactivity (MPI) based on previous researches.

Lee (2005) identified (1) user control, (2) responsiveness, (3) personalization, and (4) connectedness as important components to interactivity in a mobile commerce setting has particular relevance to the current work. We adopt these three components: user control, responsiveness, connectedness, to fit on the website environment. User control refers to the user's ability to control the information display and content. Responsiveness refers to the site as being able to respond to user queries. Finally, perceived connectedness refers to whether customers share experiences regarding products or services offered with other visitors to the mobile site.

2.2   Consequence of Perceived Interactivity

Users visit websites not only for information, but also for entertainment. Utilitarian performance results from user visiting a site out of necessity rather than for recreation; therefore, this aspect of performance is judged according to whether the particular purpose is accomplished (Davis et al. 1992; Venkatesh 2000).

The hedonic aspect of Web performance is the evaluation of a website based on the assessment by users regarding the amount of fun, playfulness, and pleasure they experience or anticipate from the site. It reflects a website's entertainment value derived from its sensory attributes, from which users obtain consummatory affective gratification (Batra and Ahtola 1990).

Thus the hypothesis formulate as follow:

Hypothesis 1a. Higher levels of user perceived interactivity will have positive evaluate on perceived utilitarian. Hypothesis 1b. Higher levels of user perceived interactivity will have positive evaluate on perceived hedonic.

Hypothesis 2a. Higher levels of user perceived utilitarian will have positive evaluate on perceived satisfaction. Hypothesis 2b. Higher levels of user perceived hedonic will have positive evaluate on perceived satisfaction.

2.3   Socialness

While B2C Internet sales continue to increase, the rate of increase in online sales is slowing. Bhatnager et al. (2000) argued that positive attitudes toward and acceptance of e-commerce may be inhibited by a lack of product 'touch'. Jahng et al. (2007) pointed out lack of interaction with a representative from the organization may be the reason, too. Wakefield et al. (2011) found that if websites infused with cues that express familiarity, helpfulness and intelligence (for example) generate a social response from users of the site can leading to greater enjoyment of the website.

Prior research has demonstrated that virtual environments are designed to promote social interaction. Moon (2000) defined social response as people tend to treat computers as social actors even when they know that machines do not possess feelings, intentions, selves, or human motivations. In this study we utilize Moon's concept of attraction (likeable, friendly, kind, helpful), reciprocity (socially appropriate sequence), intimacy to measure socialness in website interaction. Hypothesis 1c. Higher levels of user perceived interactivity will have positive evaluate on perceived socialness. Hypothesis 2c. Higher levels of user perceived socialness will have positive evaluate on perceived satisfaction.

2.4   Website Satisfaction

Satisfaction is a post-consumption evaluation based on the comparison between the expected value in the pre-consumption stage and the perceived post-consumption value after the purchase or after the use of services or products (Oliver 1981; Ravald and Gröroos 1996). This is especially true for companies selling goods and services on their websites. Customers must be satisfied with their experience with the website or they will not return. Barnes and Vidgen (2002) argues that socialness has a strong association with satisfaction, but how about it for ACG users on entertainment information still not clear. Hypothesis 1d. Higher levels of user perceived interactivity will have positive evaluate on perceived satisfaction.

2.5   Internet Users' Searching Behavior

Product information seeking often is portrayed as a critical early stage in the consumer buying process (Haubl and Trifts 2000).

Novak et al. (2003) drawing nine distinctions between goal-directed and experiential behavior is particularly important in online environments, because the experiential process is, for many individuals, as or even more important than the final instrumental result. Thus we propose hypothesis 1: goal-directed and experiential users have different online searching experience on the same ACG portal site. Hypothesis 3. Goal-directed and experiential users have differences online searching experience on ACG portal site.

3   Method

3.1   Measures

To test the hypothesis, three popular ACG portal sites ranked by alexa were selected in Taiwan. A pilot test was conducted with 148 undergraduate students from vocational universities of north Taiwan. Additionally, the interviewees' compeers who confirmed to the characteristics of cosplay groups were invited to participate in the questionnaire investigation. Two groups of goal-directed (score ≤ 21) and experiential (score ≥ 27) were differentiated with their reports score of six questions, the sample size of goal-directed is 65 the other one is 83. They all visited three selected ACG websites before.

To analyze the relationship among these variables and examine the fitness of the conceptualized framework, this study conducts Structural Equation Modeling (SEM). The questionnaire is designed in Likert 7 point scale and adjusted according to the pilot test. Participants are asked to fill in the questionnaire and indicate their current situation for each variable item (1 = strong disagreement and 7 = strong agreement).

3.2 Model Evaluation and Modification

Based on literature reviewed, a structural equation modeling was conducted to evaluate the fit of the research model (Fig. 1).

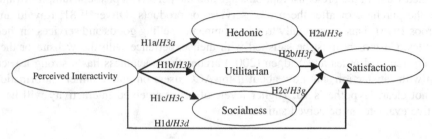

Fig. 1. Research model

4 Item Purification

Some of the measurement items may not be relevant to the scale, hence a "purification" process is needed to identify the effective items by eliminating the relationship between the individual item and the entire scale. The coefficient alpha and the item-to-total correlation for each item were computed, then the items whose item-to-total correlations were low and whose removal increased the coefficient alpha were deleted. In addition, squared multiple correlation for each item, the multiple R^2 from the regression analysis with the very item as the dependent variable and all other items as independent variables, was also computed to determine if the item should be deleted due to its low value. Thus, the internal consistency of the set of items was examined.

5 Result

After item purification by pilot test, the questionnaire is proposed as Table 1.

Table 1. Questionnaire for survey

(1) Online searching experience Items Based on (Novak et al. 2003)
Q1_1. I visit an ACG portal site, most of the reason by my extrinsic motivation or intrinsic motivation Extrinsic or Intrinsic
Q2_1. I visit an ACG portal site, cause of the reason by its instrumental orientation or my ritualized orientation Instrumental or Ritualized
Q3_1. I visit an ACG portal site, cause of the reason by its situational involvement design or my enduring involvement Situational or Enduring
Q4_1. I visit an ACG portal site, cause of the reason by its utilitarian benefits/value or hedonic benefits/value? Utilitarian or Hedonic
Q5_1. I visit an ACG portal site, cause of the reason by my directed search or non-directed browsing? Directed (pre-purchase) or Non-directed (ongoing) search
Q6_1. I visit an ACG portal site, cause of the reason by its cognitive reason or emotional affect? Goal-directed choice or Navigational choice

Construct	Question
(2) User Control	UCL1. I was in control over the content of this website that I wanted to see
	UCL2. I was in control over the information display format, condition when using this website
	UCL3. I was in control over the order of this web pages that I wanted to browse
	UCL4. I was in control over the personal homepage of this web site for my revisit next time
	UCL5. I was in control over the clips sharing what I want
(3) Responsiveness	RES1. The information shown when I interacted with the site was relevant
	RES2. The information shown when I interacted with the site was appropriate
	RES3. The information shown when I interacted with the site met my expectations
	RES4. The information shown when I interacted with the site was useful
	RES5. The information feedback instantly when I interacted with the site
(4) Connectedness	CON1. Customers share experiences about the product or service with other customers of this website
	CON2. Customers of this website benefit from the community visiting the website
	CON3. Customers share a common bond with other members of the customer community visiting the website
	CON4. Customers share opinions from the video annotation tool of this website
	CON5. Customers affect wider searching from the online discuss of this website
(5) Utilitarian	UTI1. I accomplished just what I wanted to do on this searching trip

(Continued)

Table 1. (*Continued*)

	UTI2. While searching, I found just the item(s) I was looking for UTI3. While searching, I found the information update instantly UTI4. The rankings I found has significant influence
(6) Hedonic	HED1. I continued to search online, not because I had to, but because I wanted to HED2. During online searching, I felt the excitement of the hunt HED3. During online searching, I was able to forget my problems HED4. The community discussions I found were interesting
(7) Socialness	SOL1. Attraction/likeable SOL2. Attraction/friendly SOL3. Attraction/kind SOL4. Attraction/likeable, SOL5. Reciprocity (socially appropriate sequence), SOL6. Intimacy
(8) Satisfaction (Based on Yoo et al. 2010)	SAT1. Overall of this website searching was good decision SAT2. Overall of this website searching was satisfying SAT3. Overall of this website searching was enjoyable SAT4. Overall of this website searching was easy to find information SAT5. Overall of this website service was satisfying

References

Babin, B.J., Darden, W.R., Griffen, M.: Work and/or fun: measuring hedonic and utilitarian shopping value. J. Consum. Behav. **20**, 644–656 (1994)

Barnes, S.J., Vidgen, R.T.: An integrative approach to the assessment of ecommerce. J. Electron. Commer. Res. **3**(3), 114–126 (2002)

Batra, R., Ahtola, O.: Measuring the Hedonic and Utilitarian sources of consumer attitude. Mark. Lett. **2**(2), 159–170 (1990)

Bhatnager, A., Misra, S., Rao, H.R.: On risk, convenience, and internet shopping behavior. Commun. ACM **43**(11), 98–107 (2000)

Bloch, P.H., Richens, M.L.: Shopping without purchase: an investigation of consumer browsing behavior. In: Bagozzi, R.P., Tybout, A.M. (eds.) Advances in Consumer Research, vol. 10, pp. 389–393. Association for Consumer Research, Ann Arbor (1993)

Davis, F.D., Bagozzi, R.P., Warshaw, P.R.: Extrinsic and intrinsic motivation to use computers in the workplace. J. Appl. Soc. Psychol. **22**(14), 1111–1132 (1992)

Moon, Y.: Intimate exchanges: using computers to elicit self-disclosure from consumers. J. Consum. Res. **26**, 323–339 (2000)

Novak, T.P., Hoffman, D.L., Duhachek, A.: The influence of goal-directed and experiential activities on online flow experiences. J. Consum. Psychol. **13**(1-2), 3–16 (2003)

Fornell, C., Larcker, D.F.: Evaluating structural equation models with unobservable variables and measurement error. J. Mark. Res. **18**, 39–50 (1981)

Hancock, G.R., Nevitt, J.: Bootstrapping and the identification of exogenous latent variables within structural equation models. Struct. Equ. Model. **6**, 394–399 (1999)

Haubl, G., Trifts, V.: Consumer decision making in online shopping environments: the effects of interactive decision aids. Mark. Sci. **19**(1), 4–21 (2000)

Hirschman, E.: Experience seeking: a subjectivist perspective of consumption. J. Bus. Res. **12**, 115–136 (1984)

Jahng, J., Jain, H., Ramamurthy, K.: Effects of interaction richness on consumer attitudes and behavioral intentions in e-commerce: some experimental results. Eur. J. Inf. Syst. **16**(3), 254–270 (2007)

Johnson, G.J., Bruner, G.C., Kumar, A.: Interactivity and its facets revisited. J. Advertising, **35**(4), 35–52 (2006)

Lee, J., You, M.: The role of interactivity in information search on ACG portal site. In: Nah, F.F.-H. (ed.) HCIB/HCII 2014. LNCS, vol. 8527, pp. 194–205. Springer, Switzerland (2014)

Lee, T.: The impact of perceptions of interactivity on customer trust and transaction intentions in mobile commerce. J. Electron. Commer. Res. **6**(3), 165–180 (2005)

McMillan, S.J.: The researchers and the concept: moving beyond a blind examination of interactivity. J. Interact. Advertising **5**(1) (2005). http://jiad.org

Oliver, R.L.: Measurement and evaluation of satisfaction process in retail settings. J. Retail. **57**(3), 25–48 (1981)

Ravald, A., Grönroos, C.: The value concept and relationship marketing. Eur. J. Mark. **30**(2), 19–30 (1996)

Rowley, J.: Product search in e-shopping: a review and research propositions. J. Consum. Mark. **17**(1), 20–35 (2000)

Rust, R.T., Varki, S.: Rising from the ashes of advertising. J. Bus. Res. **37**(3), 173–191 (1996)

Sangani, K.: Otaku world. Eng. Technol. **3**, 94–95 (2008)

Schlosser, A.E., Kanfer, A.: Interactivity in Commercial Web Sites: Implications for Web Site Effectiveness. Working Paper, Vanderbilt University (1999)

Srinivasan, S.S., Anderson, R., Ponnavolu, K.: Customer loyalty in ecommerce: an exploration of its antecedents and consequences. J. Retail. **78**(1), 41–50, Spring 2002

Stromer-Galley, J.: Online interaction and why candidates avoid it. J. Commun. **50**(4), 111–132 (2000)

Venkatesh, V.: Determinants of perceived ease of use: integrating perceived behavioural control, computer anxiety and enjoyment into the technology acceptance model. Infor. Syst. Res. **11**, 342–365 (2000)

Wakefield, R.L., Wakefield, K.L., Baker, J., Wang, L.C.: How website socialness leads to website use. Eur. J. Inf. Syst. **20**(1), 118–132 (2011)

Yoo, W.S., Lee, Y., Park, J.: The role of interactivity in e-tailing: creating value and increasing satisfaction. J. Retail. Consum. Ser. **17** (2010)

Criss-Crossing Idea Landscapes via Idea Networks in Knowledge Forum

Leanne Ma[✉]

Ontario Institute for Studies in Education, University of Toronto, Toronto, Canada
leanne.ma@mail.utoronto.ca

Abstract. Knowledge Building pedagogy engages students directly in continual idea improvement through progressive inquiry, with the ultimate goal of creating knowledge of value to the community. Knowledge Forum technology serves as the community space for creative work with ideas, where students design views (i.e., idea landscapes) to explore ideas, refine ideas, and synthesize ideas, with supports in place for criss-crossing these idea landscapes with ease. This study explores next-generation designs for visualizing idea landscapes in Knowledge Forum. Whereas in a typical view, explicit idea connections via build-on notes are automatically displayed, implicit idea connections via keyword tagging are not immediately accessible to students. Semantic analyses were conducted on student notes in Knowledge Forum in order to identify 'big ideas' in the student discourse and compare word cloud visualizations with idea network visualizations of the community knowledge. Implications of these designs are discussed within the context of education for knowledge creation and innovation.

Keywords: Knowledge building · Knowledge forum · Knowledge creation · Idea network · Semantic analysis · Network analysis · Data visualization

1   Introduction

The emergence and rapid proliferation of information communication technologies have drastically transformed the way in which we communicate, collaborate, and learn in our everyday lives, resulting in the rise of digital literacy as an educational priority for the 21st century (Voogt and Knezek 2008). Studies in the field of learning sciences consistently demonstrate that computer-supported collaborative learning environments facilitate students' development of traditional learning skills and new digital literacies (see Stahl et al. 2006 for review). Of particular educational importance is new competences for knowledge creation, such as generating new ideas, searching for related ideas, identifying promising ideas, developing criteria to evaluate multiple sources, and creating coherence amongst diverse ideas, in order for students to engage in knowledge creation and innovation for public good (Goldman and Scardamalia 2013). In other words, education for knowledge creation must socialize students into a pervasive culture of productive work with ideas so that they may improve their own ideas for their own learning, as well as connect to and extend the ideas of others for knowledge creation.

© Springer International Publishing Switzerland 2016
C. Stephanidis (Ed.): HCII 2016 Posters, Part II, CCIS 618, pp. 44–49, 2016.
DOI: 10.1007/978-3-319-40542-1_7

2   Current Study

2.1   Knowledge Building Pedagogy and Technology

Knowledge Building pedagogy and Knowledge Forum technology provide students with opportunities to work creatively with ideas, "exploring idea landscapes, criss-crossing them in every direction" (Scardamalia and Bereiter 2016, p. 3), which in turn facilitates the development of digital literacies and competencies essential to knowledge creation and innovation. Knowledge Building is synonymous with knowledge creation: It is the collective endeavor of advancing collective understanding through the production of knowledge of value to the community (Scardamalia and Bereiter 2014a; 2006). Much like rapid prototyping in the field of HCI design, Knowledge Building involves continual development and refinement of ideas – a process that is highly collaborative, iterative, non-linear, and ever-changing. The technological challenge is to design environments that support complex, emergent interactions and self-organization (Scardamalia and Bereiter 2014b).

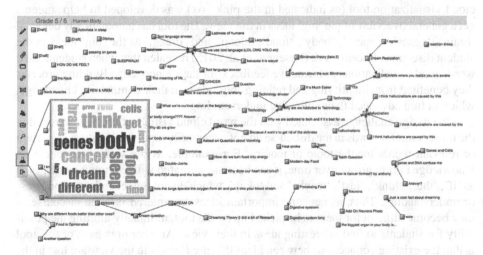

Fig. 1. Grade 5/6 human body view in knowledge forum and word cloud visualization of student discourse.

Knowledge Forum is a networked online learning environment optimized to support collaborative knowledge creation (Scardamalia 2004). In Knowledge Forum, students design idea landscapes, called views (see Fig. 1), so that their ideas have a place to live and grow. In a given view, students contribute ideas as notes, sketches, images, videos, and other multimedia, which then become objects of the community, so that other students can build on, cite, annotate, tag, and even synthesize ideas in the form of rise-above notes. Whereas in a typical view, explicit connections are made between ideas via build-ons, implicit connections, such as keyword tags, are not immediately accessible; therefore, embedding analytic tools can make such connections visible to students. Guided by the Knowledge Building principles of *epistemic agency, idea diversity*, and *rise above* (see Scardamalia 2002 for overview), this study aims to explore designs for visualizing idea landscapes in Knowledge Forum, so that students may discover hidden connections between ideas in the community knowledge and find new ways to create conceptual coherence across idea landscapes.

2.2   Knowledge Forum Next Generation Designs

When students are working in a view in Knowledge Forum, the view is synchronized in real-time as a dynamic community space. The Knowledge Building process can be visualized in real-time as the view changes when new ideas are added, existing ideas are edited, ideas are moved around and connected together, and so forth. Over time, the view can become a cluttered space, making it difficult to navigate and search for ideas. Figure 1 shows a view in Knowledge Forum for a grade 5/6 class studying the human body over the span of a week. Though it cannot be seen clearly in Fig. 1, several themes have already emerged in the student discourse, such as sleep and dreams, puberty and aging, food and digestion, cancer and illnesses, and evolutionary psychology. The word cloud visualization tool (as indicated in the pink box) was developed to help students get a general overview of the 'big' ideas in the view. The tool has automatically detected 'brain', 'genes', 'cancer', 'body', 'food', 'sleep', and 'dream' as the 'big' ideas in the student discourse. Recent work (Resendes et al. 2015) revealed that when students used word cloud visualizations as formative feedback for their Knowledge Building process, they benefited from identifying and refining 'big' ideas in their community knowledge, which in turn advanced their collective understanding.

One design challenge associated with the word cloud visualization, however, is that the most common words in the discourse do not necessarily represent the most important or relevant words for the topic of inquiry. For example, as the student discourse on Knowledge Forum grows over time, it can become saturated with common words, such as 'if', 'the', 'think', 'just', 'maybe' and 'okay', which do not reflect collective progress or understanding. Thus, as new and important ideas are entered into the discourse, it may become difficult for them to be picked up by the tool, ultimately limiting the possibility for students to find interesting ideas in their view. Another drawback of this tool is that the existing connections between ideas that are already in the view are lost in the word cloud visualization, which reduces the conceptual coherence that is already created in the view. Looking at the word cloud, it is difficult to see which 'big' ideas are connected to one another and which ones are not.

One way to address these design challenges is to create idea network visualizations of student discourse in Knowledge Forum, as shown in Fig. 2. The idea network was created based on keyword tagging of student notes, followed by thematic coding of keyword tags (see Appendix for themes and associated keywords). Whereas each circle represents one theme related to the topic of the human body, each square represents a note containing keywords related to that theme. For example, a student working on the topic of sleep can search for related ideas by clicking on the 'neuroscience' theme, which is also connected to the 'evolution' and 'nervous system' themes. Notes connected to these themes cover issues such as stages of sleep, dreams and consciousness, brain processes, and bodily growth. Whereas in Fig. 1, notes about REM, sleepwalking, dreaming, and consciousness are placed in various locations on the view, in Fig. 2, the idea network visualization, brings all these ideas together based on both explicit connections (i.e., build-ons) and implicit connections (i.e., keyword tags). This then allows students to explore and create unexpected connections between ideas. For example, the pink box in Fig. 2 shows one student's note about dreaming, which lies at the intersection of the 'neuroscience' and 'evolution' themes. Though this student is simply sharing information, their note represents a significant contribution to the community because they are reframing the discussion about the human body in terms of its evolutionary history and purpose, and in turn, advancing the collective understanding of sleep by discussing its role in the history of the human species. The ability to find and make serendipitous connections between ideas is invaluable to the Knowledge Building process, and the idea network visualization has the potential to support students in engaging creatively with ideas in Knowledge Forum.

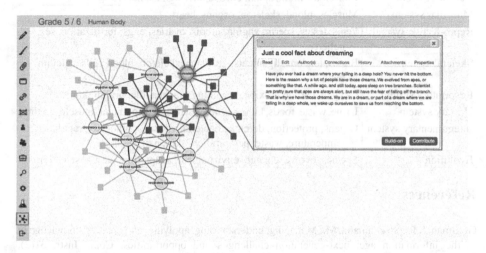

Fig. 2. Idea network visualization of Grade 5/6 human body view in Knowledge Forum and one student's note.

3 Design Implications

In this study, word cloud and idea network visualizations were designed to facilitate criss-crossing idea landscapes and connecting ideas in a view in Knowledge Forum. It is expected that "idea networks" will help students reach higher levels of explanatory coherence amongst diverse ideas in their community knowledge and support the role of serendipity in identifying promising ideas for their knowledge work – both of which are essential digital literacies for knowledge creation. Knowledge Building pedagogy and Knowledge Forum technology represent one avenue for schools to move from the periphery to the center of the Knowledge Society, preparing students to participate in the growing need to innovate and create knowledge for public good (OECD 2015).

Appendix

Table 1. Themes and keywords related to grade 5/6 human body

Theme	Keywords
Circulatory system	Blood, nutrients, oxygen, carbon dioxide, hormones, heart,, cardiac, vessels, arteries, veins
Digestive system	Organs, food, waste, mouth, esophagus, stomach, small intestine, large intestine, rectum, anus, liver, pancreas
Endocrine system	Glands, hormones, blood, regulation, metabolism, growth, sex, puberty
Immune system	Bacteria, virus, pathogens, lymph nodes, spleen, bone marrow, lymphocytes, white blood cells, infection
Nervous system	Conscious, brain, spinal cord, spine, signals, nerves
Muscular system	Muscles, blood, skeleton, organs, heart
Reproductive system	Penis, testes, sperm, vagina, uterus, ovaries, eggs, fertilization, sex, puberty
Skeletal system	Bones, tendons, ligaments, cartilage, skeleton, blood cells, calcium, teeth
Respiratory system	Oxygen, carbon dioxide, breathing, trachea, diaphragm, lungs
Urinary system	Urine, waste, foods, kidneys, ureters, bladder, sphincter, muscle, urethra
Integumentary system	Organs, protection, defense, bacteria, viruses, pathogens, regulation, temperature, waste, perspiration, skin, hair, nails
Evolution	Species, evolve, change, environment, adaptation, natural selection

References

Goldman, S.R., Scardamalia, M.: Managing, understanding, applying, and creating knowledge in the information age: next-generation challenges and opportunities. Cogn. Instr. **31**(2), 255–269 (2013)

OECD: The Innovation Imperative: Contributing to Productivity, Growth and Well-being. OECD Publishing, Paris (2015)

Resendes, M., Scardamalia, M., Bereiter, C., Chen, B., Halewood, C.: Group-level formative feedback and metadiscourse. Int. J. Comput.-Support. Collaborative Learn. **10**(3), 309–336 (2015)

Scardamalia, M.: Collective cognitive responsibility for the advancement of knowledge. In: Smith, B., Bereiter, C. (eds.) Liberal Education in a Knowledge Society, pp. 67–98. Publishers Group West, Berkeley (2002)

Scardamalia, M.: CSILE/Knowledge Forum®. In: Kovalchick, A., Dawson, K. (eds.) Education and Technology: An Encyclopedia, pp. 183–192. Santa Barbara, ABC-CLIO (2004)

Scardamalia, M., Bereiter, C.: Knowledge building: theory, pedagogy, and technology. In: Sawyer, K. (ed.) Cambridge Handbook of the Learning Sciences, pp. 97–118. Cambridge University Press, New York (2006)

Scardamalia, M., Bereiter, C.: Knowledge building and knowledge creation: theory, pedagogy, and technology. In: Sawyer, K. (ed.) Cambridge Handbook of the Learning Sciences, pp. 397–417. Cambridge University Press, New York (2014a)

Scardamalia, M., Bereiter, C.: Smart technology for self-organizing processes. Smart Learn. Environ. **2014**(1), 1 (2014b)

Scardamalia, M., Bereiter, C.: Creating, criss-crossing, and rising above idea landscapes. In: Huang, R.H., Kinshuk, A., Price, J.K. (eds.) ICT in Education in Global Context: Comparative Reports of K-12 Schools Innovation, pp. 3–17. Springer-Verlag, Berlin (2016)

Stahl, G., Koschmann, T., Suthers, D.: Computer-supported collaborative learning: An historical perspective. In: Sawyer, R.K. (ed.) Cambridge Handbook of the Learning Sciences, pp. 409–426. Cambridge University Press, Cambridge, UK (2006)

Voogt, J., Knezek, G. (eds.): International Handbook of Information Technology in Primary and Secondary Education, vol. 20. Springer Science+Business Media, New York (2008)

NatureNet: An Interaction Design with a Focus on Crowdsourcing for Community

Mary Lou Maher and Sarah Abdellahi[✉]

Software and Information Systems Department, University of North Carolina at Charlotte,
Charlotte, NC, USA
{m.maher,sabdella}@uncc.edu

Abstract. Citizen science projects adopt a crowdsourcing model for collecting and analyzing scientific data for the purpose of improving science and encouraging non-scientists to participate in science projects. For example, the iNaturalist model relies on crowds of citizen scientists to scale both the detection and identification of species from photo vouchers. EBird, as another example, crowd sources bird observation data. Both of these projects leverage community interactions for effective data collection and validation, where the data is used to support environmental sustainability research [1]. In NatureNet, the interaction design has a focus on creating an online community around informal learning about environmental sustainability issues and on engaging the community to extend and customize the design of the technology to better support their environmental sustainability projects.

Keywords: Crowdsourced design · Citizen science · Sustainability

1 Introduction

NatureNet is a citizen science project that creates community around informal learning about environmental sustainability issues and engages the community to customize the design of the technology to better support their environmental sustainability projects. NatureNet is deployed via a multi-platform application delivered on a multi-user, touch-based tabletop display, smart phones, and a web site [7]. The NatureNet mobile app allows a park naturalist or visitor to record biodiversity data while in the park. The biodiversity data collected by individuals through the mobile app are loaded into a database and can be viewed and discussed by other visitors and naturalists on the website in addition to on the tabletop station in the park.

What distinguishes NatureNet from other biodiversity projects such as iNaturalist or eBird is its focus on community and the crowd's participation in both scientific contributions and design of the technology used by the online community.

In NatureNet, creative development of the design happens by individuals suggesting design ideas for extending or modifying the features of the interaction design or adding new features of the system, commenting and having discussions around the ideas and voting on the ideas. Based on a synthesis of crowdsourced comments and votes, strong

© Springer International Publishing Switzerland 2016
C. Stephanidis (Ed.): HCII 2016 Posters, Part II, CCIS 618, pp. 50–55, 2016.
DOI: 10.1007/978-3-319-40542-1_8

ideas are selected by the design team and integrated into the next version of the platform [3–5].

While a great amount of crowdsourcing literature has focused on crowdsourcing as a strategy to either collect scientific data or collect designs, what we focus on in NatureNet is forming community around the science projects as well as the design of NatureNet system. This will enable the users of online communities to iteratively re-design the community platform and projects to meet their latest needs and improve collaboration in their field of interest [2].

NatureNet is being deployed in three communities focused on environmental sustainability: NatureNet for ACES, a community of visitors to the Aspen Center for Environmental Studies in Aspen Colorado. NatureNet for AWS, a community focused on protection of Anacostia watershed in Maryland. NatureNet for Reedy Creek, a community of Reedy Creek Park visitors in Charlotte North Carolina.

In the following sections, we present the NatureNet platform design and how the design elements support different types of collaboration to serve the online community dynamics.

2   NatureNet Interaction Design

A quick look at different types of services provided in form of crowdsourcing highlights the difference between NatureNet and other citizen science projects. Vuković [6] categorized the way crowdsourcing platforms manage needs into two general groups, "Crowdsourced Function" and "Crowdsourcing Mode". Crowdsourced function represents the part of the product and/or service lifecycle that is being crowdsourced. Crowdsourced function may take one of the following forms: design, development and testing, data collection, marketing and sales and support. The second category of crowdsourcing activities is Crowdsourcing mode. Crowdsourcing mode identifies whether a decision is acceptable by potential users or not. Crowdsourced mode includes voting and evaluation provided by crowd as is commonly used in marketplace and competitions.

2.1   NatureNet and Crowdsourced Function

The crowdsourced function of data collection has been regularly used in citizen science projects. As an example, eBird utilizes volunteers to collect observations of birds. The crowdsourcing function of design engages the creativity of crowds. Members of the crowd can contribute their own design ideas, before the design team proceeds with new product development.

Crowdsourced function in form of design is way of doing business among enterprises such as Threadless.com. The crowd is responsible for contributing t-shirt designs before mass production [6]. In Threadless, the crowdsourced mode includes comments for evaluating a design and voting for a design.

NatureNet includes crowdsourced functions of design and scientific data gathering. NatureNet data gathering happens with contributions to observation activities and design happens with contributions of design ideas. Figure 1 shows the part of the web site in which users can review projects and contributions. The community can also explore the crowd's contributions via an interactive map, as shown in Fig. 2. The map feature allows the crowd members to explore other's contributions that are located nearby. This feature is developed as environmental matters and activities in an individual's local environment would be more perceptible and motivating for them to contribute with the community.

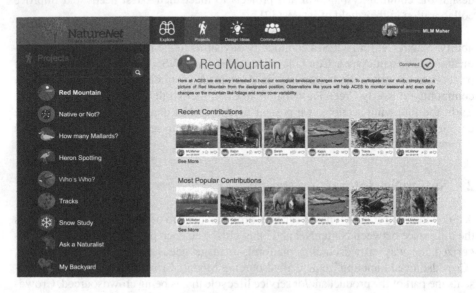

Fig. 1. NatureNet projects and associated contributions

The website and mobile app design include a specific section called "design ideas", shown in Fig. 3, where community members can suggest new design features, changes in the technical platform, new projects, or even suggest new ways to use NatureNet. One of the main considerations in design of NatureNet platform is having this design idea section easily accessible all over the platform. This allows users to see design as one of the main contributions from the community and not a side activity. In addition, the platform facilitates description of design ideas for non-designer crowd members by allowing them to upload pictures to describe their ideas, and providing them examples of design ideas created by NatureNet design team and/or other visitors.

Fig. 2. NatureNet interactive map feature for location base exploration of observations

Fig. 3. Design ideas section on NatureNet website

2.2 NatureNet and Crowdsourced Mode

In NatureNet, crowdsourced mode is developed to facilitate community formation and cohesion by encouraging the community members to collaborate around their own projects and design ideas. The crowd can influence which design ideas are to be implemented for their own use. The design idea section of the website and mobile application allow users to comment, like, or dislike ideas submitted by other members of the community. The voting process helps the community members to feel they can be involved in community decision making even if it is through very small contributions such as liking a design idea (Fig. 4).

Fig. 4. Voting and commenting functionalities available to discuss community design ideas on NatureNet platform.

In addition to feedback on the submitted ideas, NatureNet users have the option to like or comment on the observations submitted by others. These likes and comments are sources for NatureNet naturalists to know which activities were more interesting for the community, and what is crowd's understanding of different environmental topics. Based on this, they can decide what new activities could be of benefit, and what sort of information should be provided to the visitors of the Nature preserve or online community.

Finally, project and design submissions with highest number of contributions are displayed in different places on NatureNet website. This works as a motivation for community members for more collaboration around the activities as it gives them the feeling their contributions are important and would be seen by other members of the community.

3   Discussion

NatureNet is a citizen science project which encourages the crowd not only to participate in environmental data collection and validation, but also in developing community around learning about environmental sustainability and contributing to the design of the interaction for community awareness [8].

The benefits to the crowdsourcing model defined by the NatureNet project as a citizen science project are:

- Create a community of people around environmental sustainability activities.
- The community becomes a stakeholder of the system by playing a role in the design and development, thereby engaging them to contribute more towards its success.
- The community feels at home for having a say in designing the system for their activities.
- The system design is dynamic and open for the community to change as new needs or interests arise.
- The overlap among the designers and community members reduces the gap between the user and designer mental models.

Acknowledgements. NatureNet is funded by the National Science Foundation (IIS-1221513) in a grant to the University of North Carolina at Charlotte, the University of Maryland, and the University of Colorado. We thank our colleagues Carol Boston, Jennifer J. Preece, Tom Yeh, Kazjon Grace, Jin Goog Kim, Jinyue Xia, Mohammad J. Mahzoon, Marina Cascaes, Abigale Stangle, Tammy Clegg, Travis Christian, Daniel Pauw, Jacqueline Cameron, Naturalists at ACES,

Naturalist at Reedy Creek Park Charlotte, and Naturalists at Anacostia watershed in Maryland, who provided insight and expertise that greatly assisted the design of NatureNet and this research.

References

1. Bonter, D.N., Cooper, C.B.: Data validation in citizen science: a case study from project FeederWatch. Front. Ecol. Environ. **10**(6), 305–307 (2012)
2. Grace, K., Maher, M.L., Preece, J., Yeh, T., Stangle, A., Boston, C.: A process model for crowdsourcing design: a case study in citizen science. In: Gero, J.S., Hanna, S. (eds.) Design Computing and Cognition 2014, pp. 245–262. Springer International Publishing, Switzerland (2015)
3. Maher, M.L., Preece, J., Yeh, T., Boston, C., Grace, K., Pasupuleti, A., Stangl, A.: NatureNet: a model for crowdsourcing the design of citizen science systems. In: Proceedings of the Companion Publication of the 17th ACM Conference on Computer Supported Cooperative Work & Social Computing, pp. 201–204. ACM (2014)
4. Preece, J., Boston, C., Yeh, T., Cameron, J., Maher, M., Grace, K.: Enticing casual nature preserve visitors into citizen science via photos. Extended Abstract and Poster to be presented at: Conference on Computer-Supported Cooperative Work and Social Computing, San Francisco, 29 February 2016
5. Preece, J., Boston, C., Maher, M., Grace, K., Yeh, T.: From crowdsourcing design to participatory design and back again! Paper to be presented at: European Conference on Social Media, Caen, France, 12–13 July 2016
6. Vuković, M.: Crowdsourcing for enterprises. In: 2009 World Conference on Services-I, July 2009, pp. 686–692. IEEE (2009)
7. NatureNet citizen science platform for the public to participate in NatureNet project. http://www.nature-net.org
8. Research conducted under NatureNet grant. http://research.nature-net.org/

Estimation Models of User Skills Based on Web Search Logs

Asuka Miyake$^{(\boxtimes)}$, Yuji Morinishi, and Masahiro Watanabe

NTT Service Evolution Laboratories, Kanagawa, Japan
{miyake.asuka,morinishi.yuji,watanabe.masahiro}@lab.ntt.co.jp

Abstract. The number of Internet users has been increasing in Japan, especially the elderly. Even though there are differences in the skills of the elderly, no effective method of personalizing the user interface to suit skill level has been proposed. To solve this problem, conventionally, questionnaires or tests are used to evaluate user skills, but users find them burdensome. In order to evaluate user skills automatically, we focus on the logs of user operations. This study uses machine learning to build models that can estimate skill level from operation logs on tablet PC. First, we investigate and identify the 6 key skills necessary for effective Web search. Second, the skill evaluation tasks and the Web search tasks are created and then performed by elderly users. During the Web search tasks, the operation logs such as screen touch behavior are gathered by the Web browser. Finally, decision tree-based estimation models of the 6 skills are built. The results confirm that models can very accurately estimate skill level.

Keywords: Skill · Operation logs · Tablet PC · Decision tree

1 Introduction

The number of Internet users continues to increase in Japan, especially the elderly. Due to individual differences such as experience and cognitive ability, it is essential that we provide personalized user interfaces, or recommend services that suit the user's skills. To achieve it, we urgently need efficient method of evaluating the user's skills. However, unfortunately, the conventional approach of using questionnaires or tests are not user friendly. In order to evaluate the user's skills without burden and automatically, we focus on the logs of user operations.

Previous studies have examined Web search and estimated user satisfaction [1], success or lostness [2] from the logs of user operations. However, few studies have attempted to estimate skill level from these logs. Our solution is to use machine learning to build estimation models of the skills from operation logs. We focus on the situation in which evermore elderly people will use tablet PCs for online shopping. This study will lead to the personalization of user interface to suit skill level.

© Springer International Publishing Switzerland 2016
C. Stephanidis (Ed.): HCII 2016 Posters, Part II, CCIS 618, pp. 56–62, 2016.
DOI: 10.1007/978-3-319-40542-1_9

2 Definitions of Skills

In this study, we identify the 6 key skills necessary for effective Web search based on previous studies as shown below.

Attitude. Attitude toward technology, in particular, anxiety and self-efficacy affect the breadth of Web use [3]. Having a positive attitude and trust toward the Web are necessary for using Web sites.

Experience. Web experience is correlated with Web search performance [4]. If users use the Web for a long time and frequently, they can search information efficiently by using correct knowledge and an appropriate mental model.

Spatial Ability. Spatial ability is generally defined as the ability to perceive and transform visual patterns [5]. Many previous studies showed that spatial ability is related to Web search performance [4,6–8].

Processing Speed. Processing speed is defined as the ability to acquire, interpret, and respond to information quickly and accurately. Many previous studies showed processing speed is related to Web search performance [4,6–8].

Working Memory. Working memory is the active storage and manipulation of information to perform a task. Many previous studies showed working memory is related to Web search performance [4,6–8].

Motor Ability. Motor ability is the ability to move hands or fingers quickly and accurately. Takahashi et al. reported that motor ability is related to Web search performance [7].

3 Experiment

We conducted an experiment to give participants the labels of skill level and to obtain the operation logs. We recruited participants who were not biased against the use of Information and Communication Technology. 16 elderly people, 10 men and 6 women participated in the experiment. Ages ranged from 65 to 75 years. All participants have a computer, 6 participants have either smartphone or tablet PC. 6 participants have online shopping experience.

Participants operated tablet PC (8.9 inch Android Nexus9, 320 dpi) on their lap. During the experiment, audio and video were recorded for later analysis. The experiment consisted of 3 parts: (1) Operational practice on the tablet PC (2) Skill evaluation task (3) Web search task.

3.1 Skill Evaluation Task

In order to give participants the labels of skill level, evaluation tasks were created and then performed by the participants.

Attitude. Participants completed an Internet attitude questionnaire [9] that was translated into Japanese. Attitude towards Internet was tested using 40 questions with a 4-point Likert-type response scale (for instance, "I have never been frustrated with Internet. Strongly disagree = 1, Disagree = 2, Agree = 3, and Strongly Agree = 4"). A higher score indicated a more positive attitude.

Experience. Participants completed a WWW experience questionnaire [4,6] translated into Japanese. Experience was measured by 4 questions: the number of hours per week spent using the WWW, the number of years of WWW experience, the number of Web sites developed, and the number of different Web sites visited per week. Principal components analysis was conducted and it produced one significant component that accounted for 80 % of the variance in all the questions. A higher score based on component loadings indicated more experience.

Spatial Ability. Spatial ability was measured using the ETS Cube Comparison test and the ETS Paper Folding test [5]. The Cube Comparison test consists of drawings of pairs of cubes. Participants compare the two cubes and judge whether the two are the same or different. The Paper Folding test consists of drawings of square piece of paper being fold and punched. Participants decided which unfolded paper is correct. The mean of each individual's normalized score on these tests was used as an index of spatial ability.

Processing Speed. The visual search task was used to measure processing speed as previous study [7]. A double conjunction (Shape: circle or square × Color: blue or orange) visual search task was performed in 36 trials on the tablet PC. Participants searched and tapped a target object with a unique feature (for instance, the orange circle is the target in Fig. 1a). If the target was absent, participants tapped an absence button. A target was present in 50 % of trials, and display size was set at a constant 11 elements. Mean reaction time on target-present trials was used as an index of processing speed.

Working Memory. Working memory was estimated with a reading span test following study [7]. Participants were told to read aloud a series of Japanese sentences (2–4 sentences) and remember a target word (bold, underlined) in each sentence at the same time. Task was performed in 10 trials using 30 sentences. The number of words correctly recalled was used as an index of working memory.

Motor Ability. Motor ability was measured on the tablet PC (see Fig. 1b) following study [7]. Participants tapped two targets labeled "1", "2" in order as fast as possible in 72 trials. Target size was 30, 40, or 50 px, and distance between the two targets was 300, 400, or 500 px. Mean time from target 1 tapped to target 2 tapped was used as an index of motor ability.

3.2   Web Search Task

In order to obtain the operation logs, Web search tasks were created and then performed by the participants. We developed an online shopping Web site for tablet PC use that provides daily necessities (see Fig. 2). The Web site had 4 layer structure and included navigation menu, breadcrumb list and back/forward button. Each item page included a picture, information of price, stock,

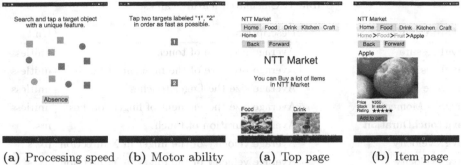

(a) Processing speed   (b) Motor ability   (a) Top page   (b) Item page

Fig. 1. Skill evaluation task. (Color   **Fig. 2.** Online shopping web site
figure online)

and rating. In the Web search task, participants were required to compare three
items and add the appropriate one to the shopping cart (for instance, "compare prices of noodles, vegetable juice and pen, then add the cheapest one to
shopping cart"). There were 2 test trials after practice, and each trial started
from the top page. We also developed a custom Web browser that collected the
operation logs such as screen touch behavior, accessed Web pages, and menu
button interactions. Then, feature values were calculated (see Table 1).

4 Estimation Model

4.1 Analysis

Skill scores of the participants were calculated from the results of the skill evaluation tasks for the 6 skills. 8 participants whose score was lower than a median
were labeled low-skill, while higher than a median were labeled high-skill. Trials
in which the participant could not complete a task or ignored instructions in the
Web search task were excluded from the analysis. Eventually, 23 trials from 14
participants were used for building the estimation models.

Decision tree-based estimation models of the 6 skills were built by using
the labels of skill level and the feature values. Due to the interpretability and
simplicity of the CART algorithm, we adopted it as the basis of the decision
tree. In order to avoid over-fitting, trees were pruned and the right-sized tree
was selected in accordance with the 1 SE rule. Leave-One-Out Cross Validation
was used in order to measure the accuracy.

4.2 Results and Discussion

All 6 estimation models and accuracies are shown in Fig. 3. All models are simple and could very accurately estimate skill level, in particular experience and
processing speed.

The level of experience was estimated from AccessedPageCount with 86.95 %
accuracy. The results showed that the level of experience is high if the count

Table 1. Calculated feature values

Feature name	Description	Unit
avgPressure	Average pressure of touch	unitless
avgPressureMoment	Average pressure of the moment of touch	unitless
avgSize	Average size the finger touches	unitless
avgSizeMoment	Average size the moment of finger touches	unitless
avgTouchDuration	Average duration of touch	ms
avgXVelocity	Average velocity of the finger in X direction	px/s
avgYvelocity	Average velocity of the finger in Y direction	px/s
avgTimeInterval	Average time interval of touch	ms
TouchesCount	Count of touches	times/s
ScrollsCount	Count of scrolls	times/s
TapsCount	Count of taps	times/s
LongtapsCount	Count of long taps	times/s
DoubletapsCount	Count of double taps	times/s
AccessedPagesCount	Count of unique accessed Web pages	pages/s
TotalAccessedPagesCount	Count of total accessed Web pages	pages/s
avgPageDisplayedTime	Average time of page displayed	ms
TappedBackButtonsCount	Count of tapped back buttons	times/s
TappedForwardButtonsCount	Count of tapped forward buttons	times/s
TappedBreadcrumbsCount	Count of tapped breadcrumbs	times/s
TappedNavButtonsCount	Count of tapped navigation menu buttons	times/s
TappedImagesCount	Count of tapped images	times/s

of unique accessed Web pages per second is high. This can be interpreted as saying that users who have more experience move to new Web pages rapidly due to their quick operation based on past experience.

The level of spatial ability was estimated from TotalAccessedPageCount with 69.56 % accuracy. The level of spatial ability is high if the count of total accessed Web pages per second is high. Users who have high spatial ability move among Web pages rapidly because they understand the structure of Web site.

The level of motor ability was estimated from TappedBackButtonsCount with 73.91 % accuracy. The level of motor ability is high if the count of back button taps per second is low. Users who have high motor ability tapped the back button less often because they tend to make correct selections.

The models of the other skills could also estimate skill level with high accuracy, but more analysis is needed to interpret the structure.

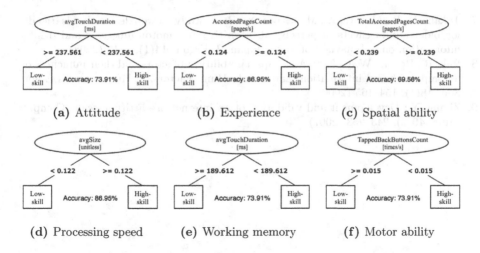

(a) Attitude   (b) Experience   (c) Spatial ability

(d) Processing speed   (e) Working memory   (f) Motor ability

Fig. 3. Estimation models of 6 skills

5   Conclusion

To build estimation models of the key skills of the elderly for accessing online shopping Web sites, we conducted experiments and gathered operation logs. We applied machine learning to the logs to build decision tree-based estimation models of 6 skills. Test results show that our models could very accurately estimate skill level; for example, the level of experience was estimated with 86.95 % accuracy from the count of unique accessed Web pages per second. Seeking other effective feature values is needed to optimize the models, and further experiments are required to validate the models' performance in other situations.

References

1. Fox, S., Karnawat, K., Mydland, M., Dumais, S., White, T.: Evaluating implicit measures to improve web search. ACM Trans. Inf. Syst. (TOIS) **23**(2), 147–168 (2005)
2. Gwizdka, J., Spence, I.: Implicit measure of lostness and success in web navigation. Interact. Comput. **19**(3), 357–369 (2007)
3. Czaja, S.J., Charness, N., Fisk, A.D., Hertzog, C., Nair, S.N., Rogers, W.A., Sharit, J.: Factors predicting the use of technology: findings from the center for research and education on aging and technology enhancement (CREATE). Psychol. Aging **21**(2), 333–352 (2006)
4. Hudson, C.E., Scialfa, C.T., Diaz-Marino, R., Laberge, J., MacKillop, S.D.: Effects of navigation aids on web performance in younger and older adults. Gerontechnology **7**(1), 3–21 (2008)
5. Ekstrom, R.B., French, J.W., Harman, H.H., Dermen, D.: Manual for Kit of Factor-Referenced Cognitive Tests. Educational Testing Services, Princeton (1976)
6. Laberge, J.C., Scialfa, C.T.: Predictors of web navigation performance in a life span sample of adults. Hum. Factors: J. Hum. Factors Ergon. Soc. **47**(2), 289–302 (2005)

7. Takahashi, R., Murata, A., Munesawa, Y.: Basic study on web design that is friendly for older adults effects of perceptual, cognitive and motor functions and display information on web navigation time. Japan. J. Ergon. **44**(1), 1–13 (2008)
8. Pak, R., Rogers, W.A., Fisk, A.D.: Spatial ability subfactors and their influences on a computer-based information search task. Hum. Factors: J. Hum. Factors Ergon. Soc. **48**(1), 154–165 (2006)
9. Zhang, Y.: Development and validation of an internet use attitude scale. Comput. Educ. **49**(2), 243–253 (2007)

Facilitating Analysis of Audience Reaction on Social Networks Using Content Analysis: A Case Study Based on Political Corruption

Stefanie Niklander[1], Ricardo Soto[2,3,4(✉)], Broderick Crawford[2,6],
Claudio León de la Barra[2], and Eduardo Olguín[5]

[1] Universidad Adolfo Ibañez, Viña del Mar, Chile
stefanie.niklander@uai.cl
[2] Pontificia Universidad Católica de Valparaíso, Valparaiso, Chile
{ricardo.soto,broderick.crawford,cleond}@ucv.cl
[3] Universidad Autónoma de Chile, Santiago, Chile
[4] Universidad Científica del Sur, Lima, Peru
[5] Universidad San Sebastián, Santiago, Chile
[6] Universidad Central, Santiago, Chile
eduardo.olguin@uss.cl

Abstract. Today, once a political corruption case takes place, it is rapidly viralized along the Internet where people can react by posting their opinions through social networks. Such audience reaction is clearly interesting but complex to analyze as people employs stereotypes, metaphors, and ironies expressed in an informal language hard to interpret. In this paper, we present how content analysis can help us to uncover the hidden meaning of a message. We focus here on the automated analysis of two political corruption cases and its corresponding opinions through social networks. In particular, one case involves the current government while the second one mostly involves the opposite side. Interesting results are gathered where the use of Content Analysis allows us to easily process the social network information in order to provide clear feedback.

Keywords: Social networks · Content analysis · Mass media

1 Introduction

Today, once a political corruption case takes place, it is rapidly viralized along the Internet where people can react by posting their opinions through widely used social networks such as Facebook and Twitter. Such audience reaction is clearly interesting and useful information for several institutions such as the government and of course for the opposite side. However, this information is complex to analyze as the audience employs stereotypes, metaphors, and ironies expressed in an informal language full of chat abbreviations, emoticons, and slang words hard to interpret.

© Springer International Publishing Switzerland 2016
C. Stephanidis (Ed.): HCII 2016 Posters, Part II, CCIS 618, pp. 63–66, 2016.
DOI: 10.1007/978-3-319-40542-1_10

In this paper, we present how content analysis can help us to uncover the hidden meaning of a message. Content analysis is a research technique for the objective, systematic and quantitative description of the manifest content of a given communication. We focus here on the automated analysis of two political corruption cases and its corresponding opinions through Twitter. The analysis period begins in September 2014 and ends in May 2015. The first one is the Penta case, concerned with the irregular financing for political campaigns, where a party from the right side was primarily involved. The second one is the Caval case, which is about influence peddling exerted by Natalia Compagnon and her husband Sebastián Dávalos, son of the president of the Chilean Republic, Michelle Bachelet. We present interesting results where the use of Content analysis allows us to easily process the social network information in order to provide clear feedback.

This paper is organized as follows: Sect. 2 presents the problem, results and discussion, followed by the conclusions and some lines of future directions.

2   Results and Discussion

Research in social networks began in the 90 s and one of the pioneers in the study of this research area were Wasserman and Faust [8]. This work can be seen as a framework for analyzing related data in social networks. However, limited work can be encountered in this context. Some related examples can be seen in [4] and in [1]. In the first one authors analyze social networks in the periods of the political campaign of Barack Obama, while the second one is focused on the wrong use of microblogging by mayors.

This article proposes the use of content analysis as a research technique to observe and reveal how the audience reacts to the publication of the news of corruption in Chile. The goal of Content Analysis is to fundamentally develop and process relevant data about conditions in which the text has been produced. According to Piñuel [7], content analysis aims to achieve the emergence of the latent meaning of the message, de-hiding the unapparent elements of every message. This research tool will allow us to make inferences from data collected and provide new knowledge of the visibilized reactions of a given audience.

Content analysis is considered as a privileged platform to access messages, since through a systematic and objective procedure we can describe the content of the messages [2]. The study of tweets offers us the opportunity to investigate the nature of the message, since it is possible to know how is the emitter and its associated thinking and ideologies [6]. As mentioned by Bartolomé [3] in this type of analysis we should avoid to make the following major mistake: removing the words of context. One word out of context says nothing about it nor about who produced it. Therefore, all our analysis will be carried out always taking into consideration who produced and communicated the message.

When content analysis is applied to messages, we are getting knowledge of who issues the message, as the discursive work is the product of his thinkings. Thus, judgments and comments issued by the producer allow us to decode their ideological structure, its context and its cultural heritage. After applying the content analysis to the tweets, as Piñuel [7] points out, we achieve the emergence of the latent sense of all social practice.

When analyzing the people reactions in the two corruption cases analyzed, we found the same act is repeated: The strategy used was the positive self-presentation and negative presentation of the other ones [5]. The reactions are performed by people who defend their political sector, which led to highlight corruption cases from the opposite side in order to diminish or soften the crime of their political sector.

In these cases we found that discussions through social networks are carried out just to remember the crimes committed by the opposite political side, without commenting on the current news published. Therefore, the strategy used relies in defending the own political sector, attacking the contrary. Thus the discussion is built around the axis Good\Bad and most of reactions analyzed are stated in that line.

Another theme present in the reactions is the impunity of political crime. It is observed that there is a discontent among citizens about how politicians are treated w.r.t a crime in contrast to the rest of citizens. The existence of two citizen classes is manifested, a first one fully of privileges and impunity which most politicians belong to, and second class fully of complications with no privileges for most common citizens.

3 Conclusion

In this paper we have analyzed the reactions that people post on social networks about two major corruption cases in Chile. We found that regardless of political party, people tend to have the same reaction when defending their sector. In addition, reactions are unrelated to the news and the space is only used to criticize and besmirch the opposing side. No real discussion is presented, but only constant attacks from both sectors can be visualized. As future work we aim at analyzing other similar thematics to see if this same phenomenon is repeated. To study the form in which content analysis techniques can be integrated in text mining software could be another interesting direction for future work as well.

References

1. Fernández-Fernández, J.G., García, B.C., Cruz-López-de-Ayala-López, M.: Twitter como plataforma de los alcaldes para la comunicación pública. Estudios sobre el Mensaje Periodístico 21(2), 757–772 (2015)
2. Bardin, L.: Análisis de Contenido. Akal, Madrid (1986)
3. Bartolomé, P.: Estudios y experiencias sobre educación en Valores. Narcea, Madrid (1981)
4. Cogburn, D.L., Espinoza-Vasquez, F.K.: From networked nominee to networked nation: examining the impact of web 2.0 and social media on political participationand civic engagement in the 2008 obama campaign. J. Polit. Mark. 10(1–2), 189–213 (2011)

5. Van Dijk, T.A.: Ideological discourse analysis. New Courant (English Dept, University of Helsinki) Special Issue Interdisciplinary Approaches to Discourse Analysis, vol. 4, pp. 135–161 (1995)
6. Holsti, O.: Content analysis. In: The Handbook of Social Psychology, vol. II, 2nd edn., pp. 596–692. Addison-Wesley, Reading (1968)
7. Pinuel Raigada, J.L.: Epistemología, metodología y técnicas del análisis de contenido. Estudios de Sociolingüística 3(1), 1–42 (2002)
8. Wasserman, S., Faust, K.: Análisis de redes sociales. Métodos y aplicaciones. Centro de Investigaciones Sociológicas, Madrid (2013)

Towards the Easy Analysis of Celebrity Representations Through Instagram: A Case Study

Stefanie Niklander[1], Ricardo Soto[2,3,4]([✉]), Broderick Crawford[2,6],
Claudio León de la Barra[2], and Eduardo Olguín[5]

[1] Universidad Adolfo Ibañez, Viña del Mar, Chile
stefanie.niklander@uai.cl
[2] Pontificia Universidad Católica de Valparaíso, Valparaíso, Chile
{ricardo.soto,broderick.crawford,cleond}@ucv.cl
[3] Universidad Autónoma de Chile, Santiago, Chile
[4] Universidad Científica del Sur, Lima, Peru
[5] Universidad San Sebastián, Santiago, Chile
eduardo.olguin@uss.cl
[6] Universidad Central, Santiago, Chile

Abstract. This paper focuses on the analysis of celebrity representations through Instagram. We refer to representation of a person as the set of concepts, images, ideas and emotions that this person transmit to the world. Representations transmit useful information for fans, but also for the entities related with the involved person. However, the representation exposed by posted images is hard to automatically process as depend on several variables which are complex to interpret. We propose then to employ discourse analysis in order to facilitate the analysis of such people representations. Discourse analysis is a qualitative and interpretive methodology for analyzing social phenomena through any communication mechanism. We illustrate interesting results where the use of discourse analysis allows us to easily process representations through images.

Keywords: Social networks · Discourse analysis · Mass media · Instagram

1 Introduction

Instagram is a widely used online mobile and social networking service based on the interchange of photos and videos. It has rapidly emerged during the last years having as distinct feature its interesting capabilities for the easy retouching of photos. Currently, it has about 400 million monthly active users and several celebrities post their photos and videos in order to instantly inform their fans about their activities. In this paper, we focus on the analysis of famous people representations through this social network. We refer to representation of a person as the set of concepts, images, ideas and emotions that this person transmit

© Springer International Publishing Switzerland 2016
C. Stephanidis (Ed.): HCII 2016 Posters, Part II, CCIS 618, pp. 67–70, 2016.
DOI: 10.1007/978-3-319-40542-1_11

to the world. This representation varies depending, among others, on the gender, country, religion, role and activities of people, and it is constructed according to a given socio-cultural context. Representations transmit useful information for fans, but also for the entities related with the involved person. Indeed, a brand promoting sports and healthy life do not want to see their ambassadors drinking alcohol or eating fast food in social networks. However, the representation exposed by posted images is hard to automatically process as depend on several variables which are complex to interpret.

In this paper, we illustrate how the use of discourse analysis can facilitate the analysis of people representations. Discourse analysis is a qualitative and interpretive methodology for analyzing social phenomena through any communication mechanism. It allows us to understand the way people behavior is reproduced and enacted in the social context. We present a case study where this methodology is effectively used to gather and analyze representations from Paris Hilton's and Justin Bieber's Instagram profiles. We illustrate interesting results where the use of discourse analysis allows us to easily process the social network information in order to provide clear feedback.

This paper is organized as follows: Sect. 2 presents the problem, results and discussion, followed by the conclusions and some lines of future directions.

2   Discussion and Results

Social networks are currently the most visited Internet websites [2], this is known to be a phenomenon emerged in the Web 2.0. These platforms of social interaction are devoted to users who generate and provide information which will be then shared, commented, and discussed by the other members of the network. The rapid penetration of social networks has led to change habits of people. Indeed, as McClure [3] states: "We are not only addicted to the network, we have become the network". This quote highlights the relevance that social networks have acquired and as a consequence the importance to study them.

Instagram, the popular photo-sharing social network is one of the most used sites for teens, soccer and television stars to expose their lives through an image. Our goal is to analyze the images that celebrities published through their accounts by observing what situations, experiences and/or objects they want to visibilize. In this way, we will be able to reveal their interest and the form in which they want to be exhibited to the world.

The study was conducted on the profiles of Paris Hilton and Justin Bieber and all images they published were analyzed for a month. Paris Hilton is a businesswoman and model, known for being the great-granddaughter of Conrad Hilton (founder of Hilton Hotels). She became known in 2003 for distributing a sex tape on the Internet. Justin Bieber is a Canadian singer-songwriter who has been nominated and awarded numerous times. The instrument we use for our study is the Discourse Analysis. We note that this technique understood the discourse not only as a text, but also as all that transmit meanings and proposes certain behaviors. Therefore, our task is to show the meanings behind the publication of these images, which are trying to transmit or communicate at the time of publication. Likewise, we see how these celebrities are represented [1] through this social network.

Paris Hilton Profile. After analyzing the images published by Paris Hilton we note that:

1. This celebrity uses this platform for publicizing products related to her brand.
2. She uses Instagram as a exhibition mean.

In this analysis we mainly focus on the second point. In this sense, we observed that she communicate and image where she can be viewed or perceived as a sexual object. In most photographs, she appears posing, with a sexy attitude, hair in the wind, smiling and scantily clad. In the society where we live, all the aforementioned features configure Paris Hilton as a sexual object. In addition to this configuration, we observe that Paris Hilton is infantilized through the images of her profile. This is done by the usage of elements that make to perceive her as little girl. She constantly employs pink dresses, with "Barbie" clothes (just as done by a child), but always maintaining a provocative attitude. The childishness of the woman figure is generally related to a woman who is not responsible for their acts, however, in the case analyzed is she who builds the image in that way.

Justin Bieber Profile. Now, when we analyze the images of Justin Bieber, we conclude the following:

1. This celebrity uses this platform for exhibiting his daily life activities.
2. She uses Instagram for posting some photos of his concerts.

In this analysis we will focus on the first point. Unlike the previously analyzed profile, this Canadian singer tries to show him through the social network as an ordinary young man. He posts pictures eating with friends, fishing on a lake and admiring different landscapes. He show only common activities that will do any common person. Only by images of his concerts we can deduce that is a celebrity, but other publications suggest a very normal young man.

3   Conclusion

After applying discourse analysis to the Instagram images we can conclude that these profiles have a completely different purpose, despite belonging both profiles to world famous celebrities. Paris Hilton tries to appear as someone unattainable, as a person located at the top level, like a diva. She boasts about her glamorous lifestyle and luxes she have access to. By contrast, Bieber exhibits a normal life performing common teenager activities. As future work we aim at analyzing other similar profiles to identify new social network phenomena. To study the form in which discourse analysis techniques can be integrated in mining software could be another interesting direction for future work as well.

References

1. Moscovici, S.: El psicoanálisis, su imagen y su público. Buenos Aires, Huemul (1979)
2. Serrano, M.: La producción social de la comunicación. Alianza, Madrid (1979)
3. Weinbergt, T.: The New Community Rules: Marketing on the Social Web. O'Reilly Media, Sebastopol (2009)

Playful Interactions for the Citizens' Engagement. The Musical Language as a Possible Application

Antonio Opromolla[1,2(✉)], Valentina Volpi[1,2], and Carlo Maria Medaglia[1]

[1] Link Campus University, Rome, Italy
{a.opromolla,v.volpi,c.medaglia}@unilink.it
[2] ISIA Roma Design, Rome, Italy

Abstract. The human side of the city is taking more and more importance. It allows to create a positive human experience and to evaluate what people feel and what are their emotions in the city during the interaction with services and spaces. Moreover, in order to make the cities more "human", an active citizens' involvement in design processes is more and more considered as a necessary factor. However, the mere existence of tools that can engage people does not ensure real and effective actions. This work proposes to consider the dissemination of game elements in the city environment (exploiting the physical affordances of the urban pattern) as a possible approach to enhance the citizens' engagement, and discusses the related technological and interaction issues. The musical language is proposed as a possible language related to the game context that we would apply to city for engagement purposes in the urban environment.

Keywords: Human smart city · Gamification · Musical language

1 Introduction

The human side of the urban environment is taking more and more importance both in the academic debate [1] and in the practical applications [2]. Indeed, the people quality of life is an increasingly central concept focusing on creating a positive human experience and on evaluating what people feel and what are their emotions in the urban context during the interaction with services and spaces. In order to make the cities more "human", an active citizens' involvement in design processes is more and more considered as a necessary factor. As an example, the co-design practice aims to involve people in designing solutions on the basis of emerging wants and needs.

However, the mere existence of tools that can engage people in the city matters does not ensure a real and effective action by people. The main reasons are related to the lack of openness from citizens, their perceived difficulty in meeting the needs of all the people, and their lack of experience in these processes. So, it is important to find specific solutions that facilitate these engagement processes.

This work proposes to consider the application of game elements in the city environment, as a possible approach to enhance the citizens' engagement. In details, in the second section we identify how the game could improve the engagement processes; in the third section we propose the dissemination of game elements in the urban

C. Stephanidis (Ed.): HCII 2016 Posters, Part II, CCIS 618, pp. 71–76, 2016.
DOI: 10.1007/978-3-319-40542-1_12

environment as a strategy to really engage people; in the fourth section we show how the music, as one of the languages related to the game context, can be applied for engagement purposes in the urban environment; in the fifth section, we focus on the role of the digital technologies in these processes; finally, in the sixth section, the conclusion and the future work.

2   The Game in the Urban Environment

In general the freedom which characterises the game makes it applicable to more and more complex environments, for example with the aim to help people in representing and understanding the events in a more easy way or in bonding them with other people [3, 4]. It is a positive element increasingly present also in the city environment, since it is able to create a suspension of the monotonous urban continuity.

The "gamification", which is defined as the application of game elements in non-game contexts [5], can be intended as an approach that allows not only to better live in the city, but also to really engage people in the city issues.

In details, the application of the game in the urban environment can be applied in order to achieve five main goals:

1. Offering the people an active and positive experience in the city environment. In this case the city becomes an active territory, more lived and practiced, increasing as a consequence its attractiveness for other people.
2. Encouraging people to approach to the territory issues, by making them aware of the meaning of specific things (social consciousness), of the main city problems, and of the importance of their behaviour to change a current situation.
3. Encouraging people to make positive actions and to adopt sustainable behaviours in the city environment (for example concerning the transportation or the environment issues).
4. Encouraging people in strengthening relationships with other people, for example with other citizens or the Public Administrations.
5. Pushing people in finding and designing solutions for communal problems, by contributing with their ideas (crowdsourcing approach).

These list of goals can be intended as a "flow" concerning citizen engagement, starting from the less to the most committed behaviour, which requires people an always deeper involvement and activity. Indeed, the highest level is represented by the fifth point of the list, since in this case the citizens are asked to intervene in order to transform their city according to their needs and desires. Of course, these points are strongly dependent on one another and they influence each other: they have in common the fact that they have both an element of "content" (because the citizens' actions leads to create something) and an element of "relation" (because the citizens' actions also implicate a contact with someone). For example, the point number four is strictly related to the point number five, since, in order to build a shared vision of the territory, it is important to have a strong relationship with the other people who live in it.

So, the game can be a useful approach to make our cities more "human" and activate people in different ways. Nowadays these principles are mainly applied in online and only-digital platforms. For example, Thiel [6] argues that mobile applications with game elements are important enablers for the citizen involvement in local issues. Moreover, Rehm et al. [7] designed a mobile application which supports civic engagement and civic collaboration through the gamification approach. However, the use of digital interfaces not adequately integrated and connected to the urban environment risks to create a deeper separation between the citizen and the context.

However, the majority of these applications do not lead to a real and high citizen engagement. So, it is important to rethink and improve the application modes of the game elements in the urban environment.

3   Rethinking Game for the Citizen Engagement

The assumption at the basis of this work is that the city environment itself can be intended as an application field of the game elements that lead to a better citizen engagement. In fact, we believe that the elements of the city could be used as enablers of the game itself, especially by exploiting their physical affordances as game tools. The described process aims to encourage the citizen to make specific actions and to assume specific behaviours according to the goals of engagement defined in the previous section.

In order to do that, we need to consider the different game elements through which we can "gamify" the urban environment. Hunicke et al. [8] identified three main game components: mechanics (the rules of the game), dynamics (the run-time behaviour of the mechanics acting on the player over time, e.g. progression, rewards, identity, etc.), and aesthetics (the emotional responses evoked in the player, e.g. challenge, fellowship, expression, etc.). In detail, in the city environment the mechanics might correspond to the actions of people in the game itself (e.g. "go", "turn", "move"), the dynamics might be the output of the action for the single player and in general for the city (e.g. to obtain a reward, to pass the level, etc.), and the aesthetics might be the specific reached benefits both for the people and for the whole community.

Clearly, the focus is on the exploitation of the morphological elements of the urban pattern. In fact these elements, while maintaining their original characteristics, turn into something else, giving them a new meaning. Considering the semantic categorization of Floch [9], with this approach the urban elements are deprived of their utilitarian value acquiring a non-utilitarian and playful connotation (e.g. a square can become a game table, a road can become a path obstacle, the bricks of a wall can become a puzzle, etc.). With these interventions, the urban space is completely re-articulated, re-produced, re-semantised, and re-told. In fact, a new story of the city is created and consequently a new overall citizen experience emerges. Sánchez Chillón [10] talks about the city as a platform for the innovation, able to build the "citizentrism", that is to say the centrality of the citizen in the urban context, and to improve the social consciousness and the co-responsibility in communal aims. The author focuses on the importance of gamification in doing that, talking about "civic gamification" as the methodology for the civic engagement in city issues.

4   The Music Language as an Application of Game Elements in the Urban Environment

The music is one of the languages related to the game context that we are trying to apply to the city for engagement purposes in the urban environment. In details, we are considering how the musical language can be "disseminated" into the city for encouraging people not only to make positive actions, but also to express their experience in the city and to share ideas for an improvement of the territory. In fact, we are thinking how the affordances of specific elements of the urban environment can be used to produce a collective musical composition that represents the shared vision of the city. The basic elements of the musical language (e.g. rhythm, harmony, melody, timbre, dynamic, etc.) can express this shared vision. In this work a process of double re-sematisation will occur: the first is addressed to the specific city elements disseminated in the urban environment that become game and musical tools that allow to express a feeling, a mood, an idea, etc.; the second is addressed to the musical composition itself, that surpasses its artistic value to become a content strictly connected with the people city perception. In general the game process of this application could be: 1. the single person will "play" a specific city elements (mechanics); 2. the action will create or transform the collective music composition (dynamics), 3. a stronger sense of community is created (aesthetics).

The consideration of the city as a musical instrument is also present in the work of Gaye et al. [11], who designs a wearable device that considers the urban environment as a musical interface and the mobility as an interaction model. Moreover, in the work of Petrovki et al. [12] the elements of the urban environment (e.g. buildings, paths, gaps, etc.) are translated in sounds with interventional design purposes.

5   Digital Technologies and HCI in Citizen Engagement Through the Game

The re-semantisation of the city as a playground where people can be engaged requires a transformation of the city allowing people to consider the city elements in a different way. This process is necessary, since otherwise people will continue to have only a utilitarian vision of the city excluding the ludic (and more engaging) one.

Regarding this, the use of digital technologies really allows to "augment" the environment. Violi [13] focuses on the importance of Information and Communication Technologies in re-defining the urban context, transforming non-human in human places.

However, in the case discussed in this paper it is essential to replace personal devices, as smartphones or tablets, with diffused devices embedded in the real world and belonging to the city itself. This change requires a technological shift, which consists in the application of the "smart objects" paradigm. In fact, the city elements become augmented objects used by people and able to make something when used. In general, the integration of electronic devices (e.g. RFId tags, sensors, actuators, etc.) in the objects transforms them, making them able to understand and interpret the human behaviors and activities [14]. It is an important requirement for our aims. Furthermore, the digital fabrication approach, which consists in using different manufacturing techniques and "open" software and hardware to build physical objects, can be a useful methodology to transform the city elements according to this vision.

Moreover, it is fundamental to think how people interact with these re-semantised city elements, in order to identify the input, output, control, and feedback processes. In this case, the main change is related to the shift from the Graphical User Interface (GUI) to the Natural User Interface (NUI) paradigm, where people interact with a system or a service, but the interface is totally invisible. In fact, the user interaction with these interfaces occurs through actions related to the natural human behavior. So, the interaction is not perceived by the user and the actions required by the digital systems are totally integrated into the daily activities. Concerning the specific elements of our topic, a useful definition derives from Sakamoto and Nakajima [15] who talk about "persuasive digital affordances" to mean the operation of digital objects into the real environment as tools to "inform, persuade, and inspire human behaviors".

So, the user interaction occurs in parallel with the actions commonly performed by people in the city environment. This is important because it allows people to decide when they want play. In effect, the intensity of the engagement (and so the choice to take part in specific processes) is a very important factor. In detail, the moments when they can play can be identified considering some specific variables regarding the people interaction within the city. These main variables are: action (he/she moves; he/she is stopped); goal (he/she moves to go to work; he/she moves home; he/she move to another place of his/her personal life; he/she moves heading for a public place; he/she walks; he/she moves for relaxation; he/she visits places of culture; he/she goes shopping; he/she waits something; etc.); used means of transportation (public transport; private transport; walking movement; etc.); location (street; square; park; waiting areas; public places; etc.). On the basis of these moments, specific occasions of citizen engagement through game elements can be identified.

6 Conclusion

In this paper we propose to apply the game elements in the urban environment to engage people in the territory. This approach shows new paths for the use of the territory that are related to game patterns. So, the game becomes a city language that allows to understand the territory and to communicate with it. It also allows to metadesign the environment. As Van Onck sustains [16] the metadesign is a structural element of the design that defines the rules within which the individual elements of design can move. Indeed, it defines the set of possibilities for the future design, the variables for the future projects. So, if we consider the game as a framework of metadesign for the city, we define the different possibilities of design and of transformation of the urban environment.

In the future work of this study, the observation of the urban environment will allow to define the possible modes of use of the city elements according to the game concepts, to identify the relationship of these elements with the people and their interaction. The study of the structures, the textures, and the forms of organization of the city elements will be the starting point of these future steps.

References

1. de Oliveira, Á., Campolargo, M., Martins, M.: Constructing human smart cities. In: Helfert, M., et al. (eds.) Smartgreens 2015 and Vehists 2015. CCIS, vol. 579, pp. 32–49. Springer, Heidelberg (2015).
2. Livework, liveworkstudio.com
3. Turner, V.: From Ritual to Theatre. The Human Seriousness of Play. Performing Arts Journal Publication, New York (1982)
4. Mead, G.H.: Mind, Self and Society. The University of Chicago Press, Chicago (1934)
5. Deterding, S., Sicart, M., Nacke, L., O'Hara, K., Dixon, D.: Gamification. Using game-design elements in non-gaming contexts. In: CHI 2011 Extended Abstracts on Human Factors in Computing Systems, pp. 2425–2428. ACM, New York (2011)
6. Thiel, S.K.: Gamified participation: encouraging citizens' involvement in local governments. In: Conference for E-Democracy and Open Government, pp. 433–438. MV-Verlag (2015)
7. Rehm, S., Foth, M., Mitchell, P.: Gamifying collective intelligence for the common good. In: Schuler, D., De Cindio, F., De Liddo, A. (eds.) Proceedings of the Workshop "Encouraging Collective Intelligence for the Common Good", Limerik, Ireland (2015)
8. Hunicke, R., LeBlanc, M., Zubek, R.: MDA: A formal Approach to Game Design and Game Research. In: Proceedings of the AAAI-04 Workshop on Challenges in Game AI, pp. 1–5 (2004)
9. Floch, J.M.: Sémiotique, Marketing et Communication. Puf, Paris (1990)
10. Urban   360.   https://urban360.me/2012/08/24/if-urban-life-is-a-game-smart-cities-are-the-playgrounds
11. Gaye, L., Mazé, R., Holmquist, L.E.: Sonic city: the urban environment as a musical interface. In: Proceedings of the 2003 Conference on New Interfaces for Musical Expression, pp. 109–115. National University of Singapore, Singapore (2003)
12. Petrovski, P., Parthenios, P., Oikonomou, A., Mania, K.: Music as an interventional design tool for urban designers. In: ACM SIGGRAPH 2014 Posters, Article 21. ACM, New York (2014)
13. Violi, P.: Smart City between Mythology, Power Control and Participation. EC-AISS (2014)
14. Kortuem, G., Kawsar, F., Sundramoorthy, V., Fitton, D.: Smart objects as building blocks for the internet of things. IEEE Internet Comput. **14**(1), 44–51 (2010)
15. Sakamoto, M., Nakajima, T.: Gamifying smart city services to flourish our society. In: Adjunct Proceedings of the 2015 ACM International Joint Conference on Pervasive and Ubiquitous Computing and Proceedings of the 2015 ACM International Symposium on Wearable Computers, pp. 1515–1518. ACM, New York (2015)
16. Van Onck, A.: Metadesign. Edilizia Moderna, 85 (1965)

Consideration of the Loyal Customer Sub-communities in a Consumer Community Through Analysis of Social Networking Services

A Case Study of a Fashion Brand

Kohei Otake[1](✉), Tomofumi Uetake[2], and Akito Sakurai[3]

[1] Faculty of Science and Engineering, Chuo University, Tokyo, Japan
otake@indsys.chuo-u.ac.jp
[2] School of Business Administration, Senshu University, Kanagawa, Japan
uetake@isc.senshu-u.ac.jp
[3] School of Science for Open and Environmental Systems, Keio University,
Kanagawa, Japan
sakurai@ae.keio.ac.jp

Abstract. Widespread popularization of social networking services (SNSs) promoted, many studies about marketing activities using SNSs. But, there are a few studies focused on tendencies of consumer communities on SNSs. In this paper, we focus on a fashion brand and "Instagram". And we study about tendencies of consumer communities on SNSs to present necessary information for users effectively. From the results of our analysis, we found that there was a community which was formed of users who had high degree of loyalty in "Fashion Brand A". Moreover, as the result of analysis of user behavior, the presence of loyal customers in the community was confirmed.

Keywords: Consumer community · Marketing · Social networks · Network analysis · Instagram

1 Introduction

Recently, Social Networking Services (SNSs) have been growing. Users can communicate with friends about their preference and favorites using SNSs. So, there are many consumer communities that are defined as a group of users who have same interests. In this situation, there have been many studies about marketing activities using SNSs [1, 2]. In particular, targeting ads that are based on a user's action history (e.g. access logs and share-post) have been the main research concern [3]. But, there are a few studies focused on tendencies of consumer communities on SNSs. We think it is effective to present necessary information for users by using the tendencies of consumer communities.

In this paper, we focus on "Fashion Brand A," where A is an anonymous brand name as a case study. Additionally, we focus on "Instagram" which is a photograph-sharing SNS, because users often watch and upload photos and videos of products (e.g. clothes, shoes, etc.) as well as their coordinated outfits.

© Springer International Publishing Switzerland 2016
C. Stephanidis (Ed.): HCII 2016 Posters, Part II, CCIS 618, pp. 77–81, 2016.
DOI: 10.1007/978-3-319-40542-1_13

2   Purposes of This Study

Purposes of this study are (1) to analyze consumer communities on SNSs, (2) to clarify the tendencies of consumer communities, and (3) to propose a method to present necessary information for users by using the tendencies of consumer communities.

3   Analysis of "Fashion Brand A"

At first, we clarify the current conditions of "Fashion Brand A". "Fashion Brand A" is a popular fashion brand for young women in Japan. "Fashion Brand A" has 40 actual stores in various places in Japan and has following tendencies.

1. "Fashion Brand A" uses SNSs such as Instagram, Facebook and Twitter for advertising actively.
2. Consumers of "Fashion Brand A" often share information about products, discount sales information and their coordinated outfits on SNSs. They often use Instagram that can be shared their photos and videos easily.

To study the communities of their brand, we interviewed the staff for "Fashion Brand A". We also interviewed the staff for "Fashion Brand A" to clarify their advertising methods.

3.1   Community Structure of a "Fashion Brand A"

By the interview, we specified that communities of "Fashion Brand A" can be divided into two types; the sales community and the consumer community. The sales community consists of goods producers, brand models and shop staff. Moreover, the consumer community can be divided into following three sub-communities based on the level of loyalty for "Fashion Brand A" (see Fig. 1).

- Core community (Loyal Customers)
- Fan community (Supporters)
- (General) Consumer community.

3.2   Advertising Methods in "Fashion Brand A"

Next, we clarified the advertising methods of "Fashion Brand A". By the interview, we identified 4 main sources of advertisement; Mass media, Fashion events, SNSs, and Customer service in the shop.

In "Mass media", the product is advertised in fashion magazines or portal sites. As a result, the product is visible to a larger audience, not just consumer community of "Fashion Brand A". In "Fashion events", the "Fashion Brand A" holds a pre-sale event to promote and advertise products. The exclusive brand models wear the products on the runway for display. Only loyal customers are invited to these events. Many of the

Brand Intelligibility

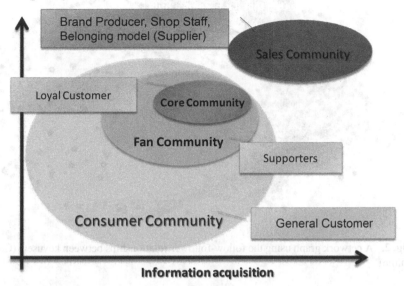

Fig. 1. Overview of the consumer community of "Fashion Brand A"

participants upload photos and videos of these events on SNSs. In this way the people who were not invited or could not attend the event can see the products. In "SNSs", the staffs of "Fashion Brand A" posts photographs of coordinated outfits every 2–3 days. From the photographs posted by the staff, the consumers can see new products and trends. The consumers can go to the shops to see the new products, and talk to the staff about coordinating outfits and new trends. Additionally, the consumers can take photographs together with the staff and can share them on SNSs. Therefore, in the next section, we clarify the correspondence relationship between the actual community and the community which is formed on Instagram.

4   Analysis of the Network of Consumer Community on SNSs

In this section, we analyze the network of consumer community on SNSs.

At first, we collect 4015 posts containing "Brand A" tags (2015/11/3 to 2015/12/25) from Instagram. The data collected consists of; Content of the post, Attributes of the user who made the post, Attributes of said user's follow-follower relationship. We also collect 2,301,974 follow-follower relationships from these posts. The details of the collected information are shown in Table 1.

We call the person who made a post as a Keyuser. The friends are people that Keyuser follows. The followers are people who follow Keyuser. The exchange users are people who follow and are followed by the Keyuser.

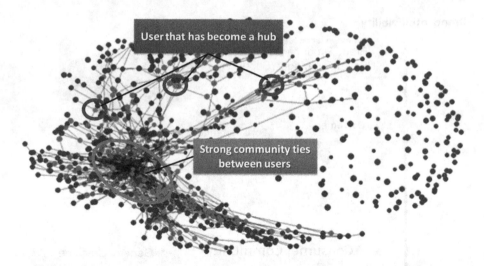

Fig. 2. A network graph using the follow-follower relationships between keyusers (Color figure online)

Table 1. Overview of the acquired follow-follower relationship information from posts on instagram.

	Friends	Followers	Exchange users
Average (SD)	212.4 (323.8)	453.7 (1360.6)	102.6 (117.8)
Median	156	134	77
Mode	94	17	1

Next, we performed network analysis on Keyusers and the follow-follower relations. We visualized the network using the "Fruchterman Reingold model" [4]. In this model, Keyusers with similar attributes are visualized closer to each other. During visualization, we surveyed the degree of the nodes and assigned colors based on the degrees.

(1) Blue: 1–4
(2) Green: 5–19
(3) Red: 20+.

The maximum degree was 190, and the minimum was 2. The results are shown in the Table 2 and Fig. 2.

Table 2. Overview of the network indicators

Total nodes	1395
Total arcs	4150
Average degree	5.949
Density	0.002

From the Table 2, density is very low and the network is sparse. From the network graph, we learned that there is a large community which is formed by users who had high degree (red user) in red circle. We extracted members at the center of this large community; we got feedback from the shop staff about these users. From a result, the presence of loyal customers in the community was confirmed. On the other hand, on the whole, users who have low degree (blue user) were not connected to a large community. For that reason the network was sparse as a whole.

A few users who had high degree were displayed in remote location from large communities (blue circle). These users were connected with blue users who did not belong to large community. Therefore, these users are thought to be in the role of a bridge (network hub) in the network.

Through the results, we think there is a community which is formed by a loyalist sub-community of "Fashion Brand A" on Instagram. The sub-community's central gathering exists in the overall community.

5 Conclusion and Future Works

In this paper we reported the results of network analysis, targeting on "Fashion Brand A". From the results of network analysis using the follow-follower relationships, there was a community which was formed of users who had high degree. Moreover, as a result of analysis of user behavior, the presence of loyal customers in the community was confirmed.

In our future works, we will analyze the contents (tags, replies, location…) of the posts on Instagram. Moreover, we will propose the visualization methods using the attribute information of the users.

Acknowledgements. We would like to thank Rooter Inc. for research funding and providing the data for this study.

References

1. Yadav, M.S., Valck, K., Thurau, T.H., Hoffman, D.L., Spann, M.: Social commerce: a contingency framework for assessing marketing potential. J. Interact. Mark. **27**(4), 311–323 (2013)
2. Reddy, A.S.S., Kasat, P., Jain, A.: Box-office opening prediction of movies based on hype analysis through data mining. Int. J. Comput. Appl. **56**(1), 1–5 (2012)
3. Okuda, T., Yasuda, T., Mizuno, M.: "Research into the impact on sales caused by the spread of information on SNS: Correlation between number of tweets on Twitter and sales of mobile application on iTunes AppStore," IEICE Technical report, Software Science, vol. 111, no. 268, pp. 1–6 (2011) (in Japanese)
4. Fruchterman, T.M.J., Reingold, E.M.: Graph drawing by force-directed placement. Softw. Pract. Experience **21**(11), 1129–1164 (1991)

The Advanced Exploitation of Mixed Reality (AEMR) Community of Interest

Maria Olinda Rodas$^{(\boxtimes)}$, Jeff Waters, and David Rousseau

Command and Control Technology and Experimentation Division,
Space and Warfare System Center Pacific (SSC Pacific), San Diego, CA, USA
{maria.rodas,jeff.waters,david.rousseau}@navy.mil

Abstract. The AEMR community of interest was developed to foster collaboration and innovation in the area of virtual reality and augmented reality. The community has over 250 representatives from entities from government, industry and academia both locally and internationally.

Keywords: Military · Community · Virtual reality · Mixed reality · Pattern recognition

1 Introduction

The Advanced Exploitation of Mixed Reality Community of Interest (AEMR COI) is an initiative that started as an effort from the Battlespace Exploitation of Mixed Reality (BEMR) Laboratory at SSC Pacific to create a community of interest in the research area of mixed reality technology. This includes the spectrum of technologies ranging from virtual reality to augmented reality. The AEMR COI is designed to include all government and non-government organizations or entities holding a significant stake in mixed reality activities, including smart avatar development, augmented and virtual reality research development, and any mixed reality related technology. The goal of the AEMR COI is to discuss, explore, and demonstrate augmented and virtual reality technology, applications, standards, use cases, and to provide appropriate guidance with recommendations to ensure effective and efficient community interoperability and collaboration. The community started in June of 2015 and has quickly grown to over 250 representatives from organizations representing nine different countries across government, industry, and academia. The community is organized into four major working groups focused on User Requirements, Technology, Human Performance, and Smart Avatars. Upcoming emerging working groups include Models, Information Exchange, and Reference Implementation Frameworks.

© Springer International Publishing Switzerland 2016
C. Stephanidis (Ed.): HCII 2016 Posters, Part II, CCIS 618, pp. 82–91, 2016.
DOI: 10.1007/978-3-319-40542-1_14

2   Community Approach

The community intends to further evolve science and technology in the virtual reality and mixed reality domain by: (1) Encouraging scientists to discuss current development, immediate and potential uses, advantages and limitations; (2) Establishing potential collaborations; and (3) Identifying community standards such as interoperability and technology evaluation tools. This community also intends to identify and evolve potential research areas for further development by: (1) Establishing a platform for research sponsors to present their needs to the scientific community; (2) Developing research gap analyses in different areas such as smart avatar, human performance, and technology assessment; and (3) Generating research ideas and proposals to foster innovative research.

3   Mission and Venue

The community mission is to foster innovation, collaboration, and interoperability in the community. Moreover, the mission is to also guide the development of new technologies towards areas of interest. The community intends to facilitate a collaborative environment to explore the rapidly evolving mixed reality technologies and facilitate their application into different domains. The mission includes facilitating the implementation of mixed reality technology in operational and support (maintenance, logistics, and training) environments by demonstrating those technologies and applications to industry leaders, technical specialists, academia, and government program managers and officials. The community will assess the technical requirements necessary to bring these capabilities to the operational domain, and support tasks that would benefit substantially from them.

The AEMR COI uses the All Partners Access Network (APAN) site to host its community. APAN is the Unclassified Information Sharing Service for the U.S. Department of Defense. Information about the community, related videos, documentations, and wikis are being held in this website. Discussions, news, updates, and other important information can also be found in this site. Meetings are being held over a telecom number and screen sharing is being offered over Defense Collaboration Services (DCS). Members are kept informed via email subscription to the different working groups, and the overall group distribution list.

4   Working Groups

There are four active working groups which concentrate their efforts in determining use cases and vignettes, evaluating current technologies, finding research gaps, determining useful metrics and tools to evaluate performance with VR technologies, and developing smart avatar technology. These four working groups were developed to support each other in their mission to enhance the community knowledge and practice in this research domain.

4.1 The User Requirements Working Group (URWG)

The User Requirement Working Group unites experts in industry, academia, and defense to explore how virtual and augmented technologies are, or can be, applied to real word problems to enhance human performance. Core themes have centered on disaster relief, manufacturing, medical, and military applications. The group is currently collaborating to document use cases and vignettes for different areas and applications, as well as to highlight the research gaps for each application. Discussions include ongoing work in the medical field. For instance, at Naval Health Research Center, virtual reality technology is used in operationally relevant ways, to define capabilities and limits of the warfighter, as well as to help wounded warriors to heal. The Computer Assisted Rehabilitation Environment (CAREN) system is being used to enhance performance of injured and healthy warfighters. This includes measurements of performance, both cognitively and physically, of persons with lower limb amputation and traumatic brain injury, as well as healthy warfighters who may show performance deficits due to wearing gear (PPE), loads carried, or fatigue. The researchers take what they learn in the lab to the field, where only a handful of things can be measured, but using this technique they can draw parallels between the two phases of testing [1, 2] (Fig. 1).

Fig. 1. The CAREN system being used at the Naval Health Research Center[1]

In the maintenance world, there is now considerable effort being devoted to this technology. This is due, in large part, to the introduction of augmented reality HMDs (i.e., MicroSoft HoloLense, PLATS, and other types) where the Computer Generated Imagery (CGI) is either presented on a display system with see-through lenses (or on a display-visor) such that the CGI is superimposed over the real world, or the CGI is combined with real-world imagery from HMD-mounted cameras. In other application areas, such as disaster relief, the participants in the system can be in different physical locations while collaborating on brining in rescue teams and coordinating resource distribution. The shared environment database is transmitted to each participant prior to the meeting, and stored locally for use when needed. This approach dramatically reduces bandwidth requirements, and only requires the real-time transmission of avatar movement and position data, interactions with the virtual environment, including the addition of features and objects, and voice communications (Fig. 2).

Fig. 2. Maintenance application demonstrations at the BEMR's Laboratory [3]

4.2 The Technology Assessment Working Group (TAWG)

The Technology Assessment Working Group unites experts in industry, academia, and government to explore, evaluate, and assess virtual and augmented reality technologies. Members share the latest ongoing activities in augmented and virtual reality technology, and discuss the uses and advantages of that technology. Core themes are centered on evaluating a wide range of technologies, products, and applications in virtual and augmented reality. The group is currently collaborating to create VR resources that members have developed or improved on in their own work. This catalogue includes the Berkeley Teleimmersion experience, which uses 3D cameras for creating a dynamic avatar in real time, and projecting it at the remote location into a shared virtual environment, to facilitate an experience similar to face-to-face interaction [4]. The users can take advantage of 3D interaction and display technologies to collaborate with their remote partners. Moreover, it also includes discussions on alternatives to control virtual and augmented reality via gesture and LED tracking solutions by Phase Space [5], and light field near-eye displays developed by Stanford Computational Imaging Laboratory at Stanford University [6]. A key concern has been the need for a new human-computer interface for the new generation of 3D augmented and virtual reality technologies (Fig. 3).

Fig. 3. Teleimmersion experience designed at UC Berkeley [4]

4.3   The Human Performance Working Group (HPWG)

The Human Performance Working Group unites experts in industry, academia, and government to explore how virtual and augmented technologies can enhance different facets of human endeavor. This group provides the human factors engineering perspective on performance measures and evaluation techniques that can be used for assessing the benefits of using mixed reality technologies to improve human performance. Core themes have centered on virtual reality and augmented reality based training platforms, user interfaces, research tools, and human-autonomy teaming. The group is currently collaborating to create a compendium of new and existing virtual reality resources that members have developed or improved in their own work. This catalogue includes innovative biosensing devices such as the EEG enhanced Oculus-based Samsung Gear VR system. This device was recently created at the Swartz Center for Computational Neuroscience at University of California, San Diego (UCSD) to record EEG and eye movement using a smart phone during full body engagement in a virtual environment [7]. A second example by UCSD is the Chronoviz, which supports the analysis and annotation of videographer data synchronized with other simultaneously recorded time-series measures [8]. Also included in the catalogue are guidance and tools on topics such as agent transparency and trust [9], and decision making performance changes following motion sickness [10]. A key concern that has been raised is the transfer of virtual reality-based learning to a real-world context (Fig. 4).

Fig. 4. UCSD Samsung Gear VR goggle adapted with integrated EEG sensing technology and eye movement system [7].

4.4   The Smart Avatar Working Group (SAWG)

The Smart Avatar Working Group unites experts in industry, academia, and government to explore and advance the discussion and documentation of the state-of-the-art smart avatar technology, key components, gaps in related technologies, and standards of interoperability requirements which can then be aligned with ongoing partner and community efforts to develop mixed reality solutions and improved information sharing and inter-operability. Reusability and interoperability are key goals for this group. The group is currently collaborating to create virtual technology resources that members have developed or improved in their own work. This includes innovative software systems such as the Virtual Human Toolkit by the Institute for Creative Technologies (ICT) at University of Southern California (USC) [11], which enables the creation of nuanced virtual characters who move, talk, and interact in true to life forms. It also includes telepresence medical applications by Capitola Netherlands which allows doctors to follow elderly patients around in their daily life to assess the impact of their activities on their health [12]. Various relevant topics were also discussed during the meetings, including machine learning techniques for intelligent systems [13] (Fig. 5).

Fig. 5. USC ICT Virtual Human Toolkit [11]

5 Future Working Groups

There is a plan to open more working groups as the community expands; the groups below are just some examples of future working groups. Notice that the working groups are linked and developed in order to help support each other.

5.1 Models and Algorithms Working Group (MAWG)

The MAWG participants would collaborate on the development and evaluation of the algorithms and theoretical models used to identify and track objects, predict their trajectories, and predict potential conjunctions. These algorithms, and the object identification taxonomy, are part of the foundation of the AEMR community.

5.2 Adoption and Best Practices Working Group (ABPWG)

The ABPWG would coordinate the AEMR COI activities such as managing the COI Wiki, managing member list and associated e-mail groups, and producing the newsletter. The ABPWG would also run the COI configuration management effort, as well as related efforts, and tasks. They would use JIRA to oversee the changes to the data model, ensuring that the correct version of the data model is saved in the Document Library. They would conduct outreach efforts to other entities (e.g., U.S. Government organizations, NGAs, industry, academia, etc.) and coalition partners (e.g., AUS, CAN, NZ, UK, etc.) to enlist new contributors to the community, and identify conference and training opportunities for COI participants. The ABPWG would also support the creation and management of a common 3D model repository for U.S. Government users to minimize the duplication of effort and cost associated with creating, or buying, the 3D models needed by each virtual environment developer.

5.3 Data Model Working Group (DMWG)

The DMWG would include personnel from different organizations, including government and contractor computer scientists, who analyze the details of the XML, schema, etc. used by the legacy systems. One of the significant problems in the application of virtual reality and augmented reality technology is the large number of different data-formats for 3D models. The goal of the DMWG is to identify duplication, or similarity, of actual data models formats and descriptions. They would then resolve these overlaps to satisfy the functional requirements. The DMWG members would coordinate with the MAWG, URWG, and the ABPWG to ensure that the existing and future requirements are integrated.

6 Community Roadmap

The AEMR roadmap illustrates the flow of products and information across the AEMR community working groups. The requirements emerging from the User Requirements group inform the technologists and vice-versa. The human performance metrics and insights from the Human Performance group are combined with the avatar improvements from the Smart Avatar group which together provide the needed input to the Model and Algorithms and Data Model groups to produce interoperability solutions for models and applications. To validate the usability of the community recommendations and guidance, a reference implementation is needed. This example implementation of the core components can support community wide demonstrations and experiments in a virtual, distributed, interoperability testbed. The recommendations, guidance, and results can be packaged in various forms of documentation (briefs, documents, wiki entries, and videos) to assist with education and outreach by the Adoption and Best Practices group. Finally, the documentation stored in APAN can feed member repositories, such as the DoD Data Services Environment (Fig. 6).

One of the long terms goals of the community is to organize the research domain effectively so that past research can be used to support future research. In order to do that, the community would have to support the development of an Enterprise Data Model (EDM). The EDM will provide a framework for a common data model enabling net-centric information exchange among the AEMR Stakeholders. The Common Data Model refers to data

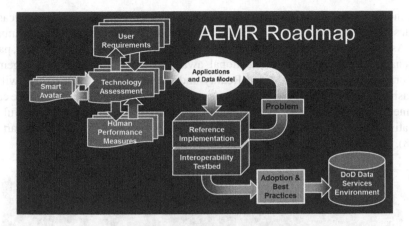

Fig. 6. AEMR COI roadmap

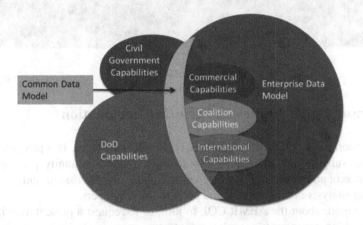

Fig. 7. Enterprise Data Model

structures, definitions, attributes, XML schema, WSDLs, namespace, etc. which are common across multiple virtual reality and mixed reality systems (Fig. 7).

7   Community Opportunities

The AEMR community will be represented at the RIMPAC 2016 exercise as part of the SSC Pacific Battlespace Exploitation of Mixed Reality (BEMR) capability demonstration. The Rim of the Pacific Exercise (RIMPAC) is the world's largest international maritime exercise and is hosted by the U.S. Navy's Pacific Fleet. Held every two years in the June July timeframe, the 2014 RIMPAC includes 22 nations, 49 surface ships, 6 submarines, more than 200 aircraft, and 25,000 personnel. RIMPAC is a unique training opportunity that helps participants foster and sustain the cooperative relationships that are critical to ensuring the safety of sea lanes and security on the world's oceans.

At the upcoming RIMPAC 2016 exercise, BEMR representatives will be showcasing the latest AR and VR gear, along with demonstrations tailored for common Humanitarian Assistance and Disaster Relief (HADR) use-cases such as en-route training, parts-maintenance repair and setup, situational awareness, and emergency management collaborations. The value of Mixed Reality and the community partnerships will be emphasized when BEMR representatives describe the equipment, capabilities, use cases and emerging standards. The AEMR community is a great example of successful and innovative collaboration across industry, academia, government, and coalition partners (Fig. 8).

Fig. 8. RIMPAC exercise

8   Sponsor Opportunities and Contact Information

Funding opportunities are available through our sponsor program. This program enables sponsors to support this community in exchange for a community package which includes areas of potential interest, with goal-oriented group discussion, and deliverables such as gap analysis in that domain, and potential white papers.

To hear more about the AEMR COI, to join, or to request a presentation in one of our four working group meetings, please contact us at aemr-admin@spawar.navy.mil.

Acknowledgements. This project was sponsored by the Office of Naval Research (ONR) and the BEMR laboratory at SSC Pacific. We would like to thank the support of our volunteer chairs for our working groups: Dr. Allen Yang from UC Berkeley, Dr. Ying Choon from UC San Diego, Dr. Luca Bertuccelli from United Technologies, and Mr. Terry McKearny from The Ranger Group.

References

1. Collins, J.D., Markham, A., Service, K.A., Reini, L.S., Wolf, E., Sessoms, P.H.: A systematic literature review of the use and effectiveness of the computer assisted rehabilitation environment for research and rehabilitation as it relates to the wounded warrior. Work **50**(1), 121–129 (2014)

2. Sessoms, P.H., Gottshall, K.R., Collins, J.D., Markham, A.E., Service, K.A.: Improvements in gait speed and weight shift of persons with traumatic brain injury and vestibular dysfunction using a virtual reality computer-assisted rehabilitation environment. J. Mil. Med. **180**(3), 143–149 (2015)

3. The Battlespace Exploitation of Mixed Reality Laboratory (BEMR) at SSC Pacific. http://www.public.navy.mil/spawar/Pacific/BEMR/Pages/default.aspx

4. Kurillo, G., Bajcsy, R.: 3D teleimmersion for collaboration and interaction of geographically distributed users. Virtual Reality **17**(1), 29–43 (2013)

5. Phase Space, Work conducted for Navy STTR with Mark Bolas from USC ICT. http://www.phasespace.com/

6. Konrad, R., Cooper, E.A., Wetzstein, G.: Novel optical configurations for virtual reality: evaluating user preference and performance with focus-tunable and monovision near-eye displays. In: Proceedings of the ACM, Conference on Human Factors in Computing Systems (2016)

7. Zao, J.K., et al.: Augmenting VR/AR applications with EEG/EOG monitoring and oculo-vestibular recoupling. LNCS (in press)

8. Fouse, A.S., Weibel, N., Hutchins, E., Hollan, J.D.: ChronoViz: a system for navigation of time-coded data. In: CHI 2011 Extended Abstracts on Human Factors in Computing Systems, pp. 299–304. ACM (2011)

9. Mercado, J.E., Rupp, M.A., Barnes, M.J., Chen, J.Y.C., Barber, D., Procci, K.: Intelligent agent transparency in human-agent teaming for Multi-UxV management. Hum. Factors **58**(3), 1–15 (2016)

10. Shattuck, N.L., Shattuck, L.G., Smith, K., Matsangas, P.: Changes in reaction time and executive decision-making following exposure to waterborne motion. Hum. Factors **57**(1), 1987–1991 (2013)

11. Hartholt, A., Traum, D., Marsella, S.C., Shapiro, A., Stratou, G., Leuski, A., Morency, L.-P., Gratch, J.: All together now. In: Aylett, R., Krenn, B., Pelachaud, C., Shimodaira, H. (eds.) IVA 2013. LNCS, vol. 8108, pp. 368–381. Springer, Heidelberg (2013)

12. Capitola Coders and Creatives, The Netherlands. http://capitola.nl/

13. Reeder, J.: Team search tactics through multi-agent HyperNEAT. In: Lones, M., Tyrrell, A., Smith, S., Fogel, G. (eds.) IPCAT 2015. LNCS, vol. 9303, pp. 75–89. Springer, Heidelberg (2015)

Gesture and Motion-Based Interaction

Synthesis-Based Low-Cost Gaze Analysis

Zhuoqing Chang(✉), Qiang Qiu, and Guillermo Sapiro

Electrical and Computer Engineering, Duke University, Durham, NC, USA
{zhuoqing.chang,qiang.qiu,guillermo.sapiro}@duke.edu

Abstract. Gaze analysis has gained much popularity over the years due to its relevance in a wide array of applications, including human-computer interaction, fatigue detection, and clinical mental health diagnosis. However, accurate gaze estimation from low resolution images outside of the lab (in the wild) still proves to be a challenging task. The new Intel low-cost RealSense 3D camera, capable of acquiring submillimeter resolution depth information, is currently available in laptops, and such technology is expected to become ubiquitous in other portable devices. In this paper, we focus on low-cost, scalable and real time analysis of human gaze using this RealSense camera. We exploit the direct measurement of eye surface geometry captured by the RGB-D camera, and perform gaze estimation through novel synthesis-based training and testing. Furthermore, we synthesize different eye movement appearances using a linear approach. From each 3D eye training sample captured by the RealSense camera, we synthesize multiple novel 2D views by varying the view angle to simulate head motions expected at testing. We then learn from the synthesized 2D eye images a gaze regression model using regression forests. At testing, for each captured RGB-D eye image, we first repeat the same synthesis process. For each synthesized image, we estimate the gaze from our gaze regression model, and factor-out the associated camera/head motion. In this way, we obtain multiple gaze estimations for each RGB-D eye image, and the consensus is adopted. We show that this synthesis-based training and testing significantly improves the precision in gaze estimation, opening the door to true low-cost solutions.

1 Introduction

Gaze tracking is the process of analyzing human eye movement. There has been a great increase of interest in this area over the last decade due to its relevance in a wide range of applications, including human-computer interaction, fatigue detection, and clinical mental health diagnosis. In many of these applications, gaze tracking needs to be performed either from a distance or in a non-intrusive manner, therefore limiting the resolution of the acquired eye images. In this common low-resolution scenario, appearance-based methods, which use the eye appearance image to estimate gaze directly, are more popular compared to model-based methods, which use derived geometric features as input.

The advantage of appearance-based methods is that no small-scale feature need to be extracted since the high-dimensional eye image is directly mapped

© Springer International Publishing Switzerland 2016
C. Stephanidis (Ed.): HCII 2016 Posters, Part II, CCIS 618, pp. 95–100, 2016.
DOI: 10.1007/978-3-319-40542-1_15

to the low-dimensional gaze direction, allowing the use of low resolution images. However, the biggest limitation of appearance-based methods is that variation in eye images arise from factors other than gaze, head motion being a major contributor. In general, appearance-based methods require a large amount of training data to cover the eye appearance space. For example, Zhang *et al.* [8] collected more than 200,000 images over a 3-month period to train a deep neural network.

In this paper, we propose an appearance-based approach for gaze estimation using synthesized eye images to efficiently address the problem of acquiring large amounts of data. Sugano *et al.* [5] proposed a synthesis approach to generate multiple views of the eye from a 3D reconstruction of the face. However, their method is only able to synthesize eye appearance changes due to head motion and not the (gaze-related) eye movement itself. In addition, they use eight industry-level cameras for the multi-view reconstruction requiring complex calibration and high cost. In contrast, we use one Intel RealSense 3D camera [1], a low-cost commercial RGB-D camera similar to Microsoft's Kinect but better in short range capabilities, to acquire 3D surface data of the face, from which multiple views of the eye are synthesized. We show how the RealSense can be used to accurately align and segment eye images automatically. In addition, we propose a novel approach to synthesize eye appearance changes due to eye movements using a linear method. Finally, we demonstrate that a test-by-synthesis approach is able to further improve the gaze estimation performance.

2   Methods

Given the RealSenses pre-registered RGB images and 3D point clouds, our synthesis-based gaze estimation approach can be summarized in four steps: face alignment, head pose synthesis, eye movement synthesis, and random forest regression. Face alignment normalizes the head pose to a canonical viewpoint, from which multiple pose eye images are generated by projecting the 3D eye surface in different directions. Within each pose, a linear approach is used to synthesize eye appearance changes to further increases the number of training (and then testing) samples. A random forest is trained for each pose to learn the mapping from the eye appearances to the gaze directions.

2.1   Face Alignment

The main goal of face alignment is to rectify the head pose to a canonical viewpoint and scale such that the eye appearance variation is not affected by head motion. Accurate alignment also allows for consistent segmentation of the eye region, which is critical in appearance-based methods.

Our method first locates facial landmarks of the face in the RGB image using Intraface [7], from which 3D landmark points are derived by mapping the 2D points to the 3D point cloud. With the 3D landmark points, the region between the forehead and mouth is cropped as the face model. We chose to use this region since it is robust to occlusion and expression changes. A frontal facing frame is used as a reference model and all other frames are aligned to it using a two step approach. First a rigid transformation is obtained by aligning 11 facial landmarks to the corresponding reference model landmarks. The rigid transformation is used to approximately align the facial point cloud to the reference model, after which Iterative Closest Point (ICP) [4] is used to further refine the alignment. Since the point clouds are from the same person, we achieve near perfect alignment using this method. The alignment process is shown in Fig. 1.

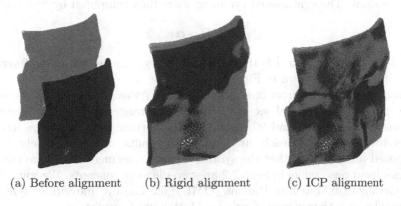

(a) Before alignment   (b) Rigid alignment   (c) ICP alignment

Fig. 1. Face alignment process. (Color figure online)

2.2   Head Pose Synthesis

We use an approach similar to [5] to generate different views of the eye by projecting the point cloud in different directions. The projection angle was chosen to be from −10 to 10 degrees with 5 degree intervals in both the horizontal and vertical direction, yielding a total of 25 different views. This range was chosen such that eye appearance changes due to head pose variation were clearly noticeable, but at the same time not distorting the eye images to an extent where gaze information is lost. A fixed eye region could be defined for each projection angle since the projections are aligned. Eye images are then sampled within the region at a fixed resolution of 24 × 40 pixels (Fig. 2a). Our proposed method is able to handle scaling and multi-resolution images by tuning the sampling resolution within the defined eye region.

2.3   Eye Movement Synthesis

We synthesize different eye appearances for a given head pose using a linear approach. Lu *et al.* [3] showed that gaze positions and eye appearances have a similar manifold when the head is static, and that gaze could be computed as a linear combination of a sparse set of training samples. We reverse this idea and use the linearity of gaze directions to synthesize eye images.

For a set of eye images $\{x_i\} \in \mathbb{R}^d$, their corresponding 3D gaze direction is denoted as $\{g_i\} \in \mathbb{R}^3$. Let $\{\tilde{g}_j\} \in \mathbb{R}^3$ denote the set of gaze directions for which we wish to synthesize eye images $\{\tilde{x}_j\} \in \mathbb{R}^d$. The idea is to solve

$$\min |\alpha_j|_1 \quad s.t. \quad \tilde{g}_j = D_g \cdot \alpha_j \tag{1}$$

for the sparse weight vector $\alpha_j \in \mathbb{R}^n$. $D_g = [g_1, g_2, \ldots, g_n]$ is the dictionary of gaze directions. The synthesized eye images are then computed by

$$\tilde{x}_j = D_x \cdot \alpha_j \tag{2}$$

where $D_x = [x_1, x_2, \ldots, x_n]$ is the dictionary of eye images. Samples of synthesized eye images are shown in Fig. 2b.

The range of gaze directions to synthesize $\tilde{g}_j$ was chosen to be the same as the range of the original set g_i. Typically the range is about 40 degrees in the horizontal direction and 20 degrees in the vertical direction. The interval was set to 0.2 degrees in each direction which results in approximately 20,000 synthesized images. Note that the synthesis gaze range mentioned here and the synthesis head pose range in Sect. 2.2 are two different concepts. We solve Eq. 1 using Orthogonal Matching Pursuit (OMP) [6]. The eye movement synthesis process takes less than a second using a Matlab implementation.

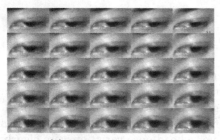 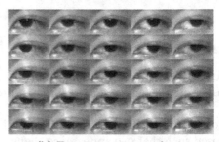

(a) Head pose synthesis   (b) Eye movement synthesis

Fig. 2. Synthesized eye images using (a) head pose synthesis, and (b) eye movement synthesis

2.4   Gaze Estimation Using Random Forests

We chose to use random forests [2] to learn the mapping between eye appearance and gaze direction because it has been shown to work well in related tasks [5,8]. Each eye image is converted to grayscale, raster-scanned to form a feature vector and normalized to have unit length. The gaze direction is defined as a unit vector that points from the center of the eye, an arbitrary fixed point relative to the face model, to the visual target.

We do not cluster samples according to head poses as in [5,8] since we only have 25 discrete head poses after face alignment and head pose synthesis. We instead train a random forest for each head pose, which we then use to independently estimate the corresponding synthesized testing image. The gaze output for each random forest is compensated by the head pose synthesis angle and the face alignment angle before being aggregated to get the final estimation.

3 Experiments

3.1 Data Collection

The data collection system consists of a 14 inch laptop with a 1600×900 display and a RealSense camera. RGB images captured by the RealSense were set to 1920×1080 pixels while the point cloud resolution was limited to 640×480. The two devices have been pre-calibrated such that pixel coordinates on the laptop screen can be mapped to its 3D coordinate in the camera reference system.

During recording sessions, 3 participants, 2 male and 1 female, were asked to sit approximately 40 cm in front of the laptop and look at 60 visual targets that appeared randomly on the screen. Participants were allowed to have there head relaxed and natural but were told to refrain from making large head movements. After post processing, 10 frames were kept for each visual target per participant. Half of the data is randomly selected as the training data and the other half as the testing data.

3.2 Results

We evaluated the performance of our proposed method by comparing three sets of experiments: no-synthesis, half-synthesis, and full-synthesis. The no-synthesis experiment is used as a baseline comparison, where only the normalized eye images are used for training and testing. The half-synthesis experiment uses eye movement synthesis on the training set to train a larger regression forest on which the testing set is tested. The full-synthesis experiment uses both eye movement and head pose synthesis on the training set to train 25 regression forests corresponding to different head poses. Head pose synthesis is also used

Table 1. Comparison of gaze estimation error

Participant	No-synthesis	Half-synthesis	Full-synthesis
1	$1.32 \pm 1.54°$	$1.18 \pm 1.37°$	$0.85 \pm 0.98°$
2	$1.40 \pm 1.73°$	$1.25 \pm 1.48°$	$1.07 \pm 1.29°$
3	$1.25 \pm 1.51°$	$0.91 \pm 1.09°$	$0.77 \pm 0.93°$
Average	$1.32 \pm 1.59°$	$1.11 \pm 1.31°$	$0.90 \pm 1.07°$

on the testing set to generate different views of each testing image which is then tested using the corresponding regression forest. After compensating the output of each regression forest with its associated pose angle, the median is adopted as the final gaze angle. The estimation errors are given in Table 1.

4   Conclusion

We proposed a novel synthesis-based approach for gaze analysis using a low-cost commercial 3D camera. We synthesize eye appearance changes due to both head motion and eye movement to dramatically increase the amount of training data. In the testing stage, we use synthesis to obtain multiple gaze estimates. Moreover, our approach works with low resolution images and is able to handle slight natural head motion. The reported results demonstrate that synthesis can be used to compensate the lack of calibration data and greatly improve gaze estimation accuracy and stability, justifying the feasibility of low-cost gaze analysis.

Acknowledgments. Work partially supported by NSF, ONR, ARO, NGA, and AFOSR.

References

1. Sugano, Y., Matsushita, Y., Sato, Y.: Learning-by-synthesis for appearance-based 3D gaze estimation. In: 2014 IEEE Conference on Computer Vision and Pattern Recognition (CVPR), pp. 1821–1828, June 2014. doi:10.1109/CVPR.2014.235
2. Intel   RealSense   3D   Camera.   http://www.intel.com/content/www/us/en/ architecture-and-technology/realsense-overview.html. Accessed 07 Apr 2016
3. Xiong, X., De la Torre, F.: Supervised descent method and its applications to face alignment. In: IEEE Conference on Computer Vision and Pattern Recognition (CVPR) (2013)
4. Zhang, X., Sugano, Y., Fritz, M., Bulling, A.: Appearance-based gaze estimation in the wild. In: Proceedings of the IEEE International Conference on Computer Vision and Pattern Recognition (CVPR), pp. 4511–4520 June 2015
5. Rusinkiewicz, S., Levoy, M.: Efficient variants of the ICP algorithm. In: 3-D Digital Imaging and Modeling, pp. 145–152. IEEE (2001)
6. Lu, F., Sugano, Y., Okabe, T., Sato, Y.: Adaptive linear regression for appearance-based gaze estimation. IEEE Trans. Pattern Anal. Mach. Intell. **36**(10), 2033–2046 (2014)
7. Tropp, J.A., Gilbert, A.C.: Signal recovery from random measurements via orthogonal matching pursuit. IEEE Trans. Inf. Theory. **53**(12), 4655–4666 (2007)
8. Breiman, L.: Random forests. Mach. learn. **45**(1), 5–32 (2001)

Outdoor Gesture Recognition System Using Accurate Absolute Position Coordinates

Tomohiko Hayakawa[✉] and Masatoshi Ishikawa

The University of Tokyo, Bunkyo, Japan
{Tomohiko_Hayakawa,Masatoshi_Ishikawa}@ipc.i.u-tokyo.ac.jp

Abstract. In this paper, we propose a gesture recognition system using accurate absolute position coordinates, which are acquired by an Real Time Kinematic Global Navigation Satellite System(RTK-GNSS) sensor. The RTK-GNSS sensor is not affected by sunshine and does not need to be calibrated; additionally, drift does not occur, even for long-term use. The system consists of an antenna, a 10-Hz RTK-GNSS processor, and a PC. The user wears the antenna connected to the processor on the back of the hand and may freely move the hand when the antenna receives satellites signals. As an experiment, we implemented gesture-sensing trials using our system to input a line and an arbitrary path. As a result, they were well observed with an accuracy on the order of a centimeter, even outside without any calibration. Through this experiment, our system has great potential to be used for gesture recognition system in flexible outdoor environments.

Keywords: Gesture sensing · GNSS · Outdoor environment · Absolute position coordinates · Wearable device

1 Introduction

Recently, various gesture recognition systems have been proposed for human–computer interaction using sensors such as a depth camera [1,2] and an accelerometer [3,4]. These systems are sold as products, even for end users, as a user interface. Additionally, the range of their applications extends from fixed indoor environments to flexible outdoor environments. However, the vision sensor has disadvantages due to sunshine, occlusion, and calibration for the extended environment. Moreover, the accelerometer has disadvantages due to drift, which results in a lower accuracy. On the other hand, the number of GNSS satellites is increasing [5], and the accuracy of the absolute position coordinates is improving more and more. A GNSS antenna has the advantage of outside use, and it complements conventional gesture sensing systems.

2 Method

Our gesture-sensing system is based on an Real Time Kinematic Global Navigation Satellite System (RTK-GNSS) sensor using accurate absolute position coordinates.

© Springer International Publishing Switzerland 2016
C. Stephanidis (Ed.): HCII 2016 Posters, Part II, CCIS 618, pp. 101–106, 2016.
DOI: 10.1007/978-3-319-40542-1_16

An RTK-GNSS sensor has a good accuracy, does not need to be calibrated, and is not affected by sunshine. Additionally, even for long-term use drift does not occur. The entire system consists of a wearable antenna, a 10-Hz RTK-GNSS processor, and a PC.

To demonstrate our strategy, we use a high-accuracy GPS device (Topcon GB-3) and the RTK-GPS method; therefore, it is possible to achieve an absolute position of ± 10 mm + 1 ppm horizontally and ± 15 mm + 1 ppm vertically in the RTK-GPS mode in an ideal situation. The user wears the antenna connected to the processor on the back of the hand and may freely move the hand when the antenna receives satellites signals. We set up the system on the roof of the four-story 6th engineering building at the University of Tokyo in Japan (latitude: 139.761142, longitude: 35.714122). A few tall buildings surround this building, but we were able to verify that around 10 satellites were detected at all time.

As an experiment, we implemented gesture-sensing trials using our system to input a line and an arbitrary path. In the first trial, we prepared a slider with an antenna to input a line path. As illustrated in Fig. 1(a), we mounted a GPS antenna onto the slider. For acquisition under motion, we loosened the screws and moved the slider linearly and smoothly by hand. The antenna orientation was fixed using screws, and everything was mounted onto a heavy surface plate to remove measurement errors. Moreover, we placed the entire system on a heavy table lift. The table height of the lift can be set arbitrarily from 0.3 m to 1.5 m. We set the height around 1.0 m to reduce errors caused by the multipath problem.

In the second trial, we prepared a wearable antenna system (see Fig. 1(b)). The arbitrary path is controlled by the user's gesture for the input. Note that the angle of the antenna should be upside to maintain the best conditions for obtaining satellite numbers.

3   Results

Figures 2 and 3 show the basic accuracy of our system. In Figs. 2 and 3, the units were converted from absolute coordinates to millimeters to discuss the accuracy. As a result, the mean distance from the linear regression line to the original points is 5.52 mm. Hence, the accuracy was usually well observed within the order of a centimeter or less, even outside without any calibration.

On the other hand, Figs. 4 and 5 show an arbitrary path for gesture sensing. The initial point is indicated by the blue cross, and the end point is indicated by the red cross.

4   Discussion

From the results of the experimental trials, our system demonstrates considerable potential to be used for gesture recognition systems in flexible outdoor environments. In particular, it is possible to improve the accuracy by using other methods [6]; however, in this research, we could not compare with other methods such as a distance sensor and an accelerometer. The characteristics of our

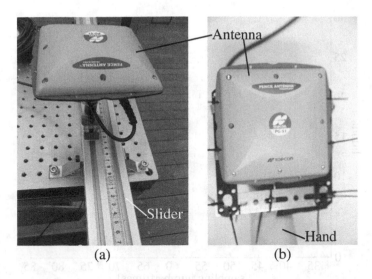

Fig. 1. System setup: (a) antenna placed on a slider to check the accuracy of the system and (b) wearable gesture sensor held by a human hand

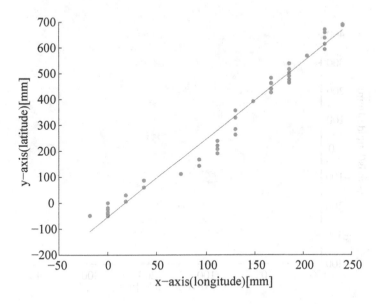

Fig. 2. Original data (green points) of a line path and a linear regression line (red line). (Color figure online)

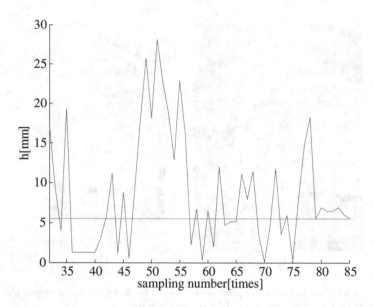

Fig. 3. Mean distance from the linear regression line (red) and each distance (blue). (Color figure online)

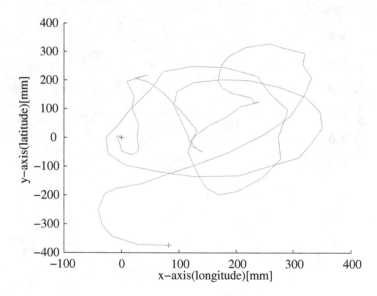

Fig. 4. The first arbitrary path is indicated by a green line. The initial point is indicated by the blue cross, and the end point is indicated by the red cross. (Color figure online)

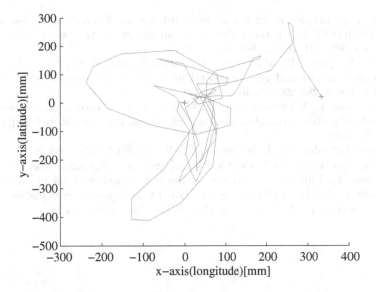

Fig. 5. The second arbitrary path is indicated by a green line. The initial point is indicated by the blue cross, and the end point is indicated by the red cross. (Color figure online)

system are suitable for flexible outdoor environments, and our system does not need to rely on other sensors.

5   Conclusion and Future Work

We proposed a gesture recognition system using accurate absolute position coordinates, which are acquired by an RTK-GNSS sensor. As an experiment, we implemented gesture-sensing trials using our system to input a line and an arbitrary path. As a result, the accuracy was well observed on the order of a centimeter, even outside without any calibration. From the experimental results, we validated that our system has great potential to be used for gesture recognition systems in flexible outdoor environments.

Additionally, we used absolute position coordinates in our research; this has the potential to interact with absolute coordinates. In future work, we will demonstrate that this system can interact with local information on a map for augmented reality.

References

1. Ren, Z., Meng, J., Yuan, J.: Depth camera based hand gesture recognition and its applications in human-computer-interaction. In: 2011 8th International Conference on Information, Communications and Signal Processing (ICICS), pp. 1–5. IEEE, New York (2011)

2. Liu, X., Fujimura, K.: Hand gesture recognition using depth data. In: Proceedings of the Sixth IEEE International Conference on Automatic Face and Gesture Recognition, pp. 529–534. IEEE, New York (2004)
3. Kela, J., Korpipaa, P., Mantyjarvi, J., Kallio, S., Savino, G., Jozzo, L., Marca, D.: Accelerometer-based gesture control for a design environment. Pers. Ubiquit. Comput. **10**(5), 285–299 (2006)
4. Liu, J., Zhong, L., Wickramasuriya, J., Vasudevan, V.: uWave: accelerometer-based personalized gesture recognition and its applications. Pervasive Mob. Comput. **5**(6), 657–675 (2009)
5. Hofmann-Wellenhof, B., Lichtenegger, H., Wasle, E.: GNSS - Global Navigation Satellite Systems: GPS, GLONASS, Galileo, and More. Springer, Wien (2007)
6. Hayakawa, T., Ishikawa, M.: GPS error range reduction method based on linear kinematic model. In: 2015 IEEE International Conference on Automation Science and Engineering (CASE), pp. 1515–1520. IEEE, New York (2015)

Development of Gesture Recognition-Based STEAM Educational Games Focused on Korean Traditional Archery

Hyung Sook Kim[1,3], Su Hak Oh[1,2], and Yong Hyun Park[1(✉)]

[1] Department of Human Art and Technology, Graduate Program in Robot Engineering,
Inha University, Incheon, Republic of Korea
{khsook12,suhakoh}@inha.ac.kr, yhpark81@gmail.com
[2] Department of Physical Education, Inha University, Incheon, Republic of Korea
[3] Department of Kinesiology, Inha University, Incheon, Republic of Korea

Abstract. The purpose of this study was to develop the gesture recognition-based STEAM educational game focused on Korean traditional archery. The game adopted the story of the Korean movie *War of the Arrows* and included educational contents based on the scientific principles of archery to help users shoot well in archery games. The game was demonstrated at the exhibition booths in the BIFF Village during the 2015 Busan International Film Festival (BIFF). Learning through body movements based on scientific knowledge could be a good approach for designing STEAM education program. The program's contents include the scientific principles of archery, such as kinetic energy, kinematics of projectile motion, and predicted aiming method. The first key issue in the development was the robustness and usability of the gesture recognition system for on-site installation. The second key issue was the customized content for immediately increasing the interests of users. The difficulty of the game was determined by the archery target size and control. The user controlled the game with his or her own gestures: Aim was controlled by the user's left hand, and the firing gesture required putting the user's right hand up. We tested the gesture recognition-based art education game with many participants at the exhibition. Participants' reaction was very favorable. Most people could play the game easily and intuitively. After the experience, users' feedback was almost entirely positive. However, kids younger than six years old and elderly people over sixty-five could not play the game as easily. These facts should be considered for an educational game design.

Keywords: Gesture recognition-based game · NUI · Korean traditional archery · STEAM education · Science · Kinect

1 Introduction

Nowadays, the use of an interactive digital game as educational media has been expanded [1]. The entertainment characteristics of digital games help improve self-active learning [2]. Many researchers have investigated the advantages of educational games on students' learning in a variety of subjects. Digital games are also a powerful

© Springer International Publishing Switzerland 2016
C. Stephanidis (Ed.): HCII 2016 Posters, Part II, CCIS 618, pp. 107–111, 2016.
DOI: 10.1007/978-3-319-40542-1_17

tool for the visualization of learning contents. The importance of active learning has been reported by educational professions and teachers [3]. Digital games are a useful tool for self-active learning. When users play a game, they are learning, acting, and interacting with the contents.

Archery is a good sport for mental and physical health and fitness. Consequently, many people enjoy archery games. The Korean traditional archer aims without using additional means like eyeholes and targeting tools. Achieving good shooting results requires much experience and practice. However, opportunities to experience and practice Korean traditional archery are rare. Thus, many novice players have trouble with the difficulty of learning how to aim and shoot. Therefore, game-based learning in archery aiming has benefits without costs (e.g., time, money) [4].

The purpose of this study is to develop the gesture recognition-based STEAM educational game focused on Korean traditional archery. To promote learners' interest, the game borrowed the story of the Korean movie *War of the Arrows*. In addition, it included not only fun factors, but also educational contents based on scientific principles of archery to help users achieve good results in archery games. The game was demonstrated at an exhibition booth during the 2015 Busan International Film Festival (BIFF) at the BIFF Village installed at the Haeundae beach entrance. Visitors to the BIFF Village were able to experience and learn archery through interactive games based on gestures. In the process, such an experience could also provide PR and promotion for the Korean traditional archery.

2   STEAM Education

This application could be utilized in science, technology, engineering, art, and mathematics (STEAM) education programs, which provide scientific knowledge and specific experience of learning through bodily movements. Nowadays STEAM fields have become essential because game-based education offers opportunities for students to develop their creativity and imagination [5]. Learning through bodily movements based on scientific knowledge could be a good approach for designing STEAM education programs. The contents of the program under study include scientific principles of archery (e.g., kinetic energy, kinematics of projectile motion, predicted aiming method) that make the game much more interesting and real. Users' experiences improved their understanding of the skill of archery.

3   Development of Game

3.1   System Architecture

Our system consists of a Kinect sensor, a laptop PC, and a TV kiosk. In order to develop the game and implement the logics, we utilized Zigfu, a programming development toolkit, and Unity, a cross-platform game creation system [6]. Figure 1 shows the system architecture and user interface of this system.

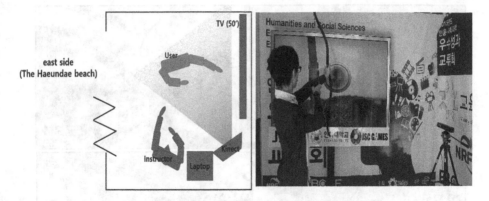

Fig. 1. System architecture and user location. The game system is configured with Kinect, a laptop PC, and a large LCD TV

3.2 Game System Setting

The issues that should be considered in the development are, first, robustness and usability of the gesture recognition system for on-site installation and, second, customized content to increase the interests of users at once because our booth was installed at the Haeundae beach entrance to the BIFF Village, where the sunlight lit up the booth each morning.

The difficulty of the game was defined by the archery target size and control (big → small, fixed → slow movement → fast movement). Archery operations applied to this game were divided into firing using the right hand and aiming using the left hand. The user moved his or left hand up, down, left, and right to aim the bow in the game. Right-hand shooting was implemented through the operation of lifting the hand over the head.

4 Exhibition Lesson and Users' Feedback

We tested the gesture recognition-based art education game with many participants at the exhibition, whose reaction was very favorable. Learning how to play the archery game was very easy. People of all ages could easily and intuitively play the game, the users' feedback was almost unanimously positive. However, kids younger than six years old and elderly people over sixty-five years old indicated some difficulty playing the game. They complained about the difficulty in understanding how to use the gesture-based control in the game. This is because the natural user interface (NUI) is not natural (Fig. 2).

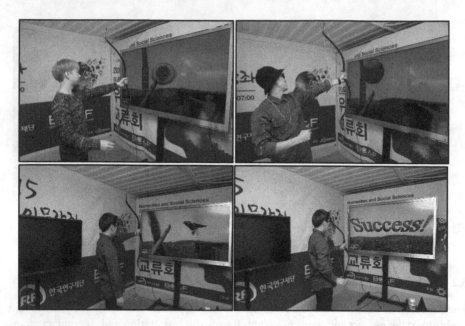

Fig. 2. Three different targets had different difficulty levels. (Upper left) The fixed circle shaped target (Upper right). The slow moving pot. (Lower left) The fast flying bird. (Lower right) The pop-up image after hitting the target.

5   Conclusion and Discussion

In this paper, we proposed a gesture recognition-based STEAM educational game focused on the Korean traditional archery. To promote learners' interest, the game borrowed the story of the Korean movie *War of the Arrows* and included not only fun factors, but also educational contents based on scientific principles of archery to help users get good results in the archery games. The game was demonstrated at an exhibition booth in the BIFF Village installed at the Haeundae beach entrance during the 2015 BIFF. Visitors to BIFF Village were able to experience and learn archery through interactive games based on gestures. In the process, Korean traditional archery could receive PR and promotion. Participants' reactions to the educational game were very favorable. Learning how to play the archery game was very easy. People of all ages could play the game easily and intuitively. After the experience, the feedback of almost every user was positive.

Acknowledgement.   This work was supported by the Industrial Strategic technology development program (10059090, 'Service Solution Development for Children's Physical Activity Convergence Contents and Health Care Service Platform Using Gesture Recognition-based Interactive Technology') funded By the Ministry of Trade, Industry & Energy(MI, Korea)

References

1. Miller, N.: Games in the Classroom. Indiana Libr. **33**, 61–63 (2014)
2. Beetham, H., Sharpe, R.: Rethinking Pedagogy for a Digital Age: Designing for 21st-Century Learning. Routledge, Abingdon (2013)
3. Freeman, S., Eddy, S.L., McDonough, M., Smith, M.K., Okoroafor, N., Jordt, H., Wenderoth, M.P.: Active learning increases student performance in science, engineering, and mathematics. Proc. Nat. Acad. Sci. **111**, 8410–8415 (2014)
4. Miles, H.C., Pop, S.R., Watt, S.J., Lawrence, G.P., John, N.W.: A review of virtual environments for training in ball sports. Comput. Graph. **36**, 714–726 (2012)
5. Taylor, P.: Transformative steam education for the 21st century. In: Proceedings of The Australian Conference on Science and Mathematics Education (formerly UniServe Science Conference). (Year)
6. http://en.wikipedia.org/wiki/Unity_%28game_engine%29

Motion Detection and Sound Effect Game for Daily Jogging

Yang Kyu Lim[1(✉)], Eun Ju Lee[1], Hyun Chun Jung[1], Seong Kuk Park[1],
and Jin Wan Park[2]

[1] Graduate School of Advanced Imaging Science, Multimedia and Film,
Chung-Ang University, Seoul, South Korea
lim0386@gmail.com, eunju.hd@gmail.com,
{jhc06,visualizator}@naver.com
[2] Integrative Engineering Technology, Chung-Ang University, Seoul, South Korea
jinpark@cau.ac.kr

Abstract. The benefits of daily jogging are already proved by many researchers. But, it is challenging to get people to keep working out. We made a motion detection and sound effect based game -*Escape Runner: Junk Buster*- to make more fun and interesting daily jogging. The game will add fun into exercise, helping the user to lose body fat and maintain good health. Because *Escape Runner* provides auditory information rather than visual information, it reduces the risk of accidents caused by inattention. The level of intensity is determined based on the individual's BMI (Body Mass Index), calculated using one's height and weight, and the intensity of the exercise increases appropriately as the user proceeds through the stages, while the user's fitness also gradually improves. The sound of junk food monsters attacking from every side makes the user feel as if they are in the virtual gaming space, which in turn increases absorption in the game and makes the exercise more effective. And the sound of junk foods comically rushing to provide entertainment, which even small children can experience. Although it is not visual, one can experience thrilling by dodging the junk foods rushing in through sound. The user will face increasing levels of difficulty according to the 8 week jogging program. The user will soon find himself in a much healthier shape. The final score can be uploaded online to share with friends. The user can compete with friends to see who has the highest score. Goal of *Escape Runner* is to complete all the courses of the 8-Week Beginner's Program. This method was proven by many other research. And *Escape Runner: Junk Buster* has been entered a competition *Game 4 Health 2015* in Utah.

Keywords: Game · Jogging · Smartphone · Health

1 Introduction

A sound-based game system is rather incorporated into the dull process of jogging, making jogging more fun and interesting. The game will add fun into exercise, helping the user to lose body fat and maintain good health. Because it provides auditory information rather than visual information, it reduces the risk of accidents caused by inattention. The level of intensity is determined based on the individual's BMI (Body Mass Index), calculated using one's height and weight, and the intensity of the exercise

C. Stephanidis (Ed.): HCII 2016 Posters, Part II, CCIS 618, pp. 112–116, 2016.
DOI: 10.1007/978-3-319-40542-1_18

increases appropriately as the user proceeds through the stages, while the user's fitness also gradually improves. Each time a target score is reached, the user can proceed upwards in the ranking system, and soon the user will find themselves in a much healthier shape. In addition, the game can be connected with an SNS to compete with friends.

2   Previous Study

Our work was motivated by *Shake It Up*: Exercise Intensity Recognizing System. It is smartphone-based exercise intensity recognizing system that we made for the HCI International poster session. After finishing our work, we focused on making exercise game with these materials. However, there are several similar ideas already in the market. We develop and use a surround sound based motion detecting system.

3   Design and Implementation

Our goal of the game is using surround sound system to fill like Junk foods are rushing into the user. The user must run away from the attack of junk foods coming in from all sides like a swarm of bees. The final goal of this game is to jog in order to run away from the attack of the junk foods sound. When attacked by junk food, fat point is accumulated in the body, and the fat can be removed through a given mission.

3.1   Design

We use *The 8-Week Beginner's Program* by *Runner's World*. It is one of the most common and effective way to keep healthy (Table 1).

We have 8 enemies expended upon junk food. Each character has taken off the original snacks name. Russian character MMM is Chocolate, Japanese character Kendai Suitsu is Candy, American character Pop C is Coke, Argentinian Springle Rays is Potato Chip. And there is also ice cream, Ruskin Barbars (US), Doughnut, Mrs. Dounafire (Netherlands), Pizza, Papa Domingo Jonhnes (Italy), and hamburger, Buggie Kim (Fig. 1).

The *ER: Junk Buster* is an iOS8-based application that can be used on the iPhone. We used smartphone gyroscope sensor to detect the swing of the arm same as our previous work *Shake it up* [2]. This algorithm is measuring man's movement similar to the pedometer. It is a device that counts each step a person takes by detecting the motion of the person's body. Our goal is detecting the moment of the motion and reflecting the game situation (Fig. 2).

Table 1. The *8-Week Beginner's Program* by *Runner's World* [1]

Wk	Mon	Tues	Weds	Thurs	Fri	Sat	Sun
1	Run & Walk / Run 1 min / Walk 2 min / Repeat 10X	Walk / Walk easy 30 min	Run & Walk / Run 1 min / Walk 2 min / Repeat 10X	Walk / Walk easy 30 min	Run & Walk / Run 1 min / Walk 2 min / Repeat 10X	Run & Walk / Run 1 min / Walk 2 min / Repeat 10X	Rest
2	Run & Walk / Run 2 min / Walk 1 min / Repeat 10X	Walk / Walk easy 30 min	Run & Walk / Run 3 min / Walk 1 min / Repeat 7X / Run 2 min	Walk / Walk easy 30 min	Run & Walk / Run 4 min / Walk 1 min / Repeat 6X	Run & Walk / Run 4 min / Walk 1 min / Repeat 6X	Rest
3	Run & Walk / Run 5 min / Walk 1 min / Repeat 5X	Walk / Walk easy 30 min	Run & Walk / Run 5 min / Walk 1 min / Repeat 5X	Walk / Walk easy 30 min	Run & Walk / Run 6 min / Walk 1 min / Repeat 4X / Run 2 min	Run & Walk / Run 6 min / Walk 1 min / Repeat 4X / Run 2 min	Rest
4	Run & Walk / Run 8 min / Walk 1 min / Repeat 3X / Run 3 min	Walk / Walk easy 30 min	Run & Walk / Run 9 min / Walk 1 min / Repeat 3X	Walk / Walk easy 30 min	Run & Walk / Run 10 min / Walk 1 min / Repeat 2X / Run 8 min	Run & Walk / Run 11 min / Walk 1 min / Repeat 2X / Run 6 min	Rest
5	Run & Walk / Run 12 min / Walk 1 min / Repeat 2X / Run 4 min	Walk / Walk easy 30 min	Run & Walk / Run 13 min / Walk 1 min / Repeat 2X / Run 2 min	Walk / Walk easy 30 min	Run & Walk / Run 14 min / Walk 1 min / Repeat 2X	Run & Walk / Run 15 min / Walk 1 min / Run 14 min	Rest
6	Run & Walk / Run 16 min / Walk 1 min / Run 13 min	Walk / Walk easy 30 min	Run & Walk / Run 17 min / Walk 1 min / Run 12 min	Walk / Walk easy 30 min	Run & Walk / Run 18 min / Walk 1 min / Run 11 min	Run & Walk / Run 19 min / Walk 1 min / Run 10 min	Rest
7	Run & Walk / Run 20 min / Walk 1 min / Run 9 min	Run & Walk / Run 20 min / Walk 1 min / Run 9 min	Run & Walk / Run 22 min / Walk 1 min / Run 7 min	Walk / Walk easy 30 min	Run & Walk / Run 24 min / Walk 1 min / Run 5 min	Run & Walk / Run 26 min / Walk 1 min / Run 3 min	Rest
8	Run & Walk / Run 27 min / Walk 1 min / Run 2 min	Walk / Run 20 min / Walk 1 min / Run 9 min	Run & Walk / Run 28 min / Walk 1 min / Run 1 min	Walk / Walk easy 30 min	Run & Walk / Run 29 min / Walk 1 min	Run & Walk / Run 30 min	Rest

Fig. 1. 8 enemies from *ER: Junk Buster*

Fig. 2. User can play *ER: Junk Buster* both indoor and outdoor [3]

3.2 Scenario

The sound of junk foods attacking from every side makes the user feel as if they are in the virtual gaming space, which in turn increases absorption in the game and makes the exercise more effective. The final score can be uploaded online to share with friends. The user can compete with friends to see who has the highest score.

The sound of junk foods comically rushing in provides entertainment, which even small children can experience. Although it is not visual, one can experience thrilling by dodging the junk foods rushing in through sound.

Because the user must jog while playing the game, without knowing, the user will soon find themselves in a much healthier shape. The user will face increasing levels of difficulty according to the 8-week jogging program. User can build themselves to dodge the incoming rush of junk foods becoming stronger every stage. The game applies a system that recognizes body motion using smartphone sensors.

4 Evaluation and Conclusion

A free trial version of *Escape Runner: Junk Buster* will first be made available on the Apple appstore to increase brand recognition among users. Afterwards, a paid pro-version will be released with newly added features, and the revenue generated from the pro-version will become the main source of revenue. The pro-version will not only measure walking speed and the number of steps, but it will also have features that measure ECG and EMG by coupling with Smart Band, which allows us to collect medical data. An Item Market will be added, where users can buy add-in features such as tracking oxygen consumption through sensors, which will make additional profits. As a result, users will be able to obtain various data, and by presenting a detailed explanation of the changes in the users' body in objective measures, we will be able to provide reliability to the users. Furthermore, a millage system will be available, and when the users play the game and reach a certain level, health food discount coupons will be issued. Some examples of healthy food would be tea, salad, nuts, and fruit, which are desserts that are low in fat and high in nutrition. We will generate additional profit from commission on the sales in health food franchises. Lastly, cute characters appearing in the app will later be made into animation, or made into figures, cups, and plates through 3D printing, available for purchase.

References

1. Runner's World. http://www.runnersworld.com/getting-started/the-8-week-beginners-program. Accessed Apr 2016
2. Lim, Y.K., Shim, B.K.: Shake it up: exercise intensity recognizing system. In: Stephanidis, C. (ed.) HCI 2014, Part II. CCIS, vol. 435, pp. 355–360. Springer, Heidelberg (2014)
3. Escape Runner: Junk Buster. https://youtu.be/JK3vY_hYYWw. Accessed Apr 2016

User Performance of Gestural and Non-gestural Operations in a Mixed Computer Task Under Different Multi-touch Screen Configurations

Cheng-Jhe Lin[✉]

Industrial Management, National Taiwan University of Science and Technology,
Taipei, Taiwan
Robert_cjlin@mail.ntust.edu.tw

Abstract. Multi-touch screens are the fastest growing main stream technology for human-computer interaction and gestural operation usually accompanies their use. Research has shown that configuring single-touch screens at greater tilting angles might optimize manual operation. Furthermore, gestural operation, given its direct-manipulating nature, may enable better performance in object manipulation tasks. The current study recruited 20 volunteer participants to perform a mixed computer task by 4 modes of operations on a multi-touch screen at 2 display positions. The results showed that display position optimized for manual operation did not improve user performance. KM mode (participants used keyboards/mice) generated the best overall performance. Gesture mode enabled participants to have comparable precision to that of KM mode in sizing the picture, while Touch mode completed the task in a shorter time. All mode that allowed mixed use of all types of operations did not outperform using traditional keyboards/mice.

Keywords: Gesture operation · Multi-touch screens · Display configuration

1 Introduction

As technology advances, multi-touch screens become the fastest growing technology among those main stream devices and gestural operation usually accompanies their use. Research has shown a touch display positioned at a lower angle from the horizon could reduce fatigue in touch operation and was preferred by the users [1]. For gestural operation, users need to perform more complicated finger/hand activity on a multi-touch screen for a longer time. It is therefore expected that a horizontal position optimized for gestural operation should improve user performance in computer tasks using multi-touch screens. Such an assumption has not received much attention in literature.

To further investigate the effect of gestural operations on user performance under different touchscreen settings, the interactions between tasks and operational modes must be considered. Direct operations using touchscreens and indirect operations using keyboards/mice may affect user performance in different types of tasks. For example, data entry tasks, e.g. word processing, require a larger amount of typing. Since typing involves repetitive clicking, it is expected that indirect operations using keyboards/mice will generate better performance. In contrast, object manipulation such as photo editing,

© Springer International Publishing Switzerland 2016
C. Stephanidis (Ed.): HCII 2016 Posters, Part II, CCIS 618, pp. 117–123, 2016.
DOI: 10.1007/978-3-319-40542-1_19

requires users to acquire and translate target objects. On one hand, direct operations can generate comparable performance to that of indirect operations [2]. However, if the target size is apparently smaller than the user's finger, the performance of direct operations becomes worse because of biomechanical disadvantages that are caused by longer distance in operations and the "fat-finger" effect signifying the target being blocked by the finger [3]. On the other hand, the performance of dragging objects is determined by the precision requirements of the task. When the requirement is not excessive, direct manipulation by gestural operations possesses advantages in that it can translate and scale the object at the same time and control the object directly with immediate response.

The research objectives of this study is to investigate whether touch and gestural operations can be superior than traditional keyboard/mouse operations in computer tasks under two display configurations, optimized for viewing and manual operations respectively. In particular, the investigator of this study is interested in knowing whether gestural operation, in comparison with single-touch operation and traditional operation with keyboards/mice, is advantageous in object manipulation, and whether gestural operation can be facilitated by the display setting optimized for manual operation. The results altogether can provide recommendations and guidelines of future HCI design using multi-touch technology.

2   Methodology

Twenty students aged from 18- and 35-years old voluntarily participated in the experiment. The experimental task was implemented through a c# program that simulated word processing software (Fig. 1). The task was composed of two parts: text editing and picture manipulation.

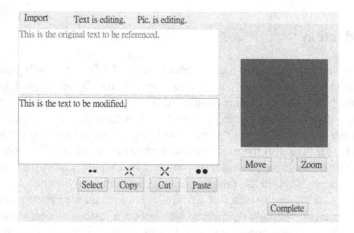

Fig. 1. Experimental program

In text editing, the task goal is to modify the text in the bottom-left column (working text) so that it would be identical to the text in the top-left column (original text).

The original text to be referenced was adopted from English textbooks for senior high schoolers. The working text was modified from the original text to a limited extent so that participants might use only copy, cut and paste functions to complete editing while s/he could still opt to type if s/he wanted. In picture manipulation, participants were instructed to import a picture by clicking the "import" button on the menu and use a mouse, touch buttons or gestural operations to match its position and size with the gray area (target) on the right side of the program. The participants were instructed to complete the experimental task in three operational modes.

1. Keyboard/Mouse (KM) mode: participants used a physical keyboard and a mouse to complete the task.
2. Touch mode: participants used touch buttons and single-touch actions on the screen to complete the task. For text editing, participants used a Windows® embedded touch keyboard to type, and click on "Select," "Copy," "Cut" and "Paste" buttons to perform corresponding functions. For picture manipulation, participants need to click "Move" button under the target area first, then single-click on the touchscreen to move the picture to a new location. Similarly, to adjust the size of the picture participants need to click on the picture first, click "Zoom" button to set the picture to the zooming mode, and then single-click on the touchscreen to set a new location for the control point. The picture would in turn change its size according to the new location of its control point.
3. Gesture mode: participants used touch buttons and a pinch gesture to complete the task. For text editing, participants also used an on-screen keyboard to type, but gestural operations were used to perform select, copy, cut and paste functions. To select, participants needed to swipe (Fig. 2) to the right or the left of the I-beam cursor, and then click on the end position of the selection. To cut or copy the selected text, participants used pinch-out and pinch-in gesture (Fig. 2) respectively. To past the selected text, participants tapped both their index and middle fingers on the touchscreen (2-finger tap, Fig. 2). For picture manipulation, participant could translate and adjust the size of the picture simultaneously by using the pinch gesture. The size of the picture would change according to the change of the finger span and the location of the picture would follow the move of the finger locations.

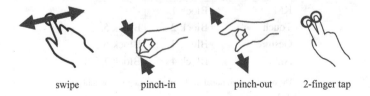

swipe   pinch-in   pinch-out   2-finger tap

Fig. 2. Gestural operations

4. All mode: participants were allowed to use all functions/operations in three previously mentioned modes. Participants, however, were told to not rely one operational mode and encouraged to mix modes for optimal performance.

Furthermore, the touchscreen was set into two different positions: a vertical position for optimal viewing (OPView), and a horizontal position for optimal manipulation (OPManu). At OPView position, the touch screen was placed on the upper part of the ergonomic desk and tilted at 75° from the surface (Fig. 3 left). At OPManu position, the touch screen was placed on the lower part of the ergonomic desk and tilted at 15° from the surface (Fig. 3, right). The height of the table and the tilt angle of the screen could be easily adjusted based on participants' preference. Since the upper part of the table was farer from the participants' sitting points and the lower part was nearer, participants were told to optimize the OPView position for their viewing from a distance and the OPManu position for their manual operation around they hands and forearms.

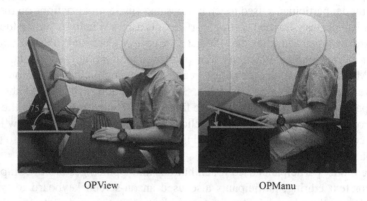

OPView   OPManu

Fig. 3. Display positions

There were 7 experimental conditions (blocks) as shown in Table 1. The participants performed 1 practice and 4 repetitive trials sequentially in each block according to its designated condition, and they executed blocks randomly.

Table 1. Experimental conditions

Operational mode[a]	Touchscreen position	
	OPView	OPManu
KM	Block 1	-[b]
Touch	Block 2	Block 5
Gesture	Block 3	Block 6
All	Block 4	Block 7

[a]The order of operational modes were randomized within block.
[b]User rarely use a keyboard/mouse at OPManu position in reality.

Their performance in terms of time spent in completing the entire work, editing text and manipulating pictures was recorded by the experimental software. Accuracy of picture manipulation including the deviation of the picture's center to the target center and the difference of the picture's size to the size of the target area was also recorded.

Accuracy of text editing, however, was manually processed by comparing the original text and the working text to compute the ratio of the correctly typed characters to the total number of characters in the designated materials.

3 Results

Both operational modes and display positions significantly affect task completion time. Analysis of variance (ANOVA) revealed that operating by KM or All mo at OPView position took significantly shorter time to complete the task (both p-value < 0.001, see Fig. 4). Further decomposition of the task completion time into text editing and picture manipulating time showed similar results. Based on Tukey's post-hoc analysis, however, Touch mode was superior to Gesture mode in picture manipulation regardless of display position.

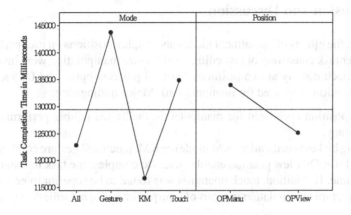

Fig. 4. Main effect plots for task completion time

The user performance in terms of accuracy was measured by ACC% (the ratio of correctly edited characters in the designated text), deviation (the Euclidean distance between the picture's center and the target center) and size difference (the product of errors in horizontal and vertical dimension of the manipulated picture). Based on ANOVA, ACC% was not significantly affected by any of the factors studied. However, both operational modes and display positions significantly affected deviation (both p-value < 0.01, see Fig. 5). As for size difference, only operational modes were proved significant (p-value < 0.001).

Further post-hoc analysis using Tukey's method showed that participants performed rather similarly in All, KM and Gesture mode. Touch operation was inferior to operations in All and KM mode in terms of sizing pictures accurately.

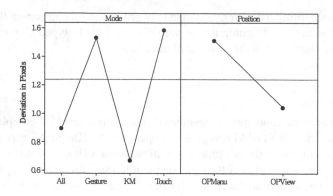

Fig. 5. Main effect plots for deviation

4 Conclusion and Discussion

In this study, the effects of operational modes and display positions on user performance in a computer task consisting of text editing and picture manipulation were investigated on a multi-touch display at two positions (vertical position optimized for viewing vs. horizontal position optimized for manipulation). Major findings are:

1. Display position optimized for manipulation facilitated neither performance time nor accuracy.
2. Operating by keyboards/mice (KM mode) or KM, touch and gesture combined mode (All mode) at OPView position enabled users to complete the task in a significantly shorter time. In addition, touch operation was found to be superior to gestural operation in picture manipulation in terms of time performance regardless of touchscreen positions.
3. Users using gesture operation were able to produce comparable precision in sizing pictures to operations in KM and All mode.

From the results it was easy to see that users were still strongly influenced by their past experience in human-computer interaction, relying heavily on keyboards/mice. This phenomenon may also explain users' inferior performance on the touchscreen at OPManu position- they just did not get used to it. These findings proposed challenges to future computer workstation design for multitouch-enabled computers. It was also noted that gestural and touch operation was different in their effects on users' precision in manipulating objects. Future study may reference to this noticeable finding to further investigate how to optimize the use of the gestural operation in object manipulation tasks that require accuracy, and the use of the touch operation in quick translation.

References

1. Sears, A.: Improving touchscreen keyboards: design issues and a comparison with other devices. Interact. Comput. **3**(3), 253–269 (1991)
2. Chung, M.K., et al.: Usability evaluation of numeric entry tasks on keypad type and age. Int. J. Ind. Ergon. **40**(1), 97–105 (2009)
3. Lin, C.-J., Wu, C.: Reactions, accuracy and response complexity of numerical typing on touch screens. Ergonomics **56**(5), 818–831 (2013)

A Support Tool for Analyzing the 3D Motions of Sign Language and the Construction of a Morpheme Dictionary

Yuji Nagashima[1(✉)], Keiko Watanabe[1], Mina Terauchi[2], Naoto Kato[3],
Tsubasa Uchida[3], Shuichi Umeda[3], Taro Miyazaki[3], Makiko Azuma[3],
and Nobuyuki Hiruma[3]

[1] Kogakuin University, 2665-1, Nakano-machi, Hachioji-shi, Tokyo 192-0015, Japan
nagasima@cc.kogakuin.ac.jp
[2] Polytechnic University, 2-32-1 Ogawanishi, Kodaira-shi, Tokyo 104-0061, Japan
[3] NHK Science & Technology Research Laboratories, 1-10-11, Kinuta, Setagaya-ku,
Tokyo 157-8510, Japan

Abstract. The present paper describes a support system for analyzing and notating the three-dimensional (3D) motions of sign language unit of frames that are obtained through optical motion capturing. The 3D motion data acquired involve Manual Signals (MS) and Non-Manual Markers (NMM). The 3D motion data acquired have two basic parts MS and NMM. This system enables users to analyze and describe both MS and NMM, which are the components of sign, while playing back the motions as a sign animation. In the analysis part, being able to step through a motion frame by frame, forward and backward, would be extremely useful for users. Moreover, the motions can be observed from given directions and by a given magnification ratio. In the description part, NVSG model, the sign notation system we propose, is used. The results of the description serve as a database for a morpheme dictionary, because they are stored in SQLite format. The dictionary that enables sign language to be looked up based on the motions and motions to be observed based on the morphemes is the first of its type ever created, and its usability and practicability are extremely high.

Keywords: Sign language · 3D animation · Morpheme dictionary

1 Introduction

A Sign Language is a visual language that uses a system of MS and NMM as the means of communication. MS consist of four components -handshape, movement, location, and orientation. NMM consist of the various facial expressions, head tilt, shapes of the mouth, and similar signals except MS. Morphemes are composed of these multiple elements. Right and left hands can also independently express morphemes by combining these elements, which makes morphological structure more complicated. Therefore, it must be analyzed by viewing it as

C. Stephanidis (Ed.): HCII 2016 Posters, Part II, CCIS 618, pp. 124–129, 2016.
DOI: 10.1007/978-3-319-40542-1_20

sign language, which is one reason why analysis of sign language structure is more difficult. ELAN is a tool for the creation of complex annotations on video resources [1]. However, the ELAN cannot support analysis and the description of the morpheme level of the sign language. In addition, spoken languages such as Japanese and English have their own writing systems. For this reason, there are superior many multilingual dictionaries exist in a spoken language. On the other hand, sign language has no standard writing system. Existing sign language dictionaries have been compiled with the use of pictures, photos and videos. There are no dictionaries that allow users to view Sign motions based on units of phonemes, morphemes and words in 3D animation from any viewpoint. Considering this situation, we construct a support system for analyzing and notating. Notation results automatically become a morpheme dictionary that uses 3D animation.

2   NVSG Element Model [2]

Among elements, MS are described in an N element and V element, while NMM are described in an S element and G element. Items related to hand shape, palm direction and hand position are described in the N element, while movement items are described in the V element. Among non-manual markers, sightline is most important, so items regarding sightline are described in the S element, while other non-manual signals are described in the G element. Table 1 shows the description items of each element of the NVSG element model.

Table 1. The items of NVSG element model

Element	Items described
N element (nominal)	Hand shape (+hand position)
V element (verbal)	Movement
S element (sightline)	Sightline
G element (grammatical)	Non-manual makers (NMM) except sightline

3   Systems that Support the Analysis and Notation of the 3D Motions of Sign

There is software that analyzes motions by using 3D motion data that are obtained through optical motion capturing in various fields, including the rehabilitation and medical fields. And, in the field of the dialogue analysis, the ELAN is a tool for the creation of complex annotations on video resources. However, there are no systems that are capable of supporting the analysis and notation of the 3D motions of sign language in the linguistic sense. This paper examines a support system for analyzing and notating the 3D motions of sign language unit of frames that are obtained through optical motion capturing. The data of the 3D motions are in BVH format. The proposed system is composed of the sign language processing part that supports analysis and NVSG notation, and the morpheme dictionary part that display and searches the results of morpheme notation.

3.1   Sign Language Processing Part

The analysis of sign language is carried out by monitoring 3D animation unit frames by using data in BVH format. TVML, which is under development by NHK STRL, is used as a tool for processing the animation [3]. The animation processing part is described in Fig. 1.

(a) Processing control: The A area in the frame on the bottom left of Fig. 1 controls playback. The → and ← keys on the keyboard are used for playback forward and backward by a frame unit. Click ① on the top right of Fig. 1, and the position of the camera is able to be controlled. By using functions in the B area in the frame on the top right of the figure, analyzers are able to view sign language animation from any viewpoint positions and magnification percentages.

(b) Information notation of BVH data: Click ② on the top right of Fig. 2, and the details of BVH data under analysis are able to be notated. The information notated here is the names of words under analysis, morpheme starting and ending frame number, and in-transition and out-transition frame number. Moreover, as information on the words under analysis, the structure of the words, such as simple word, compound word and collocation, is also notated. In addition, the structure of words is able to be entered by directly inputting terms using the keyboard or by selecting terms from the pull-down menu.

(c) Morpheme information notation: Click ③ on the top right of Fig. 3, and the morpheme structure of BVH data under analysis is able to be notated. The NVSG element model is used for the notation of the morpheme structure. When extracting data in BVH format, specify the extraction section in area C of Fig. 3. The function of extracting the BVH data is used when complex words are extracted based on a morpheme unit and new words that have not yet been registered in a dictionary are generated through morpheme composition.

By using the NVSG element model, the details of the morpheme structure are notated based on a phonetic unit in the D area of Fig. 3. The notation of N and V elements is carried out in accordance with the NVSG rule sheet [2]. In this support system, in each element, for items in which values that are required to be notated have been decided, elements are selected from the pull-down menu. Using the pull-down menu makes it possible to minimize the individual sways of notation. Moreover, S and G elements are notated by using sIGNDEX [4]. All the notation items of these elements are selected from the pull-down menu based on the sIGNDEX rule sheet. Table 2 shows the list of items that are required to be notated in the D area. Moreover,

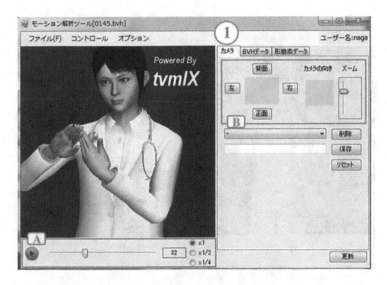

Fig. 1. Animation processing part

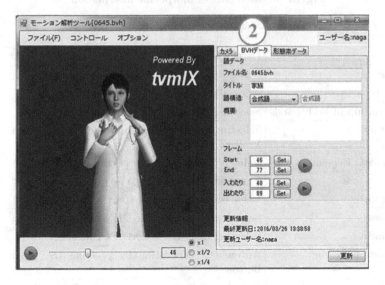

Fig. 2. Detailed information description part of the BVH data under the analysis

when the data of one word are composed of more than one morpheme, it is possible to notate a multiple number of morphemes independently in the D area.

3.2 Morpheme Dictionary Part

The results of the description in Sect. 3.1 serve as a database for a morpheme dictionary, because they are stored in SQLite format. The morpheme

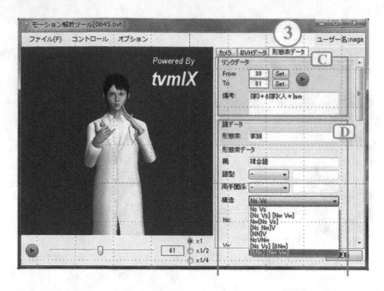

Fig. 3. Notation part of morpheme information

Table 2. Morpheme data notation items

Item		Details of notation
Genus		Concept of morpheme category items
Word type		Affix, allomorph, assimilation, etc.
Relationship of both hands		Selecting the relationship of both hands
Structure		Selecting the relationship of the N element and the V element
N element	Eement	Value of the N element (partial selection type)
	@	Expression position
V element		Value of the V element (partial selection type)
S element		Selecting from the sIGNDEX rule sheet
G element		Selecting from the sIGNDEX rule sheet
Complete notation		Automated generation by pressing the generation button
Meaning		Notation of dictionary meaning and the differences in words with the same motions but different meanings

dictionary part provides the list display of the morpheme dictionary and carries out searches.

For one unit of data, the list display is capable of providing 44 items, including the names of BVH files, the names of Japanese words, the time structure of words, each value of NVSG elements, the notation results of NVSG elements, supplementary information and update dates. Moreover, if one unit of data consists of more than one morpheme, it is possible to easily understand the spatial structure and time structure of the composition. In searching, it is possible to undertake an AND/OR search with the random details of 44 items, including each NVSG element.

As a result, because a search is able to be undertaken from the NVSG elements in this dictionary, it is possible to search meanings in Japanese from the expression of the sign language. The search key allows users to set up more than one condition.

4   Conclusion and Future Issues

This paper has described the construction of a system that supports the analysis and notation of words of sign language by using 3D motion data in BVH format. The NVSG element model is used for notation. Because the notation results are stored in SQLite format, it is possible to construct a morpheme dictionary database. In this dictionary, the N element notates the shape of the hands, and the V element notates the details of the motions. As a result, it is possible to use the dictionary as a reverse dictionary in which the meanings of sign language are able to be searched from the shapes and motions of the hands. Moreover, because 3D motion data and the morpheme time structure are linked to each other one by one in the database, it is possible to view sign language based on the morphemes. There have been no sign language dictionaries available with these functions before. The usability and practicality of the dictionary are extremely high. Approximately 2,000 words in the general and the medical field, etc. have been described in the morpheme dictionary thus far.

We are proceeding with a further study on how to synthesize new words that are not found in the current dictionary by taking advantage of this morpheme dictionary described using NVSG elements.

Acknowledgment. Part of this study was subsidized by a Grant-in-Aid for Scientific Research (A) 26244021, a scientific research grant by the Ministry of Education, Culture, Sports, Science and Technology.

References

1. Hellwig, B.: ELAN - Linguistic Annotator, version 4.9.2 (2015). https://tla.mpi.nl/tools/tla-tools/elan/
2. Watanabe, K., Nagashima, Y., et al.: Study into Methods of Describing Japanese Sign Language. CCIS **435**, 270–275. Springer (2014)
3. Hiruma, N., Shimizu, T., et al.: Automatic generation system of CG sign language animation. J. Inst. Image Electr. Eng. Jpn. **41**(4), 406–410 (2012) (in Japanese)
4. Kanda, K., Ichikawa, A., Nagashima, Y., Kato, Y., Terauchi, M., Hara, D., Sato, M.: Notation system and statistical analysis of NMS in JSL. In: Wachsmuth, I., Sowa, T. (eds.) GW 2001. LNCS (LNAI), vol. 2298, pp. 181–192. Springer, Heidelberg (2002)

Real-Time Japanese Sign Language Recognition Based on Three Phonological Elements of Sign

Shinji Sako[✉], Mika Hatano, and Tadashi Kitamura

Nagoya Institute of Technology, Jokers-cho, Showa-ku, Nagoya 466-8555, Japan
{s.sako,kitamura}@nitech.ac.jp, pia@mmsp.nitech.ac.jp

Abstract. Sign language is the visual language of deaf people. It is also natural language, different in form from spoken language. To resolve a communication barrier between hearing people and deaf, several researches for automatic sign language recognition (ASLR) system are now under way. However, existing research of ASLR deals with only small vocabulary. It is also limited in the environmental conditions and the use of equipment. In addition, compared with the research field of speech recognition, there is no large scale sign database for various reasons. One of the major reasons is that there is no official writing system for Japanese sign Language (JSL). In such a situation, we focused on the use of the knowledge of phonology of JSL and dictionary, in order to develop a develop a real-time JSL sign recognition system. The dictionary consists of over 2,000 JSL sign, each sign defined as three types of phonological elements in JSL: hand shape, motion, and position. Thanks to the use of the dictionary, JSL sign models are represented by the combination of these elements. It also can respond to the expansion of a new sign. Our system employs Kinect v2 sensor to obtain sign features such as hand shape, position, and motion. Depth sensor enables real-time processing and robustness against environmental changes. In general, recognition of hand shape is not easy in the field of ASLR due to the complexity of hand shape. In our research, we apply a contour-based method to hand shape recognition. To recognize hand motion and position, we adopted statistical models such as Hidden Markov models (HMMs) and Gaussian mixture models (GMMs). To address the problem of lack of database, our method utilizes the pseudo motion and hand shape data. We conduct experiments to recognize 223 JSL sign targeted professional sign language interpreters.

Keywords: Hidden Markov models · Sign language recognition · Phonetic systems of sign language · Depth sensor

1 Introduction

In general, sign is represented by combinations of posture or movement of the hands and facial expressions such as eyes or month. These representations of sign are happen both sequentially and simultaneously. Communication between

C. Stephanidis (Ed.): HCII 2016 Posters, Part II, CCIS 618, pp. 130–136, 2016.
DOI: 10.1007/978-3-319-40542-1_21

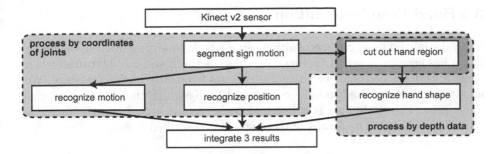

Fig. 1. Overview of the whole system

the hearing people and the deaf can be difficult, because the most of hearing people do not understand sign language. To resolve a communication problem between hearing people and deaf, projects for automatic sign language recognition (ASLR) system is now under way.

One of major problem of current ASLR system is performing small vocabulary. Corresponding to the unknown vocabulary is also important from the view of practical aspect. It is said that the number of JSL vocabulary is over 3,000. In addition, a new sign is introduced to adjust the situation. Obviously, it is inefficient to perform the recognition on an individual sign units.

From the point of view, we employ a database JSL dictionary and notation system proposed by Kimura [1]. Our system is based on three elements of sign language: hand motion, position, and pose. This study considers a hand pose recognition using depth data obtained from a single depth sensor. We apply the contour-based method proposed by Keogh [2] to hand pose recognition. This method recognizes a contour by means of discriminators learned from contours. To recognize hand motion and position, we adopted statistical models such as Hidden Markov models (HMMs) and Gaussian mixture models (GMMs). To address the problem of lack of database, our method utilizes the pseudo motion and hand shape data. We conduct experiments to recognize 233 JSL sign targeted professional sign language interpreters.

2   Overview of the System

An overview of our proposed system is shown in Fig. 1. The feature parameters of sign motion are captured by using Microsoft Kinect v2 sensor [3]. At first, time series of feature parameter is cut outed into moving segment. Second, the three phonological elements are recognized individually. Finally, the recognition result is determined by the weighted sum of each score of three elements. The recognition process of the hand pose and other two components employs depth data of the hand region and coordinates of joints, respectively.

We used JSL dictionary proposed by Kimura [1]. In this dictionary, hand poses are classified by several element as shown in Table 1. These elements are also illustrated in Fig. 2. Currently, the vocabulary of this dictionary is approximately 2,600.

3 Hand Pose Recognition

Several study on hand pose recognition using a technique of estimating the finger joints has been proposed [4,5]. However, these methods still has difficulties when some fingers are invisible. This situation occurs frequently in sign language. We adopt the contour-based technique proposed by Keogh [2] in order to recognize hand pose. This technique is considered to be robust even when the finger is partially occluded. The details of the method is described below.

Table 1. List of sign in the dictionary

Sign	SL type	Hand type	Palm direction	Position	Motion
love	3	B	down	NS	circle
between	4	B	side	NS	down
blue	1	B	back	lower face	back
red	1	1	back	lower face	right

⋮

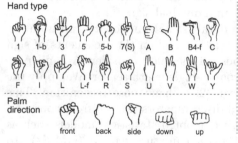
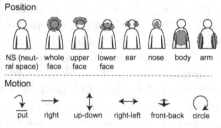

Fig. 2. List of sign elements

3.1 Feature Extraction

Hand shapes can be converted to *distance vectors* to form one-dimensional sequence. Figure 3 shows the procedure to extracting a distance vector from a hand image. At first, the center point of the hand region is determined by distance transform. Distance transform convert one pixel value of the binary image with the distance between the nearest zero value pixel. Next, each distance from the center point to every pixel on the contour is calculated. The distance vector represents a series of these distances.

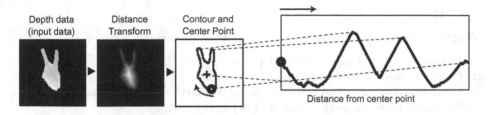

Fig. 3. Calculate distance vector from depth data

3.2 Calculation of Distance

A distance D between two distance vectors $P = \{p_0, p_1, \ldots, p_n\}$ and $Q = \{q_0, q_1, \ldots, q_n\}$ is calculated according to the followings.

$$D(P,Q) = \sqrt{\sum_{i=1}^{n}(p_i - q_i)^2} \tag{1}$$

If the length of two distance vectors is different, dynamic time warping (DTW) should be used to adjust for size variations. To simplify, we adjust length of vector to be same in advance for computation time reason.

We can compare contours by calculating their distances or using classifiers generated from contours. These classifiers are called *wedges*. Wedges have maximum and minimum values at each point. If a contour is located inside a wedge, the distance is zero. The distance D between a wedge W ($U = \{u_0, u_1, \ldots, u_n\}$ is its top, $L = \{l_0, l_1, \ldots, l_n\}$ is its bottom) and a contour $P = \{p_0, p_1, \ldots, p_n\}$ is calculated by following equation.

$$D(W,P) = \sqrt{\sum_{i=1}^{n}\begin{cases} (p_i - u_i)^2 & (p_i > u_i) \\ (p_i - l_i)^2 & (p_i < l_i) \\ 0 & (otherwise). \end{cases}} \tag{2}$$

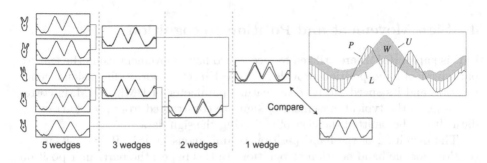

Fig. 4. How to compare wedge and belt

3.3   Generate Wedges

Wedges are generated according to the following procedures.

1. Extract feature parameter from depth data
2. Calculate distances of all contours
3. Unify two contours in ascending order of distances. The set of maximum and minimum values of merged contours become a wedge
4. Repeat third process until the predecided number of wedges

The process of generating wedges are also illustrated in Fig. 4. We prepare various wedges to recognizing each hand type.

Table 2. Experimental settings

Number of samples	223 sing × 2 signers × 2 takes = 892 samples
Number of shape	24
Depth data	120 × 120 pixel
Training data	150 (per one shape)
Number of belt	Number of shape × palm direction
Length of belt	30
Number of position	8
Training data	6 (per one position)
Feature parameters	3-dimensional hand position
Number of mixture	1 – 6
Number of motion	40
Number of training sample	10 sample per 1 motion
Feature parameters	3-dimensional hand position + direction
Number of state (HMM)	5 – 18
Number of mixture (HMM)	1

4   Sign Movement and Position Recognition

In this paper, HMMs are utilized to recognized hand movement using the feature parameter of hand position provided by the Kinect sensor. 3-dimensional hand position and its speed are used as feature parameter of HMMs. HMMs corresponding to the typical movement of sign are constructed from pseudo-training data. It can be omitted the cost of collecting the sign data.

The definition of the hand position is ambiguous in JSL. It is necessary to consider for the hand position recognition. In this paper, the particular position of the hand in sign is modeled by GMMs. 3-dimensional hand position are used as feature parameter of GMMs. GMMs corresponding to the typical position of sign are also trained from pseudo-training data.

5   Experiment and Results

We conducted experiments to recognize 223 JSL sign performed by two professional sign language interpreters. Experimental conditions are listed in Table 2. These sign are extracted from the basic JSL sign that corresponds to Japanese Sign Language Proficiency Test grade 5.

The recognition result is determined by the weighted sum of each score of three elements. Optimal weight parameter of three elements are determined by grid search in the training data.

The results of the hand shape recognition in the three data sets are shown in Fig. 5. From this result, recognition rate can be improved according to the number of wedge. Recognition results of sign and optimal weight are also listed in Table 3. The recognition rate for unknown sign which does not include training data was obtained 33.8 %. One of the reason recognition rate was low is fluctuations in the hand shape in real sign motion.

Table 3. Recognition results

	Hand shape	Hand position	Hand movement	Sign
Recognition rate (%)/Weight	28.7 (0.1)	78.3 (0.4)	60.0 (0.5)	33.8

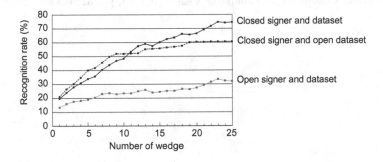

Fig. 5. Result of hand shape recognition

6   Conclusion

In this paper, we proposed a real-time Japanese sign language recognition system based on three elements of sign language: motion, position, and pose. This study examined hand pose recognition by means of contour-based method proposed by Keogh using depth images obtained from a single depth sensor. We conducted experiments on recognizing 24 hand poses from 223 typical Japanese sign.

The recognition rate for an unknown sign which does not include training data was obtained 33.8 %. To increase recognition performance, we have to increasing the learning data of the wedge. Expansion of vocabulary can also be considered as a future work.

Acknowledgement. This research was supported in part by Japan Society for the Promotion of Science KAKENHI (No. 25350666), and Toukai Foundation for Technology.

References

1. Kimura, T., Hara, D., Kanda, K., Morimoto, K.: Expansion of the system of JSL-Japanese electronic dictionary: an evaluation for the compound research system. In: Kurosu, M. (ed.) HCD 2011. LNCS, vol. 6776, pp. 407–416. Springer, Heidelberg (2011)
2. Keogh, E., Wei, L., Xi, X., Lee, S.H., Vlachos, M.: LB_Keogh supports exact indexing of shapes under rotation invariance with arbitrary representations and distance measures. In: 32nd International Conference on Very Large Data Bases (VLDB2006), pp. 882–893 (2006)
3. Microsoft Kinect for Windows. http://kinectforwindows.org
4. Liang, H., Yuan, J., Thalmann, D.: Parsing the hand in depth images. IEEE Trans. Multimedia **16**(5), 1241–1253 (2014)
5. Tang, D., Yu, T.H., Kim, T.K.: Real-time articulated hand pose estimation using semi-supervised transductive regression forests. In: Proceedings of the 2013 IEEE International Conference on Computer Vision (ICCV), pp. 3224–3231 (2013)

Documentation Generation Tool
for Motion-Based Interactions

Kristof Stahl, Bashar Altakrouri, Daniel Burmeister, and Andreas Schrader[✉]

Ambient Computing Group, Institute of Telematics,
University of Luebeck, Luebeck, Germany
schrader@itm.uni-luebeck.de
http://www.ambient.uni-luebeck.de

Abstract. Human Computer Interaction based on gestures offers enormous potential for designing ergonomic user interfaces in future smart environments. Although gestures can be perceived as very natural, the specific gesture set of a given dedicated interface might be complex and require some kind of self-description of expected body movements. We have therefore developed a machine-readable XML-based model of Labanotation, a camera-based movement analysis engine for automatic model creation, as well as a graphical editor for supporting manual design of gestures. In this paper, we present a tool for automatic generation of multimodal human-readable gesture documentation based on the XML-model. Currently, the tool supports text and 3D model animation and can be expanded to other modalities.

Keywords: Gesture interfaces · Documentation · Labanotation

1 Introduction

In recent years, many innovative human computer interaction methods have been proposed. Natural User Interfaces (NUI) try to reflect human traditional interaction with physical elements and are comprising of whole body elements including finger (touching), eye (tracking), body (moving) and even brain (signaling). In motion-based interactions, more and more full-body interactions are supported and many innovative interaction devices started entering the market (e.g., Myo, Leap Motion). With an increasing number of devices and plethora of interaction patterns, formal modelling of body movements has become essential. Interaction devices benefit from machine-readable descriptions for pattern detection and exchange in the Internet of Things with potentially several devices used as interaction ENSEMBLES [1]. Users benefit from human-readable modelling of body movements for learning the requirements of the interaction for (often varying) devices in use. Designers benefit by being enabled to describe and exchange design patterns during construction of innovative products.

Body movements for interaction can be considered as special forms of dance. Like musical scores can be used to compose and perform music, dance scores

© Springer International Publishing Switzerland 2016
C. Stephanidis (Ed.): HCII 2016 Posters, Part II, CCIS 618, pp. 137–143, 2016.
DOI: 10.1007/978-3-319-40542-1_22

are used by theatre and music professionals to compose and perform dances. We propose to map this approach for HCI and have developed various methods and tools with the help of a modified version of Labanotation [2,3].

2 Modelling Motion-Based Interactions with Labanotation

Labanotation is a movement language developed by Rudolf Laban in 1928, revised and improved multiple times, most notably at the Dance Notation Bureau [4]. Labanotation is very similar to music notation languages and notes body positions and movement commands on time lines. The symbol set covers all relevant body parts and joints and describes relations between each other as well as the position in space. It supports the notation of multiple motions in parallel and can therefore be used for simple but also quite complex interaction movements. It is therefore commonly used by professional choreographers and dancers.

By focusing on and extending essential structural elements, it is perfectly suited to describe body movements even in fine-granular movements. The use of Labanotation for the purpose of designing motion-based interaction has been suggested [5] and XML-based machine-readable implementations have been proposed as well (e.g., LabanWriter [6], Tiniklink/MovementXML [7], LabanEditor [8]).

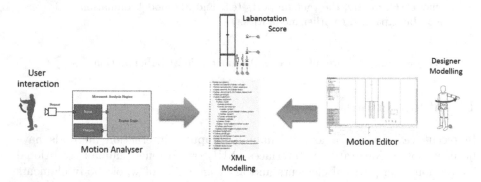

Fig. 1. Designer and Analyser tools for creating and editing the XML model of the Labanotation score.

Current methods used to describe and share interactions suffer from a number of problems, including the inability to capture a detailed description of the movements required and the inability to illustrate the timing and dynamic flow of said movements adequately. We have therefore developed an extended version of Labanotation based on XML, which also supports physical ability profiles in order to enhance the adaptability of movement-based interactions to a user's individual physical context [9]. We have also developed tools for manually designing motion-based interactions using a graphical Editor [10] and an Analyser for automatic analysing interaction performances using cameras based on depth sensors (Kinect, OpenCV) [11]. Both tools can be used to create and edit XML-based models of interaction, either by conceiving movements using the editor or by observing movements using the analyser (Fig. 1).

3   Labanotation Visualisation

XML-based descriptions might be appropriate for machines for exchanging patterns between interconnected HCI devices in interactive IoT-scenarios (Internet of Things) and graphical visualisation of the Laban scores might be appropriate for skilled designers of interaction schemes. But end-users need a more intuitive representation of the expected body movements.

Literature reports about some early approaches to generate animations from Labanotation, mostly with the goal to ease the design of movements and give direct feedback to the user on a Labanotation score. The LabanEditor [8] animates Laban scores, but was designed with a specific focus on dance applications and does not support other output modalities. It also only supports a reduced set of symbols and the code is not publically available. The Mocap Data Editing approach [12] converts from motion captured (mocap) material to Labanotation and from there to animation. This gives the ability to edit motion captured sequences via Labanotation and can be used for motion editing. Since their framework uses the mocap data to extrapolate the Labanotation it functions on already given data and does not entirely create a new data set for animation.

4   Generator

We therefore have developed a new flexible system architecture in Java allowing for the creation of arbitrary modalities (Fig. 2). Our current implementation supports text and 3D character animations, but can easily be extended to other modalities, like e.g., speech output or graphical projections of cartoon animations on ambient displays in the respective smart space, etc. The systems contains an XML parser which converts the model into a set of serialized objects in the Movement Generator Engine. The parser is taken from our Editor [10] in order to guarantee interoperability. Every Labanotation symbol is taken with its parameters and type to create a new BodyPartMovement or JointMovement object to relate to a body part or joint and written into a list to keep the constraints of parallel and consecutive movements. The representation contains the direction and amount to be moved and the duration the whole motion should take to have a primitive representation for one motion. To represent a whole movement with these motions a correlation with each other is encoded.

The Engine is then configured to convert these objects into the modality of choice. Depending on the context, the resulting media output stream can either be stored in a local file or transmitted to other entities for further processing or visualisation. For this, a set of generator types can be utilized in the system.

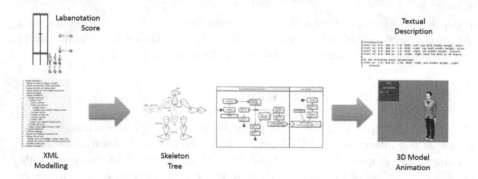

Fig. 2. Creating human-readable visualisation using the Generator. (Color figure online)

4.1 Generating Text

Textual description can suffice for a basic understanding of the required movement for simple interaction schemes. Nevertheless, describing multiple parallel movements with natural languages can result in confusing long sentences as all related movements need to be named and put in relation with each other. Therefore some type of text formatting might be an option to separate different blocks of parallel movements with appropriate keywords to signal the parallelism.

One feature of Labanotation is that the side of a limb, its height or general direction and the limb itself can be obtained from a stage without much effort. The columns are used to indicate sides. The limbs used can be obtained by the presign of a symbol or from the current column. With the given model for movements a primitive text generation can be implemented by reading the data and paraphrase them directly with the given limbs. Due to the differentiation between turn movements and translating movements a keyword of either 'turn' or 'move' can be added to the text. The qualitative direction stored in the movement model, as obtained through the Laban symbols, can be given to describe the movements direction. The narrative of the given motions creates a movement path, which is not always particularly detailed due to the range of detail in Labanotation. Furthermore, the user reenacting the movement will not always be following the directions perfectly, but usually the general directions of movements are relevant and not the exact distance or points travelled to.

An example on how the text is displayed below. First the user is given his starting position. Then each block of synchronous movement is listed:

```
1 Startposition:
2 Start at: 0.0. End at: 1.0. MOVE: left leg hold middle height, place.
3 Start at: 0.0. End at: 1.0. MOVE: right leg hold middle height, place.
4 Start at: 0.0. End at: 1.0. MOVE: right arm middle height, forward.
5 Start at: 0.0. End at: 1.0. JOINT: right hand low hold at 90 degree.
6 Do the following moves synchronous:
7 Start at:1.0. End at: 1.98. MOVE: right arm middle height, right - forward.
```

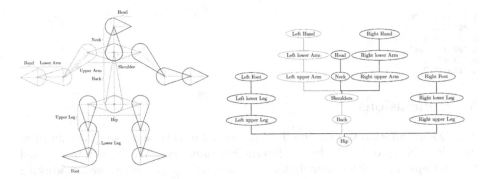

Fig. 3. Kinematic skeleton with highlighted kinematic chain in 2D (left) and as tree structure (right). (Color figure online)

4.2 Generating Animations

Animations using human-like figures support a more intuitive description of required movements, especially for more complex patterns and parallel movements of several body parts. Even though Java provides libraries for 3D rendering, the possibilities are limited. We therefore use a more general approach of generating a movement description that can be used as input for any 3D graphic engine. This even allows for distributing the Generator and the rendering processes to different devices, which might be useful in some scenarios, where the interactive device could delegate the render process to some cloud server. As an example rendering engine we deployed Unity3D. The Unity3D engine uses the MonoDevelopment API which can be compile to different platforms, including Windows, MacOS and Linux.

To create an animation model, a kinematic skeleton is needed. The kinematic skeleton is an unsorted tree whose root is usually the hip. The hip is a particularly suited root node since it is the centre of mass of the human body. Movements within the body can be related to the hip, while a movement of the whole body, usually walking, can be represented by the translation of the hip, since all other joints are attached to this node. Combined these can be seen as a walking animation where the legs propel the body.

The Generator creates a kinematic skeleton tree from scratch by adding vectors ('bones') including the position and orientation of the human bones (see Fig. 3 with a kinematic chain outlined in red as a subtree of the overall body tree). With the paths inside the subtrees, the inverse kinematic algorithm can determine the angles of each bone for a specific endpoint position in each node. For this, the 'vecmath' library of Java is used. The objects and parameters of the resulting animation is then compiled into JSON strings, serialized using the 'fastjson' library and send to our Rendering Engine using a TCP socket connection using the Mono (.NET) API of Unity3D. Deserialisation is based on the 'MiniJSON' library. The following listing shows an example object:

```
1 { "Angle":90.0,
2 "BodypartType":1,
3 "Duration":1.99,
4 "MotionType":1,
5 "Side":1,
6 "Start":2 }
```

5 Conclusions

The Documentation Generation Tool presented in this paper supports an intuitive learning process for future interactive interfaces. We have implemented two example modalities, namely text and animation. Currently, we are working on combining modalities to further increase usability, e.g., animation with oral explanations. We are also extending the system towards an ambient reflection framework [13] supporting self-describing interface devices and automatically combined multimodal rendering processes in ambient spaces.

References

1. Altakrouri, B.: Ambient Assisted Living with Dynamic Interaction Ensembles. Ph.D. dissertation, University of Lübeck, Germany, August 2014
2. Altakrouri, B., Gröschner, J., Schrader, A.: Documenting natural interactions. In: CHI 2013 Extended Abstracts on Human Factors in Computing Systems, CHI EA 2013. ACM, New York, May 2013
3. Altakrouri, B., Schrader, A.: Describing movement for motion gestures. In: 1st International Workshop on Engineering Gestures for Multimodal Interfaces (EGMI 2014) at the 6th ACM SIGCHI Symposium on Engineering Interactive Computing Systems (EICS 2014), Italy, June, Rome, June 2014
4. Hutchinson, A.: Labanotation. The System of Analyzing and Recording Movement, 4th edn. Routledge, New York (2005)
5. Loke, L., Larssen, A.T., Robertson, T.: Labanotation for design of movement-based interaction. In: Proceedings of the Second Australasian Conference on Interactive Entertainment (IE 2005), Sydney, Australia, 2005
6. LabanWriter. Ohio State Department of Dance (2000). http://dance.osu.edu/labanwriter. Accessed 7 Apr 2016
7. Hatol, J.: MovementXML: A Representation of Semantics of Human Movement based on Labanotation. Simon Fraser University (2006)
8. Nakamura, M., Hachimura, K.: An XML representation of Labanotation, LabanXML, and its implementation on the notation editor LabanEditor2. In: Review of the National Center for Digitalization, Faculty of Mathematics, Belgrade (2006)
9. Altakrouri, B., Schrader, A.: Towards dynamic natural interaction ensembles. In: Proceedings of the Fourth Workshop on Physicality, Co-located with British HCI 2012, Birmingham, UK, September 2012
10. Altakrouri, B., Gröschner, J., Schrader, A.: Documenting natural interactions. In: ACM SIGCHI Conference on Human Factors in Computing Systems (CHI 2013), Work in Progress Section, Paris, France, 2013
11. Kordts, B., Altakrouri, B., Schrader, A.: Capturing and analysing movement using depth sensors and labanotation. In: 7th ACM SIGCHI Symposium on Engineering Interactive Computing Systems EICS 2015, Duisburg, Germany, June 2015

12. Shen, X., Li, Q., Yu, T., Geng, W., Lau, N.: Mocap data editing via movement notations. In: Ninth International Conference on Computer Aided Design and Computer Graphics (CAD-CG 2005), Hong Kong, China, December 2005
13. Burmeister, D., Altakrouri, B., Schrader, A.: Ambient reflection: towards self-explaining devices. In: Proceedings of the 1st Workshop on Large-scale and Model-based Interactive Systems: Approaches and Challenges (LMIS 2015) Co-located with 7th ACM SIGCHI Symposium on Engineering Interactive Computing Systems (EICS 2015), Duisburg, Germany, June 2015

A Comparative Study of Applying Low-Latency Smoothing Filters in a Multi-kinect Virtual Play Environment

Tiffany Y. Tang[✉] and Relic Yongfu Wang

Media Lab, Department of Computer Science, Wenzhou Kean University, Wenzhou, China
{yatang,wangyon}@kean.edu

Abstract. The Skeleton Tracking System in Kinect is known for being noisy and unstable, hence, in practice, a noise reduction filter or smoothing filter needs to be employed before consuming the data in order to obtain smooth joint position data over time. In this paper, we present a comparative study on applying four different smoothing filters (Simple Moving Average Smoothing, Savitzky–Golay filter, Exponential filter, and Double Exponential filter) in "Alone Together" (Tang et al. 2015), a virtual play environment augmented with multiple sets of Kinects. Overall, among the four filters, the Exponential Smoothing Filter yields the best results in the game. The comparative study only provides quantitative observations on the four smoothing filters, the qualitative examination in terms of player satisfaction remains unclear, which is one of our immediate future research paths in this direction.

Keywords: Kinect · Smoothing filter · Comparative · Motion-sensor

1 Introduction and Background

Microsoft Kinect for Windows is a motion capture sensor, integrated with a build-in color camera, an infrared (IR) emitter, and a microphone array; it is capable to track up to six people simultaneously, and full skeleton with 25 joints can be tracked for two users (Tang et al. 2015). Hence, as a relatively low-cost skeleton tacking and uninstrumented sensor, the popularity of its integration into video games have sour especially with its high promise in home entertainment (Harper and Mentis 2013). However, the Skeleton Tracking System in Kinect is known for being noisy and unstable (Microsoft white paper 2005; Yang et al. 2013), hence, in practice, a noise reduction filter or smoothing filter needs to be employed before consuming the data in order to obtain smooth joint position data over time (Edwards and Green 2014; Yang et al. 2013; Harper and Mentis 2013). In practice, it had led to perceived latency which was reported in our mix-reality multiplayer Kinect game "Alone Together" (Tang and Wang 2015a). In order to overcome this issue and considering the balance between the smoothing effect and filtering delay particularly in "Alone Together", two filters were applied:

Savitzky-Golay smoothing filter (Microsoft white paper 2005) and simple moving averaging filter (Microsoft white paper 2005). Both filters are known as low-latency

© Springer International Publishing Switzerland 2016
C. Stephanidis (Ed.): HCII 2016 Posters, Part II, CCIS 618, pp. 144–148, 2016.
DOI: 10.1007/978-3-319-40542-1_23

filter (Edwards and Green 2014; Yang et al. 2013), which is suitable for animating a person's avatar. We made a comparison for both filters, the video demonstrating the differences can be watched at: http://youtu.be/jMz0GhI6UTo.

The results showed no significant improvement before and after the filters were employed (Tang et al. 2015b).

This paper presents the comparison of four smoothing filters introduced in (Microsoft White Paper 2005), specifically, Simple Moving Average Smoothing, Savitzky–Golay filter, Exponential filter, and Double Exponential filter; the first two are known as low-latency filter (Edwards and Green 2014; Yang et al. 2013). We applied the four filters in our game "Alone Together" (Tang et al. 2015b) and report our comparative results here.

2 Experiment Methodology and Discussion

Experiment Environment and Methodology. In order to make valid comparison across four different types of the smoothing filters, Kinect Studio V1.8.0 (Fig. 1) was implemented in our experiment. Kinect Studio V1.8.0, an extension for Kinect SDK 1.8, has the capability of recoding, fine-tuning and adjusting raw Kinect streams data including color and depth streams which can be utilized to retrieve skeleton data. Furthermore, through repeated play of the recorded data, Kinect Studio can further inject raw information into Kinect applications without revising the code, which allows developers to share the same original data streams across different applications implemented with different filters (Edward and Greens 2014).

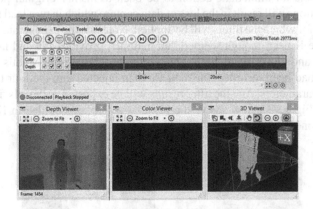

Fig. 1. Kinect Studio with the recorded Color and Depth Stream Data (Color figure online)

In our experiment, we use our game "Alone-Together" (Tang et al. 2015b) as the sample video game application. "Alone-Together" is a Kinect-based multiple player ball-passing game which enables up to three players to interact with each other among certain distance. The game played in motion can be watched at: https://www.youtube.com/watch?v=SYE2mFqOBMo&fe.

Figure 2 (Tang and Wang 2015a) shows the game moment where players' physical environment was also mirrored behind their virtual play environment in the last version of the system.

Fig. 2. Game play moment in "Alone Together" where players' physical and virtual environments interact

The "Alone-Together" game was further revised to integrate with four types of filters without other adjustments.

Experiment Procedure and Data Collection. A player will first be invited to play "Alone Together" as a warm-up session. The experiment starts after he/she is familiar with the game. The player is first instructed to play the game normally; he/she will then be required to perform some extreme movements such as a sudden approach to the Kinect sensor and an immediate action to be back to his/her original position. Such exaggerated actions will result in the loss of data capture which in turn lead to data signal jitter and noise for which the filters will be applied. Note that the exaggerated movements acquired by the Kinect, though seemed "un-natural", provides fun and laughter especially in home and close-friend-circle entertainment (Harper and Mentis 2013). After player actions had been recorded, the data are then injected into the four type of filters with different parameters. And the filter results will be exported as the .xls file for further interpretation. Figure 3 below shows the player's action as recorded in Kinect Studio and its corresponding 3D view.

 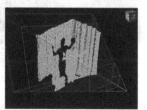

Fig. 3. Testing moment showing the test player's: (left) depth data (right) 3D view

Data Tuning and Evaluation Protocol. In our experiment, the x coordinate value of the left wrist is interpreted for analyzing the filter result. Due to the nature of the fact that "Alone-Together" is a ball game, the hand position with the wrist will be vital to the whole system. However, it is known that the hand position tracked by Microsoft Kinect Version 1 is much less stable than those tracked in the wrist, therefore, 3D coordinates of the left wrist position is the considered in the filter.

"Alone-Together" is as a ball game, the hand position with the wrist will be vital to the whole system. However, it is known that the hand position tracked by Microsoft Kinect Version 1 is much less stable than those tracked in the wrist, therefore, 3D coordinates of the left wrist position is the considered in the filter.

3   Brief Discussion on Experiment Results and Concluding Remarks

Unlike previous studies measuring the sensory-motor performance mainly in terms of movement smoothness (Hogan and Sternad 2009, Edwards and Green 2014), the aim of our study is to ensure lower latency incurred from the possible noisy raw Kinect data so as to increase player engagement in such an online multiplayer game as "Alone Together". Hence, we introduced the latency per unit frame as a measurement to compare the four filters. Through comparing the results from different filters from the exported files, the peak of each curve was marked. The distance (in frame) of the relative closest peak between the raw input data and the filter result is counted as the latency. Based on the latency value, a table with the filter and latency was generated (see Table 1).

Table 1. Average latency per frame for the four filters

Filter		Latency (Unit: Frame)
SG Filter	Length=7,order=2	2
SMA Filter	Length=5	1
Double Exponential Smoothing Filter	Smoothing = 0.5, Correction = 0.5, Prediction = 0.5, JitterRadius = 0.05, MaxDeviationRadius = 0.04	0
Exponential Smoothing Filter	Alpha=0.01	10
	Alpha=0.1	4
	Alpha=0.5	0
	Alpha=0.9	0

From the table, we can observe that the Double Exponential Filter, Exponential Filter (With alpha = 0.5) and Exponential Filter (With alpha = 0.9) have the least latency which have the value in 0, though the smoothing effects are not satisfactory. Overall, the exponential smoothing filter (with alpha = 0.1) leads to the best smoothing results in "Alone-Together."

The comparative study only provides quantitative observations on the four smoothing filters, the qualitative examination in terms of player satisfaction remains unclear, which is one of our immediate future research paths in this direction.

References

Microsoft Kinect White Paper. Skeletal Joint Smoothing White Paper (2005). https://msdn.microsoft.com/en-us/library/jj131429.aspx#ID4EQMAE. Accessed 04 Nov 2015

Yang, N., Duan, F., Wei, Y., Liu, C., Tan, J.T.C., Xu, B., Zhang, J.: A study of the human-robot synchronous control system based on skeletal tracking technology. In: Proceedings of ROBIO 2013, pp. 2191–2196. IEEE Press (2013)

Edwards, M., Green, R.D.: Low-latency filtering of kinect skeleton data for video game control. In: Proceedings of 29th International Conference on Image and Vision Computing New Zealand, pp. 190–195. ACM Press (2014)

Tang, T.Y., Wang, Y.: Alone together: multiplayer online ball passing using kinect - an experimental study. In: Proceedings of the 18th ACM Conference Companion on Computer Supported Cooperative Work & Social Computing (CSCW 2015 Companion), pp. 187–190. ACM, New York (2015a)

Tang, T.Y., Winoto, P., Wang, R.Y.: Having fun over a distance: supporting multiplayer online ball passing using multiple sets of kinect. In: CHI 2015 Extended Abstracts, pp. 1187–1192. ACM Press, New York (2015b)

Harper, R., Mentis, H.: The mocking gaze: the social organization of Kinect use. In: Proceedings of CSCW, pp. 167–180. ACM Press, New York (2013)

Hogan, N., Sternad, D.: Sensitivity of smoothness measures to movement duration, amplitude, and arrests. J. Mot. Behav. **41**(6), 529–534 (2009)

An Analysis of Accuracy Requirements for Automatic Eyetracker Recalibration at Runtime

Florian van de Camp[2(✉)], Dennis Gill[1], Jutta Hild[2], and Jürgen Beyerer[1,2]

[1] Karlsruhe Institute of Technology (KIT), Karlsruhe, Germany
florian.vandecamp@iosb.fraunhofer.de
[2] Fraunhofer IOSB, Karlsruhe, Germany

Abstract. The initial calibration of an eye-tracker is a crucial step to provide accurate gaze data, often as a position on a screen. Issues influencing the calibration such as the user's pose can change while using the eye tracker. Hence, recalibration might often be necessary but at the expense of interrupting the user executing the working task. Monitoring interactions such as clicks on a target or detecting salient objects could provide recalibration points without deliberate user interaction. To gain insight into how accurate recalibration points must be localized to ensure that gaze estimation accuracy is improved, we conducted a user study and examined the effect of correct as well as erroneous localization of recalibration points. The results show that even a localization error of 1.2 degrees of visual angle induces an error of less than 0.5° to the estimated gaze position on screen. Our results indicate the necessary requirements any method automatically providing recalibration points has to fulfill.

1 Introduction and Related Work

Video-based eye-tracking devices estimate the gaze direction from the users pupil center and corneal reflection. Gaze estimation uncertainty, often referred to as accuracy of an eye-tracker, is determined by the offset between the measured gaze direction and the actual gaze direction. Today, many eye-tracker manufacturers claim an accuracy of 0.5° of visual angle. Sitting in front of a desktop monitor at a typical distance of about 60 cm, 0.5° of visual angle correspond to about 0.5 cm on screen. Accordingly, eye-trackers propose to provide measured gaze positions off the actual gaze positions by 0.5 cm. To achieve this accuracy for an individual user, the user has to perform a calibration procedure before using the eye-tracker. This is necessary as the parameters influencing the geometrical components of the gaze direction calculation like eyeball radius, eyeball shape or glasses differ between users; besides, iris color and texture, head pose, viewing angle and lighting conditions influence the gaze direction calculation [HJ10]. Typically, the calibration procedure requires the user to look at a number of predefined calibration points covering the screen (or the area on the screen where

© Springer International Publishing Switzerland 2016
C. Stephanidis (Ed.): HCII 2016 Posters, Part II, CCIS 618, pp. 149–154, 2016.
DOI: 10.1007/978-3-319-40542-1_24

gaze data will be of interest). Common numbers are 5 or 9 [BHND14]. Various contributions proposed several methods to achieve a good calibration; they propose repeating calibration until the offset between calibration point positions and corresponding estimated gaze positions is under, e.g., 0.5° [Tat07], local recalibration for selected calibration areas [Jac90], participant-controlled calibration [HMAvdW11], or using an extra step taking 80–120 s to complete which is used for post-calibration regression [BHND14]. However, the cited contributions address the calibration process as a separate part, required initially but also during operation as the user behavior, particularly, the change of the users head pose, influences calibration. Hence, gaze estimation might deteriorate if head movements are allowed. To keep gaze data quality high, recalibration in suitable intervals is required; however, conducted like the initial calibration it would be annoying for the user [HH02]. [LKRK16] show that cute spreading of the recalibration points can reduce the number to only two. However, it seems more compelling to utilize targets provided on the screen during the working task for unobtrusive recalibration. If the system knows about the position of such targets, those might be utilized to relate gaze position and target position, and calibration would be improved at runtime without disturbing the user. Monitoring interactions such as clicks on a target or salient objects [LYS+11] in the user's field of view could provide this kind of information but without any guarantees in terms of accuracy. Using a target the user did not focus at all could not only fail to improve the current calibration, but even deteriorate it. For further research on methods of obtaining such recalibration points automatically, it is of importance to know how accurately those have to be determined to avoid a degradation of the initial calibration.

2   User Study and Results

We conducted a user study with 16 participants (aged 21–32, no glasses, four with contact lenses, one female) that had to go through a 9-point calibration

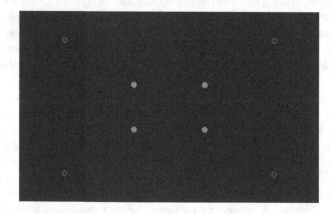

Fig. 1. Corner points of the 16-point grid (green) and the four central points (orange) utilized for recalibration. (Color figure online)

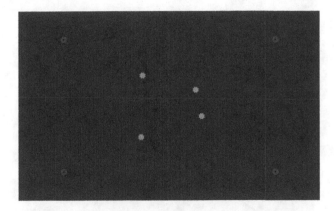

Fig. 2. Shifted recalibration points (orange) generated by randomly applying an offset to their original locations. (Color figure online)

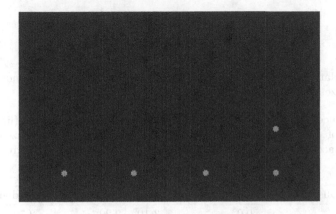

Fig. 3. Points used for evaluation of the accuracy degradation caused by the simulated recalibration point relocation. The five points were chosen as evaluation points as the participants fixated them after they fixated the recalibration points in the 16-point calibration validation step.

procedure using an infrared-based eye-tracker [BMvdC+16]. After this initial calibration, the participants performed a calibration validation step by looking sequentially at the 16 points of an evenly spaced grid on the screen.

Figure 1 shows the corner points of the 16-point grid in green and the four center points of the grid used for recalibration in orange. For recalibration, we used the corner points of the original 9-point calibration in combination with the four recalibration points. The eye-tracker we used allows to record and replay full video data of experiments. Using this feature, we reran the calibration on the recorded video data while systematically introducing offsets to the four recalibration points (Fig. 2), mimicking their erroneous localization. We tested the result of this new calibration on the remaining five points of the 16-point grid (Fig. 3).

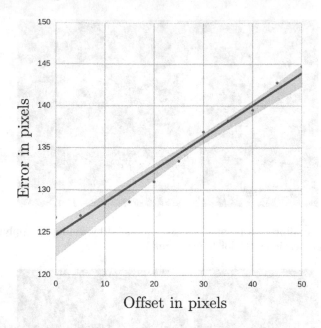

Fig. 4. Correlation between the offset (in pixels) and the resulting error induced to the estimated gaze position on screen (in pixels).

Table 1. Induced localization errors for the recalibration points (in pixels (first column) and degrees of visual angle (second column)) and their impact on the gaze estimation uncertainty (accuracy) as mean, standard deviation and median (in degrees of visual angle).

x (Offset in pixel)	Offset in degree	Mean	Std. Deviation	Median
0	0.0°	3.10°	2.20°	2.70°
5	0.11°	3.10°	2.21°	2.71°
10	0.23°	3.13°	2.23°	2.73°
15	0.35°	3.14°	2.24°	2.72°
20	0.47°	3.20°	2.30°	2.76°
25	0.59°	3.26°	2.36°	2.79°
30	0.71°	3.34°	2.41°	2.85°
35	0.83°	3.37°	2.43°	2.88°
40	0.95°	3.40°	2.46°	2.90°
45	1.07°	3.48°	2.52°	2.92°
50	1.19°	3.53°	2.53°	3.00°

The results are presented in Table 1 showing the gaze estimation uncertainty, or accuracy, as mean, standard deviation, and median for the different induced offsets. Due to the location of the evaluation points at the bottom of the screen, the mean gaze estimation uncertainty is high compared to typical results for the whole screen. However, of major importance are the relative differences between the result with no offset (baseline) and the results with an offset > 0. Figure 4 shows a linear correlation between the localization error for the recalibration points (offset) and the resulting error of gaze point estimation. Overall, the correlation between the error for localizing the recalibration point (x) and the resulting error for gaze estimation is promising as only large offsets significantly deteriorate the gaze position estimation. Even localizing with an erroneous offset of as much as 50 pixels ($1.21°$) deteriorates gaze estimation causes than $0.5°$. The fact, that the recalibration is error tolerant to a certain degree shows that techniques such as saliency detection might be suitable for the localization of recalibration points.

3   Conclusion and Future Work

The results of our study indicate which requirements any method automatically providing recalibration points has to fulfill. The next step will be to gather potential points for recalibration automatically. As mentioned in the introduction, monitoring interactions like clicks on a target or salient objects in the user's field of view could provide this kind of information but without any guarantees in terms of accuracy. For example, using Microsoft Windows 8.0, stationary targets like desktop icons cover $1.5\,cm \times 3\,cm$ ("small size"), the CLOSE-button of a window covers $0.5\,cm \times 1.0\,cm$, the MINIMIZE-button covers $0.5\,cm \times 0.6\,cm$. Assuming that the user focuses the center of a button or icon in order to make sure he will hit it with the pointer, it is reasonable to use the target center as recalibration point. Hence, detecting that the user looked at the MINIMIZE-button (as this item was clicked) introduces a maximum offset between estimated and actual gaze position of $0.5\sqrt{0.5^2 + 0.6^2} = 0.4°$, if the user actually was focussing one of the corner points. Considering the desktop icon, the maximum offset is $0.5\sqrt{1.5^2 + 3^2} = 1.7°$. Overall, it seems likely that these methods might be used to obtain points for recalibration and will need to be put to a test to examine the real-world implications of recalibration at runtime.

Acknowledgement. The underlying projects to this article are funded by the WTD 81 of the German Federal Ministry of Defense as well as by Fraunhofer IOSB in-house funding. The authors are responsible for the content of this article.

References

[BHND14] Blignaut, P., Holmqvist, K., Nystrm, M., Dewhurst, R.: Improving the accuracy of video-based eye tracking in real time through post-calibration regression. In: Current Trends in Eye Tracking Research, pp. 77–100 (2014)

[BMvdC+16] Balthasar, S., Martin, M., van de Camp, F., Hild, J., Beyerer, J.: Combining low-cost eye trackers for dual monitor eye tracking. In: HCI International (HCII) (2016)

[HH02]   Hornof, A.J., Halverson, T.: Cleaning up systematic error in eye-tracking data by using required fixation locations. Behav. Res. Methods Instrum. Comput. **34**(4), 592–604 (2002)

[HJ10]   Hansen, D.W., Ji, Q.: In the eye of the beholder: a survey of models for eyes and gaze. IEEE Trans. Pattern Anal. Mach. Intell. **32**(3), 478–500 (2010)

[HMAvdW11]   Holmqvist, K., Nyström, M., Andersson, R., van de Weijer, J.: Participants know best: the effect of calibration method on data quality. InVision Science Society (2011)

[Jac90]   Jacob, R.J.: What you look at is what you get: eye movement-based interaction techniques. In: Proceedings of the SIGCHI Conference on Human Factors in Computing Systems, pp. 11–18 (1990)

[LKRK16]   Lander, C., Kerber, F., Rauber, T., Krger, A.: A time-efficient recalibration algorithm for improved long-term accuracy of head-worn eye trackers. In: Proceedings of the Ninth Biennial ACM Symposium on Eye Tracking Research & Applications, pp. 213–216 (2016)

[LYS+11]   Liu, T., Yuan, Z., Sun, J., Wang, J., Zheng, N., Tang, X., Shum, H.-Y.: Learning to detect a salient object. IEEE Trans. Pattern Anal. Mach. Intell. **33**(2), 353–367 (2011)

[Tat07]   Tatler, B.W.: The central fixation bias in scene viewing: selecting an optimal viewing position independently of motor biases and image feature distributions. J. Vis. **7**(14), 1–17 (2007)

Expressions and Emotions Recognition and Psychophisiological Monitoring

Enhancing Emotion Recognition in VIPs with Haptic Feedback

Hendrik P. Buimer[1]([✉]), Marian Bittner[1], Tjerk Kostelijk[2],
Thea M. van der Geest[3], Richard J.A. van Wezel[1,4], and Yan Zhao[1]

[1] Department of Biomedical Signals and Systems, MIRA Institute,
University of Twente, Enschede, The Netherlands
h.p.buimer@utwente.nl
[2] VicarVision, Amsterdam, The Netherlands
[3] Department of Media, Communication and Organization,
University of Twente, Enschede, The Netherlands
[4] Biophysics, Donders Institute, Radboud University Nijmegen,
Nijmegen, The Netherlands

Abstract. The rise of smart technologies has created new opportunities to support blind and visually impaired persons (VIPs). One of the biggest problems we identified in our previous research on problems VIPs face during activities of daily life concerned the recognition of persons and their facial expressions. In this study we developed a system to detect faces, recognize their emotions, and provide vibrotactile feedback about the emotions expressed. The prototype system was tested to determine whether vibrotactile feedback through a haptic belt is capable of enhancing social interactions for VIPs.

The system consisted of commercially available technologies. A Logitech C920 webcam mounted on a cap, a Microsoft Surface Pro 4 carried in a mesh backpack, an Elitac tactile belt worn around the waist, and the VicarVision FaceReader software application, which recognizes facial expressions.

In preliminary tests with the systems both visually impaired and sighted persons were presented with sets of stimuli consisting of actors displaying six emotions (e.g. joy, surprise, anger, sadness, fear, and disgust) derived from the validated Amsterdam Dynamic Facial Expression Set and Warsaw Set of Emotional Facial Expression Pictures with matching audio by using nonlinguistic affect bursts. Subjects had to determine the emotions expressed in the videos without and, after a training period, with haptic feedback.

An exit survey was conducted aimed to gain insights into the opinion of the users, on the perceived usefulness and benefits of the emotional feedback, and their willingness of using the prototype as assistive technology in daily life.

Haptic feedback about facial expressions may improve the ability of VIPs to determine emotions expressed by others and, as a result, increase the confidence of VIPs during social interactions. More studies are needed to determine whether this is a viable method to convey information and enhance social interactions in the daily life of VIPs.

Keywords: Sensory substitution · Wearables · User-centered design

© Springer International Publishing Switzerland 2016
C. Stephanidis (Ed.): HCII 2016 Posters, Part II, CCIS 618, pp. 157–163, 2016.
DOI: 10.1007/978-3-319-40542-1_25

1 Introduction

The rise of smart technologies, such as smartphones, smartwatches, and other wearables has led to new ways of conveying information to users. In the current paper, we present a wearable system to support visually impaired persons (VIPs). Previously, interviews were conducted amongst VIPs in The Netherlands to determine the biggest problems and challenges they face in daily life, after which a survey was held to rank activities of daily life on both perceived difficulty and perceived importance. One of the issues addressed, and ranked highest on difficulty in the survey, was the recognition of persons [1]. An example of such problems is the inability to determine facial expressions which others are displaying during social interactions [2]. Therefore, we developed an assistive aid, based on the notion of sensory substitution, to support VIPs with the recognition of facial expressions of others.

Sensory substitution, in which real world information is transferred to the human sensory interface by using artificial sensors, is not a new development, with Braille (developed in the 19th century) being one of the most famous examples to date [3]. In the late 60's Bach-y-Rita proposed that sensory substitution is possible, and dependent on available artificial receptors [4]. Later studies indeed demonstrated that the human brain has the ability to adapt to artificial receptors through a tactile machine interface [3]. In other words, with the right artificial receptors, it should be possible to give VIPs visual information by conveying it through another sense.

Several studies have proven that haptic feedback around the waist can be used to convey specific information, such as interpersonal distance or locations of persons, to visually impaired users [2, 5, 6]. However, to our knowledge, no one has tried to convey facial expressions and associated emotions through such a system.

To create new assistive technology for the blind and visually impaired we linked existing technologies. A Logitech C920 webcam, mounted on a cap, was used to capture images of the conversation partner of the user. FaceReader software (VicarVision, Amsterdam), which ran on a Microsoft Surface Pro 4, then analyzed the images in real time and categorized the facial expressions displayed as one of six basic emotions (e.g. anger, disgust, fear, joy, sadness, surprise) [7]. The emotion recognized by the software was conveyed using a haptic belt with six tactors, worn around the waist (Elitac, Utrecht). Each tactor was assigned to one emotion, whereas vibration intensity represented the intensity with which an emotion was displayed according to the software (see Fig. 1). A more detailed description can be found in the method section.

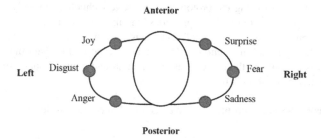

Fig. 1. Location of the tactors and the emotion assigned to it across the waist

In the current study we want to determine to what extent tactile-vision sensory substitution by means of vibrotactile feedback through a belt around the waist can support VIPs' ability to determine facial expressions and related emotions of conversation partners.

2 Method

2.1 Apparatus

The system consists of a webcam, a tablet running FaceReader software, and a haptic belt. The FaceReader software, running on the tablet, analyzes webcam content approximately at a rate of 5–6 frames per second. The software finds a face, models it, and then classifies the facial expressions of the face into one of seven emotions, which are: neutral, anger (*angry*), disgust (*disgusted*), fear (*scared*), joy (*happy*), sadness (*sad*), and surprise (*surprised*) [8–13].

This information is then conveyed through an Elitac haptic belt that was connected to the tablet by means of a Bluetooth connection. In the current setup six tactors are used to convey emotion information. On recognition of a face, all tactors on the belt activate at the same time with two bursts of 150 ms and a break of 50 ms in between. 200 ms after the two bursts, the tactor associated to the displayed facial expression, as recognized by FaceReader, will vibrate as long as a face is detected. The intensity of the displayed emotion determines the intensity of the vibration, which has 15 levels of intensity. In case of a neutral facial expression, no tactors are activated. Once a face is no longer detected, the tactors will vibrate for 300 ms.

2.2 Subjects

Preliminary tests were performed with one blind and three fully sighted subjects. Besides visual impairments, subjects included in the study had no other sensory or cognitive impairments. All subjects were in their 20 s and were university students.

2.3 Materials

Each subject was confronted with 108 stimuli (60 pictures, 24 videos without audio, and 24 videos with audio), equally representing six basic emotions [7]. Validated sets of actors displaying emotions were used: 48 videos from Amsterdam Dynamic Facial Expression Set [14]; 60 pictures from the Warsaw Set of Emotional Facial Expression Pictures [15]. Due to the fact that both the pictures and the videos were not accompanied with audio, audio was added to half of the videos, using two validated sets of nonlinguistic affect bursts [16, 17]. The affect bursts and videos were matched based on the emotions expressed and the intensity of the emotion, creating a stimulus that was as natural as possible. Before the experiment, all the stimuli were analyzed with the FaceReader software; only stimuli for which FaceReader was able to determine the emotion were included during testing.

2.4 Psychophysical Testing

Testing was divided into three phases (baseline, training, and experiment) and lasted about one and an half hour with short breaks in between. During the baseline phase 36 different stimuli, consisting of 12 pictures, 12 videos without audio, and 12 videos with audio were shown to the subject without additional feedback (Fig. 2). Each basic emotion was represented 6 times per phase. Before each stimulus the subjects heard a beep to indicate a new facial expression will be shown for about six seconds. After the end of each stimulus the subject was asked to indicate whether the displayed emotion was positive of negative, which emotion was displayed, the intensity of the emotion, and on which sensory input their conclusion was based. The stimuli lacking audio were also briefly shown to the visual impaired in order to acquaint them with the setup of the study.

The training phase was used to allow the subjects to familiarize themselves with the vibrotactile system. First, the desirable minimum and maximum vibration intensity, and the just notable difference between vibrations were determined. After calibrating the belt, the sighted subjects were blindfolded. The examiner gave a brief explanation on which tactors were assigned to each emotion. Next, the subjects were shown 12 pictures sorted by emotion and were told what emotion was displayed. Afterwards, 12 pictures were shown in a random order of emotions after which the subject reported which emotion they thought were displayed in the stimulus. The examiner either corrected or confirmed the answer the subject gave. Finally, the subject was shown 12 more pictures in a random order to train without confirmation from the examiner.

During the experiment phase, subjects were asked to determine the emotions in the stimuli using the system relying on all their available senses, as well as the vibrotactile belt. The procedure of the experiment phase is the same as the baseline phase. However, different stimuli were used and the subject was additionally asked to indicate after each stimulus the location where the vibration was felt.

After the three phases the subject completed a short questionnaire on how information was conveyed (example statement: "I could easily determine which tactor was vibrating"), on a five-point Likert scale (1 totally disagree, 2 disagree, 3 neutral, 4 agree, and 5 totally agree). In addition, open questions were asked about the ease of use of the system and whether the subject saw potential in the system for future usage.

Baseline phase	Training phase	Experiment phase
12 Pictures	12 Pictures	12 Pictures
12 Videos without audio	12 Pictures	12 Videos without audio
12 Videos with audio	12 Pictures	12 Videos with audio

Fig. 2. Study design

3 Preliminary Results

The preliminary tests with three sighted subjects and one visually impaired user showed that subjects were fairly quick in learning to interpret the information conveyed by the vibrotactile belt. In the pre-test a 21 year old sighted respondent stated "it was difficult to understand in the beginning, but once you know where everything is located you can quickly learn to interpret the system." The system even assisted a sighted subject when the displayed emotion was ambiguous: "I noticed I was looking for confirmation by the system [...], in some cases I found it difficult to decide, and then the system recognized anger, so I agree with the system (24 year old, sighted female, pre-test)."

The first visually impaired subject was a 27 year old fully blind male university student. In the experiment phase he correctly interpreted 66.7 % of the emotions displayed. He was able to successfully determine 83.3 % of the conveyed emotions by the vibrotactile belt, as detected by FaceReader (correctly interpreted emotions displayed in the validated set in 75 % of the stimuli). Considering the fact that it was physically impossible for him to detect any emotion using the non-audio stimuli without the system, this is a major improvement. For the audio stimuli, the subject slightly improved, agreeing on nine out of twelve times without the system and eleven out of twelve times while wearing the system. A schematic overview of the scores by the visually impaired user can be found in Table 1.

Table 1. Agreement between validated sets and the visually impaired user

Baseline phase				Experiment phase		
P	VWOA	VWA	Training phase	P	VWOA	VWA
0%	0%	75%		75%	50%	91.7%

Note. P = pictures, VWOA = videos without audio; VWA = videos with audio

Whereas the sighted subjects saw potential for VIPs rather than for themselves, the visually impaired subject stated that he does not expect to use a specific system for emotion recognition –as it is now– on a daily basis: "I think that if I could use it only for this purpose [emotion detection], I would not use it that quickly." However, he stated that he saw future potential for the system as a whole: "A belt like this could be worn for multiple reasons, such as a navigation aid. And when you are wearing the system already, how difficult could it be to turn on an app to recognize emotions once you are in a meeting? I think I would use it then, and I am sure I will try it out, just of curiosity."

In general, the subjects were positive about the system. The tactors were well placed and the subjects were able to distinguish vibrations originating from different units. The vibration intensity and associated sounds were acceptable in the current situation. However, the visually impaired subject stated that the sounds might be annoying in situations where everyone is rather quiet, such as in work related meetings.

4 Discussion

In the current study, we investigated whether tactile-vision sensory substitution by means of vibrotactile feedback through a belt around the waist can help people to determine the facial expressions and recognize emotions of their conversation partners. The preliminary results would seem to suggest that this is indeed possible with the system developed.

Although the system can detect faces and classify emotions reasonably well, its performance is impacted by lighting conditions and contrast of the test environment. FaceReader was capable of determining the correct facial expressions when videos were directly loaded into the software. However, during the actual experiment, where faces presented in a real time video feed were analyzed, FaceReader was less successful.

Thus, a possible limitation of the study is a lack of generalizability to real life situations. The study contents and procedure were setup to investigate whether both visually impaired and sighted persons were able to use the system and interpret the information conveyed through vibrotactile feedback in a controlled setting, using validated facial expressions stimuli, artificial lighting conditions, and a limited set of facial expressions consisting of six basic emotions. Therefore, it remains unknown how well the system will perform in real life, with ever changing lighting conditions and a wider range of facial expressions than the six basic emotions used in this study.

We plan to expand the current study with more subjects, after which we will investigate how the system and its users behave in real life situations. The current system is not always accurate in detecting the right emotion in suboptimal lighting conditions and lacks consistency. While sighted people can correct for these errors by using their sight, it is interesting to study how VIPs cope with such flaws in the system.

While the information conveyed by the system was limited to six basic emotions, the software used is capable of providing much more detailed information, based on a circumplex model that combines valence and arousal. Therefore, it should be further investigated how the amount of information conveyed though the haptic belt can be increased in order to cover a greater range of emotions.

Finally, it is interesting to investigate whether sensory substitution occurs over time and if users of the system unconsciously interpret the information conveyed by the system, thus enabling VIPs to actually feel others' emotions.

In conclusion, there are indications that users are able to quickly learn and interpret the information conveyed through the haptic belt. The system presented in this paper seems to confirm Bach-y-Rita and Kercel's predictions considering the possibility to substitute functions of the human sensory system with artificial receptors as long as those are up for the task [3]. We believe, the system presented can support VIPs with the recognition of facial expressions and associated emotions, while showing great potential for expansion to other functionalities, e.g. detecting gestures and gaze direction, socially accepted behavior, and navigation tasks.

References

1. Van der Geest, T.M. Buimer, H.P.: User-centered priority setting for accessible devices and applications. in Mensch und Computer 2015. Stuttgart: De Gruyter, Oldenbourg (2015)
2. Krishna, S. et al.: A systematic requirements analysis and development of an assistive device to enhance the social interaction of people who are blind of visually impaired, in Computer Vision Applications for the Visually Impaired, Marseille, France (2008)
3. Bach-y-Rita, P., Kercel, S.W.: Sensory substitution and the human-machine interface. Trends Cogn. Sci. 7(12), 541–546 (2003)
4. Bach-y-Rita, P.: Sensory plasticity: applications to a vision substitution system. Acta Neurol. Scand. 43, 417–426 (1967)
5. McDaniel, T. et al.: Using a haptic belt to convey non-verbal communication cues during social interactions to individuals who are blind. In: HAVE 2008, Ottawa (2008)
6. McDaniel, T. et al.: Heartbeats: a methodology to convey interpersonal distance through touch. In: CHI, Atlanta, Georgia, USA (2010)
7. Ekman, P.: An argument for basic emotions. Cogn. Emot. 6(3/4), 169–200 (1992)
8. Bishop, C.M.: Neural Networks for Pattern Recognition. Clarendon Press, Oxford (1995)
9. Cootes, T., Taylor, C.: Statistical Models of Appearance for Computer Vision (2000)
10. Viola, P., Jones, M.: Robust real-time face detection. Int. J. Comput. Vis. 57(2), 137–154 (2004)
11. van Kuilenburg, H., Wiering, M.A., den Uyl, M.: A Model Based Method for Automatic Facial Expression Recognition. In: Gama, J., Camacho, R., Brazdil, P.B., Jorge, A.M., Torgo, L. (eds.) ECML 2005. LNCS (LNAI), vol. 3720, pp. 194–205. Springer, Heidelberg (2005)
12. Denu Uyl, M.J., Van Kuilenburg, H.: The FaceReader: online facial expression recognition. In: Measuring Behaviour. Wageningen, The Netherlands (2005)
13. Van Kuilenburg, H., et al.: Advances in face and gesture analysis. In: Measuring Behavior. Maastricht, The Netherlands (2008)
14. Van der Schalk, J., et al.: Moving faces, looking places: validation of the Amsterdam dynamic facial expression set (ADFES). Emotion 11(4), 907–920 (2011)
15. Olszanowski, M., et al.: Warsaw set of emotional facial expression pictures: a validation study of facial display photographs. Front. Psychol. 5, 1516 (2015)
16. Hawk, S.T., et al.: "Worth a thousand words": absolute and relative decoding of nonlinguistic affect vocalizations. Emotion 9(3), 293–305 (2009)
17. Lima, C.F., Castro, S.L., Scott, S.K.: When voices get emotional: A corpus of nonverbal vocalizations for research on emotion processing. Behav. Res. Methods 45, 1234–1245 (2013)

Recognizing Emotional States Using Physiological Devices

Ali Mehmood Khan[✉] and Michael Lawo

TZi-Universität Bremen, Bremen, Germany
{akhan,mlawo}@tzi.de

Abstract. Emotional computing is a field of human computer interaction where a system has the ability to recognize emotions and react accordingly. Recognizing Emotional states is becoming a major part of a user's context for wearable computing applications. The system should be able to acquire the user's emotional states by using physiological sensors. We want to develop a personal emotional states recognition system that is practical, reliable, and can be used for health-care related applications. We propose to use the eHealth platform which is a ready-made, light weight, small and easy to use device for recognizing few Emotional states like Sad, Dislike, Joy, Stress, Normal, NoIdea, Positive and Negative using decision tree classifier. In this paper, we present an approach to build a system that exhibits this property and provides evidence based on data for 8 different emotional states collected from 24 different subjects. Our results indicate that the system has an accuracy rate of approximately 91 %. In our work, we used three physiological sensors (i.e. BVP, GSR and EMG) in order recognize Emotional states (i.e. Stress, joy/Happy, sad, normal/Neutral, dislike and no idea).

Keywords: Emotional states · Electromyogram · Blood volume pulse · Galvanic skin response · Skin temperature · International Affective Picture System · Machine learning classifier · User studies

1 Introduction

It is hard to express your own emotions; no one can accurately measure the degree of his/her emotional state. According to Darwin, "….the young and the old of widely different races, both with man and animals, express the same state of mind by the same movement" [16]. According to Paul Ekman, there are seven basic emotions which are fear, surprise, sad, dislike, disgrace, disgust and joy [14]. The concept behind emotional states (also known as affective computing) was first introduced by Rosalind Picard in 1995 [2]. Since then the affective computing group have produced novel and innovative projects in that domain [3]. Emotional states recognition has received attention in recent years and is able to support the health care industry. Emotions and physical health have a strong link in influencing the immune system too [15]. Due to untreated, chronic stress; occurrence of an emotional disorder is more than 50 % [6]. According to Richmond Hypnosis Center, due to stress; 110 million people die every year. That means, every 2 s, 7 people die [4]. According to American Psychological

© Springer International Publishing Switzerland 2016
C. Stephanidis (Ed.): HCII 2016 Posters, Part II, CCIS 618, pp. 164–171, 2016.
DOI: 10.1007/978-3-319-40542-1_26

Association, in 2011 about 53 percent of Americans claimed stress as a reason behind personal health problems [5]. According to Dr. Alexander G. Justicz, in the 21st century, stress is a huge problem for men [9]. Stress affects our health negatively, causing headaches, stomach problems, sleep problems, and migraines. Stress can cause many mouth problems, the painful TMJ (temporomandibular joint) syndrome, and tooth loss [7]. "Stress has an immediate effect on your body. In the short term, that's not necessarily a bad thing, but chronic stress puts your health at risk" [8]. Long term and intense anger can be caused of mental health problems including depression, anxiety and self-harm. It can also be caused of "high blood pressure", "cold and flu", "coronary heart disease", "stroke", "cancer" and "gastro-intestinal problems" [13]. "If you have a destructive reaction to anger, you are more likely to have heart attacks" [12] whereas "an upward-spiral dynamic continually reinforces the tie between positive emotions and physical health" [17]. Although the negative effects of stress are known to people, they choose (deliberately or otherwise) to ignore it. They need to be forcefully notified, that they must shrug off negative emotions; either by sending them calls or some video clips/text messages/games [10]. According to number of studies, negative thinking or depression can adversely affect your health [19]. Probably automatic and personal applications can be very helpful if it can monitor one's emotional states and persuade people to come out of negative emotional states. According to William Atkinson; "The best way to overcome undesirable or negative thoughts and feelings is to cultivate the positive ones" [18]. Emotional recognition technology can tackle this problem as it is able to monitor an individual's emotional states. This kind of system can also send an alarming call to a person when he is in a negative emotional state for long time or notify the caregivers or family members. The system can also log an individual's emotional states for later analysis. In some cases, especially in heart diseases, emotional states are also required along with the physical activities and physiological information for doctors in order to examine their patient's conditions when he is away from the doctor's clinic [11]. We want to develop a system for recognizing emotional states using physiological sensors which should be able to identify a few emotional states like sad, dislike, joy, stress, normal, no-idea, positive and negative.

2   Related Work

Recognizing emotional states by using automated systems have increased in recent years. Researchers developed systems for recognizing emotional states using speech [23–25], facial expressions [26–28] and physiological devices [20–22, 29, 30]. In this research, we want to recognize different emotional states using body worn physiological devices (EMG, BVP, GSR and temperature). Researchers used physiological devices in order to recognize for different emotional states like sad [20–22, 30], joy/happy [20–22, 30, 31], normal/neutral [21, 30, 31], negative [29] etc. However, the aforementioned researches have used different physiological devices in their work. For example; some researchers recognized emotional states using EEG, GSR and pulse sensor and they recognized joy, anger, sad, fear and relax. Audio and visual clips were used as a stimulus for eliciting the emotions [20]. Some researchers recognized emotional states using ECG and they recognized Happiness, Sad, Fear, Surprise, Disgust, and Neutral. Audio and visual clips were used as a stimulus for eliciting the emotions [21]. Some researchers recognized emotional states using ECG, EMG, skin conductance, respiration sensor and they recognized Joy, anger, Sadness and Pleasure. Music songs were used as a stimulus for eliciting the emotions [22]. In another case, researchers gathered the data from the "blood volume pulse", "electromyogram", "respiration" and the "skin conductance sensor". They conducted 20 experiments in 20 consecutive days, testing around 25 min per day on each individual. They figured out neutral, anger, hate, grief, love, romantic, joy and reverence emotion states from the data. They got 81 % classification accuracy among the eight states [31]. Different techniques can be used as a stimulus for eliciting the emotions i.e. pictures, video clips, audio clips, games etc. In our work, we used International Affective Picture System (IAPS) for stimulation. IAPS is widely used in experiments studying emotion and attention. The International Affective Picture System (IAPS) provides normative emotional stimuli for emotion and attention under experimental investigations. The target is to produce a large set of emotionally-evocative, standardized, color photographs, inter nationally-accessible that includes contents under semantic categories [32]. Above mentioned researchers used different parts of body but in our research we used only left arm for the sensor placement.

3 Hypothesis

The physiological data measured by wearable devices (EMG, blood volume pulse, and skin conductance sensor) indicate which emotion state (Sad, Dislike, Joy, Stress, Normal, NoIdea, positive, Negative) the person is in using machine learning classifier (J48 and IBK).

4 Experimental Methodology

We developed following systems for the user study.

4.1 eHealth Platform and Application

We used eHealth platform [1] in order to recognize emotional states (Fig. 1) and connected Raspberry Pi [41] to eHealth platform (Fig. 2).

The eHealth sensor comes with few sensors like 2D Accelerometer sensor, Blood pressure sensor (Breathing), Pulse and oxygen in blood sensor, body temperature sensor, airflow sensor, Electrocardiogram sensor (ECG), Electromyography sensor (EMG) and Galvanic skin response sensor. We used Galvanic skin response sensor, body temperature sensor, Electromyography sensor (EMG) and we used another blood volume pulse sensor [40]. We connected 'GSR, 'EMG' and 'BVP' to the board. We wrote a piece of code which reads the values from the aforementioned sensors and writes it to a network port.

Fig. 1. eHealth platform

Fig. 2. Raspberri pi with eHealth platform

4.2 IAPS and Its Application (Application Stimulus)

We got an access to IAPS [32] images and these images are already used by several researchers for emotional computing [33–39]. We implemented an application in C#. net that shows participants' IAPS images in a sequence in order to change participants' emotional states and also states the starting and ending time for each IAPS image during experiments. After showing participants five different images from each group, our application used to ask participants about their current emotional state by using the Likert scale (as shown in below figure) approach. We chose 100 IAPS images from different categories and presented it in following order.

1. Sad (5 images) Questionnaire Dislike (5 images) Questionnaire Joy (5 images Questionnaire Stress (5 images) Questionnaire

2. Dislike (5 images) Questionnaire Joy (5 images Questionnaire Stress (5 images) Questionnaire Sad (5 images) Questionnaire

3. Joy (5 images Questionnaire Stress (5 images) Questionnaire Sad (5 images) Questionnaire Dislike (5 images) Questionnaire

4. Stress (5 images) Questionnaire Sad (5 images) Questionnaire Dislike (5 images) Questionnaire Joy (5 images Questionnaire

5. Stress (5 images) Questionnaire Joy (5 images Questionnaire Dislike (5 images) Questionnaire Sad (5 images) Questionnaire

The images were shown as a slide show with a timer of 5 s for each image. For the questionnaire we used radio buttons and participants had to choose one emotional state, the application also stores the participants' personal information i.e. age, gender, height and weight. Participants were asked to wear sensors on their left arms, palms and fingers (Fig. 3). They were also required to perform the experiments twice; the first experiment was useful in getting the participants to familiarize themselves with the setup, while the second attempt was actually used for analyzing their data.

Fig. 3. Participant is wearing sensors

5   Results and Analysis

We recruited 26 participants (21 males, 5 females) for our experiment setup; two of them could not complete the experiments so we ended up with 24 participants (19 males, 5 females). The range of participants' age was from 20 to 44 (mean 26.17, SD 5.14) and ranged in BMI (body mass index) from 18.7 to 26.6 (mean 21.44, SD 2.17). Participants were required to conduct the experiment twice and on different days. They were asked to choose one of the following 'Emotional states' during experiments:

Normal, Sad, Dislike, Joy, Stress and No-Idea

We received values from three sensors i.e. EMG, GSR and BVP where sample rate was around 650 Hz. Our experimental setup was able to change participants' emotional states. Only four of the participants chose all of the given emotional states. This was due to the fact that it was hard for the participants to distinguish between sad, dislike and stress. Also being asked to distinguish between joy and normal during experiments was not a straightforward task. That also explains why some emotional states were ignored by participants. *"As everyone knows, emotions seem to be interrelated in various but systematic ways: Excitement and depression seem to be opposites; excitement and surprise seem to be more similar to one another; and excitement and joy seem to be highly similar, often indistinguishable"* [43]. Therefore, we generated another dataset from our experimental data; we categorized emotional states into two collections:

• Positive {Joy, Normal}
• Negative {Sad, Dislike. Stress}; 'No-Idea' is excluded

Now, we have the following types of datasets:

• Type1: It contains {Normal, Sad, Dislike, Joy, Stress and No-Idea}
• Type2: It contains {Positive and Negative}

Due to the fact that it was a huge dataset, it was not possible for WEKA [44] application to process the data of all 24 participants together. Therefore, we chose small portions of data randomly pertaining to each emotional from each participant. We got two types of data i.e. "Two-Class" and "Six-class". We applied J48 and IBK classifiers with 10-fold cross validation.

Our results show that J48 and IBK classifiers were able to classify the instances with the accuracies of 97.7584 % and 95.4684 % respectively for 'Two-Class'. J48 and IBK classifiers were also able to classify the instances with the accuracies of 96.5014 % and 91.9333 % respectively for 'Six-Class' (Tables 1 and 2).

Table 1. Confusion Matrices; Two class

	a	b
J48	394817	20401
	9917	927355
IBK	384330	30888
	30402	906870

a = Positive;
b = Negative

Table 2. Confusion Matrices; Six class

	a	b	c	d	e	f
J48	239926	4133	2313	1455	588	273
	3780	419739	4174	3533	1861	617
	2279	5123	268858	2955	683	320
	1543	4199	2577	245845	484	232
	606	2128	842	572	130597	255
	309	704	433	341	251	62123
IBK	227624	8887	5627	3826	1982	742
	9218	400731	10389	7895	4142	1329
	5882	11613	254002	5741	2222	758
	4024	8568	5841	233997	1748	702
	1613	3800	1989	1513	125707	378
	753	1241	789	670	395	60313

a = Sad; b = Dislike; c = Joy; d = Stress; e = Normal;
f = NoIdea

6   Conclusion and Future Work

Our system was able to recognize the aforementioned emotional states by using physiological devices and J48 (decision tree) and IBK classifiers with high accuracies. Results have shown that few physiological devices are enough for recognizing required emotional states ('Sad', 'Dislike', 'Joy', 'Stress', 'Normal', 'No-Idea', 'Positive' and 'Negative'). This prototype is only a "proof of concept" and our results show that our approach can identify the above mentioned emotional states independent of BMI (body mass index) and age group. The physiological sensor has to be fixed properly on the participants' skin in order to predict their emotional states successfully. We will conduct more user studies where we will use physiological data and facial expressions for recognizing these emotional states.

References

1. Cooking Hacks: e-Health Sensor Platform V2.0 for Arduino and Raspberry Pi [Biometric/Medical Applications]. http://www.cooking-hacks.com/documentation/tutorials/ehealth-biometric-sensor-platform-arduino-raspberry-pi-medical#step4_9
2. Picard, R.W.: http://web.media.mit.edu/~picard/index.php
3. Affective Computing: Publications. http://affect.media.mit.edu/publications.php
4. Richmond Hypnosis Center. http://richmondhypnosiscenter.com/2013/04/12/sample-post-two/
5. American Psychological Association: The Impact of Stress. http://www.apa.org/news/press/releases/stress/2011/impact.aspx
6. WebMD: Stress Management Health Center. http://www.webmd.com/balance/stress-management/effects-of-stress-on-your-body
7. Krifka, S., Spagnuolo, G., Schmalz, G., Schweikl, H.: A review of adaptive mechanisms in cell responses towards oxidative stress caused by dental resin monomers. Biomaterials **34**, 4555–4563 (2013)
8. Healthline: The Effects of stress on the Body. http://www.healthline.com/health/stress/effects-on-body
9. Miamiherald: Chronic stress is linked to the six leading causes of death. http://www.miamiherald.com/living/article1961770.html
10. Online Stress Reliever Games. http://stress.lovetoknow.com/Online_Stress_Reliever_Games
11. Khan, A.M.: Personal state and emotion monitoring by wearable computing and machine learning. In: BCS-HCI 2012, Newcastle, UK (2011)
12. WebMD: Stress Management Health Center. http://www.webmd.com/balance/stress-management/features/how-anger-hurts-your-heart
13. BetterHealth: Anger - how it affects people. http://www.betterhealth.vic.gov.au/bhcv2/bhcarticles.nsf/pages/Anger_how_it_affects_people
14. Ekman, P.: Basic emotions. In: Dalgleish, T., Power, M. (eds.) Handbook of Cognition and Emotion (PDF). Wiley, Sussex (1999)
15. Health and Wellness: Are Happy People Healthier? New Reasons to Stay Positive. http://www.oprah.com/health/How-Your-Emotions-Affect-Your-Health-and-Immune-System
16. Darwin, C.: The Expression of the Emotions in Man and Animals. John Murray, London (1872)
17. Kok, B.E., Coffey, K.A., Cohn, M.A., Catalino, L.I., Vacharkulksemsuk, T., Algoe, S., Brantley, M., Fredrickson, B.L.: How positive emotions build physical health: Perceived positive social connections account for the upward spiral between positive emotions and vagal tone. Psychol. Sci. **24**(7), 1123–1132 (2013)
18. Atkinson, W.W.: Thought Vibration or the Law of Attraction in the Thought World (1908)
19. Rush, A.J., Beck, A.T., Kovacs, M., Hollon, S.D.: Comparative efficacy of cognitive therapy and pharmacotherapy in the treatment of depressed outpatients. Cognit. Ther. Res. **1**, 17–38 (1977)
20. Remarks on Emotion Recognition from Bio-Potential Signals: research paper (2004)
21. Emotion Recognition from Electrocardiogram Signals using Hilbert Huang Transform (2012)
22. Emotion Pattern Recognition Using Physiological Signals (2014)
23. Sendlmeier, W., Burkhardt, F.: Verification of Acoustical Correlates of Emotional Speech using Formant-Synthesis, Technical University of Berlin, Germany
24. Dellaert, F., Polzin, T., Waibel, A.: Recognizing Emotion in Speech
25. Dai, K., Fell, H.J., MacAuslan, J.: Recognizing Emotion in Speech Using Neural Networks

26. Recognizing Emotion From Facial Expressions: Psychological and Neurological Mechanisms Ralph Adolphs, University of Iowa College of Medicine
27. Busso, C., et al.: Analysis of emotion recognition using facial expressions, speech and multimodal information. In: Proceedings of the 6th International Conference on Multimodal Interfaces, ICMI 2004, State College, PA, USA, 13–15 October 2004 (2004)
28. Perikos, I., Ziakopoulos, E., Hatzilygeroudis, I.: Recognizing Emotions from Facial Expressions Using Neural Network
29. Monajati, M., Abbasi, S.H., Shabaninia, F., Shamekhi, S.: Emotions States Recognition Based on Physiological Parameters by Employing of Fuzzy-Adaptive Resonance Theory
30. Selvaraj, J., Murugappan, M., Wan, K., Yaacob, S.: Classification of emotional states from electrocardiogram signals: a non-linear approach based on hurst
31. Healey, J., Picard, R.W.: Eight-emotion Sentics Data, MIT Affective Computing Group (2002). http://affect.media.mit.edu
32. The Center for the Study of Emotion and Attention. http://csea.phhp.ufl.edu/Media.html#topmedia
33. Cuthbert, B.N., Schupp, H.T., Bradley, M.M., Birbaumer, N., Lang, P.J.: Brain potentials in affective picture processing: covariation with autonomic arousal and affective report. Biol. Psychol. 52(2), 95–111 (2000)
34. Keil, A., Bradley, M.M., Hauk, O., Rockstroh, B., Elbert, T., Lang, P.J.: Large-scale neural correlates of affective picture processing. Psychophysiology 39(5), 641–649 (2002)
35. Lang, P.J., Bradley, M.M., Fitzsimmons, J.R., Cuthbert, B.N., Scott, J.D., Moulder, B., Nangia, V.: Emotional arousal and activation of the visual cortex: an fMRI analysis. Psychophysiology 35(2), 199–210 (1998)
36. Bradley, M.M., Sabatinelli, D., Lang, P.J., Fitzsimmons, J.R., King, W., Desai, P.: Activation of the visual cortex in motivated attention. Behav. Neurosci. 117(2), 369–380 (2003)
37. Sabatinelli, D., Bradley, M.M., Fitzsimmons, J.R., Lang, P.J.: Parallel amygdala and inferotemporal activation reflect emotional intensity and fear relevance. Neuroimage. 24(4), 1265–1270 (2005). Epub 7 Jan 2005
38. Sabatinelli, D., Lang, P.J., Keil, A., Bradley, M.M.: Emotional perception: correlation of functional MRI and event-related potentials. Cereb. Cortex 17(5), 1085–1091 (2007). Epub 12 Jun 2006
39. Bradley, M.M., Codispoti, M., Lang, P.J.: A multi-process account of startle modulation during affective perception. Psychophysiology 43(5), 486–497 (2006)
40. Maker Shed: Pulse Sensor AMPED for Arduino. http://www.makershed.com/products/pulse-sensor-amped-for-arduino
41. Raspberry Pi. https://www.raspberrypi.org/
42. Muthusamy, R.P.: Emotion Recognition from Physiological signals using Bio-sensors. https://diuf.unifr.ch/main/diva/sites/diuf.unifr.ch.main.diva/files/T4.pdf - Submitted for Research Seminar on Emotion Recognition on 15 Feb 2012
43. Russel, J.A., Bullock, M.: Multidimensional scaling of emotional facial expressions. J. Pers. Soc. Psychol. 48, 1290–1298 (1985)
44. Hall, M., Frank, E., Holmes, G., Pfahringer, B., Reutemann, P., Witten, I.H.: The WEKA data mining software: an update. SIGKDD Explor. 11(1), 11–18 (2009)

From Physiological Measures to an Automatic Recognition System of Stress

Nicolas Martin[✉] and Jean-Marc Diverrez

Uses & Acceptability Lab, b<>com, Cesson-Sévigné, France
{nicolas.martin, jean-marc.diverrez}@b-com.com

Abstract. Evaluation of stress is mainly based on standardized scales [1]. However, fill out questionnaires can be incompatible with several situations (e.g. during chirurgical intervention) [2] and offers only subjective and punctual data. Physiological measures, which provided real-time and objective data [3], can be used to cope with these constrains. To be effective, physiological data need to be related to human feeling. One solution is to build an automatic recognition system of stress based on supervised machine learning. Thereby, to acquire physiological data, we built stressful situation in laboratory. From physiological data (respiratory, cardiac and electrodermal measurement) of 24 participants, we built a model that recognizes stress with an accuracy of 70 %.

Keywords: Stress · Physiological measurement · Automatic recognition · Machine learning

1 Introduction

Stress is a serious concern facing our world today. We need to develop a better and objective understanding of this concept, through the use of non-intrusive means for stress recognition, and without troubling natural human behavior. The human body undergoes several physiological changes when exposed to acute stressors. More precisely, electrodermal activities, heart rate activities, and respiration activities data are commonly used to measure short-term emotional and cognitive stress. The goal of the current study is to build an automatic recognition system of stress from physiological measures based on supervised machine learning. For this, annotated data are required [8]. For the same reason that scales are not always adapted to evaluate stress, construct an annotated database in real situation can be very complex. One solution is to build stressful situations in laboratory and collect data. We selected this solution to induce stress and to construct our annotated database. More precisely, we proposed two types of situations (stressful or not stressful) to participants and measured physiological indexes during the experiment.

1.1 Stress Measurements

To recognize stress, it is first necessary to be able to measure it. Currently, evaluation of stress is mainly based on two methods: standardized scales [1] and physiological data [e.g. 4].

© Springer International Publishing Switzerland 2016
C. Stephanidis (Ed.): HCII 2016 Posters, Part II, CCIS 618, pp. 172–176, 2016.
DOI: 10.1007/978-3-319-40542-1_27

Subjective Evaluations. Standardized scales are the most commonly used method to evaluate stress. Scales have several advantages: they are ease to use, free and provide rapid results. However, it can be complex under several circumstances. Thereby, asking individuals to fill scales can be incompatible with several situations (e.g. during chirurgical intervention) [2]. Moreover, per definition, data from scales are subjective and punctually acquired. To cope with these two constrains, physiological measures have been developed.

Physiological Measurements. Physiological measurements, unlike subjective measurements, can provide real-time and objective data [3]. Thereby, many studies have explored the link between physiological responses and stress. Such responses may be modifications and variability of heart rate, modifications of breathing rate, blood pressure and galvanic skin activity [5]. For example, Shi et al. [4] showed a strong correlation between stress levels and electrodermal activity (EDA). Healey et al. [6] showed a correlation between breathing rate and stress levels. Lastly, Sierra De Santos et al. [7] showed the relevance of measuring stress by measurements of electrodermal and heart activity.

2 Method

2.1 Material

In previous research, several paradigms have been used to induce stress: ranging from simple tracking tasks [9] to more complex methods like the Montreal Imaging Stress Task [10]. In our experiment, induction of stress is based on the procedure proposed by Campbell [11] to investigate the effect of time pressure on simple mathematical operations. Thereby, we created stressful situations where individuals had to carry out additions under time pressure. Two conditions were created:

- *Condition 1 – Not stressful situation*: participants had to answer following a beep sound occurring 2650 ms after the calculation was presented.
- *Condition 2 – Stressful situation*: participants had to answer before a beep sound and the beep occurred 900 ms after the calculation was presented.

For each experimental condition, there were 36 trials (2 conditions: 72 trials per participant). Each trial consisted of a simple mathematical sum, such as "2 + 7" or "5 + 8".

2.2 Physiological Measurement

The following physiological indexes were measured: cardiac, respiratory and electro-dermal responses. Biopac Bionomadix MP150 was used to measure physiological responses. To build our automatic recognition system of stress, we used the following indexes on physiological data: electrodermal activities (EDA), heart rate activities (ECG RR/ECG R Wave) and respiration activities (Respiratory Rate). For each index, we computed the mean and standard deviation by trial.

2.3 Subjective Measurement

After each condition, participants filled out two standardized scales to ensure of the effect of induced stress on subjective feeling. The first questionnaire is the Short Stress State Questionnaire (SSSQ) [12] that evaluates 3 aspects of the feeling of stress (Engagement, Distress and Worry). The second questionnaire is the Raw-TLX (RTLX) [13], a simplified version of the NASA Task Load Index . The RTLX assesses the perceived workload of a task as a simple sum of 6 dimensions (mental demand, physical demand, temporal demand, performance, effort, and frustration). The choice of these 2 questionnaires allows us to assess different aspects of the feeling of stress in our participants.

2.4 Participants

24 participants took part in the study and received in exchange a coupon for €15. All participants signed up with informed consent before beginning the experimental procedure and were informed about the goals of the study, procedures, cautions and ethical issues for the participation in the study.

2.5 Procedure

The following procedure was used during the experiment: before starting calculation, a baseline for physiological measurement is recorded. After, participants start calculation and all pass the 2 conditions (within-subject design). Between each condition, a break is observed to reduce stress level. To avoid order effect, the presentation of condition is counterbalanced and the presentation of the calculations is randomized.

3 Results

3.1 Induction of Stress

To ensure that induction of stress is perceived by participants, we compare the subjective evaluation between the two conditions. Comparisons of models showed significant differences (see Table 1) for all dimensions of RTLX. For SSSQ, only distress is evaluated as significantly different between conditions.

3.2 Machine Learning

Several methods of machine learning have been tested on physiological indexes: all these learnings have been conceived to be person-independent. To train the model and test the performance, the dataset was subset into a training dataset (75 %) and testing dataset (25 %). During the training, cross-validation was used and several algorithms have been tested. The Table 2 presented the comparison of this training. From these results, random forest was selected (accuracy ≈ 73.01 %). Finally, we tested the accuracy of the selected model on testing dataset with an accuracy of 70 %.

Table 1. Descriptive statistics (Mean and Standard Deviation) for subjective measurement

Scale	Variable	Condition 1		Condition 2		Chi-square
		Mean	S.D.	Mean	S.D.	
RTLX	Mental demand	16.46	19.86	57.29	36.77	$\chi^2 (1) = 24.22$ ***
	Physical demand	13.54	17.16	38.54	32.01	$\chi^2 (1) = 14.73$ ***
	Temporal demand	22.50	26.91	78.12	19.10	$\chi^2 (1) = 43.82$ ***
	Effort	18.75	23.69	68.96	24.14	$\chi^2 (1) = 43.80$ ***
	Performance	21.25	19.80	66.46	23.01	$\chi^2 (1) = 37.31$ ***
	Frustration	19.38	15.90	60.42	22.89	$\chi^2 (1) = 42.52$ ***
SSSQ	Engagement	30.12	5.79	29.38	4.75	$\chi^2 (1) = .85$ NS
	Worry	13.04	4.64	13.79	5.35	$\chi^2 (1) = .60$ NS
	Distress	10.00	1.67	16.29	6.48	$\chi^2 (1) = 18.58$ ***

*Signifiant codes: ***: $p < .001$; NS : Non-Signifiant*

Table 2. Benchmark of machine learning algorithms

Method	Accuracy for cross-validation
Random forest	73.01 % (S.D. = .05)
Naïve bayes	69.38 % (S.D. = .05)
Neural network	68.05 % (S.D. = .06)
kNN	63.24 % (S.D. = .05)
Support vector machine	63.02 % (S.D. = .05)

4   Discussion and Conclusion

Results indicated that machine learning algorithms offer a good framework to recognize stressful situation from physiological sensors. However, the sample is relatively small. Thus, to ensure of the reliability of our model, we need to conduct new studies on more participants. Moreover, in this study, the generation of stressful situation is only based on time pressure. It can be interesting to induce stress by imposing cognitive tasks on the individuals with the aim of exploring eventual specific physiological patterns.

In the future, this type of recognition system could be used to evaluate stress in real situation. Moreover, we planned to use this system to develop augmented Human-computer interaction (AHCI). For example, we can imagine a medical interface which is automatically adapted to the user's stress level.

Acknowledgements.   We thank all those who participated in any way in this research. This work was carried out within the Institute of Technological Research b<>com and it received support from the French government under the program Future Investments bearing reference ANR-07-A0-AIRT.

References

1. Nübling, M., Stößel, U., Hasselhorn, H.-M., Michaelis, M., Hofmann, F.: Measuring psychological stress and strain at work - Evaluation of the COPSOQ questionnaire in Germany. GMS Psycho-Soc. Med. **3** (2006)
2. Ryu, K., Myung, R.: Evaluation of mental workload with a combined measure based on physiological indices during a dual task of tracking and mental arithmetic. Int. J. Ind. Ergon. **35**, 991–1009 (2005)
3. Rieder, R., Kristensen, C.H., Pinho, M.S.: Identifying relationships between physiological measures and evaluation metrics for 3D interaction techniques. In: Campos, P., Graham, N., Jorge, J., Nunes, N., Palanque, P., Winckler, M. (eds.) INTERACT 2011, Part III. LNCS, vol. 6948, pp. 662–679. Springer, Heidelberg (2011)
4. Shi, Y., Ruiz, N., Taib, R., Choi, E., Chen, F.: Galvanic Skin Response (GSR) as an index of cognitive load. In: CHI 2007 Extended Abstracts on Human Factors in Computing Systems, pp. 2651–2656. ACM, New York (2007)
5. Pickering, T.G., Devereux, R.B., James, G.D., Gerin, W., Landsbergis, P., Schnall, P.L., Schwartz, J.E.: Environmental influences on blood pressure and the role of job strain. J. Hypertens. Suppl. Off. J. Int. Soc. Hypertens. **14**, S179–S185 (1996)
6. Healey, J.A., Picard, R.W.: Detecting stress during real-world driving tasks using physiological sensors. IEEE Trans. Intell. Transp. Syst. **6**, 156–166 (2005)
7. de Santos Sierra, A., Avila, C.S., Bailador del Pozo, G., Guerra Casanova, J.: Stress detection by means of stress physiological template. In: 2011 Third World Congress on Nature and Biologically Inspired Computing (NaBIC), pp. 131–136 (2011)
8. Kotsiantis, S.B.: Supervised machine learning: a review of classification techniques. In: Proceedings of the 2007 Conference on Emerging Artificial Intelligence Applications in Computer Engineering: Real Word AI Systems with Applications in eHealth, HCI, Information Retrieval and Pervasive Technologies, pp. 3–24. IOS Press, Amsterdam (2007)
9. Rubio, S., Diaz, E., Martin, J., Puente, J.M.: Evaluation of subjective mental workload: a comparison of SWAT, NASA-TLX, and workload profile methods. Appl. Psychol. **53**, 61–86 (2004)
10. Dedovic, K., Renwick, R., Mahani, N.K., Engert, V., Lupien, S.J., Pruessner, J.C.: The Montreal imaging stress task: using functional imaging to investigate the effects of perceiving and processing psychosocial stress in the human brain. J. Psychiatry Neurosci. **30**, 319–325 (2005)
11. Campbell, J.I.D., Austin, S.: Effects of response time deadlines on adults' strategy choices for simple addition. Mem. Cognit. **30**, 988–994 (2002)
12. Helton, W.S., Naswall, K.: Short stress state questionnaire: factor structure and state change assessment. Eur. J. Psychol. Assess. **31**, 20–30 (2015)
13. Hart, S.G., Staveland, L.E.: Development of NASA-TLX (Task Load Index): results of empirical and theoretical research. In: Hancock, P.A., Meshkati, N. (eds.) Human Mental Workload, pp. 139–183. North-Holland, Oxford (1988)

Physiological and Psychological Evaluation by Skin Potential Activity Measurement Using Steering Wheel While Driving

Shogo Matsuno[✉], Takahiro Terasaki, Shogo Aizawa, Tota Mizuno, Kazuyuki Mito, and Naoaki Itakura

Graduate School of Informatics and Engineering,
The University of Electro-Communications, 1-5-1 Chofugaoka, Chofu, Tokyo 182-8585, Japan
m1440004@edu.cc.uec.ac.jp

Abstract. This paper proposes a new method for practical skin potential activity (SPA) measurement while driving a car by installing electrodes on the outer periphery of the steering wheel. Evaluating the psychophysiological state of the driver while driving is important for accident prevention. We investigated whether the physiological and psychological state of the driver can be evaluated by measuring SPA while driving. Therefore, we have devised a way to measure SPA measurement by installing electrodes in a handle. Electrodes are made of tin foil and are placed along the outer periphery of the wheel considering that their position while driving is not fixed. The potential difference is increased by changing the impedance through changing the width of electrodes. Moreover we try to experiment using this environment. An experiment to investigate the possibility of measuring SPA using the conventional and the proposed methods were conducted with five healthy adult males. A physical stimulus was applied to the forearm of the subjects. It was found that the proposed method could measure SPA, even though the result was slightly smaller than that of the conventional method of affixing electrodes directly on hands.

Keywords: Skin potential activity · Mental workload · Mental state · Safety driving

1 Introduction

The likelihood of car accidents is largely dependent on the physiological and psychological states of drivers. According to a survey, half of all car accidents occur because of the violation of safe driving. The likelihood of this violation is affected by the mental workload of drivers [1, 2]. Therefore, it is important to evaluate the physiological mental state of drivers in order to prevent accidents. In particular, an accumulation of mental workload while driving adversely affects the physiological and psychological states of the driver. Therefore, in this study, we aim to evaluate the physiological and psychological states of the driver by measuring skin potential activity (SPA) during vehicle operation.

Sweating of the palms and soles of the feet is one of the indicators used to evaluate mental workload. Skin potential activity (SPA) can be measured as a method of detecting

C. Stephanidis (Ed.): HCII 2016 Posters, Part II, CCIS 618, pp. 177–181, 2016.
DOI: 10.1007/978-3-319-40542-1_28

mental sweating. SPA is a physiological index to electrically measure the sweat gland activity under sympathetic innervation. Conventional SPA measurements are taken by applying electrodes to three positions on the arm. These three positions represent an exploration, a reference, and a ground electrode. The exploration electrode is placed on the palm, the reference electrode is place on the forearm, and the ground electrode is placed on the forearm flexor. The potential difference between these electrodes is used as physiological index. However, this method is difficult to practically use during vehicle operation, because it is requires installation of the mounting type of electrode to the forearm for every ride. Furthermore, a sense of discomfort from the attachment and detachment of electrodes may be experienced.

Thus, we have devised a method of acquiring SPA measurements without causing discomfort to the driver by placing the electrodes on the car steering wheel. In this study, we propose a method of measure SPA through installation of the electrodes to the vehicle steering wheel, and we examine whether or not it is possible to use this method of SPA evaluation by experiment.

2   Measuring SPA Through the Steering Wheel

Evaluating the psychophysiological state of the driver while driving is important for accident prevention [3, 4]. We investigated whether the physiological and psychological states of the driver can be evaluated by measuring SPA while driving. Figure 1(a) shows the typical placement of electrodes for SPA measurement. The electrodes are placed on the flexor region of the forearm, and their potential difference is used as the evaluation index. However, this method inconveniences the driver; hence, a new method of measuring SPA was devised, in which the electrodes are placed on the car's steering wheel as illustrated in Fig. 1(b). The electrodes are made of tin foil and they were placed along the outer periphery of the wheel. It should be noted that their positions while driving were not fixed. The potential difference was increased by changing the impedance through changing the width of the electrodes.

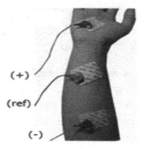 

Fig. 1. Sample data waveform of AC-EOG

3 Experiment

We conducted an experiment to verify whether or not SPA can be measured using the proposed method as well as the conventional method. In this experiment, subjects were five healthy adult males.

3.1 Experimental Procedure

First, the subjects gripped a steering wheel and rested for approximately three minutes. Then, the subjects were stimulated three times through use of a rubber ring to stress the forearm. The subjects then waited with their eyes closed so as not to know the timing of the stimulus. Electrodes were placed on the right forearm of subjects based on a feature method, and attached to the steering wheel based on the proposed method. Experiments were conducted when the wheel was grasped with both hands and when the wheel was gripped with the left hand. Figure 2 shows the experimental environment.

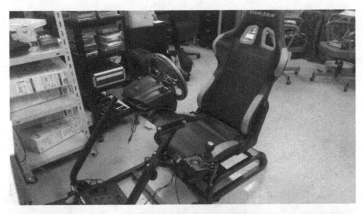

Fig. 2. Experimental environment

3.2   Evaluation of the Experimental Results

Experiments to investigate the potential of measuring SPA using the conventional and the proposed methods were conducted with five healthy adult males. A physical stimulus was applied to the forearm of the subjects, and their reactions were compared (Fig. 3 shows an example of the resulting waveform). Table 1 shows the experimental results. Variation in the signal amplitude was observed in the resulting waveforms for all subjects. This paper demonstrates the feasibility of acquiring SPA measurements via the proposed method by comparing the results with those of the conventional method. In this experiment, the amplitude ratio tended to increase in one and both hands together. Additionally, the measurement accuracy was expected to improve by changing the electrode conditions. However, the overall standard deviation ratio increased using the proposed method. This means that the amplitude of artifacts is increased as compared with the conventional method. The cause is thought to be that the artifact amplitude and reaction amplitude both increased because of the large potential fluctuation on the side of a lot of perspiration quantity.

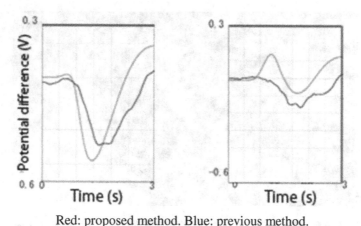

Red: proposed method. Blue: previous method.

Fig. 3.   Example of SPA waveform with stimulations (Color figure online)

Table 1.   Evaluation results

Subjects	One hand		Both hands	
	Amplitude ratio	SD ratio	Amplitude ratio	SD ratio
A	1.07	4.60	0.64	2.01
B	2.42	1.79	2.33	8.76
C	0.51	1.07	0.50	1.08
D	0.93	2.22	0.48	0.22
E	0.60	13.36	0.52	7.34

4   Conclusion

In this paper, we proposed a new method for practical skin potential activity (SPA) measurements while driving a car by installing electrodes on the outer periphery of the steering wheel. An experiment using the method was conducted with five subjects. It was found that the proposed method could measure SPA, even though the signal amplitude were slightly smaller than that of the conventional method of affixing electrodes directly on hands.

In the future, we will verify the combination of impedances of the electrodes, and aim to achieve more accurate measurements. In addition, we will improve the accuracy by correlating the individual difference with noise. Subsequently, we intend to evaluate the mental workload while holding the car's steering wheel.

References

1. Nachreiner, F.: International standard on mental work-load – the ISO 10075 series. Ind. Health **37**(1), 125–133 (1999)
2. Selye, H.: The Stress of Life, p. 1956. McGraw-Hill, New York (1976)
3. Shirai, K., Yamamoto, Y., Okuda, H.: Consideration of formative mechanism of electrodermal activity – skin potential activity and skin impedance change. J. Int. Soc. Life Inf. Sci. **21**(1), 231–239 (2003)
4. Vivek, D.B.: Ergonomics in the Automotive Design Process, pp. 105–126. CRC Press Taylor and Francis Group, Boca Raton (2012)

Support System for Improving Speaking Skills in Job Interviews

Tetsu Tanahashi$^{(\boxtimes)}$, Yumie Takayashiki, and Tetsuro Kitahara

Nihon University, 3-25-40, Sakurajosui, Setagaya-ku, Tokyo, Japan
{tanahashi,takayashiki,kitahara}@kthrlab.jp

Abstract. Speaking in an appropriate manner is important in job interviews because the interviewer's judgment sometimes depends on the impression created by the speaker's eyes, facial expressions, and voice. It is therefore important to practice speaking for job interviews, but it is not easy to practice it alone. In this paper, we propose a support system for improving speaking skills in job interviews by taking into account the emphasis required in this particular type of presentation. We conducted an experiment to test whether the judgment of the system is consistent with human judgment. The correlation coefficients for intonation and emphasis were 0.68 and 0.42, respectively. However, those for the other features were below 0.2. This is because the current system assumes reading style speaking. In the future, we aim to collect spontaneous speeches in realistic job interview situations and use them as reference data.

1 Introduction

The speaker's facial expression, eyes, and prosody are as important as the content of the speech in job interviews. It is, however, not easy to practice these aspects alone. Systems for improving speaking skills for oral presentations or job interviews have been developed [1–6], but these systems do not judge whether the user emphasizes those phrases that should be emphasized.

In this paper, we propose a support system for improving speaking skills in job interviews. The user speaks sentences specified by the system, and the system analyzes the user's eyes, facial expression, and prosody. In the specified sentences, words that should be emphasized are colored red, and the user is requested to emphasize them. The system evaluates the user's speech from six viewpoints (the eye, facial motion, smile, speaking rate, intonation, and emphasis) by comparing the user's features with those extracted from skillful speakers (called reference data here). The result of the evaluation is displayed on a scale of zero to four. By seeing this evaluation feedback, the user will realize what accepts of speech should be improved.

2 Proposed System

2.1 System Flowchart

We developed a support system for improving speaking skills in job interviews. The flow of the system is shown in Fig. 1. The user is first requested to speak

© Springer International Publishing Switzerland 2016
C. Stephanidis (Ed.): HCII 2016 Posters, Part II, CCIS 618, pp. 182–187, 2016.
DOI: 10.1007/978-3-319-40542-1_29

a specified self-promotional sentence. The system records the speech and then extracts some features from six viewpoints: the user's eyes, facial motion, smile, speaking rate, intonation, and emphasis. The extracted features are compared with reference data. The system judges the speech to be appropriate when the features closely resemble the reference data, and provides feedback on a scale of zero to four (Fig. 2).

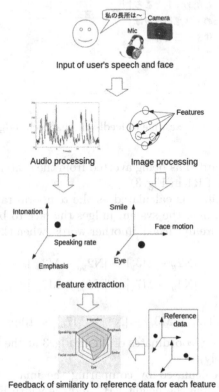

Fig. 1. The system flowchart

2.2 Image Processing

Every second, the image of the user's face is obtained through the PC's web camera. From this image, 50 facial features, shown in Fig. 3, are extracted with the "detectface();" Web API [7]. From these 50 facial features, three higher-level features representing the line of sight, facial motion, and smiling are calculated.

The line of sight represents the temporal ratio in which the line of sight is averted from the center. When

$$\left| |ER1_x - PR_x| - |PR_x - ER4_x| \right| > 2[px] \tag{1}$$

and

$$\left| |EL4_x - PL_x| - |PL_x - EL1_x| \right| > 2[px], \tag{2}$$

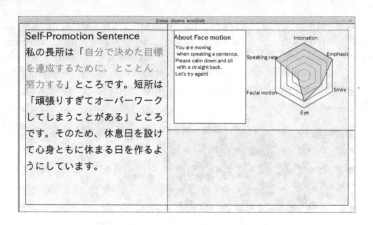

Fig. 2. An example of feedback of speech judgment

the line of sight is regarded as being averted from the center ($ER1_x$, for example, is the x-coordinate of ER1 in Fig. 3).

The feature of smiling is calculated as the temporal ratio in which the face is smiling. For each frame, the system judges the face to be smiling when both corners of the mouth are upturned, in other words, when the following equations are satisfied:

$$|N2_y - M3_y| > |N2_{y_0} - M3_{y_0}|, \tag{3}$$

$$|N4_y - M7_y| > |N4_{y_0} - M7_{y_0}|, \tag{4}$$

and

$$\left||N2_y - M3_y| - |N4_y - M7_y|\right| < 10[\text{px}] \tag{5}$$

($N2_y$ and $N2_{y_0}$ are the y-coordinates of N2 in Fig. 3 at the target frame and the first frame, respectively).

Facial motion is calculated by comparing the image with the one at the previous frame. We define the height FH_y and the width FW_x of the face as

$$FH_y = F6_y - F1_y \tag{6}$$

and

$$FW_x = F9_x - F3_x \tag{7}$$

When the temporal difference in each of FH_y, FW_x, $F3_x$, and $F1_y$ is larger than five pixels, that is,

$$FH_y - FH'_y > 5[\text{px}], \tag{8}$$

$$FW_x - FW'_x > 5[\text{px}], \tag{9}$$

$$F3_x - F3'_x > 5[\text{px}], \tag{10}$$

and

$$F1_y - F1'_y > 5[\text{px}] \tag{11}$$

($FH1'_x$ is the FH of the image at the previous frame), the system detects facial motion.

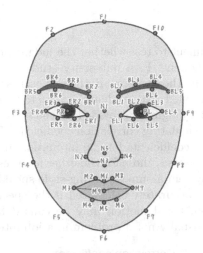

Fig. 3. Facial features obtained with Web API "detectface();" [7]

2.3   Audio Processing

The speaking rate, degree of overall intonation, and degree of emphasis are extracted from the user's speech. First, the speech-to-text alignment is performed using Julius [8]. Next, the duration of the speech is calculated from the times of the first and last words. The speaking rate is defined as:

$$(\text{Speaking rate}) = \frac{(\text{number of vowels})}{(\text{duration of speech})}. \tag{12}$$

The system calculates the fndamental frequency (F0) and amplitude of the recorded sound every 5 ms. For calculating the F0, DIO [9] is used. The degree of intonation is defined, for each of the pitch (F0) and intensity (amplitude), as the interquartile range of the temporal trajectory of the F0 or amplitude.

The degree of emphasis is calculated by comparing the F0 and amplitude in the emphasizing phrase with those in the previous phrase. The temporal medians of the F0 and amplitude in the emphasizing phrase and the previous phrase are calculated. The differences between the medians of the two phrases are calculated as the degree of emphasis for the pitch and intensity.

2.4   Comparison with Reference Data and Feedback

The user's speech features are compared with the reference data, that is, the features of the speech of skillful speakers. In the current implementation, the reference data were extracted from two people (one male and one female) who act as amateur announcers in a university's broadcasting club. For each of the six viewpoints, the distance between the user's feature and reference data is calculated and discretized on a scale of zero to four (discretization for the intonation and emphasis is performed separately for the pitch and intensity) It is fed back to the user as shown in Fig. 2.

3   Experiment

We conducted an experiment to test whether the judgment of the system is consistent with human judgment. Five university students used the system and obtained judgments from the system on their speeches. Eight students (not including the aforementioned five students) evaluated the speeches from the same viewpoints, and the judgment provided by the system and human evaluation were compared by calculating correlation coefficients. The results are shown in Fig. 4. The correlation coefficients for the intonation and emphasis were 0.68 and 0.42, respectively. However, those for the other features were below 0.2. This is because the current system assumes reading-style speaking. For example, the speaking rate cannot be accurately calculated if the speech includes humming and hawing. In addition, facial motion may be caused by both nodding and restlessness; nodding is usually not a problem in a job interview.

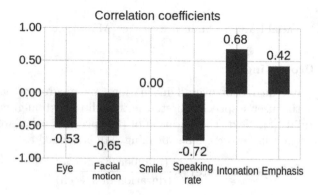

Fig. 4. Correlation coefficients of the system's judgment and human evaluation

4   Conclusion

We proposed a support system for improving speaking skills in job interviews. We particularly focused on whether the user emphasizes the phrase that should be emphasized, and achieved moderate correlation (0.68 for the intonation and 0.48 for the emphasis) compared to human evaluations. However, the ideal prosodies for emphasizing a particular phrase may depend on the characteristics of the speaker's voice. In future, we plan to improve the method for analyzing the prosody in addition to increasing the volume of reference data.

References

1. Kurihara, K., Goto, M., Oogata, J., Matsuzaka, Y., Igarashi, T.: Presentation sensei: a presentation training system using speech and image processing. In: ICMI 2007 Proceedings of the 9th International Conference on Multimodal Interfaces, pp. 358–365 (2007)

2. Kojima, A., Ito, K.: Computer aided training for acquisition of focus on presentation. Inf. Process. Soc. Jpn. 5P–07 (2015)
3. Intelligence Ltd.: VR Job interview-interview with Ryoma Sakamoto (2016). http:// doda.jp/promo/campaign/mirainomensetsu/
4. Barur, T., Ionut, T., Patrick, G., Kaska, P., Elisabeth, A.: A job interview simulation: social cue-based interaction with a virtual character. In: IEEE International Conference on Social Computing (SocialCom2013), pp. 220–227 (2013)
5. Matthew, J., Laura, B., Micael, F., Neil, J., Michael, A., Emily, J., Katherine, W., Dale, O., Bell, M.D.: Virtual reality job interview training for veterans with posttraumatic stress disorder. J. Vocat. Rehabil. **42**, 271–279 (2015)
6. Tanaka, H., Sakti, S., Graham, N., Toda, T., Negoro, H., Iwasawa, H., Nakamura, S.: Automated social skills trainer. In: IUI 2015 Proceedings of the 20th International Conference on Intelligent User Interfaces, pp. 17–27 (2015)
7. Increment Corporation: Face detection library detectFace() (2016). http://www. increment.co.jp/product/detectFace/index.html
8. Akinobu, L., Kawahara, T.: Recent development of open-source speech recognition engine Julius. In: Asia-Pacific Signal and Information Processing Association Annual Summit and Conference, Sapporo, Japan (2009)
9. Morise, M., Kawahara, H., Katayose, H.: Fast and reliable F0 estimation method based on the period extraction of vocal fold vibration of singing voice and speech. In: AES 35th International Conference, CD-ROM, London UK (2009)

An Affect Extraction Method in Personal Fabrication Based on Laban Movement Analysis

Kazuaki Tanaka[1], Michiya Yamamoto[2(✉)], Saizo Aoyagi[2],
and Noriko Nagata[2]

[1] Graduate School of Engineering Science, Osaka University, Osaka, Japan
tanaka@sys.es.osaka-u.ac.jp
[2] School of Science and Technologies,
Kwansei Gakuin University, Hyogo, Japan
{michiya.yamamoto,aoyagi,nagata}@kwansei.ac.jp

Abstract. Affect extraction in personal fabrication will become indispensable in enhancing the recent advances in the field, because we can provide that information to the fabricators and let the fabricators enjoy the experience. In this study, we proposed an extraction method of affect in personal fabrication based on Laban Movement Analysis by using the motion data of fabricators. As a result of evaluation, the average of the correctly extracted affects was approximately 80 %.

Keywords: Laban Movement Analysis · Personal fabrication · Decision tree

1 Introduction

A revolution in manufacturing is approaching, and it could change the style of fabrication. Extracting affects in personal fabrication will become indispensable in enhancing the recent advances in the field, because we can provide that information to the fabricators and let the fabricators enjoy the experience. In this study, we proposed an extraction method of affect in personal fabrication based on Laban Movement Analysis (LMA) [1] by using the motion data of fabricators.

2 Related Studies

Many studies on extracting an affect in various situations have been performed, but most of them limit the target situations. This means that such studies are not sufficiently suitable for personal fabrication, where we use various tools and various movements are dependent on the tools.

LMA is known as a method for interpreting human movement. It is a tool used by dancers and actors. Moreover, it can be applied to movement generation of CG characters and robots. For example, Chi et al. have developed EMOTE, which is a 3D character animation system based on LMA [2]. Nakata et al. have adopted the method for generating the motions of a robot and analyzed its impressions [3]. Here, we should note that both studies are applied to generating motions.

© Springer International Publishing Switzerland 2016
C. Stephanidis (Ed.): HCII 2016 Posters, Part II, CCIS 618, pp. 188–193, 2016.
DOI: 10.1007/978-3-319-40542-1_30

However, though LMA was proposed as a method to extract affects from body movement, it has been difficult. LMA was composed of several characteristic elements, such as Space (Direct/Indirect), Weight (Light/Strong), and Time (Sudden/Sustained), although they were not defined numerically. Recently, as the technology on motion sensors has shown progress, research has been conducted on analyzing motions and computing the elements [4]. In addition, some methods of extracting affects are reported [5, 6]. However, they could not be applied to personal fabrication.

3   Experiment

We conducted an experiment on personal fabrication before proposing an extraction method because we do not have data sets of motions and affects. Here, we performed an experiment by using the electronic building blocks termed littleBits. We asked participants to arrange their original synthesizer in pairs by using littleBits. We shot the motions of participants by using a motion capture system (Bonita 10, Vicon) and video camera (HVR-A1J, SONY), as shown in Fig. 1. We also measured the heart rate of the participants (WHS-2, UNION TOOL). The participants were six male and six female Japanese students.

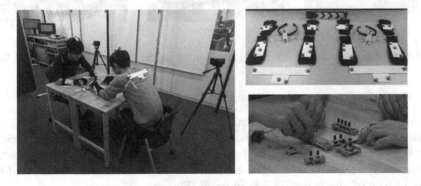

Fig. 1. Example scene of making synthesizer

We classified affects by using the affect grid by Russel [7], and asked participants to recall and select a suitable affect and its intensity (5 grades) after fabrication. Figure 2 shows an example of the result. We classified the results into strong and weak based on the average intensity. The blue bar shows a strong affect by one of the participants.

4   Affect Extraction Method

4.1   Amount of Characteristics of Laban Movement Analysis

We then defined the amount of characteristics of Laban Movement Analysis, Space, Weight and Time as shown in Fig. 3. Space was computed by the area between the

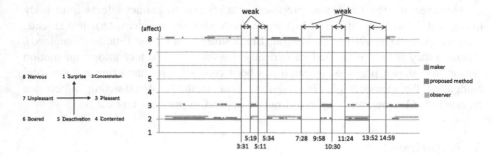

Fig. 2. An example of affect (Color figure online)

head and both wrists. Weight was the vertical position of head. Time was the sequence of the speed of the wrists for 60 s.

|Space|Weight|Time|

Fig. 3. The amount of characteristics for Laban Movement Analysis; Space, Weight and Time

4.2 Estimation of Interval of Strong Affect

First, we estimated the interval of a strong affect. Here, we used the parameters of 4.1 and heart rate. We introduced a decision tree by using the value of Space, Weight, Time, and heart rate for each person. For each value, we normalized all the parameters in advance. We used Weka and J48 decision tree. As a result, the estimation of the strong interval of affects was 71.3 % of recall (Fig. 4).

4.3 Classification of Affect

We then classified the affects by using a decision tree based on Space, Weight and Time for each participant. Figure 5 shows an example of the tree. As shown in the figure, we could classify different motions at the same affect. As a result, the average of the correctly classified instances was 58.1 %. In addition, 46.2 % of incorrect results were observed when the affect of the participants changed. This means that the correctly extracted affect would be approximately 80 %.

Table 1 shows the result of the classified affect. As shown in the table, concentration and boredom could be classified at approximately 70 %. However, classifying surprise was difficult.

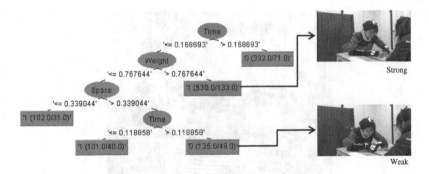

Fig. 4. Example of estimation of strong affect

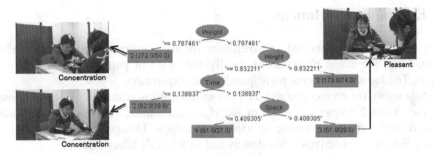

Fig. 5. An example of the decision tree

Table 1. Classified affect by proposed method

| | | | Total | Classified value | | | | | | | |
| | | | | 1 | 2 | 3 | 4 | 5 | 6 | 7 | 8 |
				Surprise	Concentration	Pleasant	Contented	Deactivation	Bored	Unpleasant	Nervous
		Total	8165	694	3249	1279	514	0	1425	653	351
			100.0%	8.5%	39.8%	15.7%	6.3%	0.0%	17.5%	8.0%	4.3%
True value	1	Surprise	799	296	256	63	19	0	50	81	34
			9.8%	37.0%	32.0%	7.9%	2.4%	0.0%	6.3%	10.1%	4.3%
	2	Concentration	2757	108	2037	259	31	0	151	105	66
			33.8%	3.9%	73.9%	9.4%	1.1%	0.0%	5.5%	3.8%	2.4%
	3	Pleasant	1324	89	400	647	74	0	29	75	10
			16.2%	6.7%	30.2%	48.9%	5.6%	0.0%	2.2%	5.7%	0.8%
	4	Contented	656	7	158	114	271	0	82	19	5
			8.0%	1.1%	24.1%	17.4%	41.3%	0.0%	12.5%	2.9%	0.8%
	5	Deactivation	58	10	0	2	2	0	36	8	0
			0.7%	17.2%	0.0%	3.4%	3.4%	0.0%	62.1%	13.8%	0.0%
	6	Bored	1326	86	146	84	74	0	908	28	0
			16.2%	6.5%	11.0%	6.3%	5.6%	0.0%	68.5%	2.1%	0.0%
	7	Unpleasant	658	24	76	90	37	0	108	323	0
			8.1%	3.6%	11.6%	13.7%	5.6%	0.0%	16.4%	49.1%	0.0%
	8	Nervous	587	74	176	20	6	0	61	14	236
			7.2%	12.6%	30.0%	3.4%	1.0%	0.0%	10.4%	2.4%	40.2%

(frame)
(%)

Fig. 6. Experimental scenery

5 Estimation by Human

As a reference, we performed an experiment for affect estimation by human participants. Here, we asked observers to classify the affect of participants, as shown in
Fig. 6. Ten Japanese students participated in the experiment.

As a result, the correct rate was 21.1 %, which was lower than that of the proposed
method. Table 2 shows the result of the classified affects. As shown in the table,
humans could classify pleasant or unpleasant affects. However, it was difficult to
distinguish between activated and deactivated in Russel's affect grid.

Table 2. Classified affect by human

| | | | Observed value | | | | | | | |
| | | | 1 | 2 | 3 | 4 | 5 | 6 | 7 | 8 |
		Total	Surprise	Concentration	Pleasant	Contented	Deactivation	Bored	Unpleasant	Nervous
		Total	1970	44	1026	334	35	33	366	34	98
			100.0%	2.2%	52.1%	17.0%	1.8%	1.7%	18.6%	1.7%	5.0%
True value	1	Surprise	250	3	137	55	5	1	26	4	19
			12.7%	1.2%	54.8%	22.0%	2.0%	0.4%	10.4%	1.6%	7.6%
	2	Concentration	580	8	323	100	7	10	96	14	22
			29.4%	1.4%	55.7%	17.2%	1.2%	1.7%	16.6%	2.4%	3.8%
	3	Pleasant	410	15	194	92	12	7	62	5	23
			20.8%	3.7%	47.3%	22.4%	2.9%	1.7%	15.1%	1.2%	5.6%
	4	Contented	120	2	54	31	2	2	26	0	3
			6.1%	1.7%	45.0%	25.8%	1.7%	1.7%	21.7%	0.0%	2.5%
	5	Deactivation	20	2	10	4	3	0	1	0	0
			1.0%	10.0%	50.0%	20.0%	15.0%	0.0%	5.0%	0.0%	0.0%
	6	Bored	250	5	112	28	2	5	77	8	13
			12.7%	2.0%	44.8%	11.2%	0.8%	2.0%	30.8%	3.2%	5.2%
	7	Unpleasant	190	5	100	13	2	5	49	2	14
			9.6%	2.6%	52.6%	6.8%	1.1%	2.6%	25.8%	1.1%	7.4%
	8	Nervous	150	4	96	11	2	3	29	1	4
			7.6%	2.7%	64.0%	7.3%	1.3%	2.0%	19.3%	0.7%	2.7%

(frame)
(%)

6 Summary

We proposed a novel affect extraction method in personal fabrication based on Laban Movement Analysis by using the motion data of fabricators. We proposed a method for extracting affects by defining the amount of characteristics of LMA, and by introducing a decision tree. The method was relatively simple, and the results of the experiments demonstrated the effectiveness of the method.

Acknowledgement. This research was partially supported by JST COI Program "Center of Kansei-oriented Digital Fabrication", and JSPS KAKENHI 16H03225, etc.

References

1. Bartenieff, I., Lewis, D.: Body Movement: Coping with the Environment. Science Publishers, Gordon & Breach (1980)
2. Diane, C., Monica, C., Liwei, Z., Norman, B.: The EMOTE model for effort and shape. In: Proceedings of the 27th Annual Conference on Computer Graphics and Interactive Techniques (SIGGRAPH 2000), pp.173–182 (2000)
3. Nakata, T., Mori, T., Sato, T.: Analysis of impression of robot bodily expression. J. Robot. Mechatron. 14(1), 27–36 (2002)
4. Maranan, D.S., Alaoui, S.F., Schiphorst, T., Pasquier, P., Subyen, P., Bartram, L.: Designing for movement: evaluating computational models using LMA effort qualities. In: Proceedings of the SIGCHI Conference on Human Factors in Computing Systems, pp. 991–1000 (2014)
5. Haris, Z., Christos, G., Yiorgos, C., Andreas, A.: Emotion recognition for exergames using laban movement analysis. In: Proceedings of ACM Motion on Games (MIG 2013), Article 39 (2013)
6. Woo, H.K., Jeong, W.P., Won, H.L., Myung, J.C.: LMA based emotional motion representation using RGB-D camera. In: Proceedings of the 8th ACM/IEEE International Conference on Human-Robot Interaction (HRI 2013), pp. 163–164 (2013)
7. Russell, J.A.: A circumplex model of affect. J. Pers. Soc. Psychol. 39, 1161–1178 (1980)

Qualitative Model for Neuro-Functional Mechanism Inducing Human Error Detection to Humanlike Agents Based on Cortico-Cerebellar Function

Yoshimasa Tawatsuji[1(✉)] and Tatsunori Matsui[2]

[1] Graduate School of Human Sciences, Waseda University, Saitama, Japan
wats-kkoreverfay@akane.waseda.jp
[2] Faculty of Human Sciences, Waseda University, Saitama, Japan
matsui-t@waseda.jp

Abstract. The uncanny valley is a major phenomenon that occurs during the implementation of facial expressions in a humanlike agent. Recent studies have explained that the negative impression of the agent's expressions is a "prediction error." We hypothesized that the prediction error stemmed from the differential output of dual processing, - that is, emotional and rational processing, - and it negatively affected a person's impression of the facial expression of the agent, which was similar to that when perceiving an eerie sensation. A qualitative computational model was proposed to clarify this mechanism according to cortico-cerebellar function to compute the prediction of the humanlike agent's facial movement. Thus, rapid emotional processing was indispensable with the thalamus playing an essential role in the processing.

Keywords: Uncanny valley · Brain functional connection · Cerebellum

1 Introduction

1.1 Background

The improvement of 3D computer graphics and robotics has gradually affected our lives by introducing humanlike agents, such as androids. In the field of human computer interaction or human agent interaction, it has been pointed out that these agents require the implementation of human (or user)-centered or human-friendly functions. Therefore, to familiarize these agents with human beings, they must be replicated into a genuine person. That is, along with their appearance, their functions should mimic those of a human. One of their important functions is the "facial expression," which conveys much information, such as emotional, social and health. However, it has been criticized that extraordinary resemblance of agents to humans elicits negative impressions by humans (ref. "the uncanny valley" [1]). One critical factor of such negative impression against agents is the complex muscle system of the facial expressions in humans. In this paper, we focused on the slight differences in the agent's facial expression that cause the negative emotional response from humans.

© Springer International Publishing Switzerland 2016
C. Stephanidis (Ed.): HCII 2016 Posters, Part II, CCIS 618, pp. 194–200, 2016.
DOI: 10.1007/978-3-319-40542-1_31

1.2   Previous Study Related to Inconsistencies with the Prediction

Previous studies have implied the importance of the "prediction error" framework. Here, "prediction" implies the fast emotional response toward the visual information of humanlike agent imprecisely captured by the retina as if it were a human. This predictive response can be modified by slow and detailed processing of the information because "it is not a human." The inconsistency switches on the negative emotional processing (e.g. the eerie feeling).

According to Seyama et al. [2], the extraordinary expansion of the humanlike agent's eye-size induced negative impression on an observer. Contrary to the observer's prediction of balance between facial feature and its component (eye) size, the extraordinary eye-size negatively affected the impression. Saygin et al. [3] conducted experiments in which the participants observed the actions, such as waving of a hand, by three types of agents – a person, humanlike android, and mechanical android. The participants' reactions were scanned through fMRI to analyze the physiological (blood oxygenation level dependent: BOLD) responses to each agent. The results indicated that compared with the actions of a person or a mechanical android, the BOLD response increased when observing the actions of the humanlike android. The results were explained as follows: the humanlike android which would typically not move mechanically is not predictable and then an error signal occurs as a prediction error [3].

As suggested in the previous study, the prediction error framework must contribute to our understanding of the mechanism inducing the uncanny valley phenomenon. Thus, we adapted the framework to account for elicitation of the negative emotional response against the facial expression of humanlike agents.

1.3   Purpose

In this paper, we propose a functional brain-model of the mechanism that generates negative emotions against the facial expressions of humanlike agents. We focused on the facial expression "smile," involving the zygomatic muscle movement.

Most importantly, we modeled the functional brain model not on the biological level but the systematic level. The biological model helped understand the details of the neuronal connection and the way in which the ionic transition is achieved. However, this model cannot explain more than how each region is connected and what architecture it has. Many brain areas should be engaged in the process of generating an eerie feeling in order for us create a bran model in the appropriate systematic level. We thus constructed the brain model through qualitative description of functional connectivity of each system.

2   Previous Model

In this section, we introduce and briefly describe some tasks of the previous model [4]. The previous proposed model provided an abstract neural-based explanation for the occurrence of the uncanny valley. We hypothesized that information processing resulted in emotional and cognitive responses until the occurrence of the eerie feeling,

196   Y. Tawatsuji and T. Matsui

well known as the uncanny valley. This basic concept of dual parallel information processing is based on the "dual pathway of emotion" [5], and the differential processing results signal an alert [4] (see also: [6]). In this concept, the emotional information processing which is rapid and imprecise, generates an immediate response toward the humanlike agent as if it were a person. Contrastively, the cognitive information processing that is processed more slowly and in detail, generates a rational response toward the agents. The emotional information processing undergoes without the cortical modulation yet, and the cognitive information processing resulted through cortical networks such as visual pathways. This dual parallel information processing model is expected to fit the "prediction error" framework.

The model has a limitation in that the input of the model is defined as the degree of abnormality of the ad hoc facial component (eyes, nose or mouth) features, which in turn, reflects the omission of the computational process for the abnormality in the model. Here, the abnormality should be the result of error calculation between prediction and perception. Therefore, in this study, we explain the error detection process. Figure 1 depicts our entire model.

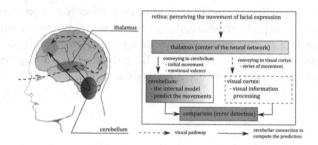

Fig. 1. Brain area contributing to prediction and error detection (Color figure online)

3   Error Detection Mechanism Subserved by Cerebellar Function

3.1   Calculation of Error Detection

First, we formulated the calculation method of the degree of abnormality. Generally, abnormality should be perceived after the error for an event is detected. The error detection can be calculated using the following two methods. The first method realizes error detection by pre-learning of the association of a certain event (stimuli itself) with a response (e.g. fear conditioning). The other method realizes error detection by detecting the deviation from a possible event (prediction): this method should correspond to predicted error detection. Therefore, we adopted the second calculation method.

The calculation of error detection requires a deviation between the predictive and actual perceived zygomatic muscle movements, that is, m^* and m, respectively. The degree of abnormality is qualitatively proportional to the deviation d, and is defined as

$$d(m^*, m)(t) = \frac{\|m^*(t) - m(t)\|}{\|m^*(t)\|}. \tag{1}$$

3.2   Neural System Subserving Calculation for Generating Facial Movement

Before proposing the computational neural system for predicting how a humanlike android's facial muscles move, we introduce the qualitative model representing facial movement in humans. In this model, the main functional brain system subserves the internal model preserved in the cerebellum (to predict the muscle movement) through the functional connectivity between the cortex and the cerebellum via pontine nuclei.

Both the inverse and forward models should be a prerequisite for predicting how a person moves his or her facial muscle. Such a model is expected to be implemented in the cerebellum [7]. Gomi [8] clarified that "the cerebellum (the burst of Purkinje cell) should code the dynamical components, such as acceleration and velocity of voluntary eye movement" (original in Japanese).

Researchers have argued about the roles of the cerebellum on emotional expressions in the pseudobulbar affect, in which the cortico-pontine-cerebellar connectivity plays an important role in modulating the emotional expressions [9]. According to Ahmed et al. [9], the pseudobulbar affect is "characterized by uncontrolled crying or laughing which may be disproportionate or inappropriate to the social context." The cerebellum modulated the motor information relayed by the motor cortex in consistent with the emotional information relayed by frontal and temporal cortex to output. In addition, the facial expressions comprised the various combinations of facial muscles. The facial nucleus to which facial muscles belong is located at the caudal pontine [10]. Thus the facial expression is executed as follows: (i) the cerebral cortex determines the emotional states, (ii) the cerebellum modulates the motor commands appropriately to a social context, and (iii) the pontine receives the modular commands to move facial muscles.

In study, we modeled the cortico-cerebellar function to modulate the motor commands in accordance with the social context by using the following qualitative differential equation:

$$\frac{d^2m}{dt^2} + \lambda_1(x)\frac{dm}{dt} + \lambda_2(x)m = 0 \tag{2}$$

where the parameters λ_1 and λ_2 represent the modulating velocity and acceleration of facial muscle movement, dependent on emotional states x. Gomi [8] experimentally demonstrated that the inverse dynamics model with a second order differential equation for determining the eye direction was persuasive in representing the burst patterns of Purkinje cells.

Define y and ξ as satisfying $y = \frac{dm}{dt}$, $\xi = (m\ y)^T$ (where x^T denotes for transpose of vector x), then Eq. (2) can be transformed into

$$\frac{d\xi}{dt} = \Lambda\xi, \text{ where } \Lambda = \begin{pmatrix} 0 & 1 \\ -\lambda_2(x) & -\lambda_1(x) \end{pmatrix}. \tag{3}$$

Let z be an output representing the state of facial muscles, then Eq. (3) and $z = m$ can be regarded as the equation of states in the framework of control theory, where Λ represents the internal model generating the series of facial movements. Hence, we introduced the model generating the emotional facial movement according to the cortico-cerebellar function.

3.3   Proposal for the Mechanism to Predict the Facial Movement of Other's

Prediction processing requires immediate processes for how the agent should move the muscles, especially before the movement is perceived. Let us assume that self-internal model Λ should be applied to the other's internal model Λ^*, that is, $\Lambda^* = \Lambda$. Then, for perceiving the agent's facial movements at the initial momentary duration $\xi^*(0) = (m(0) \quad y(0))^T$, the state of facial muscles at the arbitrary time can be easily calculated analytically by using Eq. (3). In this case, this application means the prediction.

4   Qualitative Model Representing the Transition of Emotional States

The dynamical system framework is an elaborate approach to model the transitioning of emotional states, especially considering the implementation of emotional states into the robot [11]. We introduce a model not only represents the transitioning of emotional states but also comprising valid neuropsychological knowledge.

The transition of emotional states is mathematically written as

$$\frac{dx}{dt} = f(x) + u(t). \tag{4}$$

As is shown in the equation, emotional state $x(t)$ transits in accordance with the unknown function and the given input $u(t)$. In this study, the emotional states represents the physiological state determined by the states of certain neural systems.

Posner et al. [12] proposed the neural systems of the circumplex model proposed by Russell. In their proposal, a mesolimbic dopamine system plays a role in emotional valence, and reticular formation in arousal. These neural structures are an efficient clue in characterizing the function f in Eq. (4).

5   Discussion

On the basis of the qualitative model for prediction, Eq. (3) requires rapid information processing of emotions, as Λ is dependent on variable x. This rapid emotional processing is expected to be relayed through "low-road" route [4]. Here the thalamus, which is a transit point between sensory receptor and the amygdala [4], should play an important role in processing emotional information.

We focused on the thalamus because of two main reasons. First, the absence of neural projections between the amygdala and cerebellum causes the more latency to convey emotional information to the cerebellum. Second reason is the thalamus is connected to various regions such as amygdala, cerebellum, basal ganglia and cortical area [10]. Pessoa et al. discussed the role that the pulvinar plays in human visual emotional processing [13]. The pulvinar is the part of the thalamus connected to the amygdala. In particular, the thalamus rapidly processes the emotional information to determine the internal model as the functional center of the entire brain networks.

6 Conclusion

In this paper, we proposed the functional brain model for the mechanism generating negative emotion in response to the facial expressions of the humanlike agents. The model was constructed based on the internal model of the cerebellum. The model implied the existence of rapid emotional processing and the role of the thalamus in such emotional processing.

Acknowledgement. We would like to thank Editage (www.editage.jp) for English language editing.

References

1. Mori, M.: The uncanny valley (2012). http://www.getrobo.com/. Accessed 16 Feb 2013
2. Seyama, J., Negayama, R.S.: The uncanny valley: effect of realism on the impression of artificial human face. Presence Teleoperators Vis. Environ. **16**(4), 337–351 (2007)
3. Saygin, A.P., Chaminade, T., Ishiguro, H., Driver, H.J., Frith, C.: The thing that should not be: predictive coding and the uncanny valley in perceiving human and humanoid robot actions. Cogn. Affect. Neurosci. **7**(4), 413–422 (2012)
4. LeDoux, J.: The Emotional Brain: The Mysterious Underpinnings of Emotional Life. Simon & Schuster Paperbacks, New York (1996)
5. Tawatsuji, Y., Muramatsu, K., Matsui, T.: Qualitative description representing brain functional connection for human emotional states toward human-like agents. Trans. Jpn. Soc. Artifi. Intell. **30**(5), 626–638 (2015)
6. Shimada, M., Minato, T., Itakura, S., Ishiguro, H.: Uncanny valley of androids and its lateral inhibition hypothesis, Robots and Human Interactive Communication. In: The 16th IEEE International Symposium on RO-MAN 2007, pp. 374–379 (2007)
7. Kawato, M.: Nou no Keisan Riron [Computational Theory of Brain]. Sangyo Tosho, Tokyo (1996)
8. Gomi, H.: The cerebellar role and computational model for reflective eye movement. Vis. J. Vis. Soc. Jpn. **6**(4), 153–160 (1994). (in Japanese)
9. Ahmed, A., Simmons, Z.: Pseudobulbar affect: prevalence and management. Ther. Clin. Risk Manag. **2013**(9), 483–489 (2013)

10. Fujiyama, F., Nishimura, Y., Yamao, Y., Shibata, J., Usami, K., Matsumoto, R. Trans.: In Principles of Neural Science Fifth Edition, Medical Science International, pp. 335–365 & 999–1015 (2014)
11. Miwa, H., Itoh, K., Takanobu, H., Takanishi, A.: Development of a human-like head robot for emotional communication with human: 3rd Report, Introduction of the equations of emotion and robot personality. Trans. Jpn. Soc. Mech. Eng. C **70**(699), 3244–3251 (2004)
12. Posner, J., Russell, J.A., Peterson, B.S.: The circumplex model of affect: An integrative approach to affective neuroscience, cognitive development, and psychology. Dev. Psychopathol. **13**(3), 715–734 (2005)
13. Pessoa, L., Adolphs, R.: Emotion processing and the amygdala: from a 'low-road' to 'many roads' of evaluating biological significance. Nat. Rev. Neurosci. **11**(11), 773–783 (2010)

Effectiveness of Analysis with Near-Infrared Spectroscopy for EFL Learners in Japan

Rumi Tobita[✉]

Engineering Department, Ashikaga Institute of Technology, Tochigi, Japan
rtobita@ashitech.ac.jp

Abstract. This study examined the effectiveness of analysis with near-infrared spectroscopy (NIRS) for English as foreign language (EFL) training, from a brain science perspective. The experiment presented in this paper analyzed the amount of blood flow in the brain while learners were training to improve their English listening skills. The experiment attempted to ascertain the preferable combinations of learners' characteristics and teaching materials when learners are completing training in English listening. This was done by comparing the brain activities of learners from different English proficiency levels. The data suggests that the analysis, using Functional Near-Infrared Spectroscopy (fNIRS), enabled the proposition of an effective course design for EFL learners.

Keywords: NIRS (Near-Infrared Spectroscopy) · fNIRS (Functional Near-Infrared Spectroscopy) · Brain activities · EFL · English conversation skill · ATI (Aptitude-Treatment Interaction)

1 Introduction

In light of the ever increasing globalization of our society, the development of English communication skills is considered crucial in Japan. However, recently it has been noted that Japanese students' English skills have been declining [1]. Therefore, designing and developing an effective course design to meet ELF goals for the acquisition of English communication skills has become a critical need. To solve this dilemma, this study examined the effectiveness of analysis using NIRS (fNIRS) for EFL listening training, from the perspective of brain science in order to propose a well-matched combination of learners' characteristics and listening training. The goal of the analysis is to create an effective course design for EFL learners.

2 Instructional Strategy

In the field of educational technology, Aptitude-Treatment Interaction (ATI) is an important element in the planning stages of developing an effective course design. As ATI's concept and theoretical framework suggest that the effectiveness of instructional strategies' for individuals is dependent on their specific abilities, optimal learning is achieved when the course design matches the learner's aptitude [2]. As such, appropriate training is required for the less motivated EFL learners [3].

© Springer International Publishing Switzerland 2016
C. Stephanidis (Ed.): HCII 2016 Posters, Part II, CCIS 618, pp. 201–206, 2016.
DOI: 10.1007/978-3-319-40542-1_32

Although the effectiveness of various teaching methods and materials has improved overall in Japan, assessments that are based on traditional paper and pencil tests have limitations [4]. Recently, brain activity has become subject to monitoring by technologically innovative instruments [5]. These technologies provide data that reveals the results of teaching and learning; therefore, it could be said that this data can be utilized to assess the effectiveness of EFL teaching in Japan. Alongside this newly developed technology, this study examined the effectiveness of analysis using Near-Infrared Spectroscopy (NIRS) for EFL listening training from the perspective of brain science, in order to propose a well-matched combination of listening materials and training methods for EFL learners [6].

3   Application of NIRS to Course Design

The present study used NIRS to analyze the amount of blood flow in the brain while learners are training in English listening skills. It then examined the relationship between brain activity and learning outcomes in order to identify the most effective combinations of learners' characteristics and, consequently, English listening teaching materials.

NIRS is widely recognized as a practical, non-invasive optical technique that is used to detect the hemoglobin density dynamics response during functional activation of the cerebral cortex, as shown in Fig. 1. The primary application of NIRS to the brain uses the fact that the transmission and absorption of NIR light in human body tissues contains information about the changes that occur in hemoglobin concentration. When a specific area of the brain is activated, the localized blood volume in that area quickly changes [7].

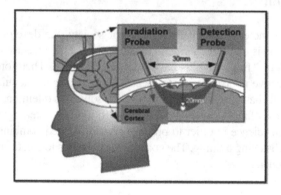

Fig. 1. Route of near-infrared (Source: modified from Shimadzu)

The greater the amount of blood flow, the greater the hemoglobin oxygenation increases. Measuring the amount of blood can thus indicate the state of brain activation caused by differences among teaching materials and learners' characteristics. This experimental technique indicated a well-matched combination of listening materials and training for EFL learners. As these new technologies could improve the accuracy in terms of evaluating the integration of English materials and methods, such technologies have further potential for improving effectiveness when it comes to curriculum development.

4   ATI Based Experiment Using FNIRS

The purpose of this study was to examine the effectiveness of analysis with fNIRS by comparing the activity of cerebral parts for more effective course design for EFL learners. This study proposes well-matched combination of EFL learners' characteristics and English listening trainings. fNIRS is the use of NIRS for the purpose of functional neuroimaging and in this study FOIRE-3000 (SHIMADZU, fNIRS) was used to measure 45 channels including Broca's area and Wernicke's area within the Broadmann area, which are all related to language learning [8, 9] [Appendix 1, 2 and 3].

To resolve the purpose, an ATI-based experiment was planned and conducted to examine the interactions of learners' aptitudes, materials and tasks, as per Fig. 2.

Rest (1 min.)	⇨	Training (3 min.)	⇨	Rest (1 min.)	⇨	Post-Test

Fig. 2. Experimental Protocol

Ten healthy subjects participated in (mean age 20.6 years old; all males; 9 right-handed and 1 left-handed) the experiment, which was conducted with the consent of each participant. They were divided into two groups; group A as higher level of proficiency (5 males) and group B as lower level of proficiency (5 males) as assessed by a listening comprehension test given one week before the experiment. After setting the holder and probes, each participant was given the same experimental listening task and post-test.

5   Results and Concluding Remarks

Comparing the average amount of change per second of deoxy-hemoglobin and oxy-hemoglobin in each channel during the training (see Fig. 3); several significant interactions between learners' characteristics and training were found, as shown in Table 1.

In Group A, regardless of their high score in the post-test results, if the material was too easy or not interesting for them, the brain activity showed up as moderate during the listening activity, as shown in Fig. 3(a). In contrast, if the material was rather difficult, more active brain activity was detected, as shown in Fig. 3(b). However, if the task was too difficult, brain activity was moderate in Group B.

Table 1. Significant Results

Proficiency	Brain activation	Average of post test score (/15)	Statistical analysis of post test score (t-test)
Group A: Higher	Moderate or None	7.8/15	t (8) = 3.111
Group B: Lower	Activate or Moderate	2.4/15	p < .01

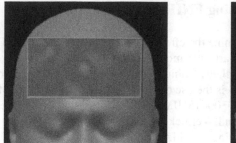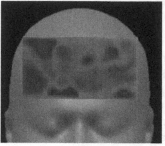

Fig. 3. Brain Activity : (a) Moderate Activity (b) Active Activiry

Comparing the average amount of change per second in deoxy-hemoglobin of Group B with that of Group A, significant differences can be seen, as per the colored channels in Fig. 4.

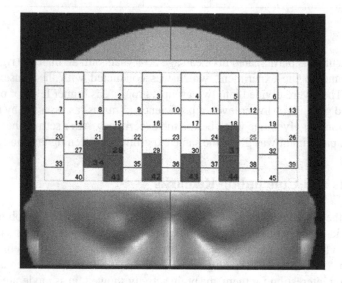

Fig. 4. The channels where significant differences were shown relating to the learners' characteristics.

These results demonstrated that the level of training and the content of materials should be considered, and using analysis of NIRS for EFL learners could be a useful method in the development of effective English courses. Moreover, teachers should consider the effectiveness of the interaction between learners' characteristics and materials, as well as the application of new technologies, in order to organize and utilize the available resources to develop the most effective curricula for EFL learners.

Acknowledgments. This study was supported by a Grant-in-Aid for Scientific Research (C) (No. 26370672), from 2014 to 2016.

Appendix

Appendix 1. fNIRS (FOIRE-3000 by SHIMADZU) [7]

Appendix 2. Measured Channels

Appendix 3. Broadmann Area [9]

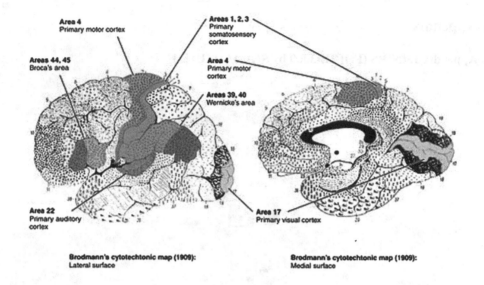

Area 4
Primary motor cortex

Areas 1, 2, 3
Primary
somatosensory
cortex

Areas 44, 45
Broca's area

Area 4
Primary motor
cortex

Areas 39, 40
Wernicke's area

Area 22
Primary auditory
cortex

Area 17
Primary visual cortex

Brodmann's cytotechtonic map (1909):
Lateral surface

Brodmann's cytotechtonic map (1909):
Medial surface

References

1. Ministry of Education, Culture, Sports, Science and Technology, Japan. Survey on the Five Proposals and Specific Measures for Developing Proficiency in English for International Communication. http://www.mext.go.jp/b_menu/shingi/chousa/shotou/102/houkoku/attach/1352464.htm. Accessed 30 Jan 2016
2. Cronbach, L.J., Snow, R.E.: Aptitudes and Instructional Methods: A Handbook for Research in Interactions. Wiley, New Jersey (1977)
3. Tobita, R., Fukuda, Y.: An experimental study on the combination of treatments and tasks in listening practice. Lang. Lab. **36**, 117–127 (1999)
4. Tobita, R.: An experimental study on the use of metacognitive learning strategies of reading comprehension in english learning. Bull. Saitama Women's Junior Coll. **13**, 207–234 (2002)
5. Shimura, T. (ed.): Prefrontal Lobe Measurement Using Near Infrared Spectroscopy – Evaluation of Early Detection Methods and Rehabilitation Methods of Dementia. Corona Publishing (2009)
6. Perani, D., Abutalebi, J.: The neural basis of first and second language processing. Curr. Opin. Neurobiol. **15**(2), 202–206 (2005)
7. Shimadzu. LABNIRS. http://www.an.shimadzu.co.jp/bio/nirs/nirs2.htm. Accessed 30 Jan 2016
8. Functional near-infrared spectroscopy. Wikipedia. https://en.wikipedia.org/wiki/Functional_near-infrared_spectroscopy. Accessed 30 Jan 2016
9. Brodmann area. Wikipedia. https://en.wikipedia.org/wiki/Brodmann_area. Accessed on 30 Jan 2016

Technologies for Learning
and Creativity

A Tangible Art Learning Tool with a Behavioral Metaphor

Chun-Wen Chen[✉] and Yan-Yu Chen

Taipei National University of the Arts, Taipei, Taiwan
junbun@ahe.tnua.edu.tw, yanyanchenbabo@gmail.com

Abstract. The use of metaphors is an important approach in interactive design. A metaphor uses a vehicle to carry a similar concept from another commonly unrelated topic to facilitate understanding. A behavioral metaphor is a kind of metaphor combining referred objects and related action. For teaching and learning in an art course, two famous paintings were converted into two three-dimensional settings. Each setting represents a state of human consciousness or unconsciousness. The changes in position and rotation of objects in the settings may represent a story or mind state. To apply the concept of behavioral metaphor, an interactive tool with a tangible user interface was designed with wood-framed boxes, tangible objects, and interactive media software/hardware consisting of magnetic sensors, a microcontroller, and a tablet display.

Keywords: Metaphor · Tangible user interface · Interaction design · Learning tool

1 Introduction

The use of metaphors is an important approach in interactive design. A metaphor uses a vehicle to carry a similar concept from another commonly unrelated topic to facilitate understanding. In a graphic user interface (GUI), the metaphor is widely utilized as a basic design method. The computer desktop environment is the most successful example of a metaphor. It helps users easily understand a new concept from previous experience [6]. The goal of a tangible user interface (TUI) is to connect the digital and physical space [4]. It also utilizes metaphors to facilitate the perceptual and representational abilities of human beings. The object meaning in a TUI can affect the understanding of operations [3, 8].

Previously, Chen et al. developed an information space navigation system with a TUI [1, 2]. To compare the effects of metaphors between a TUI and GUI, the system utilized a common noun metaphor. A noun metaphor is related to the original object/concept by a similar or typical object. In this research, we focus on the verb metaphor and the behavioral metaphor to develop a tangible user for an information navigation system. A verb metaphor is the movement or operation that is related to the original concept of movement/operation. For example, we use a trashcan to represent a container to store unwanted data. When we remove garbage from the trashcan, we clear the data. This research uses behavioral metaphor to represent a metaphor that combines noun and

C. Stephanidis (Ed.): HCII 2016 Posters, Part II, CCIS 618, pp. 209–214, 2016.
DOI: 10.1007/978-3-319-40542-1_33

verb metaphors. Users can operate it with a similar form and operation that is related to the original concept.

In most arts education curricula, digital media are only used to present traditional course content. It is possible to integrate the content and digital media to develop new forms of curriculum. While young students engage with new media, it can encourage active learning in an art course [7]. In the present research, a course and its interactive teaching tool are developed to illustrate the concept of art and society and to provide the opportunity to let students tell their own stories.

2 Method

For teaching and learning in an art course, two famous paintings were converted into three-dimensional (3D) settings. Each setting represented a state of human consciousness or unconsciousness. The change in position and rotation of objects in the settings may represent a story or mind state. To apply the concept of behavioral metaphor, an interactive tool with a TUI was designed with wood-framed boxes, tangible objects, and interactive media software/hardware consisting of magnetic sensors, a microcontroller, and a tablet display.

2.1   Course Development

Overview and Purpose. This lesson is a unit of a visual art course for Grade 7. It explores the relationship between art and society. The purpose of the lesson includes art form's construction, cultural attribute, creation, and spatial representation.

Objectives. Students can understand the relationship between art creation, society, and culture. Students can identify and apply the social and cultural meaning of arts. Students can have habit of art appreciation.

Material. Paintings of Joan Miró (Fig. 1) and Van Gogh (Fig. 2) are selected to make a pair of boxed settings representing outer and inner space. The two settings were connected through a door.

Fig. 1.   Joan Miró: The Tilled Field (Source: www.guggenheim.org)

Fig. 2. Vincent van gogh: the bedroom (Source: www.artic.edu)

Information. Background knowledge about personal information and artwork of Joan Miró and Van Gogh is provided. Detailed contents of Miró's The Tilled Field and Van Gogh's The Bedroom are helpful for a better understanding.

Activity. After introducing the artists and their artwork, students tell their own story based on the two settings formed from the paintings. Objects, such as animals and furniture, can be used as characters to perform actions and emotions.

Verification. From the recounted stories, the structure and content can show the students' ability to identify and apply the social and cultural meaning of forms.

2.2 Conceptual Design

The two settings were made of wood-framed boxes with open ceilings and movable front and side walls. Objects (animals and furniture) in the paintings were made of models with 3D printing technology. The paintings were image processed as a background to the settings after removing the objects. A tablet computer could display images outside of windows as interactive feedback (see Fig. 3).

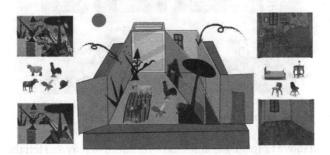

Fig. 3. Two boxes setting the stage

2.3 Interaction Design

Tools. Tablet-size (15 × 20 cm) magnetic sensors (GaussToys: GaussSense) were used as the main sensors to perceive the objects' position and rotation. An Arduino micro-controller was used as the I/O interface. Processing programming language integrated the input information and generated the image output. A tablet was used as the output display and computer.

Design. Two wood-framed boxes were used as containers of the settings. 3D objects (animals and furniture) attached with magnets were used as the TUI. The magnetic sensors were installed in a platform under the boxes (see Fig. 4) and could receive different input signals (see Fig. 5). The display changes the color temperature of the background according to the distance among animals (The Tilled Field) or order of furniture (The Bedroom). A closer or more orderly state results in a warmer background color.

Fig. 4. Installation design

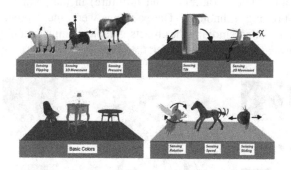

Fig. 5. Input signals received by the magnetic sensors

Use. Users could move or rotate the animals or furniture to play and tell their own story. The image and background of the display respond to changes in shape and color as feedback.

3 Results

In the preliminary test by the researchers, the settings in the teaching tool were used as miniature stages and users manipulated the characters by hands. Through playing with the paintings, details can be observed and perceived with more concentration and sensibility. From the converted and interactive 3D setting, we could see how original images are formed. The energy and atmosphere in the paintings could be imagined vividly, leading to a better discussion of the meaning and possibility of the paintings. We also found that sounds can be an important part of storytelling. We can simulate sounds of animals or other sound effects to play and tell the story (Fig. 6).

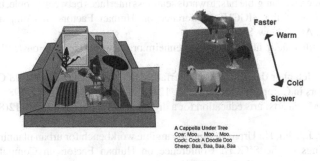

Fig. 6. A sample storytelling

4 Discussion

The form and manipulation of tangible objects can reflect behavioral metaphors in narrated stories, showing that metaphors in artwork do not have only *symbolic* or *operational* meanings. From the corresponding display feedback, the manipulation of the animals and furniture could be recognized as status/attitude/intention of the outer/inner human mind. Unpredictable patterns attract users to try to identify the rules behind the phenomena, especially when the feedback is not so linearly direct. A method to probe the mind of artwork or artists as if to have a conversation with them would be interesting and educational.

The stories that are created by using the tool could introduce more and richer imagery about the artwork. More details and associated concepts will guide a more open perspective about the artwork and will help create original work. The context created in this research is about the topic of social and personal relationships. This model can be applied to other topics in teaching art.

Acknowledgments.   This research was partly sponsored by grants (MOST 104-2410-H-119-012) from the Ministry of Science and Technology, Taiwan.

References

1. Chen, C.-W., Tseng, K.C., Chang, S.: Modeling a tangible user interface for navigation in an information space. In: Advances in Human Factors and Ergonomics 2014: Proceedings of the 5th International Conference on Applied Human Factors and Ergonomics, pp. 5612–5619. AHFE, Krakow, Poland (2014)
2. Chen, C.-W., Tseng, K.C., Kao, Y.-F.: Single tap hierarchy-structured zoom as interface for interactive indoor wayfinding map for elderly users. In: Stephanidis, C., Antona, M. (eds.) UAHCI 2013, Part II. LNCS, vol. 8010, pp. 42–50. Springer, Heidelberg (2013)
3. Fishkin, K.P.: A taxonomy for and analysis of tangible interfaces. Pers. Ubiquitous Comput. **8**(5), 347–358 (2004)
4. Ishii, H., Ullmer, B.: Tangible bits: towards seamless interfaces between people, bits and atoms. In: Proceedings of the SIGCHI Conference on Human Factors in Computing Systems, pp. 234–241. ACM, New York (1997)
5. Miró, J.: The tilled field. http://www.guggenheim.org/new-york/collections/collection-online/artwork/2934
6. Marcus, A.: Metaphor design for user interfaces. In: Proceedings of CHI 98 Conference on Human Factors in Computing Systems, pp. 129–130. ACM, New York (1998)
7. Peppler, K.: Media arts: arts education for a digital age. Teach. Coll. Rec. **112**(8), 2118–2153 (2010)
8. Underkoffler, J., Ishii, H.: Urp: a luminous-tangible workbench for urban planning and design. In: Proceedings of the SIGCHI Conference on Human Factors in Computing Systems, pp. 386–393. ACM, New York (1999)
9. Van gogh: the bedroom. http://www.artic.edu/aic/collections/artwork/28560

Android Accessible m-Learning Application for People with Hearing and Physical Disabilities

Thiago Alves Costa de Araujo[1], Francisco Carlos de Mattos Brito Oliveira[2],
Marcela Lopes Alves[3], Maikon Igor da Silva Soares[1],
Anderson Severo de Matos[3], Adriano Tavares de Freitas[4(✉)],
and Lidiane Castro Silva[1]

[1] Computer Science Department, State University of Ceará, Itaperi Campus,
Fortaleza, Brazil
thiago.ac.araujo@gmail.com, maikonigor@gmail.com, lidcastro@gmail.com
[2] Computer Science Department, University of Fortaleza, Fortaleza, Brazil
fran.oliveira@unifor.br
[3] Institute for Studies, Research and Projects (IEPRO), Fortaleza, Brazil
lopesalves.marcela@gmail.com, andersonsevero@gmail.com
[4] Computing Department, Federal Institute of Ceará, Maracanaú Campus,
Maracanaú, Brazil
adriano.freitas@ifce.edu.br

Abstract. The Brazilian companies must comply with the Quotas Law for People with Disabilities (PwD). However, it is difficult to recruit PwD with required qualifications. In this context, we have developed a mobile solution based on Android platform, accessible and integrated into our existing Accessible Learning Management System (ALMS). This tool, dedicated to distance learning and based on mobile learning methodology, offers training in software development technologies. Its user interface supports special requirements of accessibility and the content of classes is also adapted for PwD. The application is also integrated with a chat and forum, helping the communication among students and tutors. The solution is designed to facilitate and spread the access to knowledge for PwD anywhere and anytime. We expect to motivate PwD students, supporting various types of learning from existing technologies, and creating engagement opportunities in an interactive and stimulating way.

Keywords: Android application · Accessibility · m-Learning

1 Introduction

According to the Quotas Law [1], in Brazil, from 2 % to 5 % of the total jobs in a large company (100 or more employees) must be dedicated to people with disabilities (PwD). The problem comes up against the difficulty of recruiting PwD with the required qualifications for these job opportunities.

The number of people which uses a cell phone is about 125 millions in Brazil. In 2015, the number of smartphone users reached 61 % of this population [2].

© Springer International Publishing Switzerland 2016
C. Stephanidis (Ed.): HCII 2016 Posters, Part II, CCIS 618, pp. 215–220, 2016.
DOI: 10.1007/978-3-319-40542-1_34

Within this context, a mobile solution for learning presents itself as a good way to train and reach a great number of learners, including PwD.

Based on the Android platform, we have developed a mobile application (app) which is also accessible. The user interface in our app supports special requirements of accessibility, such as:

- voice commands,
- setting up the position of buttons,
- font size setting and
- high contrast.

Since the goal of the app is training people in software development technologies using an accessible manner, the classes of a Java program, for example, are also adapted for PwD, providing translation to sign language for deaf people.

Our solution is integrated into our existing Accessible Learning Management System (ALMS). This way, a chat and a forum are also offered, facilitating the communication among students and tutors. If necessary, this communication can be mediated by a interpreter of sign language.

This approach maximizes technological qualification and employment opportunities in the Information Technology (IT) job market through a solution supported by the features of internet on mobile devices. We expected to motivate PwD students, so they can be inserted into the labor market.

The structure of this work is as follows: we describe the requirements gathering process in Sect. 2. Then we present the prototyping process in Sect. 3. The aspects of the app development are shown in Sect. 4 and in Sect. 5 we present our final considerations.

2   Requirements Gathering

At the requirements gathering process, we interviewed a group of 53 people with disabilities. A Brasilian sign language interpreter worked along with us to provide an effective communication among deafs and the development team.

These interviews aimed to understand the experience of each PwD using smartphones, tablets and their operational systems. The secondary goal was discovering what they think about mobile education. At last, we needed to find out how easy or hard is the use of common mobile applications like email, instant chat messaging or social networks.

Figure 1 shows, on the left, that 81 % of the group has a mobile device with the Android operating system. That is why, among other reasons, we choose to start the application development using native programming for Android, instead of other platforms or even a hybrid approach.

One of the interview questions reveals the concern with Internet access and data consumption on mobile depending on where they are going to use the mobile device. This can be seen in Fig. 1 on the right, where we can see the ranking of the main answers given by the respondents.

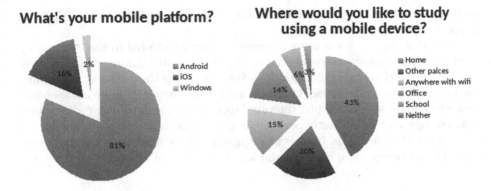

Fig. 1. Interview answers (Color figure online)

Having these information about PwD user experience, we were able to produce an application which supports the special requirements of accessibility, creating a tool which can be used easily by anyone, PwD or not.

At the end of this process, we have built a package of important requirements which includes most people to learn in the app. The system can separate some profiles. The profile for people with hearing disabilities, for example, has access to all texts in Brazilian sign language using videos. For students with physical or low sight problems, the application provides actions or shortcuts associated to buttons. This way, all actions can be accessed with a minimal effort.

3 Prototyping

The prototyping process was conducted in early stages of the project, and involved not only design professionals but mainly the PwD team, which could better tell what kind of features and accessibility items the application should have.

We had two groups of people with distinct disabilities: the first composed by physically disabled people and the second composed by hearing impairment people. Each group was exposed to the same 10 selected scenarios, they could discuss among themselves all the ideas and decide which features were relevant for a prototype. Then they produced 40 paper low fidelity models, 4 for each scenario including both cell phone and tablet screen sizes in portrait/landscape orientations.

The whole concept behind this prototyping process is bound on the participative design methodology. Participative design suggests that after a first typical requirements gathering phase, the prototyping phase must include participation of individuals who better understand the proposed object goals or that will directly interact with this object [5], in this case the mobile application. The idea is to collect the most closer to real user reactions and interests about the application, and more than this, because of the inclusive nature of the project, their main difficulties and suggestions about how the interface should behave in order to better help them in everyday use.

After this process, a few more requirements were delivered to the PwD team, after their first contribution over the prototype. The participatory design process proved itself very useful and trustable, because it brings the final user vision into the design of application users interface and features when its more cheaper and easier to manipulate and apply: the very beginning of the project. Studies shows that changes cost significantly more in time and complexity at a given stage on the project than it did on its previous stage, so applying the right concepts on early phases brings more stability and lower costs to the project.

4   Software Development

The team involved in the software development and content production consists of researchers in Human-Computer Interaction, systems analysts, pedagogues, professors, software testing analysts, developers, sign language interpreters, project managers and PwD.

In addition to inicial software requirements, new ones were added during the development process. This process was favored due to the physical proximity to the PwD, even though the requirements have previously been gathered and all the prototypes were made before the beginning of the software development. Several requirements have been adapted over the development process. Because of this proximity to PwD, the testers could be observed, and we noticed that features related to the interface are very sensitive depending on the user's disability. For example, an optional reverse position for main menu was created because one of the PwD testers claimed that the default position (left side of the screen) was not comfortable for people who have only one arm. This improvement was only possible due to the inclusion of PwD in the development process.

The software release is generated every two months. Once the test version is launched, the acceptance test is applied. This test aims to verify the solution meets the business rules and their requirements, as they are related to functionality, usability and accessibility. The testing team consists of 50 testers: 32 deaf, 16 physically disabled, 1 with low vision, 1 blind person, 2 test analysts and 2 sign language interpreters. The interpreters were responsible for coordination and translating the tests.

A test case document was created with all scenarios that should be tested, according to the type of users disability. Since it is necessary to test features, understanding the content, accessibility and usability is crucial. So testers were and have being trained constantly. The training involves issues management, Nielsen heuristics [6] and accessibility guidelines defined by the Web Content Accessibility Guidelines - WCAG [3,4].

The mobile application was developed as a native application on the Android platform, aiming the mobile learning (m-learning) methodology, and integrated platform to our ALMS via REST services. The application implemented its own accessibility features: high contrast; increase and decrease the font size; video download with sign languages; enabling the student to schedule a study time; and study even if there is not Internet connection available. The app also uses native accessibility features of the mobile Android system: voice command and caption to buttons to make it possible to use the Android talk back function.

The application also allows the configuration of forms of notification and download videos and learning objects. If the user has available space on disk, the user can download the videos or watch online. This feature is shown in Fig. 2.

All management of files that user downloads is managed within the application itself. Videos and metadata downloaded to the user's device can be deleted using the File Manager, one of the application's features. The application also communicates with the platform through Google's messaging service (Google Cloud Messaging - GCM) for sending and receiving notification messages. The app can also be installed on devices android up to the Android 3.1 Honeycomb (API level 12) version and to suit different screen sizes (smartphones and tablets). The app provides tools such as chat, forum, and its own mail messages so that students feel part of a community and that they feel assisted by course tutors and system support team.

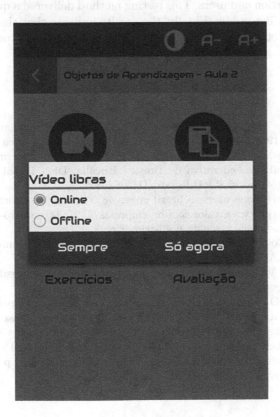

Fig. 2. The application

5   Conclusion

The research project responsible for the requirements gathering, prototyping and software development has been working with PwD for 2 years. Although we consider all the points of the end user during prototyping and survey requirements, it was necessary to have constant feedback to improve the software. We realized that the inclusion of two physical disabled people in the test process to work with the developers brought greater quality to the software. This quality was noted through higher quality in the technical error reports and, at the same time, through empirical suggestions to improve the system. The PwD were included in more technical processes such as video editing.

Another lesson learned during the application development process is that the test team should be as diverse as possible. Including people of different ages, different cultural and education backgrounds. This diversity made possible the content to be understood by this target users and that the application was becoming more intuitive over the releases launches.

The testing process and requirements gathering involved a PwD community similar to application end users. This testing method delivered a qualified content to a very demanding public. Finally, the results indicate that the community of PwD are attracted by accessible resources and the usability provided by our application.

References

1. Brazilian decree no. 3298 of 20 december 1999. regulates brazilian law no. 7,853, of 24 October 1989, provides for the national policy for the integration of people with disabilities, consolidates the rules of protection and other measures. Diario Oficial da Republica Federativa do Brasil - Brasilia, DF - Brazil (1999). http://www.planalto.gov.br/ccivil_03/decreto/D3298.htm
2. Number of smartphone users in brazil grows 48% in the 3rd quarter. Valor Econmico (2015). http://www.valor.com.br/empresas/4327844/numero-de-usuarios-de-smartphones-no-brasil-cresce-48-no-3-trimestre
3. Caldwell, B., Cooper, M., Reid, L.G., Vanderheiden, G.: Web content accessibility guidelines (WCAG) 2.0, vol. 11. W3C (2008)
4. Chisholm, W., Vanderheiden, G., Jacobs, I.: Web content accessibility guidelines 1.0. Interactions 8(4), 35–54 (2001)
5. e Silva, C.R.D.O.: Pedagogical, ergonomic basis for design and evaluation of computerized educational products (1998). Title in portuguese: Bases pedagógicas e ergonômicas para concepção e avaliação de produtos educacionais informatizados
6. Nielsen, J., Molich, R.: Heuristic evaluation of user interfaces. In: Proceedings of the SIGCHI Conference on Human Factors in Computing Systems, pp. 249–256. ACM (1990)

Mining Prerequisite Relationships Among Learning Objects

Carlo De Medio[1,2], Fabio Gasparetti[1(✉)], Carla Limongelli[1],
Filippo Sciarrone[1], and Marco Temperini[2]

[1] Department of Engineering, Roma Tre University, Via della Vasca Navale 79, 00146
Rome, Italy
carlo.demedio@uniroma3.it, {limongel,gaspare,sciarro}@ing.uniroma3.it
[2] Department of Computer, Control and Management Engineering,
Sapienza University, Via Ariosto, 25, 00184 Rome, Italy
marte@dis.uniroma1.it

Abstract. The process of carefully choosing and sequencing a set of
Learning Objects (LOs) to build a course may reveal to be quite a challenging task. In this work we focus on an aspect of such challenge, related
to the verification and respect of the relationships of pedagogical dependence that holds between two LOs added to a course (meaning that if a
given LO has another one as "pre-requisite", then any sequencing of the
LOs in the course will need to have the latter LO taken by the learners
before of the former). An innovative Machine learning-based approach
for the identification of these kinds of relationships is proposed.

Keywords: Learning objects · Sequencing · Prerequisite relationships

1 Introduction

In the case of online courses, a Learning Object (LO) can be seen as a digital
object that is used for achieving a desired learning outcome or educational goal.
With the ever-increasing use of learning management systems (LMS), repositories of LOs to be considered in specialized training are getting popular and
heterogeneous w.r.t. covered disciplines. They encourage the instructors to adopt
(and adapt) such LOs while building their education courses. Popular examples
are Connexion[1], Ariadne[2] and Merlot[3]. Autonomous crawling techniques can
also help building these repositories by sifting through hypertext resources on
the web [1,2].

Several factors inhibit a more widespread use of such paradigm of course
development. Often LOs follow poorly, or not at all, the expected standardized

---

[1] Connexions is a Learning Object Repository, available at http://www.cnx.org
(Accessed 27 January 2016).
[2] Ariadne Foundation, available at http://ariadne-eu.org (Accessed 27 January 2016).
[3] Merlot is a Learning Object Repository, available at http://www.merlot.org
(Accessed 27 January 2016).

© Springer International Publishing Switzerland 2016
C. Stephanidis (Ed.): HCII 2016 Posters, Part II, CCIS 618, pp. 221–225, 2016.
DOI: 10.1007/978-3-319-40542-1_35

meta-tag or classification scheme, and badly needed references to other LOs are missing. This could negatively impair the vision of LOs as resources that, once created, can be quickly retrieved and used several times in different contexts, compensating the high cost of production.

Promising research activities are studying ontologies and Semantic Web technologies, allowing to address these issues, and capable to support the development of next generation LO repositories [3]; yet, creating education ontologies remains a time-consuming and error-prone task.

On the other side of the same coin, building an e-learning course by a sequence of LOs, i.e. by selecting didactic resources and designing their organization in the course, is a multi-level, multi-faceted and iterative process, in which different skills and knowledge are required. In this kind of task, recommender and filtering tools can be of substantial help [4–7].

In our approach the sequencing of LOs in the course can still be managed by the instructors, basing on their taste and preferences, yet they can be also helped by a set of suggestions, related to the pre-requisite relationships holding among the LOs selected for the course. Such relationships can be automatically computed and provide the instructor with significant help and guidance. We show a light-weight formalization of the LO, and how it can be represented by a set of WikiPedia articles; then we show how such set of topics can help deciding on the dependence relationship holding between two LOs. In this endeavor we exploit the classification in categories available for the WikiPedia articles, and obtain interesting results for our framework, in terms of precision and recall of the dependence relationships.

2   Related Works

Wikipedia offers a quantity of high quality content resources in terms of presentation [8]. The openness, easy availability, and freshness of data make Wikipedia of interest in a variety of research activities, such as natural language processing and translation tools. Links, categories and information in templates provide structured content, which can be retrieved from raw XML dumps or Application Program Interface calls.

While some attempts aim at incorporating selected Wikipedia content into the curriculum as a collaborative environment [9] or for categorizing learning resources [10], to our knowledge our approach is novel w.r.t. inferring dependency relationships between LOs.

An interesting case-based reasoning approach, following a self-directed learning paradigm in assisting users to build sequences of elements out of user-defined libraries, is proposed in [11].

An evaluation of the hypotheses that motivated this research has been previously discussed in the following works: [12–14].

3   Mining Prerequisites

The current proposal consists in a traditional Machine Learning (ML) approach [15] applied to a dataset of LOs by performing a comparative analysis of several features of the LOs. The dataset is composed by LOs coming from five web-based courses we managed, on a wide variety of subject matters.

The presented approach is implemented in a software system that supports the following process. Firstly the set of LOs is textually analyzed, and each LO is associated to a Wikipedia page (*topic*): the set of topics is considered representative of the set of LOs. Then, the fact that a LO is represented by a topic allows to quantify the values of a set of features of the LO, by computing them on the associated topic.

We define the features according with peculiar aspects of the representative topics such as content length, generality, or specialization. Namely, given two learning objects LO_i and LO_j, we have: (1) the two average lengths of the text of the Wikipedia topics associated to the pair defined in terms of words obtained by a text tokenization process, (2) the number of links in the first section of the Wikipedia topics, (3) the average number of links in the topics associated to the LOs, (4) the number of distinct nouns in the LOs extracted by a part-of-speech tagger, (5) the intersection of the two sets of nouns extracted from the two LOs, (6) similar to the features #1 but limited to the first section of Wikipedia and (7) the intersection between the set of nouns used in links to other topics in the topics associated to LO_i, and the nouns extracted from LO_j.

So then, the topics are analyzed and the related LOs features computed. Finally the dependency relation between two LOs is inferred taking their features under consideration: this computation is obtained by feeding the features into a ML-based classifier.

4   Empirical Evaluation

In data mining, a decision tree is a predictive model that can be used to represent both classifiers and regression models. J48 is the implementation of C4.5 algorithm [16] developed by J. Ross Quinlan. C4.5 algorithm produces decision tree classification for a given dataset by recursive division of the data and the tree is grown using Depth-first strategy. Pruning methods have been introduced to reduce the complexity of tree structure without decreasing the accuracy of classification. Subtree raising is the followed pruning support procedure, that is, moving nodes upwards toward the root of tree and also replacing other nodes on the same way [17].

JRip is the propositional rule learner based on the Repeated Incremental Pruning to Produce Error Reduction (RIPPER) [18]. Starting with the less prevalent classes, the algorithm iteratively grows and prunes rules until there are no positive examples left. It tries every potential value of each attribute and selects the condition with highest information gain. The minimum description length is considered as stopping criterion when new conditions are sequentially added to a rule.

These two ML algorithms have been considered for the classification task, where the following measures can be defined:

- tp: the number of identified dependencies that are also expected in the test set;
- fp: the number of dependencies returned by the classifier but missing in the test set;
- fn: the number of expected dependencies that the classifier misses to identify.

and, consequently, the performances can be evaluated with the standard measures of Precision (**Pr**) and Recall (**Re**).

$$Pr = \frac{tp}{tp + fp} \qquad\qquad Re = \frac{tp}{tp + fn}$$

that is, the precision and the recall.

Five course materials with various levels of difficulty, conveying different random topics, e.g., scientific, archaeological, cinematography and art; have been considered for the evaluation. A domain expert manually identified the expected dependencies among LOs.

The average precision (**Pr**) reaches 0.828 and 0.736, for J48 and JRip, respectively. The recall (**Re**) values range from 0.811 (J48) and 0.756 (JRip). Each approach is validated following a 10-fold cross-validation. The outcomes prove that the hypothesis of a classifier trained on features extracted from two LOs has the chance to correctly identifying prerequisites among them.

5   Conclusions

We have presented and evaluated a Machine learning-based approach for mining prerequisite relations between learning objects. It can be used in a more comprehensive approach for helping teachers in searching relevant content and assisting them during the course development.

In our future work, we plan to continue evaluating the precision of the proposed approach in different domains of interest. In some circumstances (e.g., Mathematics and Statistics courses), the semantic annotation does not successfully associate relevant topics to the learning objects. Alternative approaches must be considered in order to overcome this issue and categorize the features exatracted from the LOs [19]. Preferences of teachers manifested through the course development can also be studied and combined, for example by monitoring the browsing behaviour on learning objects represented by hypertext resources [12].

References

1. Gasparetti, F., Micarelli, A.: Adaptive web search based on a colony of cooperative distributed agents. In: Klusch, M., Omicini, A., Ossowski, S., Laamanen, H. (eds.) CIA 2003. LNCS (LNAI), vol. 2782, pp. 168–183. Springer, Heidelberg (2003)

2. Micarelli, A., Gasparetti, F.: Adaptive focused crawling. In: Brusilovsky, P., Kobsa, A., Nejdl, W. (eds.) Adaptive Web 2007. LNCS, vol. 4321, pp. 231–262. Springer, Heidelberg (2007)

3. Raju, P., Ahmed, V.: Enabling technologies for developing next-generation learning object repository for construction. Autom. Constr. **22**, 247–257 (2012). Planning Future Cities-Selected papers from the 2010 eCAADe Conference

4. Limongelli, C., Sciarrone, F., Starace, P., Temperini, M.: An ontology-driven olap system to help teachers in the analysis of web learning object repositories. Inf. Syst, Manag. **27**(3), 198–206 (2010)

5. Limongelli, C., Lombardi, M., Marani, A., Sciarrone, F., Temperini, M.: A recommendation module to help teachers build courses through the moodle learning management system. New Rev. Hypermedia Multimedia **22**, 58–82 (2015)

6. Limongelli, C., Sciarrone, F., Temperini, M.: A social network-based teacher model to support course construction. Comput. Hum. Behav. **51**, 1077–1085 (2015)

7. Revilla Muñoz, O., Alpiste Penalba, F., Fernández Sánchez, J.: The skills, competences, and attitude toward information and communications technology recommender system: an online support program for teachers with personalized recommendations. New Rev. Hypermedia Multimedia **22**, 83–110 (2015)

8. Mesgari, M., Okoli, C., Mehdi, M., Nielsen, F.Å., Lanamki, A.: The sum of all human knowledge : a systematic review ofscholarly research on the content of wikipedia. J. Assoc Inf. Sci. Technol. **66**(2), 219–245 (2015)

9. Forte, A., Bruckman, A.: From wikipedia to the classroom: exploring online publication and learning. In: Proceedings of the 7th International Conference on Learning Sciences, ICLS 2006, pp.182–188. International Society of the Learning Sciences (2006)

10. Meyer, M., Rensing, C., Steinmetz, R.: Categorizing Learning Objects Based On Wikipedia as Substitute Corpus. CEUR Workshop Proceedings, September 2007

11. Gasparetti, F., Micarelli, A., Sciarrone, F.: A web-based training system for business letter writing. Knowl. Based Syst. **22**(4), 287–291 (2009)

12. Gasparetti, F., Micarelli, A., Sansonetti, G.: Exploiting web browsing activities for user needs identification. In: 2014 International Conference on Computational Science and Computational Intelligence (CSCI), vol. 2, pp. 86–89, March 2014

13. Gasparetti, F., Limongelli, C., Sciarrone, F.: A content-based approach for supporting teachers in discovering dependency relationships between instructional units in distance learning environments. In: Stephanidis, C. (ed.) HCII 2015 Posters. CCIS, vol. 529, pp. 241–246. Springer, Heidelberg (2015)

14. Medio, C.D., Gasparetti, F., Limongelli, C., Sciarrone, F., Temperini, M.: Automatic extraction of prerequisites among learning objects using wikipedia-based content analysis. In: Proceedings of the 13th International Conference on Intelligent Tutoring Systems, ITS 2016. Springer (2016)

15. Mitchell, T.M.: Machine Learning, 1st edn. McGraw-Hill Inc., New York (1997)

16. Witten, I.H., Frank, E.: Data Mining: Practical Machine Learning Tools and Techniques. Morgan Kaufmann Series in Data Management Systems, 2nd edn. Morgan Kaufmann Publishers Inc., San Francisco (2005)

17. Zhao, Y., Zhang, Y.: Comparison of decision tree methods for finding active objects. Adv. Space Res. **41**(12), 1955–1959 (2008)

18. Leon, F., Aignatoaiei, B., Zaharia, M.: Performance analysis of algorithms for protein structure classification. In: 20th International Workshop on Database and Expert Systems Application, 2009, DEXA 2009, pp. 203–207, August 2009

19. Gentili, G., Marinilli, M., Micarelli, A., Sciarrone, F.: Text categorization in an intelligent agent for filtering information on the web. IJPRAI **15**(3), 527–549 (2001)

Evaluating Software for Affective Education: A Case Study of the Affective Walkthrough

Reza GhasemAghaei[✉], Ali Arya, and Robert Biddle

Carleton University, Ottawa, ON K1S 5B6, Canada
Reza.GhasemAghaei@carleton.ca
http://hotsoft.carleton.ca/

Abstract. We present and discuss the use of a proposed walkthrough method to evaluate the affective design of an educational multimodal software system. We conducted a case study using the walkthrough. The software we studied was designed to support an educational objective of making the learners more engaged and reflective, and the software's aim was to use narrative to help the learners tell a visual story. We recruited participants to apply the method, and we observed the evaluation process. Our findings were that the evaluation method was effective, but we observed a number of effects that suggested necessary improvements.

Keywords: Multimodality · Affect · Educational software · Evaluation

1 Introduction

Interactive narratives are a form of digital entertainment that allow users of software to interact and change stories according to their own desires and participate in a collaborative experience [9]. In a multimodal learning environment, educational elements can be presented in more than one sensory mode such as audio, music, text, picture, etc. to overcome the limitations of each modality alone [10]. Many multimodal learning environments have been developed, but there has been little work on evaluating their design [8]. As far as we know, no single walkthrough technique considers learner's emotion in educational technologies. Earlier, we proposed a walkthrough technique for evaluating multimodal educational software by considering emotional aspects of the learners [6]. In this paper we examine our proposed evaluation technique with a case study of software for exploring a museum, and then we refine the technique.

Our evaluation technique is based on our model [5] that was inspired by *Bloom's taxonomy* [1]. We adapted the three domains (cognitive, affective and psychomotor), we considered the *multiple sensory* and *quasi-sensory modalities*, and our particular focus is on the affective domain. Our model is called the MADE *(Multimodal Affect for Design and Evaluation)* Framework. In this model the instructors' learning objective is shown as involving cognitive and affective aspects, and leads to linkages with sensory and quasi-sensory modalities. By quasi-sensory modalities we refer to concepts such as narrative and persuasion.

C. Stephanidis (Ed.): HCII 2016 Posters, Part II, CCIS 618, pp. 226–231, 2016.
DOI: 10.1007/978-3-319-40542-1_36

2   Case Study

Our case study is of software designed to apply narrative to help students visiting a museum. This software, Museum Explorer, was developed by Jesse Gerroir as part of a Master's thesis [3]. The software was designed for making visits to museums better by providing narrative visualizations. Narrative should support continuity, storytelling and excitement [4]. The software supports an objective, common in relationship to field trips, to help students engage more with the subject matter by planning and reflection.

We use this software as a case study for our MADE evaluation technique called the *MADE Walkthrough*. This is based on Wharton et al.'s cognitive walkthrough [11], and Dormann and Biddle's affective walkthrough [2]. It follows Kort et al.'s affective model [7]. This identifies four phases of learning and the affective character of each. The first phase is encouraging exploration with positive affect. The second phase introduces challenges, and negative affect is expected. The third phase is to support overcoming challenges and reduce the negative affect, and the fourth phase is to affirm learning and restore positive affect. In the MADE Walkthrough, the role of the evaluator is to go through some tasks, while looking at four questions.

To examine the effectiveness of the walkthrough, we recruited participants to use our technique to evaluate the software. We recruited only people with Human-Computer Interaction (HCI) evaluation experience, but not members of our own research group. We applied a qualitative approach, audio recorded and took notes for our detail analysis to identify software issues.

The participants applied the walkthrough to evaluate the software. The facilitators first started the process and gave the tasks that were chosen for testing. One person operated the software on a big screen, while the others discussed what to do and what they found. They walked through the software, answering each of the questions and considering the modalities and the teaching objectives. Figure 1 shows the Museum Explorer. On the top is a map of the visited areas and on the bottom is the visualization selection, including: the *Slideshow*, which is meant to display pictures in a way that is commonly used as a presentation, the *Categorical,* where information is arranged by the topic of the locations, the *Sequential,* which focused around giving a sense of time and place, and the *Dramatic*, to give a sense of the user's personal experience.

3   Findings

With the first participants we ran into issues where they were focused on the *usability* rather than the affective dimensions, and found that the MADE Walkthrough [6] was too concerned with usability. The importance of a need for better solutions with regards to evaluating software systems beyond just their usability was clear. Therefore, to bring more emotional aspects of the users into focus (and not usability), we emphasized Kort et al.'s affective model [7] more and modified the wording in our technique, and identified new walkthrough steps.

Fig. 1. The Museum Explorer with the four visualization styles.

Kort et al.'s model highlights the relationships between emotions and learning, and was built on Russell's circumplex model. This model focuses on what emotional state the learner is in, and from that, what help he/she needs, and attempts to link the emotion and the cognitive aspects of the learning process. This gave the modified MADE walkthrough (Version 2) in Table 1. We used these modifications for later participants. For each walkthrough question we now present some of the participants' comments, highlighting those that we felt reflected on the effectiveness of the walkthrough.

First Question: Does the system use positive emotions to encourage the user to explore the learning environment? Participants typically disagreed, and their

Table 1. The MADE walkthrough Version 2

	Walk through the system answering each of the questions considering the new modalities and the teaching objectives
1st	Exploring: Does the system use positive emotions to encourage the user to explore the learning environment?
2st	Challenging: Does the system provide more difficult material to challenge the user?
3st	Overcoming: Does the system allow the user to persevere and overcome challenges?
4st	Affirmation: Does the system gives positive affective feedback to affirm successful learning?

comments showed the question did influence them to consider the appropriate issues. — *P3: The user has a fair amount of freedom to explore. But counteracting that is the lack of clear goals that would provide the motivation to explore. Also visualization is boring and like a form, nice to have a drag and drop interface here.* — *P1 & P2: There is not much information presented about the exhibits. I am wondering why we adding to the itinerary, what it does? Why we are doing it? Not clear why the need of these functionalities.* — *P1: Give a dynamic sort of feel, for example using animations, as circle moving to itinerary, expands up or somethings that feels it is living more.* — *P4: Dramatic slideshow encourages students to seek what they have missed out on and what to look for in the future. (Other participants saw this as a weakness in the software instead of a challenging experience for the learner.)*

Second Question: Does the system provide more difficult material to challenge the user? The participants again did understand the intent and offered insightful comments. — *P5: The act of exploring the exhibits is not challenging in itself. P3: The activities are a little bit passive, because all they doing is just clicking on things and they probably are not even reading them.*

Third Question: Does the system allow the user to persevere and overcome challenges? Their comments were similar: — *P3 & P5: There are no challenges to overcome inherent in freely exploring a virtual museum.* — *P4: It does not prod you to think about these challenges to overcome. It does present data to you, does not seem challenging at all. It does not help you string together a story. Categorical visualization provides a holistic view of the material and then its individual break down by exhibit, and it prompts learning "learn more here". Allows for a holistic narrative, by theme instead of exhibit.*

Fourth Question: Does the system give positive affective feedback to affirm successful learning? The participants explained: — *P3: I do not remember any instance of positive feedback during the process of exploring the museum or creating the visualization.* — *P2: I expected music in dramatic, the name of dramatic more interactive entertaining.* — *P4: It is good for individual exhibits, but not so much as an overall theme of learning. Provides tools for students to seek out learning, no direct feedback but it encourages learning by having shareable content. Multimedia could also help with this (music, videos, YouTube links).*

Overall, the participants understood how to apply the walkthrough. They were able to imagine themselves in the place of the learners and consider which of the four questions related to each situation. Despite not being familiar with the work of Kort, the participants quickly understood the steps, their rationale and the connection between affect and learning. Moreover, they were able to connect the questions with the narrative quasi-sensory modality.

4 Discussion

The participants, using our inspection method, found a number of issues in the software that might lead to significant improvements. For example: they found the software did encourage at the beginning and provide a sense of completion at the end, but had no engaging challenges in between. They also identified many places where multimodality (animation, music, video) would have been beneficial, but was not provided. The participants found the software seemed surprisingly passive and even boring (just adding pictures and comments, but no humor, no music, no video), and did not bring the engagement expected from narrative. They also found inconsistencies and lack of continuity in the interface, which also detracted from engagement. Moreover, the participants also thought the design would not be motivating for users. For example, when some participants understood the visual story idea, they responded by commenting: "*it should be exciting like making a movie.*"

However, as our sessions progressed, we discovered several important ways to improve our inspection methods. In a normal cognitive walkthrough there are four questions that apply to each task. In our modified MADE walkthrough (Version 2), the questions were more holistic. That is to say that in the beginning of each session the evaluators should have a general idea of the system and the tasks, as the walkthrough is following four steps of learning: exploring, challenging, overcoming, and affirmation. For each task only one of those steps might be appropriate. This perhaps caused the walkthrough to be more difficult.

Once our participants understood this, they could make helpful comments. For example, where a task clearly related to exploring, one participant said: "*Yes, I think the software encourages the user to learn by providing positive emotions, it says the task I want is available to me and I can do something with it...*". Moreover, where participants recognized that the task should be more challenging, to ensure real learning was taking place, they identified that the Museum Explorer did not really have any challenges: "*There are no achievements or challenges to complete... I thought it was just filling in what I visited (or what I plan to visit), which would be the closest thing to a challenge.*" However, because there were no challenges, there was nothing to overcome, and therefore, it was hard to evaluate persuasion and encouragement. This can require delicate design, because different learners will find different levels of challenge possible. We felt that it would be better if all the questions applied at every step, as happens with a cognitive walkthrough.

Therefore, we propose the final version (Version 3) shown in Table 2 that can confidently be used to evaluate an educational system.

Table 2. The MADE walkthrough Version 3

Walk through the system answering each of the questions considering the new modalities and the teaching objectives	
1st	What is the learning goal of this task?
2st	Where in affective cycle of learning is this task? (i.e. exploring, challenging, overcoming, and affirmation)
3st	Is the appropriate affective support provided?
4st	Does the affective support work as intended?

5   Conclusions

This paper focused on an evaluation technique for affect in educational technology development. The proposed evaluation method was assessed through a case study. Our participants used the technique to evaluate Museum Explorer software, which featured narrative and visual stories to support greater engagement and reflection. Participants could apply the technique and make useful comments to significantly improve the software. However, by using qualitative analysis of our observations and transcripts of participant think-aloud comments, we were able to identify several ways to improve our inspection technique. We identified a need to de-emphasize ordinary usability, and state explicitly the teaching objectives, the educational strategies and modality advantages involved.

Acknowledgments. We thank the participants, lab colleagues for comments, and acknowledge funding from an NSERC Discovery Grant, and the Industry Canada GRAND NCE.

References

1. Bloom, B.S.: Taxonomy of educational objectives: the classification of education goals. In: Cognitive Domain. Handbook 1. Longman (1956)
2. Dormann, C., Biddle, R.: Understanding game design for affective learning. In: Proceedings of the 2008 Conference on Future Play: Research, Play, Share, pp. 41–48. ACM (2008)
3. Gerroir, J.: Constructing Visual Narratives of Museum Experiences. Master's thesis, Carleton University Ottawa (2015)
4. Gershon, N., Page, W.: What storytelling can do for information visualization. Commun. ACM **44**(8), 31–37 (2001)
5. GhasemAghaei, R., Arya, A., Biddle, R.: The MADE framework: multimodal software for affective education. In: EdMedia: World Conference on Educational Media and Technology, vol. 2015, pp. 1864–1874 (2015)
6. GhasemAghaei, R., Arya, A., Biddle, R.: Multimodal software for affective education: UI evaluation. In: EdMedia: World Conference on Educational Media and Technology, vol. 2015, pp. 1851–1860 (2015)
7. Kort, B., Reilly, R., Picard, R.W.: An affective model of interplay between emotions and learning: reengineering educational pedagogy-building a learning companion. In: ICALT, p. 43. IEEE (2001)
8. Kühnel, C.: Evaluating multimodal systems. In: Kühnel, C. (ed.) Quantifying Quality Aspects of Multimodal Interactive Systems, pp. 13–21. Springer, Heidelberg (2012)
9. de Lima, E.S., Feijó, B., Barbosa, S., da Silva, F.G., Furtado, A.L., Ciarlini, A.E., Pozzer, C.T.: Multimodal, multi-user and adaptive interaction for interactive storytelling applications. In: SBGAMES, pp. 206–214. IEEE (2011)
10. Turk, M.: Multimodal interaction: a review. Pattern Recogn. Lett. **36**, 189–195 (2014)
11. Wharton, C., Rieman, J., Lewis, C., Polson, P.: The cognitive walkthrough method: a practitioner's guide. In: Nielsen, J., Mack, R.L. (eds.) Usability Inspection Methods, pp. 105–140. Wiley, New York (1994)

The Pyramid Assessment Framework
for 'Competence Developing Games'

Johannes Alexander König and Martin R. Wolf[(✉)]

Laboratory for IT Organization and Management,
Aachen University of Applied Sciences, Aachen, Germany
{koenig,m.wolf}@fh-aachen.de

Abstract. There are different types of games that try to use the motivation of a gaming situation in a learning context. All these different types are considered separately these days. This paper introduces a new terminology 'Competence Developing Game' (CDG) as an umbrella term. Furthermore, a new assessment framework is presented that provides a standardized and comparable evaluation of all kind of CDGs. With this new framework, different types of games can be assessed, compared and optimized in a focused and effective way.

Keywords: Competence Developing Games · Serious Games · Gamification · Business Simulations · Assessment

1 Introduction

Using gaming concepts for teaching approaches provides the advantage of transferring the motivation of a gaming situation into a learning situation [1]. In addition, games provide a safe room which gives players the possibility to explore new behaviors or strategies without taking any risks on their healthiness or their (business) environment [2].

There are three major kind of games that are used within teaching context: Serious Games, Business Simulations/Games and the approach of Gamification. Despite the increasing importance of this kind of games, there is a lack of assessment tools [3]. According to current knowledge, there is no framework or tool that provides the capability to assess Serious Games, Business Simulation/Games and gamified applications. An assessment framework providing the capability to compare all three types of games is valuable to identify generic key quality criteria needed to increase the quality of future games. Further it bridges the gap between the different game kinds. By this it provides the capability to transfer quality criteria between them, which means that research results about the different kind of games can be unified.

1.1 Competence Developing Games – A Definition

A variety of publications tries to define the terms: Serious Games, Business Simulations/Games or Gamification [4–6]. Furthermore, there are a lot of game concepts that are relatively close to Serious Games (Gamebased Learning for example). By now, some authors argue that these relatively close concepts are more or less equal to

C. Stephanidis (Ed.): HCII 2016 Posters, Part II, CCIS 618, pp. 232–237, 2016.
DOI: 10.1007/978-3-319-40542-1_37

Serious Games [7]. Other authors try to define differences between these concepts [8]. However, a framework with the ability to work with all kind of above mentioned games requires an umbrella term. Following characteristics had to be explored for development of this term: All games in this scope try to teach someone something. By comparing various games, different teaching approaches can be identified. There are very simple designed games that teach only pure information e.g. a vocabulary trainer. A vocabulary trainer may have a small pedagogic concept but has no nameable Game Design, Game Mechanics etc. So applications like these are not inside the framework scope because they are no "real" games. Extending the vocabulary trainer with a ranking system or with a dynamic vocabulary in simulated conversations, you get a gamified application that starts touching the target field of the assessment framework. A vocabulary trainer teaching the vocabulary inside a 3D world while telling a dis-coverable story would be a Serious Game and of course inside the target field. This kind of games has one critical property. They do not only transport information, instead, they transport information and teach how to use them.

The European Parliament published a recommendation for the definition of the term 'competence' based on the work of the European Universities Continuing Education Network. They are defining 'competence' as follow:

"'Competence' means the proven ability to use knowledge, skills and personal, social and/or methodological abilities, in work or study situations and in professional and personal development..." [9].

This definition of competence describes the idea behind -transporting knowledge and how to use it- in a sophisticated way. Games are powerful and have the ability to teach knowledge, skills, methodological abilities and how to use them. If needed, they can even teach attitudes [4]. So "Competence Developing Games" seems to be a suitable umbrella term. The following definition of "Competence Developing Game" is based on the definition of 'Competence' above:

A Competence Developing Game (CDG), is a game that has the primary purpose to teach knowledge, skills and personal, social and/or methodological abilities, in work or study situations and in professional and personal development of the game player, by retaining the motivation of a gaming situation.

2 Framework Structure and Framework Use

With "The Pyramid Assessment Framework for 'Competence Developing Games'" (short PACDG-Framework) CDGs are evaluated from a "Designer" and a "Player" perspective in seven separated steps that build up on each other (hierarchical structure). The basic idea of having a designated "Designer"-Layer is to evaluate the game's potential by investigating the integral game components and the game's goals. The main goal of the "Player"-Layer is to investigate the effect on the players during and after playing the game.

However, the resulting PACDG-Framework is the first assessment framework which gives the possibility to handle all kinds of Competence Developing Games. It provides 7 steps grouped in 2 the layers "Designer" and "Player". The first layer "Designer" contains the steps: "Problem", "Learning Goals", "Story & Pedagogy" and

"Game Design & Aesthetics". The second perspective "Player" contains the steps: "Experience", "Aftereffect" and "Impact". Figure 1 illustrates the framework and described the framework steps.

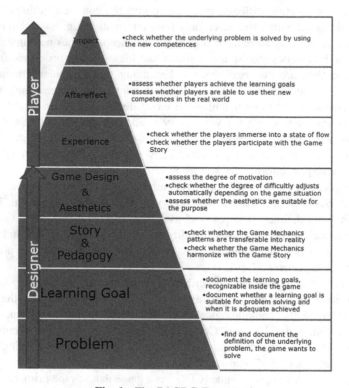

Fig. 1. The PACDG-Framework

Using the framework means to execute the illustrated steps from bottom to top. Each layer focuses on another game part. Due to the hierarchical structure, causes for failures or unwanted effects can be found in each underlying step. Every step requires different assessment operations. These operations are described on the right hand site.

There are up to three operations describing the test procedures that need to be handled in each step. All operations in the "Designer" layer refer to the design perspective of a game. Executing operations inside this layer is possible as desk work by reading manuals, checking the game material, playing the game yourself, watching recorded game sessions, etc. Verifying the test steps inside the second group needs another testing approach. Within the layer "Player" the subject of investigation is the effect on the players while and after they played the game. For this reason, it is necessary to collect relevant data by observing/ asking subjects who are playing/played the game.

3   How the PACDG-Framework Has Been Derived

Today, there are various assessment frameworks available. The MDA-Framework [10] is designed to analyze regular games. Based on the MDA-Framework, Winn developed the DPE-Framework [11] for discussing Serious Game design. Another approach developed for Serious Game assessment is the "Serious Game Design Assessment Framework" [3]. The "Eight fields instrument: analyses framework for training effects" focuses on the player (respectively the learning results) and is designed for Business Simulations/Games [2]. "Annetta's Framework for Serious Educational Game Design" [12] is another assessment approach for Serious Games. These approaches focus on only one kind of games. However, they have been widely reviewed and thus represent an excellent starting point for the derivation of a generic assessment framework.

Beside these game focusing concepts, there are solutions that deliver a measurement tool for learning outcomes. A famous one is "Bloom's taxonomy of the Cognitive Domain" [13]. Based on Krathwohls work [14], Bloom's taxonomy was taken into account and his idea of measuring learning outcomes was integrated into the PACDG-Framework. The PACDG-Framework is inspired by all of these approaches; details are shown in Table 1.

Table 1. Derivation of the PACDG-Framework

Base framework/Approach	PACDG-Framework step	Further main ideas | Notes
Bloom's taxonomy	Impact	Learning goal rating
Annetta's framework	Experience game design	Defined after analyzing related structures from four elements in Annetta's framework
DPE framework	Game design & Aesthetics	Designer & Player perspective added (based on MDA Framework) | Extend game design
	Story & Pedagogy	
SDGA framework	Learning goals	Conformation of some already adapted layers
Eight fields instrument	Aftereffect problem	–

4   Evaluation

As shown in this paper, the PACDG-Framework is developed from different approaches around gaming, serious gaming and general learning. Developing a new approach out of many established approaches ensures a sophisticated level of validity in its theoretical concepts. However, this new framework is based on two main ideas. First, it is practicable for every kind of CDG and second, it presents a hierarchical cause and effect relationship. In fact, the PACDG-Framework was already applied to Business Simulation/Games and to Serious Game without any limitations. But the second point, the hierarchical relationship, requires further investigation.

Table 2. Framework hierarchy validation

Validation of the hierarchic structure	Thesis/Theses
Problem → Learning goal	1, 2
Learning goal → Story & Pedagogy	3, 4
Story & Pedagogy → Game design & Aesthetics	5
Experience → Aftereffect	6, 7
Aftereffect → Impact	8

For validation of the hierarchical structure, collection of primary data is necessary. Due to the fact that (Serious) gaming experts already have a substantial influence on the PACDG-Framework, it was decided to collect data from teaching experts – teachers (High-School level). Eight theses were developed, all of them in teacher suitable wording. The teachers were asked to rate each thesis on a scale from 1 (min) to 5 (max). Table 2 shows which thesis supports which hierarchal level.

Totally 39 (German) teachers participated in the study (20 Female, 19 Male). On average the surveyed are ∼43 years old and have 13 years personal experience (trainees are included in this statistic with 0 years personal experience). Table 3: 'Evaluation of the questionnaire' shows the results. Table 3 'Graphic Evaluation of the questionnaire' shows the study results as a diagram. With a median and average of four or higher, all theses except thesis 5 are fully accepted. Thesis 5 shows a strong expression in the neutral range, but has a median inside the 'agree' range and is therefore accepted with limitations. This means, the hierarchy 'Story and Pedagogy' → 'Game Design & Aesthetics' is accepted with limitation (maybe further investigation is needed). However, besides this small limitation the results show that the hierarchical structure is valid.

Table 3. Study results

Thesis	1	2	3	4	5	6	7	8
x̄	5	4	5	5	4	4	4	4
x̄	4,46	4,08	4,77	4,26	3,44	4,28	4,08	4,03
σ	0,6	0,98	0,48	0,91	1,02	0,79	0,81	1,04

5 Conclusion

There are a lot of different game types with teaching intentions, which leads to the existence of different game assessment approaches. Although some of these approaches are well working for a special kind of game there was no approach working for different game types. Among other, the reason for this shortage is that there was no uniform terminology for such games. The term 'Competence developing game', defined and explained in this paper, provides some remedy. Further "The PACDG-Framework for 'Competence Developing Games'" provides a handle for the whole CDG concept. It represents the first tool that delivers the capability to analyze different game kinds in a standardized way. This enables the creation of comparable assessments helpful for the further development of game theories inside the CDG category.

References

1. Sanchez, E.: Key criteria for Game Desing, France (2011). http://archives.reseaucerta.org/meet/Key_criteria_for_Game_Design_v2.pdf. Accessed 03 2016
2. Kessels, J.W.M., Keursten, P., Smit, C.A.: The Eight Field Instrument: Analysis Framework for Training Effects. Kessels & Smit, The Learning Company, Utrecht (1996)
3. Mitgutsch, K., Alvarado, N.: Purposeful by design?: a serious game design assessment framework. In: Proceedings of the International Conference on the Foundations of Digital Games. Raleigh, North Carolina, pp. 121–128 (2012)
4. Michael, D., Chen, S.: Serious Games: Games That Educate, Train, and Inform. Thomson Course Technology PTR, Boston (2005)
5. Blötz, U.: Planspiele und Serious Games in der beruflichen Bildung. Bertelsmann, Bielefeld (2015)
6. Schulten, M.: Gamification in der Unternehmenspraxis: Status quo und Perspektiven. In: Dialogmarketing Perspektiven 2013/2014. Springer, Wiesbaden (2014)
7. Corti, K.: Gamesbased Learning a serious business application. PIXELearning Ltd. (2006)
8. Lampert, C., Schwinge, C., Tolks, D.: Der gespielte Ernst des Lebens - Bestandsaufnahme und Potenziale von Serious Games (for Health). MedienPädagogik (2009)
9. EUCEN: European Universities Continuing Education Network (2009). http://www.eucen.eu/EQFpro/GeneralDocs/FilesFeb09/GLOSSARY.pdf. Accessed 03 2016
10. Hunicke, R., Leblanc, M., Zubek, R.: MDA: a formal approach to game design and game research. In: Proceedings of the Challenges in Games AI Workshop, Nineteenth National Conference of Artificial Intelligence (2004)
11. Winn, B.M.: The design, play, and experience framework. In: Ferdig, R.E. (ed.) Handbook of Research on Effective Electronic Gaming in Education, 3rd edn, pp. 1010–1024. Information Science Reference, USA (2009)
12. Annetta, L.A.: The "I's" have it: a framework for serious educational game design. In: Gerianne, A. (eds.) Review of General Psychology, Special Issue: Video Games: Old Fears and New Directions, vol. 14, nr. 2, pp. 105–112 (2010)
13. Sitte, W., Wohlschlägl, H. (eds.): Beiträge zur Didaktik des "Geographie und Wirtschaftskunde"-Unterrichts, 4th edn. Department of Geography and Regional Research, University of Vienna, Vienna (2001)
14. Krathwohl, D.R.: A Revision of Bloom's Taxonomy: An Overview. In: Theory Into Practice, vol. 41. College of Education, The Ohio State University (2002)

Advancing Writing Work with Handwriting-Learning System for Students with Intellectual Disabilities

Iwao Kobayashi[1][(✉)], Kiwamu Sato[2], Ayumi Sugisawa[2], Gou Inoue[3],
Naohito Ogasawara[2], and Hiroshi Nunokawa[2]

[1] Center for the Research and Support of Educational Practice,
Tokyo Gakugei University, Tokyo, Japan
iwan@u-gakugei.ac.jp

[2] Faculty of Software and Information Science, Iwate Prefectural University, Iwate, Japan
nunokawa@nunokawa.jp

[3] Special Needs School Attached to Tokyo Gakugei University, Tokyo, Japan
gogomc5@u-gakugei.ac.jp

Abstract. For this research, the authors identified writing-learning system requirements for words and sentences written by learners with intellectual disabilities. The requirements can be involved in their daily work composing letters and papers, and can be used to develop a system prototype. The implemented prototype was evaluated by expert-review examinations in this study, in which four expert teachers at a school for students with intellectual disabilities participated. Furthermore, the prototype was used at the school for system evaluation. This paper presents results and describes the system's educational effects and expected difficulties related to future use.

Keywords: Handwriting-learning system · Intellectual disabilities · Tablet PC

1 Introduction

Handwriting tends to pose a daunting challenge to students who receive special needs education (SNE). The authors have investigated the use of tablet computers with a handwriting-learning system for special needs education [1, 2]. Especially for education for students with intellectual disabilities, the outcomes of learning with such systems are expected to be related directly with their actual daily life. Therefore, the authors' earlier research has been augmented to identify writing-learning system requirements for words or sentences written by learners with intellectual disabilities that can be involved in their daily work such as in letters and papers, and to develop a system prototype [3]. However, the prototype has not been evaluated in any educational scene. In this research, the implemented prototype was evaluated based on expert-review examinations. It was used at the school for system evaluation.

C. Stephanidis (Ed.): HCII 2016 Posters, Part II, CCIS 618, pp. 238–242, 2016.
DOI: 10.1007/978-3-319-40542-1_38

2   System Development

The prototype system was developed by expanding our previous handwriting-learning systems, which were intended for handwriting-learning of words and sentences [1, 2]. System development was based on an Android tablet PC (Excite Write; Toshiba Corp.) including an electromagnetic-guidance digitizer.

When conducting this research, we devoted attention to the reuse of learning outcomes for producing new documents or works in real life. In SNE schools for students with intellectual disabilities in Japan, sometimes handwriting-learning outcomes were reused to produce documents or works. For example, SNE teachers prepare writing-sheets including some support-lines of character boxes or traced characters. Then they instruct their students to write words and sentences on the sheets. Subsequently, teachers erase the support-lines, cut out the written words and sentences, and put them on a template of letters or papers. However, much time and effort of teachers are required for such procedures [3]. Therefore, we tried to develop a prototype system by which all of the above procedures can be done. In other words, the prototype system in this study is intended for the following.

- It is useful for including letters or papers of the ultimate objective.
- It is useful for educating people to understand sentences and words.
- It is useful for learning handwriting.
- It is useful for the saving and reuse of produced texts.

In addition, the required system function has the following five points.

- User Interface: setting of the user interface (e.g. hand dominance, contrast of display, and line width)
- Template creation: image of the end objective is included in the system. It is used as a template.
- Word/Sentence input: setting the location of words or sentences on the letters or papers of the end objective
- Input supporting: setting of the support line, e.g., character box or traced characters
- Saving outcome: saving of the written outcome with erased support lines; saving the file as printable.

3   System Evaluation

3.1   Expert Review

Expert reviewers were four SNE teachers (one was female, three were male) in a SNE school in Japan. They were 20–49 years old. All had sufficient experience of at least five years using ICTs for SNE.

Four questions were used to assess 10 items. Question 1 included five items related to the participant himself. All items were closed-ended questions. Question 2 included two items (one was a closed-ended question of five-grade evaluation; the other was an open-ended question) related to system purposes from learner and educator perspectives.

Question 3 involved two items for system functions (one was a closed-ended question of five-grade evaluation; the other was an open-ended question). Question 4 was designed to elicit other opinions along with a written response.

The interviewer explained the purpose of the expert review to teachers. Then the interviewer demonstrated the system prototype and explained it. Subsequently, teachers were able to use the system freely. The interviewer received questions on the system. In the end, the interviewer gave teachers a questionnaire sheet and asked them to fill it out.

For data analysis of items with five-grade evaluations, we scored answers of "insufficient" as one point, "somewhat insufficient" as two points, "neutral" as three points "somewhat sufficient" as four points, and "sufficient" as five points. Mean scores of four teachers were required for each item. Table 1 presents mean scores assigned by the four teachers to system purposes (Qu. 2). Table 2 shows those assigned to system functions (Qu. 3).

Table 1. Mean scores assigned by four expert reviewers of system purposes

Evaluation item	Learner	Educator
1. For including letters or papers of the end objective	4.3	4.3
2. For educating to understand sentences and words	4.0	4.0
3. For learning of handwriting	3.8	3.8
4. For saving and reuse of outcomes	5.0	5.0
5. Total evaluation	4.0	4.0

Table 2. Mean scores assigned by four expert reviewers of system functions

Evaluation item	Mean score
1. User interface	3.5
2. Template creation	4.3
3. Words/sentence input	4.5
4. Input supporting	4.3
5. Saving outcome	5.0

In addition, from data analysis of the description items (Qu. 2 and 3), many positive opinions related to the prototype system were pointed out. Some needs of system improvements were confirmed, such as the user interface and support of learning.

3.2 System Usage

Among the expert reviewers above, one teacher cooperated with the system use for education of his student in the SNE school. The student was an eleventh-grade boy who was diagnosed as having autism and intellectual disability. Regarding handwriting, he was able to write his own name perfectly. He was also able to write other characters, but not perfectly, as long as he had a sample text. Moreover, he was unable to understand the meanings of the words and sentences the he had read.

   The teacher used the system for the student's learning for a month to make two end objectives. One was a presentation draft. The other was group efforts for graduates. After the usage, the teacher reported that the student was able to write more beautiful characters using the system than when using a previous method (paper with pen). Moreover, although the workload for preparation was increased slightly, that for the students' support to achieve the ultimate objectives was reduced considerably.

4   Discussion

Regarding expert reviews, mean scores assigned by the four reviewers were over 4.0 for 4 items among 5 items of system purposes as well as 4 items among 5 items of system functions. Results showing a high score of more than 4.0 were shown for many items, implying high educational effects of the prototype system. Especially, for the item of "for saving and reusing of outcome" in the evaluation of system purposes and that of "saving outcome" in the evaluation of system function, all reviewers assigned the highest score. Such usable aspects of the items can be regarded as a good point of the prototype system. However, lower mean scores of less than 4.0 were found in the item of "for handwriting learning" on system purposes and that of "user interfaces" on the system function. In relation with the former, the needs of real-time feedback were pointed out. With the latter, needs of much easier operation to realize users' required works were shown as the opinions of reviewers. It is expected to be necessary to improve the system from such points of view in the future.

   Regarding educational use in an SNE school, the teacher reported that the prototype system was useful for work not only of students but also of the teacher himself. Especially, from the teacher's report, the workload for the students' support to achieve the end objective was greatly reduced compared to the previous method of paper with pen. These results imply the educational effects of the prototype system. However, further system improvements are necessary on some points such as the user interface for words/sentence input. Therefore, we would like to try to improve the system, considering such opinions.

5   Conclusion

This research examined development of a prototype system for writing-learning of words or sentences for learners with intellectual disabilities. Such words and sentences can be involved in their daily work, perhaps as letters or papers of the end objective. The prototype was developed based on an android tablet PC. Then it was evaluated by expert-review examinations in which four expert teachers at an SNE school for students with intellectual disabilities participated. Moreover, the prototype was used in a class of an expert teacher of the above for additional system evaluation. Results demonstrated the educational effects of the prototype system overall. However, requests for improvements were pointed out considering the user interface and support of learning. In future studies, we would like to undertake improvements and further examination of educational uses for many students and teachers.

References

1. Watanabe, K., Sato, K., Nemoto, N., Kobayashi, I., Nunokawa, H., Ogasawara, N.: The handwriting learning support application for special needs education. In: Proceedings of 77th National Convention of IPSJ, vol. 4, pp. 829–830. Information Processing Society of Japan, Tokyo (2015) (in Japanese)
2. Kobayashi, I., Nemoto, N., Sato, K., Watanabe, K., Nunokawa, H., Ogasawara, N.: Japanese sentence handwriting learning system for special needs education. In: Proceedings of ASSETS 2015, pp. 325–326. ACM, Portugal (2015)
3. Sato, K., Sugisawa, A., Kobayashi, I., Ogasawara, N., Nunokawa, H.: Development of teaching material application for applying learning outcomes to the real life for students with intellectual disabilities. JSiSE Research Report, vol. 30, no. 4, pp. 39–42. Japanese Society for Information and Systems in Education, Tokyo (2015) (in Japanese)

A Conceptual Model of Instructional Thematic Game for Children with Intellectual Deficiencies

Dandhi Kuswardhana[1]([⊠]) and Shinobu Hasegawa[2]

[1] School of Information Science, Japan Advanced Institute
of Science and Technology, Ishikawa, Japan
dandhi.kuswardhana@jaist.ac.jp
[2] Research Center for Advanced Computing Infrastructure,
Japan Advanced Institute of Science and Technology, Ishikawa, Japan

Abstract. In this paper, we propose a conceptual model for instructional thematic game offered as one of solutions to children with intellectual disabilities since they cannot understand something in abstract. The model is embedded through the game to make the children feel pleased to play with.

Keywords: Intellectual deficiencies · Instructional thematic game

1 Introduction

Education is really important for everyone, it should be accessed by all the people, including to those students classified as children with intellectual deficiencies (ID). Specifically, most of them have low Intellectual Quotient (IQ) under the average and diverse limitations in their daily life. For instance, some of them only have thought abstractly, others have difficulty in arranging the concept, in recalling back the information from what they had memorized, in paying attention for someone else, in making speech and in having sensor integration related to the coordination of their hands or feet [1–3]. They need some practices to increase their capability [4], exercise will increase their motoric sensor through some movements and improve concentration by doing exercising of selecting picture [5]. In making such exercise, the children with ID need learning media for training to be motivated. Learning media based on computer games have positive opinions to make the exercise [6]. Kinect sensors are used as supported interaction devices for exercise, learning, and rehabilitation. The experts on special education claimed that their interaction has an important role to increase their interest to the exercise to be learnt through the game play [7–9]. In order to encourage their self-confidence and to improve their skill and understanding, we propose a concept model of the rehabilitation process based on instructional thematic game (ITG) implemented in various types of games. Specifically, if it is used in the serious game to support the educational media in assistive technology system for the children with ID.

C. Stephanidis (Ed.): HCII 2016 Posters, Part II, CCIS 618, pp. 243–248, 2016.
DOI: 10.1007/978-3-319-40542-1_39

2 Instructional Thematic Game Model

Figure 1 shows a basic design of the proposed model which refers to the concept of the instructional thematic game. It is the game which has an attribute to represent the certain theme for each part of the game topic and is strongly relation to the curricula in improving learning process at school, this part represents the layer of the school instructional program or curricula. It gives a rule for them to learn everything from the single topic of subject by associated to diverse view points from the lesson subject. On the other side, an abstract layer represents that the children with ID could not differentiate the subject of lessons at school i.e. mathematics, science, etc. Those things are too abstract for them since they only know something in reality. It implies that they would know something appearing in front of them visibly. In the last one is a game layer which delivers the requirement of instructional theme to the children with ID in the form of game application. Therefore, from this concept, they could learn how to practice the subject from the single topic without ignoring the meaning of each subject of the lesson.

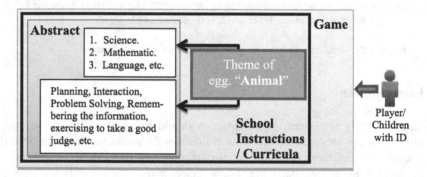

Fig. 1. Concept of instructional thematic game model

3 Game Design

The design of the proposed game based on the ITG model as shown in Fig. 2. It is modified from the game architecture design according to Garris et al. [6]. The difference is emphasized significantly on the input and process part. The components of the design are divided into 3 parts, namely input, process, and output. Each part has different function.

The first part of the game is input whose architecture design is the data input regarding to the whole game. It consists of 4 components, namely instructional program, game character, player data and devices. The instructional program is oriented as the theme to deliver the game based on curricula. It has a relation to the lesson topic at the schools. The game characteristic used in this game is a narrative game learning [10], where it can give narration to the children related to the topic carried out. They can learn firstly through this section. Player data is the variable which can be filled out to represent the condition of the children with ID. This section should be used to make the game deserves to their age and capability. The devices are the peripheral used by the children to access the game. Due to their shortcomings, if the children with ID hold a console of the game devices, it will risk for them. Therefore, it should be put sensor to displace the console devices to detect their motions to play the game such as Kinect.

The second part of the game is process which is designed to give facilitation to the players to reach their ability adaptively. The model of process has 5 main components. First one is the players' functions which perceive play history as the level of competencies. It provides appropriate functions depending on the level of the children with ID. These functions are regarded as planning, interacting, remembering on information, exercising good judgement, etc. The second one is player's tasks. These are transformed from the players' functions as the list of competencies. The player's tasks are more specific on activity of the game. We describe 3 kind of games based on ITG as the sample due to the player's functions and tasks in detail as shown in Table 1. The third one is a system feedback relating to assessment of the game progress (scoring) and oriented to be as the output indicator. Fourth one is a player judgement corresponding to the result of the game application for the players themselves. The last is the adaptive system. This is a set of entities which can respond to its adaptation [11]. In this case, it is divided into 2 categories. These are user adaptation and game adaptation. User adaptation is implemented to propose the appropriate game for the particular children with ID and game adaptation is implemented to make interaction between the children with ID as the player character (PC) and the game object as non-player character (NPC). Hence, such game would become more interesting, and attracting and hold the attention of the children with ID [6, 9] and they would be motivated deeply to improve their skill through the game.

The third part of the game is output which is learning outcomes. It comprises 3 categories, namely, cognitive, affective, and motoric skill-based. These categories were delivered from the system feedback. The cognitive outcomes relate to the skill in analyzing the problem. The affective outcomes refer to the intension, and response of the players. And the other, the motor skill-based outcomes were oriented to exercise motoric skill.

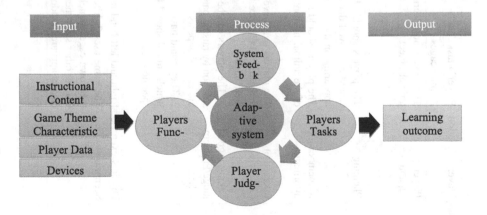

Fig. 2. Game Model based on ITG

Table 1. Player's Functions and Tasks

No	Player's function	Player's task		
		Animal cages	Interactive animal	Interactive animal (voice)
1	Player's capabilities	The player could learn how focus on the animal object	They could make indirect communication non-verbally with the animal as a part of motoric skill exercising	They could learn how to use their voice to articulate some words
2	Planning	The players should plan which hand would be moved due to the animal appearing on the game	They should determine the way to go toward the animal closely	They would be stimulated to have a plan by following the game
3	Remembering information	The players should remember the name of the animal in front of them	They should recall all the information relating to the interaction with the animal	They should memorize some animals' name then articulate them again by repeating
4	Interaction	The players may have any interaction to make the NPC move through raising their hand	They could move their body orientation to control the NPC	They could use their voice to give commands to the NPC by talking with the object
5	Taking a good judge/Problem solving	1. The players can be trained to give solution by raising particular hand where the animal appears 2. They could have an understanding which animal should be taken by a specific cage	1. They could be trained to give the solution by positioning or synchronizing position between PC and NPC 2. They should play with the animal when it comes toward the PC by making the animal body orientation wherever they go	1. They could be trained to give solution by articulating the names of some objects 2. They give a chance to calculate quantity of the animal foods
7	Physical exercise	Right and left hand raising	Body direction	Voice, right and left swiping
8	Scenario	The game uses 2 different animals with their own cage, namely horse and lion. On the other side, there would be an animal appeared randomly at the starting	The indirect interaction built on this system is nonverbal communication between the PC controlled by the players (the children with ID) positioned at the	The object on the starting point should have its own cage due to the animal appearing randomly. Such animal must come into its cage by voice ordering

(Continued)

Table 1. (*Continued*)

No	Player's function	Player's task		
		Animal cages	Interactive animal	Interactive animal (voice)
		point. Every animal goes to either cage by initiating in players' gesture. It would be detected in two modes, left and right rising hand. Left hand is oriented to move horse to the cage B and another is oriented to move lion to the other cage. For instance, when an animal appears at the starting point, the players raise their hand. If their gesture is correct, it goes toward cage B. If not so, system would give an alert by popping words	starting point and the animal as one of the NPCs. We use horses as the targeted NPCs positioned at its cage. This indirect interaction should be natural for both the PC and the NPCs. If the PC comes closer to the NPCS, for instance, the NPCs pay attention back to the PC by coming toward him/her. Afterward, the NPCs follow wherever the PC moves	from the players. They must direct the animal to its cage in diverse ways. In the way to go through, the animal should take a number of foods
9	Game design			

4 Conclusion

The main target of this research is to improve concentration, capability and some skills based on the player's functions by developing of learning media based on instructional thematic game for the children with ID through rehabilitation. The significance of the research is to improve and enhance the ways of interaction (target children) with others through exercises so that they can live normally like most of usual people.

Acknowledgement. We would like to thanks to Indonesia government for the scholarship from Ministry of Research, Technology and Higher Education and also Indonesia University of Education (UPI) for your supporting.

References

1. American Psychiatric Association: Diagnostic and Statistical Manual of Mental Disorders, p. 991. American Psychiatric Association, Arlington (2013)
2. Seay, O.J.: Evaluating Mental Retardation For Forensic Purposes. J. Appl. Psychol. Crim. Justice **2**(3), 52–81 (2006)
3. Deuel, R.K.: Mental Retardation: Definition, Classification, and Systems of Supports (10th ed). J. Pediatr. Neurol. **29**(1), 80 (2003)
4. Kamfiroozie, A., Zohari, M., Dehbozorgi, F.: Using kinect in teaching children with hearing and visual impairment. In: 4th International and The 7th National e-Learning and e-Teaching Conference, ICELET 2013, pp. 86–90 (2013)
5. Kuswardhana, D., Hasegawa, S.: Improving concentration through picture selecting game based on kinect sensor for student with intellectual deficiencies. In: 7th International Conference on Information Communication Technology and System, pp. 133–136 (2015)
6. Garris, R., Ahlers, R., Driskell, J.E.: Games, motivation, and learning: a research and practice model. J. Simul. Gaming **33**(4), 441–467 (2002)
7. Hsu, H.J.: The potential of kinect in education. J. Inf. Educ. Technol. **1**(5), 365–370 (2011)
8. Kuswardhana, D., Hasegawa, S.: Animal thematic game based on kinect sensor for mental retardation rehabilitation. In: 23rd International Conference on Computers in Education. China: Asia-Pacific Society for Computers in Education, pp. 509–514 (2015)
9. Hsu, H.J.: The potential of kinect as interactive educational technology. In: 2nd International Conference on Education and Management Technology, pp. 334–338 (2011)
10. Ayramo, S.: Narrative' in serious or learning game design. In: 2nd ENN Conference Kolding 2011 (2011)
11. Glass, A.: Explanation of Adaptive Systems. Ph.D. Dissertation, p. 173 (2011)

Preliminary Quantitative Evaluation of Effect of Learning from Text, Illustrations, and Animations on Understanding

Taiki Maruya[✉], Shun'ichi Tano, and Tomonori Hashiyama

Graduate School of Information Systems, University of Electro-Communications,
1-5-1 Chofugaoka, Chofu, Tokyo 182-8585, Japan
maruya@media.is.uec.ac.jp, {tano,hashiyama}@is.uec.ac.jp

Abstract. Animation is often used to aid understanding of information and to facilitate learning. However, in many studies, the benefits of animation have not been proved. There is also a problem that information contained in one sort of content might not match that of another sort of content. In this study, three experiments were conducted to investigate the effect of the sort of presentation of learning content on understanding. The animations and illustrations used in the experiments included all of the information of the text. The posttest scores from the first two experiments confirmed the benefits of the animation presentation. However, experiment 3 using a dual-task methodology to assess the cognitive load did not show benefits of animation presentation. However, using a visual stimulus in a secondary task was found to have a significant effect. This effect will be considered in the next experiment.

Keywords: Animation · Multimedia learning

1 Introduction

Animation is often used to help learners understand information and facilitate learning. Animated explanations of concepts and mechanical structures have become common in educational content thanks to the spread of e-learning. Animated explanations help to improve or speed up the learner's understanding of the concepts and structures being taught; they can even be used to illustrate abstract concepts that cannot be easily visualized. However, many studies have failed to show any benefits of animation, or sometimes have shown benefits only under certain conditions. There is also the problem that the information depicted in the different content does not match [1, 2]. It is necessary to verify the benefits of the animation under general conditions and animations must be compared with informationally equivalent illustrations and text. In this study, three experiments were conducted using carefully designed content to investigate the effect of the presentation of the learning content on understanding.

© Springer International Publishing Switzerland 2016
C. Stephanidis (Ed.): HCII 2016 Posters, Part II, CCIS 618, pp. 249–254, 2016.
DOI: 10.1007/978-3-319-40542-1_40

2   Experiment 1

This experiment was conducted to verify two hypotheses:

1. Presentation of animation reduces the time required to understand difficult content compared with presentation of text and illustrations.
2. Presentation of animation improves understanding of difficult content compared with presentation of text and illustrations.

2.1   Design and Materials

The participants were nine graduate students (males) from the University of Electro-Communications. Experiment 1 tested different combinations of learning content (three levels of difficulty) and presentation method (three kinds: text, text + illustration, and text + animation). The participants were assigned three combinations randomly (Latin-square design). Three pieces of learning content with different difficulties were created in text format and then three illustrations and three animations were created based on the text content. The learning content described a method for setting up an imaginary machine to prevent the effect of prior knowledge. In addition, the illustrations and animations were created to include all of the information of the text. Table 1 shows the levels of difficulty of the learning content, and Fig. 1 shows a screenshot of the animation used in Experiment 1.

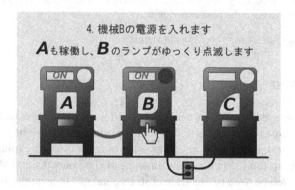

Fig. 1.   Screenshot of the animation in Experiment 1

Table 1.   Elements of learning contents in Experiment 1

Difficulty	Included content
1	3 procedures + 2 notices
2	5 procedures + 3 notices
3	7 procedures + 4 notices

2.2 Procedure

One combination of difficulty and presentation method was selected and presented to the participants. The participants were required to understand the content as quickly as possible and to report when they understood it. The text and illustration were presented on paper, and the animation was presented on an iPad. After reporting that they understood the content, the participants were required to answer posttest questions immediately. This process was performed three times per subject. The dependent variables were the time taken for understanding and posttest score.

2.3 Results and Discussion

Figure 2 shows the results of Experiment 1. The time taken for understanding and points scored in the posttest were recorded, and the three presentation methods were compared using ANOVA on these values. The results showed that there were no significant differences between the three methods. However, the time taken for understanding with the animation presentation tended to be shorter than those of the other methods for difficulty level 3. On the other hand, the posttest score was higher for all of the difficulty levels. These results show the possibility that the difficulty of the learning content was low overall, so it might be necessary to use more difficult content.

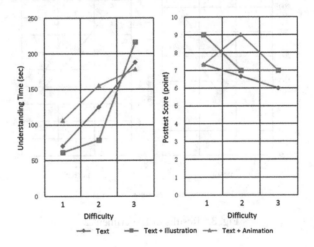

Fig. 2. Results of Experiment 1

3   Experiment 2

3.1   Design and Materials

The participants were the same eight male graduate students who had participated in Experiment 1. The learning content from Experiment 1 was used. The illustrations and animation were created in the same way as in Experiment 1. Table 2 shows the levels of difficulty of the learning content. The procedure was the same as that of Experiment 1.

Table 2. Elements of the learning content in Experiment 2

Difficulty	Content included
1	6 procedures + 3 notices
2	9 procedures + 5 notices
3	12 procedures + 7 notices

3.2   Results and Discussion

Figure 3 shows the results of Experiment 2. Regarding the time taken for understanding, there were no significant differences between the three presentation methods. On the other hand, the posttest score of the animation presentation method was significantly higher than those of the other presentation methods ($p < 0.05$). These results support hypothesis (1) and indicate the benefit of presenting animation to support understanding of difficult learning content.

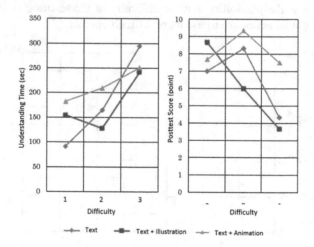

Fig. 3.   Results of Experiment 2

4   Experiment 3

Despite that there was no difference in the time needed for understanding in Experiment 2, there remained a possibility that the animation presentation method had a low cognitive load even though it did not reduce the time needed for understanding. Therefore, a new hypothesis was created.

1. Presentation of animation reduces the cognitive load of understanding difficult content more than does the presentation of text and illustrations.

In Experiment 3, a dual-task methodology was used to test this hypothesis. This methodology is promising for assessing cognitive load induced by multimedia learning systems [3]. The participants were nine male graduate students who had not participated in Experiments 1 and 2.

4.1 Procedure

As the primary task, the participants were required to perform the same task as in Experiment 2 (understanding the learning content). Additionally, they were required to press a foot switch immediately when a stimulus (a red frame) appeared on the screen to indicate the secondary task. The primary task and secondary task were performed simultaneously, except for during the posttest. The stimulation of the secondary task was presented within a random time interval. In this experiment, all of the contents were displayed on a single tablet (20 inch screen) for the secondary task. The dependent variables for the primary task were the time taken for understanding and posttest score, and the dependent variable for the secondary task was reaction time.

4.2 Results and Discussion

Figure 4 shows the results of Experiment 3. Regarding the time taken for understanding and posttest score, there were no significant differences between the three presentation methods. However, the understanding time of the animation presentation tended to be shorter than those of the other methods at difficulty level 3. It is possible that the small number of participants and small number of attempted tasks affected the results of the posttest score.

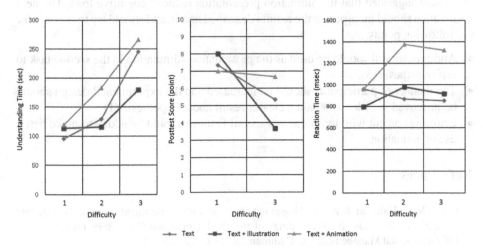

Fig. 4. Results of Experiment 3

The reaction time results in the secondary task indicated that the animation presentation had the longest reaction times for difficulty levels 2 and 3. These results were contrary to hypothesis (3).

The behaviors of the participants during the experiment were analyzed. It was found that the gaze of the participants was concentrated on the screen when they were looking at the animation, and they were unaware of peripheral stimuli. Figure 5 shows the relationship between the reaction time of the secondary task and the content being gazed at. It was inappropriate to use a visual stimulus in the secondary task.

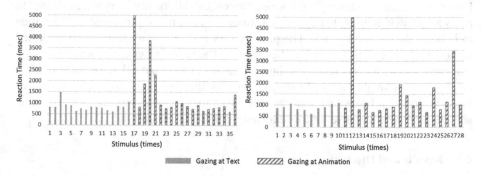

Fig. 5. Relationship between reaction time and content being gazed at

5   Conclusion and Outline of Next Experiment

The three experiments confirmed the benefits of an animation presentation. In particular, the results suggested that the animation presentation reduced cognitive load. The next verification should incorporate the results described herein and should try to account for the following points.

- Auditory stimuli should be used as the presentation stimulation in the second task to test hypothesis (3).
- The number of participants should be increased and the experimental design should be improved in order to obtain a clearer result about hypothesis (1).
- Learning content with temporal and spatial features should be added to make better use of animation.

References

1. Riaza, M.R., Halimah, B.Z.: Looking at the effects of various multimedia approach in student learning: a case study. In: Proceedings of the 7th International Conference on Ubiquitous Information and Management and Communication, vol. 27 (2013)
2. Tversky, B., Bauer-Morrison, J., Betrancourt, M.: Animation: Can it facilitate? Int. J. Hum. Comput. Stud. **57**, 247–262 (2002)
3. Brünken, R., Steinbacher, S., Plass, J.L., Leutner, D.: Assessment of cognitive load within multimedia learning by the dual task methodology. Exp. Psychol. **49**, 109–119 (2002)

Don't Read My Lips: Assessing Listening and Speaking Skills Through Play with a Humanoid Robot

Panayiota Polycarpou[1(✉)], Anna Andreeva[2], Andri Ioannou[1], and Panayiotis Zaphiris[1]

[1] Cyprus Interaction Lab, Department of Multimedia and Graphic Arts,
Cyprus University of Technology, Limassol, Cyprus
{yiota.polycarpou,andri.i.ioannou,
panayiotis.zaphiris}@cut.ac.cy
[2] Department of Logopedics, South West University "Neofit Rilski",
Blagoevgrad, Bulgaria
anna_andreeva@swu.bg

Abstract. This study investigates the potential of using the humanoid robot, NAO, as a playful tool for assessing the listening and speaking skills of seven hearing-impaired students who use cochlear implant(s) and sign language as their main communication modality. NAO does not have a human mouth and therefore, students cannot do lip-reading; we considered this to be a unique characteristic of the technology that can help make the assessment of listening and speaking skills efficient and accurate. Three game-like applications were designed and deployed on NAO for the purpose of this study. Results demonstrated how NAO was successfully used in this context. Our results, although preliminary, should encourage future research in the area of listening and speaking assessment for hearing impaired children, as well as speech enhancement via play with social robots.

Keywords: NAO · Humanoid robot · Social robot · Robotics · Special education · Listening skills · Speaking skills · Speech assessment · Hearing impairment · Deaf

1 Introduction

The assessment of the listening and speaking skills of students who use cochlear implants (CIs) is an essential task that should take place frequently and accurately. Typically, the speech therapists and audiologists use assessment tasks that include different ways to stimulate the students' auditory comprehension. Beyond the spoken instructions given to the child, a task may involve the use of sounds from the environment such as, the sound of a closing door or vocalizations of emotions; the child must derive meaning from the sounds and pronounce the respective word(s) [1]. The "auditory-verbal method" is a characteristic method for the development of verbal communication for users of CIs; it is a very strict approach which does not allow the use of lip reading (i.e. receiving visual information from the lips of the others [2]).

C. Stephanidis (Ed.): HCII 2016 Posters, Part II, CCIS 618, pp. 255–260, 2016.
DOI: 10.1007/978-3-319-40542-1_41

During the therapy sessions, speech therapists often cover their mouths in order to make the child use their amplification device (hearing aid/cochlear implant) to hear the speech sound [1]. Emerging technologies of the new era, might be able to assist such processes and assessment methods.

This exploratory study investigated the potential of using the humanoid robot, NAO, as a tool for assessing the listening and speaking skills of seven hearing-impaired students, through play. NAO does not have a human mouth and therefore, students cannot do lip-reading; we considered this to be a unique characteristic of the technology that can help make the assessment of listening and speaking skills efficient and accurate. Further, NAO has been successfully used in previous studies for play [3], assessment, therapy and education of children with special educational needs [4–6]. Yet, there is virtually nothing on the use of humanoid robots for the assessment of listening and speaking skills of hearing impaired children. As opposed to using a humanoid robot, [7] for example, used a robotic voice simulator for rehabilitation of the speech of hearing impaired people [7]. Also, a couple of studies have focused on teaching sign language using NAO [8] or other robotic platform [9]. The present study appears unique in the arena of listening and speaking assessment.

2 Method

Participants. Seven students participated, after consent forms by their parents were obtained. This was an exploratory investigation; therefore, participants were children of various ages and different levels of listening and speaking skills. The profile of the participants is presented in Table 1. All students had one or two CIs. Based on input from the school experts, P1, P2, P4, P5 had a successful CI(s) surgery and could potentially hear, learn and understand the verbal language even though, they chose to communicate in sign language. Yet, there were cases with unsuccessful CI surgery (P6 and P7) or delayed surgery (P3) (e.g., the recommended time for the surgery is between 12 and 18 months of age) resulting to failure in the efficient use of the CI. Overall, the sign language was the preferred method of communication for all the participants, leaving their speaking skills underdeveloped.

Activities and Setting. The study was conducted at the School for the Deaf in Nicosia-Cyprus with the permission of the school director. The robot used for the study

Table 1. Students' Profile

Participant	Age	Gender	CI(s)	School Grade
P1	5	M	2	K/pre-primary
P2	10	F	1	K-2/2nd grade
P3	10	F	1	K-2/2nd grade
P4	14	M	1	K-7/middle school
P5	14	F	2	K-7/middle school
P6	15	M	1	K-7/middle school
P7	15	M	1	K-7/middle school

was NAO by Aldebaran Robotics, a 58 cm tall humanoid robot that exhibits human-like features. Among others, it has the ability to recognize images, faces and objects as well as respond to speech and other sounds of the environment. NAO was positioned on a table and the participant was seated facing NAO (see Fig. 1). The sign language interpreter was present in the room, in case the children needed sign language or verbal language support for instructions. Upon responding to each activity, the sign language interpreter provided feedback to the participant, as needed.

Three game-like applications were developed and deployed on NAO for the purpose of this work. Each game involved a series of tasks to help assess students' listening, understanding of the verbal language and speaking skills:

Shapes. This game involved listening and following spoken instructions. Two shape-images were positioned in front of the student for each piece of instruction. The participant listened to NAO's instructions, selected an image and positioned it within NAO's hands (see Fig. 1). Instructions consisted of two pieces of information: shape and color (e.g. "Give me the shape which has four equal sides and has the color of the sea").

Emotions. This game involved the recognition of everyday emotions, derived from sounds. NAO asked "How do I feel now?" while he played the sound of an emotion (e.g. yawning) and demonstrated the respective gesture or bodily movement (see Fig. 1). For each emotion, two images were positioned in front of the student as visual clues to help them decide on the correct emotion and say it loud (pronunciation).

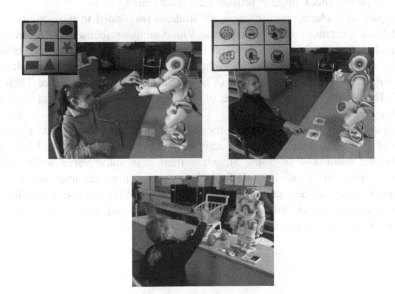

Fig. 1. Student selects the blue square according to NAO's instructions (up-left); NAO yawning – child saying which is the demonstrated emotion (up-right); NAO needs to brush teeth – child placing products in the cart (bottom). (Color figure online)

Shopping. The game involved understanding of spoken instructions; recognition of everyday sounds in the environment; familiarity with vocabulary linked to everyday routines; and speaking (pronunciation). For each piece of instruction, a total of six different products were placed in front of the student so that she/he could select the ones NAO needed and say them loud (pronunciation). For the first part of the game, two instructions were given; NAO played two sounds (sounds of running shower and brushing teeth) and demonstrated the respective bodily movement e.g., teeth brushing; in this case the student put the toothbrush, toothpaste and dental floss in the cart (see Fig. 1). For the second part of the game, three instructions were given with NAO requesting some products e.g., "I love honey cake, so please place in my shopping cart the products I need to cook it, and tell me their names"; in this case, the student selected the correct products, said their names loud, and placed them in the shopping cart (e.g., honey, flour, sugar and a cake box).

Data Collection. Data were collected in three forms: (i) an attitudinal questionnaire administered to the students right after the completion of the activity; (ii) video recordings of the activity; and (iii) interview sessions with the special education teachers of the School, the sign language interpreter and the technology (IT) teacher who had the opportunity to observe the study.

3 Results

In this poster, we elaborate on students' performance data as well as, the attitudinal questionnaire on their experience. The results from the full data corpus are presented elsewhere (please check http://cyprusinteractionlab.com/).

In regard to students' performance, all students responded to the activities, often beyond the expectations of their teachers. Video analysis focused on recording the number of correct answers (on their 1st try), the correctly pronounced emotions or products, and times the participant sought help, either in the form of sign language (SL) interpretation or verbal language (VL) repetition of instructions (see Tables 2, 3 and 4). The results provided evidence of the most and least competent students in performing each activity.

With regards to the attitudinal questionnaire data on the participants' experience, the use of NAO and associated game-activities were positively endorsed by the participants (see items 1–4 of Table 5), while there was some variation in students' responses based on items 4–7 of Table 5 about hearing and understanding. The questionnaire also included an open-ended question for additional comments; here, two high performing students (P4, P5) reported that they would like NAO to speak at a slower pace, in order to clearly hear his instructions.

Table 2. Performance on *Shapes* game – Pick the correct shape (N = 7)

	P1	P2	P3	P4	P5	P6	P7
Correct shape selected	4/6	0/6	0/6	5/6	4/6	0/6	0/6
Times seeking help	2(VL)	6(SL)	6(SL)	1(SL)	2(VL)	6(SL)	6(SL)

Table 3. Performance on *Emotions* game – Tell me how NAO feels (N = 7)

	P1	P2	P3	P4	P5	P6	P7
Correct emotion recognized	0/6	3/6	0/6	3/6	2/6	0/6	1/6
Correctly pronounced	0/6	3/6	0/6	5/6	1/6	1/6	1/6
Times seeking help	0	3(SL)	7(SL/VL)	2(VL)	0	9(SL/VL)	8(SL/VL)

Table 4. Performance on *Shopping* game – Fill in NAO's shopping cart (N = 7)

	P1	P2	P3	P4	P5	P6	P7
Correct product recognized	12/22	10/22	0/22	17/22	19/22	7/22	7/22
Correctly pronounced	12/22	10/22	0/22	17/22	19/22	4/22	0/22
Times seeking help	0	0	5(SL)	3(SL)	2(VL)	4(SL)	6(SL/VL)

Table 5. Questionnaire results on participants experience (N = 7)

Questionnaire items	😊	😐	😞
1. Did you like the games with NAO?	P1–P7		
2. Did you like the *emotions* game?	P1–P7		
3. Did you like the *shapes* game?	P1–P5, P7	P6	
4. Did you like the *shopping* game?	P1–P7		
5. Did you clearly hear what NAO was saying?		P1, P2, P5, P4	P6, P3, P7
6. Did you understand all his sayings?	P4–P2	P1, P2	P6, P3, P7, P5
7. Did you like his voice?	P5	P1, P2, P4	P6, P3, P7

4 Discussion and Conclusion

The assessment of the listening and speaking skills of students who use CIs is an essential task that should take place frequently and accurately. Emerging technology, such as humanoid robots, might hold promise in this area. This exploratory study assumed the potential of NAO as a playful tool for assessing the listening and speaking skills of hearing-impaired students; the absence of a human mouth on NAO prevents lip-reading and therefore makes him an ideal tool for this task. Findings from this work, suggest that NAO was successfully used in this context, with all participating students responding to activities, even beyond the expectations of their teachers. Moreover, NAO was positively endorsed by the participants, which confirms previous research findings on the use of humanoid robots with children [3, 4]. Future research should continue to examine the unique characteristic of this technology that can help make the assessment of listening and speaking skills efficient and accurate in addition to fun. A full report of our results, including findings from our interview data are presented elsewhere. Our results, although preliminary, should encourage future research in the area of assessment as well as speech enhancement via play with social robots.

Acknowledgements. This work is supported by the Short Scientific Mission program of the "Cost Action No TD1309: Play for Children with Disabilities".

References

1. Welling, D.R., Ukstins, C.A.: Fundamentals of Audiology For The Speech-Language Pathologist. Jones & Bartlett Learning, Burlington (2015)
2. Barnett, S.: Communication with deaf and hard-of-hearing people: a guide for medical education. J. Assoc. Am. Med. Coll. **77**, 694–700 (2002). Lippincott Williams & Wilkins, Philadelphia
3. Ioannou, A., Andreou, E., Christofi, M.: Preschoolers' interest and caring behaviour around a humanoid robot. TechTrends **59**, 23–26 (2015). Springer, US
4. Ioannou, A., Kartapanis, I., Zaphiris, P.: Social robots as co-therapists in autism therapy sessions: a single-case study. In: Tapus, A., et al. (eds.) ICSR 2015. LNCS, vol. 9388, pp. 255–263. Springer, Heidelberg (2015). doi:10.1007/978-3-319-25554-5_26
5. Robins, B., Dautenhahn, K., Boekhorst, R., Billard, A.: Robotic assistants in therapy and education of children with autism: can a small humanoid robot help encourage social interaction skills? Univ. Access Inf. Soc. **4**, 105–120 (2005). Springer, Heidelberg
6. Arendsen, J., Janssen, J.B., Begeer, S., Stekelenburg, F.C.: The use of robots in social behavior tutoring for children with ASD. In: Proceedings of the 28th Annual European Conference on Cognitive Ergonomics, pp. 371–372. ACM, New York (2010)
7. Sawada, H., Kitani, M., Hayashi, Y.: A robotic voice simulator and the interactive training for hearing-impaired people. J. Biomed. Biotechnol. **28**, 7 (2008). Hindawi Publishing Corporation, New York
8. Kose-Bagci, H., Yorganci, R.: Tale of a robot: humanoid robot assisted sign language tutoring. In: 11th IEEE-RAS International Conference on Humanoid Robots, pp. 105–111. IEEE, Bled Slovenia (2011)
9. Uluer, P., Akalin, N., Kose, H.: A new robotic platform for sign language tutoring humanoid robots as assistive game companions for teaching sign language. Int. J. Soc. Robot. **7**, 571–585 (2015). Springer, Netherlands

A New Design of an Automated Remote Lecture System in Japanese 18 Universities in 2015

Takeshi Sakurada$^{(\boxtimes)}$, Kazuhiro Mishima, and Yoichi Hagiwara

Information Media Center, Tokyo University of Agriculture and Technology,
2-24-16, Naka-cho, Koganei-shi, Tokyo, Japan
{take-s,three,hagi}@cc.tuat.ac.jp

Abstract. In this paper, we describe a new design of an automated remote lecture system in Japanese national 18 universities. Our current high-definition automated remote lecture system that was constructed in 2009 has many life-expired hardware. Thus we design a new remote lecture system for replace current system. In our design, new system controls room equipment automatically by reservation, connects rooms and mobile environment seamlessly. The designed system is expected to build actually with the goal of full-scale operations in 2016.

Keywords: Remote lecture system · Teleconference system · System automated · Mobile environments connection

1 Introduction

Since 1997, most Japanese universities have performed a remote lecture using SCS (Space Collaboration System) [1, 2]. SCS used satellite link, satellite link was often down and equipment had many failures in aging. In Addition, SCS did not support to the full HD resolution videos. Therefore, we decided to design and build a new system.

Thus we build a remote lecture system [3] in 2009. In 2009 system (hereinafter referred to as "current system"), we connected 18 national universities in Japan (Obihiro University of Agriculture and Veterinary Medicine, Hirosaki University, Iwate University, Yamagata University, Ibaraki University, Utsunomiya University, Tokyo University of Agriculture and Technology, Gifu University, Shizuoka University, Tottori University, Shimane University, Yamaguchi University, Ehime University, Kagawa University, Kochi University, Saga University, Kagoshima University, University of Ryukyu). These universities constitute six of the United Graduate School of Agricultural Science jointly. Remote lectures connecting several universities are always performed. Additionally, in June and November every year, 3 days remote lectures connected all universities are performed.

Equipment of the current system also failure began to occur in aging. Thus we have decided to update the system.

In this paper, we first describe design and operation of a current remote lecture system for Japanese 18 national universities. Then we describe a new system design of remote lecture system.

© Springer International Publishing Switzerland 2016
C. Stephanidis (Ed.): HCII 2016 Posters, Part II, CCIS 618, pp. 261–265, 2016.
DOI: 10.1007/978-3-319-40542-1_42

2 Current System

Because operation of the videoconference system equipment is very difficult, the current system is controlled automatically from a reservation system. The previous system requirements in design are as follows:

- Many universities (more than 18 universities/23 rooms) can join same lecture
- Multi-directional communications at the same time
- Simple machinery operation
- Interoperability with the other videoconference systems
- Supported two screens with high-definition
- Provide high quality videos and sounds (HD 720p)
- Support large room (Resolve sound loop)

To connect plural videoconference devices at the same time, MCU (Multipoint Control Unit) are necessary. Internal MCU of videoconference devices is only accepting 4–6 connections. We must connect over 20 rooms, we should use outside MCU device. Equipment at each rooms and MCU are controlled by reservation system. In the current system, a user can make a reservation through the web and each room is connected automatically by the system at reservation time. Figure 1 shows overview of current system.

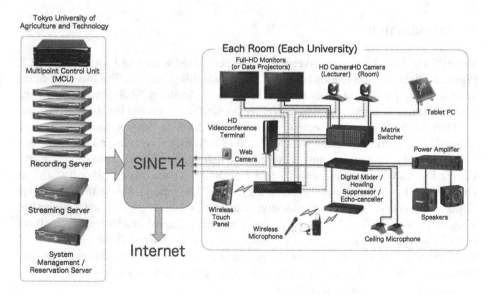

Fig. 1. Current system diagram

This automation mechanism is a good reputation from users. Lectures and meeting have been held 2 times per day in average. The system is also used in admissions as well as remote lectures and meetings. In addition, it has been well utilized to create a virtual room to connect the nearby room (Fig. 2).

Fig. 2. Connecting nearby room

3   Problems of Current System and a New System Design

3.1   Problems of Current System

Equipment of the current system began to failure in aging. In addition, dissatisfaction of the system had been out of the user:

- Not Full HD, PC screen is support XGA/15fps resolution. Cannot support digital input.
- Cannot connect from out side of the room. (Can not connect from mobile environments)
- Network is not stable in some universities, distance learning is sometimes cannot be held stable.
- Often occur charging out of the wireless touch panel.
- Higher equipment maintenance fee.
- User wants to watch the screen that user oneself is taken.

3.2   Requirements of a New System

Based on the feedback from users of the current system, we decide the requirements of the new system. Since the budget is not enough with the new system, it will replace the 23 rooms that were initially built in the current system.

- Support a digital input (HDMI)
- Support 3 screens (instructor video, PC video, local feedback video)
- Support Full HD resolution and high frame rate (Dual streams: 1080p/30fps + 1080p/30fps)
- Participation from the mobile devices
- Reduction of maintenance costs
- Easy to use

- To continue the mechanism of reservation and automation
- Control the room of current system (not replaced) with the new system.

3.3 Design of a New System

To realize the first three items of above requirements, replace to the new videoconference device. Since the maintenance costs are high it cuts the unnecessary functions. As an example, it cuts a small MCU with a built-in videoconference terminal of each room. MCU of purchase costs and maintenance costs are expensive. Connection from the mobile shall not use a dedicated software. It is a new system to allow connections from Android and iOS as well as from the notebook PC.

Figure 3 shows a design of a new system. Reservation system also controls mobile connection not only room connection at the same time. Thus the reservation system will be built from scratch.

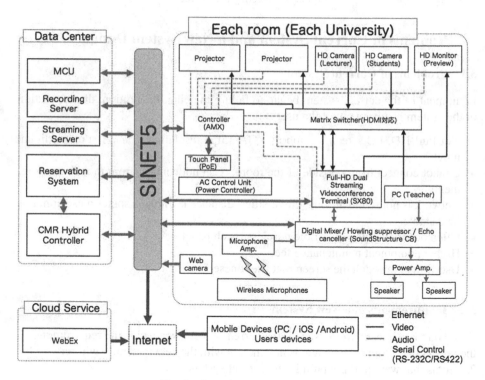

Fig. 3. Overview of a new system

4 Conclusion

In this paper, we described the new automated remote lecture system. This new system is going to build and test towards the running of spring, 2016. In the new system, we realize the high resolution and high frame rate of the video transmission. The user can only make a reservation from the Web, the new system is the same as performed in the automatic control of the equipment as before. For this reason, it is an easy-to-use system for users who are not familiar with the equipment operation.

Normal videoconference system at a room and mobile environments assumes the few participants from each room. It is possible to connect a large classroom (several hundred students) and a small number of mobile environments seamlessly in this system. This style would go become common. In the future, we hope that the new teaching style using this system appeared.

References

1. Kimio, K., Noritake, O.: Results of the operation of satellite collaboration network (SCS). IEIC Tech. Rep. **106**(1), 197–201 (2006)
2. National Institute of Multimedia Education Space Collaboration System. http://www.nime.ac.jp/SCS/
3. Sakurada, T., Hagiwara, Y., Furuya, T.: Construction of a Dual-HD videoconference system for remote lectures connecting 18 National Universities. In: 13th IASTED (The International Association of Science and Technology for Development) International Conference Internet and Multimedia Systems and Applications (IMSA 2009), pp. 124–130, August 2009. ISBN 978-0-88986-804-5

Designing a Teacher-Friendly Editor for Configuring the Attention-Aware Smart Classroom

Evropi Stefanidi, Maria Doulgeraki, Maria Korozi, Asterios Leonidis[(✉)], and Margherita Antona

Foundation for Research and Technology – Hellas (FORTH), Institute of Computer Science, N. Plastira 100, Vassilika Vouton, 700 13 Heraklion, Crete, Greece
{evropi,mdoulger,korozi,leonidis,antona}@ics.forth.gr

Abstract. Technological advancements and contemporary learning theories have redesigned the school environment to embed ICT technology in many aspects of the learning process. In particular, ICT technology can be exploited to monitor learners' behaviour during learning activities, for example to identify whether a learner is paying attention to the lecture. This poster presents the functional requirements of a visual tool for the smart classroom, which allows teachers to view and customize the attention monitoring subsystem for each individual student and for the classroom as a whole, in order to improve the educational process. Preliminary usability findings regarding its design are reported, as collected through a cognitive walkthrough evaluation with HCI experts.

Keywords: Smart classroom · Ambient intelligence · Attention monitoring · User interface evaluation · Teacher-friendly UI

1 Introduction

Attention is often considered as a fundamental prerequisite of learning, both within and outside the classroom environment, since it plays a critical role in issues of motivation and engagement. Given that the average class size worldwide is 23 students [17], obtaining and maintaining the students' attention is an important task in classroom management [10], and teachers apply various techniques for this purpose. However, currently only limited technological support is available to monitor attention levels of students and assist teachers in obtaining optimal attention for each classroom activity. The emergence of smart classrooms, where learning activities are enhanced with the use of pervasive computing [13, 14], makes it possible to identify whether a learner is paying attention to the lecture through behavior monitoring.

Despite the fact that an attention-aware smart classroom will be able to identify some cues whether the learners are inattentive or not, the expertise of a human instructor is irreplaceable. Therefore, teachers need to be involved in the customization of classroom monitoring. To this end, this work presents the design of an editor which allows teachers to view and customize: (i) the attention monitoring subsystem and (ii) the intervention mechanism that aims to re-engage students. Preliminary evaluation findings are also reported.

© Springer International Publishing Switzerland 2016
C. Stephanidis (Ed.): HCII 2016 Posters, Part II, CCIS 618, pp. 266–270, 2016.
DOI: 10.1007/978-3-319-40542-1_43

2 Related Work

ICT has become an integral part of modern educational environments with positive benefits [5, 21]. Educators acknowledge its added value in organizing their classroom activities and saving them time [7] to spend on meaningful learning-oriented activities across a range of subjects [18], via various technological applications such as educational games [7, 11] or fully-featured Learning Management Platforms [2, 6, 15], while the physical environment can employ attention-aware artifacts [3] in order to deliver targeted interventions when necessary [1, 4].

Besides classroom management though, ICT has generated monitoring tools which can provide valuable information about the students' learning processes, allowing the identification of difficult or inappropriate learning material, and can therefore significantly contribute to the design of improved student support, including analysis of students' logged behavior to provide information about their learning processes [9], activity classification in classroom discourse [20], and automatic learning styles identification and modelling [8].

All these data however would be worthless without proper visual tools that facilitate their exploration. Therefore, many GUI applications have been developed to simplify classroom management activities such as communication between students and teachers [2], management of learning assets [6, 15], distant learning [19], real-time activity monitoring [16], and on-the-fly creation of educational software [12].

3 Functional Requirements of the GUI Application

The work reported in this article is part of a larger smart classroom suite that incorporates the necessary hardware and software infrastructure to monitor students' behavior and determine their level of attention. The tool under development offers the following facilities: (i) an overview of the attention level of the entire class that could also facilitate focusing on particular students, (ii) a mechanism that asks the teacher's opinion on ambiguous behaviors, (iii) a rule editor that simplifies the formulation of new and the modification of existing rules that signify inattention, (iv) an intervention editor that facilitates the management of the available interventions and the creation of new ones, (v) an intervention-oriented rule editor that controls which intervention should be applied in any given case, and (vi) a control panel through which the teacher can manually override the system's decisions and modify the selected pedagogical activity on demand. In that particular case, the system automatically attempts to identify potential patterns that could support such a decision and request the teacher's confirmation to append them to the active set of rules.

4 Interface Design and Evaluation

A cognitive walkthrough was conducted by three (3) Human Computer Interaction experts in order to uncover any usability errors and identify problems users would have as they try to use the interface using paper prototypes (Figs. 1 and 2 present indicative mockups).

Firstly, the evaluators were asked to browse through the paper prototypes and express their thoughts and questions about the design, while two coordinators were taking notes of their comments. Secondly, they were given a scenario with some tasks to complete and they were asked to follow the Thinking-Aloud protocol and pinpoint any usability-related issues that they identify. Finally, as soon as their comments were consolidated in a single list, they

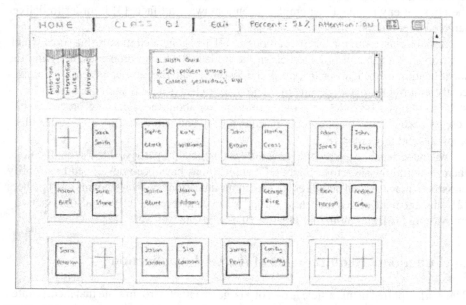

Fig. 1. Paper-based mockup of the classroom overview (including attention-oriented visual cues).

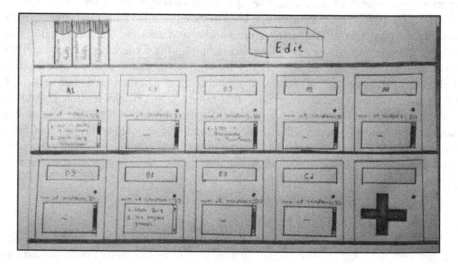

Fig. 2. Paper-based mockup that displays the classes that an individual teacher has under his jurisdiction and the available administrative actions.

were asked to grade them in terms of severity so as to compile a prioritized list with the issues that have to be addressed.

The evaluation process uncovered various problems regarding not only the design of the User Interface, but also regarding the overall concept. The major findings are summarized below:

- The functionality available to the teacher during class hour should be limited to configuring the attention and intervention mechanisms. Other operations could possibly overwhelm the user while they would take over much of the teaching hour. For example, adding students to the class and rearranging their positions should be performed during the teacher's spare time or, even better, a secretary should be responsible for such activities.
- The edit button was used to reveal the delete and add buttons, while the edit screen of an item (e.g., a classroom, a student, a rule) is displayed when clicking on its name, independently of the "edit" button, which affects the consistency and the expected behavior of the visual interface.
- One out of three evaluators thought that the "classroom" metaphor (doors, books, desks, board) that is used throughout the design would be cumbersome for a teacher that uses the system on a daily basis and wants to concentrate on important and time-critical tasks.
- All evaluators pointed out that the lists displaying the rules and interventions should be accompanied by a rich filtering mechanism to assist the educators in finding whatever they want quickly.

5 Conclusions and Future Work

This work presents the preliminary design and evaluation findings regarding a visual tool for the smart classroom, which allows teachers to view and customize the monitoring of attention levels of each individual student and of the classroom as a whole, in order to improve the educational process. The major findings were mostly related to the complexity of the most frequently used screens, and secondly to the metaphors used in the design, suggesting their refinement in order to simplify the interaction paradigm used to execute time-critical or common functions expected to occur on a daily basis and minimize visual clutter.

Future work will aim to refine the design based on the evaluation findings, while a functional prototype is currently being developed in order to be evaluated in-vivo by teachers, educational experts and school students of various ages.

Acknowledgements. This work is supported by the ICS-FORTH internal RTD Programme "Ambient Intelligence".

References

1. Archer, K., et al.: Examining the effectiveness of technology use in classrooms: a tertiary meta-analysis. Comput. Educ. **78**, 140–149 (2014)

2. Beatty, I.D.: Transforming student learning with classroom communication systems. arXiv preprint physics/0508129 (2005)
3. Borner, D., Kalz, M., Specht, M.: Lead me gently: Facilitating knowledge gain through attention-aware ambient learning displays. Comput. Educ. **78**, 10–19 (2014)
4. Cain, J., Black, E.P., Rohr, J.: An audience response system strategy to improve student motivation, attention, and feedback. Am. J. Pharm. Educ. **73**(2), 1 (2009)
5. Chung, C., Ackerman, D.: Student reactions to classroom management technology: learning styles and attitudes toward moodle. J. Educ. Bus. **90**(4), 217–223 (2015)
6. Cole, J., Foster, H.: Using Moodle: Teaching with the Popular Open Source Course Management System. O'Reilly Media, Inc., Sebastopo (2007)
7. Donnelly, D., McGarr, O., O'Reilly, J.: A framework for teachers' integration of ICT into their classroom practice. Comput. Educ. **57**(2), 1469–1483 (2011)
8. Graf, S., Liu, T.-C.: Supporting teachers in identifying students' learning styles in learning management systems: an automatic student modelling approach. J. Educ. Technol. Soc. **12**(4), 3 (2009)
9. Graf, S., et al.: AAT: a tool for accessing and analysing students' behaviour data in learning systems. In: Proceedings of the 1st International Conference on Learning Analytics and Knowledge. ACM (2011)
10. Grossman, H.: Classroom Behavior Management for Diverse and Inclusive Schools. Rowman & Littlefield Publishers, Toronto (2003)
11. Korozi, M., et al.: Ambient educational mini-games. In: Proceedings of the International Working Conference on Advanced Visual Interfaces. ACM (2012)
12. Lee, Y.-J.: Empowering teachers to create educational software: a constructivist approach utilizing Etoys, pair programming and cognitive apprenticeship. Comput. Educ. **56**(2), 527–538 (2011)
13. Leonidis, A., et al.: A glimpse into the ambient classroom. Bull. IEEE Tech. Committee Learn. Technol. **14**(4), 3 (2012)
14. Leonidis, A., Antona, M., Stephanidis, C.: Enabling programmability of smart learning environments by teachers. In: Streitz, N., Markopoulos, P. (eds.) DAPI 2015. LNCS, vol. 9189, pp. 62–73. Springer, Heidelberg (2015)
15. Loving, M., Ochoa, M.: Facebook as a classroom management solution. New Library World **112**(3/4), 121–130 (2011)
16. Mathioudakis, G., Leonidis, A., Korozi, M., Margetis, G., Ntoa, S., Antona, M., Stephanidis, C.: AmI-RIA: real-time teacher assistance tool for an ambient intelligence classroom. In the Proceedings of the 5th International Conference on Mobile, Hybrid, and On-line Learning (eLmL 2013), Nice, France, 24 February–1 March, pp. 37–42 (2013)
17. Organization for Economic Co-Operation and Development (OECD). Education Indication in Focus – September 2012 (2012b)
18. Sutherland, R., et al.: Transforming teaching and learning: embedding ICT into everyday classroom practices. J. Comput. Assist. Learn. **20**(6), 413–425 (2004)
19. Turoff, M., Hiltz, S.R.: Software design and the future of the virtual classroom®. J. Inf. Technol. Teacher Educ. **4**(2), 197–215 (1995)
20. Wang, Z., et al.: Automatic classification of activities in classroom discourse. Comput. Educ. **78**, 115–123 (2014)
21. Wood, D., Underwood, J., Avis, P.: Integrated learning systems in the classroom. Comput. Educ. **33**(2), 91–108 (1999)

The Development of a Game-Based Storytelling Support System that Incorporates Creative Activity and Motion Control

Hiroshi Suzuki(✉) and Hisashi Sato

Information Media, Kanagawa Institute of Technology, Atsugi, Japan
{hsuzuki,sato}@ic.kanagawa-itac.jp

Abstract. In previous studies, we developed the Shadow Robot System, which makes use of papercraft models. So far, we have carried out workshops using this system at science museums across Japan. The system receives very favorable reviews from participants. However, these workshops have been unable to provide the collaborative work that is one of the key merits of a workshop setting. In response to this challenge, we extended the Shadow Robot System in this study to create a storytelling system. In this system, children are encouraged to work collaboratively to craft their own stories. The system serves to support children's story telling ability. In this paper, we first describe the details of the system we developed, and then explain the effects of the system on the children we observed during the course of our workshops.

Keywords: Papercraft · Children · Drawing · Storytelling · Video games

1 Introduction

The author's previous work includes the development of the Shadow Robot System [1], which incorporates experiential games and papercraft models, as well as the implementation of the system through events at various educational institutions. The Shadow Robot System allows children to design the texture (i.e. surface design) of a robot by drawing on a papercraft schematic. Moreover, by incorporating these designed robots as characters in a video game, we were able to harness the appeal of games to encourage children to actively participate in the creative process of papercraft modeling.

While events using this system received a favorable reception from participating children, the activities were limited individual tasks such as drawing, participating in video games, and creating papercraft models. As a result, the system failed to take advantage of the potential for teamwork and that is inherent in a group event. To remedy this issue, we attempted to develop a storytelling extension to the Shadow Robot System that allows children to create stories through a collaborative process and helps participants to explain them to each other.

Storytelling is defined as the process of creating original stories and communicating them to others [2]. This process is thought to be effective in promoting language development, organizational ability, and imaginative ability in children. The traditional

© Springer International Publishing Switzerland 2016
C. Stephanidis (Ed.): HCII 2016 Posters, Part II, CCIS 618, pp. 271–276, 2016.
DOI: 10.1007/978-3-319-40542-1_44

storytelling process often uses physical objects such as puppets, dolls, or characters drawn on paper as stand-ins for the characters in the story. The description of the characters is one of the fundamental ingredients of a story, and the system that we developed divides the tasks that are necessary to create a story including the creation of the protagonist, antagonist, and setting, among a group of children.

2   Related Research

There have been a number of previous efforts to use ICT in a storytelling system, and these efforts have approached the problem using a variety of forms. In the Zootown [3] system, children place animal-shaped robots on a projection-capable table and manipulate movements such as walking and turning their necks. By projecting images onto the table that match a story, the system aims to spark the creation of new stories. In the Gentoro [4] system, a handheld projector is used to project a field onto a physical space. The story is performed on the projected image through the control of robots.

Kidpad [5] seeks to create a collaborative storytelling environment by using hyperlinks to connect dialogue with pictures drawn by participating children. Similarly, FeTe2 [6] makes it possible to create stories through network access to a virtual world. Jabberstamp [7] allows children to associate recorded dialogue with their own drawings, helping to create stories through the process of making the drawings.

The Story Mat [9] system uses a mat that displays interactive images. Children manipulate toys on top of the mat and can record the movements or dialogue to create a story. Additionally, children are able to play/edit the stories created by other children.

The primary difference between our system and those described above is the fact that we employ the design of videogame characters as a way to provide subject matter for the creation of new stories. While systems such as Kidpad [5] and Jabberstamp [7] are centered around drawing and attempt to support children's story-making endeavors in this way, our study seeks to provide children with a storytelling framework within which we encourage the children to exercise their creativity. Similarly, while systems such as Zootown [3] and Gentoro [4] provide a storytelling framework, these systems place robots within a physical space whereas our system is based on the virtual space of a videogame.

3   System Overview

By extending the Shadow Robot System to a storytelling context, we developed a system that we call the Shadow Robot System for Storytelling (SRSS). A schematic overview of the system is shown in Fig. 1. First, the children draw designs onto six papercraft schematic pages depicting elements such as the protagonist, antagonist, and buildings, while at the same time describing the scene or overall story with text. Next, the schematic pages are read into a computer using a scanner, and the appropriate sections are extracted as textures. In the game, these textures are placed onto pre-made 3D models to create the original characters. By taking screenshots during the game, the children are able to assemble the various scenes of the story that they created. At the end of the game, these screenshots are assembled together and outputted as a single story paper. We expected that the children would use this story paper to explain the stories they created.

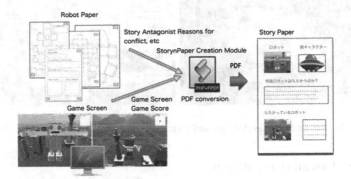

Fig. 1. Schematic overview of the SRSS system

4 Storytelling Workshops

4.1 Workshop Overview

We implemented a series of storytelling workshops using this system. The workshops were carried out on May 2nd and 5th, 2015, at the main branch of the Mitsukoshi Department Store as part of the workshop event titled "Play in the Future With Toshiba: Fight! Shadow Robots, Story-Making Edition." Each workshop lasted approximately 60 min and was held once a day. Each event accommodated 12 participants, for a total of 24 participants. Because the event was somewhat shorter than is the norm for such events, we anticipated that it could be difficult for the children to finish their stories within the allotted time. Therefore, we assigned one staff member to assist each group of three children. We administered a post-workshop survey to determine participant responses.

4.2 Workshop Execution

Once the workshop commenced, a supporting staff member directed the discussion among the children in each group to decide on the details of the protagonist and other characters that would appear in the videogame. Figure 2 shows pictures taken during the workshop. Once the story was decided upon, the support staff were put in charge of writing the text in the space reserved for describing the story while the children were put in charge of designing the robot and antagonist. While there was some variation in timing between groups, finishing all of the schematic pages took approximately 35–40 min. Once the schematics were scanned into the computer, the children took part in the game with great enthusiasm. Moreover, after the conclusion of the game, we observed the children reading the story papers and trading thoughts on the robots or characters that they created.

Fig. 2. Scenes from the workshops and Examples of story papers created by children

4.3 Survey Execution and Results

We collected information about the participants as well as impressions about the event after the workshop ended. The survey questions and results are shown in Table 1.

Table 1. Survey questions and results collected at the end of the workshop

	Question	Yes	No	Neither
Q1	Have you previously played a game using a computer?	100 %	0 %	0 %
Q2	Have you previously played games where you can control motionusing your body, such as with the Kinect or Wii?	67 %	33 %	0 %
Q3	Have you participated in storytelling before?	47 %	53 %	0 %
Q4	Did you have fun during today's workshop?	87 %	7 %	7 %
Q5	Please score your enjoyment of these activities on a scale of 1–5 (where 1 means the activity was boring and 5 means it was fun)	Score		
Q5-1	The game that you could control with your body	67		
Q5-2	Thinking up a story	60		
Q5-3	Designing the robot and the enemies	66		
Q5-4	Making things together with your friends	56		
Q5-5	Having the robots that you made appear in the game	64		

We obtained 15 survey responses, of which 11 were boys and 4 were girls. The average age of the respondents was 8.73 years.

From the questions asking about previous experience with computer games, we learned that all of the respondents had experience using some variety of computer-based game. The proportion of those who had experience with games that incorporate motion control, however, was around 70 %. Furthermore, the proportion of those who had no experience in story-making games was approximately 50 %. 90 % of the respondents stated that they enjoyed the workshop. Respondents were asked to name specific activities that they enjoyed in survey question 5, and the results are shown in Table 1. These results revealed that the survey respondents most strongly enjoyed the activity wherein they used their bodies to control the motion of the game.

5   Discussion

We can conclude from survey questions 4 and 5 that, while the participants in our workshop enjoyed the activities, the main reason for this was the motion control aspect of the game. This result confirms those obtained from our previous studies of the Shadow Robot System, which forms the basis of our current system, and shows that the opportunity to participate in the game is a motivating factor for the children. Moreover, the fact that an equivalent amount of enjoyment seems to have been derived from the ability to freely design the robots and have the robots appear in the game is also consistent with our results from the Shadow Robot System. On the other hand, the lowest levels of enjoyment were indicated for the collaborative nature of the activities, which is an important characteristic of the workshop we designed for this study. It is possible that this is due to the fact that the overwhelming proportion of the children that participated in our workshop were meeting each other for the first time, and consequently they were unable to carry out adequate discussions with their group members. This inability to express their opinions to a satisfactory extent may have caused them to become unsatisfied with the collaborative activities themselves. However, the responses to question 5–2 do not show a pronounced decline in enjoyment, and some of the responses to the open-ended questions identified the process of creating the stories as a reason for their enjoyment. Furthermore, we observed the children reading their story papers after the conclusion of the game, and it appeared that they were happy with the stories they had created. These results suggest that the system we developed is effective in helping to foster storytelling in children.

6   Conclusions and Future Work

In this study, we developed the SRSS as a proactive method of stimulating the collaborative activities that are characteristic of the workshop setting.

The storytelling workshops that we implemented using this system were rated highly by the participants with regards to the gaming system, as was the case with the Shadow Robot System. Furthermore, we learned that the participating children were able to have fun while engaging in the storytelling process. However, with regards to the question of whether we were able to accomplish the core aim of encouraging collaborative activities among the participants, there are a number of areas that require improvement.

While the workshops that we implemented brought together children who had largely never met each other before and directed them to engage in the storytelling process by deciding on the characters that appear in the games as well as their backstories, it was difficult to accomplish all of these tasks in the relatively short time (60 min) that was available. Therefore, it is important in future iterations to set aside time for the children to introduce themselves to each other and to break the ice so as to make the collaborative activities easier.

The act of storytelling through the video game itself was quite popular with the participants overall. Therefore, the improvements described above are likely to result in an even more effective storytelling workshop.

References

1. Susuki, H., Sato, H., Hayami, H.: The development of a 3D gaming system that motivates children to participate in papercraft modeling. Inf. Process. Soc. Jpn. Tech. Rep. **3**(1), 10–19 (2015)
2. Sato, T.: Development of software that supports young children's narrative productions. Jpn. J. Edu. Tech. **32**(1), 33–42 (2008)
3. Horiuchi, N., Hoshino, J.: The animal robot activates infantile storytelling. Information Processing Society of Japan Technical Reports, vol. 2012-HCI147, no. 17, pp. 1–6 (2012)
4. Toshitaka, I., Nguyen, T.N., Sugimoto, M., Inagaki, S.: Gentoro: a system for supporting children's storytelling using handheld projectors and a robot. Int. Conf. Interact. Des. Child. **50**(12), 2819–2830 (2009)
5. Hourcade, J.P., Bederson, B.B., Druin, A., Taxen, G.: KidPad: collaborative storytelling for children. In: Proceedings of CHI 2002 Extended Abstracts, Minneapolis, WI, pp. 500–501 (2002)
6. Garzotto, F., Forfori, M.: FaTe2: storytelling edutainment experiences in 2D and 3D collaborative spaces. In: Proceedings of IDC 2006, Tampere, Finland, pp. 113–116 (2006)
7. Raffle, H., Vaucelle, C., Wang, R., Ishii, H.: Jabberstamp: embedding sound and voice in traditional drawings. In: Proceedings of IDC 2007, Aalborg, Denmark, pp. 137–144 (2007)
8. Bobick, A.F., Intille, S.S., Davis, J.W., Baird, F., Pinhanez, C.S., Campbell, L.W., Ivanov, Y.A., Schutte, A., Wilson, A.: The KidsRoom: a perceptually-based interactive and immersive story environment. Presence: Teleoperators Virt. Environ. **8**(4), 369–393 (1999)
9. Ryokai, K., Cassel, J.: StoryMat: a play space with narrative memories. In: Proceedings of CHI 1999, Pittsburgh, PA, pp. 272–273 (1999)

Eye Movements of Hearing Impaired Students in Self-practice to Learn How to Use Graphic Software

Takuya Suzuki[1,2(✉)], Makoto Kobayashi[1], and Yuji Nagashima[2]

[1] Tsukuba University of Technology, Tsukuba City, Ibaraki, Japan
suzukit@a.tsukuba-tech.ac.jp, koba@cs.k.tsukuba-tech.ac.jp
[2] Kogakuin University, Shinjuku-ku, Tokyo, Japan
nagasima@cc.kogakuin.ac.jp

Abstract. This study investigates where hearing impaired students see when they try to learn how to use graphical drawing software with subtitled educational video material in case of self-practice situation. An experiment was conducted to ten students with hearing impaired using eye tracking system. The data from the system showed that students who needs more time to learn it had tendency to consume long time to read explaining subtitles in the video material and it causes to miss out to see important operation.

Keywords: Eye movement · Hearing impaired students · Self-practice

1 Introduction

The first author and the second author are teaching staff of a special university for students who have a visual impairment or a hearing impairment. The university has a department of synthetic design which is only for hearing impaired students including deaf students. When a teacher of this department conducts a lecture to these students, the teacher uses a sign language, subtitled educational materials, and communication tools such as a whiteboard or a chatting software in usual case. If the teacher is part-time staff or does not have enough skill of sign language, a subtitle translation service will be provided. Such educational techniques are useful and effective for our students with hearing impairment to study.

However, in practical lectures such as teaching how to use a computer software or how to draw a picture, sign language and subtitle translation service are not so effective compare with using them in other normal classes. For example, when a teacher explain a difficult part of how to use a software with showing a model operation, the teacher encounters a problem. At first, he/she cannot produce his/her own sign language and the computer operation at a same time. Second, students cannot see the model operation and the explaining sign language or subtitle sentences simultaneously if they will have translation services. They should see them alternately. Third, these translation has time delay even in the highest quality service and it confuses the explanation with showing the model operation because the sign or subtitle describes slightly before operation.

To solve the problem mentioned above, we developed a teaching support software called "SynchroniZed Key points Indication Tool: SZKIT" [1, 2]. The software is

C. Stephanidis (Ed.): HCII 2016 Posters, Part II, CCIS 618, pp. 277–281, 2016.
DOI: 10.1007/978-3-319-40542-1_45

composed of icons and a subtitle text window, and basically it always exists around a mouse cursor to avoid eye motion between a position of the subtitle and the model operation. These icons represent a mouse and modifier keys. They will appear when a teacher clicks a mouse button or presses modifier keys so that students can understand when the teacher clicks a mouse button or presses a key. For example, an icon of mouse with colored left button and an icon of shift-key and alt-key appear around the mouse cursor when the teacher clicks left mouse button with pressing a shift-key and an alt-kay. If the teacher makes a dragging action after that, these icons are kept to be displayed and students can understand the teacher keeps to pressing the mouse button and the shift-key. Figure 1 shows appearance of SZKIT in example described above. Addition to it, the subtitle text window shows explanation of the operation by sentences. The explanation texts are prepared in advance and are changed by the teacher arbitrarily. Hence it is not a translation software and there is no time delay.

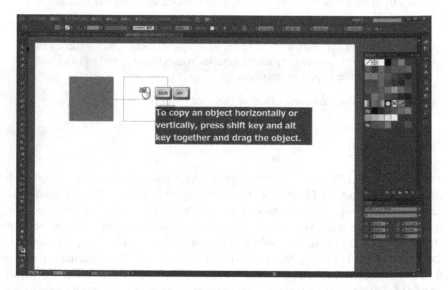

Fig. 1. Appearance of Synchronized Key points Indication Tool: SZKIT

Moreover, using SZKIT in practical lectures has another important advantage. That is every teacher can make a subtitled educational video material without any difficulty, by just recording a desktop of a computer during the lecture. The first author uses SZKIT in his class in which students learn how to use an "Adobe Illustrator," and record his operation during the lecture to make video materials. The produced video are used for revising in self-practice by students who could not understand the contents of the lecture. Nevertheless such a revising, it was clear that some students had difficulty to understand new technique of Illustrator. Therefore, we decided to investigate where the students see when they learn new technique by the revising video by recording eye movement.

2   Experimental Procedure

Experimental circumstance was computer with dual display. One of them is for operation by subjects and the other display is for video material that explain how to use an Illustrator. This circumstance is a usual setting of the practical lecture in our university and that is the reason why we prepared them. The number of participated students who has hearing impairment is ten. The experimental procedure with which these subjects tried to do is as follows.

At first, these subjects watched a video material continuously without returning to the same segment. The material was made with SZKIT which adds subtitles around a mouse cursor. The purpose of this procedure is that we would like to observe how students see the model operation and how they make their own operation in passive studying. After that, they took an examination to clear where the point they cannot understand well was. Next to the examination, they watched the same video material again and in this time they were allowed to return to any segment they wanted, to observe where they see in active studying. During both experimental procedures, the eye movement data in the display for video material were recorded by the eye tracking system in front of them and the operating sequences were recorded by a desktop capture software and the position of mouse pointer is considered as eye focusing point if it moves (Fig. 2).

Fig. 2. Experimental circumstance for watching eye movement of hearing impaired students when they tried to study how to use an Illustrator.

3   Results and Consideration

The result data from eye tracking system showed that some students who had a difficulty to learn tend to take more time to read explanation subtitles than to see model operation and it causes to miss out to see important operation in the video material.

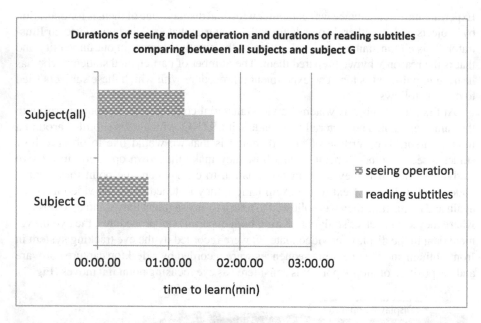

Fig. 3. Durations of seeing model operation and durations of reading subtitles comparing between all subjects and subject G.

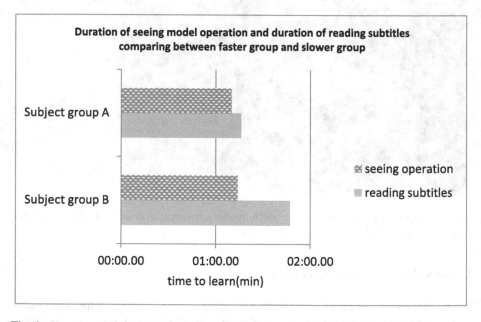

Fig. 4. Duration of seeing model operation and duration of reading subtitles comparing between faster group and slower group.

Figure 3 shows average durations of all subjects and one subject named G, who needed more time to acquire the new skill and who marked lower score in the examination compare with other subjects. In this graph, upper graphs represent durations of seeing the model operation and lower graphs represent durations of reading subtitles in the text window of SZKIT. The average time shows that all of them needed more time to read subtitles though, the subject G marked especially long time to read subtitles and the duration to see the model operation is short. The same tendency was able to be seen in other subject who needed more time to learn.

Figure 4 also shows average durations of seeing model operation and reading subtitles by two groups. Members of group A are students who took less than 10 min to acquire the skill and members of group B are students who took more than 10 min. The number of the group A is three and the number of the group B is seven. By this graph, it is clear that slower members took more time to read subtitles.

References

1. Kobayashi, M., Suzuki, T., Wakatsuki, D.: Teaching support software for hearing impaired students who study computer operation - SynchroniZed Key Points Indication Tool: SZKIT. In: Miesenberger, K., Karshmer, A., Penaz, P., Zagler, W. (eds.) ICCHP 2012, Part I. LNCS, vol. 7382, pp. 10–17. Springer, Heidelberg (2012)
2. Suzuki, T., Wakatsuki, D., Kobayashi, M.: Effects of SZKIT in the designing software lecture for hearing impaired students. In: Proceedings of Universal Learning Design International Conference 2013, pp. 57–63 (2013)

How to Teach Young Kids New Concepts with Interactive Videos and Visual Recognition

Quan H. To, Ba-Huu Tran[✉], and Minh-Triet Tran

Faculty of Information Technology, University of Science, VNU-HCM,
Ho Chi Minh City, Vietnam
{thquan,tbhuu}@apcs.vn, tmtriet@fit.hcmus.edu.vn

Abstract. Advances in modern computing technology have enabled a wide variety of applications in many areas. Realizing that mobile devices such as smartphones and tablets are great learning platforms for educating young children, the authors create an interactive system that helps young kids learn new concepts via videos. By allowing kids to choose objects in the video that they are watching, the system provides relevant information about those objects. It has the effect of enhancing young kids' understanding about new concepts in the video. The system employs Cross-based Local Multipoint Filtering (CLMF) for object selection and Support Vector Machine (SVM) for recognition. Experimental results show that our system has achieved 95 % recognition accuracy.

Keywords: Learning platform · Educational technology · Interactive system · Visual recognition · Human computer interaction

1 Introduction

Getting to know the world around them is essential to young kids' mental development, especially in the early years [9]. During this critical period, young kids learn new concepts (such as toys, animals, flowers...) in many ways. They observe the scenery, read picture books and listen to stories told by their parents, watch videos... As a result, there are various means of education to enrich kids' understanding of the world. One of the most popular means to educate kids is by using printed or digital books, because books can capture children's attention with beautiful pictures. The authors explore a way to enhance the interaction between young kids and the teaching materials, as well as to get them more engaged, thereby helping kids learn more effectively.

In this paper, we propose an innovative and interactive system for young kids to learn new concepts on mobile devices, such as tablets and smartphones. This system enables young kids to interact with the videos that show different concepts and objects in the real world. Videos can easily capture children's attention via motions, sounds, and colors. Another advantage of using videos is that it can teach kids about the context of each concept; e.g. animals live in their natural habitats, food is made in the kitchen...

When kids watch a video, they see many interesting things and would want to know more about them. To learn about a certain object in the video, they simply draw a loose boundary around that object. Our system would automatically highlight that object

C. Stephanidis (Ed.): HCII 2016 Posters, Part II, CCIS 618, pp. 282–286, 2016.
DOI: 10.1007/978-3-319-40542-1_46

around its natural border, instead of using the traditional rectangular bounding box, which may include the background and minor artifacts. The background and minor artifacts may not be what kids want to learn about and could confuse or distract them. The system accomplishes this task by using the CLMF algorithm. CLMF helps identify the main object appearing in the selected area. As a result, the system can get an appropriate shape of that object. This allows young kids to know the real shape of the object that they wish to learn about.

Next, the system employs recognition algorithm to recognize the object bounded by its natural border. By removing the background and irrelevant artifacts that might appear near the object of interest, the authors can enhance the accuracy of object recognition. After that, the system displays the name of the highlighted object. It can also provide relevant information such as songs, stories, videos... about that object.

The main contributions of our paper are as follow:

- First, we propose an idea and implement the system on mobile devices to teach young kids new concepts via interacting with objects in video.
- Second, we propose using CLMF to determine the natural border corresponding to the actual shape of an object (animals, toys, trees...) that appears in the region of interest. This way, young kids can know exactly the actual shape of the object.
- Third, by removing irrelevant information in the region selected by young kids and keeping only the main object itself, we can enhance the accuracy of object recognition. Therefore, we can provide relevant information about that object to the young kids.

2   Related Works

2.1   Cross-Based Local Multipoint Filtering (CLMF) [1]

Edge-aware filtering (EAF) techniques are widely used in many areas of image processing. Two of the most popular EAF processes are bilateral filter (BF) [2] and guided filter (GF) [3]. However, both of them have their own weaknesses. For example, BF produces staircase effect and gradient reversal artifacts while GF generates undesired fuzzy boundary. CLMF could overcome the weaknesses of both BF and GF. Therefore it emerged as a better alternative because of its fast performance and high quality.

2.2   Bag-of-Words Model

Usually, hand-crafted descriptors such as SIFT [4], SURF [5] are used to represent object's local features. The extracted features are then clustered to build the visual vocabulary. In the Bag-of-Words model, objects are represented by a histogram of quantized local features, i.e. the frequencies of the visual words [6, 7]. After all the description vectors have been computed, they serve as the training examples for the Support Vector Machine (SVM). Finally, the SVM model returns the label of the object we want to classify. The Bag-of-Words model has been used extensively in computer vision to solve a wide variety of recognition problems with remarkable results.

3   Proposed System

3.1   Overview

Figure 1 illustrates the overview of the whole system. First, young kids simply open the application on a mobile device and choose an arbitrary video that they want to watch. The video shows wonderful things that exist in this world. Naturally, the kids would love to know more information about various objects that they see in the video. We enhance the interactivity of the video by letting the kids select any object within that video. To do that, they simply use their fingers to draw a free closed shape around that object. Our system will automatically identify the region in which the kids are interested; and then show a natural border around the interested object. With this, the young kids would be excited because the object of interest is highlighted with a natural border that closely corresponds to its actual shape in reality. Additionally, the object is extracted without unnecessary background and irrelevant artifacts, i.e. minor objects that is not of the kids' interest. The system then classifies the chosen object using an object classification module. The output of this module is the label of the class to which this object belongs. Finally, the system provide appropriate augmented information on screen. The augmented information could be in different formats; including texts, 3D models, video clips, audio clips, web pages...

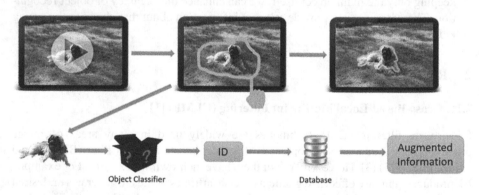

Fig. 1. Overview of our proposed system

3.2   Determining the Natural Border of an Object

Figure 2 represents how the system can approximate the natural border of an object. After the kids have drawn the free closed boundary around the object, the area inside this boundary forms the region of interest. The region of interest is used to create a binary mask. However, this binary mask is not well-aligned with the natural border of the object that the kids choose. As a result, we apply CLMF to transform the binary mask. CLMF uses the original image to guide the process of turning the mask into a shape that aligns more closely with the chosen object. After this process, the binary mask now looks like the object that the kids are interested in. Finally, the system uses the resulting mask to highlight the object in the frame, as well as to extract the object for classification.

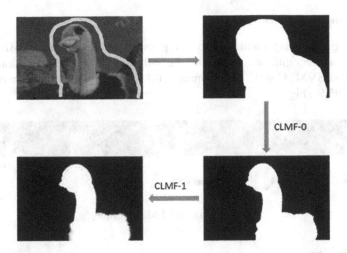

Fig. 2. Approximating object's natural border with pre-drawn boundary and CLMF

3.3 Object Classification with Support Vector Machine

Dense-SIFT features and Bag-of-Words model are used to represent the objects produced by CLMF algorithm. The authors employ multi-class Support Vector Machine (SVM) for object classification. SVM is a popular supervised learning model. The set of training examples is fed into the SVM. Each example is represented as a point in space and is marked as either positive or negative. SVM aims to solve the problem of finding a hyperplane that separates the positive and negative examples by a margin that is as wide as possible. New examples are then classified as belonging to one category or the other. By combining multiple two-class SVMs, we obtain a multi-class SVM that can recognize many types of object [8].

4 Experiment

4.1 Experiment Setup

To demonstrate the use of CLMF algorithm, the authors perform experiment on a set of five images with pre-drawn boundary. CLMF would determine the border of the object so that it is as close to the shape of the object as possible.

In the next part of the experiment, five short videos about several objects are selected for visual recognition. In each video, 10 frames are sampled and divided equally for the training and testing sets. There are 5 object classes, which are giraffe, cheetah, elephant, squirrel, and bird. The training set is fed into the SVM as examples. The authors then measure recognition accuracy on the testing set.

4.2 Experiment Results

Here is the original images and corresponding results when applying CLMF:

In the visual recognition experiment, the authors set the following parameters for the multi-class SVM: C = 0.2 and Gamma = 0.15. The system achieves a recognition accuracy of **95** % (Fig. 3).

Fig. 3. Results of CLMF algorithm

5 Conclusion

In this paper, we propose a system to help kids learn new concepts via interactive videos. Young kids can draw a boundary around an object in the video to know more about it. By highlighting the object around its natural border, we can increase both kids' perception of the object; as well as the accuracy of object recognition. The system aims to educate and enrich young children's understanding of the world around them.

Acknowledgement. This research is supported by research funding from Advanced Program in Computer Science, University of Science, Vietnam National University - Ho Chi Minh City.

References

1. Lu, J., Shi, K., Min, D., Lin, L., Do, M.N.: Cross-based local multipoint filtering. In: CVPR (2012)
2. Tomasi, C., Manduchi, R.: Bilateral filtering for gray and color images. In: ICCV (1998)
3. He, K., Sun, J., Tang, X.: Guided image filtering. In: Daniilidis, K., Maragos, P., Paragios, N. (eds.) ECCV 2010, Part I. LNCS, vol. 6311, pp. 1–14. Springer, Heidelberg (2010)
4. Lowe, D.: Distinctive image features from scale-invariant keypoints. IJCV **60**, 91–110 (2014)
5. Bay, H., Tuytelaars, T., Van Gool, L.: SURF: speeded up robust features. In: Leonardis, A., Bischof, H., Pinz, A. (eds.) ECCV 2006, Part I. LNCS, vol. 3951, pp. 404–417. Springer, Heidelberg (2006)
6. Sivic, J., Zisserman, A.: Video google: a text retrieval approach to object matching in videos. In: International Conference on Computer Vision (2003)
7. Chatfield, K., Lempitsky, V., Vedaldi, A., Zisserman, A.: The devil is in the details: an evaluation of recent feature encoding methods. In: BMVC (2011)
8. Weston, J., Watkins, C.: Support vector machines for multi-class pattern recognition. In: ESANN (1999)
9. Shonkoff, P.: From neurons to neighborhoods: the science of early childhood development (2000)

Mobile Assisted Language Learning Applications for Health Care Sciences Students: A User Experience Study

Ilana Wilken[1,2(✉)], Febe de Wet[1], and Elsabé Taljard[2]

[1] Human Language Technology Research Group, Meraka Institute, CSIR,
Pretoria, South Africa
{iwilken,fdwet}@csir.co.za
[2] Department of African Languages, University of Pretoria,
Pretoria, South Africa
elsabe.taljard@up.ac.za

Abstract. South Africa has 11 official languages and speakers of different languages communicate with each other on a daily basis, especially at hospitals and clinics. Sometimes it is difficult for a patient to find a health professional that speaks a language he/she understands. The University of Pretoria addresses potential language barriers in the health care professions by teaching students from the Faculty of Health Care Sciences Sepedi as an additional language. This study aimed to assist the university in its endeavor, by providing students enrolled for the Sepedi language module with three custom-designed Sepedi mobile assisted language learning (MALL) applications to be used as supplementary tools for their studies. The students used the applications over nine weeks after which they completed a questionnaire. The questionnaire was used to determine if the students thought the applications were useful and whether or not they had a clear preference for one application in particular.

Keywords: Mobile assisted language learning · Sepedi · User experience · Health care sciences

1 Introduction and Contextualization

South Africa is a multilingual country with 11 official languages. The country's language diversity does not occur in only one part of the country or affect only a specific section of the population. It has an impact on everyone in South Africa, particularly when people want to have a conversation in their first language or if they wish to have a conversation with someone with whom they do not share a language. The health-care sector in South Africa is one area where the country's language diversity and the associated communication barriers are especially difficult to cope with.

South Africa's health-care sector can be divided into three levels, namely clinics and Level 1 hospitals (district), Level 2 hospitals (regional) and Level 3 hospitals (central) [1]. The structure of the health-care sector provides clinical care that increases in terms of speciality and intensity according to level [1]. The ideal is that patients first visit a

© Springer International Publishing Switzerland 2016
C. Stephanidis (Ed.): HCII 2016 Posters, Part II, CCIS 618, pp. 287–292, 2016.
DOI: 10.1007/978-3-319-40542-1_47

district hospital or clinic before they visit a regional hospital, but many patients do not adhere to this process due to weaknesses in the referral system and limited hospital coverage in their area [1]. Many South Africans living in rural areas only have access to district hospitals [2] and due to the location of the hospitals, the patients generally speak the language spoken by the communities in the area.

New medical graduates are required to complete a mandatory period of community service and they are mostly assigned to hospitals and clinics in remote areas [3]. When studying, the health professionals live in cities or large towns, where most of the universities offering qualifications in the health care sciences are situated [4] and where the language of instruction is English [5]. Because of this situation, a communication barrier often exists between the patients and the health professionals and only a few professionals are able to speak their patients' languages.

A number of South African universities have taken note of the communication barrier and try to address it by teaching students in the health care sciences an additional language. The language taught is the language spoken by the majority of the patients in a specific area and forms part of the course curriculum. A section of the language modules focuses on the acquisition of basic communicative skills in the target language, including everyday expressions as well as high frequency vocabulary for everyday clinical situations. After achieving the outcomes of the modules, students are able to engage with patients to either retrieve information from patients or to communicate information to patients.

The learning of a new language consists of a combination of specific language subsystems, including grammar, phonology and vocabulary [6]. Vocabulary is of vital importance when learning a new language, but it often gets neglected and more focus is placed on grammar and phonology [6]. Due to time constraints during lectures, it is not always possible for lecturers to focus on vocabulary acquisition and students are often expected to learn vocabulary in their own time. Because vocabulary forms such an important part of language acquisition, a different approach is needed to assist students with learning vocabulary.

2 Application Design and Development

This study aims to assist students with their vocabulary acquisition by offering three mobile assisted language learning (MALL) applications that focus solely on vocabulary acquisition. The study was conducted at the University of Pretoria where the health care science students enroll for a Sepedi[1] module in their second year of studies.

The applications were designed, developed and evaluated in an attempt to determine whether or not students perceive them as being useful in acquiring vocabulary and if they have a clear preference for a specific MALL application.

---

[1] Sepedi (also known as Northern Sotho) is one of the regional languages spoken in the Pretoria area and the Limpopo province. It belongs to the Sotho language group, and is mutually intelligible with Tswana and Southern Sotho, the other two members of the Sotho group.

2.1   Applications Design

The three MALL applications are:

- Silent (vocabulary acquisition with text and graphics only)
- Listen (vocabulary acquisition with text, graphics and pre-recorded audio clips)
- Speak (vocabulary acquisition with text, graphics, pre-recorded audio clips and record-and-playback)

The three applications share basic functionalities, but each application can be seen as an application on its own. This offers students a variety in vocabulary learning tools. The design also aimed to determine if the students prefer using a specific application and the reason(s) behind their choice, should there be any.

2.2   Applications Functional Description

The Silent application is the application with the most basic functionality. The Listen application is an extension of the Silent application and plays an example pronunciation of the target word. The Speak application is an extension of the Silent and Listen applications and offers users a chance to record and listen to their own pronunciations of the target word. A summary of the functionalities of all three applications is shown in Fig. 1.

Silent Application. The user is given an English word (question), a matching picture and three Sepedi words (possible answers). One of the possible answers in Sepedi is the correct translation (answer) of the English word. The user has two attempts to choose the correct answer. If the user answers correctly, the answer is displayed on the screen and he/she can proceed to the next question. If the user fails to answer correctly on the first attempt, a message is displayed prompting another attempt. If, after two attempts, the user has still not chosen the correct answer, the correct answer is shown and the user can proceed to the next question.

Listen Application. The Listen application shares the Silent application's functionalities, but when the user answers correctly, a pre-recorded audio version of the answer is played along with the answer displayed on the screen. Users can listen to the pronunciation as many times as they like before moving on to the next question. If the user does not choose the correct answer after two attempts, the answer is shown on the screen and the pre-recorded audio version of the answer is played. Users can then also listen to the pronunciation as many times as they like before moving on to the next question.

Speak Application. The Speak application shares the Listen application's functionalities. When the user answers correctly, the pre-recorded audio version of the answer is played. They may listen to it as many times as they like. The user then has to record his/her pronunciation of the answer and listen to it, before they can move on to the next question. If the user still does not choose the correct answer after two attempts, the audio version of the answer is played and again they have to record their own pronunciation of the answer and listen to it before moving on to the next question.

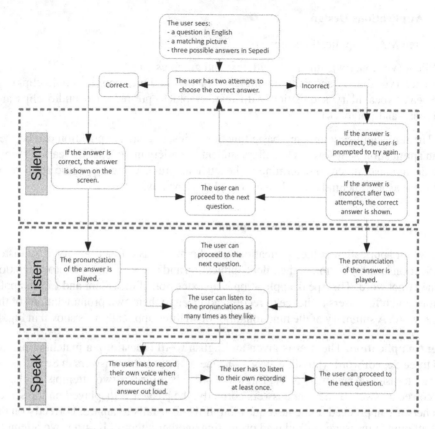

Fig. 1. Functional description of the three applications

2.3 Applications Development

The applications were designed and developed for mobile devices running version 4 and later of the Android operating system and were developed in collaboration with Geckotech[2], a software development company. The devices used in the study are Asus Google Nexus 7 tablets.

3 Evaluation of the Applications

Eighty health care sciences students from the University of Pretoria were enrolled for a Sepedi module in the second semester of 2015. They were identified as ideal candidates to evaluate the applications. However, only 36 students volunteered to participate in the study.

---

[2] http://www.geckotech.nl.

3.1 Intervention

The students had weekly scheduled lectures for the Sepedi module. During the last 30 min the students used the applications at random and completed as many lessons on the applications as possible.

Due to unforeseen circumstances, only five sessions with the students over a period of nine weeks could take place. At the end of the intervention, 20 students had used each application at least once and completed a questionnaire on their experience with the applications.

3.2 Results

The students had a largely positive experience with the applications, with 80 % thinking the applications were very easy to use and 40 % enjoying the intervention with the applications. The majority (58 %) of the students also indicated that they would use the applications if they formed part of the Sepedi module and almost 70 % said they would recommend the applications to other students learning Sepedi.

The students were also asked to indicate which of the three applications they preferred to use overall by giving the applications a rating of 1 to 3, with 1 being the most preferred. The Listen application was rated as the students' first preference, with 39 %, the Silent application was second with 35 % and the Speak application was third with 26 %.

Because of the importance of determining the usefulness of the applications, it was decided to include a question on the applications' availability on the Google Play Store. If the applications were made available on the Play Store, 70 % of the students indicated that they would download them; however, only 5 % were willing to pay for the download. This is contrary to the findings of a study done at the Carnegie Mellon University in the United States of America, where non-native English students evaluated an application used during the preparation of scientific presentations [7]. The students thought the application could be used in real-life situations and they were willing to pay between $1 and $2 for it [7].

A possible motivation behind the South African students' unwillingness to pay for the applications is that they might be prepared to pay for only one application, but not all three. Further investigation into this matter is warranted as well as how to create free and useful language learning applications for the South African languages.

4 Conclusion

The feedback received from the questionnaire indicated that the students had a positive experience with the applications and that they perceived the applications as being useful as a supplementary tool for Sepedi vocabulary acquisition. The students also indicated throughout the questionnaire that the Listen application was their firm favorite.

5   Future Work

During the design process, it was decided to keep the applications as technologically simple as possible. This was done to ensure honest feedback from the students with regards to supplementary language learning applications without their opinions being influenced by the performance of the technology in any way.

Future versions of the applications will include text-to-speech (TTS) and automatic speech recognition (ASR) technologies. TTS can be used to automate the generation of the example pronunciations of target words which will save time and effort when new content is added to the applications, and ASR will provide users with immediate feedback on their pronunciation.

References

1. von Holdt, K., Murphy, M.: Public hospitals in South Africa: stressed institutions, disempowered management. In: State of the Nation: South Africa 2007. HSRC Press, Cape Town (2007)
2. Cullinan, K.: Health services in South Africa: a basic introduction. In: Health-e News Service (2006)
3. Abdool Karim, S.S.: Medical education after the first decade of democracy in South Africa. Lancet **363**, 1395 (2004)
4. SouthAfrica.info: The Languages of South Africa. http://www.southafrica.info/about/people/language.htm#.VsrfNPl96Uk
5. Ministry of Education: Language Policy for Higher Education (2002)
6. de Groot, A.M.B., van Hell, J.G.: The learning of foreign language vocabulary. In: Handbook of Bilingualism: Psycholinguistic Approaches. Oxford University Press, Inc., New York (2009)
7. Davis, E.M., Saz. O., Eskenazi, M.: POLLI: a handheld-based aid for non-native student presentations. In: Speech and Language Technology in Education (SLaTE), Grenoble, France, pp. 43–47 (2013)

Health Applications

Towards the Design of a Cross Platform Solution for Efficient Colorimetric Tests

Subrata Acharya[1(✉)], Gabriel Susai[1], and Kelly M. Elkins[2]

[1] Department of Computer and Information Sciences,
Towson University, Towson, MD, USA
sacharya@towson.edu, garoanl@students.towson.edu
[2] Department of Chemistry, Towson University, Towson, MD, USA
kmelkins@towson.edu

Abstract. Every year millions of crime related events are reported, many of which are drug-related. Illegal drugs are among the prime factors for criminal activity, making illicit drug evidence an important type of chemical evidence. Identifying the exact drug is difficult since majority of the seized substances are in the form of white powders. Colorimetric drug tests are used to tentatively identify the substances. We report an automated application using the Android platform for interpretation of presumptive drug test results.

Keywords: Colorimetric · Android · Identification · Interpretation · Drug testing

1 Introduction

Every year millions of crime related events are reported, many of which are drug-related [1]. Illegal drugs are among the prime factors for criminal activity, making illicit drug evidence an important type of chemical evidence [2]. Identifying the exact drug is difficult since majority of the seized substances are in the form of white powders. Herein we present an automated method using an Android app to identify a substance based upon inputting the color observed after a prescribed time upon testing it with a chemical test [3] and searching a library [4]. Currently, interpretation of the color is reported using a *Munsell* color swatch [5] or by matching colors imprinted on the surface of commercial, premade, single use test kits. However, both positive and negative color interpretation is often reported differently depending upon the specific user and lab notebooks and case reports are difficult to interpret without the knowledge of the recording analyst. As these tests are often performed in poor visibility conditions such as at night or under a streetlight or flashlight, and individual differences in eye physiology and working color terminology, these concerns are likely underrepresented. The method is designed to reduce investigator skill level, interpretation error, and report time while preserving test records, improving data sharing, and improving data security. The digital database library is comprehensive, searchable, and easily accessible, secure and easily updated. It includes quantitative measures of the color using the RGB (red, green, blue) color system. The software will improve the reliability, reproducibility, selectivity and

© Springer International Publishing Switzerland 2016
C. Stephanidis (Ed.): HCII 2016 Posters, Part II, CCIS 618, pp. 295–300, 2016.
DOI: 10.1007/978-3-319-40542-1_48

sensitivity of colorimetric testing for controlled substances. The software will run on portable smartphones or a separate portable device such as a Raspberry Pi B + [6].

2 Framework Design

Presumptive tests are used to determine the tentative identity of a substance in crime scene investigation and for obtaining a search warrant for further searches. Today presumptive drug testing is conducted using a color test reagent; the reagent is mixed with suspected illicit substances as specified by a protocol [3]. The resulting color of the mixture is used to interpret the tentative identity of the substance by mapping it to a color library [4]. But the result depends on the color visualized within the limitations of crime scene, constraints due to human vision, and training and experience of the individual who is conducting the test. To overcome these hurdles, we have applied smartphone technology to automate the color interpretation to reduce the subjective interpretation, investigation time, variable investigator training and skill, and improve test accuracy and data security.

There are various apps available in the marketplace which can label, by name or numerical value, the color of a substance using the camera available in the phone. One method of reporting color use through the use of the RGB three point numerical color system. However, the RGB value of a substance will drastically vary depending on the projection of light on the substance. The Android app will accept the RGB color value from a colorimetric chemical drug test, perform a Euclidian distance (or other best) algorithm [4, 7, 8] and find the closest set of RGB values in a database [4], sort them by closest to the farthest against a predetermined value and store the result on a server for a fixed timeframe. The Android app allows the user to view the previous test results by date and time. By using technology we can map the color of a suspected material evaluated using a specific test to an illicit or legal substance with high accuracy. The overall framework diagram is presented in Fig. 1. During evaluation, the application is trained with multiple sets of input values to produce results with higher accuracy. The application will be tested in terms of input, processing, storing the result and the output to provide desired results.

The presumptive drug testing is done in two phases:

- Phase I – Identification: In this phase the application will search a comprehensive database based upon the color response displays the matched results.
- Phase II – Interpretation: In this phase the application will use distance vector (or other best) algorithm to find the self-similarity substances and suggest drugs in rank order that match the parameters for the specific test.

The first interaction with the application is using Android app. The end user application was built using the Android 5.0 Lollipop operating system [9]. The Android application communicates with the service layer using JSON (JavaScript Object Notation). The service layer is built using Microsoft ASP.NET WEB API 2 which is an ideal platform to create light weight HTTP services [10]. The service layer communicates with the ASP.NET Entity Framework. Entity framework is very helpful to handle SQL server database tables as objects and creates a wrapper around the

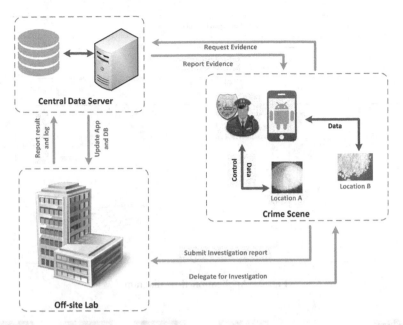

Fig. 1. Framework diagram

database. Using Entity Framework we wrote various LINQ (*Language INtegrated Query*) [11] queries to fetch, modify and store the information in the database. SQL Server 2012 is used as a backend database to store all the data which can be accessed by the application. Figures 2 and 3 present the application flow diagram and database design respectively. The Android application will authenticate the user by validating the login credentials by communicating with *WebAPI* [10]. This is the service layer which receives the request from the Android application, executes the business logic using data from database and sends the appropriate response back to android application. The credentials are securely stored in the database using SHA512 Hashing algorithm and appended with a 4 byte salt.

3   Evaluation

Once the user (either from the Crime Lab or the Crime Scene) has successfully authenticated into the application, s/he may choose to conduct the following operations: *Create a new case*; *Conduct more tests with existing case* and/or *View previous test results*. User can key in all the necessary information to identify the drug substance (Fig. 4). The user is presented with the option to choose one of the methods to use to conduct the test, *i.e.* is the RGB value based on (i) *Color Assist* (ii) *Color Assist with Light* and/or (iii) *Spectrophotometer* [11] method. The user then makes the selection for the type of test to be conducted and enters the corresponding Red, Green and Blue values in the given input controls. Figure 4 presents the procedure for creating a new case in the application.

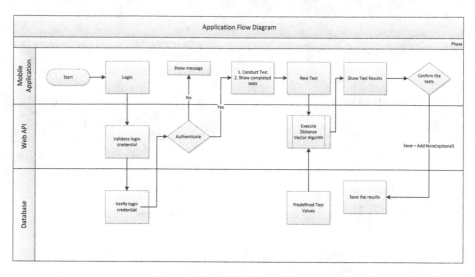

Fig. 2. Application flow diagram

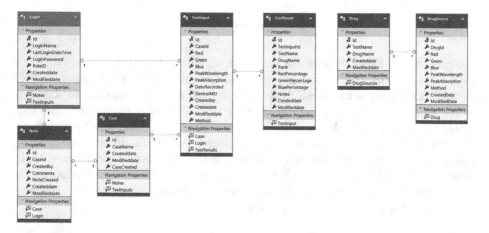

Fig. 3. Database design

The results are presented to the user after each test and the suggested drug identity is suggested in a sorted rank order (with accuracy of prediction). Users can also add notes to the entire case and save these results. These results can be accessed both at the crime scene and later in the crime lab in order to analyze the results and conduct additional tests, if necessary. Each note is stored and mapped to the logged in user. This helps in identifying the owner of the notes, date and time created, and actual note information for effective case analysis. Figure 5 presents the review of a previously created case for further analysis and recommendation for jurisdiction.

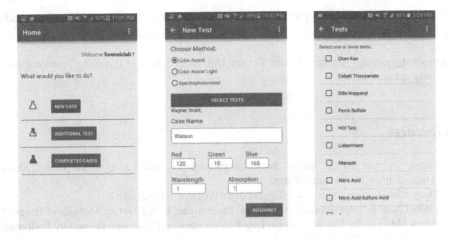

Fig. 4. Application (new case creation)

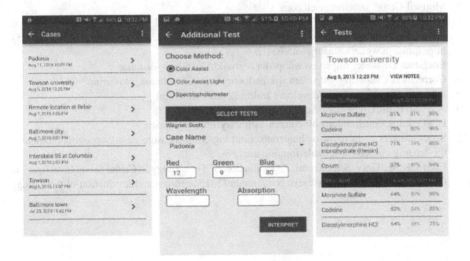

Fig. 5. Application (prior case review)

4   Conclusion

This research presents a novel automated approach to interpret colorimetric test results. It adds a new technology tool to the several solutions available to help crime scene investigators [13]. The Android application is currently available for testing by crime laboratories and investigators. The goal of the application is to improve the accuracy of interpretation phase and help the crime scene investigator conduct more reliable and cost effective examinations to be effectively used in legal proceedings. As future research, the team is working to incorporate various other algorithms [12] and methods [6, 12] to conduct effective automated crime scene investigation.

Acknowledgements. Funding from the Towson University School of Emerging Technologies is gratefully acknowledged.

References

1. Crime in the United States. https://en.wikipedia.org/wiki/Crime_in_the_United_States Android. https://www.android.com/
2. Drug-related crime. https://en.wikipedia.org/wiki/Drug-related_crime
3. United Nations International Drug Control Programme, Rapid Testing Methods of Drugs of Abuse: Manual for Use by National Law Enforcement and Narcotics Laboratory Personnel, United Nations, Vienna (1995)
4. Elkins, K.M., Weghorst, A., Quinn, A.A., Acharya, S.: Color quantitation for chemical spot tests for a controlled substances presumptive test database. Drug Test. Anal. (2016). doi:10.1002/dta.1949
5. Munsell Color. http://munsell.com/
6. Acharya, S., Khatiwada, S., Elkins, K.M.: CSI-Pi: a novel automated secure solution to interpret on-site colorimetric tests. Colonial Acad. Alliance Undergraduate Res. J. 5 (2015). http://publish.wm.edu/caaurj/vol5/iss1/2/
7. Euclidian Distance. https://en.wikipedia.org/wiki/Euclidean_distance
8. Correlation Clustering. https://en.wikipedia.org/wiki/Correlation_clustering
9. Android Developer. http://developer.android.com/index.html
10. ASP.NET. http://www.asp.net/web-api
11. LINQ. https://msdn.microsoft.com/en-us/library/bb397926.aspx
12. Spectrometers. http://www.hunterlab.com/blog/color-measurement-2/spectrophotometers-the-leading-choice-for-reliable-forensic-analysis/
13. Elkins, K.M., Gray, S.E., Krohn, Z.: Evaluation of Technology in Crime Scene Investigation. CS Eye (2015). http://www.cseye.com/content/2015/april/research/evaluation-of-technology

When It Comes to Depression, ICT Use Matters: A Longitudinal Analysis of the Effect of ICT Use and Mattering on Depression Among Older Adults

Jessica Francis[✉], Travis Kadylak, Shelia R. Cotten, and R.V. Rikard

Department of Media and Information, Michigan State University, East Lansing, MI, USA
{franc202,kadylakt,cotten,rvrikard}@msu.edu

Abstract. Information and communication technologies (ICTs) provide numerous benefits to older adults' well-being, such as reducing feelings of depression. Previous studies show that ICTs are effective in promoting a sense of mattering, which has also been inversely related to feelings of depression. Our analysis examines the effect ICTs have on older adults' sense of mattering and, ultimately, depression. We examine these relationships through longitudinal regression and the Sobel-Goodman Mediation Tests. Our results show that the effect of ICT use on depression among older adults is partially mediated by mattering over time.

Keywords: Older adults · Icts · Mattering · Geriatric depression

1 Introduction

Between 5 and 10 million adults, aged 50 and older, experience feelings of depression, a condition that can lead to decline in overall well-being [1, 2]. Studies attribute the prevalence of depressive symptoms to the decrease in social interaction, which often results from retirement and age related physical and cognitive decline. All of these may lead to increased loneliness, isolation, and depression [1, 3]. In recent years, there has been an increase in studies focused on how information and communication technology (ICT) use may mitigate such threats through the building and bolstering of social networks [1, 4–7]. Furthermore, ICT use can be especially beneficial among older adults with limited mobility and access to face-to-face interactions and may promote an individual's sense of mattering [8–10]. Mattering, or one's perception that they are important to, acknowledged by, and relied upon by others, is a key mechanism to reduce depression [11–13].

To date, the relationship between ICT use and mattering has received limited scholarly attention [8–10]. The current research, however, proposes mattering as a mechanism through which ICT use may decrease feelings of depression and promote well-being among older adults by forging and strengthening social networks and providing platforms for the communication of importance, commitment, and dependence. For the purposes of our study, we empirically examine how ICT use and mattering affect depression among older adults.

© Springer International Publishing Switzerland 2016
C. Stephanidis (Ed.): HCII 2016 Posters, Part II, CCIS 618, pp. 301–306, 2016.
DOI: 10.1007/978-3-319-40542-1_49

Mattering is posited as a mechanism tied to both stress-buffering and the reduction in depressive feelings [11–14]. Conceptually, mattering can be broken down into three main tenets: attention, importance, and dependence and refers to the belief that one is the object of another's concern and relies on one to fill some sort of need [11–18]. Mattering may be especially relevant to older adults as it is proposed that the sense of mattering evolves over the life course as individuals experience and obtain different role obligations [14, 16, 18]. For instance, an individual may experience a decrease in their mattering level upon retirement, as they may perceive that fewer people rely on them to fill a specific role [16, 18]. Likewise, perceived decreases in mattering may occur when an individual experiences personal role changes, such as losing a spouse [16, 18]. A decrease in mattering can, in turn, lead to increased feelings of depression [11–13].

There is some limited research to suggest that ICTs promote mattering among younger adults and minorities [8–10]. There is a dearth of research, however, regarding ICTs and mattering among older adults. Furthermore, the effect of the relationship of ICT use and mattering on older adults' depressive symptoms has yet to be empirically examined. To this end, we hypothesize the following:

H1: ICT Use will be Inversely Associated with Symptoms of Depression.
H2: The Association between ICT Use and Symptoms of Depression will be Mediated by Perceived Mattering.

2   Data and Methods

Our data come from an ICT and Quality of Life Study, a multi-site randomized controlled trial. The goal of the study was to investigate how ICT use might affect quality of life among older adults. Study participants resided in assisted and independent living communities (AICs) in a mid-sized metropolitan city located in the Deep South region of the United States. AICs were randomized into one of three study arms: ICT, Activities Control (AC), and True Control (TC). Participants in the ICT arm of the study received an 8-week computer and Internet training course. Study personnel conducted activities such as trivia and sing-alongs for participants in the AC arm. Participants in the TC arm received no intervention. Prior to the intervention the Mini-Mental State Examination [19] was employed to screen each potential participant for cognitive impairment. Results of the screening yielded an initial n of 313 participants: 101 participants in the ICT arm, 112 participants in the AC arm, and 93 participants in the TC arm.

During the 8 week ICT training program, participants met twice a week for 90 min at which time they received introductory information and training about using computers, email, online searching, social networking, and various recreational websites. Graduate students led each of the courses and supplied participants with training materials and manuals that they were allowed to keep for reference. To ensure that participants had sustained access, each AIC was supplied with desktop computers for use outside of the allotted training time.

Despite availability of both qualitative and quantitative data, our research focuses on the quantitative data for purposes of analyses. Our analyses focuses on data pulled from five in-person surveys. The surveys were administered over the course of 14 months. Data was collected at baseline prior to the ICT training, post-intervention at eight weeks after baseline, and at 3-, 6-, and 12-month intervals following the post-test. For the purposes of this study, we use 5 waves of longitudinal data for our analyses. The surveys included questions regarding topics such as health and overall well-being, social connections, ICT use, as well as basic demographic characteristics.

2.1 Measures

We measured ICT use with a twelve item scale that asked participants to address the frequency with which they performed specific online activities such as: "Go online to check Eons, Facebook, or MyVillage," "Go online to visit websites that family or friends have created," "Go online to send or receive an e-mail." The original response options were ranged from 1 (*Several times a week*) to 6 (*Never*). We recoded these response options into dichotomous categories due to low response frequencies resulting from a skip pattern in the questionnaire. Response categories 1 through 5 were recoded to 1 and response category 6 (i.e., *Never*) was recoded as 0. Responses were summed to reflect higher values, indicating greater ICT use (α reliabilities > .9 at each wave).

We assessed perceived mattering with Rosenberg and McCullough's (1981) mattering scale ($\alpha = .78$). This scale contains five items and asks respondents to rate their answers to questions such as: "How much do you feel other people pay attention to you?", "How important do you feel you are to other people?", and "How much do you feel other people depend on you?" Response options were set on a four point scale and ranged from 1 (*Not at all*) to 4 (*Very much*). Responses were summed to reflect higher values indicating higher levels of mattering (α reliabilities > .7 at each wave).

To assess our outcome of interest, we used the Geriatric Depression Scale [20]. Participants were asked to respond to questions such as, "Do you feel pretty worthless the way you are now?", "Do you often feel helpless?", and "Are you basically satisfied with your life?" Items were recoded so that positive responses for depression are *No* to the first question and *Yes* for all subsequent questions. The GDS has a high level of sensitivity, specificity, and overall accuracy [20–22].

We controlled for respondent's age, living facility (Assisted Living vs. Independent Living), and study arm. Age was measured as number of years at the time of intervention. Respondents' living facilities were dummy coded and Independent Living facility served as the excluded category in this analysis. Study arm was also dummy coded and TC served as the excluded category in this analysis.

3 Results

We employ a random effects linear regression panel model to examine the impact of ICT use over the five periods of data collection. A random effects model is preferable to fixed effects given that the estimation is more efficient, the effects of time invariant variables are estimated, rather than controlled for, and the standard errors of estimates are smaller. In Model 1, ICT use among older adults significantly decreased depression

($\beta = -0.0278$, $p < 0.05$) over the duration of the project and accounts for approximately 5.0 % of the variation in depression.

Model 2 includes the activities and ICT study arms, residence in an assisted living compared to independent living communities, participant's age, and the measure of mattering. Note that ICT use is not significant in Model 2 ($\beta = -0.0183$, $p < 0.137$). However, participants living in an assisted living community experienced significantly greater levels of depression ($\beta = .390$, $p < .001$) compared to participants in independent living communities. In addition, mattering significantly decreased depression ($\beta = -.0448$, $p < .001$) over the duration of the project. Model 2 accounts for 11.3 % of the variation in depression. We employed the Sobel-Goodman Mediation Test to determine if mattering mediates the effect of ICT use on depression over time. The Sobel-Goodman Mediation tests whether a mediator carries the influence of the predictor to the outcome of interest. The Sobel-Goodman Mediation estimates were significant and mattering mediated 12.5 % of total effect of ICT use on depression over time.

4 Discussion and Limitations

Our findings support previous research on both mattering and ICT use with regards to reduction of depressive symptoms [1, 11–13]. Our results' contribute to the extant literature by demonstrating that mattering serves as a mechanism through which ICT use reduces depression among older adults over time. Though our ICT use measure is broad in nature, we suggest that by using ICTs to communicate with family and friends, older adults may gain access to valuable social network support. By utilizing online activities such as email, social network sites, and other various avenues of Internet communication, older adults are afforded platforms through which they may receive meaningful communication of attention and importance, which leads to increased perceptions of mattering [14]. Additionally, ICTs serve as channels through which older adults maintain and develop significant roles in the lives of their social connections, the understanding of which can also promote mattering and, in turn, decrease feelings of depression among older adults [11–14, 17].

Interestingly, our results suggest that older adults who live in assisted living facilities were more likely to experience depression than older adults residing in independent living facilities. The difference between living facility may be due to any number of age-related factors such as declining health, limited mobility, and reduced access to social networks. For this reason, we assert that ICTs are an especially valuable and crucial tools for older adults residing in assisted living facilities, as ICT usage allows older adults to overcome both social and spatial barriers to connection with loved ones [7]. For residents of assisted living communities, ICTs may become a primary channel of communication with their loved ones, which is essential to mitigating the effect of depression.

There are some potential limitations to our study. First, our ICT use measure assessed the total number of online activities, instead of frequency or duration of use. For future research, a more robust measure of ICT use might assess uses and activities with different types of ICTs. Finally, data was collected in the Deep South, which may limit generalizability.

Despite the limitations, our study makes a valuable contribution to the research on older adults' ICT use and well-being. Our findings suggest that mattering serves as a mechanism though which ICT use may reduce symptoms of depression. By developing a deeper insight into the psychosocial benefits yielded by ICT use, it is our aim that ICTs be implemented in ways that truly matter for the well-being of older adults.

References

1. Cotten, S.R., Ford, G., Ford, S., Hale, T.M.: Internet use and depression among retired older adults in the united states: a longitudinal analysis. J. Gerontol. Ser. B Psychol. Sci. Soc. Sci. **69**(5), 763–771 (2014)
2. Hoyert, D.L., Kochanke, K.D., Murphy, S.L.: Deaths: Final data for 1997. National Vital Statistics Reports. National Center for Health Statistics, Hyattsville (1999)
3. Cacioppo, J.T., Hughes, M.E., Waite, L.J., Hawkley, L.C., Thisted, R.: Loneliness as a specific risk factor for depressive symptoms: cross sectional and longitudinal analyses. Psychol. Aging **21**, 140–151 (2006)
4. Blit-Cohen, E., Litwin, H.: Elder participation in cyberspace: a qualitative analysis of israeli retirees. J. Aging Stud. **18**(4), 385–398 (2004). doi:10.1016/j.jaging.2004.06.007
5. Cotten, S.R., Anderson, W.A., McCullough, B.M.: Impact of internet use on loneliness and contact with others among older adults: cross-sectional analysis. J. Med. Internet Res. **15**(2), e39 (2013). doi:10.2196/jmir.2306
6. Choi, M., Kong, S., Jung, D.: Computer and internet interventions for loneliness and depression in older adults: a meta-analysis. Health Inf. Res. **18**(3), 191–198 (2012)
7. Winstead, V., Anderson, W.A., Yost, E.A., Cotten, S.R., Warr, A., Berkowsky, R.W.: You can teach an old dog new tricks: a qualitative analysis of how residents of senior living communities may use the web to overcome spatial and social barriers. J. Appl. Gerontol. **32**(5), 540–560 (2013). doi:10.1177/0733464811431824
8. Chew, H.E., Ilavarasan, V.P., Levy, M.R.: Mattering matters: agency, empowerment, and mobile phone use by female microentrepreneurs. Inf. Technol. Dev. **21**(4), 523–542 (2015). doi:10.1080/02681102.2013.839437
9. Cotten, S.R.: Students' technology use and the impacts on well-being. New Dir. Stud. Serv. **2008**(124), 55–70 (2008)
10. Watulak, S.L., Wang, Z., McNary, S.: Facebook and mattering: how can instructors make the most of undergranduates' Facebook use? In: Searson, M., Ochoa, M. (eds.) Proceedings of Society for Information Technology and Teacher Education International Conference 2014, pp. 914–919. Association for the Advancement of Computing in Education (AACE), Chesapeake (2014)
11. Dixon, A.L.: Mattering in the later years: older adults' experience of mattering to others, purpose of mattering to others, purpose in life, depression, and wellness. Adultspan J. **6**(2), 83–95 (2007)
12. Rosenberg, M., McCullough, B.C.: Mattering: inferred significance and mental health among adolescents. Res. Community Ment. Health. **2**, 163–182 (1981)
13. Taylor, J., Jay Turner, R.: A longitudinal study of the role and significance of mattering to others for depressive symptoms. J. Health Soc. Behav. **42**(3), 310–325 (2001)
14. Thoits, P.A.: Mechanisms linking social ties and support to physical and mental health. J. Health Soc. Behav. **52**(2), 145–161 (2011). doi:10.1177/0022146510395592

15. Elliott, G., Kao, S., Grant, A.-M.: Mattering: empirical validation of a social-psychological concept. Self Identity **3**(4), 339–354 (2004). doi:10.1080/13576500444000119
16. Fazio, E.M.: Sense of mattering in late life. In: Avison, W.R., et al. (eds.) Advances in the Conceptualization of the Stress Process: Essays in Honor of Leonard I. Pearlin, pp. 149–175. Springer, New York (2009)
17. Schieman, S., Taylor, J.: Statuses, roles, and the sense of mattering. Sociol. Perspect. **44**(4), 469–484 (2001). doi:10.1525/sop.2001.44.4.469
18. Thoits, P.A.: Multiple identities and psychological well-being: a reformulation and test of the social isolation hypothesis. Am. Psychol. Rev. **48**(2), 174–187 (1983)
19. Folstein, M.F., Robins, L.N., Helzer, J.E.: The mini-mental state examination. Arch. Gen. Psychiatry **40**(7), 812 (1983). doi:10.1001/archpsyc.1983.01790060110016
20. Rinaldi, P., Mecocci, P., Benedetti, C., Ercolani, S., Bregnocchi, M., Menculini, G., Catani, M., Senin, U., Cherubini, A.: The satisfaction with life scale. J. Pers. Assess. **49**(1), 71–75 (1985)
21. Marquez, D.X., McAuley, E., Motl, R.W., Elavsky, S., Konopack, J.F., Jerome, G.J., Kramer, A.F.: Validation of geriatric depression scale-5 scores among sedentary older adults. Educ. Psychol. Measur. **66**(4), 667–675 (2016)
22. Song, H.J., Meade, K., Akobundu, U., Sahyoun, N.R.: Depression as a correlate of functional status of community dwelling older adults: utilizing a short-version of 5-item geriatric depression scale as a screening tool. J Nutr. Health Aging **18**, 765–770 (2014)

Method for Preventing Imposter Fraud During Blood-Pressure Measurement

Kaori Fujimura[✉], Haruka Suzuki, Gen Takahashi, Toru Nakamura,
and Kazuhiro Hayakawa

NTT Secure Platform Laboratories, Tokyo, Japan
{fujimura.kaori,suzuki.haruka,takahashi.gen,nakamura.toru,
hayakawa.kazuhiro}@lab.ntt.co.jp

Abstract. With the recent rapid growth in personal devices, the amount of data generated by individuals is increasing. When third parties think of using such data for their services, it is important to ensure that the data is authentic. As the first step in achieving this, we previously developed a system to ensure the authenticity of an legitimate person's blood-pressure data using pulse waves. However, if a user measures his/her blood-pressure with this system, it is necessary to keep touching the authentication device during measurement.

To improve the usability of this system, we evaluated the feasibility of a pulse-wave extraction method using face sequence images. We conducted a pulse-wave-extraction experiment in August 2015. From the results of the experiment, we found that we should use a video camera with a high frame rate and remove the effects of face movement.

Keywords: Data authenticity · Imposter prevention · Non-contact pulse wave extraction

1 Introduction

1.1 Necessity of Data Authenticity – Data Utilization by Third Party

Following the widespread use of personal health devices (activity monitors, blood-pressure monitors, etc.), various services for personally managing healthcare data have been launched, such as Google Fit and Apple's healthcare apps. In these services, individuals use such data for personal health management. When third parties, such as health insurance providers, want to use that data for providing lower premiums, it is important to ensure that the data is authentic. However, even if a person has been authorized using biometrics when measuring blood pressure at home, there has been no method for verifying whether subsequent measurements were done by the same person. Figure 1 shows the method of registering an imposter's blood pressure data as an authorized person's data. Suppose the authorized person had already correctly registered with the service. Usually, in healthcare apps, a user first logs in to the service then measures his/her data. Since authentication and measurement are different actions, if the imposter measured his/her blood pressure after the authorized person authenticated with a finger-vein

C. Stephanidis (Ed.): HCII 2016 Posters, Part II, CCIS 618, pp. 307–311, 2016.
DOI: 10.1007/978-3-319-40542-1_50

authentication device, then the imposter's data would be uploaded as the authorized person's data.

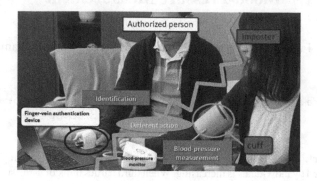

Fig. 1. Method of registering imposter's blood pressure data as authorized person's data

1.2 Our System to Ensure Blood-Pressure Data Authenticity Using Pulse Waves

To ensure the authenticity of a person's data, we previously proposed a system that enables the linking of one's authentication and measurement using pulse waves from his/her heartbeat [1].

Pulse waves obtained from the same person can be observed as a single heartbeat pattern, regardless of which part of the body the measurement was made. Using this characteristic, the system matches the time-series patterns of the pulse waves obtained separately from two locations.

Our blood-pressure measurement system is composed of a finger-vein authenticity device with a pulse-wave sensor, blood-pressure monitor, and server (Fig. 2).

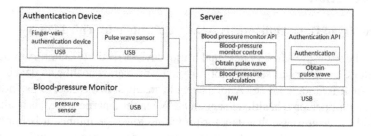

Fig. 2. Blood pressure measurement system

The blood-pressure monitor detects pulse waves during blood-pressure measurement, and the authenticity device continues to authenticate during measurement. The authenticity device also simultaneously detects pulse waves. The system then matches the two types of pulse wave data to determine whether they belong to the same person.

Figure 3 (a) shows an example of pulse-wave data obtained from the same person during personal authentication and measurement of blood pressure. It shows that peaks occurred at the same timing. Figure 3 (b) is an example of pulse-wave data obtained when a different person underwent blood-pressure measurement. Since the pulse waves from the authentication device and blood-pressure monitor were from different individuals, the timing of the peaks differed.

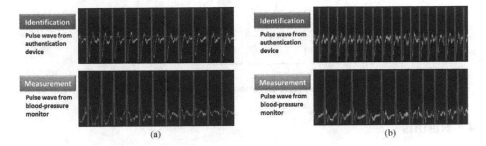

Fig. 3. Matching of the two types of pulse wave data. (Color figure online)

Since the authentication device measures pulse waves during measurement, it is necessary for a user to keep touching the sensor.

However, pulse waves can be detected from face sequence images. We believe that the usability of such a system would improve if face authentication can be combined with non-contact pulse-wave detection.

2 Pulse-Wave Extraction from Face Sequence Images

Since heartbeat widens capillaries in the face, the skin color of the face changes. There have been studies on calculating pulse by analyzing face sequence images [2, 3]. Poh [3] proposed a method of calculating heart rate by using face sequence images taken with a Web camera.

However, the method is only aimed at making simple calculations and records of pulse rate for healthcare purposes. We conducted an experiment to evaluate the feasibility of pulse-wave detection using video cameras.

3 Experiment

We conducted a preliminary experiment with a Kinect Sensor for Xbox One (Kinect) in August 2015. Participants were 5 men and 2 women. They were seated in front of a Kinect camera and wore a pulse-wave sensor on a fingertip, as show in Fig. 4. They were asked not to move for 60 s. To remove the effect of light reflection, we placed a green background behind a participant.

We compared the pulse waves from images with those measured using a pulse-wave sensor attached to an authentication device.

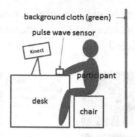

Fig. 4. Experimental environment. (Color figure online)

4   Results

Figure 5 shows the pulse waves calculated from the face sequence images (upper) and those measured using the pulse-wave sensor (lower). Small circles in the graphs are peaks detected by MATLAB. Participant No. 4 moved his/her face a little due to whispering.

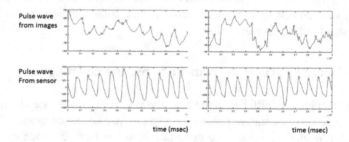

Fig. 5. Results of extracting pulse waves from face image

Figure 6 shows pulse waves of two seconds. Because the frame rate of the Kinect is up to 30 (whereas sampling frequency of the pulse-wave sensor is 409.8 Hz), peaks were detected more precisely with the pulse-wave sensor.

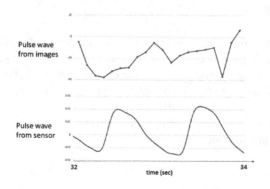

Fig. 6. Difference in smoothness of two pulse waves

5 Discussion

From the experimental results, the following problems in detecting pulse waves from face images were found.

- The peak of the pulse wave detection failed due to face movement. Therefore, we should develop a movement compensation algorithm.
- The frame rate of Kinect was not sufficient for carrying out matching; therefore, the required frame rate should be clarified.

6 Conclusion

To improve the usability of our data authentication system, we conducted an experiment to evaluate the feasibility of non-contact pulse-wave extraction. From the experimental results, we found that we should use a video camera with a high frame rate and remove the effects of face movement.

If face recognition is combined with non-contact pulse-wave detection, it will enable the guaranteeing of data authenticity using a simple device configuration composed of a smartphone and sphygmomanometer. It will also widen the possibilities for actions that can be linked to the authentication process, for example, qualifying exams and administrative procedures that do not allow proxies.

References

1. Suzuki, H., et al.: A study of attribute assurance of data generated by individuals. In: Proceedings of the 2016 IEICE G.C., D-9-18, p. 130 (2016) (in Japanese)
2. Lewandowska, M., Ruminski, J., Kocejko, T., Nowak, J.: Measuring pulse rate with a webcam - a non-contact method for evaluating cardiac activity. In: 2011 Federated Conference on FedCSIS, pp. 405–410 (2011)
3. Poh, M.-Z., McDuff, D.J., Picard, R.W.: Non-contact, automated cardiac pulse measurements using video imaging and blind source separation. Opt. Express **18**(10), 10762–10774 (2010)

Training System for Puncture Technique of Hemodialysis

Ren Kanehira[1(✉)], Atsushi Ohashi[1], and Hideo Fujimoto[2]

[1] FUJITA Health University, 1-98 Dengakugakubo, Kutsukake-cho, Toyoake,
Aichi 470-1192, Japan
kanehira@fujita-hu.ac.jp
[2] Nagoya Institute of Technology, Nagoya, Japan
fujimoto@vier.mech.nitech.ac.jp

Abstract. It is required for a clinic engineer to have highly professional knowledge as well as operation skills for different medical machines. Such knowledge and skills are normally difficult to master by teaching and practicing only at universities within a limited time. In this study, a training system with the information communication technology for clinical engineer was constructed. With the system, several problems which may most probably happen in the operating of medical machines were made clear, and solutions for such problems were proposed. The training system for Hemodialysis Apparatus was taken as an example. In more detail, a simulation circuit and an arm model for dialysis were firstly constructed. Operation data from experienced clinical engineers were quantified and taken as indicators to evaluate the training effects in combination with video texts. With the system, students carried out practical punctures and repeated practices on techniques such as needle holding or puncturing angles, under real-time judgement feedback from the system. Good effect was confirmed by questionnaire upon trained students.

Keywords: Computer training system · Skill science · Medical equipment · Clinic engineer · Support to operations

1 Introduction

With the recent progress in computer technology and multimedia, it becomes possible to provide quantities of preserved visual or other sensory information to us. Particularly, some training systems for students using e-learning technologies have obtained much attention [1, 2]. Similarly in clinical medicine, systems using advanced technologies of both information and engineering to support have been taken into account [3].

A clinical engineer has to deal with a wide range of tasks such as the operation, management, and maintenance of medical machines which requires high levels of expertise and technical capabilities. It is very difficult to master such a large sum of knowledge and skill only in university within limited times, particularly in an environment being lack of repeated operation and trouble-shooting experience [4].

In order to solve these problems, we have been carried out a series of study for the construction of educational systems with operation skills [5–7]. In this study, for a high training efficiency for the student in clinical engineering, and aiming the goal of a

C. Stephanidis (Ed.): HCII 2016 Posters, Part II, CCIS 618, pp. 312–317, 2016.
DOI: 10.1007/978-3-319-40542-1_51

computer-added training system with low cost, simulated experiences, and good repeatability, we proposed a training system for clinical engineer using the up-to-now technologies in our sequential researches on computer-added skill-training system. Special attention was paid to the training of medical operations in addition to the conventional e-learning for general knowledge [8–10].

The conventional e-learning method focuses mostly on the learning of knowledge like that from textbook, paying less attention to practical operations of medical machines. Obviously, the knowledge learnt only from textbook can hardly be comparative to that by experience (empirical knowledge), body movements (embodies knowledge), and explicit knowledge in addition to textbook [11, 12].

In this study, the training system for hemodialysis apparatus was taken as a training example. In more detail, a simulation circuit and an arm model for dialysis were firstly constructed. Operation data from experienced clinical engineers were quantified and taken as indicators for the evaluation of operation training effects. In addition, a camera and operation movement analysis software was used to construct the above training system.

2   Hemodialysis and Puncture Technique

Hemodialysis is such a medical operation to take out the blood of a patient with disabled kidney and to purify it through a dialyzer. The operation normally takes 4 h, repeated every 2 days.

The operation is accompanied firstly with a "puncture" to the blood vessel with needle. The puncture includes one to take out the blood and another to return the blood to vessel by putting needles into their special shunts prepared earlier in blood vessel. It is required to put the needle with a proper angle precisely into the shunt under the condition that the blood vessels are structurally complex and visually hidden under skin. As can be imaged, a correct puncture operation should be much difficult than a normal injection, because an erroneous puncturing may result in medical accidents such as heavy bleeding. Therefore, the puncture operation is among the most important techniques for hemodialysis.

Of course, high levels of precision and skill are required for such operation. However, it is impossible for a student to do practical puncture on a patient during his clinical training process. It can be imaged how anxiety he may be when the student faces a patient for the first time. Though, there has not yet been such a training system developed up to the present time. In order to solve the above problems, we proposed the following training system for "puncture" operation for hemodialysis.

3   Puncture Technique Training System

3.1   Construction of Simulation Circuit

The practical roller pump was used in the system. Simulated blood vessels were made, and the flow of blood was demonstrated with red-colored distilled water. The blood vessels were inserted into the arm model, further covered with silicone rubber sheet as an artificial skin. The schematic of simulation circuit was shown in Fig. 1.

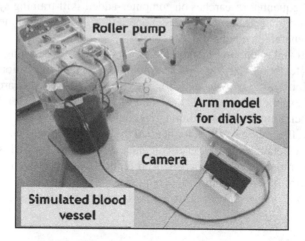

Fig. 1. Simulation circuit (Color figure online)

3.2 Determination of Teaching Data

It is necessary to prepare operation teaching data as the standard to judge student's operation. For this purpose, operations from experienced clinical engineers were recorded, analyzed quantitatively, and taken as the judgement standards. The correct insertion angle, for example, should be between 12 to 15° after analyzing several expert's operations. Textbook video was made based on the standard operations. As an example, a good holding of puncture needle is shown in Fig. 2, by which an unexpected reverse flow of blood can be viewed clearly.

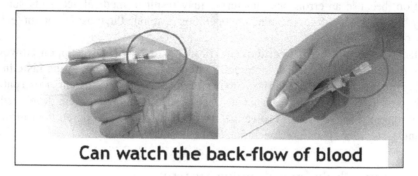

Fig. 2. A good holding of puncture needle

A teaching movie was made after recording a series of expert's puncture movements with necessary analysis, and important points for puncture were extracted to construct a teaching movie, as shown in Fig. 3.

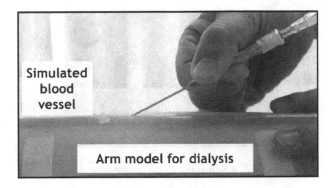

Fig. 3. Teaching video of dialysis puncture

3.3 Configuration of the Puncture Training System

The system was constructed using the simulated circuit and teaching data. The configuration and flowchart for operation and information were shown in Fig. 4.

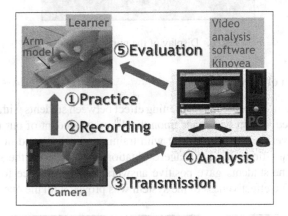

Fig. 4. Configuration of the puncture training system

Series of operations were firstly provided to the students by electronic textbook for getting the basic knowledge. After that, the students carried out puncture operations upon the arm model, and the operation movements were recorded by camera and the data were transferred to a personal computer. The operations of students were analyzed with a video analysis software "kinover", and their movements such as needle holding poses and puncture angles were superimposed and evaluated with those from the teaching data (Fig. 5). A display screen of puncture angles was shown in Fig. 6.

Fig. 5. A Superposition to the teaching data

Fig. 6. Display of the puncture angle

3.4 Verification of System

To verify the system, a comparison of training effect between students with and without the use of the proposed system was made upon the 4th grade student of our university using questionnaire. A verification experiment with training was displayed in Fig. 7. With all questions in the questionnaire, a 5 stage evaluation was made on the students. As the results, 90 % of the students gave positive answers with confidence for the use of the training system. The effectiveness of the system was proved with the questionnaire.

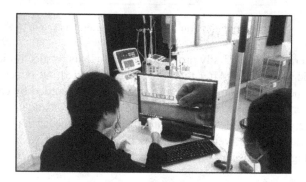

Fig. 7. Verification experiment

4   Conclusions

In this study, a training system for puncture technique of hemodialysis was proposed. A simulation circuit and an arm model for dialysis were constructed. Operation data from experienced clinical engineers were quantified and taken as indicators for the evaluation of operation training effects together with video texts. The effectiveness of the system was proved with a questionnaire upon the 4th grade students in our university.

Further improvement on the system, such as the use of new materials to construct blood vessels with high reality, and trouble-shooting with blood vessels or shunt, will be included into the system. New sensors and analysis methods with high precisions are considered also for the development of more advanced training system.

Acknowledgments. This study was supported by JSPE KAKENNHI Grant Number 25350304. I would like to thank clinical engineers and 4th grade students for cooperation of research studies.

References

1. Japan e-learning, Education IT Solutions EXPO. http://www.edix-expo.jp/el/
2. Watanabe, K., Kashihara, A.: A view of learning support research issues based on ICT genealogy. Jan. J. Educ. Technol. **34**(3), 143–152 (2010)
3. Sueda, T.: Development of a Training Simulator for Extracorporeal Circulation with a Heart-Lung Machine, Hiroshima University (2010). http://hutdb.hiroshima-u.ac.jp/seeds/view/3/en
4. Japan Association for Clinical Engineers (2014). http://www.ja-ces.or.jp/ce/
5. Kanehira, R., et al.: Development of an acupuncture training system using virtual reality technology. In: Proceedings of 5th FSKD, pp. 665–668. IEEE Press (2008)
6. Kanehira, R., Yang, W., Narita, H., Fujimoto, H.: Insertion force of acupuncture for a computer training system. In: Wang, F.L., Deng, H., Gao, Y., Lei, J. (eds.) AICI 2010, Part II. LNCS, vol. 6320, pp. 64–70. Springer, Heidelberg (2010)
7. Kanehira, R., Yang, W., Fujimoto, H.: Education and training environments for skill mastery. In: Wang, F.L., Lei, J., Lau, R.W., Zhang, J. (eds.) CMSP 2012. CCIS, vol. 346, pp. 451–458. Springer, Heidelberg (2012)
8. Kanehira, R., Narita, H., Kawaguchi, K., Hori, H., Fujimoto, H.: A training system for operating medical equipment. In: Li, S., Jin, Q., Jiang, X., Park, J.J. (eds.) Frontier and Future Development of Information Technology in Medicine and Education. Lecture Notes in Electrical Engineering, vol. 269, pp. 2259–2265. Springer, The Netherlands (2013)
9. Kanehira, R., Hori, H., Kawaguchi, K., Fujimoto, H.: Computer-supported training system for clinical engineer. In: Stephanidis, C. (ed.) HCI 2014, Part II. CCIS, vol. 435, pp. 89–94. Springer, Heidelberg (2014)
10. Kanehira, R., Kawaguchi, K., Fujimoto, H.: Learning-training system for medical equipment operation. In: Stephanidis, C. (ed.) HCII 2015 Posters. CCIS, vol. 529, pp. 321–327. Springer, Heidelberg (2015)
11. Noh, Y., Segawa, M., Shimomura, A., Ishii, H., Solis, J., Hatake, K., Takanishi, A.: Development of the evaluation system for the airway management training system WKA--1R. In: Proceedings of the Second IEEE RAS/EMBS International Conference on Biomedical Robotics and Bio mechatronics (2008)
12. Furukawa, K.: Skills Science Introduction: Approach to the elucidation of embodies knowledge. Ohmsha, Tokyo (2009)

Graphical Tools for Doctor-Patient Communication: An App Prototype Design in Children's Pain Management

Fang Suey Lin[1(✉)], Ching-Yi Lin[1], Yu Jie Hsueh[1],
Chun-Yi Lee[2], and Chun-Pei Hsieh[1]

[1] National Yunlin University of Science and Technology,
123 University Road, Sec. 3, Doului, Yunlin, Taiwan, ROC
linfs@yuntech.edu.tw
[2] Chang Bing Show Chwan Memorial Hospital, No. 6 Lugong Rd. Lukang Zhen,
Changhua County, Taiwan, ROC

Abstract. With the popularity of digital tools, such as smart phones and tablet computer, mini-applications have been developed where visualized interactive media are used to achieve the purpose of more interesting conveyance and understanding. This research project focuses on integrating medical and design professional fields to develop children's pain-related medical information and auxiliary communication tool, as well as to design and assess the children's pain APP prototype concept. The main purpose is to understand the needs for design of doctor-patient communication visualization system, as well as to develop APP prototype concept design. Based on the information on design needs obtained from the analysis on user experience design, this study may provide effective reference for future designers and researchers of relevant doctor-patient auxiliary communication systems.

Keywords: Children · Pain · Medical communication · User experience design · Interface design

1 Introduction

The suffering of children is difficult to quantify as their cognition of emotion is still evolving. The same degree of pain, stimulus or surgery does not necessarily produce the same degree of pain [4]. Effective control of pain shall be evaluated from the perspectives of physiology, spirit, and mind comprehensively with tools varying according to age [3]. Many factors affect the accurate evaluation of pain, including the children's mental and emotional state, behavior, and personality as well as the cultural background of their parents, such as, how do parents and children consider the influence on the processing of pain by their viewpoints on pain [5]. The absorption of information by children is significantly subject to their existing ideas and knowledge. Besides, children tend to have immature judgment and short attention and memory and fail to cover both reasons and consequents during their reasoning. Thus, it is difficult for them to comprehensively understand the process and reason of an event through logical thinking. Symbols refer to the exchange of items required through abstract patterns like lines, pictures, and

© Springer International Publishing Switzerland 2016
C. Stephanidis (Ed.): HCII 2016 Posters, Part II, CCIS 618, pp. 318–323, 2016.
DOI: 10.1007/978-3-319-40542-1_52

characters, which can compensate for the weakness of language reception capacity of children and extract advantage competence through visual cues. The picture exchange system proposed by Bondy and Frost adopting pictures as the media for communication has been widely studied and applied [2]. For the reliability of the self-report of pain assessment, the priority is to design sound visual patterns, colors, and numbers in order to improve the accuracy of medical staff on clinical judgment [10].

Along with the improvement of the capacity and operational capability of mobile devices and the maturity of mobile communications network infrastructure, increasing functions of e-health can be applied to mobile platform so as to make mobile-health (M-health) service the key of the applications of e-health [6]. The development of electronic pain self-assessment tool can also be used in home care while protecting the privacy of patients' information, recording the pain of patients, feed-backing to physicians during subsequent visits, and rendering convenient and appropriate communication between medical staff and patients after surgery or with chronic diseases [7]. The principle of the design of an app lies in easy operation, quick start, and simplified information. In addition, it shall streamline the commonly used functions of mobile phones, provide easy reading and easy touch operation, allow users with poor vision or reading disability, and contain all-round design [8]. This study referred to the information communication approach of AAC and EMS Symbol Board [1], centered on the icon-based understanding of the frequency of pain to develop app interfaces, considered user experience (UX), and facilitated the understanding of the feasibility, infeasibility, and effectual applicability of products [9].

This study referred to augmentative and alternative communication (AAC) to realize the four items of communication and interaction which were applied in the auxiliary communication system for medical staff and patients. The four items include (1) communicate symbol: Concepts are expressed with abstract symbols like specific vision, auditory sense, and touch. For instance, visual images and animations are adopted by a doctor to help him/her orally convey the message to a patient; (2) Communication aids: Images and animations are displayed with a computer screen to assist the conveying and communication of messages; (3) Communication strategy: The efficiency of information communication from a doctor to a patient is enhanced by images and animations which can assist the doctor's verbal communication; (4) Technical system: High-tech auxiliary devices are integrated into a communication intervention program through the design of app graphical interfaces to assist effective communication on a case-by-case basis.

2 Method

To create a testable wireframe prototype, software architecture was planned in accordance with the design theory of visual information, the design principle of micro software, user experience design, and interface design. After the planning and collection of the information related to the pain of children and the consultation with experts of medical care, the content was summarized and recorded in the database to be set up.

Conceptual Development. At the stage of conceptual development, spiral and divergent thinking method was carried out with Mandala thinking method (Fig. 1) so as to find possible innovative solutions, followed by convergence and integration. Discussion was carried out with users. The products or service mentioned in the storyboard script was specified as prototype which would serve as a reference for follow-up communication, design, and evaluation (Fig. 2).

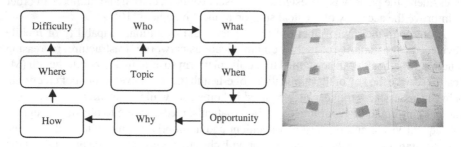

Fig. 1. Mandala thinking method

Fig. 2. Interview with the users at the Show Chwan Memorial Hospital

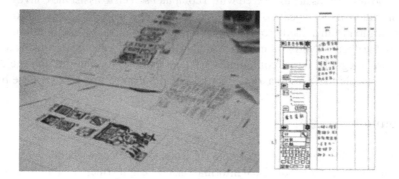

Fig. 3. Story board (produced by this study)

Script Architecture and Sketch Development. The script was designed in the way of storyboard script to develop relevant people, things, time, place, and materials into a simulation scenario of users. "Visual communication" was used to "telling stories". The images used were arranged in a chronological order (Fig. 3).

3   The Design and Evaluation of the Illustration of Children's Pain

3.1   Design and Evaluation the Icons

In accordance with the information communication approach of EMS Symbol Board [11], this study focused on the faces rating scale of children, pain frequency, and illustration of time to explore the expression of pain by children. Ten children of three to nine years old were regarded as the subjects. The purpose of the measurement was to clarify the degree of understanding of image design elements by children. After the interviews with medical staff, images were painted in accordance with their suggestions. The icons designed in this study were then assessed cognitively by students at school. The questionnaire was designed in line with ISO/9186-1 [12] with 96 children of four to nine old as subjects to observe their reaction and degree of understanding of pain. Through rigorous steps and objective assessment with 35 children of four to nine years as subjects, the overall design was improved to provide a new image system with effectiveness and consistency (Fig. 4).

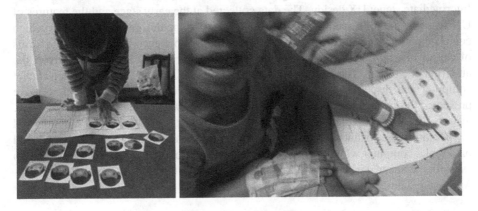

Fig. 4. Images comprehensive assessment

3.2   The Design of APP Interface

For children and caregivers, classification system must be clear with the function of rapid picture card formation, search, and conversion between images and characters. The interface design should not be too rich in case it might divert the attention of children. The interface design diagram was reflected 1:1 on a tablet computer and discussed with users. The features of concepts and conceptions were presented through the operation of simulation interface with animation so as to confirm if the design met their needs. This study also thought about how to apply the developed prototype to a tablet computer. It carried out cross-domain discussion and cooperation with the information engineering team. The actual operation of icons on a tablet computer and the functions of icon search and sentence-making could save the time to look for picture cards. The design of app interface: After entering the home page, one should select identity which contained children (or caregivers) and medical staff. After the confirmation of identity, one entered login and registration programs. After login and reading instruction, one might start to use the app by the functions on the list like selecting Faces Rating Scale, Pain Frequency, and Time (Fig. 5).

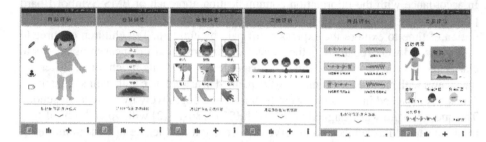

Fig. 5. APP prototype (interface design samples produced by this study)

Early stage: UX research. Design draft and discussion with users were conducted. Intermediate stage: UX design. The data collected at the early stage and the features of UX was integrated in accordance with ACC to list some design characteristics which could help children and caregivers in terms of pain experience. For instance, in terms of caregivers, the interface design should not be too rich in case it might divert the attention of children. The interface design diagram was reflected 1:1 on a 7 inchs tablet computer and discussed with users. The features of concepts and conceptions were presented through the operation of simulation interface with animation. Later stage: UX testing. After the completion of interface design draft, cross-domain discussion and cooperation were conducted with the information engineering team. Icons were operated on a tablet computer while the interviews and interaction was conducted with users so as to fine tune and adjust. Lastly, the main functions of the icon assistant learning software were defined.

4   Conclusion

The combination of the digital advantages of a tablet computer with UX design could effectively enhance learning fluency. The integration of the concept of UX into the early, intermediate, and later stages of the design could not only render user-oriented design, but also design based on the operation and experience of users who provided many positive feedback and suggestions, which could serve as a reference for the designers and researchers of the auxiliary communication system between patients and medical staff in the future. The design of auxiliary and visual communication system between patients and medical staff could be applied in clinical doctor-patient communication so as to improve doctor-patient interaction, assist children in communication, and enhance the understanding of doctors' inquires, enhance the accuracy of the information exchange between doctors and patients, and reduce their communication gap.

Acknowledgements. This study is part of the results of research project "Children Pain Scale Design and Assessment (II) – Communication Platform Development and Assessment" of the Ministry of Science and Technology, Taiwan (MOST 104-2410-H-224-022-). The support from the MOST is highly appreciated.

References

1. AAC-RERC. http://aac-rerc.psu.edu/index.php/pages/show/id/18. Communication Access for People with Limited Speech. Accessed 5 Dec 2013
2. Bondy, A.S., Frost, L.A.: Educational approaches in preschool. In: Schopler, E., Mesibov, G.B. (eds.) Learning and Cognition in Autism, pp. 311–333. Springer, USA (1995)
3. CCO (2008). http://www.cancercare.on.ca/. Cancer-related pain management: A report of evidence-based recommendations to guide practice. Accessed 27 Feb 2016
4. Cheng, S.-F., Foster, R.L., Hester, N.O., Huang, C.-Y.: A qualitative inquiry of Taiwanese children's pain experiences. J. Nurs. Res. **11**(4), 241–250 (2003)
5. Crowell, T.: (2009). http://www.aboutkidshealth.ca/en/resourcecentres/pain/painassessment/FactorsAffectingPainAssessment/Pages/default.aspx. Factors Affecting Pain Assessment, Accessed 05 December 2013
6. Liu, C., Zhu, Q., Holroyd, K.A., Seng, E.K.: Status and trends of mobile-health applications for iOS devices: A developer's perspective. J. Syst. Softw. **84**(11), 2022–2033 (2011)
7. Semple, J.L., Sharpe, S., Murnaghan, M.L., Theodoropoulos, J., Metcalfe, K.A.: Using a mobile app for monitoring post-operative quality of recovery of patients at home: a feasibility study. JMIR mHealth uHealth **3**(1), e18 (2015)
8. Shi, A.-Q.: A pilot study of using smartphone App to assist the physical and psychological disorders of adults. Ann. J. Spec. Educ. **201312**, 163–174 (2013)
9. Tech_Direct (2014). http://www.technical-direct.com/2014-03/%E4%BD%95%E8%AC%82%E4%BD%BF%E7%94%A8%E8%80%85%E7%B6%93%E9%A9%97%E5%8F%8A%E5%A6%82%E4%BD%95%E6%8F%90%E5%8D%87%E4%BD%BF%E7%94%A8%E8%80%85%E7%B6%93%E9%A9%97/. What is the user experience and how to enhance the user experience? Accessed 15 Dec 2014
10. Tyson, S.F., Brown, P.: How to measure pain in neurological conditions? A systematic review of psychometric properties and clinical utility of measurement tools. Clin. Rehabil. **28**(7), 669–686 (2014)
11. Widgit-Health. http://widgit-health.com/. First Response Communication Book. Accessed 1 Dec 2014
12. ISO 9186-1. Graphical symbols - Test methods - Part 1: Methods for testing comprehensibility (2007)

A Novel Mobile-Computing Based Assistive Approach for Knee Injury Telerehabilitation – A Preliminary Study

Tao Liu[1], Hongshi Huang[2], Gang Qian[1], Yan Zhao[3], Maria Jones[3], Wenxi Zeng[1], Justin Hampton[1], and Jicheng Fu[1(✉)]

[1] University of Central Oklahoma, Edmond, OK, USA
jfu@uco.edu
[2] Peking University Third Hospital, Beijing, China
[3] The University of Oklahoma Health Sciences Center, Oklahoma City, OK, USA

Abstract. Patients with knee injuries may not return to their pre-injury level if rehabilitation is not effectively conducted. Ineffective rehabilitation can be largely attributed to the fact that few approaches are available to assist patients in achieving goals of home-based rehabilitation, which plays an increasingly important role in modern rehabilitation protocols. In this study, we propose a novel mobile-computing based approach to assist patients in carrying out the home-based rehabilitation. Specifically, the proposed mobile application can control the inertial sensors in a smartphone to collect rehabilitation activity data. By integrating the knee rehabilitation protocol into the mobile application, it can effectively guide and remind a patient to carry out the protocol in a quality manner. We have conducted experiments by using the mobile application to capture and analyze leg extension data. Experimental results demonstrated that our proposed approach could accurately recognize the leg extension activities and identify the ones completed with poor quality that may result in harmful results. In addition, we have taken the initial step to expand the mobile application to a novel mobile cloud computing (MCC) based telerehabilitation system, in which the mobile subsystem periodically transmits data to the cloud subsystem for storage and analysis. This MCC system will provide a promising solution to assist patients in achieving effective rehabilitation while allowing healthcare providers to provide effective interventions by monitoring the recovery progress.

Keywords: Cloud computing · Knee injury · Mobile computing · Telerehabilitation

1 Introduction

Knee injury is among the most common nonfatal single injury types in work-related injuries [1]. Besides, it is also one of the most frequent sports injuries [2]. Owing to its lengthy recovery (typically more than 24 weeks), the knee injury is identified as one of the top 12 most expensive injury types in terms of total costs (average cost per claim × number of claims) [1]. The high cost tends to force patients to finish the rehabilitation protocol at home. However, the rehabilitation protocol is so complex that a patient can hardly accomplish it without professional supervision. Furthermore, the

© Springer International Publishing Switzerland 2016
C. Stephanidis (Ed.): HCII 2016 Posters, Part II, CCIS 618, pp. 324–329, 2016.
DOI: 10.1007/978-3-319-40542-1_53

assessment of adherence to rehabilitation protocols extensively relies on retrospective self-reports, which can be both inaccurate and biased [3]. As a result, many patients will not be able to return to their pre-injury level [4], thus greatly weakening their ability to participate in social activities as well as affecting their quality of life. Hence, a low-cost and effective assistive approach is highly desirable.

Armed with the cutting-edge mobile cloud computing (MCC) techniques, telerehabilitation can provide an interactive rehabilitation procedure to support a large number of patients. This not only can enable healthcare providers to remotely provide professional supervision to patients at a low cost, but can also offer instant guidance and data analysis to generate better outcomes.

Current telerehabilitation approaches are mostly built on computers with Internet connections and equipped with cameras or video game consoles. For example, the Microsoft Kinect and Xbox jointly provide an interactive model, which has been used in [5] to rehabilitate two young adults with motor impairments in a school setting. Another Kinect guided rehabilitation approach was presented in [6] as a video game, in which a player (patient) was trained to "reach" the target objects displayed in a TV monitor. The Kinect sensor could capture the patient's motions to generate a game score and performance data for post-session replay and analysis. This approach demonstrated the potential to assist patients in finishing the required rehabilitation exercises in an interactive manner. However, this approach suffers from some serious limitations that are imposed by the Kinect's space requirement and its accuracy limitation (the Kinect depicts an object's motion by a skeleton of 20 joint nodes). In [7], the MCC technique was used in an analysis oriented decision support system (AODSS), which consisted of three sides, namely, therapist-, server-, and patient-side. On the patient side, multiple sensors (e.g., Kinect/ Creative Glaze3D/Biosensor) were used to collect activity video data, which was then transmitted to the server-side database in the Cloud. Thus, the therapist could keep track of a patient's rehabilitation progress. Although a multilevel data encoding method was used to encode video data, this approach could still generate a considerable amount of data that exerts substantial influence on the network bandwidth.

Compared with existing approaches, our proposed MCC telerehabilitation system is easy to set up and easy to use. It utilizes a smartphone to collect and transmit data to the cloud for data storage and analysis. Furthermore, it provides an affordable solution to interact and guide patients to complete their rehabilitation activities.

2   Method

Figure 1 shows the framework of our proposed MCC system. The mobile subsystem collects activity data by employing the inertial sensors (i.e., the accelerometer and gyroscope) in a smartphone, which is attached to the affected leg of the user with a sports band. The mobile subsystem provides different options of sampling rates for data collection and can transmit the collected data to the cloud automatically. In case that the network connection is not available, it can also temporarily store the collected data in a local CSV file. Then, our mobile subsystem will guide the user to perform the activities (e.g., range of motion (ROM)) prescribed in the rehabilitation protocol. Novel text-to-speech and voice recognition techniques [8] are employed to interact with the user via voice alerts. Furthermore, our mobile subsystem can alert the user to slow down if the user performs a ROM activity too fast because fast ROM activities may result in harm to the healing knee.

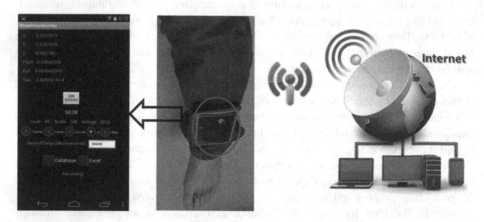

Fig. 1. The assistive system structure

Based on collected data, we will develop a data analysis application in the cloud subsystem to generate reports, which will be sent to patients regarding the number of repetitions of a ROM activity performed during an exercise and the quality of activity completion. In addition, the telerehabilitation will enable healthcare providers to monitor whether a patient has effectively carried out the home-based rehabilitation protocol, and provide necessary intervention if needed.

Figure 2(A) illustrates the three axes (i.e., x, y, and z) of a smartphone. The built-in accelerometer measures accelerations along these three axes. In addition, the angular speed of roll is also marked in Fig. 2(A). Due to the placement of the smartphone during the experiments (see Fig. 1), we use the roll data of the gyroscope to measure the leg extension

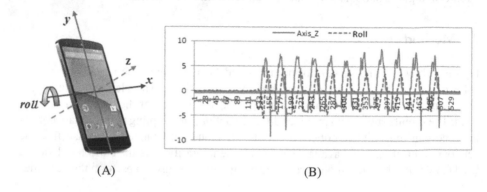

(A)   (B)

Fig. 2. Smartphone sensor dimensions and collected data

activity. Figure 2(B) shows the ROM data related to leg extension activities captured by our mobile subsystem. The blue (solid) curve represents the accelerometer data in the z-axis and the red (dashed) curve represents the gyroscope data of roll. It is clear that both of the accelerometer and gyroscope data showed clear sinusoid-like curves. In comparison, the roll data of the gyroscope demonstrated a clearer and stronger pattern, i.e., the data was not seriously impacted by noise; while the accelerometer data was drifted downward by noise. Hence, we used the gyroscope data in the subsequent analysis.

We have developed a preliminary algorithm as shown in Fig. 3 to analyze the number of ROM activities in each set of exercises, the number of sets of exercises performed in a day, and the quality of activity completion. Particularly, Fig. 2(B) shows that the collected gyroscope data was around 0 when the leg was stationary. In addition, one complete leg extension activity consists of two peak values (one positive and one negative), which can be identified by our algorithm as shown in Fig. 3. If any of the absolute peak values was found to be larger than a preset threshold (e.g. $t = 4.5$ rad/s), our mobile application would record this event and remind the user to slow down to avoid possible harms to the healing knee.

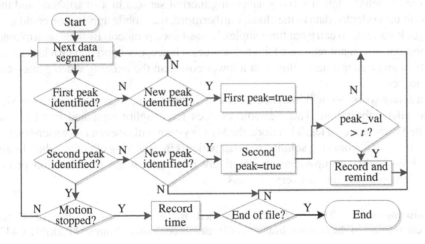

Fig. 3. ROM data analysis

3   Experimental Results

A healthy volunteer participated in this preliminary study. He conducted 6 trials of leg extension with each trial repeating the leg extension activity for 10 times. Among these leg extension activities, 10 activities were purposely finished faster than required. In order to evaluate the applicability of our approach, we used two brands of smartphones, i.e., the Samsung Galaxy SII and LG Nexus 5. Correspondingly, the experiments were conducted twice, each for a specific smartphone.

Table 1 shows the experimental results. Not only could the proposed algorithm accurately recognize all the rehabilitation activities regardless of which brand of smartphones was used, but it could also identify activities finished with poor quality that might lead to harmful consequences.

Table 1. Activity identification accuracy

	Activities		
	Recorded	Identified	Finished with poor quality
Samsung Galaxy SII	60	60	10
LG Nexus 5	60	60	10

4 Conclusions

In this paper, we presented a novel mobile computing-based application aiming to achieve telerehabilitation for knee injuries. The proposed application could collect and analyze the rehabilitation activity data using inertial sensors in a smartphone and then transmit the collected data to the cloud. Furthermore, the mobile application could assist and guide patients to carry out the complex home-based protocol. Besides smartphones, our approach does not require additional devices. Hence, our approach provides a more practical and easier to use solution at a lower cost than the existing video game-based approaches.

In future work, we will integrate wearable devices, e.g., smartwatch, into the MCC based telerehabilitation. The wearable devices have lightweight and can be easily attached to the affected leg. Therefore, the MCC system will be even more user-friendly. It will provide a promising solution to assist patients in achieving effective rehabilitation and allow healthcare providers to effectively intervene in the rehabilitation process through monitoring the recovery progress.

Acknowledgement. This study was supported by the National Institute of General Medical Sciences of the National Institutes of Health through Grant Number 8P20GM103447.

References

1. Mroz, T.M., et al.: Frequency and cost of claims by injury type from a state workers' compensation fund from 1998 through 2008. Arch. Phys. Med. Rehabil. **95**(6), 1048–1054 (2014)
2. Common Sports Injuries: Incidence and Average Charges (2014). https://aspe.hhs.gov/pdf-report/common-sports-injuries-incidence-and-average-charges
3. Brewer, B., et al.: Rehabilitation adherence and anterior cruciate ligament reconstruction outcome. Psychol. Health Med. **9**(2), 163–175 (2004)
4. te Wierike, S.C., et al.: Psychosocial factors influencing the recovery of athletes with anterior cruciate ligament injury: a systematic review. Scand. J. Med. Sci. Sports **23**(5), 527–540 (2013)
5. Chang, Y.-J., Chen, S.-F., Huang, J.-D.: A Kinect-based system for physical rehabilitation: a pilot study for young adults with motor disabilities. Res. Dev. Disabil. **32**(6), 2566–2570 (2011)

6. Lange, B., et al.: Interactive game-based rehabilitation using the Microsoft Kinect. In: 2012 IEEE Virtual Reality Workshops (VRW) (2012)
7. Li, S., et al.: A mobile cloud computing framework integrating multilevel encoding for performance monitoring in telerehabilitation. Math. Probl. Eng. **2015**, 1–14 (2015)
8. Google. Google Text-to-speech Application (2016). https://play.google.com/store/apps/details?id=com.google.android.tts&hl=en

Multiplatform Game Type of Health Survey on Cancer Patient's Stress Level

Seong Kuk Park[1(✉)], Sang Rak Jeong[2], Dong Gyun Kim[2], Jae Hee Kim[2], Yang Kyu Lim[1], Han Byul Moon[3], and Jin Wan Park[2]

[1] Graduate School of Advanced Imaging Sciences, Multimedia and Film,
Chung-Ang University, Seoul, South Korea
jrvis117@gmail.com, lim0386@gmail.com
[2] Integrative Engineering Technology, Chung-Ang University, Seoul, South Korea
{homarin,eastgerm_8}@naver.com, jaycekingkjh@gmail.com,
jinpark@cau.ac.kr
[3] Department of Psychology, Chung-Ang University, Seoul, South Korea
mhanbyul@gmail.com

Abstract. Monitoring the changing condition of cancer patients is a significant part of their treatment. Stress coming from the patient's current situation may have a great effect on the spread of cancer cells. Thus, a cancer patient's stress level is a crucial factor for doctors to refer to when deciding for an appropriate treatment. In order to gather these data, "Distress Thermometer and Problem List" distributed by NCCN (National Comprehensive Cancer Network) is used globally, but the participation rate among patients is low. This is because the survey is very tedious and provides no feedback, which makes the patients feel like it is a waste of time. This game is made based on "Distress Thermometer and Problem List", and has entered in the 2016 Game4health competition in Utah, USA under the name of "Measure Your Stress Level". This game uses fun and cute animations to identify with the patient's situation and patients can participate in the survey in a more entertaining way. Also, at the end of the survey, a stress relieving game is provided as a package in order to make the survey more engaging. The game is based on a multiplatform game engine so it can be outputted to smartphone, website, exe file making the game accessible anywhere, at any time. Thus, it will be easier for the medical staff to gather more data in less time.

Keywords: Distress survey · Multiplatform game · Game design

1 Introduction

Cancer patients not only go through physical pain, but mental anguish as well. The mental anguish that patients go through, regardless of the reason, is called "distress". Cancer patient's distress symptoms may vary from everyday emotions such as sadness, fear, dilemma to morbid conditions that damage psychological and social functions such as depression, anxiety, panic, social isolation, existence crisis. Distress is known to affect the spread of cancer cells [1] and to figure out the reasons for distress, NCCN (National Comprehensive Cancer Network) distributed a globally approved survey called

© Springer International Publishing Switzerland 2016
C. Stephanidis (Ed.): HCII 2016 Posters, Part II, CCIS 618, pp. 330–334, 2016.
DOI: 10.1007/978-3-319-40542-1_54

"Distress Thermometer and Problem List" [2]. This survey contains many items related to possible stress situations the patients may be going through. However, the survey is made up of formal questions and provides no feedback at the end, which may be the reason why many patients do not participate in the survey. Thus, it is a tiring process for the doctors who regularly require surveys to be done, and the patients who have to participate in such surveys. "Measure Your Stress Level", a multiplatform measurement game was made to induce the patients to participate in the survey more, and to offer the medical staff a more efficient data service (Fig. 1).

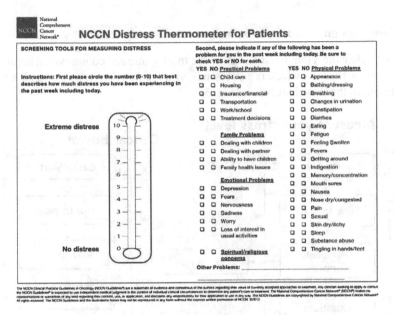

Fig. 1. Distress Thermometer and Problem List (Source: NCCN)

2 System Overview

2.1 Client-Server Model

This app is made by using a game engine called coco2d-js. Using the JavaScript properties, this engine supports cocos2d-html5 which is used for web app development and cococos2d-x which is used to develop native apps [3]. As a result, codes written in JavaScript can be outputted to web, iOS, android, exe file, resulting in a cross platform app.

The game is uploaded on a heroku server which is Paas (platform-as-a-service) base and provided to patients. After the game, the patient's data is saved by going through a server with a node.js based express module and is automatically saved on DB. The saved data is passed to another URL address through the server's router and there, it uses d3.js library to show the results using data visualization and is then offered to the medical staff (Fig. 2).

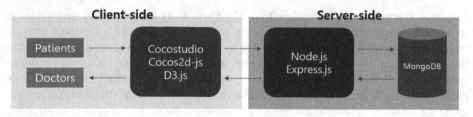

Fig. 2. App service model

2.2 Game Design

The game "Measure Your Stress Level" is the main game and comes with a bonus game called "Cancer Buster", which is a stress-relieving game. The game's overall structure is illustrated in the flowchart below (Fig. 3).

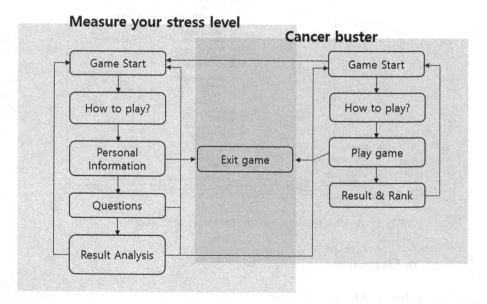

Fig. 3. Game flow chart

The Distress Thermometer and Problem List mentioned earlier is made up of 40 questions, and as it was a bit difficult to make one game scene for each question, the game uses 4 types of problem form to summarize the survey into 24 game scenes (Fig. 4).

In order to make the game less tedious, each question is made up of fun and cute images and a time limit is set so the survey can be processed more smoothly. If the time limit has passed, a doctor character shows up and asks if the player will end the game. Additionally, multiple sound effects are used to make the game livelier. After the game, the player's stress level is shown as a result of the weighted sum of each question, and the result is shown by indicating one of the 9 levels, where each level is represented to the user with a fun sprite image.

After the result is shown, the game asks the user if they will play the bonus game, Cancer Buster. Cancer buster is an arcade game and the goal is to protect the healthy cells from the cancer cells.

Fig. 4. Measure your stress level's problem form

Fig. 5. Cancer buster's game characters

The game scene is processed as illustrated in Fig. 6 - the cancer cells can be removed by using click and touch. The healthy cells that have survived from cancer cells turn into a growing cell, and if the growing cells develop into a certain size, it changes into an organ. This is counted as a game score, and the player that saves the most organs goes to the top rank. The organ characters are used in cooperation with the National Cancer Center [4], and the organs where cancer is likely to occur are used as the characters (Fig. 5).

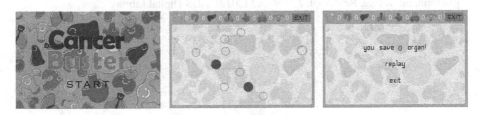

Fig. 6. Cancer buster's game scenes

As the game continues, the cells continue to grow with the ratio of growing cells at 10 %, cancer cells at 40 %, normal cells at 50 %, thus making the game harder. Also, physics engine is used to calculate the cell's collision so the cell's movement is more natural [5].

3   Conclusion and Development Plan

The project's main purpose was to gather data of cancer patients, so the game was designed to increase patient's participation. Multiplatform game engine was used to make the game more accessible to patients, and the game is easy to understand due to its simplicity and intuitive interface. Also, fun and cute characters and images, along with appropriate sound effects, and a bonus game for stress relief were used to reduce the wearisome process of the original survey. It is expected to offer great support to the medical staff who have to gather the patient's data on a daily basis. Currently, it is only a simple 2D game, but we are planning to develop it into a 3D game that can be played on a VR device. By doing this, we will focus more on the stressful situations that cancer patients go through.

Acknowledgment.   This study was funded by a grant from the Korea Creative Content Agency (R2014040055).

References

1. Caroline, P.L., Cameron, J.N., Corina, K., Edoardo, B., Jonathan, G.H., Hilmy, I., Matthew, A.P., Ming, G.C., Tara, K., Nicole, R., Giuseppe, R., Sara, G., Colin, W.P., Davide, F., Andreas, M., Steven, A.S., Erica, K.S.: Chronic stress in mice remodels lymph vasculature to promote tumour cell dissemination. Nat. Commun. (2016). NPG
2. National Comprehensive Cancer Network. http://www.nccn.org
3. Yang, L., Xiaojun, H.: Research and implementation of cross-platform engine for intelligent terminal. In: Computer Science and Applications, pp. 137–141. CRC Press, Shanghai (2014)
4. National Cancer Center. http://www.ncc.re.kr
5. Rahamathunnisa, U., Pragadeeswaran, S.: Collision detection game using cocos2Dx-A cross platform. Int. J. Eng. Res. Appl. **2**, 959–963 (2012). ADS Digital Library

Smartphone Application Content for Prevention and Improvement of Adolescents' Depression

Jung-Sun Park[1], Hyeon-Woo Bak[1], Sun-Hee Ham[1], Jae-Suk Cho[1], Hye-Ji Yoon[1],
Ji-Soo Park[2], Da-Yeon Seo[2], and Jung-A Gwon[2(✉)]

[1] Science of Education, Soonchunhyang University, Asan, Korea
[2] Youth Education and Counseling, Soonchunhyang University, Asan, Korea
hellogwon@gmail.com

Abstract. The purpose of this study was to develop the content of a smartphone application for the prevention and improvement of adolescent depression. This application has been developed by a psychology laboratory and a computer software engineering laboratory for an interdisciplinary convergence study to develop and implement the application content. For the management and treatment of depression, the theoretical basis of the content was focused on cognitive behavioral therapy. In addition, for the depression test, we used the CES-D (depression scale test).

Keywords: Smartphone application · Adolescent depression · Cognitive behavioral therapy

1 Introduction

Because adolescents' mental health affects their mental health in adulthood, its importance is becoming more recognized. Particularly, adolescent depression appears severe, as it is largely related to maladjustment in family and school life, suicide, and emotional disturbance even in adulthood [1]. Recently, demands for technology highlighting user-centered convenience are increasing; thus, smartphone applications that connect engineering with psychology are currently under development. However, most applications developed so far are just for reporting mental states after diagnosing and analyzing users on a one-off basis, which is not practical and not able to support consistent psychotherapy [2]. Therefore, with the purpose of enhancing adolescents' mental health, this research aims to develop smartphone-based application content that can provide continuous self-diagnosis and cognitive behavioral therapy-based self-practice with both individualized and specific analysis for depression, one of the main mental health problems affecting adolescents [3].

2 Application Content for Prevention and Improvement of Adolescent Depression

Among the features of adolescent depression, irritability is mainly reported first as an emotional symptom, and such irritability is displayed as rebellious and hostile behaviors.

© Springer International Publishing Switzerland 2016
C. Stephanidis (Ed.): HCII 2016 Posters, Part II, CCIS 618, pp. 335–338, 2016.
DOI: 10.1007/978-3-319-40542-1_55

Difficulty concentrating may be displayed along with feelings of worthlessness, sense of refusal, and irrational fear as major symptoms.

Based on the cognitive behavioral treatment approach acknowledged as an effective treatment method to change the maladaptive thinking and behavior problems that are related with depression, the depression symptoms are analyzed, and specific measures are employed to promote improvement. The application content developed in this research considered adolescents' preferences and interests. In addition, based on daily patterns, its components were based on cognitive behavioral therapy, which can be employed by therapists and users in group psychotherapy or counseling.

The specific measures utilized for developing the content were as follows.

2.1 Depression Test (CES-D):

- Users complete the depression test in the main menu so that they can understand their level of depression; then, they can choose an appropriate solution from the content menu.

2.2 Recommendation for Psychological Counseling:

- To be able to look back life accidents causing negative emotions and sentiments, and find automatic thinking and cognitive errors.
- To be able to change the cognitive errors to realistic thinking, find appropriate alternatives for automatic thinking.
- Content: Making life journals/thinking charts, changing negative thinking, preparing weekly schedule of positive activities.

2.3. Recommendation for Emotion Management:

- By periodic evaluation of emotional conditions to help recognition of major emotions related to their own depression and presentation of counseling treatment measure

Fig. 1. Checkup for emotion control content

suitable for each condition, allow voluntary and continuous improvement of problems in life (Fig. 1).

- Content: Daily evaluation of emotional condition, checkup for emotion control, relaxation therapy (Fig. 2).

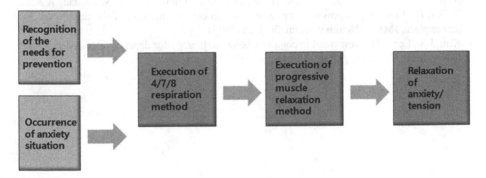

Fig. 2. Application process for relaxation therapy

3   Conclusion

The application content of this research focused on the prevention and improvement of depression, a serious mental problem that many adolescents experience. It efficiently supported adolescents' wellness by enabling them to think independently regarding problem solving and prevention plans. In addition, this application will be an important measure of adolescents' wellness, because the intercommunication created in this application can be used in group psychotherapy or counseling activities.

Future research for the evaluation of this application will be conducted through depression-related adolescent group counseling. Before using this application in group counseling, a preliminary investigation will be conducted, and we will modify and supplement it based on the investigation result.

Henceforth, we will consistently reflect users' reviews and assessments of this service as well as adolescents' preferences and demands to improve its user-centered practicality. Lastly, we plan to improve user satisfaction by providing a customized service through a variety of information and counseling strategies related to adolescent mental health.

Acknowledgements. This research was supported by the MSIP (Ministry of Science, ICT, and Future Planning), Korea, under the ITRC (Information Technology Research Center) support program (IITP-2016-H8601-16-1009) supervised by the IITP (Institute for Information & communications Technology Promotion).

References

1. Kang, H.A.: The effect of cumulative risk of adolescents on their depression and anxiety. Korean J. Youth Stud. 20(9) (2013)
2. Nelson, S., Levitan, M.-J., Johnson, A., Bender, J.L., Hamilton-Page, M., Jadad, A.A.R., Wiljer, D.: Finding a depression app: a review and content analysis of the depression app marketplace. JMIR mHealth uHealth. **3**(1), 16 (2015)
3. Kim, J.B., Lee S.H.: New trend in cognitive behavior therapy for depressive disorders. Cogn. Behav. Ther. Korea 6(2) (2006)

Challenges Involved in the Design of an e-Health Application for a Wearable Scoliosis Monitoring System

Gheorghe Daniel Voinea[(⊠)], Cristian Postelnicu, and Silviu Butnariu

Transilvania University of Brasov, Brasov, Romania
voinea.dani@gmail.com, cristian.postelnicu@yahoo.com,
butnariu@unitbv.ro

Abstract. The use of a wearable scoliosis monitoring system can improve the process of rehabilitation by offering objective information about the movement of the spine. Such a system provides a new source of knowledge to physicians and enables them to implement a more efficient treatment. The system uses magnetic and inertial measurement units (IMUs) that are placed on an adjustable frame. The main challenges for an eHealth application and a multi-criteria analysis are presented in this paper.

Keywords: e-Health · Scoliosis monitoring · Portable device

1 Introduction

Spinal disorders in particular back and neck pain are a very common situation, regardless of age, gender or social status. According to recent studies, spinal disorders affect our work capacity and consume more health care resources than any other health problems [1]. An efficient and user-friendly method to assess disability in people with spine pain is the use of Patient-Reported Outcome (PRO) questionnaires [2]. Although this method is demonstrated to facilitate patient self-management strategies [3], this might not be enough to properly monitor the effectiveness of a physical treatment. The possibility of obtaining objective data, which describe the movement of the spine while the patient is doing exercises, can help the clinician improve the rehabilitation process.

The development of Information and Communication Technologies (ICT) have enabled health and healthcare systems to improve the quality of life and bring innovative products on the health market. e-Health represents the use of ICT in health products, services and processes in order to improve the health of citizens. e-Health or health information technologies (HITs) include the interaction between patients and health-service providers, institution-to-institution transmission of data, or the peer-to-peer communication between patients and health professionals. The wellbeing and e-Health domains present a high growth potential by unlocking effective health data exchange [4].

Human Computer Interaction (HCI) involvement in eHealth will help to design more informative health records for clinicians [5], but the main opportunity is to bridge individually developed health strategies with health information provided by professionals [6].

© Springer International Publishing Switzerland 2016
C. Stephanidis (Ed.): HCII 2016 Posters, Part II, CCIS 618, pp. 339–344, 2016.
DOI: 10.1007/978-3-319-40542-1_56

The main factors that need to be evaluated in the process of designing and developing an online health application are users' needs, data security and privacy, products risks and benefits, its feasibility and user acceptance to the new technologies [7].

2   Materials and Methods

The architecture of the wearable scoliosis monitoring system is presented in the following figure (Fig. 1).

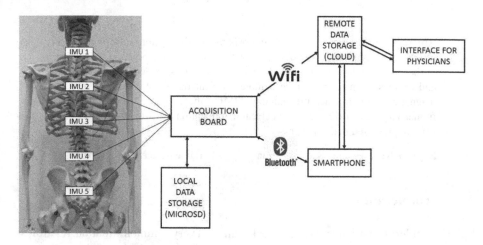

Fig. 1. The architecture of the wearable scoliosis monitoring

Regarding the communication of the system with the users and physicians, two wireless connections were implemented, Wi-Fi and Bluetooth. While Wi-Fi has the advantage of directly transmitting the information to the remote data storage, it comes with the cost of great energy consumption and is not recommended for real time monitoring. Bluetooth is preferred because it increases the autonomy of the system and the user can easily verify his recommended posture with the help of a mobile application installed on a smartphone or tablet. In order to further increase the autonomy, the information gathered from the sensors is stored locally on a microSD card and regularly transmitted to the remote data storage.

The number of sensors that can be used is limited by their size and also by the limitations of the I2C communication protocol. While a higher number of sensors enables a better detection of the movements of the spine, the number of IMUs was limited to five, which presented good results.

A key point is the adaptability and ergonomics of the system. The frame has rubber bands that can be easily adjusted to fit patients of different sizes.

A major challenge is represented by data security and privacy. As stated by the European Commission [8]: "In all countries, trust in e-Health systems by both citizens and professionals has been identified as one if not the key challenge. Privacy is recognized as the most sensitive aspect of e-Health records systems." The information gathered by the system can be accessed by the patient and his physician from any computer, by using a username and password. Access control ensures that users can only access healthcare data that they are allowed to access based on their authentication and access levels.

The mobile application for patients has two main roles: inform the patient about the recommended posture and give alerts in case of prolonged bad posture, and also transmit the information received from the acquisition board to the cloud.

The user interface of the e-Health application is designed to be easy to use by both patients and physicians and does not require a special training in order to use it. A further study is necessary to find more ways to increase motivation and improve acceptance in order to make the technology more user friendly for older people [9].

3 Challenges

The progress of health care systems has been rapidly growing thanks to the Information and Communication Technology advances. A recent trend is to use advanced equipment to monitor a patient's progress from the comfort of their own home.

The main challenges identified by Kreps [10] for designing HITs include the following: high interactivity, interoperability, dynamic and engaging design, and providing interpersonal connections that can have the reach of mass media. Interactivity factors that have the biggest influence on the quality of a web site are connectedness, playfulness and reciprocal communication [11]. Interpersonal connections can be developed by the help of artificial intelligence that can act as a guide for the rehabilitation session, although this feature will not be implemented in the present application. A direct link between the patient and physicians is facilitated by a mobile application and a web based user interface, which can only be accessed with a username and password. Interoperability represents the ability that allows distinct systems to exchange information and perform compatible transactions [12].

Other challenges that need to be addressed in order to ensure an effective communication of eHealth applications are the following: strategic design, accurate monitoring and responsive adaptation [10]. Studies have shown that communication between patients and clinicians that is based on computer applications, has the potential to enhance the confidence and knowledge of the patient [13].

Petersen et al. [14] highlighted a major challenge that appears in eHealth development, and that is how to create a connection between individuals with different backgrounds. IT professionals need to consider the point of view of the user and focus on making the applications easy to work with, in a clinical context.

In order to prioritize the technical and functional characteristics of the scoliosis monitoring system, we used competitive engineering methods. The Analytical Hierarchy Process (AHP) is used to assist researchers in finding the appropriate solution that fits their needs, but it does not guarantee that it will be the correct one. AHP offers a comprehensive and rational environment that helps in the process of decision making, by representing and quantifying the elements of the problem, correlating them to the main objectives of the system and to evaluate other possible solutions.

The software Qualica QFD [15] was used to perform the criteria-based AHP. The first step is to identify the criteria, which are entered in the 'Functional Requirements' tab. In Fig. 2 we see the matrix generated by the software, after entering the criteria. The second step requires a direct comparison between the criteria by ranking them with the help of numbers from 0 to 9 (9 – most important, 0 – less important) (Fig. 3).

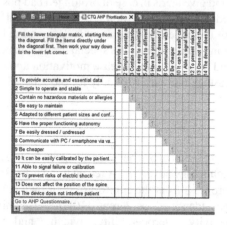

Fig. 2. Matrix criteria of Qualica QFD

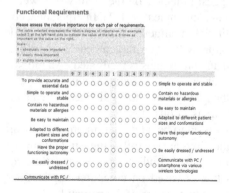

Fig. 3. Criteria assessment

The results from the prioritization process of the criteria are presented in Fig. 4. Two criteria stand out from the graphic and reveal the most important conditions that the scoliosis monitoring system must fulfill: the device should not affect the position of the spine and it must provide accurate and meaningful data regarding the movement. The criteria that are included in the 5.5–10 % interval are also crucial and refer to aspects such as ergonomics, safety, stability, adaptability and communication. The remaining six criteria should also be taken into consideration, but their impact on the overall system is less significant.

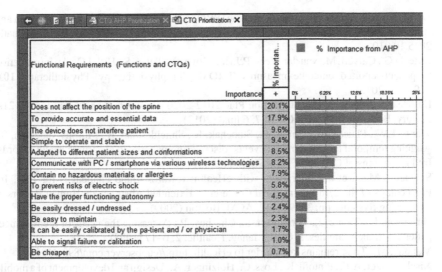

Functional Requirements (Functions and CTQs)	Importance +	% Importance from AHP
Does not affect the position of the spine	20.1%	
To provide accurate and essential data	17.9%	
The device does not interfere patient	9.6%	
Simple to operate and stable	9.4%	
Adapted to different patient sizes and conformations	8.5%	
Communicate with PC / smartphone via various wireless technologies	8.2%	
Contain no hazardous materials or allergies	7.9%	
To prevent risks of electric shock	5.8%	
Have the proper functioning autonomy	4.5%	
Be easily dressed / undressed	2.4%	
Be easy to maintain	2.3%	
It can be easily calibrated by the pa-tient and / or physician	1.7%	
Able to signal failure or calibration	1.0%	
Be cheaper	0.7%	

Fig. 4. Results of multi-criterial analysis

4   Conclusions

Health technologies are becoming more ubiquitous and are starting to become a part of our lives. By developing wearable devices that patients can use at home, with minimal intrusion in their normal lives, rehabilitation sessions may become more efficient and pleasurable. There are several mobile applications that monitor health related parameters, but they are not accurate enough to be taken in consideration by clinicians. A solution for allowing better home measurements is to use special equipment/sensors that can transfer the data straight to the Internet, where medical professionals have access. The main problem is guaranteeing the security of the data and blocking unauthorized access.

The scoliosis monitoring system uses specific sensors to measure motion and transmits the data to a paired mobile device. Patients have access to their own data and can receive a feedback regarding their posture. Patient related data is backed up regularly on a server and can only be viewed by their corresponding physician.

Acknowledgments.   This paper was realized within the Partnership Programme in priority domains - PN-II, which runs with the financial support of MEN-UEFISCDI, Project no. 227/2014, System for Diagnosis and Therapy of Spine Diseases (SPINE).

References

1. Martin, B.I., Deyo, R.A., Mirza, S.K., Turner, J.A., Comstock, B.A., Hollingworth, W., et al.: Expenditures and health status among adults with back and neck problems. J. Am. Med. Assoc. **299**(6), 656–664 (2008)

2. Leahy, E., et al.: Patient-Reported Outcome (PRO) questionnaires for people with pain in any spine region. A systematic review. Manual Ther. (2015). http://dx.doi.org/10.1016/j.math.2015.10.010

3. Kyte, D.G., Calvert, M., van der Wees, P.J., ten Hove, R., Tolan, S., Hill, J.C.: An introduction to patient-reported outcome measures (PROMs) in physiotherapy. Physiotherapy **101**, 119–125 (2015)

4. European Commision, eHealth Action Plan 2012-2020 - Innovative healthcare for the 21st century, Brussels, 6.12.2012 COM, 736 final (2012)

5. Wang, T.W., Plaisant, C., Quinn, A., Stanchak, R., Shneiderman, B., MurphyAnderson, S.: Aligning temporal data by sentinel events: discovering patterns in electronic health records. In: Proceeidngs of CHI 2008, pp. 457–466 (2008)

6. Schraefel, M.C., et al.: Interacting with eHealth: towards grand challenges for HCI. In: Proceedings of the 27th International Conference Extended Abstracts on Human Factors in Computing Systems, pp. 3309–3312. ACM, Boston (2009)

7. Gustafson, D., Taylor, J., Thompson, S., Chesney, P.: Assessing the needs of breast cancer patients and their families. J. Qual. Manag. Healthc. **2**, 6–17 (1993)

8. Mahony, M.: Trust remains key barrier to eHealth. http://euobserver.com/893/31958

9. Nischelwitzer, A.K., Pintoffl, K., Loss, C., Holzinger, A.: Design and development of a mobile medical application for the management of chronic diseases: methods of improved data input for older people. In: Holzinger, A. (ed.) USAB 2007. LNCS, vol. 4799, pp. 119–132. Springer, Heidelberg (2007)

10. Kreps, G.L., et al.: New directions in eHealth communication: opportunities and challenges. Patient Educ. Couns. **78**(3), 329–336 (2010)

11. Chen, K., Yen, D.C.: Improving the quality of online presence through interactivity. Inf. Manag. **42**(1), 217–226 (2004). ISSN 0378-7206. http://dx.doi.org/10.1016/j.im.2004.01.005

12. Rothenberg, J., Botterman, M., Oranje-Nassau C.V.: Towards a Dutch interoperability framework. RAND Europe (2008)

13. Wald, H.S., Dube, C.E., Anthony, D.C.: Untangling the web—the impact of Internet use on health care and the physician–patient relationship. Patient Educ. Couns. **68**, 218–224 (2007)

14. Petersen, L.S., Bertelsen, P., Bjørnes, C.: Cooperation and communication challenges in small-scale eHealth development projects. Int. J. Med. Inf. **82**(12), e375–e385 (2013). doi:10.1016/j.ijmedinf.2013.03.008

15. Qualica Quality Function Deployment. http://www.qualica.de/qps_qfd.html

Location-based and Navigation
Applications

Car Park Finder – Presumptive Design Brings the Best Out of It!

Damian Chen[✉], Siang Huat (Alfred) Teoh,
and Siew Ling (Cathy) Yong

Intel Microelectronics Sdn Bhd, Bayan Lepas Free Industrial Zone Phase 3,
Halaman Kampung Jawa, 11900 Penang, Malaysia
{damian.chen,alfred.siang.huat.teoh,
cathy.yong}@intel.com

Abstract. It is said that great user experience starts with great user centric design. This paper narrates how Presumptive Design (PrD), a design research technique, was used by a small UX team of 3 volunteers to rapidly and inexpensively overcome a tight schedule and come up with a UX design for project called Car Park Finder. We will explore how through some perseverance, PrD was used successfully to develop a working proof of concept that became a showcase for a Smart City solution.

Keywords: Presumptive design · User experience · Car park finder · User centered design · Smart city solution

1 Introduction

In big cities/metropolis, it takes an average of 20–30 min to find parking. All that according to a UK research [1], adds up to around 2549 h or 106 days of a motorist's life wasted searching for parking space in streets, malls or city centers. This is expected to worsen with some 1 + billion cars on roads at present and growing to 2 billion in a decade. Eliminating all this waste of time, not to mention fuel wastage and needless illegal parking issues called for an innovative, user friendly, effective and efficient solution.

Car Park Finder (CPF) is Intel's answer to this bane of urban city living. This innovative solution uses IOT gateways, magnetic sensors, and mobile APIs to enable motorist to search for car parks, reserve them and pay via e-payment. It also offers establishments opportunity to utilize parking data with BI to generate revenue. A win-win for both users who want hassle a free parking and proprietors with profits on their mind.

2 Presumptive Design (PrD): To Boldly Go

The saying "Shoot first, ask questions later" usually conjures up negative impressions and so might "Do First, Ask forgiveness later", however Presumptive design which follows that train of thought offers a different perspective. It embraces the value to be bold in delivering transformative solutions with superior customer experience.

C. Stephanidis (Ed.): HCII 2016 Posters, Part II, CCIS 618, pp. 347–353, 2016.
DOI: 10.1007/978-3-319-40542-1_57

The CPF is a collaborative project by a multidisciplinary team of Intel volunteers coming together in their spare time to figure out a novel solution for a real life problem. With just a basic scope of technologies to be used, vague ideas on desired/required features, the proof of concept (POC) for Car Park Finder was developed using a reverse design process focused on the end user's perspective, envisioned parking experience from market researched solutions and targeting prestigious establishments aiming to provide premier parking services for their customers.

The team collected lots of ideas for the solution and a method was soon needed to determine which combinations from the many ideas, works best for the least amount of time, effort and cost.

Cue Presumptive Design (PrD). This methodology uses simple prototypes and provides opportunities to experiment with designs faster to see which is most effective as it elicits user reactions, uncovering issues in the design solution while simultaneously enable requirements gathering.

Using rapid prototyping, low fidelity sketches and simple mock ups of the solution were crafted to create design blueprints for users to provide feedback and reactions on design assumptions and intentions.

During interview sessions, users were given scenarios to find out how the solution would be use to complete tasks. Through this conversations, requirement gaps and assumption faults in the solution were uncovered. This iteration with users repeats after the solution is refined based on the feedbacks. Each refined iteration improves the solution's usability until it had a very good sense of the user's actual needs and achieves the desired CPF experience (Figs. 1, 2, 3).

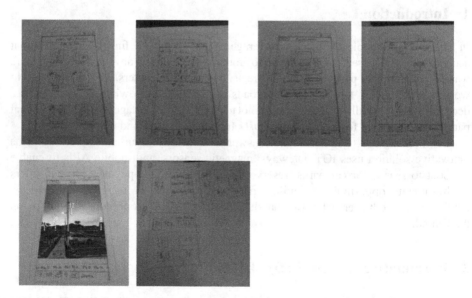

Fig. 1. The first low fidelity rapid prototype design used with users.

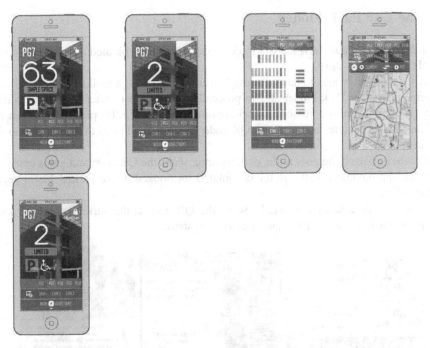

Fig. 2. The second iteration of low fidelity rapid prototype designs used with users.

Fig. 3. The final iteration of low fidelity rapid prototype designs used with users.

3 The Car Park Finder

For the simple layman, how the Car Park Finder works is explained and illustrated in a simple comic strip story.

A user, Justin, wants to have a stress free time parking at a mall over the weekend, he remembers Car Park Finder and so proceeds to book a lot. After some simple data entry, the app presents a number of parking options for Justin. He picks one. When the booking part completes he receives a QR code which he will need to gain access to the parking.

On the day itself, he goes to the parking area, scans the QR code and gains entry. At once the app navigates Justin to the designated lot booked. Once parked Justin gets a confirmation.

When Justin is ready to leave, he scans the QR code at the parking area exit point and payment is deducted from an e-payment system.

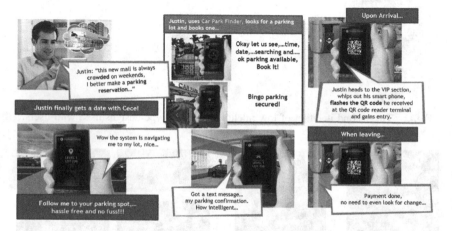

For the Geeky version what happens when a car parks in the lot involves 3 parts; the Sensor, Internet of Things (IoT) gateway and Server.

1. **Sensor to Gateway**; The Intel IoT Gateway software by IoTG (IoT Group) runs on Intel Bay Trail SoC (System on a chip) on Linux Operating System. The software enables the sensor provisioning and management via Zigbee protocol.
2. **Gateway to Sensor**; Once the sensors are provisioned, sensor information is sent back using MQTT (Message Queuing Telemetry Transport) to the IoT gateway every second.
3. **Server to external devices**; between the IoT Gateway and the web server & database server a bridge was developed for data processing and storage. This web and database servers provides the front end service for mobile devices with the information from the sensors.

The entire solution built solely on open source software tools and running on open source operating system drives a low cost of solution implementation (Fig. 4).

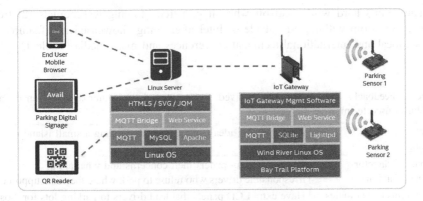

Fig. 4. Car Park Finder Technical Architecture

4 The Fruits of Presumptive Design

Abiding by Presumptive Design's 5 principles (i.e.; 1. Design for failure; 2. Create, Discover, Analyze; 3. Make assumptions explicit; 4. The faster you go, the sooner you know; 5. Iterate, iterate, iterate), the project team collaborated with end users to produce the POC in just 3 months. It wasn't easy. Nobody likes critiques. During interview/engagement sessions with users, the UCD team learnt how to take criticism from users constructively for each solution prototype. Each design flaw called out spurred the team to explore a different design approach, edging the team ever closer to an authentic solution by slowly eliminating flawed design assumptions (Fig. 5).

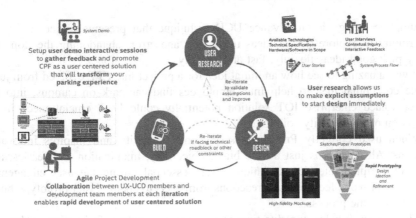

Fig. 5. The flow used abiding by Presumptive Design's 5 principles.

After 4 design iterations, the UCD team produced an end to end system flow, with futuristic bluish luminescent Tron like UI inspired by famous car marques, complete with responsive design interface and voice command notifications that works on multi form factors.

The team's hard work paid off when it garnered glowing testimonials [2] from stakeholders from within and outside of Intel after being showcased and featured in various local and international technical conferences and mass media (Table 1).

Table 1. Feedbacks and evaluation received from external and internal conferences and roadshows used to improve the system.

Chief Minister of Penang	An interesting idea to implement in Penang a small island city.
Managing director gamma solutions	Parking display panels theft concerns and what about irresponsible drivers who refuse to park where they are supposed?
CEO calms technologies	Have extra LCD panels that lead drivers to parking lots for those who do not have the navigation map when they do not book using the application
Site manager intel IT Malaysia	Eco systems needs to be considered, namely integration of premium and traditional methods
Principal engineer intel IT Malaysia	Focus should be on getting product to market first, then once the system is adopted we can really show what we have in store. Focus on how we can integrate with the existing system and get us adopted faster.
UX principal engineer intel	Top Quest or most wanted solution from IoTG.

5 Key Learnings/Conclusion

Presumptive Design is an advance UCD technique that presents project teams the opportunity to explore design ideas using trial and error, abandoning the flops and cherry pick good ideas flexibly, fast and cheaply.

It was amazing to see how an initial idea for a project like CPF evolved from just a simple conceptual idea to help Intel employees find car park on campus, into this greater valued enterprise IOT solution potentially could be a crucial piece in the realization of a smart city solution.

When used correctly PrD enables efficiency, velocity and inspires innovative solutions. All it takes is just a little bit of objectivity, imagination and fearlessness. Carefully scripted interview techniques were essential during the user engagement sessions to provoke feedback and reactions from users to enable faster prototype builds and repeat of the process.

This approach helps expedite time to market of a product, facilitating in this case our footprint expansion in IOT marketplaces by delivering the right solution to the right target user population.

Star2, WEDNESDAY 26 NOVEMBER 2014 SCIENCE 15

< P PREMIUM PARKING

🚗 BOOKED

Prestige Plaza

8.36pm, 27 March 2014

Charges from 5 Dices onwards
To your capted entrance

Autogate detect your arrival

Drive SAFE
we await your arrival!

The Car Finder app is a cool concept for locating
parking spaces, but will require collaboration with
carpark operators to become a reality.

The idea is that if you know your plans and
want to get a guaranteed parking spot instead
of spending all your time stalking the car park
for spaces, you simply pay to book a space
through the app.

People liked the idea, at both the internal
Intel fair and at the Penang Mini Makers Faire.
"Some people thought it looked like a real
product," says Ooi.

Unfortunately it's not actually a functional app: Ooi's team has the code and design
interface down, but for it to work, special
arrangements with parking operators will be
needed.

"The idea is that when you have reached
the mall, you show the QR code to the parking machine, which opens the barrier, then
the app feeds you information about where to
find your designated spot," he explains.

Ooi says the Maker Faire was a good impe-
tus for everyone to get organised enough to
complete the app, and he was impressed at
all the other creations at the fair.

References

1. Motorists spend 106 days looking for parking spots. http://www.telegraph.co.uk/motoring/news/10082461/Motorists-spend-106-days-looking-for-parking-spots.html
2. CPF solution was showcased in various internal/external forum: APAC IoT Focus Seminar for Intel Customers, IoT Transportation Day, Intel IoT Asia 2014 @ Taiwan, Intel MYS IA Maker Open Day (IMIMOD), Penang Mini Maker Faire (PMMF)

A Social Context-Aware Recommender of Itineraries Between Relevant Points of Interest

Dario D'Agostino, Fabio Gasparetti, Alessandro Micarelli,
and Giuseppe Sansonetti$^{(\boxtimes)}$

Department of Engineering, Roma Tre University, Via della Vasca Navale 79,
00146 Rome, Italy
dario.dagostino@outlook.com, {gaspare,micarel,gsansone}@dia.uniroma3.it

Abstract. In this paper, we present a personalized recommender system able to suggest to the target user itineraries that both meet her preferences and needs, and are sensitive to her physical and social contexts. The recommendation process takes into account different aspects: in addition to the popularity of the points of interest (POIs), inferred by considering, for instance, the number of check-ins on social networking services such as Foursquare, it also includes the user's profile, the current context of use, and the user's network of social ties. The system, therefore, consists of four main modules that accomplish the following tasks: (1) the construction of the user's profile according to her interests and tastes; (2) the creation of the path graph in the user's proximity; (3) the routing to locate the first k itineraries that match the query; (4) their ranking through a scoring function that considers the POI popularity, the user's profile, and her physical and social context. The proposed system was evaluated on a sample of 40 real users. Experimental results showed the effectiveness of the proposed recommender.

Keywords: Location-based services · Social networks · Recommender systems

1 Introduction

Location-based social networks (LBSNs) allow users to retrieve points of interest in the area surrounding their current location, and to share with their friends contents related to it, such as photos and geo-tagged texts. The large amount of geographical and social data made available by LBSNs offers an unprecedented opportunity to study the ways in which humans interact with their surroundings based on their social and spatial behavior [1,2]. This paper describes a recommender system of popular itineraries, which enhances the recommendation process with the user profile, the current context of use, and information extracted from social networks. For *popular* itineraries we mean tourist itineraries including venues deemed of interest by the user community. The user

© Springer International Publishing Switzerland 2016
C. Stephanidis (Ed.): HCII 2016 Posters, Part II, CCIS 618, pp. 354–359, 2016.
DOI: 10.1007/978-3-319-40542-1_58

community is extracted from *Foursquare*[1], a social networking service that allows users to share locations with their friends through the *check-in* functionality.

2   The Recommender System

In the proposed recommender system (RS) each user is profiled as a vector of weights whose values (between 0 and 1) express the user's interest in a certain category of points of interest (POIs). Such user profile is explicitly created and implicitly updated. Another crucial factor in the recommendation process is the current physical context, namely, any information that can be used to characterize the situation of an entity [3]. In this case, *entities* are the active user and the POIs, whilst *information* concerns the current location, the time of the day, the day of the week, the weather conditions, the means of transport, and so on. Almost all this information can be determined without the user's involvement. Indeed, the location is detected by the GPS sensor of the mobile device, as well as the means of transport is detected by the accelerometer. Moreover, the weather conditions are obtained from query weather services, based on the current location. Since the main goal is the recommendation of popular routes, the problem has been modeled as the search of a directed graph. Each node represents a POI (i.e., one of the Foursquare venues), each edge represents a direct link between two POIs, with a weight denoting their distance in terms of time (minutes). For the graph construction, we have to select the set of POIs, and then derive the set of edges among them. Therefore, the first step is to select the rectangular region containing those POIs, which is delimited by latitudes and longitudes of the starting point (deducted from the GPS sensor of the device), and the end point (entered by the user). After defining the region boundaries, all the POIs included in the database that fall within this area, form the graph nodes. Such POIs are then filtered based on the contextual information. For instance, time and weather conditions can be used to rule out all the POIs that would be not valid for the current situation. The edge inference and the graph construction occur as follows. The information related to an edge comprises the shortest path to get from one node to another and the traveling time, taking into account the user's means of transport. Obviously, if the user is walking, the edge weight will be increased. Such information is obtained through the Google Maps API[2]: for each pair of nodes (e_i, e_j) the system asks Google for the traveling time from e_i to e_j and the traveling time to e_j to e_i, thus creating the edge. Starting and end nodes are slightly different from the other nodes: while the latter have both incoming and outgoing edges, the starting node has only outgoing edges, the end node only incoming edges. Once inferred all the edges, a complete graph from the starting node to the end node is obtained. Then, a routing algorithm is executed on it. Such algorithm is designed based on the one presented in [4]. More specifically, starting from the itinerary comprised by the only starting and end points, further POIs are gradually inserted until all the available time has been spent. Such insertion is not random, but occurs while sorting the left POIs based on several factors, such as popularity and distance. The routing algorithm returns many itineraries from the starting node to the end node. In order to

---

[1] https://foursquare.com.
[2] https://developers.google.com/maps/.

obtain the first k of them, which maximize the user's satisfaction, the following scoring function is used:

$$score = \alpha \sum_{i=1}^{n} pop(v_i) - \beta \sum_{i=1}^{n-1} dist(v_i, v_{i+1}) + \gamma f(n) + \delta \sum_{i=1}^{n} sim(u, v_i) + \theta \sum_{i=1}^{n} soc(v_i) \quad (1)$$

Such function is made up of several terms. All of them are normalized and weighed by constants whose values were set after empirical analysis. The first term denotes the relevance/popularity level of individual POIs. The popularity level of an itinerary is calculated by summing all the users' check-ins in each POI. The second term represents the total distance of the itinerary, which is given by the sum of the traveling times of each single path. This term is the only negative one, in order to give greater relevance to the shorter routes than the longer ones. The third term takes into account the number of venues in the path. The fourth term expresses the path affinity with the user's taste: for every POI, its affinity with respect to the user's interests is assessed. Such value is computed through the cosine-similarity function between the weight vector representing the user profile and weight vector representing the POI category. The last term gives the social contribution, which includes information derived from social networks. The assumption behind this is that if some friends of the active user perform check-ins in a given POI, then such POI receives a bonus value depending on the check-ins amount.

3   Experimental Evaluation

This section summarizes the preliminary outcomes of the experimental evaluation. Tests were performed on a sample of 40 real users aged between 20 and 65 years, mostly students and academics. Almost all testers had an active account on one or more social networks. First of all, we created five different scenarios with different contexts, so as to have most possible varied situations. An example is: "suppose yourself to be in Rome, in Termini Railway Station, it is raining, on Monday, at 2 pm, by car, traffic is heavy; you have six hours to get to Piazza Navona". Each tester was presented with one of these five scenarios randomly chosen. Based on the scenario and the user profile, the systems returns the first ten itineraries, for each of which the user has to express her satisfaction through a 5-point Likert scale. Itineraries are randomly returned to the target user, so as to preserve the rating fairness. The performance of the recommender was assessed in terms of the normalized version of *Discounted Cumulative Gain (nDCG)* [5]. *nDCG* is usually truncated at a particular rank level to emphasize the importance of the first retrieved documents. To focus on the top-ranked items, we considered the *DCG@n* by analyzing the ranking of the top n itineraries in the recommended list with n from 1 to 10. The measure is defined as follows:

$$nDCG@n = \frac{DCG@n}{IDCG@n} \quad (2)$$

and the Discounted Cumulative Gain (DCG) is defined as:

$$DCG@n = rel_1 + \sum_{i=2}^{n} \frac{rel_i}{\log_2 i} \quad (3)$$

where rel_i is the graded relevance of the i-th result (i.e., $0 = non$-$significant$, $1 = significant$ and $2 = very\ significant$), and the Ideal DCG ($IDCG$) for a query corresponds to the DCG measure where scores are resorted monotonically decreasing, that is, the maximum possible DCG value over that query. $nDCG$ is often used to evaluate search engine algorithms and other techniques whose goal is to order a subset of items in such a way that highly relevant documents are placed on top of the list, while less important ones are moved lower. Basically, higher values of $nDCG$ mean that the system output gets closer to the ideal ranked output. The graph shown in Fig. 1 illustrates the average values of $nDCG$ for each position, based on the ratings of 40 users. The x-axis reports the rank (from 1 to 10), while the y-axis displays the respective value of $nDCG$. Analyzing the obtained results, we can notice how the system allowed us to achieve high $nDCG$ values, showing high accuracy performance.

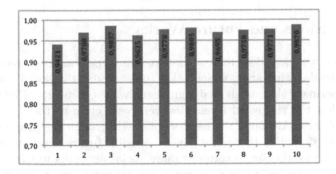

Fig. 1. Values of $nDCG$ for different rank levels.

4   Related Work

In the research literature, there are several approaches to making context-aware mobile interaction available in scenarios where users are looking for categories of points of interest (POIs), such as cultural events and restaurants, through remote location-based services [6]. Time constraints are in general more sensitive in itinerary recommendation. Determining the proper visiting time of each place and the proper transit time from one place to another is fundamental for defining route goodness functions [7]. Yoon et al. [8] explicitly model both the available time of the user and the staying time for each POI included in the itinerary. Techniques based on signal processing are proposed for including time dimension in context-aware recommendation tasks [9,10]. Online photo sharing services, such as Flickr, or real-world public datasets of rich photographers' histories are often used as sources for mining popular venues [11], travel sequences [12] or, more in general, their attractiveness [13]. The large amount of geo-tagged photos shared on SNS allow LBS to mine also demographic information about the locations by detecting people attributes by means of image analysis techniques. In [14] the authors take into consideration several visual features to classify each photo in one of the following attributes: family, friends, couple and solo traveler. By sorting the geo-tagged photos, the followed itineraries are collected and one of the above-mentioned attributes is identified and assigned to each of them. Finally, a Bayesian learning model sorts out the best itinerary given a query and the attributes representing the user profile. Local travel experts can help populate a knowledge base of popular itineraries. Manual customization of the suggested itineraries by the users can provide valuable feedback for improving the local knowledge base [15]. More complex approaches dynamically suggest new POIs according as the last visited ones, their characteristics and categories, personalizing the recommendation as the current context evolves. Multiple conflicting criteria and undesirable situations that may result in the modification of the current schedule can also be considered by monitoring the user's behavior [16].

5   Conclusions and Future Works

In this paper, we have described a context-aware, personalized, recommender system of popular itineraries, which takes into account the social contribution as well. Experimental tests showed significant values in terms of $nDCG$, thus indicating that the suggested itineraries were very close to the ones preferred by the target user. Although the results obtained through the proposed recommender are encouraging, there exist several possible future developments of this work. First, we would like to consider more social networks in the data collection, in order to further refine and customize the recommendation process. An other interesting point would be also to relate the influence of the social factor to each user. The idea is to make such weight to increase or decrease based on the user's past behavior. For instance, if in the past the user has liked the POIs visited by her friends (e.g., giving them check-ins), the value of the social factor may be consequently increased by a certain percentage. Finally, we would like to integrate the recommendation process with an analysis of the user-generated content on social networks. Indeed, in the research literature it has been shown that the accuracy of RSs can be improved by considering sentiments and opinions extracted from the user micro-posts [17–19].

References

1. Biancalana, C., Gasparetti, F., Micarelli, A., Sansonetti, G.: An approach to social recommendation for context-aware mobile services. ACM Trans. Intell. Syst. Technol. **4**(1), 10:1–10:31 (2013)
2. Biancalana, C., Gasparetti, F., Micarelli, A., Sansonetti, G.: Social semantic query expansion. ACM Trans. Intell. Syst. Technol. **4**(4), 60:1–60:43 (2013)
3. Dey, A.K.: Understanding and using context. Pers. Ubiquitous Comput. **5**(1), 4–7 (2001)

4. Hagen, K., Kramer, R., Hermkes, M., Schumann, B., Mueller, P.: Semantic matching and heuristic search for a dynamic tour guide. In: Frew, A.J. (ed.) Proceedings of the International Conference in Innsbruck, Austria, pp. 149–159. Springer, Vienna (2005)
5. Järvelin, K., Kekäläinen, J.: Cumulated gain-based evaluation of IR techniques. ACM Trans. Inf. Syst. **20**(4), 422–446 (2002)
6. Biancalana, C., Flamini, A., Gasparetti, F., Micarelli, A., Millevolte, S., Sansonetti, G.: Enhancing traditional local search recommendations with context-awareness. In: Konstan, J.A., Conejo, R., Marzo, J.L., Oliver, N. (eds.) UMAP 2011. LNCS, vol. 6787, pp. 335–340. Springer, Heidelberg (2011)
7. Hsieh, H.P., Li, C.T., Lin, S.D.: Measuring and recommending time-sensitive routes from location-based data. ACM Trans. Intell. Syst. Technol. **5**(3), 45:1–45:27 (2014)
8. Yoon, H., Zheng, Y., Xie, X., Woo, W.: Social itinerary recommendation from user-generated digital trails. Pers. Ubiquitous Comput. **16**(5), 469–484 (2011)
9. Biancalana, C., Gasparetti, F., Micarelli, A., Miola, A., Sansonetti, G.: Context-aware movie recommendation based on signal processing and machine learning. In: Proceedings of the 2nd Challenge on Context-Aware Movie Recommendation. CAMRa 2011, pp. 5–10. ACM, New York (2011)
10. Arru, G., Feltoni Gurini, D., Gasparetti, F., Micarelli, A., Sansonetti, G.: Signal-based user recommendation on twitter. In: Proceedings of the 22nd International Conference on World Wide Web, WWW 2013 Companion, pp. 941–944. ACM, New York (2013)
11. Brilhante, I., Macedo, J.A., Nardini, F.M., Perego, R., Renso, C.: Where shall we go today?: planning touristic tours with tripbuilder. In: Proceedings of the 22nd ACM International Conference on Conference on Information & Knowledge Management, CIKM 2013, pp. 757–762. ACM, New York (2013)
12. Zheng, Y., Xie, X.: Learning travel recommendations from user-generated GPS traces. ACM Trans. Intell. Syst. Technol. **2**(1), 2:1–2:29 (2011)
13. Waga, K., Tabarcea, A., Franti, P.: Recommendation of points of interest from user generated data collection. In: International Conference on Collaborative Computing: Networking, Applications and Worksharing, October 2012, pp. 550–555 (2012)
14. Chen, Y.Y., Cheng, A.J., Hsu, W.: Travel recommendation by mining people attributes and travel group types from community-contributed photos. IEEE Trans. Multimedia **15**(6), 1283–1295 (2013)
15. Schaller, R., Elsweiler, D.: Itinerary recommenders: how do users customize their routes and what can we learn from them? In: Proceedings of the 5th Information Interaction in Context Symposium, pp. 185–194. ACM, New York (2014)
16. Takayuki, S., Munenobu, N., Naoki, S., Yoshihiro, M., Keiichi, Y., Minoru, I.: A personal navigation system with functions to compose tour schedules based on multiple conflicting criteria. IPSJ Digital Courier **46**(11), 2590–2598 (2005)
17. Gurini, D.F., Gasparetti, F., Micarelli, A., Sansonetti, G.: iSCUR: interest and sentiment-based community detection for user recommendation on twitter. In: Dimitrova, V., Kuflik, T., Chin, D., Ricci, F., Dolog, P., Houben, G.-J. (eds.) UMAP 2014. LNCS, vol. 8538, pp. 314–319. Springer, Heidelberg (2014)
18. Feltoni Gurini, D., Gasparetti, F., Micarelli, A., Sansonetti, G.: Enhancing social recommendation with sentiment communities. In: Wang, J., et al. (eds.) WISE 2015. LNCS, vol. 9419, pp. 308–315. Springer, Heidelberg (2015). doi:10.1007/978-3-319-26187-4_28
19. Feltoni Gurini, D., Gasparetti, F., Micarelli, A., Sansonetti, G.: Analysis of sentiment communities in online networks. In: SIGIR (2015)

A Flexible Scenario-Based Mobile Learning System for Disaster Evacuation

Hisashi Hatakeyama[1,3(✉)], Masahiro Nagai[2], and Masao Murota[3]

[1] Library and Academic Information Center, Tokyo Metropolitan University, Tokyo, Japan
hatak@tmu.ac.jp
[2] University Education Center, Tokyo Metropolitan University, Tokyo, Japan
mnagai@tmu.ac.jp
[3] Graduate School of Decision Science and Technology, Department of Human System, Science,
Tokyo Institute of Technology, Tokyo, Japan
murota@hum.titech.ac.jp

Abstract. Disaster prevention awareness has been growing in Japan since the Great East Japan Earthquake in 2011. This research aimed to improve high school students' judgments in emergency situations by training through a scenario-based learning support system called "ES3." Groups of four to five students were presented with a hypothetical earthquake disaster scenario on Android tablets and used their own judgment to navigate routes and shelters throughout the evacuation process. Faced with certain dangers and sites of damage, the students were required to select appropriate responsive actions. During the exercise, learning logs of locations and input values were stored in the server system. Following the exercise, the students discussed their decisions and actions, completing a questionnaire on safety consciousness. The data analysis suggested that the students selected actions, shelter, and evacuation routes using their own subjective judgment, and that the evacuation training increased their consciousness of their own safety.

Keywords: Disaster management · Disaster evacuation · Mobile learning · Scenario-based learning

1 Introduction

Japan is a country frequently affected by disasters like earthquakes and typhoons. In 2011, more than 15,000 people were killed in the Great East Japan Earthquake and the accompanying tsunami, including 617 school children, with many more injured while at school. Some students avoided the danger by using their own judgment to evacuate to a safe place, rather than risking a shelter assumed by others to be safe. On the other hand, many people became victims because of delayed decisions on evacuation in areas where the tsunami was assumed not to pose a threat. Since these events, disaster prevention awareness has been growing in schools and communities.

Many schools in Japan have adopted evacuation training, such as "ShakeOut" [1], as a form of education for disaster management. Such training aims to have students memorize particular actions to ensure smooth evacuation of buildings and areas,

© Springer International Publishing Switzerland 2016
C. Stephanidis (Ed.): HCII 2016 Posters, Part II, CCIS 618, pp. 360–364, 2016.
DOI: 10.1007/978-3-319-40542-1_59

including schools, in the event of an emergency. However, it is difficult for such students to judge life preserving actions when encountering an emergency situation outside of school, because they have never pictured such a scenario.

The research reported here aimed to improve students' judgment in emergency situations. This paper presents a learning system prototype that supports student judgment training for emergency situations.

2 Training Development

Various scenarios for disaster evacuation education have been developed in similar research. Alexander reports that scenario methods are useful in developing decision making skills under stress [2]. However, such scenarios have certain limitations, such as divergent narratives based on given choices. Because of such limitations, it is difficult to train emergency judgment for situations beyond the scenario creator's assumptions.

For the purposes of this research, we developed a flexible scenario-based learning support system called the "Evacuation Scenario Simulator System" (ES3), based on an improvised situation at a real location. The scenario consists of location-based elements of the disaster situation and shelters, with certain parts of the area damaged by the disaster. The scenario includes no set route or order of events and actions, having only two types of points, namely disaster encounter points and shelters as goal points. The disaster encounter points include the first point encounter, namely the start of the training, and various secondary points of disaster encountered during the evacuation. Because it is not a pre-defined scenario with a prepared narrative, the trainee is able to experience the situation with flexibility, diverging in terms of the hypothetical disaster.

The ES3 system consists of a server and a client application run on an Android tablet connected bidirectionally to the server. Figure 1 shows a conceptual overview of the system. The main features of the application are its presentation of a hypothetical disaster scenario based on a real location, and its recording of trainees' activity logs, such as locations and input values. The scenario is pre-set on any device on which the client application is installed. Trainees bring their devices outdoors for the evacuation training. When the disaster encounter point is approached, the system shows the hypothetical disaster situation through an image on the device, and a message indicating the training is about to start. The trainee takes action using his or her own judgment to navigate routes and shelters throughout the disaster evacuation. During the evacuation, dangers are revealed at certain points along the way, upon which the trainee selects an appropriate action with a reason. The evacuation is completed when the trainee reaches a shelter as a goal point.

The server collects the activity logs recorded in each device in which the client application is installed. The collected data are stored and arranged to display as an overlay on a map of the scenario. Trainees can browse these data using a web browser to reflect on their actions after the experiential learning.

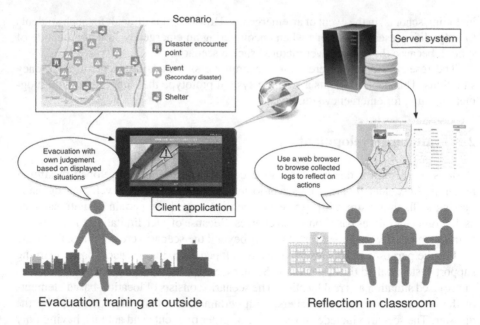

Fig. 1. Conceptual overview of ES3

3 Training Exercise

We conducted a training exercise with 111 first grade high school students in order to validate the utility of the ES3 system. The training comprised the school's integrated studies course, which aimed to allow students to learn and reflect on their actions in the event of a major earthquake. The training was carried out over four lessons conducted between September and November 2015. Each lesson was carried out at the same time for each class. The students were divided into groups of approximately four, and each group was lent an Android device.

Five training scenarios assuming the occurrence of a major earthquake, each including 50 events and reflecting the geological features of the area, were used. The scenarios were prepared with recognition of particular points and areas of safety or danger around the school, based on previous research [3].

Each of the four classes received the same four lessons. In the first lesson, the students were taught area information and basic disaster knowledge through a video, and how to operate the system through a tutorial in the schoolyard. The second and third lessons comprised the actual outdoor activities for the evacuation training outside the school. Each group conducted two outdoor activities with their devices configured for one of the five scenarios. Thus, the training was carried out twice, with a different scenario each time. Each training session took approximately 85 min, including the time taken to move from the classroom to the starting point and from the shelter at the goal point back to the classroom. Following the training, the students reflected on their results with the help of the system in the fourth lesson. They reviewed their own behaviors by browsing their trace and activity logs, which were stored in the system. They discussed standards for judgments in emergency situations following an earthquake. After this, they reviewed the training behaviors of all the groups, voting for the training route that was the closest match to the standard in order to learn optimally from the training, over and above their own experience.

4 Results and Discussion

4.1 Training Records

For each scenario, the evacuation starting point was the same. However, the final evacuation shelter and the route to it differed for each group. The time taken for evacuation also varied according to the scenario and the selected route, with many of the groups evacuating in approximately 20 min. The groups encountered an average of 4.1 events during their evacuations. Many, although not all, of the routes consisted of wide roads.

It seems that the judgments by which the students selected their evacuation routes were promoted by use of the system. After reflecting on their results in order to construct a judgment standard, their review-based votes were concentrated on a specific route. By means of this learning process, we believe that the students' judgment skills for emergency situations were improved, leading to more appropriate judgment.

4.2 Questionnaire Results

The students were required to complete survey questionnaires before and after the training in order to determine any changes in their disaster judgments skills and the learning effects of the training. The questionnaire, which contained five-point scaled items relating to awareness of disaster risk management and a sense of disaster values,

Table 1. Results for self-efficacy questions.

	N	Before		After	
		M	SD	M	SD
Can you judge which places outside the school are dangerous in the event of a major earthquake? *	107	3.20	1.120	3.54	0.984
Do you always check a shelter outside the school in the event of a major earthquake? *	107	2.57	1.150	3.21	1.172
Can you protect yourself if you feel an extremely strong vibration?	107	3.53	1.102	3.60	1.054
Can you evacuate to a shelter after the tremors of the earthquake stop?	107	3.58	1.010	3.74	0.894
Can you describe specifically where there is danger when an earthquake occurs? *	107	2.68	1.024	3.08	1.011
Can you describe specifically to where you should evacuate when an earthquake occurs? *	107	2.60	1.050	3.01	0.895

* significant at p < 0.01

H. Hatakeyama et al.

was developed by Motoyoshi et al. [4]. The questionnaire also contained additional questions relating to self-efficacy against disaster.

The questionnaire results showed improvements in average scores for most of the items, with the exception of those targeting a sense of disaster values. The change in scores was found by t-test to be significant for 11 of the 21 questions. For example, Table 1 shows the results for the questions relating to self-efficacy against disaster. The self-efficacy results show that the students' disaster consciousness was developed through the training exercise. However, no significant change in terms of a sense of disaster values was observed.

5 Conclusions

As reported above, we developed the ES3 scenario-based learning support system based on an improvised situation at a real location. The analysis of the students' actions revealed that they selected routes and shelters using their own subjective judgment. The questionnaire results showed that evacuation training in the field increased the students' consciousness of their own safety.

Acknowledgements. We would like to thank Amaha High School for their support of the training exercises described here. This work was supported by JSPS Grant-in-Aid for Scientific Research(B) Grant Number 15H02933.

References

1. ShakeOut. http://www.shakeout.org
2. Alexander, D.: Scenario Methodology for Teaching Principles of Emergency Management. Disaster Prev. Manage. Int. J. **9**, 89–97 (2000)
3. Hatakeyama, H., Nagai, M., Murota, M.: Educational practice and evaluation utilizing disaster prevention map creation support system "FaLAS". Research Report of JSET Conferences **15**, 1–6 (2015). (in Japanese)
4. Motoyoshi, T., Matsui, Y., Takenaka, I., Arai, Y., Mizuta, K., Saido, M., Shimizu, Y., Tanaka, M., Fukuoka, Y., Hori, H.: An experimental study on the educational effectiveness of simulation training of earthquake shelter program. J. Soc. Saf. Sci. **7**, 425–432 (2005). (in Japanese)

Will o'the Wisp: Augmented Reality Navigation for Hikers

Catherine S. Johnson, Shambhavi Mahajan, Mehmet Ordu,
Samyukta Sherugar[(⊠)], and Bruce N. Walker

Georgia Institute of Technology, Atlanta, Georgia
{catherine.johnson,smahajan43,mehmet.ordu,
ssherugar3}@gatech.edu, bruce.walker@psych.gatech.edu

Abstract. In this study we discuss the design of a non-intrusive navigational aid for amateur hikers and evaluate issues of trust and efficiency. We conceptualized an augmented reality interaction to project on-demand GPS directions in front of the hiker, and integrated the system into a hiking stick. We implemented an Arduino-powered prototype to evaluate the concept, interactions, and form factor. Evaluation methods include heuristic evaluations with an expert panel, followed by a round of design iteration. This was proceeded by task-based usability testing with amateur hikers. Our results confirm that hikers adapted easily to the new interaction, though trust in the device was less forthcoming. Data also confirms the efficiency of the projected cues compared to a traditional paper map.

Keywords: Augmented reality · Navigation · Hiking · Arduino · Usability testing

1 Introduction

Individuals rely on a number of wayfinding devices to assist with navigation. Today these devices most commonly include global positioning systems, mobile phones, maps and compasses [1]. Experienced hikers rely on one or even several of these devices for successful navigation [2]. However, amateur hikers, who do not always own such an array of devices, face challenges when it comes to hiking. This work started out as an exploration to find a navigational solution for amateur hikers. For the purpose of this study, an amateur hiker is defined as one who has some minimum prior experience, but is not an expert with authoritative knowledge of the domain.

In exploring potential solutions, we went through several possibilities. The existing literature in this space and our own exploration into the world of hiking led us to realize that the solution would have to be: (a) non-intrusive (b) GPS based and (c) of a favorable form factor. The rationale for this and the resultant choices made are explained below.

Non-intrusive. Devices used by hikers help them follow the trail and rely heavily on distracting visual cues. They distract the hiker's attention away from their surroundings to a map or a screen, which is risky. Auditory interfaces are also not an option as the

© Springer International Publishing Switzerland 2016
C. Stephanidis (Ed.): HCII 2016 Posters, Part II, CCIS 618, pp. 365–371, 2016.
DOI: 10.1007/978-3-319-40542-1_60

auditory sphere is a source of helpful feedback for a safe journey. Thus, direct-visual or auditory-cue based devices are not suitable for a mobile user [3]. This finding was central to our discussions and led us to move away from traditional systems of navigation. In [4], the authors found 3D virtual world representation to be quite promising upon comparing different wayfinding visualization techniques on a mobile phone. AR systems take this promise further as they have the capability of overlaying virtual information onto the real world in a natural, non-distracting manner. Thus AR emerged as an interesting space to find a fitting solution. Augmented Reality navigation systems have been discussed before [5], even in the context of AR of terrestrial navigation [6]. We take this discussion further by considering an AR display system that could work in the specific context of hiking.

GPS Based. While AR showed potential to be the display system, the source of the trail-information was yet to be determined. Traditionally, hikers rely on GPS based data to navigate as these are more reliable and do not suffer from the degree of signal issues associated with cellphones [2]. Thus we decided upon GPS based map data. Reliance on GPS is also confirmed by our study, through the participant interviews and self-reported survey data.

Favorable Form Factor. It has been found that if technologies for physical activity require the user to carry or wear devices then form factor is a critical consideration [7]. Integrating the technology into the cellphone was one option. However, it is not uncommon for users to temporarily abandon their cellphones with a desire to be unavailable and disconnected [8]. This desire is more commonly seen during outdoor activities like hiking. Further, the cellphone having functions other than navigation, tends to lose battery too soon. Thus, we needed a dedicated device which allowed the user to pursue a disconnect from the world. After considering multiple options we settled on the hiking stick- an existing component of hiking gear. Apart from a form-factor already adopted by the hiking community, it has the affordance of gripping which provides for interesting modes of interaction.

2 Conceptual Design Description

Thus, we present Will 'o the Wisp: a Hiking Stick with a GPS-based AR navigation system (see Fig. 1). The staff of the hiking stick has a projector that projects navigational cues which overlay on the environment. These navigational cues appear or disappear by the click of a button situated near the top end of the stick. It is designed to be turned on or off by the thumb. This idea was to provide choice by providing on-demand directions and to keep the interaction simple so that it does not interfere with the primary task of hiking. Users would be able to upload a GPS route to the stick beforehand.

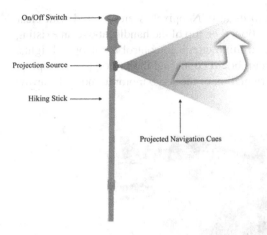

On/Off Switch

Projection Source

Hiking Stick

Projected Navigation Cues

Fig. 1. Conceptual diagram

In this conceptual design, directions are reduced to simple visual instructions. We expect these clear cues to reduce the mental load required to self-orient and navigate. They overlay on the environment and so, are non-obtrusive. Thus we hypothesize that this design would be convenient to handle while on a hike, has an interaction that is easy to use and learn, and is unobtrusive. We highlight our evaluation goals in the following section.

3 Evaluation

Participants. Fifteen (15) individuals (6 women and 9 men, ages 18–39) participated in the evaluation, including four (4) subject matter experts and eleven (11) qualified participants. Inclusion criteria required participants to be fluent in English, over 18 years old, able to see (eye glasses or contact lenses permitted), capable of providing written consent, and comfortable walking up to ten feet. Experts met the same inclusion criteria, as well as being Human-Computer Interaction, Human-Centered Computing, and Engineering Psychology graduate students, experienced/advanced hikers and having previously conducted heuristic evaluations. Participants were recruited from the Georgia Tech student and faculty populations, as well as the greater Atlanta area. Evaluations were conducted over a two week period and no compensation was provided.

Prototype. The prototype was constructed using the following components: (1) lightweight plastic mop handle, (2) clear, laser-cut acrylic arrow, electrical tape, (3) small paper coffee cup, (4) limit switch, (5) 10-foot USB cable, (6) 180° rotating servo motor, white foam core, (7) Arduino circuit, a strip of approximately fifteen neopixel lights. For testing, the fixed Arduino circuit was connected via the USB cable to a MacBook Air running Arduino software.

A 5" foam core platform supported the electronic components. Both the mop shaft and platform were covered with black electrical tape to create a uniform appearance. The shaft passed through a hole in the platform 1" from the edge. A coffee cup covered with black electrical tape covered the electrical components.

The Arduino circuit board was wired and connected to the servo motor. The board was fastened vertically against the mop handle on top of the platform. The servo motor was positioned approximately $2/3$ of the way down the platform away from the mop handle, with the acrylic arrow attached to its arm. Neopixels were secured with clear tape under the arrow. The switch was positioned on top of the handle, above an existing grip. Wires connected the switch to the Arduino circuit to control the neopixel lights. A 10-foot USB cable attached to the circuit board connected the prototype to a laptop, allowing researchers to manipulate the orientation of the servo motor to move the arrow (Fig. 2).

Fig. 2. The directional components of the hiking stick

Objectives. In addition to task-based usability testing, the evaluation focused on two research areas: (1) Did users trust the novel interaction? What was necessary for them to trust it? (2) How did the efficiency of the interaction compare to existing navigational tools?

Procedure. Evaluation sessions included four activities. Each session was conducted with two researchers present.

Activity 1 was a semi-structured interview relating to existing navigational tools. The goal was to record baseline familiarity and dependence on navigational technology. Participants were presented with images of four common navigation tools: a compass, a map, a GPS device, and a smartphone, and asked to identify each item and explain which devices they would take with them on a hike where cellphone service was not available.

Activity 2 was a fifteen question paper survey to gather demographic data and information about their hiking experiences, including expectations and equipment. Questions included Likert scales, open response and multiple choice options.

Activity 3 included two tasks: Self-Navigation and Directional Efficiency. The Self-Navigation task was a think-aloud task. Participants were instructed to follow navigational cues provided by the prototype, and discuss their thought process while using the device. Navigational cues were manipulated by a researcher from a distance of 8–10 feet. The Direction Efficiency Task measured the efficiency of identifying in which direction to proceed based on navigational cues versus a traditional map. Efficiency was defined as task completion time. Participants were presented with a map or the prototype in a randomized order. Time was recorded from the start of the task to the point they indicated which direction to go by either pointing or walking in the appropriate direction. (See [10] for similar comparison.)

Activity 4 was a semi-structured interview about navigational devices (similar to Activity 2) assuming the participant now had access to a fully functional hiking stick. The sessions concluded with a debrief discussion.

Pilot Testing and Heuristic Evaluations. A pilot session was conducted with a qualified participant to test and adjust the protocol and prototype. Iterations to the prototype included modifying the platform to be adjustable to accommodate participants of different heights, changing the arrow from blue to clear, and modifying the switch to react to a single press (rather than requiring the participant to hold the switch to keep the lights on). In addition, four (4) subject matter experts completed the Self-Navigation and Directional Efficiency tasks, and focused on five of Nielsen's 10 Usability Heuristics [9]: visibility of system status, user control and freedom, error prevention, aesthetic and minimalist design, and recognition rather than recall. Suggestions included smoother interactions when the arrow changed positions and additional features (not developed for testing purposes).

4 Results

Activity 1: Interview. Cellphone maps were the most common navigational tool used while hiking. Participants also reported relying on intuition, gut feeling, and/or other hikers for navigational assistance. Half of the participants reported using paper maps and compasses. Only one participant reported relying on trail markers.

Activity 2: Survey. Overall, participants reported that technology in general was very helpful when lost (4.5/5). 66 % of participants reported they currently used a hiking stick. 71 % of participants indicated they would be amenable with a navigational help system being embedded in their hiking stick. 42 % reported previous issues with losing service while hiking (Fig. 3).

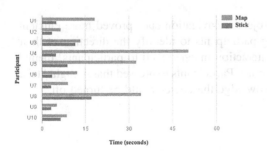

Map
Stick

Fig. 3. Task performance times

Activity 3: Directional Efficiency Task. The Directional Efficiency Task required participants to determine the direction of travel indicated by both the hiking stick and a map. In all sessions, the response times for the hiking stick were faster than the paper map.

Activity 4: Secondary Interviews. Participants were asked what they would take with them for navigation before and after using testing the prototype. Responses differed very little. Most participants reported that they would carry the same navigational tools in addition to the hiking stick (Fig. 4).

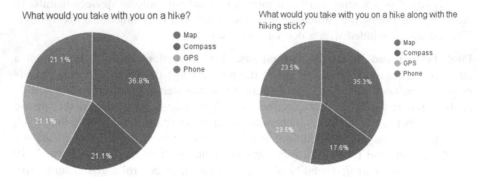

Fig. 4. Navigational tool preferences (before and after testing)

5 Discussion

Objective 1: Trust. Trust in the device, or lack thereof, was closely tied to a bigger picture view. Participants felt they were blindly following the device without a clearer understanding of their position relative to start and end points. Participants further expressed concern about electrical failures, including battery issues. Participants indicated that they could not trust such a new product without using it more consistently. These concerns led participants to confirm that they would carry additional navigational devices in addition to a functional hiking stick. Due to the high stakes nature of navigation, a low-tech solution was always preferred as a back-up, in the event of technical failures. More information would be necessary for participants to fully trust the device and rely on it for navigation. Information may include confirmation their destination was reached, warning when traveling in the wrong direction, and/or more fluid directional cues.

Objective 2: Efficiency. In all trials, projected navigation cues proved more efficient than a traditional paper map in assisting participants to identify the direction of their path. Qualitative data showed that the interaction mapped well to participants' mental models, making it simple to follow directions. Participants expressed that it might "take the adventure out of hiking" while acknowledge the device could be turned off.

6 Conclusion

This conceptual design demonstrated that projected cues may be a valuable form of navigation aid. Integrating this concept into existing navigation technologies may provide additional support for amateur hikers, due to the low learning curve. Additionally, projected navigation cues may be valuable for other scenarios and populations, including those where navigation is a cognitive burden. Potential populations include older adults with cognitive impairments and transportation operators.

Acknowledgements. Special thanks to Dr. Carrie Bruce for her insights and support throughout the project, as well as Clement Zheng and Harrison Daniels for their technical assistance with prototype development.

References

1. Darken, R.P., Peterson, B.: Spatial orientation, wayfinding, and representation. In: Handbook of Virtual Environments: Design, Implementation, and Applications, pp. 493–518 (2002)
2. Posti, M., Schöning, J., Häkkilä, J.: Unexpected journeys with the HOBBIT: the design and evaluation of an asocial hiking app. In: Proceedings of the 2014 Conference on Designing Interactive Systems, pp. 637–646. ACM (2014)
3. Heuten, W., Henze, N., Boll, S., Pielot, M.: Tactile wayfinder: a non-visual support system for wayfinding. In: Proceedings of the 5th Nordic Conference on Human-Computer Interaction: Building Bridges, pp. 172–181. ACM (2008)
4. Kray, C., Elting, C., Laakso, K., Coors, V.: Presenting route instructions on mobile devices. In: Proceedings of the 8th International Conference on Intelligent User Interfaces, pp. 117–124. ACM (2003)
5. Narzt, W., Pomberger, G., Ferscha, A., Kolb, D., Müller, R., Wieghardt, J., Hörtner, H., Lindinger, C.: Augmented reality navigation systems. Univ. Access Inf. Soc. 4(3), 177–187 (2006)
6. Thomas, B., Demczuk, V., Piekarski, W., Hepworth, D., Gunther, B.: A wearable computer system with augmented reality to support terrestrial navigation. In: Second International Symposium on Wearable Computers, 1998. Digest of Papers, pp. 168–171. IEEE (1998)
7. Consolvo, S., Everitt, K., Smith, I., Landay, J.A.: Design requirements for technologies that encourage physical activity. In: Proceedings of the SIGCHI Conference on Human Factors in Computing Systems, pp. 457–466. ACM (2006)
8. Salovaara, A., Lindqvist, A., Hasu, T., Häkkilä, J.: The phone rings but the user doesn't answer: unavailability in mobile communication. In: Proceedings of the 13th International Conference on Human Computer Interaction with Mobile Devices and Services, pp. 503–512. ACM (2011)
9. Nielsen, J.: 10 Heuristics for User Interface Design. https://www.nngroup.com/articles/ten-usability-heuristics/
10. Pielot, M., Henze, N., Boll, S.: Supporting map-based wayfinding with tactile cues. In: Proceedings of the 11th International Conference on Human-Computer Interaction with Mobile Devices and Services, p. 23. ACM (2009)

smarTactile Map: An Interactive and Smart Map to Help the Blind to Navigate by Touch

MyungJoong Lee and Jie-Eun Hwang[(✉)]

Department of Architecture, University of Seoul, Seoulsiripdaero 163,
Dongdaemun-gu, Korea
abide.nm@gmail.com, curiozen@gmail.com

Abstract. Tactile map is a popular method for the visually impaired to help their independent walking. It is made of protruding dot, line, surface and braille. Visually impaired people can recognize the structure of space by touching a tactile map. However, it is not smart enough to use in their real life. We carried on user interviews with thirty subjects of visually impaired people to define problems from the real situation. In addition, we conducted a field observation how they utilized the tactile map. We analyzed their touching behaviors and reclaimed the problems of existing tactile maps. Based on these findings, we designed prototype of new tactile map with 3D volumetric symbol system, which is potentially deployable to an interactive braille device. We proposed a new way of representing space for navigation with the 3D symbol system. The landmarks and routes are customized by the end users through dynamically scaled symbols with consistency of reading. Adapted by the user's level of vision, familiarity of the space, and the smart tactile map can customize representation of space so then reinforce perception of the place. We conducted an initial usability evaluation of the new system and discussed about fundamental benefits of such map system.

Keywords: Visually impaired people · Tactile map · Smart device

1 Introduction

1.1 Tactile Map for the Visually Impaired

Visual information is the most important element in perception of environments. Therefore, a visually impaired person has limitation in interacting one's surrounding physical space [1]. It causes limitation in independent walking. For this difficulty, a tactile map has been used to aid their mobility [2]. Tactile map is a guide map which consists of protruding dot, line, surface and braille to help the visually impaired people recognize the space. A tactile map has both short term and long term benefits in helping visually impaired children to navigate to space and to acquire spatial abilities [3]. A tactile map can provide an embodied source of spatial information which preserves all the interrelationships between objects in space [4]. In Korea, it is widely encouraged that public facilities provide the tactile map for the visually impaired. The study began by questioning whether the tactile map is useful. Our initial survey about utilization

© Springer International Publishing Switzerland 2016
C. Stephanidis (Ed.): HCII 2016 Posters, Part II, CCIS 618, pp. 372–378, 2016.
DOI: 10.1007/978-3-319-40542-1_61

of existing tactile map revealed that they didn't use tactile map almost at all when they walk or refer to spatial context.

2 Experiments

2.1 1st Experiment: Field Observation

We conducted an experiment to investigate problems of tactile maps. We separated participants into A group and B group. 5 students in Seoul National School for the Blind belong to A group and 4 members in Nowon Center for the Visually Handicapped belong to B group. We designated the two places (Purme welfare center for A group, and Nowon-gu office for B group.) where participants had never been and public tactile maps were installed (Fig. 1).

Fig. 1. Photo of existing tactile map. Left is Purme center and right is Nowon-gu office.

We assigned each group same task to observe whether the subjects could perceive spatial structure and find a way to destination by reading tactile map. The task is walking from main entrance through toilet, information room, and to the main entrance. We observed and video-recorded all behaviors such as touching the tactile map and walking in order to analyze them. We measured (1) Time of reading the tactile map, (2) Number of errors in reading the map, (3) Time of walking, (4) Number of errors in walking with different vision leveled subjects.

2.2 Results of the 1st Experiment

The average time of reading a tactile map took approximately 15 min. It was very difficult for the visually impaired to reach the final destination without mistakes and most participants easily lost orientation by one mistake, due to limited sight. A half of participants failed wayfinding, even though they read a tactile map in advance. The result of 1st experiment is shown in Table 1.

Table 1. Result of 1st experiment

		Vision level	Time of reading tactile map(sec)	Number of error in reading map	Time of walking (sec)	Number of error in walking
A group	PJH	Light perception	1,063	14	233	5
	PJY	Hand movement	576	18	108	4
	LKS	Total blindness	655	14	323	11
	DSM	Light perception	1,133	22	118	0
	LCE	Total blindness	1,782	9	120 + α	Task failed
B group	YJC	Total blindness	1,332	25	406	14
	LDS	Hand movement	906	18	160 + α	Task failed
	CSM	Total blindness	365	7	164 + α	Task failed
	PW	Total blindness	683	4	310 + α	Task failed

2.3 Finding Problems

From the measurement result and filed observation, we elaborated problems of utilizing tactile maps in four aspects.

- Difficulty of recognizing symbols in the map: It is difficult to recognize map symbols and their meanings. Irrelevant representation of spatial elements, current location, and the route consequently confuses wayfinding.
- Inefficiency in scalable representation: There are psychological and cognitive burdens to memorize all the route, landmarks and spatial structure to destination. It is impossible to control the level of detail in the static map.
- Lack of standards: Tactile map manufacturing companies have their own shapes of symbols and layout of map even if there is an official standard of tactile map.
- Wrong and fixed location of the map: Public tactile maps are usually installed at the entrance of the building as a fixture. The location is often abandoned and not relevant to where it refers.

3 Design Proposal

3.1 Design Strategy

Based on the finding problems, we proposed an interactive tactile map that can be used for wayfinding. We hypothesize that a portable device, called smarTactile map, which deploy dynamic maps will improve usability of a static tactile map. We focused on the representation of spatial information that is legible by touch as well as cognitively consistent within the machine-deployable range. Thus, we focused on three dimensional tactile expression of symbols that could be semantically legible as architectural elements, since volumetric symbols are easily identified, recognized and discriminated [5]. In this way, we can enrich spatial representation.

3.2 Prototype Design Mockup

We developed a prototype mockup of smarTactile for usability experiment (Fig. 2). To improve efficiency of reading, we developed several functions such as layer, zoom, voice mode, and navigation tools. Layer function makes users select and recognize information of layer that they want to see. Zoom function makes it possible to control level of detail that tactile map provides. The prospective major functions of the smarTactile is described as below.

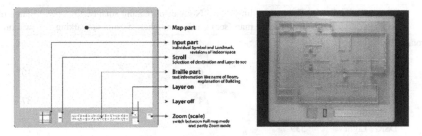

Fig. 2. Prototype design of smarTactile map

- **User setting**: First, users choose their level of vision if they are blind or low vision. Then, they select text information modes whether they prefer to braille or voice. After choosing shape types of symbols, they select protruding height of wall line, route line and other symbols. Finally, they choose shape of route, following either interior wall lines or route line.
- **Searching and exploring mode**: Users select a destination building, then a destination room in the building. Selecting a destination begins in a full map mode. Which is a searching and exploring mode. The name of destination is provided with the process of searching. After they select destination, device makes route from the main starting point to the destination automatically. Users can change starting point and destination whenever they want.
- **Walking mode vs. overview mode**: When users start walking, they switch over to a walking mode. In the walking mode, it works as egocentric like a vehicle navigation system that current location of users is static and spatial information near them move as their position changes. Users can change the setting of walking mode to overview mode.
- **Input mode**: Users can make their own symbol using input function. And they can use input function when they encountered a barrier or anything that they felt to make as a landmark. This device makes users' walking self-initiated by getting them make their own landmarks at that position.

3.3   2nd Experiment: Usability Test

We took the same group for the same task by utilizing the prototype mockup. In addition to measuring times for reading and walking, we also collected user setting configuration to user preference tendency.

3.4   Results of the 2nd Experiment

Contrary to results of 1st experiment, 2nd experiment shows that time of reading tactile map and time of walking decrease significantly, no one failed in navigation. We counted the number of re-reading smarTatile in situ to supplement the number of error in walking, since it indicated that they got lost (Tables 2 and 3).

Table 2. Result of 2nd experiment

		Vision level	Time of reading smarTactile map (sec)	Number of reading smarTactile map = number of error in walking	Time of walking
A group	PJH	Light perception	213	4	165
	PJY	Hand movement	357	6	167
	LKS	Total blindness	200	4	87
	DSM	Light perception	339	3	77
	LCE	Total blindness	528	6	176
B group	YJC	Total blindness	283	8	227
	LDS	Hand movement	272	6	101
	CSM	Total blindness	286	7	134
	PW	Total blindness	328	7	138

The result of user setting demonstrates that most participants prefer 3D shape symbol. Each participants has a different personal preference so it is essential to have them configure individualized user setting. The best advantage of smart tactile map is the function of immediate orientation in real time. And they are satisfied with individual user setting as their preference unlike existing tactile map that has unilateral interface (Fig. 3).

Table 3. Individual user setting configuration

		Text information	Height of wall	Route Mechanism	Current location	Stair	Elevator	Route	Men restroom	Women restroom
A group	PJH	Braille		Following wall						
	PJY	Braille		Following wall						
	LKS	Voice		Following wall						
	DSM	Voice		Following wall						
	LCE	Braille		Following wall						
B group	YJC	Voice		Following wall						
	LDS	Voice		Following wall						
	CSM	Voice		Following wall						
	PW	voice		Following wall						

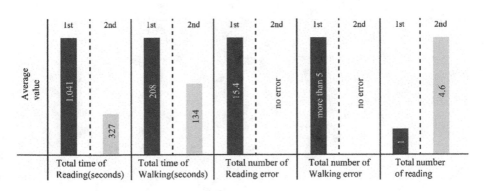

Fig. 3. Comparison result of 1st and 2nd experiments.

4 Conclusion and Future Work

Fundamentally, the combination of orientation and mobility is the most important for the visually impaired to walk independently. They have to connect spatial configuration of 'where they are', 'where destination is' and 'how they can get there' in real time at the confronted space. Two sets of experiments of field observation and usability test revealed that the portable dynamic map are much more helpful for navigation and walking, and that individual preferences to configure the map varied.

The great lessons from this study is to rethink the process of establish an accessibility policy from the real users' point of view. The visually impaired with diverse levels of vision could have different demands for navigation, therefore the standardization of the tactile map should not be the description of the shape of the map, but should be based on the ultimate experience of the users.

References

1. Lowenfeld, B.: Berthold Lowenfeld on Blindness and Blind People. American Foundation for the Blind Press, New York (1981)
2. Bentzen, B.L.: Orientation maps for visually impaired persons. J. Vis. Impairment Blindness **71**, 193–197 (1977)
3. Ungar, S.: The role of tactile maps in mobility training. Br. J. Vis. Impairment **1**, 159–161 (1993)
4. Ungar, S., Blades, M., Spencer, C.: The construction of cognitive maps by children with visual impairment. In: Portugali, J. (ed.) The Construction of Cognitive Maps, pp. 247–273. Kluwer Academic Publishers, Dordrecht (1996)
5. Gual, J., Puyuelo, M., Lloveras, J.: The effect of volumetric (3D) tactile symbols within inclusive tactile maps. In: Applied Ergonomics, vol. 48, pp. 1–10 (2015)

Adaptive Landmark-Based Pedestrian Navigation System with Hand-Held and Wearable Devices

Daeil Seo, Doyeon Kim, Byounghyun Yoo$^{(\boxtimes)}$, and Heedong Ko

Center for Imaging Media Research,
Korea Institute of Science and Technology, Seoul, South Korea
{xdesktop,ko}@kist.re.kr, ehdus0219@imrc.kist.re.kr,
yoo@byoo.net

Abstract. Mobile navigations help people to find route faster and easier. However, current pedestrian navigations provide the same route information as the instructions of car navigation with little consideration for pedestrians. Mobile pedestrian navigations should consider pedestrian walkways and device capabilities. In this paper, we propose a landmark-based navigation system for pedestrians based on the user's locational context and the capabilities of hand-held and wearable devices. The system generates turn-by-turn routes and mashups landmarks with social media contents. The system provides context clues on wearable devices, and the overall context on hand-held devices to assist pedestrians who are unfamiliar with an area.

Keywords: Pedestrian navigation · Landmark-based · Hand-held and wearable devices

1 Introduction

With the sharp increase of wearable devices connected to smartphones and tablets, pedestrian navigation systems using these devices are also on the increase. However, current pedestrian navigation instructions are similar to the instructions of car navigation except that they use the pedestrian walkways. The car navigation methods are not suitable for the pedestrian navigation, as pedestrians have more freedom of movement than drivers, and they are much slower [1]. The pedestrian navigation systems should provide information considering these new device capabilities and usage patterns of pedestrians because of the different form factors and modalities by wearable devices.

The pedestrians need detailed information about salient objects, such as landmarks, rather than road networks to reach a destination. May et al. [2] concluded that landmarks are the main navigation cues used for providing directions to the pedestrians as opposed to road junctions and signs in car navigations. The social media contents like panoramas and photos can be collected to enrich description of landmarks and give locational context cues for the users. Hile et al. [3] proposed a system that automatically generates landmark-based pedestrian navigation instructions from existing

© Springer International Publishing Switzerland 2016
C. Stephanidis (Ed.): HCII 2016 Posters, Part II, CCIS 618, pp. 379–384, 2016.
DOI: 10.1007/978-3-319-40542-1_62

collections of geo-tagged photos. Shuhui et al. [4] presented a representative image generation system using user generated geo-tagged photos based on popular shooting locations.

In this paper, we propose an adaptive landmark-based pedestrian navigation system that generates landmark-based navigation instructions using a point of interest (POI) database and augmented multimedia from social media to describe the route point. In addition, we divide navigation instructions into two steps for providing suitable navigation instructions based on the user's device capabilities and locational context: partitioning route path into landmark-based path guide (Step 1) and direction guide to the next route point (Step 2).

2   Our Method

In Fig. 1 the pedestrian route planner generates landmark-based navigation instructions for the user, and the adaptive pedestrian route handler manages the hand-held and wearable navigation views. The map server provides map tiles to render maps on the device views.

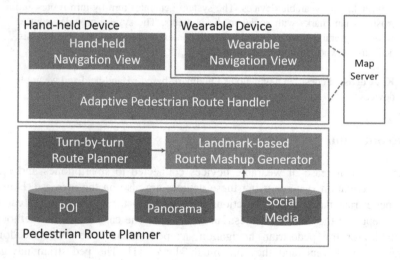

Fig. 1. Overview of proposed architecture

2.1   Landmark-Based Pedestrian Navigation Generation

When a user selects a destination POI, the system obtains the current position of the user and passes the locations to the pedestrian route planner, as shown in Fig. 1. To provide landmark-based pedestrian navigation, the landmark-selection process depicted in Fig. 2a is required for each route point. The turn-by-turn route planner passes route points to the landmark-based route mashup generator.

The route generator retrieves nearby POIs from OpenPOIs [5] as the POI database and chooses candidate POIs over the road of a route point based on the walking direction and the field of view of the user, as shown in Fig. 2a. The route generator scores and ranks the candidate POIs to choose a landmark of the route point based on the proximity of the landmark to the road and its height compared to surrounding buildings with a higher score being given to a POI that is closer to the road and taller against surrounding buildings. The orange POI in Fig. 2 is the landmark, and the green POIs are not selected as landmarks because of the height of the building is lower than the orange POI. In addition, the route generator chooses a panoramic photo based on the location of the route point from Google Street View [6] and photos taken in the blue locations in Fig. 2a and tagged by the name of the landmark POI from Panoramio [7] (a location-based social photo sharing site). According to the locational context of the user, the hand-held device renders the overall context on the map. The route generator mashups turn-by-turn route plan, the selected landmark, a photo about the landmark, and panoramic view using location information of these resources to provide landmark-based route instructions based on user's location cues and device capabilities.

2.2 Adaptive Navigation Guide for Wearable Devices

The movement from the current position to the destination POI involves going to the next target route point from the current route point in the route path, as shown in Fig. 2b. In this paper, we divide this process into two steps: landmark-based path guide (Step 1) and direction guide to the next route point (Step 2). The adaptive pedestrian route handler in a hand-held device, shown in Fig. 1 manages the navigation views of hand-held and wearable devices based on locational context. The hand-held device tracks current position of the user and compares the location to the target route point to change adaptively modes and views of the wearable device between the first and second steps based on locational context. When the user starts the movement to the

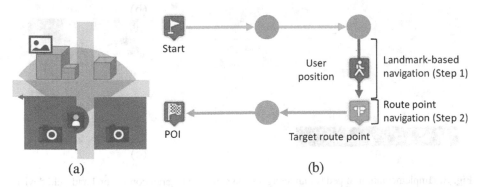

(a)   (b)

Fig. 2. Process of landmark-based pedestrian navigation: (a) landmark and social media selection-based route path and (b) partitioning route path into landmark-based path guide (Step 1) and direction guide to next route point (Step 2). (Color figure online)

target route point, the adaptive pedestrian route handler shows the first step in Fig. 2b on the wearable device. When the user arrived within a ten-meter radius, the wearable device's mode and view are changed to the second step. After changing to direction, the mode and view are changed into first step.

The goal of the first step is to move from the user's current position to the target route point. Required routing information includes the distance and direction of the target route point and a photo of the landmark at the location of the target route point. The second step begins when the user nears the target route point, and information on the direction of the next route point is provided to change the walking direction of the user. The wearable device (e.g., Google Glass) depicts the distance and direction of the target route point and a photo of the landmark in the first step. In the second step, the wearable device renders the current route path, position, and direction of the user on the map and a panoramic view, the angle of which is animated based on the user's progress toward the next route point.

3 Experimental Results

We implemented a prototype pedestrian navigation system using a Google Glass and a Google Nexus smartphone to verify the usefulness of our approach. Figure 2 shows the screenshot of the hand-held and wearable devices providing navigation information. The overall context of the route information is shown in Fig. 3a. The routing path is

(a)   (b)   (c)

Fig. 3. Implementation of pedestrian navigation system: (a) Overall context on hand-held device (Google Nexus smartphone), (b) landmark-based navigation for finding route point on wearable device (Google Glass), and (c) route point navigation for turning to next route point on wearable device. (Color figure online)

from a subway station to the Gyeongbokgung Palace in Seoul, Korea. A navigation path from the start point of the user to the destination POI is presented on the map. A gray line represents the path the user has completed, a red line represents the current path, and an orange line represents the future route path. A red marker represents the current position of the user and an orange marker represents the current target route point.

Figure 3b and 3c present navigation information on the wearable device depending on the user's context. As the user goes to the target route point, the wearable device shows landmark-based navigation information as shown in Fig. 3b (i.e., the first step in Fig. 2b). In this step, the user's direction, remaining distance, and a photo of the target route point are shown. When the user arrives at the target route point, the device then provides the direction of the next route point, the user's direction on the map, and a panoramic view of the current route point, as shown in Fig. 3c. The angle of the panoramic view is animated from the user's current progress direction toward next route point (i.e., the second step of Fig. 2b).

4 Conclusion

In this paper, we proposed an adaptive landmark-based pedestrian navigation system. Our approach separates route instructions into two steps: one for landmark selection and the other for landmark-based pedestrian instructions based on the combined capabilities of hand-held and wearable devices and the user's locational context.

Using the proposed system, a pedestrian receives route information with the overall and locational context with hand-held device. The pedestrian is aware of an overview of the whole navigation paths for overall context. On the other hand, the instructions on wearable device help people to find target route points with specified information such as landmarks and user's direction.

In the future, we will conduct a user study to evaluate our proposed system, and then we will improve our approach according to the study results.

Acknowledgments. This research was supported in part by the Korea Institute of Science and Technology (KIST) Institutional Program (Project No. 2E26450).

References

1. Millonig, A., Schechtner, K.: Developing landmark-based pedestrian-navigation systems. IEEE Trans. Intell. Transp. Syst. **8**, 43–49 (2007)
2. May, A.J., Ross, T., Bayer, S.H., Tarkiainen, M.J.: Pedestrian navigation aids: information requirements and design implications. Pers. Ubiquit. Comput. **7**, 331–338 (2003)
3. Hile, H., Vedantham, R., Cuellar, G., Liu, A., Gelfand, N., Grzeszczuk, R., Borriello, G.: Landmark-based pedestrian navigation from collections of geotagged photos. In: International Conference on Mobile and Ubiquitous Multimedia (MUM), pp. 145–152. ACM, Umeå, Sweden (2008)

4. Shuhui, J., Xueming, Q., Yao, X., Fan, L., Xingsong, H.: Generating representative images for landmark by discovering high frequency shooting locations from community-contributed photos. In: IEEE International Conference on Multimedia and Expo Workshops, pp. 1–6. IEEE, San Jose, CA, USA (2013)
5. OGC, OpenPOIs Database Homepage. http://www.openpois.net. Accessed 21 Mar 2016
6. Google, Google Street View Image API. https://developers.google.com/maps/documentation/streetview. Accessed 21 Mar 2016
7. Google, Panoramio Widget API. http://www.panoramio.com. Accessed 21 Mar 2016

Advancement of a To-Do Reminder System Focusing on Context of the User

Masatoshi Tanaka[1]($\boxtimes$), Keisuke Yoshida[1], Shogo Matsuno[2],
and Minoru Ohyama[1]

[1] Graduate School of Information Environment,
Tokyo Denki University, Chiba, Japan
{15jkm13,14jkm23}@ms.dendai.ac.jp,
ohyama@mail.dendai.ac.jp
[2] Graduate School of Informatics and Engineering,
The University of Electro-Communications, Tokyo, Japan
ml440004@edu.cc.uec.ac.jp

Abstract. In recent years, smartphones have become rapidly popular and their performance has improved remarkably. Therefore, it is possible to estimate user context by using sensors and functions equipped in smartphones. We propose a To-Do reminder system using user indoor position information and moving state. In conventional reminder systems, users have to input the information of place (resolution place). The resolution place is where the To-Do item can be solved and the user receives a reminder. These conventional reminder systems are constructed based on outdoor position information using GPS. In this paper, we propose a new reminder system that makes it unnecessary to input the resolution place. In this newly developed system, we introduce a rule-based system for estimating the resolution place in a To-Do item. The estimation is done based on an object word and a verb, which are included in most tasks in a To-Do list. In addition, we propose an automatic judgment method to determine if a To-Do task has been completed.

Keywords: To-Do · Context-awareness · Smartphone · Wi-Fi · Location-based reminder · Indoor positioning

1 Introduction

In recent years, as smartphones have become rapidly popular, various location-based services have been developed [1]. The present generation of smartphones are equipped with various sensors and functions, which can be used to simplify the task of estimating the user context [2, 3]. Moreover, smartphones have become capable of providing suitable information to users at appropriate timing by estimating the user context. Therefore, many systems that provide information by estimating user context have been studied [4, 5].

We propose a To-Do reminder system using indoor position information and moving state. In conventional reminder systems, there are two types of reminders for the user. The first concerns the deadline of a task in a To-Do list. The second is

C. Stephanidis (Ed.): HCII 2016 Posters, Part II, CCIS 618, pp. 385–391, 2016.
DOI: 10.1007/978-3-319-40542-1_63

concerned with reminding the user about the resolution place where a To-Do item is to be solved. In this study, we mainly focus on the latter type of To-Do reminders. The current conventional reminder systems require the user to input the resolution place when adding a task to the To-Do list.

We propose a new reminder system that does not require the user to input the resolution place. This system estimates the resolution place from a To-Do item based on indoor position information and moving state. We constructed the reminder system by adopting a rule-based system for estimating the resolution place. The resolution place is estimated by an object word and a verb, which are generally included in most To-Do items. In addition, we propose an automatic judgment method to determine whether a To-Do is has been performed/completed. The proposed system prompts the user whether the To-Do item can be deleted.

2   Related Works

A number of research initiatives pertaining to time- and location-based reminder systems are available in literature. We reviewed several papers that are closely related to our work.

The reminder system proposed by [6] reminds the user by using the GPS-based user position data. In this system, the user has to input the resolution place of the To-Do item.

The reminder system proposed by [7] reminds the user by using the user position obtained from the cell tower information closest to the user's phone. Moreover, in this system, the user has to input the resolution place of a To-Do item.

The system proposed in [8] generates suitable messages from the information stored in the smartphone. These messages are generated based on the user's call history, mail history, and events such as birthdays.

Moreover, the systems proposed in [6, 7] have a drawback; the user has to input the resolution place of a To-Do item. These reminder systems cannot operate indoors because they utilize GPS or cell tower information.

We propose a novel reminder system that does not require the user to input the resolution place of a To-Do item. This system estimates the resolution place of a To-Do item based on indoor position information and moving state.

3   Proposed Reminder System

The proposed reminder system has a function that estimates the resolution place of a To-Do item. This system also reminds the user when the user's position is in the vicinity of the resolution place. This section describes our proposed reminder system in detail. Furthermore, we propose a judgment function to determine whether a To-Do item has been completed.

This system comprises the following three functions.

3.1 Indoor Position Estimation

Our proposed system adopts a Wi-Fi fingerprinting method as to estimate the indoor position [9]. In the Wi-Fi fingerprinting method, the system collects RSSI (Received Signal Strength Indication) data for each Access Point (i.e. BSSID (Mac Address)) at designated places where we want to estimate. The system then adds a location name to collected RSSI data at each designated place and stores this data in a database. When estimating the position, the system compares the measured data with previously collected RSSI data in the database for each access point. The system arranges the comparison of results in descending order of RSSI similarity. Each RSSI data stored in the database has a location name. The system retrieves the location names of RSSI data in the database that are similar and estimates the location name as a user position.

The proposed reminder system deems it necessary to estimate whether the user position and resolution place are in close proximity. Since the system adopts the Wi-Fi fingerprinting method to estimate the user position, the estimated position that has the largest similarity is not always the correct position. Therefore, we conducted an experiment to evaluate if the correct answer is included in the top three ranked estimated locations. A subject carrying a smartphone was asked to walk around randomly on campus. The system estimates his positions according to the positional data obtained from the smartphone. The subject is then asked to compare the actual position with the estimated position. Table 1 shows that the probability of including a correct answer is 92 % in the top three estimated positions. Therefore, it is sufficient to adopt top three estimated positions.

Table 1. Experiment result

Rank of estimated position	1	2	3
Probability of including a correct position	59 %	82 %	92 %

3.2 Estimation of Resolution Place

Input style of a To-Do is different for each user. We surveyed twenty subjects related to the input style of To-Do and collected 140 To-Do items. These collected To-Do items can all be solved on our campus. Table 2 shows breakdown of the questionnaire.

Initially, we assumed that the input style of To-Do was composed of an object word and a verb. However, we found that input styles of To-Do items were classified into four patterns, shown in Table 3. The pattern of an object word and a verb was the highest input style, with 56 %, shown in Table 3.

(1) Object word and verb

   e.g.: Deposit $100

(2) Only object word

   e.g.: $100

(3) Only verb

    e.g.: deposit

(4) Only resolution place

    e.g.: ATM

To address the four input patterns, we constructed a rule-based system for estimating the resolution place of the inputted To-Do items. We constructed this system based on the object word and verb, which are extracted from the To-Do items collected by a questionnaire.

In addition, we added object words and verbs to the rule-based system related to each resolution place on our campus. Table 4 shows examples of the rules that were constructed in our system.

Table 2. The breakdown of questionnaires

Resolution place	Number of To-Do
ATM	60
Secretary room	20
Certificate issuance machine	20
Counseling room	20
Convenience store	20

Table 3. Analysis of questionnaire

Expression of To-Do	Example	Percentage (%)
(1) Object and verb	Deposit $100	56
(2) Object word	$100	26
(3) Verb word	Deposit	2
(4) Resolution place	ATM	16

Table 4. Examples of rules to estimate the resolution place

Object word	Verb	Resolution place
Pencil, notebook	Buy (purchase)	Convenience store
$100	Draw, deposit	ATM

3.3 Prompting the Deletion of Completed To-Do Item

Even if a user approaches a resolution place of a To-Do item, only the user knows whether the specific To-Do has been completed or not. Under normal circumstances, the user deletes the completed To-Do item manually from the To-Do List; if the user fails to delete the To-Do item the same item is reminded again. Therefore, we need a function that prompts the deletion of the solved To-Do.

We propose an automatic method that determines whether a To-Do item has been completed or not based on the moving state [2], position information [10], and dwell time at the resolution place. For example, a user has a To-Do of "draw $100". The resolution place of this To-Do is ATM. When the user's position information and moving state are aligned, it is considered that the user is going to complete the To-Do task/item. Therefore, the system regards the To-Do as solved after the following states are confirmed. The system then prompts the user to delete the solved To-Do item when user's position information is in a different place and their moving state changes.

(1) User's positional information

   $\rightarrow$ near ATM

(2) User's moving state

   $\rightarrow$Halted (dwelling time: approximately 20–120 s)

4 Experiment

We performed an experiment to confirm whether the reminded place and the reminded To-Do items are accurate. The experimental space is the first floor of the first building on our campus. Ten subjects input a To-Do item in their style to a smartphone. All inputted To-Do items are related to the resolution place of our campus, without specifying the input style of To-Do. The subjects, having a smartphone, walk along the arrow shown in Fig. 1. This system registers a total of 26 resolution places and outputs the estimated position every 1.6 s. We evaluated a total of twenty To-Do items that were inputted by the ten subjects.

As a result, our system can estimate every resolution place from inputted 20 To-Do items. As for 4 To-Do items, the proposed system can not send a reminder when the user is present at the place, because of wrong position estimation.

Radio waves emitted from the access point are fluctuated by opening/closing doors and movement of people. In addition, the environmental changes and time changes influence the estimation of the position. For example, adding and removing access points occur often. These events decrease the accuracy of estimating position. We

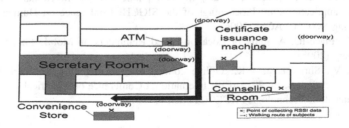

Fig. 1. Design of first floor of our college

suspect that individual differences of smartphones affect the position estimation [10]. Therefore, we believe that it is possible to reduce the number of false positives by introducing a threshold to the similarity.

Although the proposed system is customized for application to our campus, it can be easily applied to other colleges and workplaces by adding their specific rules. It can also be extended to outdoors by combining with existing systems [11] that utilize GPS.

5 Conclusion

We proposed and constructed a To-Do reminder system that makes it unnecessary to input the resolution place of a To-Do item. We tested the feasibility of the system by performing an experiment that assumes an actual user.

As part of our future work, we intend to perform a full-fledged evaluation experiment to test the applicability of the proposed system. We also plan to construct a reminder system that can be used both indoors and outdoors by combining the system with existing GPS-based systems.

References

1. Deva, B., Garzon, S.R., Schunemann, S.: A context-sensitive privacy-aware framework for proactive location-based services. In: 9th International Conference on Next Generation Mobile Applications, Services, and Technologies. IEEE (2015)
2. Keisuke, Y., Shogo, M., Minoru, O.: A study on the estimation of calories and moving state using smartphone built-in sensors. In: RISP International Workshop on Nonlinear Circuits, Communications and Signal Processing (NCSP), Hawaii, USA, March 2016
3. Ozaki, K., Ohyama, M., Matsuno, S.: Determining mobile device indoor and outdoor location in various environments - estimation of user context. In: The International Conference on Intelligent Informatics and Biomedical Sciences (ICIIBMS), Okinawa, Japan (2015)
4. Nakanishi, Y., Tsuji, T., Ohyama, M., Hakozaki, K.: Context aware messaging service: a dynamical messaging delivery using location information and schedule information. Pers. Ubiquit. Comput. 4(4), 221–224 (2000)
5. Kenta, O., Shinsuke, N., Jun, M., Shunsuke, U.: Context-aware recommendation system based on context-dependent user preference modeling. IPSJ J. Data Base 48(11), 162–176 (2007)
6. Ludford, P.J., et al.: Because I carry my cell phone anyway: functional location-based reminder applications. In: Proceedings of the SIGCHI Conference on Human Factors in Computing Systems. ACM (2006)
7. Sohn, T.: Place-Its: A Study of Location-Based Reminders on Mobile Phones. Springer, Heidelberg (2005)
8. Gaurav, V., Shrivastava, V.K.: Offline context aware computing in smart devices for intelligent reminders. In: 2015 IEEE International Conference on Electrical, Computer and Communication Technologies (ICECCT). IEEE (2015)

9. Kaemarungsi, K., Krishnamurthy, P.: Modeling of indoor positioning systems based on location fingerprinting. In: INFOCOM 2004, Twenty-Third Annual Joint Conference of the IEEE Computer and Communications Societies, vol. 2. IEEE (2004)
10. Tanaka, M., Yoshida, K., Matsuno, S., Ohyama, M.: A Location estimation method considering radio wave reception sensitivity of mobile devices. In: Proceedings of the 2015 IEICE General Conference, p. 610 (2015)
11. https://keep.google.com/

Speech Activity Detection and Speaker Localization Based on Distributed Microphones

Yi Yang[✉], Jingyun Zhang, and Jiasong Sun

Tsinghua National Laboratory for Information Science and Technology,
Department of Electronic Engineering, Tsinghua University, Beijing, China
{Yangyy, jingyun-14, sunjiasong}@tsinghua.edu.cn

Abstract. Speech activity detection aims to distinguish the speech/non-speech sections in audio data. This technology had been widely used in the scene of speech recognition, speech enhancement and speaker diarization, where most of them adopted methods of multiple threshold, reducing noise, Gaussian Mixture Model (GMM) or Deep Neural Network (DNN) as the state-of-the-art. As the front-end of these applications, the precision of speech activity detection and speaker localization will serious impact the overall system performance. But how to conquer the interference caused by indoor reverberation and environmental noise is still the bottleneck of improving the accuracy of detection by single channel. Distributed microphones are integrated with scattered microphones in the same room or space and each microphone has its own device to collect data. It can utilize the time delay of sound source to depress the interference of non-speech signals and has no prior request on location or synchronism which is strictly regulated in microphone array. For its convenience, distributed microphones system is being increasingly applied in smart home, vehicle hands-free communication and monitoring. In this paper, a method of enhanced Long Short-Term Memory Recurrent Neural Networks (LSTM-RNN) based on distributed microphones is proposed and compared with the same method on single channel. In several distributed microphones datasets, the novel method has the best twenty-four percent and eighteen percent increase in terms of precision and recall of detection. At the same time, the correct rate of 3D-coordinate speaker localization has been proved to go up thirty present than before.

Keywords: Speech activity detection · Speaker localization · Distributed microphones · LSTM-RNN · Precision and recall of detection

1   Introduction

With the rapid development of network and communication technology, how to realize multi-party dialogues under the complex acoustic environment attracted considerable attention of researchers in the speech signal processing field. The head mounted microphone, omnidirectional and directional microphone and microphone array are the general sound recording equipment. The traditional single microphone has the advantages of small size and low cost, but it does not have the ability to deal with external

© Springer International Publishing Switzerland 2016
C. Stephanidis (Ed.): HCII 2016 Posters, Part II, CCIS 618, pp. 392–400, 2016.
DOI: 10.1007/978-3-319-40542-1_64

noise or conduct with sound source localization task. Microphone array is composed of a number of omnidirectional or directional microphones which are placed by the specific geometric structure. Its capabilities include [1, 2]: sound source localization, speech enhancement, identification and separation of multiple sound sources, etc. However, the microphone array system may not share a common clock thus there may be synchronization errors [3]. In addition, the number of sound source, the microphones' location and indoor acoustic environment always are unknown in the multi-party dialogues scene, which means the absence of priori information about time and space.

The distributed microphones [4] is a signal collection system consisted by multiple single microphones. Each microphone is controlled by different each device such as mobile or other portable devices. There is no restriction on the arrangement and spacing of microphones. It has the advantages of simple structure, convenient operation and low cost, which is in accordance with the requirements of complex dialogue scene and can effectively complete various applications such as sound source localization or speaker clustering/identification.

The sound source localization method on the distributed microphones system is different with that on the microphone array system. The microphone array is required to form array according to some special display rules, or at least has the fixed spacing between microphones. The distributed microphones is more flexible for it basically has no display rules. Besides, the signal of microphone array is fully synchronized in time-domain, while each microphone is controlled by a unified clock. And the distributed microphones is not completely synchronized and has to estimate the number and relative positions of speakers and microphones, which are all or partly unknown. Another similar system, named distributed microphone arrays [5], is also different with distributed microphones: the former is composed of multiple microphone arrays and there is a unified clock to ensure the time synchronization between microphone arrays. In contrast, each microphone in the distributed microphones is controlled by one different terminal equipment, which means they use different data capture card and have the unsynchronized sample time.

Distributed microphones system can be widely used in the speaker indexing and rich transcription, the speaker segmentation and clustering helping Automatic Speech Recognition (ASR) systems and preprocessing modules for speaker-based algorithms [6]. Speech activity detection is needed to be the front-end component of these applications with no exception. Speaker's spatial position is another useful information to improve the performance in the speech recognition or speaker classification tasks.

In order to achieve the speech activity detection by single microphone, a typical system consists of two core parts: a feature extraction and a speech/non-speech decision mechanism. Such as Mel-Frequency Cepstral Coefficients (MFCC) features or autocorrelation function based features are proposed to have the discriminative characteristics [7, 8]. And existing decision making mechanisms are [9]: thresholding, statistical modelling and machine learning, which is presented by Gaussian Mixture Model (GMM) or Deep Neural Network (DNN). But the accuracy of speech activity detection is sustainable worsening for the heavy and non-stationary environmental interference noise and indoor or in-car reverberation. To enrich the discriminative information carried by the features, the asymmetric spatial feature extracted in the distributed microphones system is calculated and adjoined with the traditional features. In the decision making section, the enhanced Long Short-Term Memory Recurrent Neural Networks (LSTM-RNN) is proposed to build the refined decision making model.

The rest of this paper is organized as follows. Some related work is briefly reviewed in Sect. 2. In Sect. 3, we simply review the speech activity detection and speaker localization algorithm. In Sect. 4, we propose a novel feature method to overcome the noise and reverberation problem and extend this method by introducing a modified LSTM-RNN to deal with the decision making, and we give the log likelihood method to score this model. Experimental results on corpus recorded under real meeting scene are presented in Sect. 5 and comparing our method with other methods respectively, which is followed by the conclusions and future works.

2   Relation to Prior Work

The work presented here focused on theory and method of Speech Activity Detection (SAD) and speaker localization algorithm. The earliest SAD is determined by the short-term energy and zero-crossing rate which is useful only under the condition of almost no noise interference. The features applied in arbitrary noise or reverberation can be summarized into five categories [9]: energy-based features, spectral-domain features, cepstral-domain features, harmonicity-based features, and long-term features. The energies across different sub-bands often combine with other features such as Zero-Crossing Rate (ZCR) or Line Spectral Frequency (LSF); Assuming that the noise is additive and independent, the spectral-domain features are based on noise power estimation and subtraction; As the power spectrum of the log-power spectrum, cepstral-domain features can be used to determine the fundamental frequency for SAD; for the harmonic structure of voiced speech are preserved even in very noisy condition, the harmonicity-based features are the most powerful features; long-term features are extracted from contiguous frames and beneficial for distinguishing speech from noise. As the spatial features, Time Delay of Arrival (TDOA) features based on Multiple Distant Microphones (MDM) could provide the discriminative information of speaker's relative positions, which offers different aspects of speaker identity information from the conventional acoustic features [10].

Compared with statistical modelling and machine learning [9], most of thresholding method of SAD decision making is the hard decision. The prerequisite of statistical modelling is all the signals obey some special distribution. The classic Gaussian Mixture Model (GMM) and Neural Networks (NN) is the representative of machine learning on SAD decision making. Recently, Dahl et al. [11] proposed a novel Deep Neural Network Hidden Markov Model (DNN-HMM) model and got more than 70 % recognition rate on the dataset of large-vocabulary continuous speech recognition, in which the noise, music, spoken, and other conditions were considered. A significant advantage of DNN model is its hierarchical learning ability, which means DNN model learn common mode at low level and learn complex mode on high level. DNN can automatic learn the distinguishing features of speech/non-speech, such as energy, spectral/cepstral-domain features. Meanwhile, DNN has the ability to learn complicated classification tasks, which could be utilized to learning a variety patterns of speech and noise signal from a large amount of data. Long Short-Term Memory

(LSTM) [12] was first proposed in 1997 and one effective deep Long Short-Term Memory Recurrent Neural Network (LSTM-RNN) structure was born in 2013, which combines the hierarchical representation of LSTM with RNN's ability of utilizing the long-span context flexibly. This LSTM-RNN acoustic model has 17.1 % phoneme error rate, which is significantly better than the RNN and HMM. The similar structure with standard RASTA-PLP frontend features [13] was applied on SAD and the frame-wise Equal Error Rate (EER) was 9.6 % on synthetic test data of TIMIT and Buckeye corpora at a peak SNR of 0 dB.

3 Deep LSTM-RNN

Simple RNN structure describes the neutral network model with limited temporal dependency. However, in the RNN training process, if the gradient descent method is used to modify the weight, the gradient layer will gradually dissipate with the increasing number of network layers and its effect in the adjustment of network weights is becoming smaller. This phenomenon is known as the vanishing gradient problem.

Long Short-term Memory is an RNN architecture using context information with an improved memory, which can be adjusted by the context and previous outputs. Meanwhile, the weights of input gate, output gate and forget gate are continually adjusted to obtain the best profile from mass data. By this way, LSTM-RNN can alleviate the vanishing gradient problem of general RNN [14, 15].

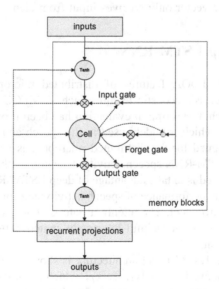

Fig. 1. Common LSTM-RNN architecture

The input signal of this architecture is defined as $x = [x_1, \ldots, x_T]$, which usually is the extracted features of each speech frame. The corresponding output the hidden layer of RNN is $y = [y_1, \ldots, y_T]$ and $h = [h_1, \ldots, h_T]$. The standard RNN equation is:

$$h_t = \text{sigmoid}(\mathbf{W}_{xh}x_t + \mathbf{W}_{hh}h_{t-1} + \mathbf{b}_h) \tag{1}$$

$$y_t = \mathbf{W}_{hy}h_t + \mathbf{b}_y \tag{2}$$

where $\mathbf{W}_{xh}$ is weight matrix between input layer and hidden layer, $\mathbf{W}_{hh}$ is weight matrix between two hidden layers, $\mathbf{W}_{hy}$ is weight matrix between hidden layer and output layer, $\mathbf{b}_h$ is hidden bia vector, $\mathbf{b}_y$ is output bia vector. On the basis of RNN, the memory cells and several gates are added into LSTM-RNN architecture to keep and use previous context information, which is demonstrated in Fig. 1. The iterative equations are [15]:

$$i_t = \sigma(\mathbf{W}_{xi}x_t + \mathbf{W}_{hi}h_{t-1} + \mathbf{W}_{ci}c_{t-1} + \mathbf{b}_i) \tag{3}$$

$$f_t = \sigma(\mathbf{W}_{xf}x_t + \mathbf{W}_{fc}h_{t-1} + \mathbf{W}_{cf}c_{t-1} + \mathbf{b}_f) \tag{4}$$

$$c_t = f_t c_{t-1} + i_t \tanh(\mathbf{W}_{xc}x_t + \mathbf{W}_{hc}h_{t-1} + \mathbf{b}_c) \tag{5}$$

$$o_t = \sigma(\mathbf{W}_{xo}x_t + \mathbf{W}_{ho}h_{t-1} + \mathbf{W}_{co}c_t + \mathbf{b}_o) \tag{6}$$

$$h_t = o_t \tanh(c_t) \tag{7}$$

where σ is the logistic sigmoid function, i, f, o, c are respectively the input gate, forget gate, output gate and cell activation vectors, all of which are the same size as the hidden vector h. The weight matrices from the cell to gate vectors (e.g. $\mathbf{W}_{xi}$) are diagonal, so element m in each gate vector only receives input from element m of the cell vector.

4   Enhanced Deep LSTM-RNN

As the basic method, TDOA features of distributed microphones were generally combined with other classic acoustic features such as MFCC or PLP. Its better performance on NIST Rich Transcription evaluation had been proved [16]. However, the deep learning method, which is widely used in the speech and speaker recognition, is still not specially designed for the distributed microphones under noisy background. The enhanced deep LSTM-RNN speech activity detection method based on distributed microphones we proposed is to take advantage of deep LSTM-RNN architecture and to deal with the drop in the performance of speech activity detection system caused by the annoying acoustic environment. The attention gate is added to adjust its threshold at any time period, which can be helpful to exactly switch between silence and voice under noisy environment.

The enhanced deep LSTM-DNN architecture is shown in Fig. 2. The input signal of this architecture is defined as $x = [x_1, \ldots, x_T]$, which usually is the extracted features of each noisy speech frame on each channel. The iterative equations are:

$$i_t = \sigma(\mathbf{W}_{xi}x_t + \mathbf{W}_{hi}h_{t-1} + \mathbf{W}_{ci}c_{t-1} + \mathbf{b}_i) \tag{8}$$

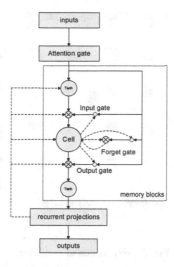

Fig. 2. Enhanced LSTM-RNN architecture

$$a_t = \sigma(\mathbf{W}_{ai} i_t) \tag{9}$$

$$f_t = \sigma(\mathbf{W}_{xf} x_t + \mathbf{W}_{fc} h_{t-1} + \mathbf{W}_{cf} c_{t-1} + \mathbf{b}_f) \tag{10}$$

$$c_t = f_t c_{t-1} + a_t \tanh(\mathbf{W}_{xc} x_t + \mathbf{W}_{hc} h_{t-1} + \mathbf{b}_c) \tag{11}$$

$$o_t = \sigma(\mathbf{W}_{xo} x_t + \mathbf{W}_{ho} h_{t-1} + \mathbf{W}_{co} c_t + \mathbf{b}_o) \tag{12}$$

$$h_t = O_t \tanh(c_t) \tag{13}$$

where σ is the logistic sigmoid function, i, a, f, o, c are respectively the input gate, attention gate, forget gate, output gate and cell activation vectors, all of which are the same size as the hidden vector h. All the weight matrices are diagonal.

5   Experimental Results

The experimental conditions (shown in Fig. 2) are designed to verify this LSTM-RNN's effect on SAD and speaker localization based on distributed microphones. The lab room's size is 9.0 m * 9.0 m * 2.7 m. There are eight single microphones (small circles) on the corner and two microphone arrays (two rectangles) on the front wall and the room's center. The 4*4 squares represent the sixteen speakers' positions when they did sound recording. Some recording requirements are set down such as each recording lasted more than ten minutes, speaker is close to the microphone when recording and intermediate of sound is less than 40 %. All the recording data include forty speech segments by one speaker and forty conversations between two speakers. Three-hundred minutes data and its annotations are provided. Some kinds of

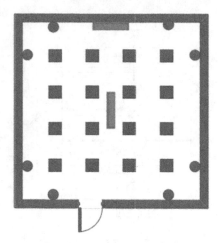

Fig. 3. Experimental conditions

noise sounds such as white noise and car noise are played by the loudspeaker on the center of ceiling. The types of noise and their Signal-to-Noise Ratio (SNR) are listed in Table 1 (Fig. 3).

On the speech activity detection task, the baseline method is common Gaussian Mixture Model (GMM). The enhanced deep LSTM-RNN method is compared with the baseline method and common deep RNN method. With the eight channel data of forty speech segments by one speaker, the average precision and recall of speech activity detection are shown in Table 2. The last method has the best twenty-four percent and eighteen percent increase in terms of precision and recall of detection. On the eight channel data of forty conversations between two speakers, the average 3D-coordinate correct rate (error is below 10 cm) of speaker localization is shown in Table 3. The common TDOA and deep LSTM-RNN method are compared. The correct rate of the last method increased more than 30 %, which shows this method has some advantage on distributed microphones system's SAD and speaker localization.

Table 1. Types of noise and their Signal-to-Noise Ratio (SNR)

Types of noise	SNR				
White noise	−20	−10	0	10	20
Car noise	−20	−10	0	10	20
Engine noise	−10	−5	0	5	10
Air-condition noise	−10	−5	0	5	10

Table 2. The average precision and recall of speech activity detection

Precision/Recall	Types of noise							
	White noise		Car noise		Engine noise		Air-condition noise	
GMM	64.03 %	72.26 %	56.64 %	69.93 %	55.12 %	68.45 %	53.74 %	64.17 %
deep RNN	81.90 %	77.58 %	75.32 %	74.08 %	70.79 %	72.54 %	68.25 %	71.43 %
enhanced deep LSTM-RNN	87.15 %	90.63 %	82.69 %	85.67 %	76.44 %	83.37 %	75.82 %	79.56 %

Table 3. The average correct rate of 3-D speaker localization

Precision	Types of noise			
	White noise	Car noise	Engine noise	Air-condition noise
TDOA	55 %	51 %	49 %	52 %
deep LSTM-RNN	86 %	78 %	77 %	74 %

6 Conclusion

Different with microphone array, distributed microphones system is composed by several independent acoustic sensor and has no regular placing rules between them. The advantage is its freedom of position and time delay vector collected from its asymmetric sensors. In this paper, an enhanced Long Short-Term Memory Recurrent Neural Networks (LSTM-RNN) based on distributed microphones is proposed. In the distributed microphones datasets, this method has some growth on precision and recall of speech activity detection and speaker localization. This kind of system can be applied in many scenes such smart home, unmanned vehicle and robots.

References

1. Ward, D.B., Williamson, R.C.: Particle filter beamforming for acoustic source location in a reverberant environment. In: Proceedings of IEEE International Conference on Acoustic Speech Signal Processing (ICASSP), Orlando, USA, pp. II1777–II1780, 13–17 May 2002
2. Benesty, J., Chen, J., Huang, Y.: Microphone Array Signal Processing. Springer, Berlin Heidelberg (2008)
3. Liu, Z.: Sound source separation with distributed microphone arrays in the presence of clock synchronization errors. In: 2008 International Workshop for Acoustic Echo and Noise Control (IWAENC 2008), Seattle, USA, 14–17 September 2008
4. Huijbregts, M., Leeuwen, D., Hain, T.: The AMI RT09s Speaker Diarization System. http://www.itl.nist.gov/iad/mig/tests/rt/2009/workshop/ami-diarization.pdf
5. Jia, Y., Luo, Y., Lin, Y., Kozintsev, I.: Distributed microphone arrays for digital home and office. In: 2006 Proceedings of IEEE International Conference on Acoustics, Speech and Signal Processing (ICASSP 2006), Toulouse, France, vol. 5, pp. 1065–1068, 14–19 May 2006

6. Miro, X.A.: Robust speaker diarization for meetings. Ph.D. thesis of Universitat Politecnica de Catalunya, Spain (2006)
7. Yoo, I.C., Lim, H., Yook, D.: Formant-based robust voice activity detection. IEEE/ACM Trans. Audio Speech Lang. Process. **23**(12), 2238–2245 (2015)
8. Savoji, M.H.: A robust algorithm for accurate endpointing of speech. Speech Commun. **8**(1), 45–60 (1989)
9. Khoa, P.C.: Noise robust voice activity detection. Master thesis of Nanyang Technological University, Singapore (2012)
10. Yang, Y., Liu, J.: Exploring the large-scale TDOA feature space for speaker diarization. In: Stephanidis, C. (ed.) HCI 2014, Part I. CCIS, vol. 434, pp. 551–556. Springer, Heidelberg (2014)
11. Dahl, G., Yu, D., Deng, L., Acero, A.: Context-dependent pre-trained deep neural networks for large-vocabulary speech recognition. IEEE Trans. Audio Speech Lang. Process. **20**(1), 30–42 (2012)
12. Hochreiter, S., Schmidhuber, J.: Long short-term memory. Neural Comput. **9**(8), 1735–1780 (1997)
13. Eyben, F., Weninger, F., Squartini, S., Schuller, B.: Real-life voice activity detection with LSTM recurrent neural networks and an application to hollywood movies. In: 2013 IEEE International Conference on Acoustics, Speech and Signal Processing (ICASSP 2013), Vancouver, Canada, pp. 483–487, 26–31 May 2013
14. Graves, A., Mohamed, A., Hinton, G.: Speech recognition with deep recurrent neural networks. In: 2013 IEEE International Conference on Acoustics, Speech and Signal Processing (ICASSP 2013), Vancouver, Canada, pp. 6645–6649, 26–31 May 2013
15. Sak, H., Senior, A.W., Beaufays, F.: Long short-term memory recurrent neural network architectures for large scale acoustic modeling. In: 15th Annual Conference of the International Speech Communication Association (INTERSPEECH 2014), Singapore, pp. 338–342, 14–18 September 2014
16. Rich Transcription Evaluation Project. http://www.itl.nist.gov/iad/mig/tests/rt. Accessed 10 Mar 2016

Smart Environments and the Internet of Things

Evaluation of the Interaction with an Internet of Things Smart Building

Rafael Bacchetti$^{(\boxtimes)}$

Eldorado Research Institute, Campinas, Brazil
rafael.bacchetti@eldorado.org.br

Abstract. The Internet of Things is transforming the way we interact with our houses and cities. The advance of technology granted a wide range of possibilities to connect virtually any device and collect data on its use; however, it seems that we are not considering the human that will interact with it. In this paper, I will present how a Human-Centered Design approach was adopted in the development of a Smart Building office.

Keywords: Internet of Things · Smart building · User experience · Heuristic evaluation · Interface evaluation

1 Introduction

The Internet of Things (IoT) comprises a variety of daily objects that acquired connectivity and computing power using sensors and actuators to enable the communication between person-to-object and object-to-object. For that reason, it is now possible to make objects smart.

This technology is present in different categories such as connected homes – that includes thermostats, lighting, and energy monitoring; wearables; medical devices; connected cars; and urban systems – that includes air quality sensors, city rental bikes, and parking meters/sensors [1]. The smart building uses a range of equipment, services and applications that work together to create an intelligent environment for different spheres including communication, comfort, security and sustainability. It uses technologies to make the building functioning more efficiently.

It is important to note, however, that the accelerated evolution of IoT brought a wide range of opportunities. Nevertheless, the focus is usually on the devices and technology needed or in the data analysis instead of its use. It seems that we are forgetting to consider the human that interacts with this technology.

This study evaluates the user experience and usability of the mobile application created to interact with the smart building that is being developed by Eldorado Research Institute. This paper is organized as follows: in Sect. 2 is presented the Eldorado Smart Building scope and the mobile application; in Sect. 3 is presented the results of the usability inspections; and in Sect. 4 is presented the discussion and conclusion of this paper.

C. Stephanidis (Ed.): HCII 2016 Posters, Part II, CCIS 618, pp. 403–408, 2016.
DOI: 10.1007/978-3-319-40542-1_65

2   The Eldorado Smart Building – "Smart Eld"

In order to take advantage of IoT technology, Eldorado Research Institute is transforming its own office into a smart building. In the first development cycle, Eldorado started to collect information of the building such as the air quality and temperature of office and meeting rooms. Therefore, it was possible to adjust the environment based on this data.

On the second cycle, it was designed a mobile application to connect people and devices. It is important to consider that it will be used by different users (personas), such as executives, managers, employees and even visitors. Furthermore, interactions with these objects may occur in a wide variety of contexts, especially for mobile devices [1]. Hence, the interface is composed according to the user context. The Fig. 1 shows the options available according to their location: (a) is the screen for a user inside a meeting room; (b) is for a user inside the office, but not in a meeting; (c) is for a user outside the building; and (d) is the screen with parking lot information.

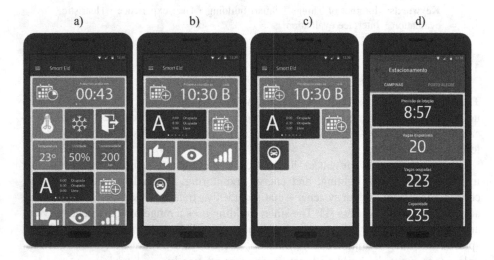

Fig. 1. Prototype of the mobile application in each context

Outside the building, the user is informed of their next meeting time, search for available rooms, schedule a new meeting and get parking lot information.

Once in the office, the user is also able to vote the subjective thermal sensation based in their location and get information of cellular signal on the building. Meanwhile, during a meeting, the user is able to see for how long the room can be used, control the lights and air conditioner, end the meeting and see information of temperature, humidity.

The parking lot information is shown on a different screen and consist of the prediction time it will be crowded, the number of available spots, number of occupied spots and capacity (as shown on Fig. 1, screen d).

The application gathered all the controllers into one mobile application where the user feels a consistence service – designing simplified mental models of the tasks, even in cases where the technology is more complicated.

3 Usability Inspection

The usability evaluation should occur during the entire development cycle and its results should be used to continuously improve and adapt the system to the user needs [2, 3]. For the first release of the mobile application, it was combined two different inspection methods: one considering the user perspective and another considering the knowledge of usability specialists. The combination of different inspection methods can help achieve better results [4].

3.1 Card Sorting

The information architecture of the mobile user interface was evaluated through a card sorting session with 15 users, as suggested by Nielsen [5]. The objective of this evaluation is to understand the mental model of the users by comprehending their expectations and understanding of the smart building interactions available. The similarity matrix (Table 1) shows the percentage of users that agree with each card pairing.

By observing the results, it is possible to infer that users tend to group the room controllers, the information of temperature, humidity and luminosity, and "end meeting" together. "Schedule a meeting" and "show meeting" rooms available is another common grouping. The final group gathers the information of cellular signal, the "vote how is the ambient temperature" option and the information of parking lot spots.

Table 1. Similarity matrix of the card sorting results

Control meeting room projector										
100	Control meeting room videoconference									
88	88	Control meeting room lights								
88	88	100	Control meeting room air conditioner							
77	77	88	88	Show meeting room temperature, humidity and luminosity						
55	55	44	44	44	End meeting					
0	0	0	0	0	44	Schedule a new meeting				
11	11	11	11	11	33	88	Show meeting rooms availability			
0	0	0	0	11	0	22	22	Information of cellular signal on the building		
11	11	11	11	11	0	22	22	44	Vote the subjective thermal sensation	
0	0	0	0	11	0	11	11	44	33	Information of parking lot spots

3.2   Heuristic Evaluation

The heuristic evaluation technique was chosen because it is fast, cheap and can raise problems that usability specialists recognize from years of user research experience. In this evaluation participated five specialists, being that two had previously contact with the smart building development.

An introductory meeting gathered the evaluators to explanation of how the system works and a dynamic prototype was sent to the evaluators with the features that will be available in the first release:

- Turn the room lights on/off;
- Turn the room air conditioning on/off;
- End the meeting;
- Schedule a new meeting (search for a vacant room);
- Look for information of the parking lot.

Each specialist conducted their own individual evaluation to find as many as usability problem as possible, regardless of its complexity. In a second meeting, each specialist presented the problems found and which heuristic were violated.

In total, 22 problems were found, although, many of them violated more than one heuristic, resulting on 34 violations (Table 2). Each of the problems were discussed to reach consensus on its severity, as listed: 4 usability catastrophes; 4 major usability problems; 4 minor usability problems; 2 cosmetic problems and 8 that are not a usability problem at all.

Table 2. Heuristic violations found and classified according to its severity rating. (The usability heuristics and severities are from Nielsen [7].)

Heuristics	Number of violations				
Severity →	0	1	2	3	4
(1) Visibility of system status	2	2	2	1	1
(2) Match between system and the real world				2	1
(3) User control and freedom					1
(4) Consistency and standards	1			1	
(5) Error prevention				1	3
(6) Recognition rather than recall		1	1		
(7) Flexibility and efficiency of use	3			1	
(8) Aesthetic and minimalist design	3		2		
(9) Help users recognize, diagnose, and recover from errors					1
(10) Help and documentation				1	
Total of violations found	12	3	5	7	7

The Usability Catastrophes. The first problem is that the interface does not show to the user when there is some downtime – if there is any connectivity issue, for instance. It is necessary to show when there is a problem and if the user is able to do anything to solve it.

Another problem is that the user can erroneously end the meeting thinking that the button calls for a different action, such as close the application. The application do not allow the user to confirm if they really intend to end the meeting and make the room available for other people.

The Major Usability Problems. There are buttons that do not have their function very clear – such as information of cellular signal and vote the subjective thermal sensation. Besides, it is not clear that the lights and air conditioner controls correspond to the room the user is using. The suggested solution for this is use labels to complement the icons and help the user recognize functionalities.

The Minor Usability Problems. Some icons are interactive, such as turning on and off the lights and air conditioner and others are simply showing information, such as temperature. However, they presentation is the same which may confuse the user.

Another problem found is the representation of light and air conditioner status (on or off). Lights on is represented with a yellow background whereas lights off is represented with a grey background. The specialists pointed out that a grey color may lead the user to believe that the functionality is unavailable.

The Cosmetic Problems. In the parking lot screen, it would be nice to have an icon on the vacant spot information and on the prediction of crowding time. The information of occupied spots and capacity are irrelevant or rarely needed.

The Ones That Are Not a Usability Problem at All. Among the problems found that are not a usability issue, the specialists listed that in the countdown is not clear if the time is represented in hours and minutes or minutes and seconds and the temperature does not have its unit (Celsius or Fahrenheit). In addition, in the parking lot screen, the information could be shown according to the user's location instead of alternating the navigation tabs to change the city. Finally, the application could be integrated into a personal assistant so the user could ask when his next meeting is or when the parking lot will be crowded.

4   Conclusion and Discussion

It is challenging to design IoT products since they incorporate thinking across different layers of design from the most visible to the user – such as interface, interaction, navigation and visual design – to the least visible – such as conceptual architecture, integration with non-digital touch points and functionality of a specific service [1]. A human-centered approach to IoT technology can help designers and developers to understand better the fusion between the virtual and physical world where the user is surrounded by many devices.

Looking at the card sorting results is possible to imagine that the users will recognize the interface organization. However, the heuristic evaluation pointed out issues that can hamper the use of the application. The user should feel confident that they will be able to accomplish the desired task, even if they are not aware of the details on how the technology will handle it.

As future work, the interface will be improved to fix the usability issues found by the specialists. A new evaluation is required to measure the effectiveness of the changes. In order to have a more complete evaluation, a third method will be used: a usability test. This method will help identify problems that will pester the actual users and, as stated by Nielsen, "data from users has an impact on the engineers developing the product that no 'expert evaluation' can equal" [6].

Acknowledgements. I would like to thank my colleagues from Eldorado Research Institute that participated on the Heuristic Evaluation and provided insight and expertise that greatly assisted the research. I would also like to thank Janaina Ruas and Daniel Costa who coordinate the implementation of the Eldorado Smart Building, and Camila Kamarad and Eduardo Tanaka for the comments that greatly improved the manuscript.

References

1. Rowland, C., Goodman, E., Charlier, M., Light, A., Lui, A.: Designing Connected Products: UX for the Consumer Internet of Things. O'Reilly, Sebastopol (2015)
2. Nielsen, J., Molich, R.: Heuristic evaluation of user interfaces. In: Proceedings of the SIGCHI Conference on Human Factors in Computing Systems, New York (1990)
3. Jeffries, R., Miller, J.R., Wharton, C., Uyeda, K.: User interface evaluation in the real world: a comparison of four techniques. In: Proceedings of the SIGCHI Conference on Human Factors in Computing Systems, New York (1991)
4. Nielsen, J.: Usability inspection methods. In: Conference Companion on Human Factors in Computing Systems, Boston (1994)
5. Nielsen, J.: Card Sorting: How Many Users to Test. https://www.nngroup.com/articles/card-sorting-how-many-users-to-test/
6. Jeffries, R., Desurvire, H.: Usability testing vs. heuristic evaluation: was there a contest. SIGCHI Bull. **24**, 39–41 (1992)
7. Nielsen, J., Mack, R.L.: Usability Inspection Methods. Wiley, New York (1994)

Reflective Interaction Capabilities by Use of Ambient Manuals for an Ambient Light-Control

Daniel Burmeister(✉), Andreas Schrader, and Bashar Altakrouri

Institute of Telematics, University of Lübeck, Lübeck, Germany
{burmeister,schrader,altakrouri}@itm.uni-luebeck.de

Abstract. Intelligent Environments like Smart Homes consist of a variety of interconnected devices, which are increasingly controlled by NUI. However, provided interaction possibilities and functionality are often not obvious to users. Illustrating such scenario, we've developed an ambient light-control using two NUI devices for interaction. Building on this, four ambient manuals reflectively explaining available interaction possibilities and functionality on different output devices were developed in a participatory design process. With a total of 60 subjects all manuals were evaluated regarding workload.

Keywords: Ambient manuals · Reflective interaction capabilities · Light-control · Natural user interfaces

1 Introduction

With proliferation of embedding digital technology in everyday objects, Intelligent Environments like Smart Homes include a growing number of intelligent interconnected devices. However, provided interaction possibilities are becoming increasingly invisible (known as the *Invisibility Dilemma* [1]), esp. with regard to the expanding utilization of natural interaction like motion-gestures [2]. Mostly, it is not obvious which gestures can be performed and what corresponding functionality is available among these devices. Smart Devices are produced by different manufacturers and are therefore highly heterogeneous in nature, protocols and functionality. In order to reduce such complexity, devices could be enabled to reflect their interaction possibilities by providing ambient manuals on available output devices [3]. Within the course of an ambient computing class at the University of Lübeck, we addressed this type of problem. Hereafter, the development process, implementation, and provision of ambient manuals on different devices based on an intelligent light-control by the use of Natural User Interfaces (NUI) will be presented.

2 Light-Control

In order to build a representative scenario of an Intelligent Environment with low complexity in functionality but heterogenous Smart Devices, three Smart

© Springer International Publishing Switzerland 2016
C. Stephanidis (Ed.): HCII 2016 Posters, Part II, CCIS 618, pp. 409–415, 2016.
DOI: 10.1007/978-3-319-40542-1_66

Lights were interconnected to an ambient light-control system, which can be operated by two different NUIs.

2.1 Used Devices

As input devices one stationary (Leap Motion) and one wearable (Myo) device were used. The Leap Motion Controller uses two infrared (IR) cameras capturing the reflection of three IR-LEDs to recognize finger and hand motion-gestures, performed within an area up to 60 cm above the device. The Myo-bracelet is worn on the users forearm at height of the anconeus. Using electromyography (EMG) sensors and an inertial measurement unit (IMU), performed hand and finger gestures can be recognized by analyzing muscle contractions, velocity and accelerations. Both devices are able to recognize a given set of gestures ex factory. Three different light sources with slightly different functionality and heterogenous protocols were used. These include two LED-stripes, namely Adafruit Neonpixel[1] and ArtNet LED Dimmer 4[2], and one light bulb, namely Philipps Hue[3]. Whereas the Adafruit Neonpixel allows to control each single LED, the ArtNet LED Dimmer as well as the Philipps Hue do not. All light sources are able to be turned on and off as well as changing their color and brightness.

2.2 System Architecture

In order to interconnect all devices mentioned in Sect. 2.1 an extensible system architecture was developed (see Fig. 1). Central input component is the *Gesture Provider*, which is responsible for setting up the connection to NUI devices and recognizing performed gestures within per device *Gesture Detectors*. All gestures are transformed into a system coherent commands and are provided to other system components via publish-subscribe-pattern using device-specific *Gesture Listeners*, if such device is available and ready for communication. Furthermore, the communication with all light sources is handled by the *Light Manager*, which subscribes to available *Gesture Listeners* and coordinates the delivery of received commands to the current selected light source by translating the commands to the needed protocol. Upon this, the current state of the light-control and detailed information about NUI devices can be accessed via the *Feedback Server*, which subscribes to *Gesture Listeners* and observes the *Light Managers'* current state. Information like selected light source, last recognized gesture, current color values, etc. can be separately retrieved by external instances like ambient manuals via HTTP in JSON format. Additional light sources and NUI devices can easily be integrated into the existing system by just developing a *Gesture Detector* resp. *Lightconnector* for setting up the connection with such devices.

---

[1] https://www.adafruit.com/, accessed 08.04.2016.
[2] http://www.dmx4all.de/, accessed 08.04.2016.
[3] http://www.meethue.com/, accessed 08.04.2016.

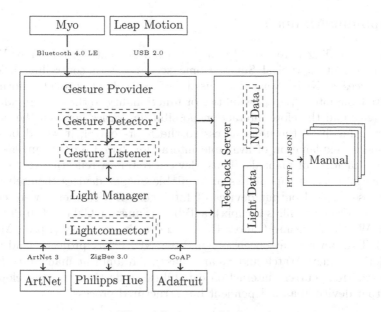

Fig. 1. System architecture

2.3 Control Capabilities

In addition to currently available functionality of commercially available Smart Lights such as switching light on and off as well as changing color and brightness, the implementation of light-control includes a mechanism to switch between light sources. All functionality were mapped to motion gestures on both NUIs. For this purpose provided gestures by the SDKs were first used (like Wave-In/Out of Myo). In order to map additional functionality, further gestures were defined (see Table 1). Light follows Hand command is just available on Adafruit Neonpixel, because its the only lamp which LEDs can be controlled individually.

Table 1. Gesture overview

Command	Leap motion	Myo
Previous light	Swipe hand left	Wave-In
Next light	Swipe hand right	Wave-Out
Toggle light	Draw circle with finger	Rotate fist
Change brightness	Move horizontal fist	Move fist vertically
Change color	Move vertical fist	Move fist horizontally
Light follows hand	Move victory sign horizontally	Move spread fingers horizontally

3   Ambient Manuals

As part of building a realistic Intelligent Environment, the developed light-control represents a typical Smart Home scenario with controlling interconnected devices by NUIs. None of the used devices is able to provide information about available interaction possibilities or functionality to the user. In addition, functionality and therefore interaction possibilities varies between the devices. In order to facilitate the users access to the light-control, it would be useful to provide an explanation of available interaction based on the current interconnection in form of manuals. Thus, devices obtain a reflective character by explaining interaction capabilities on available output devices themselves. For this purpose, typical output devices of Intelligent Environments were chosen, namely a Projector (Philips Picopix), a Tablet (Samsung Galaxy Tab Pro 12.1), a Smart Watch (Samsung Galaxy Gear), and a Smart Glass (Epson Moverio BT-200). Two devices have been assigned per NUI (Myo: projector and tablet, Leap Motion: Smart Watch and Smart Glass). An ambient manual explaining the light-controls' current interaction capabilities reflectively was developed on each output device in an independent but structured process.

3.1   Participatory Design

In order to cover potential users' needs, all manuals were developed in a participatory design process [4]. Therefore, five subjects per each device were recruited. With the purpose of giving all test persons an idea about the Invisibility Dilemmas complexity, the output devices, the NUI as well as the developed Smart Home scenario were explained to the participants. After that, all participants got the possibility to experience the NUI themselves by controlling demo applications provided from the manufacturers. Jointly with the subjects, paper prototypes of potential manuals were developed and used for further conception. As one of the most important requirements, all potential users mentioned a graphical representation of available gestures. There, representations should show a gestures motion sequence and be available as animation or video. These findings are thus consistent with [5]. In addition to systems interaction capabilities, it should be explained how to put a NUI into operation. Important information about the device' use should appear during interaction.

3.2   Visualization of Manuals

All paper prototypes resulting from the participatory design were further developed including the participants requirements and wishes. By using the light-controls provided interfaces (see Feedback Server in Fig. 1) ambient manuals on all output devices were realized. Figure 2 illustrates all manuals. In Fig. 2a, a mobile application running on a tablet, is depicted. All position of light sources are visualized within a realistic spatial model in which the current selected light is colored depending on selected color and brightness (at this point red with medium brightness). Picograms, located around the currently selected light

source, display available functionality as well as animations of corresponding gestures. As seen in Fig. 2b gestures are visualized by means of realistic animations
of hand and finger movements. Upon this, information about provided functionality of each light source is available and presented by pictograms. Instructions
about commissioning the NUI can also be accessed. Figure 2c displays the ambient manual projected on a wall. Beside a video presenting the performance of
a gesture, a pictorial as well as a textual representation is arranged next to it.
In comparison to the previous presented manuals, users are able to train how
to use the light-control by passing an interactive training mode after setting up
the device. Checkmarks below the pictorial representations indicate the amount
of correct performed gestures. Figure 2d visualizes the graphical interfaces projected into the users field of view while wearing a Smart Glass. In the radial
menus' center the current selected light source is depicted. Around this, information about available functionality is provided. Next to the device and functionality information a looped 3D rendered animation shows the to be performed
gesture within a realistic room model as the user selects it.

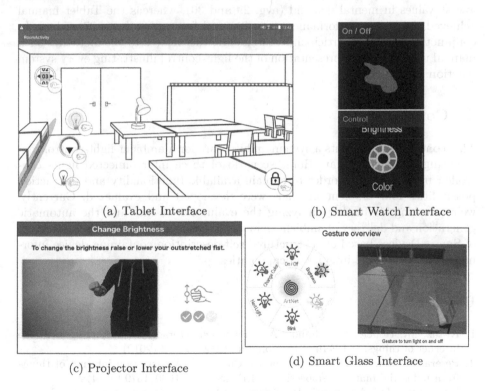

(a) Tablet Interface   (b) Smart Watch Interface

(c) Projector Interface   (d) Smart Glass Interface

Fig. 2. Ambient Manuals on different output devices (Color figure online)

3.3   Evaluation

Each manual got evaluated targeting its workload while using the light-control. In total, 60 subjects (15 each manual) aged from 13 to 61 were asked to perform the following three tasks: (1) select a light source and switch it on, (2) change the lights color and brightness, and (3) let the light follow your hand. After each task, participants filled out a NASA-TLX-questionnaire [6] on six different sub scales with values from 0 to 100 indicating the perceived workload from low to high. Upon this, participants were asked to Think-Aloud while performing the task. All participants recognized the necessity of reflective manuals within the given scenario. By using the provided manuals all participants were able to fulfill the given tasks, whereas none of them was able to do without. A preliminary analysis of the results reflects this by the lowest overall average value of 28 by the performance sub scale. Overall, an average value 30 was measured, which indicates a low perceived workload by the users in using the light control guided by reflective interaction explanations. Furthermore, both manuals using a realistic representation of a gesture performance (Projector and Smart Glass) achieved lowest values in mental demand (avg. 29 and 30), whereas the Tablet manual achieved the lowest performance (avg. 21) and frustration (avg. 27) values. In conjunction with the participants statements, this relates to the fact, that such manual uses a spatial representation of the light-control illustrating every system reaction.

4   Conclusion

This contribution presents a system architecture for a ambient light-control representing a realistic Smart Home scenario of three interconnected lights controlled by two NUI. In order to explain available functionality and interaction possibilities four ambient manuals were developed and evaluated. Currently, we're working on further analyzing the evaluation results and the automatic generation and delivery of ambient manuals by the current interconnection state of Smart Devices based on a structured self-description containing device information and available interaction capabilities.

References

1. Kranz, M., Holleis, P., Schmidt, A.: Embedded interaction: interacting with the internet of things. IEEE Internet Comput. **14**(2), 46–53 (2010)
2. Perera, C., Liu, C.H., Jayawardena, S., Chen, M.: A survey on internet of things from industrial market perspective. IEEE Access **2**, 1660–1679 (2014)
3. Burmeister, D., Altakrouri, B., Schrader, A.: Ambient reflection: towards self-explaining devices. In: 1st Workshop on Large-Scale and Model-based Interactive Systems: Approaches and Challenges; Workshop at the 7th ACM SIGCHI Symposium on Engineering Interactive Computing Systems. Duisburg, Germany, June 2015

4. Schuler, D., Namioka, A. (eds.): Participatory Design: Principles and Practices. L. Erlbaum Associates Inc., Hillsdale (1993)
5. Murao, K., Terada, T.: Evaluating effect of types of instructions for gesture recognition with an accelerometer. In: Proceedings of the 5th Augmented Human International Conference, AH 14, NY, USA, pp. 6:1-6:4. ACM, New York (2014)
6. Hart, S.G., Staveland, L.E.: Development of NASA-TLX (TaskLoadIndex): results of empirical and theoretical research. Adv. Psychol. **52**, 139–183 (1988)

Developing a the Advanced IoT (Internet of Things) Technology Based on Spatial Information

Mi Na Ra Jang, Chan Yang Suhr, and Yun Gil Lee[(✉)]

Department of Architecture, Hoseo University, Asan, Korea
{nara337337,chanyangkee}@naver.com, yglee@hoseo.edu

Abstract. This study aims to develop a location-based technology that can provide optimized information services to users depending on their location. The ultimate goal is to develop an advanced platform and service contents for location-based service (LBS) using spatial information. The proposed technology is similar to the Internet of Things (IoT) but differs by using spatial information as semantic location maps, an integrated platform, and a natural interface. This study is a basic step in the ultimate goal of realizing what is known as human-space interaction (HSI), which represents the proposed technologies in this study. This study focuses mainly on developing complete HSI frameworks and the fundamental technologies to realize this aim, such as a situation model based on spatial information, the IoT platform, a reasoning algorithm, and a natural user interface.

Keywords: Building information modeling · Internet of things · Location based service · Spatial information

1 Introduction

Several years ago, scientists expected that the Internet of Things (IoT) would grow consistently to become the next technological revolution as the trends of wireless sensor networks and ubiquitous computing dwindled. [1, 2] Recently, the IoT has been a prevailing research topic and has become the next product to lead the market share. The IoT is closely related to location based services (LBS) because both aim to provide users with advanced services that relate to their locations. Until now, IoT has focused only on information services limited to devices, but the service coverage will reach out to the whole living environment. For this reason, IoT services should focus on the user's location. One of the significant issues in the IoT research is opportunistic human activity and context recognition. [2] Location is the most important information for recognizing a user's context. However, the relationship between IoT technologies and the user's context related to his/her location is difficult to grasp.

The aim of this study was to develop a location-based technology that can provide optimized information services to users depending on their location. The ultimate goal of this research is to develop an advanced platform and service contents for LBS using spatial information. The proposed technology is similar to the IoT, but is distinct in its use of spatial information as semantic location maps, an integrated platform, and a

© Springer International Publishing Switzerland 2016
C. Stephanidis (Ed.): HCII 2016 Posters, Part II, CCIS 618, pp. 416–419, 2016.
DOI: 10.1007/978-3-319-40542-1_67

natural interface. This study constitutes a basic step toward the goal of realizing what is known as human–space interaction (HSI), which represents the proposed technologies in this study. This study focused mainly on developing a complete HSI framework and the fundamental technologies for achieving this aim, such as a situation model based on spatial information, the IoT platform, a reasoning algorithm, and a natural user interface.

2   The Concept of HIS: Human Space Interaction

Figure 1 shows the concept of the advanced IoT service based on the proposed technologies. In order to make this concept a reality, spatial information, such as semantic location maps, can be used as a resource for modeling the user's situation relative to his or her location, which provides the specific information for reasoning about the user's needs and likely next steps. The semantic location maps can be used to develop an integrated platform that manages the user's situation information and provides an advanced user service. Furthermore, though space is a natural interface, users can conveniently interact with devices and information in spaces with which they are familiar to behave in analogous ways. Therefore, a key HIS technology is semantic situation modeling. In this paper, we propose a situation model that uses ontology and is based on the spatial information model.

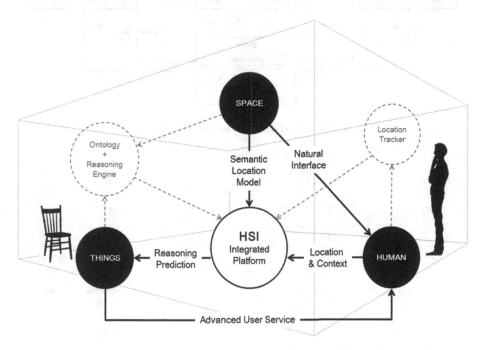

Fig. 1. The concept of the advanced IoT service based on spatial information

3   Situation Model Based on Ontology

There have been several attempts to develop a so-called semantic location model to realize an advanced LBS particularly in indoor space. [3] Location cannot be regarded as a position because location refers not only to numerical data but also to the situation related to the position. [4] To develop a location model, we needed to consider diverse layered knowledge, like position, geometrical and topological data, semantics, social relation, and so on. Ontology, a kind of descriptive language and method for complicated information, is appropriate for illustrating a situation based on location.

Figure 2 shows the overall data structure for the development of the situation model. To describe the user's situation in the built environment, we consider four elements that construct the situation—namely, building, human, device, and event. These elements

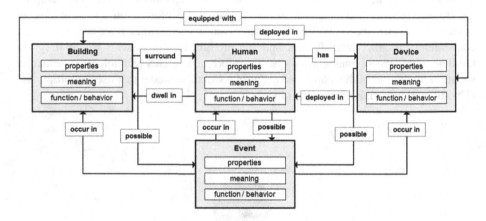

Fig. 2.   The overall data structure for situation model

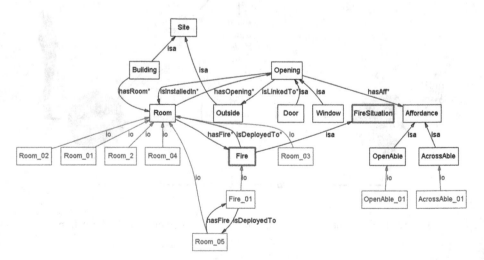

Fig. 3.   The example of the situation modeling for the fire situation

refer to the classification of all data constructing the situation and are linked to others semantically. In addition, each element contains properties, a meaning, and a function/ behavior. These can describe the characteristics of the sub-elements, and their relationship should be defined according to their semantic influence. Figure 3 provides an example of situation modeling for the fire situation. We developed it using Protégé, which is an authoring tool for ontology-related data. This model describes not only the physical condition but also the context caused by fire and the potential actions of the human by object [5].

4   Conclusion and Discussion

This study was a first step toward the ultimate goal of realizing HSI. The study focused mainly on developing the situation model using ontology. In a further study, we will improve the situation model and apply it to the IoT service scenario to evaluate the feasibility.

Acknowledgment. This research was supported by Basic Science Research Program through the National Research Foundation of Korea (NRF) funded by the Ministry of Education (NRF-2015R1D1A1A01057525).

References

1. Gubbia, J., Buyyab, R., Marusica, S., Palaniswamia, M.: Internet of Things (IoT): a vision, architectural elements, and future directions. Future Gener. Comput. Syst. **29**(7), 1645–1660 (2013)
2. Feki, M.A., Kawsar, F., Boussard, M., Trappeniers, L.: The Internet of Things: the next technological revolution. Computer **46**, 24–25 (2013)
3. Wang, X., Shang, J., Yu, F., Yan, J.: Indoor semantic location models for location-based services. Int. J. Smart Home **7**(4), 127–136 (2013)
4. Lee, Y.G., Choi, J.W., Lee, I.J.: Location modeling for ubiquitous computing based on the spatial information management technology. J. Asian Archit. Build. Eng. **5**(1), 105–111 (2006)
5. Lee, Y.G., Park, C.H., Im, D.H.: A study on the development of the user behavior simulation technology using a perceived action possibilities. J. Korea Multimedia Soc. **17**(11), 1335–1344 (2014)

The Belonging Robot (BeRo): A Hybrid Physical-Digital System to Reflect Moods

Tarek H. Mokhtar$^{(\boxtimes)}$ and Samer E. Mansour

The Intelligent Design and Art (iDNA) Research Group, Alfaisal University,
Riyadh, Kingdom of Saudi Arabia
{tmokhtar, smansour}@alfaisal.edu

Abstract. The Belonging Robot or **BeRo,** is a hybrid physical-digital art installation to develop a culture of belonging, collaboration and connectedness of the students, the professors, and the employees to their educational institution. A mobile app and in-site sensory interactions relay the collective mood of these members to the physical system by changing the system's physical configurations, in what we call the Belonging Robot (**BeRo**). BeRo's users interact with its physical environment using pressure sensors in the form of five different colored buttons corresponding to the five different moods of users; or, the users may choose to have their inputs through a mobile app buttons of these different moods. **BeRo's** configurations are to reflect the five selected moods: Very Satisfied, Satisfied, Don't Know, Somewhat Satisfied, and Not Satisfied. Based on usability engineering evaluations, we will design and prototype **BeRo,** to create a place for interaction between students, teachers, employees and their environment, literally HCI on environmental scale! Our platforms will be iteratively designed, prototyped and evaluated on real users. In this research, we will present **BeRo's** concept, motivations, scenarios of operation, architecture, and the prototype of the selected system. Finally, we will present the heuristic evaluations of BeRo from 4 experts in the field of computation, robotics, and control.

Keywords: Design · Interactive systems · Physical-digital platforms · Collective interaction · Education

1 Introduction

In addition to the challenges of the cost of Higher Education and the number of years needed to obtain a degree, lack of belonging is considered among the challenges of our educational systems. "Belonging," as suggested by the "What Works?" UK Report findings, is "at the heart of successful retention and success of students in HE" [8]. Additionally, belonging and "social support is considered one of the critical elements distinguishing those who remain healthy from those who become ill," as stated by Pelletier [6].

Our educational systems are changing rapidly, and getting more and more complex. Scientists have to rethink the role of technology in reshaping and restructuring patterns of social interactions in higher academic institutions everyday [2]. Universities should

© Springer International Publishing Switzerland 2016
C. Stephanidis (Ed.): HCII 2016 Posters, Part II, CCIS 618, pp. 420–425, 2016.
DOI: 10.1007/978-3-319-40542-1_68

include activities and interactive platforms for students to reflect their opinions and moods, and to act accordingly. Nevertheless, our universities seem quaint to these changes [1, 3]. The literature on the use of technology in public places and interactive environments is growing [2, 7]; the literature for creative, intelligent robotic collective environments has not yet been fully realized [3].

Thus, it is important for universities to provide a secure platform to understand the students' opinions/moods of their educational experiences at all times. However the current online platforms, e.g., Moodle and LMS, provide an evaluation platform for courses and instructors, they don't provide a real-time interaction on the student-university experience. The **Belonging Robot** or what we call "**BeRo**" seeks to fill this gap by focusing on how a robotic environment on an art installation scale can augment collective mood and belonging to our educational institutions.

2 Motivations

"Belonging," as a concept and a need, is associated with many ideas, such as: to connect, to memorize, to interact, to socialize, and to feel associated with a context or to be better situated [2, 5]. What an interactive experiential context can provide to enhance student-to-university belonging? We believe that the physical-digital contexts can provide multifaceted platform for engaging, learning, associating, memorizing, and more. Thus, **BeRo** is proposed as a real-time morphological presentation of the students' collective moods, a system to share the collective and to get the students to feel connected – literally, belonging.

The understanding of the movements of plants and flowers inspires **BeRo**! The concept is simple, if the flower is in a good health it will be standing still (upward), while if it gets in an unhealthy state it will fall down. Similarly, **BeRo**'s different configurations reflect the different moods of students in a university setting, as discussed below.

3 Introducing BeRo

BeRo is an interactive digital-physical environment, which will be developed through an iterative design process including designs, developments, evaluations, and refinements. The design will employ the use of three platforms, a. the digital, a web-based app; b. the physical, an interactive robotic environment; and, c. the IoT platform, a structure for communication and processing data between the digital and the physical environments through a cloud-based server.

3.1 BeRo's Digital Interface

We envision the digital interface as a web-based app to be used as the input for students to reflect their moods. It is designed using an Object Oriented Platform by which students will be able to insert their daily moods while using their notebooks or any smart device. The **BeRo**'s web-based app is comprised of five inputs designed to reflect the five moods, as described below. The research team had designed three different low-fidelity prototypes of the UI using Microsoft PowerPoint and Hyperlinks, see Fig. 1. Usability Evaluation techniques and Heuristic Evaluations had been employed to ensure good usability and functionality of the system; and for selecting and enhancing the UI design.

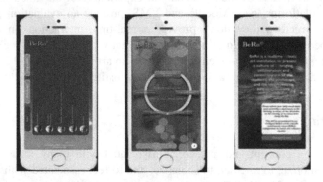

Fig. 1. BeRo's web-based app alternative designs

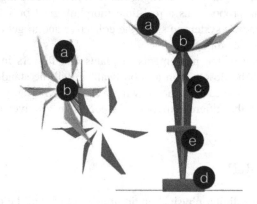

Fig. 2. Top (left) and front (right) views of BeRo's physical components

3.2   BeRo's Physical Interface

BeRo's physical platform is a robotic environment comprised of five elements: a. **BeRo**'s Six Petals; b. the Holding Crown (Kinematics placeholder); c. the Steams (the structure); d. Roots (cabinet for IT components); and, e. Mine (the sensory input platform), see Fig. 2.

BeRo's kinematics will be based on the classical tendon-based platform, in which the structure/petals is actuated using cables connected to custom made gears and driven by servos, located on the Holding Crown, see "b" on Fig. 3. **BeRo**'s Robotic elements are: a. sensors (push buttons, and proximity sensors); b. six petals actuated using cables and six servo motors with their encoding systems (encoders and IR sensors); and, c. six RGB LEDs. It will be based on an existing microcontroller platform, Arduino.

3.3 BeRo's IoT Platform

BeRo's third platform is based on an Internet of Things structure, using ASP.NET platform. It is programmed using C language, which will calculate the averages of both inputs, i.e., the web-based and the robotic sensory inputs. Accordingly, the IoT platform will collect and send real-time information through the cloud to actuate BeRo's kinematic structure, i.e. the servos and the six petals, to reflect the collective mood of the university. The IoT structure will send this information to the microcontroller to activate the five different movements and color configurations of **BeRo**, see Fig. 3.

BeRo's five configurations are as follows, a. Satisfied, where the six Petals are all the way up, and all the LEDs will turn red; b. Somewhat Satisfied, where the six Petals are 45° down from the previous configuration, and all the LEDs will turn yellow; c. Neutral, where the six Petals are horizontal, and all the LEDs will turn white; d. Somewhat Dissatisfied, where the six Petals are 45° down from the previous setting, and all the LEDs will turn blue; and, e. Dissatisfied, the six Petals are all the way down, and all the LEDs will turn green, see Figs. 3 and 4.

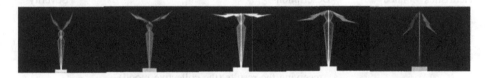

Fig. 3. BeRo's five configurations: satisfied, somewhat satisfied, neutral, somewhat dissatisfied, dissatisfied (left-right).

4 Scenarios of Operation

One morning in 2016, "Magan Morgan" and "Christopher Lee," two freshmen students, are walking in front of the BeRo's environment, and suddenly they found a plate near to it saying, "I am "BeRo"! Please enter your today's mood"! "OMG, this looks like a giant flower! It asks us to enter our today's mood ☺," Megan commenting while smiling. "What?! It seems weird to meet this guy in our first day on campus!," said Chris. Megan decided to hit the Smiley face on BeRo's plate! While they were looking into the five buttons, they heard a voice of a moving object, and the light of BeRo turned on! BeRo's six petals starts to move upward, like an ancient Egyptian guard welcoming the king! It turns red!

"This is awesome!" Chris reacted. "Wow! It understands my input," Megan explained, pointing. Chris nodded his head. "I will push the "sad face" and see what will happen," Chris responded.

Chris clicked on the sad face button. Immediately, they found the petals starts to move downward to the horizontal position, and it turns white! "Now, it looks like a sunflower in its neutral state! Does it make sense?!". "Okay! I think it is collecting our moods! That's fantastic! ☺". "Reacting to the collective mood!". "It is like a surveying system, but interactive! I hope my family had one at home to see how we feel about their decisions!," Megan smiling.

Fig. 4. BeRo's prototype: satisfied config. (right), neutral config. (middle), dissatisfied config. (left).

Table 1. BeRo's violated heuristics as identified by the experts

Task I: The virtual interface

Heuristics violated	Description	Severity ratings
User control and freedom	• After clicking the mood icon, there is a need to return to the main page	3.2
Visibility of system status	• Background should be consistent, even after receiving the results (the collective mood)	1.4
Task II: The physical interface		
Match between the system and the real world	• The faces representing the moods are not enough to understand the moods! • The choices of button colors are counter to norm of virtual interfaces!	2.5
Visibility of system status	• No feedback received after clicking the pushbuttons	3.6

5   Heuristic Evaluations of Early Prototype and Analysis

After developing a 1:2 scaled prototype as shown in Fig. 4, heuristic evaluations were employed for further design development and evaluation. All evaluations were performed in our lab. Participating in the heuristic evaluation were four "experts" from the fields of computation, robotics, and control.

We had defined two tasks to be evaluated, task one: interacting with BeRo's virtual interface to activate the robotic linkages/six petals, and receive the intended feedback; and, task two, interacting with BeRo's physical interface to activate the robotic linkages/six petals, and receive the intended feedback. The heuristic evaluations took from 45 min to 1 h for each expert. The experts were then asked to rate the severity of each problem identified, using Nielsen's five severity rating scale [4]. The average severity ratings for usability problems were used to identify priorities for improving the design of BeRo, see Table 1.

We found that there is a need for improving BeRo's Virtual Interface design by providing flexibility to undo or return to the main webpage; and, to modify the feedback page (the last webpage) and make it consistent with the other pages. For the Physical Interface, we need to add a feedback after using the push buttons, and to add more explanation of what is expected from users.

6 Conclusions

While the use of the hybrid physical-digital platforms in enhancing the sense of belonging is not yet fully experimented, the vision of the hybrid reconfigurable environment will open the possibilities for more explorations on the use of this system in public spaces to enhance human-hybrid interactions, digital and physical.

In this research, we envisioned **BeRo** as an interactive physical-digital environment, and described its three platforms, a. the digital UI, b. the robotics/physical interface, and c. the IoT platform. Also, we had described the hardware employed, the project's motivations, the likely scenarios, and the heuristic evaluations. BeRo's system suggests a novel research for designing social interactive systems for the public use, and for enhancing both the human-hybrid interactions and our educational systems. The work has the potential for full-scale realization and evaluation on real users.

Acknowledgements. The authors acknowledge support from Alfaisal University under grant number IRG. 220130101145.

References

1. Critical Art Ensemble: Electronic Disturbance. Autonomedia (1994)
2. McCullough, M.: Digital Ground: Architecture, Pervasive Computing, and Environmental Knowing. MIT Press, Cambridge (2005)
3. Mokhtar, T., Green, K., Walker, I.: Giving form to the voices of lay-citizens: monumental-IT, an intelligent, robotic, civic monument. In: Stephanidis, C. (ed.) HCII 2013. CCIS, vol. 374, pp. 243–247. Springer, Heidelberg (2013)
4. Nielsen, J.: Usability Engineering. Academic Press, Morgan Kaufmann, Boston (1993)
5. Pigozzi, O.W., Peterson, S., Mau, B., Orr, D.: The Third Teacher: 79 Ways You Can Use Design to Transform Teaching and Learning, 1st edn. Abrams, New York (2010)
6. Pelletier, K.: Sound Mind, Sound Body: A New Model for Life-Long Health, pp. 137–138. Simon and Shuster, New York (1994)
7. Robertson, T., Mansfield, T., Loke, L.: Designing an immersive environment for public use. In: The Proceedings of the Ninth Conference on Participatory Design: Expanding Boundaries in Design, vol. 1, pp. 31–40. ACM, Trento, Italy (2006)
8. Thomas, L.: What Works? Student Retention and Success Report. Paul Hamlyn Foundation, UK (2012)

Cloud Assisted IOT Based Social Door to Boost Student-Professor Interaction

Ali Asghar Nazari Shirehjini[1][(✉)], Abulsalam Yassine[2], Shervin Shirmohammadi[2], Ramtin Rasooli[1], and Mohammad Salar Arbabi[1]

[1] Ambient Intelligence Laboratory, Department of Computer Engineering,
Sharif University of Technology, Tehran, Iran
shirehjini@sharif.edu
[2] DISCOVER LAB, University of Ottawa, Ottawa, Ontario, Canada

Abstract. Face to face meetings and physical presence are important concepts in student-professor relations. Many students require flexibility in arranging meetings or the possibility of ad-hoc meeting with their professors. However, ad-hoc meetings could be difficult to arrange due to busy schedule of professors. It is not unusual for students to attempt several times in a day to catch a professor, or wait an hour behind his door. To overcome this challenge, some professors have teaching assistants (TAs) or office assistant who manage their schedule or provide students with helpful information on how to reach them or handover their documents, projects, etc. Many other professors do not have any secretary or TA.

When students look for a professor at his office and he is not there, it is common to leave a message on a whiteboard or some paper outside the office. However, by this approach professors will not be able to update their schedule dynamically or some might not will to share their schedule with public because of their privacy concerns. Some students also intend to contact with the professor by email. Professors usually get a lot of emails every day and they will not be able to read and answer to all of them, besides it will be frustrating for students too when they don't receive feedbacks from their professors.

To overcome this problem, recent technological advances could be used. We have been motivated by the problems addressed above to propose a cloud assisted IoT based cyber-physical door to boost student-professor interaction in the absence of the professor at his office. This door can be thought as a virtual secretary and an interface between students and professors to help the students to get in touch with their professors.

Keywords: Cyber-physical door · Internet of things · Student-professor interaction

1 Introduction

Normally, university professors are elusive. They are not easily found even in their offices during work hours. Students and other visitors cannot readily get hold of them. The use of computer-mediated communication (CMC) technology has dramatically

© Springer International Publishing Switzerland 2016
C. Stephanidis (Ed.): HCII 2016 Posters, Part II, CCIS 618, pp. 426–432, 2016.
DOI: 10.1007/978-3-319-40542-1_69

changed the ways for students to interact with their professors, especially for communications occurring outside the classroom.

A recent study investigated the impact of offering virtual office hours by using instant messaging (IM) software for student-faculty interaction. The study found that participants in classes that offered virtual office hours reported higher levels of satisfaction with office hours than students in classes that offered only traditional face-to-face office hours. Also revealed, however, was that students' use of virtual office hours is not significantly different from their use of traditional office hours. The study further reported that students prefer asynchronous tools such as email to communicate with the professor.

A question that comes up is why student do not use email to improve their faculty communication. Danielewicz-Betz conducted a research to examine student–faculty communication by email and the lack of clear guidelines that leads to misuse of email in student–faculty interaction. The way students communicate with faculty in higher-education, despite common usage nowadays, has not been analyzed sufficiently (Biesenbach-Lucas 2006a). Moreover, most academic syllabi lack explicit instruction in email writing. Consequently, students, growing up in the instant messaging culture, are unsure how to (or not aware that they should) modify the content of their messages when addressing professors. They often seem unaware of the fact that their emails influence professors' impressions of themselves and their academic achievements (c.f., Jessmer and Anderson 2001).

On the other hand university professor get numerous emails daily and they will not be able to answer to all of them. Besides, different students with different positions try to contact the professor by email. They may vary from undergraduate students to research assistants and PhD students. To address this challenge, we propose a collaborative system to boost the student-professor relation in academic environments. The system integrates office doors using internet of things (IoT) technology, Near Field Communication (NFC) and mobile applications. This creates a cyber-physical system that facilitates IoT enabled doors to allow asynchronous communication between students and faculty, which improves students' perceived satisfaction of student-professor-interaction experience. The system architecture and the way to interact with the system is described in detail in Sect. 3.

The reminder of this paper is as follows. Section 2 discusses related work. In Sect. 3 we describe the proposed cloud assisted IoT based cyber physical system. Section 4 concludes the paper.

2   Related Works

Many researchers studied factors affecting student satisfaction, attention and retention in academic environments, revealing that "student engagement in college activities outside the classroom and interactions with other students and faculty tends to have a substantial impact in terms of student retention, academic performance, and overall satisfaction (Astin 1999)". In his study of the effects of out of classroom experiences, Kuh (1995) found that participation in college activities, living on campus, and conversing frequently with other students and faculty positively influenced students' learning and personal development. Also different students prefer different means of communication (Kelly et al. 2004). Quite simply, reticent students tend toward the use of CMCs and it is therefore less probable that a face-to-face visit take place (Kelly et al. 2004).

Research on the effects of student-faculty interaction outside the classroom have consistently found that informal contact between professors and their students was positively associated with personal, social, and intellectual outcomes as well as students' overall satisfaction with their college experience (Pascarella 1980; Endo and Harpel 1982; Fusani 1994; Myers et al. 2005; Halawah 2006). In their meta-analysis of student faculty interaction, Kuh and Hu (2001) explored the frequency and nature of out-of-class interactions between students and faculty over a period of time and found a positive correlation between the interactions and positive student outcomes despite the myriad of changes that have taken place in higher education over time. The richness of media choice bears mention. While effective in many ways, albeit less rich, the CMC media outlet entails less feedback potential which, in some cases, may impede message transfer (Huett 2004).

Recent technological advances such as the Internet of Things, Augmented Objects, and Cyber Physical Systems bring new potentials in terms of systems that could positively influence the student-professor interaction. A research on augmenting everyday objects was made by Kawsar et al. (2005). They call the objects "sentient artifacts." These objects are everyday life objects augmented with sensors to provide added value services.

Kuniavsky defined object augmentation specifying that instead of designing new ubiquitous devices, non-digital objects could be used to gather and process information. The new object will keep all its original functionalities but will be improved with new ones. The main reasons why intentional augmentation of everyday objects works as a Ubicomp user experience design strategy are as follows: Users have familiarity with the objects, interaction patterns are already defined, when augmentation breaks the object just returns to its pre-augmented stage, and marketing of such objects can be done traditionally (Kuniavsky 2010).

While most research focused on studying different facets of student-professor interaction, to the best of our knowledge, no research contributed tools or technology-mediated tools to improve or influence the interaction quality. Considering the fact that most students use mobile phones, it seems feasible idea to use mobile interaction to improve the interaction. In addition, recent advances in IoT can be used to create a virtual representative for each faculty. Internet of things and related technologies can be used to augment office doors to represent professors during their absence and provide a tangible proxy in the student-professor interaction.

While many aspects of IoT have been well explored, the application of IoT and cyber physical systems to the above described specific problem domain has not been studied yet. In contrast, we have developed an augmented door supporting interaction between students and professors. The system has been deployed to real education settings and intensively tested.

3   The Proposed System

The concept of this work is to create a solution to support professors and students concurrently by creating an interactive smart virtual secretary on the academics office door. By definition, "A door in the physical world is a means of access, admission, or exit, it can also provide a means of access to virtual areas. By creating virtual interactivity with commonplace physical objects, the hope is to optimize the current system, and improve students' interaction with their professors."

The solution would act as an add-on service in order to encourage access to online information on demand. These micro interactions ideally would be used to leave a small notes/reminders for students to have a quick access to retrieve the professor's availability.

This system demonstrates methods of solving the communication problems using a set of low cost NFC tags that can be scanned by students' android based mobile applications which will then update them with the comings and goings of the professor whose tag is scanned. In addition we have added a series of QR codes, providing an alternative method to two access the same service for those students who will not have NFC-enabled smart phones. Figure 1 represents Smart Door's system architecture.

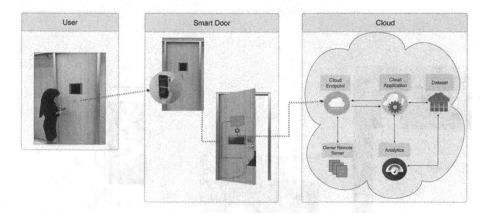

Fig. 1. Smart Door's system architecture

Using this system professors can leave specific messages for custom group of students. Students will only have access to the messages that are defined for their access level which will be granted to them on the server by the door owner himself.

Students can scan the NFC tag/QR code installed on the door that contains its virtual identity and to get connected to system's cloud server. Despite of the technology being used by the students, information will be fetched from server and will be shown on their android smart phones. Students then will be able to reply to professor's messages or to submit their presence to inform the professor of their intent to have a meeting. The system can also provide updates of all the interaction that take place at professor's door step to him by email.

The system was installed in two rooms of the CE department offering access to members of the Ambient Intelligence lab as well as all undergraduate students taking courses with the author or conducting undergraduate projects with him. An overall of 26 students subscribed, downloaded and used the system. Figure 2 illustrates two students using their mobile application to use the system.

Fig. 2. Students interacting with the smart door

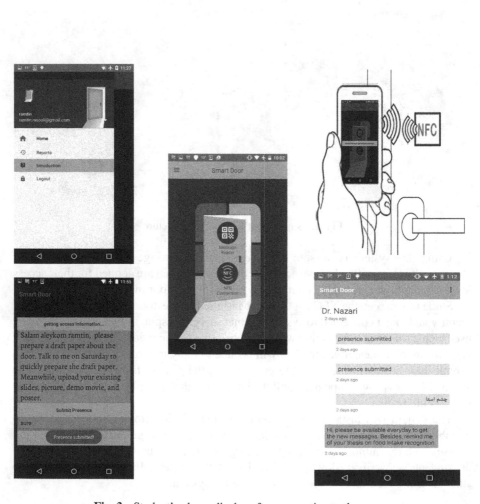

Fig. 3. Student's phone display after connecting to the serve

After the application is launched it read the door's identity with a single touch to the NFC tag or scanning the QR code. Figure 3 shows an example of students' phone display scanning being connected to the server.

4 Conclusion

We propose a system that enables a new way to interact and communicate with professors using mobile phone generating a virtual system where professors do not have to be physically present or respond. The students have the opportunity to get updates from the professor without the need to meet in person with the professors. Unlike previous attempts, the system is current and can be deployed now without expensive and time consuming installations. Students are able to deliver and retrieve information in context and the service enhances their experience within the higher education environment. The system supports student's organization of learning by utilizing pervasive mobile technologies and by disseminating information from the central information systems to the user's android based mobile devices. Door owners have full control of the system, being able to manage public and private conversations without.

Having to worry to plan their days and meetings with students in advance, solving current common issues in academic environments. The innovative approach using an actual door to enable interactions with the specific professor, the mobility and speed of the process all differ in how students are currently able to engage with their supervisors. Future work requires the evaluation from both students and faculty into the engagement of the users with the system, although fully operational; the system will be extended across differing departments in preparation for a long term study.

The goal of the system is to allow users another way to engage in higher education, collect extra materials/hints and stay motivated. Whilst lecturers have a tool they can customize to their needs and engage with their students with different techniques by allowing doors to act as an extra point of contact to deliver relevant information.

References

Jessmer, S., Anderson, D.: The effect of politeness and grammar on user perceptions of electronic mail. N. Am. J. Psychol. **3**, 331–346 (2001)

Kelly, L., Keaten, J.A., Finch, C.: Reticent and non-reticent college students' preferred communication channels for interacting with faculty. Commun. Res. Rep. **21**(2), 197–209 (2004). Spring

Huett, J.: Email as an educational feedback tool: relative advantages and implementation guidelines. Int. J. Instr. Technol. Distance Learn. **1**(6), 35–44 (2004)

Kawsar, F., Fujinami, K., Nakajima, T.: Prottoy: a middleware for sentient environment. In: Yang, L.T., Amamiya, M., Liu, Z., Guo, M., Rammig, F.J. (eds.) EUC 2005. LNCS, vol. 3824, pp. 1165–1176. Springer, Heidelberg (2005)

Kuniavsky, M.: Smart things. Ubiquitous computing user experience design. Elsevier, New York, NY (2010)

Myers, C.L., et al.: Discovery of biological networks from diverse functional genomic data. Genome Biol. **6**(13) (2005). R114

Endo, J.J., Harpel, R.L.: The Effect of Student-Faculty Interaction on Students Educational Outcomes

Fusani, D.S.: 'Extra-class' communication: frequency, immediacy, self-disclosure, and satisfaction in student-faculty interaction outside the classroom. J. Appl. Commun. Res. **22**, 232–255 (1994)

Kuh, G.D.: The other curriculum: out-of-class experiences associated with student learning and personal development. J. High. Educ. **66**, 123–155 (1995)

Halawah, I.: The Effect of Motivation, Family Environment, and Student Characteristics on Academic Achievement

Terenzini, P., Pascarella, E.T.: Student/faculty relationships and freshman year educational outcomes: a further investigation. J. Coll. Student Pers. **21**, 521–528 (1980)

Astin, A.W.: Student Involvement: A Development Theory for Higher Education

Biesenbach-Lucas, S.: Making requests in email: do cyber-consultations entail directness? toward conventions in a new medium. In: Bardovi-Harlig, K., Félix-Brasdefer, J.C., Omar, A. (eds.) Pragmatics and Language Learning, pp. 81–108. Honolulu, HI: Second Language Teaching and Curriculum Center, University of Hawai'i (2006a)

Development of Next Generation Indoor Environment Control Technology Using ICT

Toshihiro Otsuka(✉) and Kazuhiro Sadakiyo

Shimizu Corporation, 4-17 Etchujima 3-chome, Koto-ku, Tokyo, Japan
{otk,sadakiyo}@shimz.co.jp

Abstract. Smart Workplace (SWP) is a concept of an office space that meets both energy conservation and comfortability needs by delicate control of the built environment by use of information and communication technology. This concept aims to save energy by controlling the environmental conditions of only the areas occupied by office workers according to their preferences and turning off air conditioning and lighting in the vacant areas. This paper reports on the SWP system (configuration, location information system, interface), energy conservation performance and some consideration for comfort of workers.

Keywords: Workplace · Location information · RFID tag · Lighting control · Air conditioning control

1 Introduction

Various ideas have been proposed for making the spaces we live and work in by applying robotic technology [1]. It is generally believed that natural and intuitive services can be provided by using various sensors and actuators built into the interiors to understand the states and intentions of occupants according to scenarios and context [2]. This approach to providing services goes well with the individuality needs in the field of architectural environmental engineering in recent years, and possible applications include personal air conditioning and personal lighting control. The aim of these applications is to make spaces more comfortable and satisfactory and thereby enhance productivity by reflecting personal preferences in air conditioning and lighting control of the personal environment. When trying to provide such services, it is necessary to obtain information on the locations of occupants and environmental conditions such as temperature and illuminance.

With the advances in information and communication technology in recent years, monitoring technology for obtaining location information and environmental information has advanced to make our lives easier. In the area of outdoor location information acquisition, GPS (global positioning systems) have already come into widespread use. To collect indoor location information, various efforts are underway to develop technologies for acquiring location information by using such means as RFID (radio-frequency identification) tags and wireless LAN devices. To collect environmental information, wireless sensor networking technology, which is free from locational restrictions, is replacing the conventional monitoring technology that wall-mounted sensors, making

© Springer International Publishing Switzerland 2016
C. Stephanidis (Ed.): HCII 2016 Posters, Part II, CCIS 618, pp. 433–438, 2016.
DOI: 10.1007/978-3-319-40542-1_70

flexible measurement at multiple control points possible. The emerging technologies are making it possible to acquire information on the locations of occupants and their surroundings so that location-aware services can be provided to enhance the level of comfort and convenience. With these services, it is possible to control the environment according to personal preferences.

It has been reported that personal preferences vary considerably. It has also been reported that older people tend to prefer higher illuminance levels [3], and women tend to feel the cold more easily than men [4]. Conventional practice in lighting and air conditioning is to control the entire room uniformly. With the development of lighting systems and personal air conditioning systems with address control, however, it is now possible to control the environment according to personal preferences.

On the other hand, there is growing public demand for energy-efficient buildings as a means of combating global warming. Uniform energy reduction in a uniformly controlled indoor environment may result in a decrease in the comfort and productivity of office workers. Proposing the "Smart Workplace" (hereinafter referred to as "SWP") concept of next-generation environmental control aiming to achieve the conflicting goals of comfort and energy conservation, we have developed and have been using an SWP system embodying that concept.

This paper reports on the SWP system (configuration, location information system, and interface), energy conservation performance and some consideration for worker's comfort.

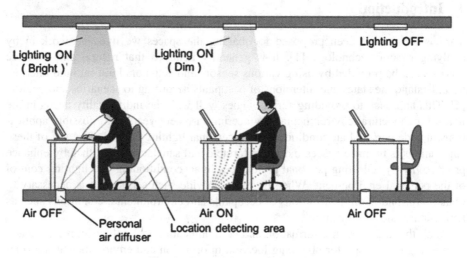

Fig. 1. Control image of the SWP

2   Concept and Configuration of SWP

SWP is a concept of an office space that meets both energy conservation and comfortability needs by delicate control of the built environment by use of information and communication technology. Figure 1 illustrates the control concept. The SWP concept aims to save energy by controlling the environmental conditions of only the areas occupied by office workers according to their preferences and turning off air conditioning and lighting in the vacant areas. Figure 2 shows the system configuration. The system consists of a spatial information recognition system and a facility control system. The spatial information recognition system continuously monitors the environmental information (temperature, humidity, and illuminance), worker location, and electric power consumption as an indicator of the status of equipment operation. According to the information thus acquired, the facility control system controls environmental conditions such as personal air conditioning and lighting.

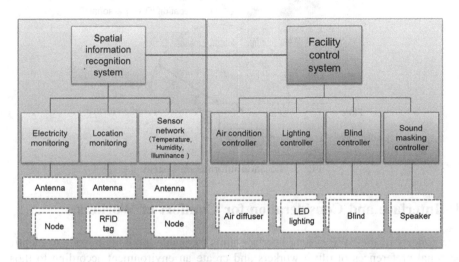

Fig. 2. System configuration

3   Location Information System

Semi-active RFID tags (hereinafter referred to simply as "RFID tags") have been adopted to acquire worker location information. This is a type of battery-powered RFID tag that transmits radio waves only when a signal has been received from an external source. Figure 3 shows the location information system. The LF (low-frequency) antenna installed between the floor paneling and the carpet tiling transmits LF radio waves carrying location ID information at certain intervals. The area in which these LF radio waves can be received is the location detection area. When a person carrying an RFID tag enters the location detection area, the RFID tag receives the LF radio waves, and this triggers the transmission by the RFID tag of UHF radio waves carrying location ID and personal ID information. The information acquired by the readers that received the UHF radio waves is collected by the server and used for facility control. The SWP system uses different LF antennas by which to receive location ID information for three applications, namely, personal space monitoring, meeting table monitoring and room entry detection.

The location information system is advantageous compared with motion sensors because not only presence/absence information but also personal ID information are made available. By referring to personal preferences based on personal ID information and controlling the environment accordingly, an environment comfortable to each person can be created.

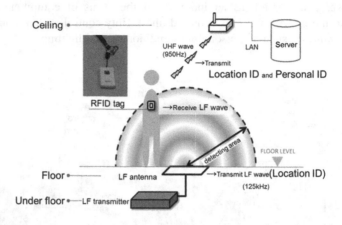

Fig. 3. Location information system

4   Interface and Consideration for Comfort of Workers

The concept of the SWP system interface aims to enable the building side to identify personal preferences of office workers and create an environment according to those preferences without making the workers aware of what is going on. Table 1 shows the interface implemented for the system, listing the user actions used for interfacing, information generated from them, and the functions that can be carried out.

Table 1. Interface of SWP system

User action	Information	Function
Carry RFID tag	Location information	Lighting and air conditioning to be operated
Operate PC dialog box	Change the set value	Change the set value of lighting and air conditioning
Power-on the projector	Electric power change	Turn off the light
ID card authentication	Attendance information	Desk area precooling

Workers always carry their RFID tags with them so that their locations can be detected by the location information system mentioned earlier and desk areas and meeting tables can be air-conditioned and lit according to their preferences. The use of location information eliminates the need to switch on and off during daily activities and prevents a failure to turn off a switch. As a result, wasteful consumption of energy due to negligence or failure on the part of workers is reduced.

Air-conditioning and lighting preferences can be set on the computer screen dialog box. In view of the fact that illuminance level needs differ between individual desk areas and meeting tables, different illuminance levels can be set for different areas.

When a projector integrated with a meeting table is activated, the resultant change in electric power consumption is detected and the ceiling lights over the meeting table are turned off automatically so that the projection screen becomes easier to view.

The air conditioning system has a desk area precooling function. When a worker returns to the office from out-of-office activity on a hot summer day and checks into the building by presenting his or her identification card (IC card), the personal air conditioning system for the worker's desk area comes into operation so that the desk area is cooled before the worker arrives there.

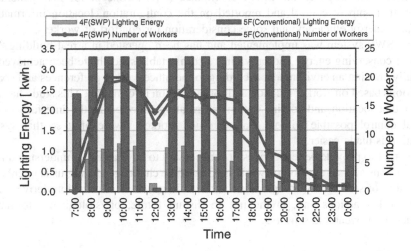

Fig. 4. Comparison of the lighting electric energy consumption and number of workers between 4F SWP and 5F workplace (conventional Lighting). (Color figure online)

5 Energy Conservation Performance

For the purpose of evaluating the energy conservation performance of the lighting control function of the SWP system, a comparison in power consumption by lighting was made with a conventionally lit, upper-floor room having the same floor area. The SWP system uses LED lighting (70 units, max. 3.6 kW) with individual control, while the conventional lighting system uses Hf fluorescent lighting (66 units, max. 3.3 kW) with three-zone ON/OFF control.

Figure 4 shows the number of workers in each office. In the morning, similar numbers of people were in the two offices. After 15:00, the number of occupants in the SWP office was slightly smaller, but still there were occupants in both offices until midnight. Figure 4 also shows electric power consumption by lighting. Since all lighting is turned off during lunch break, comparison is made with respect to the other time zones. The SWP office shows changes in power consumption by lighting proportional to the number of occupants. The office with conventional lighting, which has a zone-based ON/OFF control system, remains fully lit most of the time although only one zone or two zones are lit during early morning or midnight hours when the number of occupants is small. During the working hours (9:00–18:00), the SWP lighting system is 69 % more energy efficient. In terms of whole day energy consumption, the SWP lighting system is 78 % more efficient. These results show that the SWP lighting system is very effective during early morning and overtime working hours when the number of occupants is relatively small.

6   Conclusion

This study has proposed the Smart Workplace (SWP) concept for next-generation indoor environment control and reported on the configuration, location information, interface, energy efficiency and some consideration for comfort of workers.

The SWP system was implemented and has been operated in a real building. The goals of conserving energy and providing a comfortable space have been achieved by carefully creating an environment according to the office worker preferences and spatial conditions based on worker location and routine action information. This study has also shown that location and routine action information reflected in the interface makes natural control possible without making office workers aware of it so that system operation is made easier.

In order to provide better services, it is necessary to have a deeper understanding of the intentions and states of office workers. One of the challenges facing us is to enhance the quality of services by using context information such as information derived from office worker actions and, in the not so distant future, physiological information obtained from wearable sensors.

References

1. Hashimoto, H.: Making spaces intelligent and system integration. J. Soc. Instrum. Control Eng. **44**(8), 568–573 (2005)
2. Ronzhin, A.L., Karpov, A.A., Kipyatkova, I.S.: Designing cognition-centric smart room predicting inhabitant activities. In: Schmorrow, D.D., Estabrooke, I.V., Grootjen, M. (eds.) FAC 2009. LNCS, vol. 5638, pp. 78–87. Springer, Heidelberg (2009)
3. Otsuka, T., Furukawa, K., Igarashi, Y., Sadakiyo, K., Yamada, T.: Lighting control system using location information in office and study on technology for visual comfort. Tech. Res. Rep. Inst. Technol., Shimizu Corp. **90**, 119–124 (2013)
4. Kawahara, Y., Emura, K., Nabesima, M.: Categorical data and symmetric transformation. Rep. Sci. Living, Osaka City Univ. **45**, 65–69 (1997)

MocaBit 1.0

A Gamified Mo-cap System to Track Physical Location

Sudarshan Seshasayee[✉] and Sanghyun Yoo

School of Arts, Media and Engineering,
Arizona State University, Tempe, AZ, USA
{spseshas,cooperyoo}@asu.edu

Abstract. To define the movement, both quantitative and qualitative measurements are used. Sensors that provide such accurate data prove efficient in monitoring physical location. In this paper, we approach the study of kinesiology through vision-based technology and gamification. We conclude with an introduction to MocaBit, a new gamified mo-cap system to track physical movement in a spatially localized environment.

Keywords: Activity tracking · Mo-cap · Gamification · Kinesiology · Measurement · Human factors

1 Introduction

In recent years, the availability of new interactive technologies has enabled researchers to have more opportunities to inspect aspects of location-based activity tracking.

In this work, MocaBit, we apply the vision-based technology of a motion capture (**mo-cap**) system in a localized domain to monitor the physical movement of its users. Our main goal is to create an experimental system to track and visualize the movement data, simultaneously for multiple users in real-time.

From a user experience standpoint, we implemented a sub-level architecture to explore the capability of our system. Using gamification we study the application of intuitive interaction. By presenting a highly calibrated prototype of real-time projection mapping, users were able to visualize their movement while in the mo-cap space.

2 Related Work

Since pedometers have been around for a very long time, development of various digital platforms renewed interest in tracking activities [1]. Smartphone apps such as Nike+, Moves App, and Runkeepr enabled GPS technology to track where and how the users were running and walking in a wide-range area.

Previously, several attempts have been made to track activities using wearable hardware devices [3]. In personal activity trackers such as Fitbit, Jawbone, and Nike Fuelband, 3-axis accelerometers and altimeters are used to track speed, direction, and

© Springer International Publishing Switzerland 2016
C. Stephanidis (Ed.): HCII 2016 Posters, Part II, CCIS 618, pp. 439–444, 2016.
DOI: 10.1007/978-3-319-40542-1_71

elevation [5]. Computational interfaces and ubiquitous computing allowed us to create new forms of understanding human activities. However, due to the limitations of GPS and gyroscope technologies these devices lose accuracy in an indoor environment [8]. Daniel Victor et al. also found that users were incredulous about the accuracy of activity data from these wearable devices as they don't visualize the data in real time [11].

In contrast, these wearable devices communicate with the user through quantitative data. The user is not concerned with the cost of computation the accelerometer performs with. The system as a whole encapsulates these nuances and provides a service for motion tracking [2]. The company can delve into more non-trivial data sets as obtained from these users to deploy a complex algorithm to determine their activity.

Mo-cap environments have been developed to focus on recording the movement of subjects for various purposes [10]. Vision-based techniques are used to capture tri-dimensional body points of the users. They are widely used in entertainment, sports, industrial ergonomics, and medical applications [7]. Myroslav et al. probed the issue of using mo-cap based simulation in detecting everyday human activities [9]. They found that combination of motion capture and biomechanical simulation allows measuring of both performance and physical ergonomics in a user interface.

MocaBit, named after the combination of words mo-cap and FitBit, is a conceptual prototype that tries to track user movement and visualize the motion using a state of the art system. Our work takes a step forward, by adapting a mo-cap environment for researchers to track location-based activity data of the users. The high accuracy of the data in a localized space using a mo-cap system, overshadows this wearable technology. This strengthens the purpose of tracking movement data in an indoor space. We also imitate the works of these wearable devices at the sociological level. How the complexity of device is irrelevant to the user but the derived quantitative interpretation of the study namely calories burned or in our application, points serves a deciding factor.

3   Design and Implementation

Our goal is to simulate the advantages of live tracking with a positive feedback loop through the system. The generated output should also benefit the user. By developing an interactive experience for the user through a game, a back and forth communication is established between the system and the user. The entire project was deployed using various software toolboxes.

3.1   Mo-cap

The mo-cap stage consists of a frame mounted on the ceiling with 16 OptiTrack cameras. At the base of the hierarchy, our mo-cap system uses Motive an OptiTrack camera compatible software to obtain tracker data of the various subjects in the mo-cap stage. This then allowed a transmission of these objects in real time.

3.2   Sending Multiple Data in Real-Time

Motive has the ability to broadcast frame data. A parser script was written in python to analyze these encrypted data and subsequently, route it through a UDP protocol in a packed arrayList. UDP is a mode of connectionless transmission. It ensures immediate host-to-host connection.

The MATLAB script takes a list of strings, raw data, rotation, quaternion and other features obtained from the Motive software and converts it into decipherable data which is then packed into an array of id and numerical entries.

This data in turn is routed accordingly to Processing and unpacked into its respective coordinates and rigid body. An OSC parser script was written inside it to segregate them into an array. Additionally, the sketch also scales the incoming data stream coordinate referenced to the 12 × 24 ft of the projection space.

3.3   Visualization/Projection Mapping

Scaled data is picked up by the class where the entire UI was designed. Processing was used to design a generative art background. Further, each user was given a rigid body tracker. Each user's position in localized space calculated their nearest neighbor, using the k-Nearest Neighbor (KNN) algorithm. As this computation constantly spews out a user index as they move around, a line is drawn between them and their Nearest Neighbor (NN). Enhancing user experience in the design, if user index i's NN is j and vice versa, a double line is drawn between them. Since the IDE is based on a java wrapper, a PApplet class used as an MVC was implemented to control the inter-communication of tasks and also control the timer. A hash map was used to derive the NN using Euclidian distance and its efficiency was tested against a brute force Hamming method (Figs. 1 and 2).

$$argmin \sum_{i=1}^{k} |x_{i+1} - x_i|$$

Fig. 1. The minimum distance over the list of users

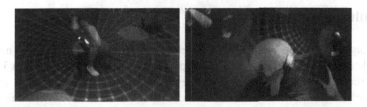

Fig. 2. Visualization of MocaBit: (a) visual feedback on the floor generated by processing, (b) visual graphics projected on the floor for user test

3.4   Gamification

In order to obtain an optimum data set to test the capability of our system, we adapted the concepts of gamification. This provided the users an incentive to move faster and more erratic.

Hespanhol and Tomitsch argue in their study of public urban spaces [4] that core concerns designing interactive experiences in spaces. To enhance user experience in multi-person interaction, it is important to give clear feedback about who is in control of the interface at any given time, and to clearly indicate the roles by users participating in the interaction zone. Spotlight type abstract images and different colors and thickness of lines are used in our design based on the user's movement. Intuitive interactive mechanisms in MocaBit easily allows participants to interact with both other users and with the system.

The point system ensures that the user does not remain idle for more than 5 s and constantly interact with a new user to attain more points. The NN users with a double connect racked up 5 points in the first second. Every second the same NN users were connected hence will add one point less. Also, if the same NN users were connected after the first 5 s it would result in a linearly proportional loss of one point (See Table 1).

Table 1. Points flow chart of MocaBit

Time (seconds)	1	2	3	4	5	6	7	8
Points		5	4	3	2	1	−1	−2	−3

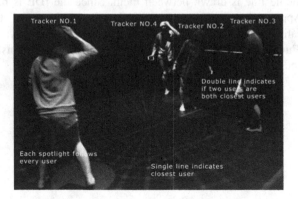

Fig. 3. Four testers interacting with MocaBit

4   Results

The primary focus of the user test was to detect substantial, fast and erratic movement of multiple users, using our system. For the purpose of the case study, we ran 3 sessions of 2 min each. The first time, we let the users try the system without any prior knowledge and also without points. The second time around, we briefed the users on how the connections were made and still without points. In the third session, we introduced the points system.

Mocabit is an installation that tested the hypothesis, which reasoned to recreate an ambience that sparked social connectedness between users and also generated useful data that can be used in future research to study patterns. The point algorithm and real-time projection mapping were a strong incentive for the users to use Mocabit. Just like the wearable counterpart, high dimensional data was recorded for research purposes and the users were provided a feedback of their performance using points as analyzed through their movement.

We observed a high intensity of movement scattered over the entire space. The response time of the system was high. This led to negligible data loss albeit the fast movement of multiple users simultaneously (See Fig. 3). The use of a mo-cap, gamification and projection mapping enhanced real-time tracking in a localized space.

From a research standpoint, it helps one better understand the correlation between movement and non-trivial data. It was widely surprising to observe the various geometric patterns that formed. As the users moved around, various connections were formed. As a by-product of the outcome, these allow us to further explore the concepts of graph theory using dynamic node (Fig. 4).

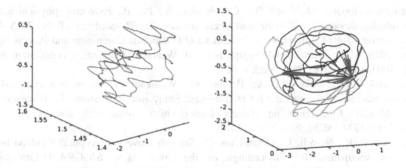

Fig. 4. User activity data of (a) single user, (b) all four users (Color figure online)

5   Discussion and Future Work

This project is an inception of plausible technologies that can derive from real-time physical tracking. This system enabled us to explore the use of a mo-cap system outside its trivial purpose of full body tracking. However, this paper can start with the simplicity of direction invariant single-point cloud data to determine the correlation between several biomechanical parameters.

Further, we can determine how a mo-cap system with high precision and negligible latency can equal the use of wearable technology to study applied kinesiology and behavioral patterns.

These patterns can help study social interactions and the effect a user has on the other. Phillips in her article [6] about how diversity makes us smarter discusses an experiment about external factors improving efficiency. Further, how a user affects the performance of another user thrives to experiment with granger causality.

References

1. Thiagarajan, A., Biagioni, J., Gerlich, T., Eriksson, J.: Cooperative transit tracking using smart-phones. In: Proceedings of the 8th ACM Conference on Embedded Networked Sensor Systems (SenSys 2010), pp. 85–98. ACM, New York (2010)
2. Bort-Roig, J., Gilson, N.D., Puig-Ribera, A., Contreras, R.S., Trost, S.G.: Measuring and influencing physical activity with smartphone technology: a systematic review. Sports Med. **44**(5), 671–686 (2014)
3. Guo, F., Li, Y., Kankanhalli, M.S., Brown, M.S.: An evaluation of wearable activity monitoring devices. In: Proceedings of the 1st ACM International Workshop on Personal Data Meets Distributed Multimedia (PDM 2013), pp. 31–34. ACM, New York (2013)
4. Hespanhol, L., Tomitsch, M.: Strategies for intuitive interaction in public urban spaces. Interact. Comput. (2015). doi:10.1093/iwc/iwu051
5. Chen, K.Y., Bassett Jr., D.R.: The technology of accelerometry-based activity monitors: current and future. Med. Sci. Sports Exerc. **37**, 490–500 (2005)
6. Phillips, K.W.: How diversity makes us smarter. Sci. Am. **311**(4), 43–47 (2014)
7. da Silva, M., Abe, Y., Popović, J.: Interactive simulation of stylized human locomotion. In: ACM SIGGRAPH 2008 Papers (SIGGRAPH 2008), 10 p., Article 82. ACM, New York (2008)
8. Randriambelonoro, M., Chen, Y., Geissbuhler, A., Pu, P.: Exploring physical activity monitoring devices for diabetic and obese patients. In: Proceedings of the 2015 ACM International Joint Conference on Pervasive and Ubiquitous Computing and Proceedings of the 2015 ACM International Symposium on Wearable Computers (UbiComp 2015), pp. 1003–1008. ACM, New York (2015)
9. Bachynskyi, M., Oulasvirta, A., Palmas, G., Weinkauf, T.: Is motion capture-based biomechanical simulation valid for HCI studies? Study and implications. In: Proceedings of the SIGCHI Conference on Human Factors in Computing Systems (CHI 2014), pp. 3215–3224. ACM, New York (2014)
10. McDonnell, R., Newell, F., O'Sullivan, C.: Smooth movers: perceptually guided human motion simulation. In: Proceedings of the 2007 ACM SIGGRAPH/Eurographics Symposium on Computer Animation (SCA 2007), pp. 259–269. Eurographics Association, Aire-la-Ville, Switzerland (2007)
11. Yang, R., Shin, E., Newman, M.W., Ackerman, M.S.: When fitness trackers don't 'fit': end-user difficulties in the assessment of personal tracking device accuracy. In: Proceedings of the 2015 ACM International Joint Conference on Pervasive and Ubiquitous Computing (UbiComp 2015), pp. 623–634. ACM, New York (2015)

Sync-BIM: The Interactive BIM-Based Platform for Controlling Data-Driven Kinetic Façade

Yang Ting Shen[1(✉)] and Tien Yu Wu[2]

[1] Department of Architecture, Feng Chia University,
Taichung, Taiwan
yatishen@fcu.edu.tw
[2] Department of Architecture, National Cheng Kung University,
Tainan, Taiwan
tyarchstudio@gmail.com

Abstract. The research presents a methodology and tool development which delineates the performance-based building active control system. We demonstrates the integration of environment sensors, the parametric engine, and interactive facade components by using the BIM-based system called Sync-BIM. It is developed by the BIM-based parametric engine called Dynamo. The Dynamo engine works as the building brain to determine the interactive control scenarios between buildings and surroundings micro-climate conditions. There are three sequent procedures including 1. data input, 2. scenario process, and command output to loop the interactive control scenarios. The kinetic façade prototype embedded with Sync-BIM system adopts the daylight values as the parameter to control the transformation of façade units. The kinetic façade units dynamically harvest the daylight via opening ratios for the sake of higher building energy performance.

Keywords: Building information model (BIM) · Adaptive building · Parametric engine · Kinetic façade · Building energy performance

1 Introduction

Performance-based building design methodologies have been investigated to deal with diverse decision variables and design objectives in various environmental issues (Machairas et al. 2014). With the rapid development of sensing and interactive technologies, several methods of BIM tools were developed to design adaptive and high performance building for complex environmental conditions. The high performance means the building interface which can take advantages from natural environment to lower artificial energy consumption. This research proposes to engage more natural energy such as the daylight using for increasing building performance. This issue is divided into two sub-issues including the development of eco-friendlier façade which can interact with its local environment, and the related smart management system which can process the environment parameters for façade eco-friendly actions.

© Springer International Publishing Switzerland 2016
C. Stephanidis (Ed.): HCII 2016 Posters, Part II, CCIS 618, pp. 445–450, 2016.
DOI: 10.1007/978-3-319-40542-1_72

2   Literature Review

2.1   Kinetic Facade with High Performance

One of the primary purposes of building façade is designed to deal with the climate conditions. Most of façade designs adopt the passive control method to response normal or routine weather conditions. However, the micro-climate around building is dynamically changed and sometimes unpredictable. Compared to a passive control building with a static shading, daylighting, or ventilating, the use of the active control methods could support more flexible interactivity to response the variability of climate conditions. It means the building can adapt even benefit from natural environment to decrease the use of artificial energy for high building performance purpose. Through the adjustable façade units and active control system, the building adapt itself to the best situation for the given environmental condition and thus increase its potential impact. Kinetic façade systems (Fig. 1) can help to mitigate environmental problems, decrease the need for mechanical systems such as HVAC systems and artificial lights.

dECOI : Hyposurface   Fox : Responsive skylights   Enric ruiz-geli : Media ICT   Aedas Architecture : Al-Bahur   Heliotrace :SOM Architects

Fig. 1. The kinetic facade with active control system to adapt the various climate conditions

2.2   BIM-Based Active Control System

Dynamo is a parametric engine which can analysis and respond building-related data in the Building Information Modeling (BIM) environment. Dynamo has a visual scripting interface for the compilation of Autodesk Revit API. It allows users to add features into the software and create customized tools. Dynamo is designed to extend Revit's functions by adding new parametric possibilities that does not exist of software. As a plug-in of Revit, Dynamo plays a crucial role to extend functions like Nurbs surface, Helix, topology to build model and synchronize with BIM model to exert more possibilities. The elements with which users interact in Dynamo engine are referred as "nodes". Each nodes can have numbers of com ports, which enable communications between nodes alone connecting lines. Com ports can only be connected to other com port whose output type matches the input type. The most import function compiled by those nodes is to set the scenarios which can interact with parametric data. According to the changes of input value, Dynamo can trigger corresponding events. For example, control the transformation of BIM model or deliver commands to the 3rd part system.

3   The Framework of Sync-BIM

3.1   Framework and Workflow

The research presents a methodology and tool development which delineates the performance-based building active control system. We demonstrates the integration of environment sensors, the parametric engine, and interactive facade components by using the BIM-based system called Sync-BIM. Sync-BIM consists of kinetic façade units and BIM-based management system. The kinetic façade was designed as modular units for mass production and consistent control logic. We use the foldable and flexible structure to shape each unit. The foldable structure facilitates the gradational transformation of façade openings. The kinetic unit can control the micro climate factors such as ventilation, ambient light, or humidity etc. via the degree of opening for several situations by climate changes or user's requirements. The ambient weather sensor embedded in each kinetic unit supports the practical parameter.

The BIM-based system works as the building brain to determine the interactive control scenarios. There are three sequent procedures including INPUT, PROCESS, and OUTPUT to loop the interactive control scenarios (Fig. 2). The workflow of interactive adaption follows the three sequent to loop the circle instantly between exterior micro-climate and interior computing-machine. At the first stage, the virtual data from internet such as the weather forecast and sensing data apply to the INPUT procedure. And the parameters were deliver to the computing engine as references and cross-compared by BIM-based system during the PROCESS procedure. After the computing engine operates multi-parameters, the computing engine were based on discriminates referred to the synthetic micro-climate conditions and compared the scenarios in the database. Once matched, Sync-BIM will trigger the following command to control the kinetic unit, and adjust the optimized building facade.

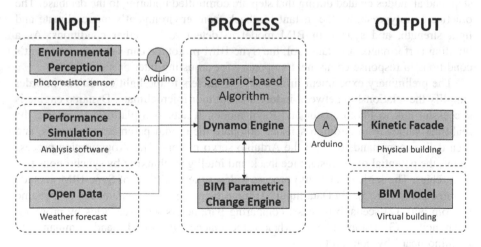

Fig. 2. The workflow of Sync-BIM

3.2   Interactive Operation Engine

Based on the Sync-BIM loop procedure, the building facade can sense and adapt the diverse micro-climate to balance the indoor and outdoor conditions. The interactive operation system depends on a simulated facade model with modular components created in Revit. The sunlight parameters inputted to Dynamo engine include real-time sunlight from physical sensors, and the simulated solar model from Autodesk Revit to trace and monitor the feedback. Each component was linked to a light level parameter from distributed Arduino Photoresistor. There are two hierarchy level of control logic for stimulating the real world daylight condition, higher hierarchy affected by the precise solar angle and daytime of the simulated model in computing machine, and the lower hierarchy decided by the value detected from real sensor which allow us to simulate the instant variations of daylight. Higher hierarchy control can prevent inappropriate opening scenarios. For example, the Sync-BIM unit should not reach the full angle in the winter due to the human perceived temperature. And the lower hierarchy provided actual micro-climate by the Photoresistor received the value of ambient environment from 0 to 255, and delivered value to Dynamo engine via Arduino instantly. For example, light level may different due to the weather issue, like cloud or occasional weather changes, lower hierarchy control could help recognizing real-time micro-climate and programmed by Dynamo engine. Dynamo has used for several applications, one of which is provided an interactive engine to synchronize BIM model and Arduino board, servo motor, and light sensors. Besides, the inner operation of connected nodes in Dynamo engine created the sequent nodes to define the interactive scenario. It consists of three steps including destroy, build and update. The destroy step is used to clean up node's temporary files. The build step regenerating Revit components based on the input connections. And the updated step is used to execute loops of programming scenarios. Dynamo engine classified data and divided to "transaction" or "non-transaction". Transactional nodes open a database transaction during their build step, and all nodes created during that step are committed updating to the database. The practice prototype shows the instant feedback from environment's micro-climate and light strength, and sync with BIM model to detect real weather conditions. As a building performance assistant tool, the Sync-BIM prototype can sense environment's conditions to response component's opening for adjusting interior's condition.

The preliminary experiment limited the parameters to the light conditions in order simplify the relationship between indoor and outdoor microclimate. Dynamo engine is successful link to Photoresistor and Revit model. It acts as a platform to receive the real-time values from Arduino sensors, compare them with parametric scenarios, and then deliver commands back to the Arduino servo motors. The Programming process shows the potential of the instant feedback and intelligent thinking by synchronous two hierarchies. The logic of Dynamo process follows the workflow of Sync-BIM, include of three parts (Fig. 3). (1) Data input: Arduino board provided parameters to Dynamo by com port, (2) scenario process: comparing parameters with scenarios by programming nodes, (3) command out: when value reached threshold, send commands to Arduino board by com port.

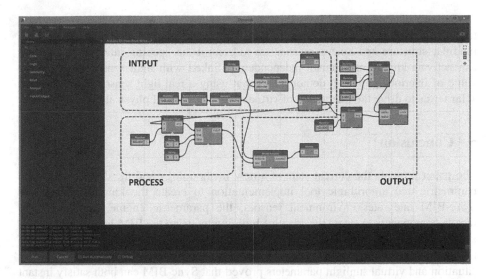

Fig. 3. The workflow of dynamo engine

4 The Practice of Sync-BIM

The Sync-BIM prototype including the physical model and the BIM-based control system is developed as Fig. 4. We design a façade unit which is a folding structure in each kinetic component to fit in curtain wall module. The rotation of servo motor can drive the folding motion to increase or decrease the opening degree. The design of kinetic components is modularizing in order to repeat and cover the whole façade to become an interface between the building and its located environment.

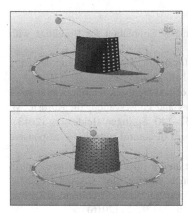
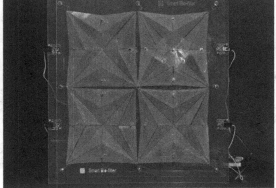

Fig. 4. The prototype of Sync-BIM

We use solar degree and strength as our parameter, and organize a façade system to test the opening degrees of each component. The prototype combined folding structure, modular structure and kinetic mechanism to control the opening ratio. Each one unit can activate kinetic mechanism independently linked with light sensor to adjust the value of interior lighting. It demonstrates that using a real light sensor plus simulated solar terms to drive the interaction of virtual Revit model and physical building facade.

5 Conclusion

The paper presents the current state of a new methodology and the development of a parametric and algorithmic tool implementation to create the kinetic façade. The Sync-BIM integrates environment sensors, the parametric engine, and interactive facade components to create the adaptive building by using the BIM-based system. The kinetic façade units dynamically harvest the daylight via opening ratios for the sake of higher building energy performance. The integration between physical environment situation and virtual sunlight parameters proved that Sync-BIM can both satisfy instant variations of microclimate and the permanent constraints of season. In the future, more quantitative data such as precise energy consumption should be measured and analyzed to validate the building performance outcome. In addition, recruit more environmental parameters is the critical work to represent the complex climate conditions. Fundamentally the future work will address on completing and analyzing Sync-BIM applications to real world projects.

Acknowledgements. The financial support from Ministry of Science and Technology (MOST) including project "Smart Bio-Filter" (102-2218-E-035-008-) and project "Urban Probe" (104-2221-E-035-024-), is greatly acknowledged.

References

Kim, H., Asl, M.R., Yan, W.: Parametric BIM-Based Energy Simulation for Buildings with Complex Kinetic Façades (2015)

Machairas, V., Tsangrassoulis, A., Axarli, K.: Algorithms for optimization of building design: a review. Renew. Sustain. Energy Rev. **31**, 101–112 (2014)

Shen, Y.T., Chen, P.C., Jeng, T.S.: Design and evaluation of eco-feedback interfaces to support location-based services for individual energy awareness and conservation. In: Kurosu, M. (ed.) HCII/HCI 2013, Part V. LNCS, vol. 8008, pp. 132–140. Springer, Heidelberg (2013)

Sterk, T.D.E.: Building upon Negroponte: a hybridized model of control suitable for responsive architecture. Autom. Constr. **14**(2), 225–232 (2005)

Shen, Y.-T., Lu, P.-W.: The development of kinetic façade units with BIM-based active control system for the adaptive building energy performance service. In: CAADRIA 2016 Proceedings of the 21st International Conference on Computer Aided Architectural Design Research in Asia, Melbourne, 30 March–2 April 2016, pp. 517–526 (2016)

The Research of Using Magnetic Pillbox as Smart Pillbox System's Interactive Tangible User Interface

Ming-Hsiang Sung[1(✉)] and Chen-Wei Chiang[2]

[1] Department of Information Communication, Yuan Ze University, Taoyuan, Taiwan, ROC
k6121761217@gmail.com
[2] Department of Product Innovation and Entrepreneurship,
National Taipei University of Business, Taipei, Taiwan, ROC
chenwei@saturn.yzu.edu.tw

Abstract. Along with the improved technology and living quality, people's lives have become more and more comfortable. The ages of patients with chronic diseases drop and the numbers year by year, therefore the demand of medication for chronic disease will keep growing. To easily record and remind the time of taking medication, the smart pillbox has been developed. However, currently most of smart pillboxes were designed for elderlies who usually stay in home. They are too large to be easily carried, with multiple buttons on their interfaces and complex steps of operation. This study introduces a smart pillbox system which applies magnet and tablet computer as its entity to be interface. The system uses 3D printing technology to produce prototype kit, and the magnet so that each cartridge is connected. Through installing Liang Rong-Hao's GaussSense to enhance its accuracy of sensor, the user can operate the tablet computer to obtain information wanted by moving, rotating and combing the pillbox. The study evaluates the practicality and feasibility through applying software prototyping method on implementation system, and its result will be the reference for future development and research.

Keywords: Tangible user interface · Interaction design · User experience

1 Introduction

1.1 Chronic Diseases and Medication

According to a report from World Health Organization in 2014 [1], it shows the ages of patients with chronic diseases are decreasing, and the numbers are becoming more and more by every year. In 2010, the top three causes of death in world's top ten are all chronic diseases [2] and currently, the most effective treatment for chronic disease will still be constant medication.

In addition, in The Smart Pill Box [3] by Brianna Abbey, it mentioned that it is actually very complicated for patients to memorize the information patients will take for taking a medication, among them there are seven properties: drug name, indication, usage, frequency of use per day, hours of use, dose and duration of treatment. The

© Springer International Publishing Switzerland 2016
C. Stephanidis (Ed.): HCII 2016 Posters, Part II, CCIS 618, pp. 451–456, 2016.
DOI: 10.1007/978-3-319-40542-1_73

complexity of information required to use drug and treatment both determine whether the patient can continue such medication.

1.2   Smart Pillbox

Smart pillbox, an electronic pillbox, is a combination of "alarm clock" and "traditional pillbox". The ordinary model adopts LCD panel as its display interface, and it is with multiple buttons for setting reminder function as various designs for selection, but there exists the complexity issue for operation on interface.

Afterwards, as to the more advanced design, A WSN smart medication system [4], it adopts main unit, pillbox that can be carried separately and combine them with wireless transmission technology to record relevant information and integrate functions more patients need. The operating also transforms from traditional button to touch-panel, which can be operated more easily. However, the size of its main unit is large and more suitable for use in home. If you go out, although you can carry the sub-pillbox, you cannot use other functions. And in The Intelligent Pill Box by Shih-Chang Huang [5], this device connects medical personnel and patient through internet communication software to let medical personnel instantly comprehend the treatment status of such patient, but it was designed hard to be carried. Therefore this study aims to combine aforementioned advantages of wireless transmission, solve the issue of hard to be carried and improve functions of displaying information and relevant operation.

1.3   Tangible User Interface and Smart Mobile Devices

As for the operation, this study attempts to adopt user interface as the operation interface of this system. The user interface applies many tangible and touchable objects for multiple users, systems or software to interact [6], such as table games [7], interactive digital games [8], the creation by controlling music [9] and other functions; Users can intuitively use both hands to touch and move objects for operating [10], and it can also give such user the instant feedback for senses of touch and vision. This study wishes to apply the traits of intuitive use and instant feedback to improve the easiness of operating the smart pillbox.

According to the latest statistic data counted by III and Mobile First in the end of 2014 [11], population with carrying smart devices in Taiwan has reached 69.1 % of total population. Smart mobile device has become the most common information display device carried in the modern age, so it will be the information display device for this system. With the result in study of Magnetic Appcessories [12] and MagGetz [13] which detected magnet around and make it as the effect of operating mobile device, pillboxes were connected to be detected by tablet computer, in order to generate various modes of interaction.

2 Design and Implement

2.1 System Structure

This study was designed a smart pillbox system which, with magnet, connects prototypes of round-shaped pillbox printed by 3D printer, and places magnets with different magnetic forces on the bottom for identification of system (Fig. 1a–c). In the study Google Nexus 7 (2013) was taken as the tablet computer for testing, and GaussSense [14] was installed behind to strengthen the stability and accuracy magnetic force acquired (Fig. 1d). Later, the information was transmitted to application coded with Unity through WIFI, and the tablet computer will show relevant information and interactive response (Fig. 2).

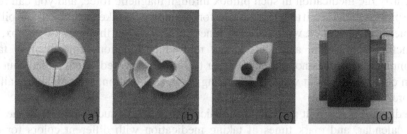

Fig. 1. (a, b, c) Pillbox prototype, and (d) Google Nexus 7 (2013) with GaussSense

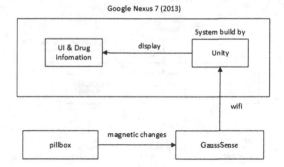

Fig. 2. System framework diagram

2.2 The Designing of the Smart Pillbox System

In this study, three functions patients with chronic diseases would need the most were practiced: Drug Information, Reminder Setting and Medication Record (Fig. 3).

- Main Menu. In the main menu, you only need to simply place such pillbox on the screen of tablet computer to let the program of rotating pillbox select function required. After required functions have been selected, you can enter the interface of such function by removing pillbox from the screen.

- Drug Information. In this function, you can search features of medication taken this time, such as appearance, name, and side effect to let patient verify the proper effect and possible side effect of drug. In the past, the functions regarded to this part were seldom developed, therefore a patient could only identify medication according to medical prescription, and would not be able to easily recognize them before taking. The user would only need to place a single pillbox on tablet computer, then the screen of computer will show all relevant medication information set by such pillbox, and the user can seek for more detailed information by simply rotating pillboxes.
- Reminder Setting. To keep user from missing the time of taking medication, you can easily set alarm clock for period that requires reminding. When you are setting, you need to place two pillboxes on it, and set the data of medication and time of taking by controlling two pillboxes with your both hands. The pillbox placed on the top can identify the medication in such pillbox through magnetic force, and you can rotate the pillbox underneath to select the time for reminding. Unlike most electronic pillbox which were installed with alarming function directly on the body of pillbox, this function applies the alarm clock and reminding functions embedded in tablet computer, as it does not only allow user to set their favored sound effects, but also can combine different ways of reminding, such as vibration, sending an e-mail and more.
- Medication Record. It presents the medication status for such month with the form of calendar, and mark times of taking medication with different colors for easy comprehension. The user can switch status of taking medication between different months by simply rotating a single pillbox.

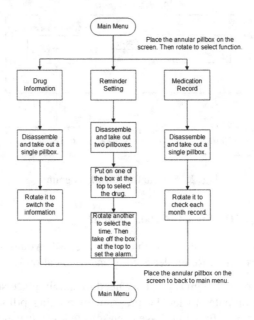

Fig. 3. Operation flowchart

2.3   System Testing

After the user place a pillbox on tablet computer, he can instantly start to select functions with rotation (Fig. 4a). After entering the function Drug Information, if the user place a single pillbox on tablet computer, system will automatically identify the medication information set by pillbox through magnetic force and displace relevant information on screen (Fig. 4b and c). While staying in the function Reminder Setting, if you place the medication set on the top, system will identify such medication in the pillbox and you can rotate underneath it to set the time for reminding (Fig. 4d and e).

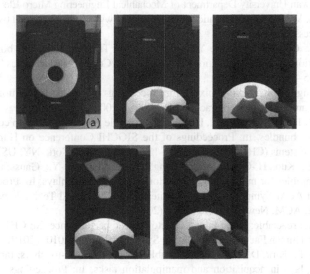

Fig. 4.   (a) Main menu, (b, c) Drug Information, and (d, e) Reminder Setting

3   Conclusion and Future Works

This study attempts to apply the latest 3D printing technology to make real prototype of pillbox, and combine the cognition of real object, possibility of operating such object to extend them to the usage of real user interface with digital content, therefore they can be directly linked with human's cognition to make such system designed as really human orientated. Due to restriction on time and resource, currently, the system still remains in a very basic status. With further testing and improvement, I believe there are more functions and concepts to be inspired, and they can all be reference and new direction for the future development of real user interface and smart pillbox connected by smart mobile device and platform.

References

1. World Health Organization: Global status report on noncommunicable diseases (2014). http://www.who.int/nmh/publications/ncd-status-report-2014/en/. Accessed 18 May 2015
2. World Health Organization, 2011: Global status report on noncommunicable diseases (2010). http://www.who.int/nmh/publications/ncd_report2010/en/. Accessed 18 May 2015
3. Abbey, B., Alipour, A., Camp, C., Hofer, C.: The Smart Pill Box. In: Proceedings of the Rehabilitation Engineering and Assistive Technology Society of North America (2012). http://resna.org/conference/proceedings/2012/PDFs/StudentDesign/1207.pdf
4. National Taiwan University Department of Mechanical Engineering Micro Electro-Mechanical Systems Lab. WSN Smart Medication System. http://www-mems.me.ntu.edu.tw/pdt_view.asp?sn=131. Accessed 18 May 2015
5. Huang, S.C., Chang, H.Y., Jhu, Y.C., Chen, G.Y.: The intelligent pill box—design and implementation. In: IEEE International Conference on Consumer Electronics-Taiwan (ICCE-TW), pp. 235–236. IEEE (2014)
6. Ishii, H.: Tangible bits: beyond pixels. In: Proceedings of the 2nd International Conference on Tangible and Embedded Interaction (TEI 2008) (2008)
7. Baudisch, P., Becker, T., Rudeck, F.: Lumino: tangible blocks for tabletop computers based on glass fiber bundles. In: Proceedings of the SIGCHI Conference on Human Factors in Computing Systems (CHI 2010), pp. 1165–1174. ACM, New York, NY, USA (2010)
8. Liang, R.-H., Kuo, H.-C., Chan, L., Yang, D.-N., Chen, B.-Y.: GaussStones: shielded magnetic tangibles for multi-token interactions on portable displays. In: Proceedings of the 27th Annual ACM Symposium on User Interface Software and Technology (UIST 2014), pp. 365–372. ACM, New York, NY, USA (2014)
9. Jordà, S.: The reactable: tangible and tabletop music performance. In: CHI 2010 Extended Abstracts on Human Factors in Computing Systems (CHI EA 2010) (2010)
10. Tuddenham, P., Kirk, D., Izadi, S.: Graspables revisited: multi-touch vs. tangible input for tabletop displays in acquisition and manipulation tasks. In: Proceedings of the SIGCHI Conference on Human Factors in Computing Systems (CHI 2010) (2010)
11. Foreseeing Innovative New Digiservices, and Mobile First (2014). http://www.iii.org.tw/m/News-more.aspx?id=1475. Accessed 18 May 2015
12. Bianchi, A., Oakley, I.: Designing tangible magnetic appcessories. In: Proceedings of the 7th International Conference on Tangible, Embedded and Embodied Interaction (TEI 2013), pp. 255–258. ACM, New York, NY, USA (2013)
13. Hwang, S., Ahn, M., Wohn, K.-Y.: MagGetz: customizable passive tangible controllers on and around conventional mobile devices. In: Proceedings of the 26th Annual ACM Symposium on User Interface Software and Technology (UIST 2013) (2013)
14. Liang, R.-H., Cheng, K.-Y., Su, C.-H., Weng, C.-T., Chen, B.-Y., Yang, D.-N.: GaussSense: attachable stylus sensing using magnetic sensor grid. In: Proceedings of the 25th Annual ACM Symposium on User Interface Software and Technology (UIST 2012), pp. 319–326. ACM, New York, NY, USA (2012)

Correction of Optical Flow Calculations Using Color Balance Change

Nami Tanaka[✉] and Hiromitsu Nishimura

Kanagawa Institute of Technology, Atsugi, Kanagawa, Japan
ntanaka732@gmail.com

Abstract. To detect the detailed motions of moving objects, we propose a new correction method for optical flow calculations based on the block matching algorithm. After first analyzing optical flow results obtained using the block matching algorithm, the three features were found. Based on these three features, we constructed a correction method for optical flow calculations. In the developed correction method, optical flow images are multiplied. Some optical flow images were calculated from an image for which the color balance was changed, while others were calculated from neighboring frames. At the multiplication stage, the vector length of the optical flows were gathered based on their frequency distribution. To evaluate the proposed method, experiments were conducted using video images in which a color checker is moving to the left or right. It is found that several erroneous optical flows are calculated in the case of the before correction, while the number of errors is drastically reduced in the case of the after correction.

Keywords: Optical flow · Color balance · Object motion detection

1 Introduction

Multiple examples of systems for tracking objects using dynamic displacement have been previously reported [1, 2]. This is important because highly accurate techniques for capturing the detailed motion of objects are essential ingredients for the design of human-computer interaction systems involving image processing. However, methods for determining the displacement of objects, including optical flow techniques [3], typically yield results contaminated by large numbers of errors.

In this study, we investigate a highly accurate computational technique for optical flow in which object motions are identified with high accuracy by merging multiple color adjusted captured images. To facilitate this, we adopt block matching as a computational technique for optical flow. The object motions we consider are restricted to translation within a flat surface.

2 Optical Flow Analysis

We begin by analyzing an optical flow obtained via block-matching methods. The images used in this analysis are shown in Fig. 1. In this figure, the image on the right is

© Springer International Publishing Switzerland 2016
C. Stephanidis (Ed.): HCII 2016 Posters, Part II, CCIS 618, pp. 457–462, 2016.
DOI: 10.1007/978-3-319-40542-1_74

shifted overall by 50 pixels to the right compared to the image on the left. In our analysis, we also constructed two modified versions of the figure at right: (1) an image in which +5 was added to the R values of all pixels, and (2) an image in which +5 was added to all RGB values of all pixels.

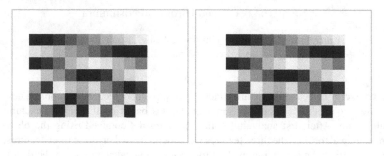

Fig. 1. Images of object moving

Figure 2 shows optical flows computed using the images of Fig. 1 and their color-adjusted versions. The left image of Fig. 2 shows the results obtained for the unmodified images, while the center and right images show results obtained for images with R values increased by 5 and with all RGB values increased by 5. The five most commonly occurring ring displacements determined from the optical flows of Fig. 2 are listed in Table 1, ranked in order of the frequency with which they occur in the images.

Table 1. Frequency of occurrence of optical flow

Rank	No change			R + 5			RGB + 5		
	dx	dy	Frequency	dx	dy	Frequency	dx	dy	Frequency
1	0	0	1546	0	0	1546	0	0	1546
2	50	0	81	50	0	99	50	0	119
3	50	−3	26	3	−3	18	45	0	28
4	50	−13	26	40	0	17	40	0	25
5	50	−23	26	48	0	17	49	0	19

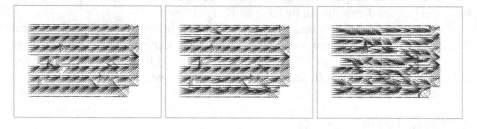

Fig. 2. Optical flow results using color balance change

The following features are evident in Fig. 2 and Table 1:

- The optical flows contain numerous displacements errors for similar color regions.
- Large numbers of correct flows are computed with high frequency, while erroneous flows are present with low frequency.
- Color-adjusting the analyzed images yields different detection results.

3 Proposed Method

Next, we propose a computational method that corrects optical flows based on the three aforementioned features observed in our analysis. The correction methods used by our proposed method may be broadly classified into three types. In this section we discuss these three methods and describe their implementation in our proposed method. Figure 3 shows the images used in this section. These images consist of a color-chart board, as captured before and after a rightward displacement of 6.5 cm, together with the corresponding optical-flow image. The displacement here corresponds to approximately 105 pixels in the images.

Fig. 3. Images of object moving and optical flow

3.1 Correction Using the Most Frequent Vector

Based on the results of the analysis of Sect. 2, we conclude that correct optical flows are computed with high frequency, while erroneous optical flows are present at low frequencies. This observation suggests the possibility of correcting errors by replacing computed optical flows with the optical flows that appear with the greatest frequency. Moreover, even in cases involving multiple duplicate objects with different displacements, we expect the optical flow that appears with the greatest frequency for each duplicate to be correct. Motivated by these observations, we attempted a correction scheme in which we replaced optical flows for each of the various edges that are present in an image, with similarly colored regions taken to delineate duplicate objects.

3.2 Correction Using Perturbations of Image Color

Based on the results of the analysis of Sect. 2, we conclude that adjusting the coloration of analyzed images yields differing results. For this reason, seems reasonable to expect that applying the correction scheme of Sect. 3.1 to coloration-adjusted images will also give rise to discrepancies. The left image of Fig. 4 shows the result of applying the correction scheme of Sect. 3.1 to an image before coloration adjustment. Similarly, the right image of Fig. 4 shows the result of applying the correction scheme of Sect. 3.1 to an image in which all R values have been increased by 5.

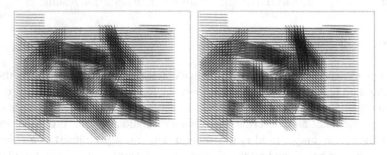

Fig. 4. Optical flow of correction result of Sect. 3.1

From Fig. 4, we see that intentionally adjusting the coloration of the image yields different results for optical-flow correction. These considerations suggest that errors may be corrected by preparing three versions of an image, with colorations intentionally adjusted, and then applying the correction scheme of Sect. 3.1 to each image. In this proposal, we use 14 coloration adjusted images together with the unmodified image, and we can select as many as three versions of each object duplicate. Next, we will compute optical flows for these three image versions and execute the correction scheme of Sect. 3.1.

3.3   Correction Using Consecutive Images

In this study, we use moving images to determine optical flows. In general, the motion of objects in moving images is continuous. Consequently, there is a high probability of finding the same vector in two consecutive images captured for optical-flow computations. For this reason, we obtain vectors using the three frames of images that follow the two consecutive images used for our optical-flow computations, and we use these vectors to assist in selecting images within the correction scheme of Sect. 3.2.

4   Comparative Experiments

To test whether or not the optical-flow correction scheme proposed in this study actually yields corrections in practice, we conducted experiments to compare corrected results to pre-correction results. In these experiments, we use moving images obtained from a single calibrated camera. We used six seconds of moving images at a frame rate of five frames per second (FPS). The content of these images consists of color-chart board held with one hand and moved from left to right in front of the camera in a room with stable illumination. Figure 5 shows two consecutive images selected at random from the set of moving images used in these experiments. In this figure, we have selected portions of the images involving the color-chart board moving in the downward left direction.

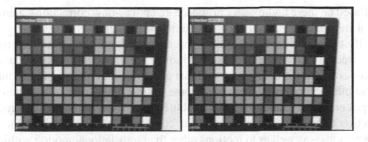

Fig. 5. Images of object moving of comparison experiment

Figure 6 shows the optical flow computed using Fig. 5. The left and right images in this figure correspond pre-correction and post-correction results, respectively. As we can see in this figure, the results of our comparison experiments demonstrate that our correction scheme successfully eliminates errors. However, there are many regions in which the optical flow has been replaced by a displacement of 0. One possible explanation for this is that, in this method, we use the Canny edge-detection technique to distinguish duplicate objects. In this method, edges are not detected in situations deemed to involve only minor variations in the gradient. Instead, such cases result in a merger with regions corresponding to other duplicate objects. For this reason, the values that occur with the greatest frequency differ from the ideal values, and are thus replaced by not ideal values.

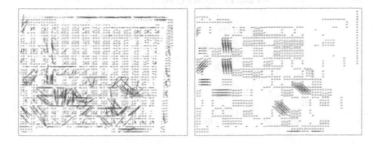

Fig. 6. Optical flow results of Fig. 5

In addition, in this study we restrict the motion of objects to translational motion in the plane. For this reason, images which a person is moving the board from left to right may include slight expansions or contractions and slight rotational motions. Thereby, it is considered that the maximal-frequency values differ from ideal values.

5 Conclusion

In this study we investigated an optical-flow correction scheme designed to improve the accuracy of optical flows. We began by attempting to detect key features present in the results of existing optical-flow computations and succeeded in identifying three such features. Based on these findings, we proposed an optical-flow correction scheme whose operational steps may be broadly classified into three categories.

To verify the effectiveness of our proposed method, we conducted experiments to compare corrected and uncorrected results. Upon drawing optical flows computed before and after our correction process, we found that our correction scheme successfully eliminated large numbers of errors. However, some optical flows were overwritten by erroneous displacements, and thus lost. We attribute these losses to the low accuracy of our edge-selection technique – which caused the correction process to fail due to mergers with other regions – as well as to motions other than translational motion within a plane in the moving images we used.

Topics for future work include efforts to improve the accuracy of our method by increasing the accuracy of our edge-selection algorithm, and to detect motions of duplicate objects other than in-plane translations, including expansion, contraction, and rotation.

References

1. Shin, J., et al.: Optical flow-based real-time object tracking using non-prior training active feature model. Real-Time Imaging **11**(3), 204–218 (2005)
2. Mikić, I., Krucinski, S., Thomas, J.D.: Segmentation and tracking in echocardiographic sequences: active contours guided by optical flow estimates. IEEE Trans. Med. Imaging **17**(2), 274–284 (1998)
3. Horn, B.K., Schunck, B.G.: Determining optical flow. In: Technical Symposium East. International Society for Optics and Photonics (1981)

Turning an Electric Cargo Vehicle into a Portable Interactive Information Kiosk

Emmanouil Zidianakis[1(✉)], George Margetis[1], Spiros Paparoulis[1],
Thanasis Toutountzis[1], Kallia Stratigi[1], George Paparoulis[1],
and Constantine Stephanidis[1,2]

[1] Institute of Computer Science, Foundation for Research and Technology – Hellas (FORTH),
70013 Heraklion, Crete, Greece
{zidian,gmarget,spirosp,atout,stratigi,groulis,cs}@ics.forth.gr
[2] Department of Computer Science, University of Crete, Heraklion, Crete, Greece

Abstract. This paper presents the conversion of an electric cargo vehicle into a portable platform for interacting with information applications. The cargo vehicle hosts 2 seats for the driver and 1 extra passenger, and 3 interactive systems installed at the cargo's right, left and back exterior side. The vehicle is intended to follow predefined routes from central ports to the nearest city center, making long term stops. During stops, embedded interactive systems entertain and provide visitors and other passersby with information of local interest. This papers focuses on the vehicle's conversion process, from the installation of the necessary hardware components needed by the interactive systems to the development of a portable control panel designed to address the driver's needs.

Keywords: User interaction on car's exterior · Electric vehicle · Cargo · Interactive applications · Ambient intelligence · Portable interactive information point

1 Introduction

There is a continuing trend to develop information kiosks, accessible in public locations (i.e. shopping malls, airports, railways stations), to deliver information and services to the general public. Early kiosks as described in [5] were typically uninteresting boxes with relatively simple interfaces, designed specifically to allow customers to conduct a simple transaction (i.e., placing an order). Latest kiosks represent a significant change of perspective. According to [6], they support four types of functionality: (a) information provision/promotion, (b) interaction, (c) transaction and (d) relationships. Usually, kiosks deliver services at the point of need (e.g. money near a shopping center, tickets in a station).

This paper presents the conversion of an electric cargo vehicle into a portable inter-active information kiosk able to deliver services while remaining stationary at various points of need (see Fig. 1). Electric vehicles enjoy great popularity because they improve fuel economy, lower fuel costs, and reduce emissions as well as levels of noise. The developed portable kiosk follows predefined routes (i.e. from central ports to the nearest

© Springer International Publishing Switzerland 2016
C. Stephanidis (Ed.): HCII 2016 Posters, Part II, CCIS 618, pp. 463–469, 2016.
DOI: 10.1007/978-3-319-40542-1_75

city center), making long term stops. During that stops, embedded interactive systems entertain and provide visitors and other passersby with information of local interest.

Fig. 1. An electric vehicle turned into an interactive information point.

Users are able to interact with the embedded interactive systems in an intuitive and seamless manner. That systems consists of three large displays enabled with touch capabilities and depth sensors. The latter led to the development of a plethora of applications enabled with recognition of gestures, gaze, body movements, etc. Regarding public displays, a large proportion of users are passers-by and thus first-time users [1]. In this context, public displays integrated in the vehicle enhances the opportunity for interaction by anyone in a walk-up-and-use manner [4]. The developed information kiosk is internet enabled via available Wi-Fi spots for real-time information provision and communication.

2   Converting an Electric Cargo Vehicle

The goal of this project was to make an electric vehicle capable of carriage and simultaneous operation of 3 interactive systems. All the necessary hardware equipment is embedded in a special designed cargo box in a way invisible to the naked eye. Figure 2 depicts the hardware setup inside the vehicle. Specifically, 6 × 12 V 200 AH deep cycle batteries (J) were selected for powering on the 3 embedded large displays (D,E,F), 3 PCs (A,B,C) and the connected peripherals required for the operation of the interactive applications such as Microsoft Kinect 2.0 sensor (K).

The installed batteries are combined into 3 groups connected in parallel. Each group contains 2 batteries connected in series increasing the voltage output up to 24 V. Figure 3 depicts this combination of series and parallel circuits which has as a result to increase both the battery current and voltage level at the same time. As opposed to using 12 V, the 24 V approach has the benefit of resulting in a lower voltage drop and thus to achieve better efficiency in energy use. Ordinary hardware components which can easily be found on the market were selected for this project. That components, such as PCs and touch sensitive displays are functioning on 220 V. For that reason, a power inverter

Fig. 2. Hardware setup for the operation of embedded interactive applications.

is used to convert the direct current of 24 V (DC) to alternating current of 220 V (AC) for the normal operation of all connected devices (Fig. 2I).

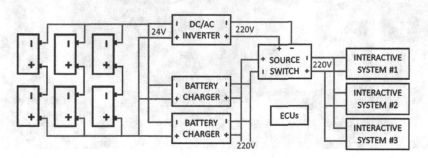

Fig. 3. High level wiring diagram

Wired batteries with total rated capacity of 600 Ah (3 × 200 Ah) are able to continuously supply a current of 24 A for almost 8 h before next charging. Various electronic control units (ECUs) monitor constantly the remaining voltage which has to be more than 19 V, otherwise, the operation of the interactive systems is suspended automatically to prevent the batteries from becoming completely discharged. When there is access to the power public corporation network (P.P.C.), the electric vehicle can be connected to it in order to charge the installed batteries. Charging is performed by 2 chargers simultaneously wired in parallel for better performance (2 × 30 Ah, Fig. 2H).

In order to achieve faster charging the functioning of the interactive systems can be isolated from the batteries. To this end, the interactive systems are able to operate directly through P.P.C. as the power source switch is set accordingly by the ECUs (see Fig. 3).

Regarding ECUs, 1 Raspberry Pi[1] (RPi) and 1 Arduino UNO[2] are used to control the car as well the interactive systems. ECUs receive data from various sensors and take actions depending on driver's input, batteries' status, temperature, current flow, vehicle status (handbrake, engine starter, doors, etc.). For example, when the temperature inside the cabinet goes high, ECUs adjust the ventilation accordingly by increasing fans speed. If needed, ECUs automatically shut down interactive systems to prevent them as well as the batteries from overheated. Lastly, RPi connects automatically to any available wireless network stations in order to route network traffic from the interactive systems and vice versa.

3   Interactive Applications on the Go

At every vehicle's stop, passersby will be able to interact with 3 systems, located on every side around the vehicle, in an intuitive and user friendly manner (Fig. 4). These systems aim to entertain and provide information about points of interest, such as historical sites, museums, landscapes, activities etc.:

Fig. 4. Interacting with the embedded applications

- **Be There NOW** is an immersive application, where users are depicted standing in front of various landscapes as if they were there. The system offers to users the ability to navigate by rotating the cube placed next to the system. In addition, users can take a snapshot and send it through e-mail to themselves or their friends, by touching the image of a camera on the nearby screen [1].
- **Infocloud** comprises a collection of keywords, images and video thumbnails displayed on a very large touch screen. When a word is selected, an information window opens, which may contain an image or video accompanied by a short textual description. When an image is selected, it becomes much bigger and a caption is added to it. When a video thumbnail is selected, it becomes bigger, and a related description is displayed along with a play button [2].

---

[1] https://www.raspberrypi.org/.
[2] https://www.arduino.cc/en/Main/ArduinoBoardUno.

- **Interactive Map** is a system that comprises points of interest shown on a map by using multi-touch technologies and gives users the opportunity to extract information in multimedia content and text form. When the user selects a predefined point on the map, an information window appears, which may contain images, videos and a short description for the selected point. The points of interest are organized in categories, allowing users to change the displayed results on the map according to their preferences [3].

4   Driver's Administration Facilities

A control panel has been developed in order to provide the driver with valuable information regarding the overview status of the vehicle as well as the operation of the interactive systems (Fig. 5). The driver is able to turn on/off the interactive systems by pressing the corresponding button. In case of failure, an alarm buzzer gives an audible signal about the problem or condition which prevents the systems from turning on in addition to the visual feedback (corresponding led flashes constantly). The same applies to the case of the vehicle's ability to move. The driver can also change the power source (Batteries or P.P.C.) as well as be informed about the battery status and internet connectivity.

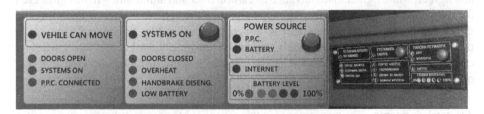

Fig. 5. Driver's control panel. (Color figure online)

Furthermore, the driver has access to detailed information using his tablet device. In detail, a mobile application running on android tablets synchronizes data through Wi-Fi (RPi runs also as Wi-Fi station) regarding the vehicle's status as depicted in Fig. 6.

Fig. 6. Screenshots of the driver's control mobile application.

The main screen of the mobile application presents an overview of the vehicle and the interactive systems, while the next tabs are associated with the interactive systems and power source accordingly. The driver is also able to control the interactive systems or change the power source and also in case of failure or temporal impossibility the specific reasons are textually elaborated. Furthermore, the driver can be informed about the remaining time left when the systems are running on batteries or the estimated time left for the batteries to be fully charged.

5   Conclusion and Future Work

This paper has presented the conversion of an electric vehicle into an interactive information kiosk. The vehicle follows predefined routes from central ports to the nearest city center and make long term stops. During that stops, embedded interactive systems entertain and provide passersby with information of local interest. The paper presented details of the implementation process from the installation part of the necessary hardware components to the driver's administration facilities. The main direction of further work is anticipated in a path towards improving the efficiency of vehicle in terms of power consumption while employing the necessary infrastructure to harness solar energy. Regarding reducing overall net weight, the batteries will be redesigned to be smaller and lighter, while lighter materials such as carbon fiber and aluminum will be considered for the vehicle's frame. Finally, the biggest part of the vehicle's exterior including the doors and the top of its cabinet will be covered with thin-film flexible solar panels in order to take advantage of Greece's abundant sunshine. Last but not least, wireless charging stations will be installed at the vehicle's stops to make charging fast and effortless.

Acknowledgements. The work reported in this paper has been conducted in the context of the AmI Programme and Smart Environments of the Institute of Computer Science of the Foundation for Research and Technology-Hellas (FORTH). Part of the work has been supported by PRODROMOS, a research project cofounded by the European Union, Greece and Cyprus, through the Greece-Cyprus Program of Transnational Cooperation (2007–2013). The authors would like to express their gratitude to Antonis Katzourakis for his graphical designs concerning the tablet application, as well as Manolis Apostolakis and Manolis Stamatakis who shaped the artistic concept and the industrial design of the vehicle's exterior.

References

1. Drossis, G., Ntelidakis, A., Grammenos, D., Zabulis, X., Stephanidis, C.: Immersing users in landscapes using large scale displays in public spaces. In: Streitz, N., Markopoulos, P. (eds.) DAPI 2015. LNCS, vol. 9189, pp. 152–162. Springer, Heidelberg (2015)
2. http://www.ics.forth.gr/ami/projects/view/All/Infocloud
3. http://www.ics.forth.gr/ami/projects/view/All/Interactive_Map
4. Izadi, S., et al.: Dynamo: a public interactive surface supporting the cooperative sharing and exchange of media. In: Proceedings of the 16th Annual ACM Symposium on User Interface Software and Technology. ACM (2003)

5. Rowley, J.: Multimedia kiosks in retailing. Int. J. Retail Distrib. Manag. **23**(5), 32–40 (1995)
6. Slack, F., Rowley, J.: Kiosks 21: a new role for information kiosks? Int. J. Inf. Manag. **22**(1), 67–83 (2002)

Design and Evaluation Case Studies

Design and Implementation of an NFC Food Labeler for Smart Healthcare

Yara Al-Tehini and Hend S. Al-Khalifa[✉]

Information Technology Department, CCIS,
King Saud University, Riyadh, Saudi Arabia
Yaraaltehini@gmail.com, hendk@ksu.edu.sa

Abstract. This paper presents the design of a smart food labeler mobile application that utilizes Near Field Communication (NFC) technology. The system aims to increase nutrition awareness and encourage food sellers to provide information about their food products in an efficient and interactive way.

Keywords: Nutrition education · Food label · NFC technology · Smart healthcare · Mobile application

1 Introduction

Human body health depends on what someone eats. Most of diseases such as Diabetes, High Blood Pressure and Digestive Diseases are caused by bad nutrition [1–3]. It is important for people to be more conscious about the food they are going to eat. One approach that helps people know about the food nutrition is food labels.

Food labels play an important role in communicating nutrition facts and health related issues where people can be aware of the food they are consuming and can make healthier choices. Food labels provide vital information about any food such as food content, ingredients, calories and fats. Knowing food ingredients help people who have food allergy to avoid the ones that are not suitable for them. Also, knowing food calories and fats help them to know how much energy and fats that their body will gain after consuming that food.

Smartphone devices with advanced features are the most growing technology in the market today. Their usage is increasing and they even become an aid in various fields of life using different apps. One of the recently emerging technologies that are integrated in smartphones is Near Field Communication (NFC). NFC is built inside more than 500 million smartphones and it is expected to be increasing for the next years [13]. In contrast to other available technology such as Quick Response (QR) codes that require additional apps installed in smartphones to read them, NFC is built inside the smartphone and does not require any additional apps to read its tags. Therefore using NFC as a medium for information storing will give the developed application a high user experience in an interactive and smart way.

C. Stephanidis (Ed.): HCII 2016 Posters, Part II, CCIS 618, pp. 473–478, 2016.
DOI: 10.1007/978-3-319-40542-1_76

2 Background

2.1 NFC Technology

Near Field Communication (NFC) is a technology that allows devices to communicate wirelessly over a short distance of few centimeters. NFC technology devices have various communication ways. One of the ways, which is for passive devices, is communicating with a reader and storing information on them but not actively reading other devices [4]. Another way is peer-to-peer communication between active devices such as smartphones, which both can send and receive information [4]. The NFC technology is widely used in payment domain such as Google wallet and Apple pay. Also in exchanging information between smartphones i.e. read and write information to NFC tags.

2.2 NFC Tags

NFC tags are chips that use NFC technology and have different forms such as stickers, labels or hangs. They are considered passive devices and can store information that can be read and written by other NFC devices like smartphones [5]. The stored information could be normal data such as text, photos or videos or it could be specific action such as turning on Wi-Fi, opening certain app, etc.

Technically speaking, there are five different types of NFC Tags defined by NFC Forum. Table 1 shows major features of the first four types. However, Type 5 has been defined recently by NFC Forum, it follows ISO/IEC 15693 standard and it is configured to store NFC Data Exchange Format (NDEF) messages [8].

Table 1. NFC forum NFC tag types [6, 7]

Features	Type 1	Type 2	Type 3	Type 4
Standard	ISO14443A	ISO14443A	Japanese Industrial Standard (JIS) X 6319-4, known as (FeliCa)	ISO/IEC14443
Memory size	96 bytes and can be expand up to 2 Kbytes	48 bytes and can be expand up to 2 Kbytes	Variable (limit 1 Mbyte per service)	Up to 32 Kbytes per service
Communication speed	106 Kbit/s	106 Kbit/s	212 Kbit/s	Between 106 Kbit/s and 424 Kbit/s
Read and write capability	Both and can be configured to become read only	Both and can be configured to become read only	Pre- configured to become both or read only	Pre- configured to become both or read only

3   Related Work

There are many available websites and mobile apps in different platforms such as iPhone and Android, which have some common features with our proposed app. We selected the most three popular from them to be compared with our app. Table 2 shows the comparison between our app and the selected apps.

Table 2. Comparison between smart food labeler app and other selected apps

Major features	ReciPal	Fooducate	Calorie counter	Smart food labeler
Diet tracking	✕	✓	✓	✕
Barcode reader	✕	✓	✓	✕
Provide huge food database	✓	✓	✓	✓
Allows to add new food	✓	✓	✓	✕
Allows to add recipes	✓	✓	✓	✓
Storing recipes in the cloud	✓	✓	✓	✓
Calculate calories	✓	✓	✓	✓
Allows to view nutrition information	✓	✓	✓	✓
Generate nutrition information	✓	✕	✕	✓
Support NFC	✕	✕	✕	✓

3.1   ReciPal [9]

ReciPal is a website that enables creating nutrition facts labels with FDA format. The website allows creating recipes by adding ingredients from their database or adding new ingredients by the user. All nutrition facts for the recipes are calculated when adding the ingredients. The recipes are stored in the cloud and the user can edit them or delete them any time. It provides options to hide ingredients, allergens list and business info. It provides various label styles, which the user can choose from them then save the label and print it. The website offers a free trial for three free recipes.

3.2   Fooducate [10]

Fooducate is a free mobile application available on Android and iPhone platforms. Also it has a website version. The application allows scanning food product barcode then shows whether it is healthy or not based on their grading system that grade product from A down to D. It provides food, calories and exercise tracking. Also it allows searching and adding food from their database and allows adding user recipes and food, which is stored in the cloud.

3.3   Calorie Counter [11]

Calories Counter is a free mobile application available on Android, iPhone, iPad and Windows Phone platforms. Also it has a website version. The application provides tracking of food, exercise and major nutrients such as calories, fat, protein, sugar, fiber and cholesterol. It allows scanning food product barcode. Also it allows searching and adding food from their database and allows adding user recipes and food, which all stored in the cloud.

4   System Design

Our Smart Food Labeler system is designed to help food sellers provide their customers with information about their food products efficiently. The system consists of three essential components which are NFC food labels, smart food labeler app and cloud backend, as shown in Fig. 1.

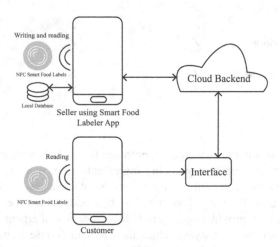

Fig. 1. System architecture

The system works as follows: a seller uses the App to add her/his food products information and retrieve the ingredients from cloud backend database. The added food product information will be stored in the cloud backend associated with a seller ID. Then (s)he writes one of the added food products to the smart Food Label after entering activation ID which is provided to seller with smart Food Labels. The seller will place the smart Food Label on her/his food package and sell it to the customer. Then the customer taps her/his NFC smartphone to the smart Food Label and all information of that food product will be retrieved from the cloud backend through the interface to the customer.

4.1   NFC Food Labels

NFC Food label is an NFC tag that can be read and written by NFC smartphones. The label is small and suitable for all kind of food packaging. The tag type that will be used for the labels is Type 2 with ISO 14443A standard.

4.2   Smart Food Labeler App and Cloud Backend

Smart Food labeler app is an Android mobile application that enables sellers to write their food content to the NFC food labels. It allows them to add their food ingredients from comprehensive food database and automatically calculates food calories. Also it enables reading from the smart food labels.

The cloud backend is used for storing seller recipes, ingredients and contact information along with seller ID. Also, it is used for retrieving recipes and ingredients of sellers and for retrieving nutrition information of the food product to the customer.

5   Implementation

The Smart Food Labeler App is developed for Android platform using Android Studio and Android NFC library package [12] to provide NFC functionality. The cloud backend is implemented using PHP and SQL for database storage. The mobile database is implemented using SQLite to store seller's products and information and uncompleted backend processes. The interface is developed using HTML5 and JavaScript in a form compatible with mobile devices.

The application provides three main options: Write to tag, Read from tag and View all user food products, as shown in Fig. 2.

The View all user food products option allows a seller to view all his/her food products and add new one or edit/delete existing one. When a seller adds new food product, it will be provided with a user friendly form which includes the name of the

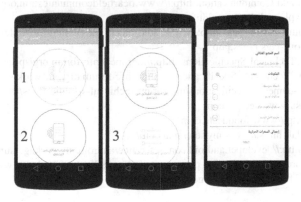

Fig. 2. Main interface in Arabic: (1) write to tag (2) read from tag (3) view all user food products and (4) add new food product interface.

product, ingredients and total of calories, as shown in Fig. 2(4). The calories will be calculated after the seller adds the ingredients using the comprehensive database that enables him to search and add the ingredients (s)he wants. For the seller property rights, the application provides hide ingredients, which hide all ingredients of the food product recipe. The write to tag option allows the seller to write food product information to the Smart Food Label. It allows seller to select one of the food products that (s)he adds in his/her list, then it will ask him/her to tap the mobile device to write on the Smart Food label. For read from tag option it will ask the user to tap his/her device to the Smart Food Label to view the information of the food product inside the Smart Food Labeler App.

6 Conclusion

This paper presented the design and development of a smart food labeler mobile app using Near Field Communication (NFC) technology. The need for such an app came from the perspective of nutrition awareness and its importance in the healthcare field; the awareness can be achieved through food labeling of homemade food.

We presented our Smart Food Labeler App in an exhibition to conduct user acceptance testing. We asked 12 persons using a questionnaire and the reviews ware very satisfactory, where 92 % said that the app was excellent and 8 % said that the app was very good.

References

1. Diabetes Causes and Risk Factors. http://familydoctor.org/familydoctor/en/diseases-conditions/diabetes/causes-risk-factors.html
2. High Blood Pressure Causes and Risk Factors. http://familydoctor.org/familydoctor/en/diseases-conditions/high-blood-pressure/causes-risk-factors.html
3. Digestive Diseases: MedlinePlus Medical Encyclopedia. https://www.nlm.nih.gov/medlineplus/ency/article/007447.htm
4. About Near Field Communication. http://www.nearfieldcommunication.org/about-nfc.html
5. NFC Tags Explained. http://rapidnfc.com/nfc_tags
6. NFC Tags and Tag Types. http://www.radio-electronics.com/info/wireless/nfc/near-field-communications-tags-types.php
7. NFC Forum: Technical Specifications. http://members.nfc-forum.org/specs/spec_list/
8. NFC Forum Technical Specifications. http://nfc-forum.org/our-work/specifications-and-application-documents/specifications/nfc-forum-technical-specifications/#tag
9. Recipal. https://www.recipal.com
10. Fooducate. http://www.fooducate.com/
11. My Fitness Pal. https://www.myfitnesspal.com/
12. android.nfc. http://developer.android.com/reference/android/nfc/package-summary.html
13. Worldwide forecast NFC-enabled phone installed base 2013–2018. http://www.statista.com/statistics/347315/nfc-enabled-phone-installed-base/

Enhancing the Customers' Experience Using an Augmented Reality Mirror

Chryssi Birliraki[1], George Margetis[1(✉)], Nikolaos Patsiouras[1],
Giannis Drossis[1], and Constantine Stephanidis[1,2]

[1] Institute of Computer Science (ICS),
Foundation for Research and Technology – Hellas (FORTH),
N. Plastira 100, Vassilika Vouton, 700 13 Heraklion, Crete, Greece
{birlirak,gmarget,patsiouras,drossis,cs}@ics.forth.gr
[2] Department of Computer Science, University of Crete,
Heraklion, Crete, Greece

Abstract. Augmented reality fitting rooms enrich customers' experience and expedite the shopping procedure. This paper presents an Augmented Reality (AR) mirror which provides motion-based interaction to the users and suggests various outfits. The proposed system can be easily installed inside or at the window of a retail shop, enabling the users to stand in front of it and see themselves wearing clothes that the system suggests while they are able to naturally interact with the system remotely, using gestures, in order to like or dislike the recommended outfit. The users can also choose to post photos wearing the proposed clothes on their social media accounts, as well as to buy the clothes either directly from the store or on-line.

Keywords: Fitting room · Virtual fitting room · Interactive · Augmented reality mirror · Microsoft Kinect · Hand tracking · Skeleton tracking

1 Introduction

Augmented reality fitting rooms facilitate the shopping experience by allowing customers to try-on apparel and/or mix and-match garments without being physically present in the retail shop [10]. They are used to improve the process of trying on clothes and maximizing time efficiency [8]. These platforms not only are powerful decision tools for the on-line shopper [3], but also contribute to the fun factor of in-store shopping. E-commerce is a strong application field for augmented reality applications. Specifically, in the area of retail, the inability of users to foresee how particular clothing items will fit them when shopping online has always been a significant weakness [11]. Fitting rooms are applications targeting at both personal computers and mobile devices [9]. The main interaction technique used by augmented reality fitting rooms is the real time detection of body and hands used to engage gesture based interaction. HD camera or/and Microsoft Kinect sensor inputs are usually used for detection [2, 6, 12]. Another interaction technique -less widespread- is spoken language. It was observed that the combination of spoken language input and virtually-real image output provides natural and robust interaction [7]. This paper

© Springer International Publishing Switzerland 2016
C. Stephanidis (Ed.): HCII 2016 Posters, Part II, CCIS 618, pp. 479–484, 2016.
DOI: 10.1007/978-3-319-40542-1_77

represents the development of an augmented reality mirror which uses Microsoft Kinect v.2 for body and hand detection in order to offer a more natural way of interaction to the user, providing new features with regards to related approaches enhancing thus the customer's shopping experience. The proposed AR mirror operates both on-line and offline and can be installed in a retail or department store as well as store in a house.

2 AR Mirror

2.1 System Description

The AR mirror comprises a large LED display, a Microsoft Kinect v.2 and a PC. The users can stand in front of the system and see themselves on the display, wearing virtual garments and accessories (Fig. 1).

Fig. 1. System setup

The initial "Welcome screen" of the system familiarizes the user - who stands in front of it - with the gestures that the system uses as the main interaction modality. In more details, aiming at the faster introduction of the user to the system and the most intuitive learning of the system's interaction, a supportive assistance system has been developed, through which step-by-step user training is performed with the aid of animations and confirmatory messages to the user about whether he/she responds correctly regarding system manipulation. This "Help system" acts as an interactive assisting tool [1] and prompts the user to interact with the AR mirror. This way, users are quickly introduced to the system's environment, which allows them to become accustomed to it and creates a sense of "early achievement" in terms of interaction.

After the user's quick training, the "Main screen" is displayed. The main screen is divided into three sections (top, middle and bottom) (Fig. 2).

The first part at the top presents the logo of each store as well as menu options, such as language, gender and clothes category (Fig. 3), while the second part in the middle is the actual AR area of the system, displaying a real-time video of the user standing in front of the system wearing virtual garments of the selected category superimposed on his/her body. This way the users perceive how they would look like if they tried them on.

Fig. 2. Main screen of the system

Fig. 3. Top section of the system. (Left) logo of the store, (right) menu options.

In the middle section there are three more options for the user: the "Like" and "Dislike" interactive buttons, as well as an information bubble (Fig. 4). By selecting the Like or Dislike button, the user declares his/her preference about the suggested outfit to the system, the system removes the current outfit, and provides a new one according to the user's their preferences (which have been defined through the options menu). On the left hand side of the user, an info bubble is presented providing information about the product the user is currently "trying on". The third section at the bottom, comprises the Buy and View Photos button (Fig. 3). The latter button displays a strip of photos of the user wearing the recommended outfits. Shots of the user's outline interacting with the system are being taken every time the garment changes and a gallery is created for the user to review what he/she "tried on" previously.

Fig. 4. "Like" and "dislike" buttons and the "info" section.

2.2 Novel Features

Beyond the help functionality described above, there are a few more features which introduce novel elements in the user's purchasing experience. For example, users are able to purchase the offered products either online or offline using a passport code.

Fig. 5. (Left) passport screen, (right) buy options

The AR mirror may be installed on retail stores or be available through on-line stores, to which each user connects through the XBOX console and a TV-mounted Kinect sensor to try on available products and buy them on demand. In the first case, each user can take the passport code written on the screen to the cashier and buy the product connected to this code. In the case of on-line stores, users can buy products via a personal web page that is generated while they try clothes on, and which contains all the outfits they liked accompanied with a link to the online shop service of the store.

Another feature of the AR mirror that enhances the user's shopping experience is the double projection when he/she tries on items. In more details, the system provides in real-time a split view of the AR area, presenting the user wearing two different outfits, having this way the opportunity to compare (Fig. 6).

Fig. 6. Augmented reality split screen feature

Another interesting feature of the system is the "Photo Gallery", which shows a strip of photos of the user wearing the recommended outfits, and a "Passport" code for retrieving these photos later on via his/her favourite browser (Fig. 5). The "Passport" is a hash code which is given to a customer, once he stands in front of the system, and is used as a unique identifier that gives access to an online html page containing all the products he liked, as well as the photos of the user taken by the system. A Passport can be also obtained through QR code, so that users can gain immediate access to their personal page through their mobile devices (Fig. 5).

The system also supports both horizontal and vertical display with automatic rearrangement of its UI components in order to fit the aspect ratio of each screen. All the features are provided equally in the two projections (Fig. 7).

Fig. 7. The vertical layout of the system

An assistive administrative environment has also been developed providing functionality such as, entry and management of products displayed by the AR mirror, management of the offers or discounts displayed, statistic insights, etc.

2.3 Interaction Techniques

Interaction with the system is achieved through gestures via hand tracking [4]. Using a Microsoft Kinect version 2 depth sensor [13], the user skeleton is acquired [5], and further recognition of the movement of his/her hand is being recognized, so that the hand movement is mapped to a virtual hand cursor (mouse emulation). Moreover, when the virtual hand cursor lies over an interactive component, a selection can be performed by leaving the cursor for a specific duration on top of the component, which is equivalent to a mouse click. Apart from hand tracking for selection, skeleton tracking is also used to calculate the minimum distance needed in order to start tracking the user and enable the application, or to know when the user has left the mirror. As well as to place the virtual clothes correctly on the user's body regarding the skeleton's joints tracked by the sensor.

3   Conclusion

An AR mirror has been presented aiming to provide virtual try on of apparel and accessory products in retail stores. This system initiates an interesting digital interaction experience for all users, through which they can snap and share their virtual fittings online while at the same time connect with the store's online presence. It can be installed in various commercial locations. Customers are able to try as many products as they wish, without waiting on fitting room queues, and buy them from the comfort of their home or while a store is closed without having to carry them. Furthermore, user's preferences and user's experience feedback is collected for evaluation purposes in order to assess the system in terms of its usability and overall user experience. Future work pursues the inclusion of the application in popular on-line stores (e.g., windows store) or their installation on alternative devices, such as XBOX or PS4 consoles, enabling this way on one hand its use by home users and on the other hand brands to merge aspects of the online and in-store shopping into one exciting solution. The product presented in this work is commercialized in collaboration with LiateR.

References

1. Birliraki, C., Grammenos, D., Stephanidis, C.: Employing virtual humans for interaction, assistance and information provision in ambient intelligence environments. In: Streitz, N., Markopoulos, P. (eds.) DAPI 2015. LNCS, vol. 9189, pp. 249–261. Springer, Heidelberg (2015)
2. Chang, H.-T., Li, Y.-W., Chen, H.-T., Feng, S.-Y., Chien, T.-T.: A dynamic fitting room based on Microsoft Kinect and augmented reality technologies. In: Kurosu, M. (ed.) HCII/HCI 2013, Part IV. LNCS, vol. 8007, pp. 177–185. Springer, Heidelberg (2013)
3. Cordier, F., Lee, W., Seo, H., Magnenat-Thalmann, N.: Virtual-try-on on the web. In: Laval Virtual (2001)
4. Drossis, G., Grammenos, D., Birliraki, C., Stephanidis, C.: MAGIC: developing a multimedia gallery supporting mid-air gesture-based interaction and control. In: Stephanidis, C. (ed.) HCII 2013, Part I. CCIS, vol. 373, pp. 303–307. Springer, Heidelberg (2013)
5. Drossis, G., Grammenos, D., Adami, I., Stephanidis, C.: 3D visualization and multimodal interaction with temporal information using timelines. In: Kotzé, P., Marsden, G., Lindgaard, G., Wesson, J., Winckler, M. (eds.) INTERACT 2013, Part III. LNCS, vol. 8119, pp. 214–231. Springer, Heidelberg (2013)
6. Giovanni, S., Choi, Y.C., Huang, J., Khoo, E.T., Yin, K.: Virtual try-on using Kinect and HD camera. In: Kallmann, M., Bekris, K. (eds.) MIG 2012. LNCS, vol. 7660, pp. 55–65. Springer, Heidelberg (2012)
7. Kawahara, T., Tanaka, K., Doshita, S.: Virtual fitting room with spoken dialogue interface. In: ESCA Tutorial and Research Workshop (ETRW) on Interactive Dialogue in Multi-Modal Systems (1999)
8. Kumari, N., Bankar, S.: A real time virtual fitting room application (2015)
9. Martin, C.G., Oruklu, E.: Human friendly interface design for virtual fitting room applications on android based mobile devices. J. Signal Inf. Process. 3(04), 481 (2012)
10. Pachoulakis, I., Kapetanakis, K.: Augmented reality platforms for virtual fitting rooms. Int. J. Multimed. Appl. 4(4), 35 (2012)
11. Pereira, F., Silva, C., Alves, M.: Virtual fitting room augmented reality techniques for e-commerce. In: Cruz-Cunha, M.M., Varajão, J., Powell, P., Martinho, R. (eds.) CENTERIS 2011, Part II. CCIS, vol. 220, pp. 62–71. Springer, Heidelberg (2011)
12. Zhang, W., Matsumoto, T., Liu, J., Chu, M., Begole, B.: An intelligent fitting room using multi-camera perception. In: Proceedings of the 13th International Conference on Intelligent User Interfaces, pp. 60–69. ACM, January 2008
13. https://en.wikipedia.org/wiki/Kinect

Sectors Chained by Design

Collaborative Development of Product Footwear and Leather Goods from the Implementation of Participatory Methodologies. Case Cluster of Footwear in the Valle Del Cauca in Colombia

Lina Olaya Muriel, John J. Cardozo V.(✉), Nélida Y.T. Ramírez,
and Víctor M. Díaz C.

Palmira's Headquarters, Universidad Nacional de Colombia, Bogotá, Colombia
{lmolayam,jjcardozov,nyramirezt,vmdiazc}@unal.edu.co

Abstract. Leather industry, footwear and leather goods in the Valle del Cauca is composed of all the links in a supply chain: suppliers of inputs, raw materials and finished products; which shows the advantages of this sector in the region; however, it lacks the necessary linkages to generate a horizontal integration, "due largely to low vocation of association in a group of entrepreneurs in this sector" (Cámara de Comercio de Cali 2013). This study develops from triple helix model of Etzkowitz, in order to stimulate the participation of companies, state institutions and the transfer of knowledge from the university.

In this sense, from the perspective of industrial design it is considered that the implementation of collaborative methods, increases the power and accelerates performance triple helix model, because it allows product development by integrating the links in the production chain. To address this complexity, methodological tools are applied, which allow defining features of design and product development in a participatory way; online platforms specializing in analysis of industry trends worldwide, are used to identify the most relevant design criteria; CAD applications are used; to integrated the technical, productive and conceptual knowledge; this allow to provide design strategies as a tool for business competitiveness.

Keywords: Productive linkages · Industrial design · Competitiveness · Soft technologies

1 Introduction

The Colombians footwear and Leather goods Industry is composed by four groups: Primary supplies (collect rawhide), secondary supplies (bought or manufactured parts and inputs for the manufacture of products), finished product manufacturers (manufacture of consumer products) and distributors (commerce of finished products). [1] This sector plays an important role in the national economy because it brings together nearly 13,000 companies linked to the processing and production of inputs and 15,000 with commerce, of which 98 % are in the micro and small enterprises group. These are located in 28 of the 32 regions of the country [2].

© Springer International Publishing Switzerland 2016
C. Stephanidis (Ed.): HCII 2016 Posters, Part II, CCIS 618, pp. 485–490, 2016.
DOI: 10.1007/978-3-319-40542-1_78

However the current context demands high levels of competitiveness in the creation of differentiated products, reducing the response time needed to adapt to market conditions [3]. Nevertheless, "in Colombia design processes and product development in manufacturing companies in the leather, footwear and leather goods sector, distinguished by the lack of value creation as a differentiating factor to respond to the demands and dynamics of global markets." [4] This is because the development of new products is based on imitation strategies or to create minimal differences in the products.

Valle del Cauca has all the links in the production chain, which makes clear the advantages of this sector in the region, however lacks the necessary linkages to generate a horizontal integration of input suppliers, raw material and finished product, this due largely to the low associative vocation from entrepreneurs [5]. In fact, the difficulty of access to a broad portfolio of supplies create a loss of opportunities, both for the development of a differentiated product and its market position.

In this sense, it is pertinent to reference the triple helix model of Etzkowitz [6] through which it such problems are solved, since its approach achieves stimulate the participation of enterprises, state institutions and the transfer of knowledge through academy; in fact, the government supports strategies for strengthening, promotion and sectoral innovation through the Productive Transformation Program - PTP[1], from which the incorporation of design is promoted as a fundamental component of enterprises at all levels.

In this sense, the project applies participatory methods in 5 companies located in the city of Cali, belonging to the sectors mentioned, which have expressed interest in creating products differentiating under a system of forecasting trends of fashion. This participatory process was achieved through 2 workshop, which aimed at integrating know-how, skills in design and development of the industrial designer's own products. From academy and specifically from the perspective of industrial design is considered that the implementation of collaborative methods, strengthen and accelerates the approaches of Etzkowitz [6], enabling the development of products that link the supplies, raw materials and finished products of the production chain (Fig. 1).

---

[1] The national Government's program to transform the Colombian industry and promote the development of enterprises of 16 strategic sectors of the national economy, so that they compete and grow. This engine of industrial policy is part of the Ministry of Commerce, industry and tourism.

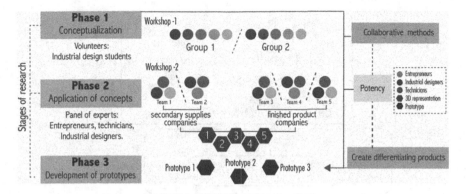

Fig. 1. Stages of research (Source: own formulation based on case cluster of footwear in the Valle del Cauca in Colombia.)

2   Materials and Methods

The conceptualization phase, looking for an initial immersion, It runs at the first workshop where the sample of participating volunteers was of 2 groups of 6 students in the last semester of career Industrial Design of the Universidad Nacional de Colombia headquarters Palmira; this phase required a record of relevant aesthetic and perceptual attributes in some traditional fruit consumption in the Valle del Cauca that will provide conceptual characteristics.

The second phase consisted of the application of the concepts on the products. That is to say, five models of three-dimensional representation based on attributes such as color, texture, shape, proportion, contrast were built; these models were produced in the second workshop by a group of 15 participants (10 experts and 5 Industrial design students); this phase required that the characteristics of the product be tangible, so that the technical features, functional and aesthetic particularities are linked each other. Consequently, established strategies for defining characteristics of design and development of products in a collective manner.

In the last phase, evaluated the formal proposals of 3 prototypes and their possible manufacturing processes, resulting in the use of soft technologies to generate quick prototypes in machining centers, cutting laser and CAD tools, allowing dynamic processes in the manufacture of prototypes.

The workshops were developed with the participation of entrepreneurs, technicians and students of Industrial Design at the Universidad Nacional de Colombia headquarters Palmira, and lasted twelve months from April 2014–April 2015. The results were five three-dimensional models (one for each participating company) where the conceptual basis proposals were reflected, and three prototypes which were performed dimensional adjustments.

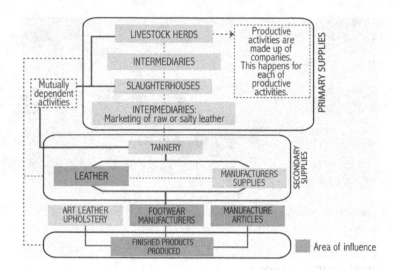

Fig. 2. Diagram general for the productive chain of the footwear, leather, manufactures and supplies. (Source: Campo, Y. 2012, p. 21)

2.1 Characterization of Companies

In the initial immersion it is noted that the selection of participating companies should be based on their influence on the manufacture of the product. The following chart presents the elements of the chain of leather, footwear and leather goods (Fig. 2):

Based on this diagram and supported by the statistical analysis by the CEPEC [5] about manufacturing firms by region and product sector in Colombia, it is identified that in the Valle del Cauca greater participation segments, represent 8 % of the domestic leather production, 15 % leather goods and 11 % represents shoemaking, becoming a representative region for the country.

In short, the selection of companies respond to a relationship of interdependence, so, if one takes inputs for component development, and at the same time, have the components ahead of time for the development of the final products, adequate responses will be taken on time in order to satisfy the final consumers.

2.2 Conceptualization

Generally the design process in the companies studied is characterized by the development of simple dynamics directly linked to the preparation of samples. These are based on reviewing sources of fashion inspiration as: magazines, national and international fairs and competitions. Then proceed with the search for raw materials, patterns and subsequent samples are reviewed and evaluated by management and finally the necessary production adjustments are made to proceed with the marketing strategy (Fig. 3).

| 1. Generation of ideas | – 2. Product selection | – 3. Construction of the prototype | – 4. Test and series production | – 5. Construction | – 6. Commercialization |
| | Preliminary design of the product | Final design of the product | | | |

Fig. 3. Overall product development process. (Source: Vega, L. 2011, p. 39)

Companies face a problem regarding the interpretation of fashion information obtained from different sources; In addition, poor anticipation of this review reflects the low priority given to studies context in which this information is produced. Fashion trends are a factor as high sensitivity and influences set out the guidelines to be followed not only manufacturers but also the entire supply chain, specialized magazines, events and fashion shows.

2.3 Results

The results were five models of three dimensional representation corresponding to each participating undertaking therein reflected the proposed conceptual bases and 3 prototypes. Below are the results obtained with the prototype 1 (Fig. 4).

Fig. 4. Results (Source: own formulation based on collaborative development of product footwear and leather goods from the implementation of participatory methodologies. 2014)

Finally, is shows that the implementation of participatory methodologies that are supported in the use of TIC strengthens alliances to the inside of the chain and promoting commercial links between suppliers, manufacturers and marketers, in conditions of formality, trust and fairness.

References

1. Ramirez, C.M.S.: Los ciclos de la moda. Enfoques teóricos y propuesta para el sector del cuero, Calzado y marroquinería., pp. 47–49. Bonaventuriana, Cali, Valle del acuca (2012)
2. Departamento Nacional de Planeación: Observatorio Económico y Social del Valle del Cauca (2010). http://www.observatoriovalle.org.co/wp-content/uploads/2012/05/PLAN-NACIONAL-DE-DESARROLLO-2010-2014T1.pdf. Último acceso: 12 Feb 2013
3. Becerra, O.E.H.: Desarrollo técnico de colecciones comerciales de moda: Cuero, Calzado y Marroquineria. Un factor clave para la generación de producto diferenciado en un entorno altamente competitivo., de Actas de Diseño 10., Buenos Aires, Argentina (2010)
4. Herreño Tellez, E., Diaz Carrero y, V.M., Hernández, D.: Metodología para el desarrollo de productos en Cuero, Calzado y Marroquinería., de *Dia de la ciencia y la tecnologia*, Palmira, Valle del cauca (2008)
5. F. C. P. d. t. p. d. R. Acicam: Plan de negocios para el sector de cuero, calzado y marroquinería, Coelho, Cali, pp. 34–35 (2013)
6. Etzkowitz, H.: The Triple Helix: University-Industry-Government Innovation in Action, p. 176. Routledge, Abingdon (2008)

Evaluating Usability of a Battery Swap Station for Electric Two Wheelers: A Case Study

Fei-Hui Huang[1], Yu-Cheng Lin[2(✉)], and Ting-Ting Lv[1]

[1] Department of Marketing and Distribution Management, Oriental Institute
of Technology, New Taipei 22061, Taiwan, ROC
Fn009@mail.oit.edu.tw

[2] Department of Computer-Aided Industrial Design,
Overseas Chinese University, Taichung 407, Taiwan, ROC
yclin@ocu.edu.tw

Abstract. This study aims to evaluate usability of BSS by using System Usability Scale (SUS), and obtain the potential needs of e-scooter riders for using the BSS. An experiment was conducted with a sample of 85 participants who had experienced a battery swapping service, operation procedure, and filled out a SUS questionnaire to evaluate the quality of using BSS. The results showed that the SUS score was 76.85. Most of participants perceived that they might use BSS frequently, and the BSS was easy to use and easy to learn. However, several participants perceived that they need to learn a lot of things or technical person support for getting going with BSS. For increasing the usability of the proposed BSS, operation procedure and user interface design should be investigated further.

Keywords: Electric two wheelers (E2Ws) · Battery swap station · Usability · SUS · Usability evaluation

1 Introduction

Taiwan has a population of 23 million, of which about 13.7 million are scooter users. Thus, one in every 1.67 people is a scooter commuter, which is the highest density in the world, and New Taipei City has the highest density in Taiwan. According to Taiwan's Environmental Protection Administration (EPA) report, emissions generated by scooters account for 330,000 tons of carbon monoxide and 90,000 tons of chemical compounds containing carbon hydroxide per year. The real-world operation of motorcycles/scooters results in a significant contribution of road transport CO and HC emissions, reaching 38 % and 64 %, respectively, to the total emissions from road transportation [1]. In order to improve the air quality, the Taiwanese government is dedicated to promoting an eco-environmental protection policy. Increasing the penetration level of electric two wheelers (E2 Ws) is one of the aims of the policy. The widespread adoption of E2 W brings potential social and economic benefits, such as reducing the quantity of fossil fuels and greenhouse gas emissions, as well as environmental benefits. However, limitations on E2 Ws batteries have meant that many people are unwilling to buy the related products. In spite of the incentives offered by

© Springer International Publishing Switzerland 2016
C. Stephanidis (Ed.): HCII 2016 Posters, Part II, CCIS 618, pp. 491–496, 2016.
DOI: 10.1007/978-3-319-40542-1_79

Taiwan's government, the penetration level of E2 W in the market is not encouraging. Only 29,942 e-scooters and 108,602 e-bikes were sold between 2009 and 2014.

A battery swapping model is proposed to overcome the battery limitations, including an expensive purchase price, short lifetime, limited driving range per charge, long charging time, and inconvenient charging, in order to improve the penetration of E2 Ws in Taiwan. This model includes providing self-service battery swap stations (BSSs). The BSS, as one promising charging infrastructure, can provide great convenience to E2 W customers without considering the all-electric range limit while the BSS is available. As of February 2014, there were 30 operational BSSs open to the public in New Taipei City, Taiwan. It is important to provide user-friendly BSS for E2 W riders to enhance their willingness to accommodate related products and service. The purpose of this experimental study is to detect user external behaviors of operating the BSS, evaluate usability of BSS by using System Usability Scale (SUS), and obtain the potential needs of e-scooter riders.

2 Literature Reviews

A battery swapping model may provide a faster charging service than even the fastest recharging stations and lower the charging cost by charging depleted batteries overnight at a discounted electricity price. In this study, the battery swapping model separates the ownership of the battery and the E2W. Using a battery leasing service may also reduce the expense incurred by E2W owners. The model provides self-service BSSs, where an owner can ride to the nearest BSS and swap to a fully-charged battery within 2 min. BSS is one of the solutions to the limitations of the E2W battery [2–5]. The concept of an exchangeable battery service was first proposed as early as 1896 in order to overcome the limited operating range of electric cars and trucks [6]. BSS can also be regarded as energy-storage power stations, which can alleviate the variability and uncertainty of power output of renewable energy [7] and improve the management of a power grid [8]. BSS is usually connected to the megavolt-ampere scale substation [9] and requires high power during a day, which may lead to network overload. However, the charging load forecasting model for a BSS has not been included in [7–9], and the BSS is not simply a storage power plant which should also satisfy the battery swapping demand of E2Ws [7, 8].

BSS can offer great convenience for travel range that is longer than the driving range per charge of the vehicle. Nielsen's system acceptability model may provide an overview of the issues that influence the service acceptance of a system. Nielsen [10] defines acceptability as "whether the system is good enough to satisfy all the needs and requirements of the user." System acceptability is the goal designers should aim for and can be achieved by meeting the social and practical acceptability objectives of the system. Hence, the Nielsen system acceptability model is a combination of social acceptability and practical acceptability. With regard to practical acceptability, it is a combination of the characteristics of the system, including its usefulness, cost/price, compatibility, reliability.

Usefulness has been identified as a key objective of practical acceptability. Usefulness refers to how well a system achieves a desired goal, and is divided into two subcategories: utility and usability [11]. Utility is the question of whether that functionality in principle can do what is needed; usability is the question of how well users can use the functionality of a system [12]. The two concepts of usability and utility are highly interrelated. A usable user interface may contribute to a service being perceived as having the utility to provide appropriate functionality. Conversely, if a service has the utility to provide appropriate functionality, but can only be used or consumed via a badly designed user interface, users may avoid using the product or service.

With regard to the definition of usability, Bevan et al. [13] focus on how usability should be measured, with a particular emphasis on either ease of use or acceptability. The usability of a product is affected not only by the features of the product itself, but also by the characteristics of the users, the tasks they are carrying out, and the technical, organizational and physical environment in which the product is used [10]. Then, Nielsen [10] further defines a usable system as a quality attribute that assesses how easy user interfaces are to use, and outlines five usability attributes: learnability, efficiency, memorability, error recovery/few errors, and satisfaction. The definition of learnability is that "how easy is it for users to accomplish basic tasks the first time they encounter the design". The definition of efficiency is that "once users have learned the design, how quickly can they perform tasks". The definition of memorability is that "when users return to the design after a period of not using it, how easily can they reestablish proficiency". The definition of errors is that "how many errors do users make, how severe are these errors, and how easily can they recover from the errors". The definition of satisfaction is that "how pleasant is it to use the design". The principles of usability are concerned with the five usability attributes, and are connected to the usefulness of a product. The International Organization of Standards (ISO) [14] defines usability as the extent to which a product can be used by specified users to achieve specified goals with effectiveness (the ability of users to complete tasks using the system, and the quality of the output of those tasks), efficiency (the level of resource consumed in performing tasks), and satisfaction (users' subjective reactions to using the system). In a specified context of use. Usability plays a role in each stage of the design process. Also, the only way to a high-quality user experience is to start usability evaluation early in the design process and to keep evaluation every step of the way. The outcome of a usability study is generally expected to be some recommendations on how to improve the product and how to make it easier and more enjoyable to use.

3   Methods

The BSS is self-service only. It is important to provide user-friendly BSS for E2W riders. This study forms investigation into user-based usability evaluation methods (UEM) based on experimental and survey studies for evaluating usability of the BSSs. The materials of the study are described as below,

- SUS evaluation contained the following 10 items that designed to collect categorical quantitative data, assessed using a 5-point Likert scale ranging from strongly agree to strongly disagree — (1) I think that I would like to use this system frequently; (2) I found the system unnecessarily complex; (3) I thought the system was easy to use efficiency; (4) I think that I would need the support of a technical person to be able to use this system; (5) I found the various functions in this system were well integrated; (6) I thought there was too much inconsistency in this system; (7) I would imagine that most people would learn to use this system very quickly; (8) I found the system very cumbersome to use; (9) I felt very confident using the system; (10) I needed to learn a lot of things before I could get going with this system.

- All of the participants have to complete the operation procedure of swapping 2 batteries for an e-scooter, after researcher introduced the experimental procedure. After make user 2 batteries has been inserted in the BSS successfully, BSS may open a track with a fully-charged battery for participant to remove it from the track to the e-scooter. After 2 nearly depleted batteries has been exchange to the 2 fully-charged batteries, participant has to fill out the SUS questionnaire.

4   Results

Of 89 surveys, 4 involved material data omission, and the effective response rate was 95.5 %. Summarized demographic information of the 85 riders is shown in Table 1.

Table 1. Demographic information of the participants (N = 85)

Frequency (n) & Sequence / Items		1	2	3	4	5
Gender	Item	Male	Female			
	Total	60	25			
	%	(70.6%)	(29.4%)			
Age	Item	<24	25-34	35-44	55-64	45-54
	Total	66	12	4	2	1
	%	(77.6%)	(14.1%)	(4.7%)	(2.4%)	(1.2%)
Education	Item	College	Senior	≥Master	Junior	
	Total	66	10	7	2	
	%	(77.6%)	(11.8%)	(8.2%)	(2.4%)	

Each item's score of SUS contribution ranged from 0 to 4. For items 1, 3, 5, 7, and 9 the score contribution is the scale position minus 1. For items 2, 4, 6, 8 and 10, the contribution is 5 minus the scale position. Each item's score is shown in Table 2. Then, multiply the sum of the scores by 2.5 to obtain the overall value of SUS. The results showed that the average SUS score to use BSS for the experimental participants was 76.85.

Table 2. Scores of each item for SUS (N = 85)

Items	$\bar{X}$	σ
1. I think that I would like to use this system frequently	3.55	0.71
2. I found the system unnecessarily complex	3.05	0.93
3. I thought the system was easy to use efficiency	3.28	0.86
4. I think that I would need the support of a technical person to be able to use this system	2.99	1.10
5. I found the various functions in this system were well integrated	3.11	0.83
6. I thought there was too much inconsistency in this system	2.94	0.87
7. I would imagine that most people would learn to use this system very quickly	3.27	0.97
8. I found the system very cumbersome to use	3.08	0.91
9. I felt very confident using the system	3.16	0.84
10. I needed to learn a lot of things before I could get going with this system	2.31	1.21

4.1   t Test

The t -test results indicated that the item 4 "I think that I would need the support of a technical person to be able to use this system" differed significantly (t = 2.135, p = .038) between men ($\bar{X}$ = 3.15, σ = 1.09) and women ($\bar{X}$ = 2.6, σ = 1.08).

5   Discussion

SUS provides to be a valuable evaluation tool, being robust and reliable. It correlates well with other subjective measures of usability. SUS has been made freely available for use in usability assessment, and has been used for a variety of research projects and industrial evaluations. In this study, the results showed that the SUS score to use BSS for the experimental participants was 76.85. Most of participants perceived that they might use BSS frequently, if they were e-scooter owners. In other words, BSS may provide an conveniently charging service, especially for the city residents. Also, most of participants perceived the BSS was easy to use and easy to learn. Therefore, they felt very confident using BSS. However, still had several participants found the BSS very cumbersome to use.

The results indicated that the major problem of using BSS was participants needed to learn a lot of things before they could get going with BSS (item 10), followed by too much inconsistency in BSS (item 6) and needed the support of a technical person to be able to use BSS (item 4). Furthermore, gender difference had been found in this study. With regard to the need of personal support for using BSS, women were more likely to need the technical person support then men needed. To sum up, the BSS may provide user an okay quality to use it. Streamline operation procedures and complexity of the interface are the way to enhance the BSS usability in the near future.

6 Conclusion

A battery swapping model has been proposed to provide a faster charging service and lower the charging cost. The model provides self-service BSSs to increase user convenience. Therefore, BSS's usability plays an important role to lead a convenient charging services and market acceptance. The results of this study indicated that the SUS score was 76.85. It shows the quality of use for BSS and the way to improve BSS. In order to increase the quality of use for the proposed BSS, operation procedure and user interface design should be investigated further.

References

1. Tsai, J.H., Hsu, Y.C., Weng, H.C., Lin, W.Y., Jeng, F.T.: Air-pollution emission factors from new and in-use motorcycles. Atmos. Environ. **34**, 4747–4754 (2000)
2. Li, J.Q.: Transit bus scheduling with limited energy. Transp. Sci. **48**(4), 521–539 (2014). doi:10.1287/trsc.2013.0468
3. Liu, J.: Electric vehicle charging infrastructure assignment and power grid impacts assessment in Beijing. Energ. Pol. **51**, 544–557 (2012)
4. Worley, O., Klabjan, D.: Optimization of battery charging and purchasing at electric vehicle battery swap stations Chicago. In: IEEE Vehicle Power and Propulsion Conference (VPPC), IL, pp. 6–9, 1–4 September 2011
5. Lombardi, P., Heuer, M., Styczynski, Z.: Battery switch station as storage system in an autonomous power system: optimization issue. In: IEEE Power and Energy Society General Meeting, Minneapolis, MN, pp. 25–29, 1–6 July 2010
6. Kirsch, D.A.: The Electric Vehicle and the Burden of History, pp. 153–162. Rutgers University Press, New Brunswick (2000)
7. Takagi, M., Iwafune, Y., Yamamoto, H., Yamaji, K., Okano, K., Hiwatari, R., Ikeya, T.: Economic value of PV energy storage using batteries of battery switch stations. IEEE Trans. Sust. Energ. **4**(1), 164–173 (2013)
8. Lombardi, P., Heuer, M., Styczynski, Z.: Battery switch station as storage system in an autonomous power system: optimization issue. In: Proceedings of IEEE Power and Energy Society General Meeting, pp. 1–6 (2010)
9. Wang, C., Yang, J., Liu, N., Mao, Y.: Study on sitting and sizing of battery-switch station. In: Proceedings of the 4th International Conference on Electric Utility Deregulation Restructuring. Power Technology, pp. 657–662 (2011)
10. Thomas, C., Bevan, N.: Usability Context Analysis: A Practical Guide. Usability Services, Teddington (1996)
11. Nielsen, J.: Usability Engineering. Academic Press, Cambridge (1993)
12. Grudin, J.: Utility and usability: research issues and development contexts. Interact. Comput. **4**(2), 209–217 (1992)
13. Bevan, N., Kirakowski, J., Maissel, J.: Proceedings of the 4th International Conference on HCI, Stuttgart (1991). http://www.nigelbevan.com/papers/whatis92.pdf
14. ISO 9241-11: International standard first edition. Ergonomic requirements for office work with visual display terminals (VDTs). Part 11: Guidance on usability (1998). http://www.idemployee.id.tue.nl/g.w.mrauterberg/lecturenotes/ISO9241part11.pdf

Proposal for a Remote Communications System Based on Proxemics Theory

Namgyu Kang[✉] and Kensaku ITO

Department of Information Architecture, Future University Hakodate, Hakodate, Japan
{kang,b1012001}@fun.ac.jp

Abstract. In recent years, it has become easy for people who are far apart to communicate by telephone or e-mail. However, neither the telephone nor e-mail can create the feeling that two people are sharing the same space. If it were possible to feel physically close to someone far away, our ability to communicate would be significantly enriched. The purpose of this study is to propose a system of communication that would enable two people to feel as if they were in the same place, despite being far apart. The first experiment was conducted using 12 types of visual information to ascertain which types of visual information most effectively created the illusion that two separated people were sharing the same space. This experiment showed that simple visual information was more effective than more complex visual information at creating the illusion of shared space. Based on these results, our research team was able to propose a new system of communication using a table and various projected visual objects. In this system, if a participant put a hot drink (for example, a cup of coffee) on the table, a red circle would appear and blink slowly in the same position on the other person's table before fading away. Conversely, if the participant put a cold drink on the table, a blue circle would be projected onto the other person's table in the same position. If the first person moved the cup or glass on his or her own table, the red or blue circle would repeat the move, blink slowly, and then fade away on the other person's table. The second experiment used 14 participants to ascertain the effectiveness of the proposed communication system. We found that 71 % of participants who used the proposed communication system felt that the person they were communicating with shared the same space. Moreover, participants felt that the proposed communication system enhanced communication, making it feel more proactive. It was clear that participants experienced this sense of a shared space more strongly when the circle moved than when it blinked or faded away. These results suggest that the proposed communication system (using a table and various projected visual objects) did succeed in creating the impression that two people in different locations were sharing the same space.

Keywords: Nonverbal communication · Proxemics · Communication system · Visual information

1 Introduction

In recent years, it has become easy for people who are far apart to communicate by telephone or e-mail. However, neither the telephone nor e-mail can create the feeling

© Springer International Publishing Switzerland 2016
C. Stephanidis (Ed.): HCII 2016 Posters, Part II, CCIS 618, pp. 497–502, 2016.
DOI: 10.1007/978-3-319-40542-1_80

that two people are sharing the same space. If it were possible to feel physically close to someone far away, our ability to communicate could be significantly enriched. According to L. B. Ray, the communicated information by language is only 35 % of entire information, while 65 % is communicated nonverbally [1]. Knapp has divided nonverbal communication into the following seven factors: (1) motion; (2) characteristics of the human body; (3) touching action; (4) sublanguage; (5) proxemics; (6) physical factors; and (7) environmental factors [2]. Proxemics expresses how we perceive each other's social or personal space and use space in our daily lives. According to Hall, Proxemics Theory defines four levels of distance in interpersonal communication: "close distance," "personal distance," "social distance," and "public distance" [3]. Nishimura has pointed out that interpersonal distance exists between avatars in a three-dimensional virtual space [4]. Many devices enable us to communicate with others who are far away by telephone or e-mail. However, neither the telephone nor e-mail can create the feeling that two people are sharing the same space. If it were possible to feel physically close to someone far away, our ability to communicate could be significantly enriched. The purpose of this study is to propose a communication system that enables people who are far apart to feel as if they were sharing the same space.

2 Method

This research was carried out in three stages. (1) The first experiment demonstrated the effectiveness of nonverbal visual information (NVI) and selected the most useful NVI system. (2) We then proposed a system of communication based on the results of the first experiment. (3) The second experiment confirmed and clarified the effectiveness of the proposed communication system.

The first experiment used 12 types of visual information (VI) to ascertain which type of NVI was most effective in creating the illusion of shared space. Figure 1 illustrates these 12 types of VI, grouped into three categories: (1) 4 types of visual information combined with a simple change that involves motion, (2) 4 types of visual information combined with ordinary changes that involve motion, (3) 4 types of visual information combined with very complex changes that involve motion. Each form of VI was shown randomly and evaluated using the pair comparison method; the 34 participants were students at Future University Hakodate (=FUN).

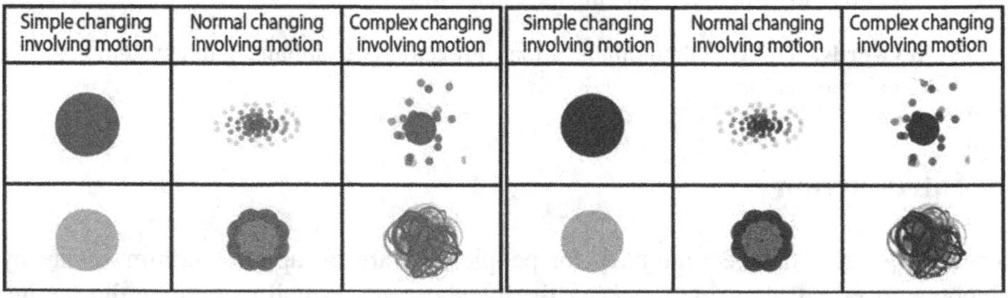

Simple changing involving motion	Normal changing involving motion	Complex changing involving motion	Simple changing involving motion	Normal changing involving motion	Complex changing involving motion

Fig. 1. 12 types of visual information (Color figure online)

We proposed a nonverbal communication system, using a table and projected VI combined with simple changes that involved motion. This system used NVI to create the feeling that two people (in reality, far apart) were sharing the same space.

If the participant put a hot drink (for example, a cup of coffee) on the table, a red circle would appear, blink slowly, and then fade away in the same position on the other person's table (Fig. 2). If the participant put a cold drink on the table, a blue circle would be projected onto the other person's table in the same position. If the first person moved the cup or glass on his or her own table, the red or blue circle would appear, move, slowly blink, and then fade away on the other person's table in the same position.

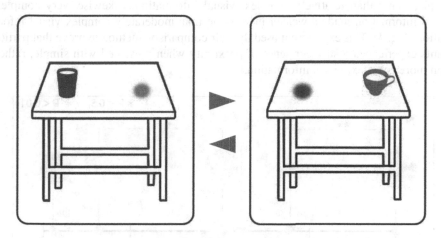

Fig. 2. The concept of the proposed system (Color figure online)

Fig. 3. The proposed system using proxemics theory

A second experiment, involving 14 FUN volunteers, confirmed the effectiveness of the proposed nonverbal communication system. Each participant used the system and then evaluated it by completing a questionnaire (Fig. 3).

3 Results

3.1 Experiment 1

Participants had a stronger impression that another person was present when they saw simple, rather than relatively complex, visual information. Likewise, very complex visual information made a weaker impression than moderately complex visual information (Fig. 4). This experiment used the pair comparison method to prove that participants experienced a stronger sense of proximity when presented with simple, rather than more complex, visual information.

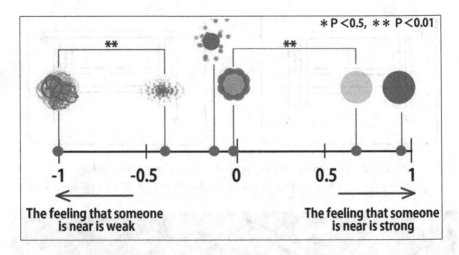

Fig. 4. Results achieved using the pair comparison method

3.2 Experiment 2

The second experiment was designed to ascertain the effectiveness of the proposed system in supporting nonverbal communication; 71 % of participants felt as if the absent person were sharing the same space (Fig. 5). They also felt that the system enhanced various types of proactive communication. It was clear that participants experienced this effect most powerfully when a circle moved, rather than blinking slowly or fading away. Figure 6 (below) illustrates these results.

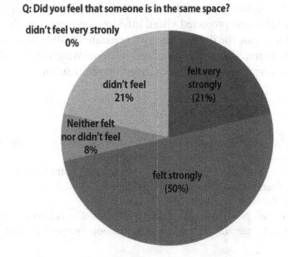

Fig. 5. Results of the second experiment

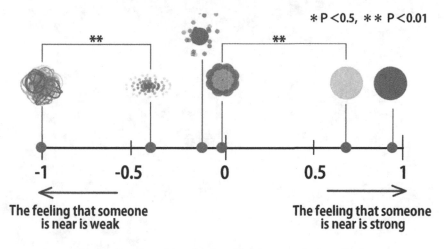

Fig. 6. Results achieved using the pair comparison method

4 Conclusion

The purpose of this study was to propose a nonverbal communication system that would allow two people who were far apart to feel that they were sharing the same space. Our first experiment showed that combining simple visual information with a small change involving motion created a stronger impression of shared space than did visual information combined with larger and more complex changes involving motion. Based on the results of the first experiment, four types of visual information (combined with small changes involving motion) were used to design a nonverbal communication system. The second experiment confirmed the effectiveness of this nonverbal communication system, by using a table and projected visual information (incorporating small changes involving motion) to create the illusion that two separated people were sharing the same space. It also demonstrated that the proposed system, which is based on proxemics theory, does enhance various types of proactive communication.

References

1. Birdwhistell, R.L.: Kinesics and Context: Essays on Body Motion Communication, pp. 157–158. University of Pennsylvania, Philadelphia (1970)
2. McCroskey, J.C., Larson, C.E., Knapp, M.L.: An Introduction to Interpersonal Communication. Prentice Hall, Englewood Cliffs (1971)
3. Hall, E.T.: Proxemics. Curr. Anthropol. **9**, 83–108 (1968)
4. Nishimura, T., Akashi, N., Handa, M., Koda, T.: Adaptation behavior of personal distance between an agent and a user. In: Human-Agent Interaction Symposium 2012, pp. 1B–2 (2012)

Developing a Design Supporting System in the Real-Time Manner for Low-Energy Building Design Based on BIM

Yun Gil Lee[✉]

Department of Architecture, Hoseo University, Cheonan, Korea
yglee@hoseo.edu

Abstract. This study intends to introduce a method for designing a low-energy building based on building information modeling (BIM) and a BIM-based application. The proposed application aims to generate an analysis report of energy-saving performance of design alternatives automatically in a real-time manner, during the architectural design process. The research focuses mainly on developing an automatic generation application for that report, using BIM concepts. The proposed technology (EBIM) is a type of design-supporting system that minimizes the time and labor needed for energy analysis and generates the optimized design alternative by automatic generation of the analysis report.

Keywords: Building information modeling · Low-energy building · Design supporting system · Real time evaluation · Architectural design

1 Introduction

Energy scarcity is a worldwide problem to which the architectural industry is not immune. Buildings are at the center of this problem, as they represent 40 % of the global energy consumption. Several governments, including the South Korean government, have established regulations for saving energy, such as the implementation of energy efficiency ratings and green building certifications. The architectural design process is one of the most vital stages of saving energy because most of a building's energy performance is fixed during that phase [1–3].

The aim of this study was to develop a method for designing a low-energy building based on building information modeling (BIM) and a BIM-based application that can generate an analysis report of the energy-saving performance of design alternatives automatically, in a real-time manner, during the architectural design process. The main focus of this research was on developing an automatic generation application for that report using BIM concepts. The proposed technology (EBIM) is a design support system that minimizes the time and labor needed for energy analysis and generates the optimized design alternative by automatically generating the analysis report. EBIM can supply an energy-saving plan and data for the energy efficiency class verification of the design alternatives, thereby enabling the architect to review and make modifications during the design phase itself. To create the EBIM, we performed several tasks, such as a user interface design, the survey and classification of the building materials, development of the standard families for external walls and windows and doors, crafting of algorithms

© Springer International Publishing Switzerland 2016
C. Stephanidis (Ed.): HCII 2016 Posters, Part II, CCIS 618, pp. 503–506, 2016.
DOI: 10.1007/978-3-319-40542-1_81

for energy performance analysis, and creation of the automatic generation module for the analysis report.

2   Implementation of EBIM

The process of architectural design involves several attempts to evaluate the energy-saving performance. [4, 5] However, there is scant research related to automatic reporting systems for energy performance analysis and architectural design. As previously stated, the aim of this research was to develop the analysis report generator of the energy-saving performance of design alternatives automatically and in real time.

Figure 1 shows the system structure of EBIM. It is a kind of plug-in module activated in Revit architecture 2014 (After Revit), one of the world's most popular BIM authoring tools. Thus, EBIM can be executed at any point during the architectural design process. EBIM consists of EBIM_Evaluator and EBIM_Reporter. EBIM_Evaluator is responsible for the energy performance evaluation of the designed alternative. Revit delivers the geometrical information of the design alternatives to EBIM_Evaluator and it calculates the energy consumption performance using a material database, which is used in both EBIM_Evaluator and BIM family library. After the calculations are done, EBIM_Evaluator delivers the evaluation result to EBIM_Reporter and it generates automatically the report of the evaluation result, which follows the format of the certificate report common to the architectural practice in Korea.

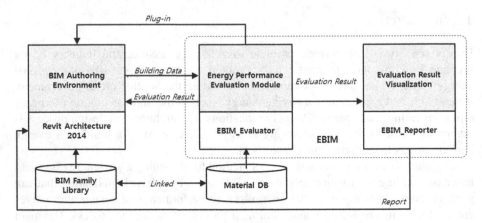

Fig. 1. The system structure of EBIM

Figure 2 shows the execution of EBIM for the automatic generation of the energy performance evaluation report. Executing EBIM then yields four kinds of real-time energy performance reports: (1) average heat transmission ratio, (2) wall area calculation table, (3) performance reports by door type, and (4) performance reports by wall type. These can be used as official documents for the eco-friendly building certification report as well as the design feedback for the improvement of the eco-friendly performance in the designed alternative.

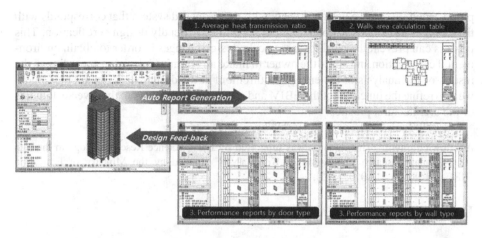

Fig. 2. Execution of EBIM for automatically generating an energy performance evaluation report

Figure 3 shows the eco-friendly architectural design process for EBIM. Conventionally, the energy performance evaluation of a design alternative is executed at the end stage of the design process, making it difficult to change the design alternatives that have already been finalized. However, it is easier to improve the energy performance and modify the design alternative because the architect can check the energy performance at an early stage of the design process. [6] With EBIM, architects can evaluate the energy performance of the alternatives at any stage of the design process, and they can make real-time decisions regarding the details of the design according to the results of the evaluation.

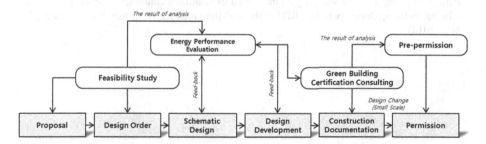

Fig. 3. Eco-friendly architectural design process using EBIM

3 Conclusion and Discussion

This study resulted in a proposed technology that can undertake the real-time evaluation of the energy performance of design alternatives. This technology is a BIM-based evaluation system, EBIM, which calculates the energy performance as well as the result report of alternatives during the design phase. This research mainly focused on the feasibility of this idea by developing the prototype for this system. Moreover, we proposed an innovative design process with the proposed system that corresponds with the changes to Korea's national regulations and eco-friendly design certification. This process can prevent the need for large-scale design changes in order to obtain environmental certification and allow the owner to make an optimized decision according to the results of the analysis of the energy requirement at the design stage. In another study, we will refine the functions of the EBIM and apply this technology to the diverse domains of the architectural practice.

Acknowledgment. This research was supported by Basic Science Research Program through the National Research Foundation of Korea (NRF) funded by the Ministry of Education (NRF-2015R1D1A1A01057525).

References

1. Ahn, K.H., Kim, H.K., Choi, Y.S.: A study on energy conservation plan of eco-friendly school by energyplus. J. Architectural Inst. Korea – Plann. Des. **27**(12), 19–26 (2011)
2. Oh, S.M., Kim, Y.J., Park, C.S., Kim, I.H.: Building energy performance assessment using interoperability of BIM-based simulation model. J. Architectural Inst. Korea – Plann. Des. **27**(6), 237–245 (2011)
3. Ko, D.H.: A study on BIM-based sustainable design process using building performances and energy efficiency evaluation. J. Architectural Inst. Korea – Plann. Des. **26**(9), 237–247 (2010)
4. Schlueter, A., Thesseling, F.: Building information model based energy/energy performance assessment in early design stages. Autom. Constr. **18**, 153–163 (2009)
5. Larsen, K., Lattke, F., Ott, S., Winter, S.: Surveying and digital workflow in energy performance retrofit projects using prefabricated elements. Autom. Constr. **20**(8), 999–1011 (2011)
6. Park, J.W., Lee, Y.G.: Developing an integrated evaluation technology for energy- and cost-efficient building design based on BIM in the real-time manner. Architectural Res. **16**(3), 93–100 (2014)

Programming of Virtual Reality System for Swimming Teaching

Ting Liao[1,2(✉)], Bin Wang[3], and Di Wu[3]

[1] School of Sports Training, Wuhan Sports University, Wuhan 430079, Hubei, China
33199579@qq.com
[2] Hubei Provincial Collaborative Innovation Center for Exercise and Health Promotion,
Wuhan 430079, China
[3] School of Physical Education, Wuhan Sports University, Wuhan 430079, Hubei, China

Abstract. As swimming is a kind of water sports, swimming teachers generally find it difficult to express demonstration actions in practice teaching by using appropriate manners. Furthermore, teaching effectiveness will be optimized by avoiding technical barriers in learning, thus realizing great transformation and innovation of swimming teaching. This research combines three-dimensional virtual reality simulation and database technology, provides precise digital management platform for real-time data acquisition and monitoring system, and lets users can control the objects as they were right on the scene. With the help of VR technology, designers can not only publicize it to the mass, but also present it to decision makers for modified opinions applied in swimming teaching area. The purpose of this research is trying to design a virtual reality system to suit the complex demand of swimming teaching and promote the outcome of the course.

Keywords: Virtual reality technology · Swimming teaching · Programming · System · VRP-SDK · Procedures of integrating database

1 Introduction

Virtual Reality (VR) technology, also called virtual environment technology, is a rapidly developed technology of computer-generated simulation. Involving computer graphics, multimedia, artificial intelligence, multi-sensor and network parallel processing, it enables computer to generate three-dimension images. By presenting visual, auditory and touching sense as graphics and animations, it can provide users with a feeling that they were right on the scene. Besides, users can also personally operate and practice this software to enjoy an interaction with the virtual environment. That is because such software has altered the passive and static information transfer of traditional computer aided design [1]. Therefore, VR can be defined as a computer system able to generate and experience a virtual world. By generating various virtual environments, such software could provide users a feeling of being right on the scene via visual, auditory and touching experience. In terms of virtual world, it refers to the set of virtual environments or given simulation objects.

C. Stephanidis (Ed.): HCII 2016 Posters, Part II, CCIS 618, pp. 507–512, 2016.
DOI: 10.1007/978-3-319-40542-1_82

2   Selection of VR Software in Swimming Teaching

VRP-SDK, developed by Vi standard Digital Technology Co., Ltd., is a powerful software tool for junior and senior virtual reality developer. It is compatible with various Windows operating systems, with friendly editing interface, effective and efficient workflow, powerful capabilities of 3D graphics and arbitrary and real-time 3D display. Besides, this software supports the simultaneous installation and usage of multiple versions of 3ds Max (3ds Max 5, 6, 7, 8 and 9). Accurate navigation map is applicable in this software, even with a precision of 9999999.00. Furthermore, angle switching is also possible in this software, and navigation map can be amplified and reduced by user-defined navigation arrow. With the attribute of efficient and precise physical collision, it is easy to realize high-precision capture. This software supports the import and export of model or animation camera. It also supports various ways of selection, such as point selection, frame selection, round selection, irregular polygon selection and anti-selection. While handling engineering document, fog effect can be used to enhance the scene depth [2]. In addition, various sun halos can be edited and selected to simulate realistic halo effect. Furthermore, abundant styles of sky boxes can be edited and selected to simulate realistic sky. This software supports the display and modification of object sizes. Besides, the object can be copied, mirrored, rotated, zoomed and translated along random reference axis. It supports multi-view display by physical display, gizmo display and point display [3]. In this software, the heights, facade materials, colors and textures of buildings can be randomly changed. It supports ATX dynamic mapping with user-defined ATX start frame and playing times. For its powerful map manager, it is easy to realize automated mapping management and optimization in this software.

3   Overall Framework of System

Data is the core of pipe network management system. Thus, using safe and efficient database technology to manage massive pipeline network is of importance to develop data pipe network information management system. Currently, the development trend of virtual reality technology is to manage data by connecting spatial data engine to a relational database [4].

In this work, actions of breaststroke teaching were named one by one to constitute the components of spatial database and relational database. Underwater scene of swimming pool was managed by VRP that redeveloped for the interaction of VRP-SDK and virtual reality model. Relevant data of any object selected by users could be searched in relational database according to the name of object. Figure 1 showed the overall framework of system.

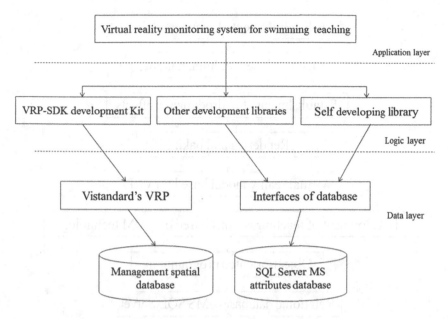

Fig. 1. Overall framework of system

4 Basic Development Flow of VR Experiment Courseware of Swimming Teaching

In this work, the optimum visual, auditory and sensory effects of breaststroke teaching were presented using a pipeline network simulation system of breaststroke teaching. Such system was built using advanced VR technology, computer graphics technology and relational database technology. Besides its decision-making function of network planning and transformation for teachers and management departments, it also provides precise digital management platform for real-time data acquisition and monitoring system. Procedures of integrating database includes modeling, material setting, light setting, camera setting, rendering and baking, exporting models to VRP and the secondary development by Borland Delphi. Figure 2 showed the basic ideas of this design.

To build this system, the procedures includes modeling, material setting, light setting, camera setting, rendering and baking, and exporting models to VRP. Then, relational database is integrated after the secondary development via object oriented development tools.

4.1 Establishment of Scene Model

After the 3D model of the whole swimming pool being pretreated by AutoCAD, the three-dimensional model was built by 3dmax. The sizes of scene model should be the real sizes of swimming pool, using the unit in millimeter.

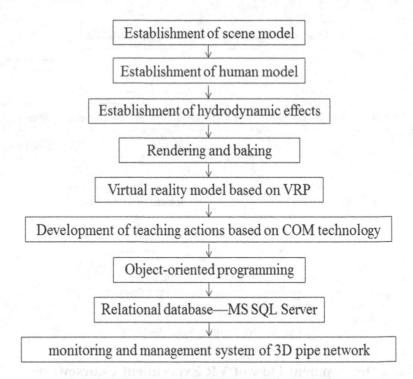

Fig. 2. Basic flow chart of research design and development

4.2 Establishment of Human Model

After the establishment of scene model, static model of human was established. Lighting Map and Complete Map were commonly used for their good compatibility. The formats of maps included jpg, bmp, tga, png and dds.

4.3 Establishment of Hydrodynamic Effects

Photorealistic rendering of swimming scene required reasonable parameters of fluid mechanics. The parameters of this system were the default settings. In this system, Target Spot and Skylight were used, and the shadow type was set as Area Shadows. Hydrodynamic parameters in this scene were set according to the standards of swimming hydrodynamics.

4.4 Rendering and Baking

Virtual reality dynamic effect of breaststroke teaching was built according to the basic actions, emphasis and difficulty of actions, as well as all the details of demonstration teaching.

4.4.1   3dsMax Rendering

After the establishment of human model and dynamic effect of breaststroke teaching, the default rendering Scanline of 3dsMax was used. The effect of rendering effect in VRP was affected by the modeling and rendering of 3dsMax, such as the quality of rendering and numbers of error.

Although advanced light rendering can generate the effect of global illumination and real diffuse reflection, the rendering effect was also good while using Scanline under standard light. To strengthen the realistic sense, advanced light rendering of Max was used in this system.

4.4.2   3dsMax Baking

Baking referred to bringing the lighting of objects in MAX to the virtual reality environment through maps, thus achieving the realistic sense. However, it was unreal if introducing objects into system without baking. The operation of baking in 3dsMax was inputting the order of "Rendering | Render To Texture".

4.5   Optimization of Virtual Reality Model Based on VRP

Using virtual reality software VRP, several modules were added to breaststroke teaching model, such as real-time rendering, skeletal animation, sound simulation, particle system and physics engine. Then, the entire scene came to be vivid and lifelike, greatly increasing users' interactivity.

4.6   Secondary Development Based on COM Technology

In this work, Microsoft's Component Object Model (COM) technology was used to integrate the optimized three-dimensional VR model of steel plant into the system. Besides, the core function and 3D engine of VRP components were used to further expand the function of three-dimensional VR model.

4.7   Object-Oriented Programming

With the help of object oriented development tool Delphi of Borland, this system was provided with an information control platform for the pipe network of breaststroke teaching. Thus, it was possible to realize the simulation of pipe network roaming based on DirectX technology, as well as combination of network layers.

4.8   Relational Database—MS SQL Server

Database of the main actions of breaststroke teaching was built to realize the dynamic management and maintenance of attributes database. Thus, it was possible to realize the inquiry of device information and spatial information of pipe network, as well as the analysis and management of assistant decisions.

4.9   Monitoring and Management System of 3D Pipe Network

In this stage, virtual experiment courseware was further perfected based on the feedback information from the test of virtual classroom and application of teaching.

5   Conclusions and Suggestions

Virtual environment was built based on the combination of real data models using VR technology, strictly following the standards and requirements of engineering project design. Traditional designs were almost presented through ichnographies, elevations, and aerial views. These expressions are flat and static, totally different from the VR environment, which is three-dimensional and dynamic. Using VR technology is an ideal way to present design results. With the help of VR technology, designers can not only publicize it to the mass, but also present it to decision makers for modified opinions. With the three-dimensional, intuitive and scientific presentations of digital visualization system, users can control the objects as they were right on the scene. Therefore, both professional and non-professionals will enjoy personal experiences and understandings in this system in project presentation, demonstration, review, publicity and reporting.

References

1. Parsons, S., Mitchell, P.: The potential of virtual reality in social skills training for people with autistic spectrum disorders. J. Intellect. Disabil. Res. **46**(Pt 5), 430–443 (2002)
2. Cromby, J.J., Standen, P.J., Brown, D.J.: The potentials of virtual environments in the education and training of people with learning disabilities. J. Intellect. Disabil. Res. **40**(Pt 6), 489–501 (1996)
3. Biocca, F., Levy, M.R.: Communication in the Age of Virtual Reality, vol. 23, pp. 546–548. L Erlbaum Associates, Hillsdale (1995)
4. Yang, Y.R., Tsai, M.P., Chuang, T.Y., Sung, W.H., Wang, R.Y.: Virtual reality-based training improves community ambulation in individuals with stroke: a randomized controlled trial. Gait Posture **28**, 201–206 (2008)
5. Laver, K.E., George, S., Thomas, S., Deutsch, J.E., Crotty, M.: Virtual reality for stroke rehabilitation. Cochrane Database Syst. Rev. (9):CD008349 (2011)

I am Ssam: Learning Benefits of the Korean Wrap Food

Yang Kyu Lim[1]([⊠]), Eun Ju Lee[1], Joo Young Ha[1], and Jin Wan Park[2]

[1] Graduate School of Advanced Imaging Science, Multimedia and Film,
Chung-Ang University, Seoul, South Korea
lim0386@gmail.com, eunju.hd@gmail.com, ihajoo0@gmail.com
[2] Integrative Engineering Technology, Chung-Ang University, Seoul, South Korea
jinpark@cau.ac.kr

Abstract. We made a mobile game -*I am Ssam*- to introduce Ssam and learn the benefits of the Korean wrap food culture using motion sensors and touch screen. This game will review all procedures and provide recipe that focuses on methods and benefits of the Ssam. In the Ssam, we sometimes add raw garlic to remove the greasy taste of meat. And also, many experiments have established the effect of raw garlic on cancer. So, we have to remember this precious fact tuck into a meal. *I am Ssam* makes the Korean food and the culture more interesting to know.

I am Ssam will work following the procedure. First, the user has to select a leaf, the main material of the Ssam. And then, select any pieces of food. Shake the smart device to wrap up the Ssam. After finishing this procedure, you will get information on the nutrition, and its effect. This can be the best chance to learn about Korean food culture and folk remedies.

Keywords: Food · Culture · Calorie · Nutrition · Ssam

1 Introduction

In recent years the popularity of Korean culture has been increased. Specially, Korean food is the real missionary of Korean culture. More and more people in the world enjoy eating Korean food. One of the major foods prepared and eaten in the world is the Bibimbap, Korean mixed rice with meat and assorted vegetables. And another food, Ssam is also becoming popular in other countries. World trend is changing to Asian food culture. Specially, Korean foods are rich in vegetables.

The meaning of 'Ssam' is 'wrapped', refers to a dish in Korean cuisine in which, usually, leafy vegetables are used to wrap a piece of meat such as pork or other filling.

I am Ssam is a handheld digital Korean wrap food simulator that can be simply used by people in order to have a Korean food Ssam. Many people in Korea are enjoying traditional Korean food Ssam. The Ssam is made with many kinds of unique vegetable from Korea such as Korean lettuce and Chinese cabbage (Fig. 1).

© Springer International Publishing Switzerland 2016
C. Stephanidis (Ed.): HCII 2016 Posters, Part II, CCIS 618, pp. 513–518, 2016.
DOI: 10.1007/978-3-319-40542-1_83

Fig. 1. Korean wrap Ssam has many vegetables

These days, the effect of the Korean wave is fast sweeping the world. Korean wave is not only K-pop and Drama but also the Korean food culture. Many people in the world already tried Bibimbap, the mixed rice with vegetables (Fig. 2).

Fig. 2. Korean favorite food bibimbap advertisement in US (left) and shape of bibimbap (right).

There are many reasons why people try to eat Korean food. The keyword is healthy. Actually, one of the well-known Korean food is the dog meat food. TV programs in other countries laugh at these food cultures in Korea. There is no truth in this rumor. We have to change the thought and also have to promote the right culture of the Korean food.

We already know about the effect of the smartphone. Nowadays, there are already various food-related applications in the market. *I am Ssam* is using the touchscreen in the smartphone to select vegetable, and any other traditional spice.

2   Related Work

Our study is similar to many applications which can teach food recipe. Our goal is calculating calorie and nutrition of the Ssam to get the right information.

Nowadays, there are special kiosk based ordering system in McDonald Korea. We call it a signature burger ordering system. Choosing bread, and any other things can be automatically ordered by this system. And also can pay with a credit card. Calorie and nutrition calculation is a matter of course [1] (Fig. 3).

Fig. 3. McDonald's new ordering system is using touch screen, pay system, and notification bell in Korea.

Noom series are food and exercise logging application. User can simply put the name of the food to automatically calculate the calorie. Using smartphone sensors to detect the activity and location of the person's daily life. When input begins, *Noom* automatically activate the calorie calculator [2–4]. This part is similar to our study. However, calculating Korean food is difficult in single *Noom* application. *Noom* is specialized in western culture. Using custom registration can make up for any other food calorie. But it is difficult and unclear for common people to use (Fig. 4).

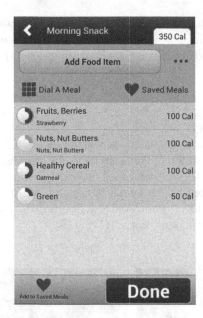

Fig. 4. Screenshot of the food calculating part in *Noom*

3 Design and Implementation

Some details of *I am Ssam* are as follows. Each of food items has own part. First, the user inputs a main wrap. Koreans are enjoying several vegetables for the Ssam wrapping (Fig. 5).

Fig. 5. Koreans love Korean lettuce, perilla leaf, Chinese cabbage, and Keil for Ssam

Second, select main dish such as pork, beef, and raw fish. Also rice is the user's choice. Also the Korean mushroom, green onion, and garlic are the most popular item for Ssam. At the end, select sauce to make rich taste. After selection, must shake your smartphone to mix your items together. Your calorie and nutrition will calculate after finish up wrapped Ssam.

I am Ssam is designed to simply and easily. The basic design of the form is a real situation that people who tried Ssam can understand already. We put simple drag and drop controlling method for the application (Fig. 6).

Fig. 6. Using I am Ssam [5]

The *I am Ssam* is a multi-platform application that can be used on any other smart devices. We used a smartphone touch screen to show the situation and any other information. The motion sensing system is a common way in these days. We used both gyroscope and accelerometer to measure the movement of eating. The hand movement can be calculated to make a funny mixing action.

4   Evaluation

We simply tested for people who are eating Ssam. We wanted to know usability and the effects of the application. Two types of *I am Ssam* user can be taken. The first is just a player who wants to get information only. Second is the user who wants to calculate the calorie and nutrition of the Ssam in the restaurant. After using *I am Ssam*, participants were interviewed. The interview inquired about their interest, and discovered things about Korean food. Many people worried about eating Ssam by hand. But in Korea, we wash our hands before eating food. This is also the table manner in Korea. This can be the best chance to learn about Korean food culture and folk remedies (Fig. 7).

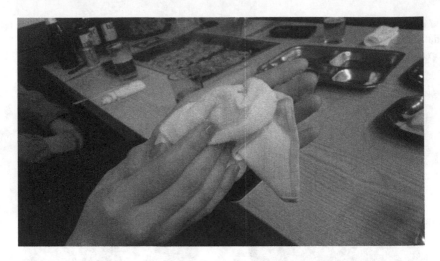

Fig. 7. Washing hands with wet towel is one of the Korean culture

5   Conclusion

I am Ssam is a system through which a person can simply and easily learn the benefits of the Korean wrap food culture. We submit an application for an open exhibition, Games4Health, University of Utah [6]. Unfortunately, the award was not ours, but the audience in Utah was kept asking of Korea and its food culture.

Knowing calories and nutrition of each item can keep healthy diet life. At this point of view, *I am Ssam* is trying with special application to overcome an unhealthy eating habits. We have to pay attention to the possibility of the future. The first is many types of items have to add. In this study, we tested only little range of Ssam items. In the future, we will expand our application to many kinds of items.

References

1. Kang, D.W.: McDonald's Signiture Burger is in Gangnam, Money Today, November 2015
2. Noom Inc. https://www.noom.com/coach, last visit April 2016
3. Noom Inc., Noom Coach: Weight Loss, Apple App Store. https://itunes.apple.com/th/app/noom-coach-weight-loss/id634598719?mt=8, last visit April 2016
4. Noom Inc., Noom Coach: Weight Loss Plan, Google Play. https://play.google.com/store/apps/details?id=com.wsl.noom&hl=en, last visit April 2016
5. Chung-Ang University, FMA Lab, [Games4Health 2016]: I am Ssam (FULL). YouTube https://youtu.be/jl5brgLtwwY, March 2016
6. Park, S.: I am Ssam, Happy Fitness, Games4Health. https://g4h2016.utah.spigit.com/Page/ViewIdea?ideaid=832&pageSize=6&pageNum=0, March 2016

Developing a Human Behavior Simulation Technology in the Real-Time Manner Based on BIM

Changhoon Park[1] and Yun Gil Lee[2(✉)]

[1] Department of Game Engineering, Hoseo University, Cheonan, Korea
chpark@hoseo.edu
[2] Department of Architecture, Hoseo University, Cheonan, Korea
yglee@hoseo.edu

Abstract. This study intends to develop a human behavior simulation system based on building information modeling (BIM) in a real-time manner in the early stages of the architectural design process. This paper introduces the system developed, named SafeBIM, and a design process based on it. The proposed system is an add-on module for Revit Architecture, one of the most popular BIM authoring tools, which supports both architectural design and real-time human behavior simulation of design alternatives. With SafeBIM, architects can perform user behavior simulations at any point in the design process, and the autonomous, human-shaped characters in SafeBIM provide important information related to human behavior by their actions. Additionally, both architects and non-professionals can participate in the design process by using an immersive head-mounted display.

Keywords: Building information modeling · Architectural design · Human behavior simulation

1 Introduction

In architectural design, the user is one of the most important factors of the design task as well as the standard for evaluating the value of the built environment after its construction. However, architectural designers conventionally evaluate performance in relation to the human behavior of design alternatives according to their own experiences or simple building codes that meet only the minimum requirements that are insufficient for generating optimized design solutions for user safety and convenience. Human behavior simulation is regarded as an especially significant factor in the design of facilities for large populations, such as rail stations, hospitals, and airports. Recently, there have been several attempts to simulate human behavior in design alternatives, but the effect of these simulations has been negligible, as they were not related to the design process; rather, they were carried out at the end of the design stage, when the designers are normally highly reluctant to change the design alternatives.

The aim of this study was to develop a human behavior simulation system based on building information modeling (BIM) in a real-time manner in the early stages of the architectural design process. This paper introduces the system, named SafeBIM, and a

© Springer International Publishing Switzerland 2016
C. Stephanidis (Ed.): HCII 2016 Posters, Part II, CCIS 618, pp. 519–523, 2016.
DOI: 10.1007/978-3-319-40542-1_84

design process that is based on it. The proposed system is an add-on module for Revit Architecture, one of the most popular BIM authoring tools that supports both architectural design and the real-time human behavior simulation of design alternatives. With SafeBIM, architects can perform user behavior simulations at any point in the design process, and the autonomous, human-like characters in SafeBIM provide important information regarding human behavior by their actions. Additionally, both architects and non-professionals can participate in the design process by using an immersive head-mounted display (HMD).

2   Performance Evaluation Methods Related to Human Behavior in Buildings

The evaluation of human behavior by observing not only physical expression but also social aspects, perception, and its meaning is one of the most complicated tasks in the architectural design field. Most architects are accustomed to relying on their experience. However, the design attempt based on their experience is insufficient for corresponding to all situations of the human response to buildings.

Two approaches to representing knowledge about the human response to buildings are currently in wide use: a normative approach and an experience-based approach [1, 2]. The normative approach uses appropriate design criteria accumulated from past experiences. Despite its limitation of explaining the human response to buildings, it is useful for architectural practice because it can be regarded as the explicit standard. However, once design criteria such as codes are codified, they become very difficult to modify. Moreover, because they illustrate average behavior, this approach cannot be modified to meet the needs and behaviors of individuals.

The experience-based approach constitutes an attempt to simulate the situations that the occupants of buildings will experience. A Post Occupancy Evaluation (POE) is one of the most conventional methods for the experience-based approach. Recently, the virtual reality (VR) realized simulation of human experience was introduced. VR enables people to experience virtual situations and interact with human-like characters generated by a computer [2–4]. Moreover, with newly developed devices like HMD, data gloves, and so on, people can be completely immersed in a virtual world created by a computer. However, if the human-like characters are not intelligent, this approach is limited, because the architect can see the pre-defined situation. That is why virtual environments like massive multiplayer online role-playing games have been developed. In the proposed system, named SafeBIM, both architects and non-professionals can participate in the design process by using an immersive HMD.

3   SafeBIM: BIM-Based Real Time Human Behavior Simulator

The evaluation system for human behavior should be strictly related to the architectural design process, because its ultimate purpose is for use in architectural design. In order to realize this idea, we established the following strategies for its development. First, SafeBIM should be used in the middle of architectural design process. Conventional human behavior simulation is not effective for realizing a well-designed alternative for human behavior because such a simulation is run at the end of the design process. To solve this problem, we developed an add-on application for the BIM authoring tool— that is, a three-dimensional modeling tool for the architectural design and real-time performance evaluation. Second, the architect can assign behavioral situations to the intelligent human-like characters. Therefore, we developed authoring functions to assign the overall mission for their behaviors. However, the user cannot define all the specific behaviors one by one. The characters should be intelligent enough to behave freely according to their assigned mission. We applied several artificial intelligence (AI) technologies in the game engineering field, such as way finding and collision detection.

Third, non-professional users can participate in the evaluation process. Most clients or occupants of the architectural design are non-professional. Since they have difficulty understanding architectural drawings, symbols, and terminology, the architects have a duty to provide intuitive information about the design alternatives. Thus, we developed a virtual environment based on HMD because non-professionals are familiar with three-dimensional environments. Furthermore, SafeBIM can connect multiple users in the same virtual environment, and immersive HMD allows both architects and non-professionals to participate in the design process (Fig. 1).

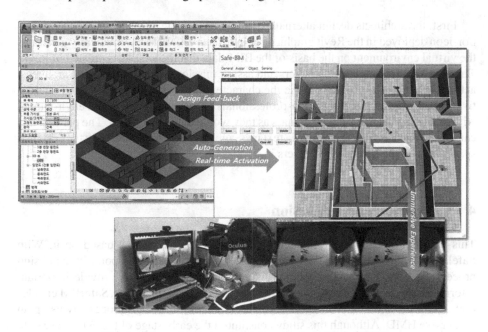

Fig. 1. Human behavior simulation process with SafeBIM

SafeBIM is developed according to the aforementioned strategies. It is a kind of add-on module based on BIM and developed using Unity3D (one of the most popular game engines) and Revit SDK (software development kit for Revit applications). Figure 2 shows the process of using SafeBIM [5].

Fig. 2. Virtual immersive experiences of the designed alternatives

First, the architects design alternatives and then execute SafeBIM using the activation icon deployed in the Revit graphic user interface. SafeBIM automatically generates the virtual environment on the basis of the BIM data that the architects created in Revit. Then the architects deploy characters and assign missions to them. Next, the architects activate the simulation and examine the characters' behaviors in the designed alternatives. Lastly, the architects and non-professionals participate in the virtual environment with HMD and behave via their avatars as they would in the real world. The participants can communicate with each other via text messages and experience not only the designed space but also the behaviors of others in it.

4   Conclusion and Discussion

This paper introduced the system SafeBIM and a design process based on it. With SafeBIM, architects can perform user behavior simulations at any point in the design process, and the autonomous, human-like characters in SafeBIM provide important information about human behavior through their actions. Furthermore, SafeBIM enables both architects and non-professionals to participate in the design process by using an immersive HMD. Although this study constituted the early stage of the entire research, there is no doubt that the result of this study can provide a comprehensive framework for developing an advanced human behavior evaluation tool based on BIM. In a future study, we will improve the intelligence of the human-like characters and investigate the performance of SafeBIM using in-depth interviews and a survey.

Acknowledgment. This research was supported by Basic Science Research Program through the National Research Foundation of Korea (NRF) funded by the Ministry of Education (NRF-2015R1D1A1A01057525).

References

1. Steinfeld, E., Kalay, Y.E.: The impact of computer-aided design on representation in architecture. In: Proceedings of ARCC Conference on Representation and Simulation in Architectural Research and Design (1990)
2. Heilbrun, A.: Virtual reality. Whole Earth Rev. (1989)
3. Tello, E.: Between man and machine. BYTE **13**(9), 288–293 (1988)
4. Foley, J.D.: Interfaces for advanced computing. Sci. Am. (1987)
5. Autodesk Developer Network. http://usa.autodesk.com/adsk/servlet/index?siteID=123112 &id=2484975

Augmented Reality Based Guidance for Solving Rubik's Cube Using HMD

Jaebum Park and Changhoon Park[✉]

Department of Game Engineering, Hoseo University, 165 Sechul-ri, Baebang-myun,
Asan, Chungnam 336-795, Korea
ppp4542@imrlab.hoseo.edu, chpark@hoseo.edu

Abstract. This paper proposes a guidance system to help to solve the Rubik's cube using Head Mounted Display (HMD) and gesture interface. Our system use augmented reality technology to recognize the placement of each square and provide intuitive and easily understandable guidance for solving procedure. Also, this system aims to improve the user experience of guidance system for solving Rubik's Cube by allowing the user pose naturally.

Keywords: Guidance system · Rubik's cube · Augmented reality · Intuitive · Head mounted display · HMD · Gesture interface

1 Introduction

We propose a guidance system to help to solve the Rubik's cube using head mounted display (HMD) and gesture interface. Rubik's Cube is a 3-D combination puzzle invented in 1974 by Erno Rubik of Hungary. The puzzle is scrambled by making a number of random twists. For the puzzle to be solved, each face must be returned to consisting of one color. There are 4.3252×1019 different states that can be reached from any given configuration [1]. Augmented reality technology is applied to recognize the placement of each square and provide intuitive and easily understandable guidance for solving procedure [2]. This paper aims to improve the user experience of guidance system for solving Rubik's Cube by allowing the user pose naturally.

2 HMD Based Guidance System

2.1 System Description

The proposed system consists of smartphone based HMD, gesture interface and $2 \times 2 \times 2$ cube. $2 \times 2 \times 2$ cube is used because the size of square is bigger than classic $3 \times 3 \times 3$ cube. The size of square is closely related to the recognition rate and speed when augmented reality works. We introduce Samsung Galaxy Note 4 and Samsung GearVR for smartphone based HMD. Video pass-through mode enables augmented reality applications, allowing to see out of the camera on the back of the Galaxy Note 4 attached to the Gear VR. The Galaxy Note 4 has a 16 MP camera and the ability to shoot video at

© Springer International Publishing Switzerland 2016
C. Stephanidis (Ed.): HCII 2016 Posters, Part II, CCIS 618, pp. 524–529, 2016.
DOI: 10.1007/978-3-319-40542-1_85

60FPS at 1080p. Gear VR includes a special IMU for head tracking which updates at a 1000 Hz, where most phone sensors only do 100 Hz or 200 Hz. This IMU is more accurate and well calibrated with lower latency than internal smartphone IMUs (Fig. 1).

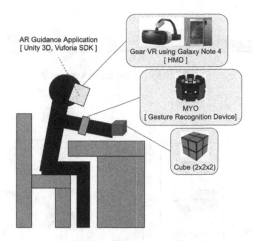

Fig. 1. System overview

The MYO armband is used as a gesture recognition device using various wrist and forearm motions. It uses a set of electromyographic (EMG) sensors that sense electrical activity in the forearm, combined with a gyroscope, accelerometer and magnetometer to recognize gestures. The MYO armband recognizes 5 pre-set gestures out of the box. In the guidance system, the MYO enables the user to use both hands for manipulating cube because it is worn on the wrist. This means that the user can control next step solution without changing both hand posture. Therefore, the user doesn't need to touch display interface any longer. This will improve the natural user experience as well as the usability of the guidance system [3].

Our system uses Vuforia SDK and Unity3d as its underlying development platform and rendering engine. For augmented reality, we use a Mobile AR SDK called Vuforia that supports iOS, Android and Unity 3D. It uses computer vision technology to recognize and track planar images and simple 3D objects in real-time. The virtual object then tracks the position and orientation of the image in real-time so that the viewer's perspective on the object corresponds with their perspective on the Image Target, so that it appears that the virtual object is a part of the real world scene. Unity3D is a cross-platform game engine with a built-in IDE. It is a very flexible engine that was used for generating and integrating richer 3D graphic.

2.2 System Operation and Procedures

Our system has three main processes like the Fig. 2. First is for the recognition of the placement of each square, the cube's six faces. If recognition is successes, colored planes are displayed in exploded views to show the result of recognition [1, 4]. Second is for solving the puzzle by using the results of first process [5, 6]. This generates a sequence of solution steps. There are 12 different kinds of solution step [1]. Third is for guidance of solving cube. Colored planes are augmented to show a series of solution steps. And, a gesture recognized by MYO is used to control the interaction of guidance system (Fig. 3).

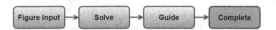

Fig. 2. Steps of guidance system

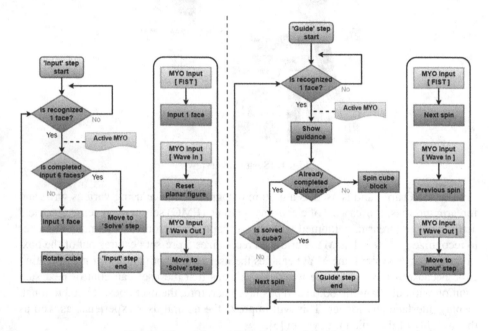

Fig. 3. Flowcharts of 'input' step and 'guide' step

3   Implementation and Results

Vuforia uses computer vision technology to recognize 2D and 3D image targets. An image target or 'Trackable' is an image that the Vuforia SDK can detect and track. In the system, a special kind of predefined markers called Frame Markers is used. Vuforia provides 512 predefined Frame Markers where each marker has an unique code of binary pattern around the border of the marker image. Decoding a Frame Marker takes relatively little processing power. In the system, we designed Frame Markers for 24 square with 6 different colors of $2 \times 2 \times 2$ cube like the Fig. 4 [1] (Fig. 5).

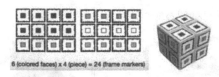

Fig. 4. Frame markers and marked cube. (Color figure online)

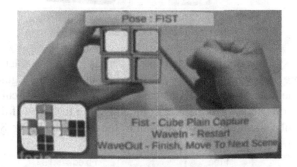

Fig. 5. Screenshot of 'input' step

In the step of input, there is an user interface for exploded views and gesture description for MYO input. Each of the cube's six faces will be recognized and displayed in exploded views. Every square has four blocks. If four blocks of one square are recognized, MYO device will be activated and the status of MYO will be displayed. Then the user can pose forearm motion to recognize next square of the cube. After recognizing all six square, the step of solving starts (Fig. 6).

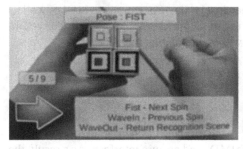

Fig. 6. Screenshot of 'guide' step and solved cube

In the step of guidance, target blocks, direction of rotation, description of MYO gesture, and current and total number of step are displayed on the HMD. For the intuitive guidance, target blocks are represented by red frame while direction of rotation is represented by arrow icon. After rotating target blocks, user can pass the next step of solution (Fig. 7).

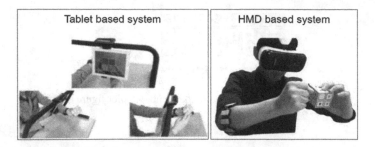

Fig. 7. Tablet based system and HMD based system

The proposed system provides a better user experience than the tablet based guidance system. In the previous system, the ipad displaying an augmented guidance is fixed, independent of the head of the user. This means that the position of cube also must be in front of the rear camera when the user is manipulating the cube. If the user want to see closely, the cube should be moved in front of the fixed tablet (Fig. 8).

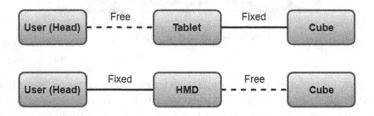

Fig. 8. Comparison of tablet based system and HMD based system

The HMD based guidance system is worn on the head. HMD has a small display optic in front of each eye. If the user's head moves, the rear camera of HMD also moves along with the head. If the user wants to see closely, the user can move head as well as the cube naturally. Moreover, the user don't need to touch for input of guidance system. Instead, the user can pose forearm motion with manipulating the cube.

4   Conclusion

This paper proposed an augmented reality based guidance system to help to solve the Rubik's cube using head mounted display (HMD) and gesture interface. As a result, the user experience of guidance system was improved by allowing the user pose naturally. This means that the system can provide an more intuitive guide by using augmented reality and HMD. And the user can use both hands for manipulating cube controlling the guidance system.

References

1. Rubik's Cube. http://en.wikipedia.org/wiki/Rubik's_Cube
2. Park, J., Park, C.: Guidance system using augmented reality for solving Rubik's cube. In: Stephanidis, C. (ed.) HCI 2014, Part I. CCIS, vol. 434, pp. 631–635. Springer, Heidelberg (2014)
3. Sathiyanarayanan, M., Mulling, T.: Map navigation using hand gesture recognition: a case study using MYO connector on apple maps. Procedia Comput. Sci. **58**, 50–57 (2015)
4. Kasprzak, W., Szynkiewicz, W., Czajka, L.: Rubik's Cube Reconstruction from Single View for Service Robots
5. Korf, R.E.: Finding optimal solutions to Rubik's cube using pattern databases. AAAI/IAAI (1997)
6. Demaine, E.D., Demaine, M.L., Eisenstat, S., Lubiw, A., Winslow, A.: Algorithms for solving Rubik's cubes. In: Demetrescu, C., Halldórsson, M.M. (eds.) ESA 2011. LNCS, vol. 6942, pp. 689–700. Springer, Heidelberg (2011)

Research on Interaction Design of Portable Body-Slimming Cabin for Female

Yang Qiao[✉] and Minggang Yang

School of Art, Design and Media, East China University of Science and Technology,
No. 130, Meilong Road, Xuhui District, Shanghai 200237, China
1042485987@qq.com

Abstract. Recently, the development of China's beauty industry is becoming more technology-based and modernized, with high-tech equipment playing a critical role in offering real solutions to body slimming. Many female consumers in modern cities are in continuous pursuit of health and beauty, looking for ways to lose weight, do plastic and aesthetic surgery, delay aging and remove skin problems. With the popularization of high-technology, various technologies are applied to the beauty industry, resulting in the emergence of equipment with different functions and appearances, which has brought China's beauty industry into the era of high-technology. Portable slimming cabin, with significant effects and comprehensive functions, is making more and more female consumers experience the significant effects of body shaping. This paper aims to have an in-depth research on the human-computer interaction design of portable slimming cabin on the basis of existing slimming cabins to make it more convenient, fully functional, more fashionable and more comfortable, making it a product that can be applied to families and beauty salons and ultimately a kind of art in the environment. Respect to human-computer interaction design, portable slimming cabin can facilitate the cooperation between slimming cabin and users so that it can be easily accepted and used. It can also provide clear interface information such as temperature control and traffic statistics etc. Meanwhile, the cabin can monitor users' physical condition and health situation and give feedbacks timely, which embodies its humanized and intelligent design. This paper summarizes the principles and elements of user experiences as well as types of interface, elaborates the expression of interface user experience and gives the concept definition of user experiences, App, interaction design and portable slimming cabin. Through the expression of user experience and an analysis of the success of the portable slimming cabin App, an app interface to user experiences model is established for portable slimming cabin. Meanwhile, enhanced scientific and technological features and sense of safety can increase users' trust in the cabin, making users better cooperate with the cabin, be familiar with their bodies and shape body with joy.

Keywords: Product design · Portable technology · Beauty technology

1 Introduction

Body slimming is internationally defined as body care and fitness that can help maintain physical and psychological health and beauty. In our body slimming market which is

© Springer International Publishing Switzerland 2016
C. Stephanidis (Ed.): HCII 2016 Posters, Part II, CCIS 618, pp. 530–534, 2016.
DOI: 10.1007/978-3-319-40542-1_86

still not mature and needs to be developed, the number of potential consumers has reached 400,000,000 and most of them are female consumers. Besides, the consumer demand in slimming, functional cosmetics, body slimming and fitness, bustier and other beauty industries reaches 900,000,000 yuan annually. There are thousands of products of different kinds in the body slimming market. The market shares of our body slimming market are mainly composed of three categories of products: the first category is health care product and medicine for body slimming; the second category is externally used special makeup for body slimming; the third category is body slimming equipment. Body slimming by equipment has accounted for over 80 % shares of beauty salons and the equipments are required to be more scientific and offer more functions. Therefore, body slimming equipments has entered the high-tech era.

Currently, people put more emphasis on heathy dietary habits and women, in particular, focus more on body slimming through healthy manners. The popular manners at present include dietary therapy, sports therapy, medicine therapy and operation therapy. The core content of these therapies is to reduce calories, namely to reduce calorie intake and increase calorie consumption. Many people choose to use body slimming equipments, making body slimming cabin a new means of body slimming.

Body slimming cabin is a kind of medical body slimming equipment applying high tech and it can be used at home, in beauty salons, hospitals and other orthopedic medical institutions. Body slimming cabins reach the aim of body slimming on the basis of physical electronic. The principle of body slimming is to cause the frequent activity of fat, make the part of body heated and perspire and finally reach the aim of body slimming. The cabin can be used to body slimming, toxin-elimination and body shaping; improve skin metabolism and systemic anti-aging; promote metabolism and accelerate the discharge of waste and moisture in body; relax muscles, relieve muscle spasm and ease muscular pain. Classified by the principle of the cabin, there are far infrared, khan steam, fumigating and hematite body slimming cabins in the market at present.

Classified by the moulding of the cabin, there are indented style, overturned style and other styles in present market. Most of these cabins are large in size and mainly used in beauty salons and some medical plastic surgery hospitals, but they are not suitable for home use or travelling, because they are not easy to carry or store. In contrast, the innovative portable body slimming cabins can be easily carried, stored and folded, so it can be used while travelling, on business trip or at home.

2 Psychoanalysis of Female

From the perspective of gender, female concern more about health than male while at the same time most females are not satisfied with their physical condition as social values resort to the media to strengthen hypnosis through tangible or intangible criterias of value. Therefore, female take being young and slim the most attractive criteria, feeling that beauty worths most. Middle-aged women pursue fashion, beauty and health and focus on the outlook and emotion of products. Because of the psychology of appreciating and pursuing beauty, female pay more attention to their body shape and appearance and they are often with more self-awareness and self-esteem.

The design of portable body slimming cabin is positioned at females who have spending powers, including young and middle-aged female consumers aging from 18 to 55 years old. Middle-aged women pursue fashion, beauty and health and focus on the outlook and emotion of products. Because of the psychology of appreciating and pursuing beauty, female pay more attention to their body shape and appearance and they are often with more self-awareness and self-esteem. Urban females spend most on beauty consumption including clothing, body slimming, special makeups, plastic surgeries and body shaping, with an average monthly spending of 3681 yuan. It can be seen that the consumer group of middle-aged female spend quite a lot on "beauty consumption". Therefore, the design of portable body slimming cabin is mainly targeted at young and middle-aged female consumers aging from 18 to 55 years old.

3   Studies on the Human-Machine Interaction of Portable Body Slimming Cabin

Interaction design is a new subject focusing on interaction experience proposed by Bill Moggridge, founder of IDEO Company at a design conference in 1984. The essence of human-machine interaction is to ensure human surpass machine and make machine serves people, thus forming interaction and communication through products and services.

The human-machine interaction design conforms to the principles of design aesthetics and interaction design.

In terms of aesthetics: as the users of the cabins are females, portable body slimming cabin should conform to the psychological characteristics of female consumers. First of all, in appearance, portable body slimming cabin is medical body slimming equipment applying high tech and it is often used by female consumers personally, therefore its appearance will influence consumers' psychology directly. Besides, as a serious medical behavior, body slimming will result in permanent sacars for any failing. Taking these factors into account, the appearance of portable body slimming cabin should bring people a sense of technology and safety, reliability and sense of trust so that consumers will have more trust in the product. Meanwhile, as the beauty industry is a industry creating the myth of youth and beauty, its consumers are generally open-minded, always lead the fashion and have certain fashion sense, with the characteristic of being fashionable, neat and decent. The cabin integrate into the home environment as an artwork and brings female comfortable and pleasant experience, therefore it has smooth curves which looks full and powerful.

Appearance and color can bring products spirit, culture, emotion and other higher level values. Therefore, in terms of color, portable body slimming cabin should fully combine color design with appearance design so that the product can present a fresh new feeling and it seems that its emotional value worth more than the prices on the tag, in this way, consumers will be attracted at the first sight. With the elegant white as its main color, the cabin can make the environment more elegant and comfortable, reducing people's physical tiredness and psychological fear. Meanwhile, the elegant white is collocated with silvery grey and blue, which makes it look more scientific and fashionable. While inheriting the sense of being scientific brought by blue and silver grey, it gets rid of the sense of heaviness brought by the two colors and adds more bright colors such as red, orange, yellow and green, bringing people a colorful and fashionable feeling.

The design modification of the product in materials can effectively improve its appearance and quality, visual sense of beauty and sense of touch. It is of equal importance with color and can help make the product more fashionable and personalized. As the economy develops rapidly and people's living standard improves, according to Maslow's hierarchy of needs, the change of consumers' demand for products from the material level to the psychological level is manifested in the images produced by the product modality. For example, some people like red while some people like green, yellow and grey, but can we say that nobody like the dull polish, delicate and woodiness feeling? Therefore, they have the same wonder with the shape, length and width in appearance. The mature use of materials can also embody the profound meaning of the product and it is one of the most important factor that industrial designers can use to reduce the conflicts between man and technology, balance their relation and make technology more humanized. The appearance of the cabin should be designed after receiving exact information about female consumers' psychological needs for its appearance, color and material, thus giving full play to the sense property of the material.

In terms of the folded structure, the surface of the body slimming cabin is made from a new type of canvas. Taking advantage of planar motion structure, the folding structure can be spread when used and be folded to put away when it is not used. It usually has more than two stable states: completely folded, completely spread and semi spread state. When the product is folded, the folded structure is usually in the shape of bundle, in stack or folded type and it is small in size, therefore it is convenient to store and transport; When consumers want to use the product, the folded structure can be spread to the working state. In the process of folding and spreading products, some product need more working states. In the process of folding and spreading products, the folded structure is a variable system and it is a mechanism. In the state of completely spread, the folded structure is a fixed geometry system which can bear the load from the outside world. Through the transformation among different states, products can present different appearance and shapes, satisfying people's various needs for the product in different periods. The folding principle of portable body slimming cabin is similar to that of tent and its material is fiberglass. Fiberglass and aluminium alloy are processed into single section rods of different lengths and with a hole in the center and their diameters range from 7 mm to 12 mm. Multiple section rods are connected together as a set by elastic cords while single section rods are connected by the method of inserting.

In terms of interface interaction, the essence of the interface design is to realize human-machine interaction. Consumers interact with the body slimming cabin through its interface while using the cabin. Interface elements are designed to make it convenient for consumers to learn about the cabin and guide them to interact by providing relevant information. Therefore, every part of the interaction interface should conform to certain principles.

First of all, maintain the consistency of interface. The consistency of interface include many aspects, from color, shapes to the overall structure, general style of windows and font. On the same user interface, all the menu options, command inputs, data displays and other functions should be consistent in style. The simple and harmonious human-machine interface which is consistent in style can bring people a sense of beauty. Secondly, the interface should be simple and clear. Simple style will can make consumers feel that the product is well-designed and improve their experience. In the details, the interface provides some simple error handling or some correcting operations. It requires consumers to confirm when it has to complete some harmful operations. The system provides feedbacks for some not commonly used and important operations to increase efficiency and avoiding make users feel at a loss.

The portable body slimming cabin should be intelligent. Connected with App on mobile phones, it can provide users with the feedback information about their physical condition every moment by monitoring users' physical condition. Consumers can adjust the temperature of the body slimming cabin and the intensity of far infrared on mobile phone when they use it.

4 Conclusion

The human-machine interaction design of the portable body slimming cabin for female targets at the need of female, with satisfying the emotional experience of consumers as its product inform. Therefore, the design focus of the portable body slimming cabin is to conform to the psychological characteristics of female and its operation interface which is simple and easy to use. When female use the product, the product will be added with emotional meaning and certain emotion of the female will be satisfied. Attractive appearance and intimate functions are the key to improving the human-machine interaction design of the portable body slimming cabin.

The body slimming cabin, simple and decent in design and elegant in appearance, is easy to carry and exists as an artwork in the environment. Meanwhile, the increased sense of high tech and safety of the cabin makes consumers have more trust in the product and reduces the indifferent sensation and the sense of fear of equipment, thus enabling female to lose weight and keep fit in a relaxing and pleasant atmosphere.

In the future, the body slimming cabin will be more light, convenient, simple and intelligent, helping female consumers get real-time information to know their physical condition. The cabin will also be connected by the Internet of Things and exist elegantly in home life as an intelligent home furnish.

References

1. Yongliang, C.: Human machine interface design of medical instrument. Jiangnan University
2. Min, J.: User-centered interface design of fitness equipment. Art and Design College of China University of Mining and Technology (2012)
3. Chao, Y.: Research on the design of digital spinning based on internet of things technology. Electron. Technol. (1), 52–56 (2015)
4. Li, L.: Design of human computer interaction interface based on the user's psychological needs. Electron. Technol. Softw. Eng. 21, 29–30 (2015)
5. Li, Y.: Research on the emotional design of female app user interface. Hubei Institute of Arts (2015)

Naturalistic Human-Robot Interaction Design for Control of Unmanned Ground Vehicles

John Kok Tiong Soo[✉], Angela Li Sin Tan, and Andrew Si Yong Ho

DSO National Laboratories, Singapore, Singapore
johnsoo@dso.org.sg

Abstract. This study explored the effectiveness of multi-modal interaction techniques to enable dismounted soldiers to manage their digital information systems and Unmanned Ground Vehicles (UGV) in urban environments. The objective of using multi-modal techniques like speech and gesture was to reduce the physical and cognitive workload of the soldier whilst controlling a UGV. An evaluation was conducted to compare multi-modal interaction against a baseline interface on a smartphone.

Keywords: Naturalistic · Multi-modal interaction · Human robot interaction · Speech · Gesture · See-through HMD

1 Introduction

Robots have been identified as key partners to the next generation of dismounted soldiers in the increasing complex battlefields of the future. However, the introduction of robots can add to the physical and cognitive loads on the soldier. This could lead to an earlier onset of fatigue for the dismounted soldier and adversely affect the accomplishment of his mission. The proposed system is designed with naturalistic interaction and information display strategies to enable the soldier to effectively control his wearable information system and robot-partner in challenging battlefield situations.

2 Objective

This study aims to explore the use of a binocular see-through HMD coupled with a multi-modal interface involving speech and gestures to enhance soldier performance and reduce workload when employing robots to perform room clearing tasks.

The multi-modal interaction approach to control the robot would be compared against a baseline interface.

3 Interface and Interaction Design

Two distinct interfaces were developed; smartphone interface as well as the multi-modal interface to enable control of the robot. The operator would be able to move the robot in four distinct directions; Forward, Pivot left, Pivot right, Reverse. The operator would also be able to adjust robot speed and camera settings.

C. Stephanidis (Ed.): HCII 2016 Posters, Part II, CCIS 618, pp. 535–540, 2016.
DOI: 10.1007/978-3-319-40542-1_87

3.1 Smartphone Interface

Smartphone control of the robot was developed as an improvement to current soldier operations of man-portable robots. The current system requires soldiers to launch the robot before employing a bulky proprietary input device to control the robot. It is envisioned that implementing robot control on the smartphone enables the soldier to operate a smaller and familiar device form factor as well as allow consolidation of robot control with other soldier information systems currently deployed on smart devices. The smartphone GUI (Graphical User Interface) design for robot control deployed on an Android OS smart device is shown in Fig. 1 below.

Fig. 1. Smartphone interface for robot control

3.2 Multi-modal Interface

The multi-modal interface enables operators to control the robots via speech and gesture. Display of robot information was presented to the operator via a GUI deployed on a binocular see-through Head Mounted Display (HMD).

GUI Design. The design of the display took into consideration system feedback with regards to speech and gesture input. The robot camera view is displayed on the central region of the GUI. Robot and input indicators were located on the peripheral of the GUI. Figure 2 shows the GUI design schematic and actual GUI when implemented.

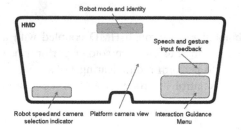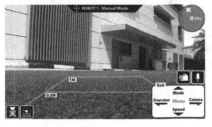

Fig. 2. (Left) HMD GUI design schematic. (Right) Actual HMD GUI design

Speech Interaction Design. Speech interfaces were explored as they are ideal for system interaction in situations where hands and eyes are otherwise occupied. The speech interface developed allows for operators to issue verbal commands to the robot to adjust speed and camera settings. It further enables operators to invoke deeply nested functions and effect system changes quickly. Speech interaction was enabled by a battlefield noise cancelling speech command recognition application.

The speech interface took into consideration the noisy operating environment as well as reduced interference to other tasks; it is thus proposed that the use of "Imperative Phrases" be employed. Imperative sentences are preferred as they are usually short, simple and direct. An example of an imperative statement would be "Shut the door" where shut is the imperative verb (Harris 2005). An example of a speech command employed is "Change Camera".

Other considerations to speech interaction design include lexical priming and lexical density that improves system learnability. Lexical priming is supported when features in the GUI cues the operator to the types and syntax of speech commands understood by the system (Estes and Jones 2010). Lexical density is supported when semantically similar words are recognised and accepted by the system (Harris 2005).

Gesture Interaction Design. A gestural interface allows for more direct interaction with the robots and eliminates the need for intermediate hand held devices/peripherals. Use of hand gestures enables greater flexibility as they do not require a pivot reference point such as those for joysticks (Baudel and Beaudion 1993; Tran 2009). Gesture interaction was enabled via an instrumented right-handed glove. This allowed for posture agnostic, non-vision based recognition of gestures.

The gestural interface allows the operator to control movement of the robots as well as perform menu navigation and item selection on the GUI. For robot movement, pantomimic gestures were used. For menu navigation and item selection, symbolic and deictic gestures were employed (Billinghurst 2009).

Robot Movement (Pantomimic Gestures). These gestures are performed simulating the use of an invisible tool or object in the user's hand. Pantomimic gestures designed allowed for the operator to move the robot forward, reverse, pivot left and pivot right. An example of a pantomimic gestures designed is shown in Table 1.

Table 1. Pantomimic gestures

No.	Description	Initial State	Final State
1	Manual Mode (Forward)	Side View	Side View

Menu Navigation and Item Selection (Symbolic and Deictic Gestures). Symbolic gestures are gestures that possess a single meaning. An example of such a gesture would be the "Ok" sign. Deictic gestures on the other hand gestures are gestures of pointing or directing attention to an event. These gestures allowed operators to navigate the GUI and invoke functions and features. An example is shown in Table 2 below.

Table 2. Symbolic and deictic gestures

No.	Description	Initial State	Final State
1	Open the Interaction Menu		NIL

4 Method

4.1 Participants

Ten male participants were recruited for the study and their ages ranged from 21 to 23. All participants have infantry operational experience. The participants have computer and console gaming experience with frequency of play ranging from weekly to monthly.

Participants were provided training on the respective smartphone and multi-modal interfaces one day prior to the study.

4.2 Experiment Scenario

The experiment was a within-subjects study where participants were required to perform close quarter navigation of the robot in a room clearing task employing the smartphone and multi-modal interface. Participants were given three minutes to clear as many rooms as possible along a corridor. An undisclosed number of targets were planted in each room and participants had to detect and report to the experimenters.

The conditions were counter-balanced to mitigate learning effects. Figure 3 shows the room clearing task during a separate exercise whilst employing the multi-modal interface.

Fig. 3. Robot operator controlling the robot via multi-modal interface

4.3   Independent and Dependent Variables

The smartphone and multi-modal interface designs were evaluated as independent variables. The dependent variables examined were participant workload and performance.

Participant workload was measured via the NASA-Task Load Index administered after each condition. Performance was measured by the number of rooms examined and cleared by the participant operating the robots within the allocated three minutes.

5   Results

A Wilcoxon Signed-Ranks Test indicated that participants cleared fewer rooms when employing multi-modal interaction (M = 1.0, SD = 1.41) compared to the runs when smartphone interaction was employed (M = 2.7, SD = 3.37), Z = −2.579, p = 0.01. On the other hand, workload experienced whilst controlling via multi-modal interaction (M = 74.13, SD = 59.94) was significantly higher as compared to controlling the robot via smartphone (M = 55.33, SD = 38.81) Z = −2.193, p = 0.028 (see Table 3).

Table 3. (Left) No. of rooms cleared. (Right) Perceived workload (NASA-TLX)

Number of Rooms Cleared			Perceived Workload (NASA-TLX)		
Sample Size, n = 10	Smartphone	Multi-modal	Sample Size, n = 10	Smartphone	Multi-modal
Minimum	1.00	0.00	Minimum	29.00	46.67
Maximum	4.00	2.00	Maximum	68.67	89.67
Median	3.00	1.00	Median	57.50	77.00
Mean	1.00	2.70	Mean	55.33	74.13
SD	3.37	1.41	SD	38.81	59.94

6   Discussion and Conclusion

The study involved the design and evaluation of a multi-modal interface to operate a robot. A multimodal interface was desirable as it reduces the hands-off weapon time for the dismounted soldier. The result unexpectedly shows a drop in performance and an increase in workload when compared to the baseline smartphone control.

This was attributed to participants unable to anticipate the robot's turning maneuvers and perform fine movement adjustments with free-form pantomimic gestures as these gestures are unconstrained. Therefore, although participants were observed to be able to learn how to control the robot via gestures, the gestures were not mapped optimally to the robot's behavior. It was thus recommended for future work to modify gesture design to increase sense of control over the robot. Current limitations of the gesture recognition glove resulted in unintended gestures being recognized due to challenges faced by the system to disambiguate the gestures. It is further recommended for future work to enhance gesture glove instrumentation as well as adjust the gesture interaction dialogue model.

Speech interaction was not frequently employed during robot room clearing as participants felt it was unnecessary to change robot speed or camera which speech interaction allows for. Participants were also not inclined to use speech as the right hand that was used to activate speech interaction was occupied to control the robot. It was thus recommended for future work to enable greater ease of access for speech interaction. It was also recommended to enhance the implemented dialogue models and explore natural/free speech interaction within the projects that follow.

Visualization of robot camera feed on the see-through HMD allowed for a hand held device free view of the robot's perspective. Participants commented that strong sunlight/ambient light adversely affected the viewing experience. There was however no reports of discomfort or nausea resulting from viewing from the see-through HMD.

References

Billinghurst, M.: Gesture Based Interaction. Extract from "Haptic Input", pp. 14.1–14.30 (2009)

Baudel, T., Beaudion, M.: Charade; remote control of objects using free-hand gestures. Commun. ACM **36**, 28–35 (1993)

Harris, R.A.: Voice Interaction Design. Morgan Kaufmann Publishers, USA (2005)

Jones, L.J., Estes, Z.: Lexical Priming: Associative, Semantic and Thematic Influences on Word Recognition, Visual Word Recognition, vol. 2. Psychology Press, Hove (2012)

Tran, N., et al.: Wireless data glove for gesture based robotic control. In: Jacko, J.A. (ed.) Human Computer Interaction. Lecture Notes in Computer Science, vol. 5611, pp. 271–280. Springer, Heidelberg (2009)

Usability of Thermal Sensation Voting Device

Eduardo Hideki Tanaka[✉], Lúcia Satiko Nomiso,
and Daniel Augusto Guerra da Costa

Eldorado Research Institute, Campinas, SP, Brazil
{eduardo.tanaka,lucia.nomiso,daniel.costa}@eldorado.org.br

Abstract. Indoor climate has a key role on the performance of office workers. To assess the thermal comfort of a room, some models have been proposed. However, even with those models, manage and control all variables related to thermal comfort is a complex task. To simplify this process, a simple device that allows workers to vote if the indoor climate is "hot", "nice" or "cold", was developed, and a usability survey was conducted to evaluate how good the proposed user interface was. A poor feedback when voting and the lack of information about how the gathered votes were used to manage the indoor thermal comfort are some of the major findings from this survey.

Keywords: Thermal sensation · Usability evaluation · Voting device

1   Introduction

More and more companies are aware of the impact of indoor climate on the performance of their workers. In fact, several studies highlight how thermal sensation influences people's productivity in a work environment [1–3]. Although models have been proposed to assess thermal sensation based on air temperature, ventilating, humidity and other factors [2, 4], it is not an easy task to set up an air conditioning system (ACS) and keep an adequate level of thermal comfort in a large building. Moreover, the complexity increases if energy consumption needs also to be taking into account when managing an ACS [5].

In order to estimate the thermal comfort in a building with dozens of rooms and hundreds of workers, a simple, low cost device has been implemented. Inspired by clickers (such as iClicker + [6], IML Click [7], and others) and Amazon Dash [8], the proposed device is a small board with some sensors as well as voting buttons to allow workers to express their opinion about the thermal comfort in a room. All data gathered by the device (voting, temperature and humidity) are used to automatically plot graphs on a Web portal created to assist ACS technicians to adjust the thermal comfort for each room.

Given that the device should be easy to use by any people, a usability evaluation was applied, especially to identify issues related to feedback and users' expectations about the device and thermal comfort of their room.

The next sections will present the device, the usability evaluation, the major results and discussions about them, finishing with the concluding remarks and future works.

C. Stephanidis (Ed.): HCII 2016 Posters, Part II, CCIS 618, pp. 541–545, 2016.
DOI: 10.1007/978-3-319-40542-1_88

2 Proposed Device

To make it feasible for any company to track thermal comfort in its building, the proposed device should be inexpensive, especially if there are dozens or even hundreds of rooms to monitor and control. Also, it should be easy to use, without too many options or configurations to be performed by the user.

As there are several variables in a room that could influence thermal comfort, such as air temperature, humidity and ventilating, the device should also be able to measure at least some of them. Although there are models to estimate thermal sensation based on these variables, they may not reflect people's opinions and the actual degree of thermal discomfort of people in a room. For example, ISO 7730 [4] is one of the main thermal comfort standards nowadays and proposes a seven-point thermal sensation scale to predict "the mean value of votes of a large group of persons" [4] as well as the percentage of "thermally dissatisfied people who feel too cool or too warm" [4], but this standard is only based on air temperature, air velocity, clothing insulation, not people's opinions. In order to assess subjective thermal comfort, there is another standard, ISO 10551 [9], which proposes to adopt some thermal sensation scales similar to ISO 7730 to ask people about indoor thermal sensation.

Then, to simplify the gathering of subjective thermal sensation, the proposed device has three voting buttons: "hot", "nice" and "cold", as shown in Fig. 1. Additionally, there are temperature, humidity and luminosity sensors in the back, so that the device can collect both key parameters required by thermal sensation models as well as the people's opinion about subjective thermal sensation. After voting, the LED (Light Emitting Diode) is turned on for a few seconds and its color is the same as the proposed scale in the device (red for "hot", green for "nice" and blue for "cold").

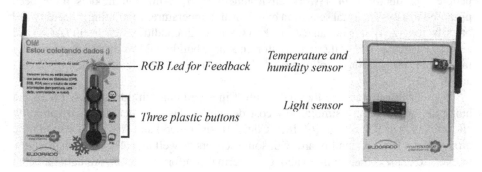

Fig. 1. Device front and back views (Color figure online)

Both data collected by the sensors and the votes are automatically sent to a server, processed and presented in a Web portal created to keep historical data of each room monitored by the devices. Real time data about temperature and humidity are also available. Figure 2 shows a screenshot of the Web portal. The content of the Web portal will assist technicians to properly adjust the ACS of the building, having in mind thermal comfort as well as energy consumption.

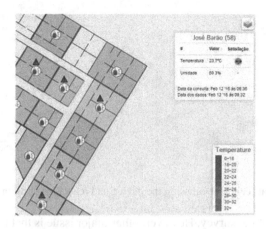

Fig. 2. Web portal to present collected data

3   Usability Evaluation

To evaluate the ease of use of the device, an online usability survey was applied to 15 people who had been using the device for at least two weeks. Before the survey was sent to the participants, it was explained the main objective of this study (to evaluate the usability of the device, not the participant) and informed that the responses would be anonymous, so that none of the participants would be identified.

The survey was composed by 21 questions divided into two major sections: in the first section, there were demographic, multiple choice questions (age, gender, profession, etc.), whereas in the second section, participants were requested to answer about the ease of use of the device, thermal comfort and subjective satisfaction. All questions of the second section were Likert scales, except the last one, which requested the participant to write their comments and suggestions about the device.

Most of the participants were male (73.3 %), with ages between 26 and 35 years old (46.7 %), working on software development area (86.7 %) and had never used a device to collect thermal sensation before (80 %). Also, based on the responses from the survey, it is possible to say that most of the participants were curious about the device when seeing it for the first time (73.3 %) and felt that thermal comfort was relevant and may have impact in work performance (80 %), which reinforces previous researches related to this topic. Some of the findings are presented in the charts of Fig. 3.

Although all participants answered that they were able to understand the meaning of the voting buttons and how the device works, 66.7 % answered that it is not easy to check if the device is turned on. In fact, this was an expected result as there is no feedback about that – the LED is turned on only after a voting button is pressed, so that it remains off most of the time. Moreover, 44.4 % of the participants answered that they couldn't identify if a vote was sent to the server even with the LED turning on.

In addition, very few participants knew about the Web portal to track the thermal comfort information (80 %). One of the hypothesis is that the URL for the Web portal was not properly informed to the participants – in fact, one of the participants commented

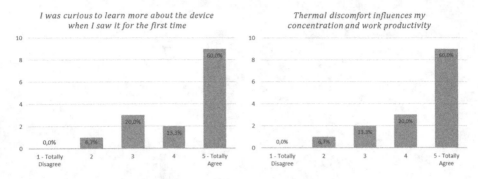

Fig. 3. Initial feeling about using the device and relevance of thermal comfort

about it at the end of the survey. However, other major issue is that there was no information about the Web portal in the device. Therefore, the device doesn't help novice users to learn about the Web portal as well as it doesn't help expert users to remember the existence of the Web portal. Figure 4 presents charts containing the responses for the questions about the Web portal and about the feedback when voting.

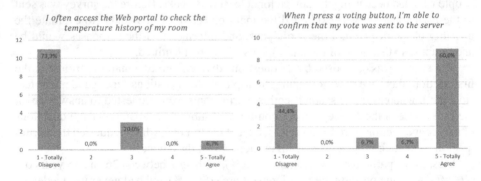

Fig. 4. Web portal access and feedback of the device when voting

In the open question that allowed the participants to write their comments and suggestions, one of the participants suggested to include in the device some clues that all data collected (temperature, humidity and thermal sensation votes) can be retrieved through the Web portal. Also, another participant complained about the weight of the device. According to this participant, as the device was too lightweight, he needed to hold the device firmly when voting, otherwise it would slip on the desk. Additionally, this participant suggested to increase the weight of the device or add cupping-glass to the device in order to keep it fixed to the desk.

4   Concluding Remarks

Given its low cost, the proposed device could be installed on all rooms in a building to track the thermal comfort, as it collects temperature and humidity as well as people's opinions about the thermal comfort. However, some usability issues were found with the applied survey. These usability issues are planned to be fixed in the next version of the device, especially to enhance overall feedback as well as provide more integration with the Web portal. As future work, the authors also intend to develop a smart ACS that automatically changes temperature and ventilating of the rooms based on the collected data and assess the usability of the Web portal.

Acknowledgments.   The authors would like to thank Eldorado Research Institute for supporting this project and all participants of the survey who contributed with valuable responses that will help to enhance the next versions of the device.

References

1. Seppänen, O., Fisk, W.J., Lei Q.H.: Effect of temperature on task performance in office environment. Ernest Orlando Lawrence Berkeley National Laboratory, Berkeley, CA (2006)
2. UK Health and Safety Executive: Thermal comfort. http://www.hse.gov.uk/temperature/thermal/. Accessed 12 Feb 2016
3. Jensen, K.L., Toftum, J., Friis-Hansen, P.: A Bayesian network approach to the evaluation of building design and its consequences for employee performance and operational costs. Build. Environ. **44**, 456–462 (2009)
4. ISO 2005: ISO 7730:2005 Ergonomics of the thermal environment – analytical determination and interpretation of thermal comfort using calculation of the PMV and PPD indices and local thermal comfort criteria
5. Kalz, D., Pfafferott, J.: Thermal Comfort and Energy-Efficient Cooling of Nonresidential Buildings. Springer, Heidelberg (2014)
6. iClicker. 2016: iClicker +. https://www1.iclicker.com/products/iclicker-plus/. Accessed 06 Mar 2016
7. IML 2016: IML Click. http://lumiinsight.com/products/iml-click/. Accessed 06 Mar 2016
8. Amazon 2016: Get to Know Your Dash Button. http://www.amazon.com/gp/help/customer/display.html?nodeId=201746300. Accessed 12 Feb 2016
9. ISO 2011: ISO 10551:2011 Ergonomics of the thermal environment – assessment of the influence of the thermal environment using subjective judgement scales

The Intuitive Human Interaction to Activate the Wetsuit Heating System

Fábio Teixeira[1], Claudia Regina Batista[2(✉)], Ambra Trotto[3],
Christoffel Kuenen[4], Claudio Henrique da Silva[2],
and Adhemar Maria do Valle Filho[5]

[1] Túnel Design Company, Caxias do Sul, Brazil
[2] Federal University of Santa Catarina, Florianópolis, Brazil
`claudia.batista@ufsc.br, design@midiak.com.br`
[3] Interactive Institute Swedish ICT and School of Architecture, Umeå
University, Umeå, Sweden
`ambra.trotto@gmail.com`
[4] Umeå University, Umeå, Sweden
`christoffel.kuenen@dh.umu.se`
[5] University of Vale do Itajaí, Itajaí, Brazil
`adhe.valle@gmail.com`

Abstract. The design process to create a wetsuit with heating system is shown in this paper. The wetsuit concept was inspired by characteristics of amphibians, so it was proposed a product that provides freedom of movement and adaptability into several environments. An intuitive interface without buttons or display based on human body language was created to activate the heating system of a wetsuit.

Keywords: Intuitive interface · Human interaction

1 Background

This paper shows the conceptual design of a wetsuit with heating system. This heating system is activated via an intuitive interface that was created based on the human body language. This design results from international workshops, realized by the Eindhoven University of Technology (Netherlands), the Industrial Design Department of the University of Florence (Italy) and Design Course of the University of South of Santa Catarina (Brazil), within the research project Rights Through Making. Here, the fourth edition of the workshop is described/commented, which took place in Florianópolis – Brazil, entitled: Rights Through Making – Cultural Waves: Extending local identities, skills and manufacturing to global markets.

2 Methods

The objective of the "Rights Through Making" Workshops is to develop products with the objective of promoting the respect of human rights, as part of daily lives of multicultural societies.

C. Stephanidis (Ed.): HCII 2016 Posters, Part II, CCIS 618, pp. 546–551, 2016.
DOI: 10.1007/978-3-319-40542-1_89

The Fig. 1 shows Rights through Making's approach of a design process. The main phase is "conceptualising by making", constituted by cycles of reflection-on-action, triggered by creative techniques and boosted by the construction of low-fi experienceable prototypes.

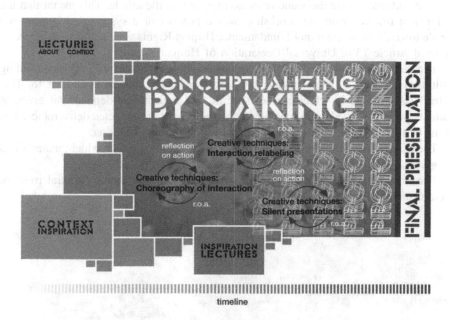

Fig. 1. The rights through making workshop's model. Source: Trotto (2011)

In addition, the following is the structure that lists the steps and the related activities that have been proposed to students to lead through the design process of the fourth workshop.

1. Theme introduction
2. Dividing into teams
3. Inspirational support/context information the essence and the state of art of wearable technologies and the role that designers play in this scenario (Stoffel Kuenen) a brief account of the indigenous pre-existence of Santa Catarina – the element of recognition that was defined as a base for the brand repositioning (Marco Aurélio Nadal De Masi - a cultural anthropologist of the University of South of Santa Catarina) Original people of Santa Catarina - Mbyá Guarani in specific. (Jaci Rocha Gonçalves)
4. Inputs from contributors
5. Applying creative techniques choreography of Interaction (Ambra Trotto) (silent) Presentations
6. Conceptualization by Making (experience able prototyping)- designing form, function, interaction
7. Results

3 Results

The workshop was articulated based on these main steps: Task, theme and assignment.

Each student team received one article of Universal Declaration of Human Rights. They should materialize the values expressed by a specific article. This meant that the design that resulted from the workshop was a product or a system that empowered people towards the realization of fundamental Human Rights. The authors of this study received Article 13 of Universal Declaration of Human Rights.

The second layer was the theme: before each workshop, coaches from both funding institutions defined a general theme that they wanted the student to address to. This theme was the field in which a most specific assignment was defined and given to students, which clarified more specifically the theme and the expected deliverables. The theme of the fourth workshop was: Cultural roots of Santa Catarina.

The assignment was to develop an intelligent wearable product, which: materialises the given UDHR article and transforms local values into fashion values.

The information connection between Article 13 and the theme Cultural roots of Santa Catarina is represented in Fig. 2.

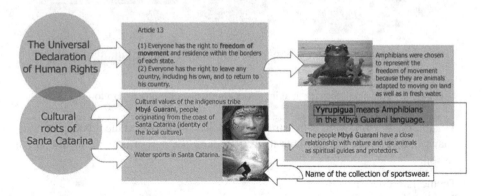

Fig. 2. Analysis synthesis about article 13 and cultural roots of Santa Catarina

3.1   Yyrupigua: A Wetsuit with Heating System

The wetsuit concept (see Fig. 3) was inspired by characteristics of amphibians, so it was proposed a product that provides freedom of movement and adaptability into several environments.

In order to add value to the wetsuit as a genuine product from Santa Catarina, it was inserted the conceptual cultural values of the indigenous tribe Mbyá Guarani (native people of the Santa Catarina coast – identity of the local culture). The Mbyá Guarani

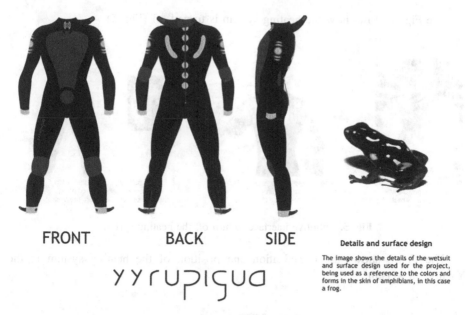

FRONT   BACK   SIDE

Details and surface design

The image shows the details of the wetsuit and surface design used for the project, being used as a reference to the colors and forms in the skin of amphibians, in this case a frog.

yyrupigua

Fig. 3. Yyrupigua Wetsuit

have a close relationship with nature and use animals as spiritual guides and protectors; therefore, this wetsuit model was named Yyrupigua, which in the Mbyá language means amphibian.

3.2 An Intuitive Interface Based on Human Body Language

The activation of the heating system made through an intuitive interface without buttons or display. The idea of the interface resulted from the observation of human body language, as shown in the figure below:

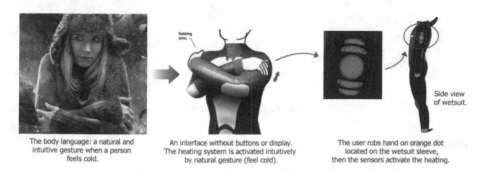

The body language: a natural and intuitive gesture when a person feels cold.

An interface without buttons or display. The heating system is activated intuitively by natural gesture (feel cold).

The user rubs hand on orange dot located on the wetsuit sleeve, then the sensors activate the heating.

Side view of wetsuit.

Fig. 4. Intuitive interface to active heating system

The Fig. 4 shows how the heating system is turned off (Fig. 5).

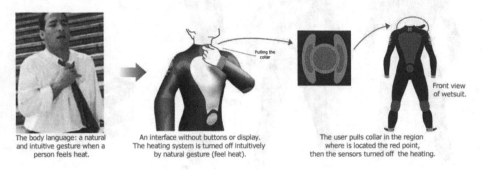

The body language: a natural and intuitive gesture when a person feels heat.

An interface without buttons or display. The heating system is turned off intuitively by natural gesture (feel heat).

The user pulls collar in the region where is located the red point, then the sensors turned off the heating.

Fig. 5. Intuitive interface to turn off the heating system

The Fig. 6 shows the organization and position of the heating system in the Yyrupigua wetsuit.

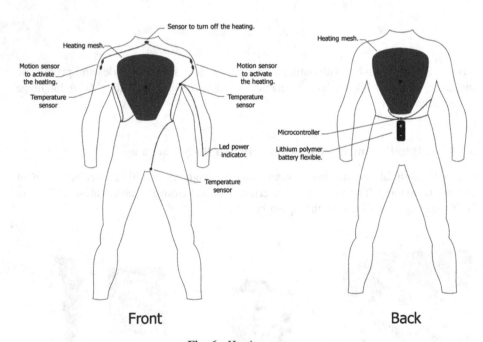

Fig. 6. Heating system

References

Norman, D.A.: The Design of Future Things. Basic Books, New York (2009)
Seymour, S.: Fashionable Technology: The Intersection of Design, Fashion, Science and Technology. Springer, Vienna (2009)

Trotto, A.: Rights through Making – 9 projects. In: Proceedings of Smart Textiles Salon, Ghent, Belgium, 25 September 2009

Trotto, A.: Rights through making: skills for pervasive ethics, Eindhoven University (2011)

Trotto, A., Hummels, C.C.M., Overbeeke, C.J., Cianfanelli, E., Frens, J.W., Goretti, G. (eds.): Rights Through Making (Ethics in Design). Edizioni Polistampa, Firenze (2008)

Trotto, A., Hummels, C.C.M., Overbeeke, C.J., Cianfanelli, E., Frens, J.W. (eds.): Rights Through Making: Wearing Quality (Ethics in Design). Edizioni Polistampa, Firenze (2009)

Trotto, A., Hummels, C.C.M., Overbeeke, C.J., Cianfanelli, E., Frens, J.W. (eds.): Rights Through Making: Bionic Wearables and Urban Lights. Edizioni Polistampa, Firenze (2010)

Nail Art Design System Using Interactive Evolutionary Computation with VR

Masataka Tokumaru$^{(\boxtimes)}$ and Ayataka Yonezawa

Kansai University, 3-3-35 Yamate-cho, Suita-shi, Osaka 564-8680, Japan
{toku,k474496}@kansai-u.ac.jp

Abstract. In this study, we have developed an interactive design support system with virtual reality (VR) devices. This system automatically creates nail art painting images on a three-dimensional (3D) finger model. A system user can put on a head-mounted display and look at these images in VR space. They can control the 3D finger model in VR space using their hands and observe the nail art designs from various angles. The system provides various nail designs to the user and optimizes the designs according to the user's evaluation using an interactive genetic algorithm (IGA), which is one of the major methods for interactive evolutionary computation. To build the system, we implemented a tournament-style evaluation method for IGA that we proposed in a previous study. This method provides a simple paired comparison judgment to the user evaluating the candidates. In this system, the candidates are the nail art designs. The nail art design system creates various French nail designs that have different colors with the same basic design. The system allows users to easily and quickly select their favorite design. In the system, the user can choose two different nail art designs, one of which is painted on the 3D finger model on the left hand and the other of which is painted on the right hand. The users can then easily evaluate the candidates by comparing the two designs in detail in VR space.

Keywords: Interactive evolutionary computation · Tournament-style evaluation · Virtual reality · Nail art design

1 Introduction

Interactive evolutionary computation (IEC) is one of the major methods to automatically create designs that suit a user's preference via human computer interactions [1,2]. This method is effective for candidates that are difficult to evaluate in a strictly quantitative value due to human emotions. Recently, several researchers have developed various IEC systems, such as sound generation systems [3], clothing retrieval systems [4], clothing [5], and interior [6] design support systems.

One of the major problems of IEC systems is how to maintain the user's motivation to use the system. In general IEC systems, users need to evaluate multiple candidates, which are automatically created by the system. The system

© Springer International Publishing Switzerland 2016
C. Stephanidis (Ed.): HCII 2016 Posters, Part II, CCIS 618, pp. 552–557, 2016.
DOI: 10.1007/978-3-319-40542-1_90

usually creates approximately ten candidates in one generation and requires the user's evaluation of each candidate. In an evaluation with only one generation, the user can easily provide evaluations without stress. However, the IEC system needs to repeat the evaluation process ten or more times because it evolves candidates by combining several candidates that have obtained high evaluations from the user. This iteration process tires the user and reduces their motivation.

Another problem contributing to the user's fatigue when using an IEC system is the difficulty in comparing similar candidates. In the early generations, the system provides candidates whose similarity levels are low. During the repeating evolution process, the similarity levels become higher and the user needs to evaluate these similar candidates by considering their slight differences.

To solve these problems, our previous study proposed a tournament-style evaluation method for IEC systems [7,8]. This method provides users with a simple and easy evaluation wherein they can simply compare two candidates at a time and select their favorite one. This method effectively reduces the evaluation load on the user and maintains their motivation.

In this study, we propose a new system using IEC with a tournament-style evaluation method with the aim of eliminating the difficulty in comparing two similar candidates using virtual reality (VR) devices. VR provides users with actual images of candidates and makes it easy to compare two candidates in detail. Therefore, it is possible for the users to maintain their motivation while using the system for a long time. In this study, we developed a nail art design system as an example of the tournament-style IEC system with VR and conducted a performance evaluation of the system.

2   Tournament-Style Evaluation

Even though the tournament-style IEC system creates several candidates in one generation, it shows only two candidates to the user during each evaluation.

Figure 1 shows the candidates' progress during a tournament-style evaluation. We use a genetic algorithm and create eight candidates labeled $p_1 - p_8$, which are randomly arranged in a tournament table. During each round, the user selects two candidates on the basis of the pairing in the tournament table in Fig. 1 and judges their superiority or inferiority. First, the user judges the superiority and inferiority of p_1 and p_2. Next, the user judges the superiority and inferiority of p_3 and p_4. In this case, because p_2 and p_4 win the first round, they reach the semi finals. The round is completed by comparing p_7 and p_8. Next, the semi finals are conducted, starting the round by evaluating p_2 and p_4. When the final round is completed, each candidate is assigned an evaluation value.

This system assigns evaluation values according to the number of victories for each candidate. In Fig. 1, because p_4 is the winner of the tournament, it is assigned a value of 10. Because p_7 won in the semi finals but lost in the final of the tournament competition, it is assigned a value of 8. Similarly, because p_2 and p_5 lost in the semi finals, they are assigned a value of 6. The remaining four candidates defeated during the first round are assigned a value of 4.

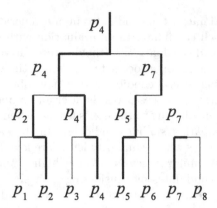

Fig. 1. Tournament-style evaluation.

Because the best candidates are assigned high evaluation values, the tournament-style evaluation determines the best candidates to be used for the next generation of evaluation with a high probability. For eight candidates, the conventional IEC evaluation method requires eight evaluations in each generation, whereas the tournament-style evaluation, which applies paired comparisons, requires seven evaluations. To compare two candidates in each round, the tournament-style evaluation requires 14 choices in each generation. However, in the conventional IEC evaluation, the user rarely chooses each candidate only once to assign an evaluation value. In general, the user chooses candidates several times and often revises their evaluation values. Furthermore, when a user evaluates objects such as music or animation, because the user must sequentially confirm eight patterns, evaluating the candidates is very difficult. In this case, when the tournament-style evaluation is used, the user compares only two patterns and determines only the superiority or inferiority of the candidates. This simple evaluation method reduces the evaluation load on the user.

3   Nail Art Design System

3.1   Outline of the System

We developed a nail art design system as an application of the tournament-style evaluation IEC system with VR devices. The system uses a head mounted display (HMD) and a real-time motion capture device to enable users to observe virtual images of fingers with nail art designs in detail with VR.

Figure 2 shows an example image that the user sees in virtual space when using the HMD. First, the system randomly creates eight nail art designs as candidates and arranges them in a tournament table. In the first round, the design of candidate A is painted on the fingernails of the left hand while the design of candidate B is painted on the fingernails of the right hand. The user can control both hand images to examine the two nail art candidates in detail by moving their hands. After judging their superiority or inferiority, the user moves the hand with their favorite nail art design over a black button on a table in VR space. Then, the system moves on to the next round and other candidates are shown to the user.

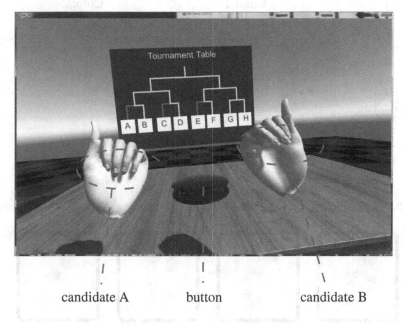

candidate A   button   candidate B

Fig. 2. Nail art design system.

3.2 Three-Dimensional Model of Nail Art Design

The system uses a three-dimensional (3D) hand model with 3D nails. Candidates for IEC are translated into 3D nail models according to a design table. Figure 3 shows an example of design tables for French nail designs. The French nail design is a popular nail art pattern and has a straight borderline that divides the nail area into two or four areas, which are painted with different colors.

The French nail design in the system was coded using a design table with 22 bits. The first two bits are used to decide the basic design of the nail art from four different French nail patterns: simple, skewed, double, and cross. The next two bits are used to decide the color of the borderline. There are four colors available for the borderline. The remaining 18 bits are used to decide the two main colors for the nail art. Each color is selected from 512 colors described using RGB, each of which has eight values with three bits.

Figure 4 shows the examples of nail art designs created by the system. When the simple or skewed design is selected, because a single color is painted, the last

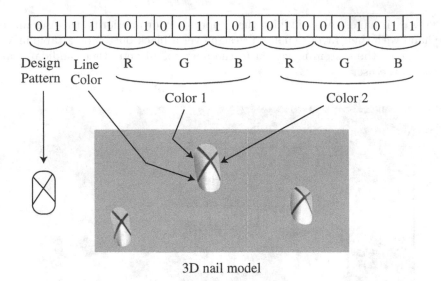

3D nail model

Fig. 3. An example of a design table for a French nail design. (Color figure online)

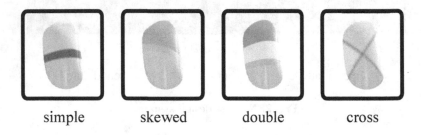

simple   skewed   double   cross

Fig. 4. Examples of 3D nail art designs. (Color figure online)

nine bits for the second color are ignored. As a result, 4,096 different color patterns can be created in the simple or skewed designs, whereas 2,097,152 different color patterns can be created in the double or cross designs.

4   Conclusion

In this study, we developed a nail art design system using the tournament-style evaluation in an IEC system with VR devices. The system has the possibility of enabling a user to easily determine their favorite nail art design without an evaluation overload, which is a serious problem in conventional IEC systems. A usability evaluation of the proposed system by users will be conducted in future studies.

Acknowledgement. This research was partially supported by a MEXT-supported Program for the Strategic Research Foundation at Private Universities, 2013–2017 from the Ministry of Education, Culture, Sports, Science, and Technology.

References

1. Unemi, T.: SBArt4 for an automatic evolutionary art. In: 2012 IEEE Congress on Evolutionary Computation in 2012 IEEE World Congress on Computational Intelligence (WCCI 2012), pp. 2014–2021 (2012)
2. Takagi, H.: Interactive evolutionary computation: fusion of the capabilities of EC optimization and human evaluation. Proc. IEEE **89**(9), 1275–1296 (2001)
3. Miki, M., Orita, H., Wake, S.H., Hiroyasu, T.: Design of sign sounds using an interactive genetic algorithm. In: Proceedings of 2006 IEEE International Conference on Systems, Man and Cybernetics (SMC 2006), pp. 3486–3490 (2006)
4. Urai, T., Tokumaru, M.: User kansei clothing image retrieval system. J. Adv. Comput. Intell. Intell. Inform. **18**(6), 1044–1052 (2014)
5. Sugihara, M., Miki, M., Hiroyasu, T.: Design of japanese kimono using interactive genetic algorithm. In: Proceedings of 2008 IEEE International Conference on Systems, Man and Cybernetics (SMC 2008), pp. 185–190 (2008)
6. Bamba, Y., Kotani, J., Hagiwara, M.: An interior layout support system with interactive evolutionary computation using evaluation agents. In: Proceedings of Joint 2nd International Conference on Soft Computing and Intelligent Systems and 5th International Symposium on Advanced Intelligent Systems (SCIS&ISIS 2004), WE2-4 (2004)
7. Takenouchi, H., Tokumaru, M., Muranaka, N.: Tournament-style evaluation using kansei evaluation. Int. J. Affect. Eng. **12**(3), 395–407 (2013)
8. Takenouchi, H., Tokumaru, M., Muranaka, N.: Tournament evaluation system applying win-lose result presumption considering kansei evaluation by multiple people. J. Adv. Comput. Intell. Intell. Inform. **16**(3), 453–461 (2012)

An Android Application for Supporting Amateur Theatre

Yuya Toyoda, Saori Nakajo, and Tetsuro Kitahara(✉)

College of Humanities and Sciences, Nihon University,
3-25-40, Sakurajosui, Setagaya-ku, Tokyo 156-8550, Japan
{toyoda,nakajo,kitahara}@kthrlab.jp

Abstract. This paper proposes an Anrdoid application for supporting amateur theatre. Amateur theatre mainly has three difficulties:
1. it is difficult for an actor to grasp beforehand what kind of acting there will be during the performance,
2. it is difficult for staff to picture the performance plan in their hand,
3. it is difficult to share the image each performer/staff has of the performance with other people.

Towards resolving all of these problems, we develop an Android application that has the following functions: 3D visualization of the stage in which the user can place and check actors and stage sets, simulation of lighting and sound effects, and sharing of the performance information through the Internet. Experimental results showed that the simulation of lighting and sound effects was useful but the implementation should be improved for other functions.

1 Introduction

Amateur theatre is a highly popular and creative activity. Acting, lighting and sound, among other various elements mutually affect each other in a theatrical performance. As such, actors, actresses and staff need to move forward with preparations while communicating with each other to have a successful performance. However, that is not an easy thing to do. It is thought that amateur theatre mainly has the following three difficulties.

Difficulty 1. It is difficult for an actor to grasp beforehand what kind of acting there will be during the performance.
Difficulty 2. It is difficult for staff to picture the performance plan in their head.
Difficulty 3. It is difficult to share the image each performer/staff has of the performance with other people.

There has been research that supports creative activities up to now. For example, Kato *et al.* used pictures to develop a system for supporting story production [1]. A user provides the facial orientation and expressions of characters with pictures, then the system analogizes the relationships of characters, extrapolates the behavior of each character using a database, and makes proposals to

© Springer International Publishing Switzerland 2016
C. Stephanidis (Ed.): HCII 2016 Posters, Part II, CCIS 618, pp. 558–563, 2016.
DOI: 10.1007/978-3-319-40542-1_91

the user. Nevertheless, there are only a few studies that were aimed to support amateur theatre. Lewis developed the Bown Virtual Theatre system, in which actors and stage art are arranged in an imaginary space with three-dimensional graphics and a stage can be checked virtually by entering lighting information [2]. Slater *et al.* developed a system in which actors can rehearse in a virtual reality space [3]. In addition, Horiuchi *et al.* developed a system in which the stage conditions and performance plan can be shared using a table top interface [4].

There have been several studies that focused on amateur theatre, in this way, but they did not aim to resolve all three of the aforementioned problems. The premise of Lewis's system [2] was use by one person. As such, there is no assumption that there will be sharing of performance images with other people. Slater *et al.*'s system [3] is effective since instructions for acting are given and used by the director. However, the user cannot enter/check the lighting and acoustic performance. The premise of Horiuchi *et al.*'s system [4] has people surrounding a table top interface and is large-scaled and places all relevant parties in the same space. Information cannot be shared unless every member is present.

An Android application that can solve these three difficulties is being proposed here. This application has the following three functions:

1. The stage and stage setting are displayed with 3D graphics. Actors are represented as 3D objects in this space. As such, the user can expect to be able to rehearse while imagining the actual space even in an environment that is not the same as the actual performance.
2. The lighting and sound performance information is reproduced with 3D and audio functions. These will help the user think about the performance, make it easier to understand the performance plan and can be conveyed to other staff.
3. This information is shared with multiple devices through a network. There will be a smooth transmission of performance images among staff. In addition, the user can expect to be able to share information more easily with people who are not participating in meetings and rehearsals.

2   Application Overview

In this application, the left half of the screen will be the stage area and the right half will be the performance editing area (Fig. 1). The stage area will show 3D models. A menu button will be placed on the right end for the performance editing area and, if the user taps that, a performance editing panel which responds to functions assigned to each button will be displayed in the lower part of the performance editing area. A script will be displayed on the upper part. When editing the performance information, the user enters the view of the stage in the left-side stage area and the lighting and sound performance information in the right-side performance editing area.

2.1   Stage Area

The stage reproduced with 3D graphics will be displayed on the left side of the screen and this will be the stage area. The contents will be expressed in that area when performance information is entered in each function that will be explained later. The user can freely control the visual camera that shows the stage when dragging to this area and check the different points of view from the spectator seats and an actor's viewpoint also. In addition, zoom-in and zoom-out with the pinch control and a switch to a full screen display of the stage area with long tap will become possible.

2.2   Performance Editing Area — Lighting

There are two lighting functions installed, lighting function 1 and lighting function 2. They are used separately according to the objective. The lighting function 1 performance editing panel will be displayed by tapping the "Light 1" button from the menu (Fig. 1 top-left). The same number of slide bars as light stands in a theater are installed in lighting function 1 and the intensity of the light stand beams changes according to the control of each bar. There are white, red, green and blue buttons on the left end of the performance control panel with which the user can change the light color. Since the information change will be reflected in the stage area, he/she uses this function when he/she wants to check the conditions of a stage due to a change in lighting. The lighting function 2 performance editing panel will be displayed by tapping the "Light 2" button from the menu (Fig. 1 top-right). Lighting function 2 selects the light stands that the user want to edit from a drop-down list and determines the intensity of the light by moving the displayed graph with a dragging motion. The horizontal axis on this graph is related to the script and the vertical axis indicates the light intensity.

2.3   Performance Editing Area — Sound

The sound performance editing panel will appear by tapping the "sound" button from the menu (Fig. 1 buttom-left). The user selects a song or a sound effect from the drop-down list and decides the volume by moving the displayed graph with a dragging motion. There are play, pause and stop buttons. The bar that displays the current playing position will flow from the right side when the user taps the play button and all the songs edited and set for the performance will play accordingly.

2.4   Performance Editing Area — Stage Set, Actors

The stage set performance editing panel will be displayed by tapping the "stage set" button from the menu (Fig. 1 buttom-right). The user can select the type of stage set, push the position button and a stage set will be generated in the central stage area. Currently, there are only three types of cubic stage settings. The user can also place an actor in the form of a person by selecting the actor button. The colors will change by tapping on stage sets produced in stage areas and actors and their positions can be freely changed by dragging.

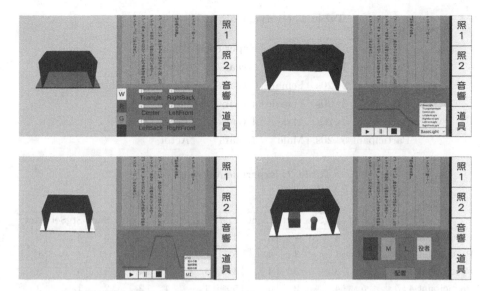

Fig. 1. Screenshots of our application. The screen of our application consists of the left-side stage area and the right-side performance editing area. The panel on the performance editing area can be switched between *Lighting 1* (top-left), *Light 2* (top-right), *Sound* (buttom-left), and *Stage Set* (buttom-right). (Color figure online)

2.5 Information Sharing Between Devices (Data Transmission)

The performance information entered into each device is shared real-time with other devices through a server using the Internet. With the production of a stage set by users and objects of actors, the information of each object is shared with other devices. The information received and sent between the devices are the positions of each object within a virtual space and the values of the size of objects. When all the devices are disconnected from the server, the information of each object stored in the server will be annulled.

3 Experiment

3.1 Experimental Conditions

Evaluation experiments were carried out to verify the effectiveness of the application in actual public performances. We asked five participants (Table 1), who were in a drama circle at their university, to briefly address everyone on an actual stage. Ten days before the actual performance, we lent an Android tablet, which had the application we developed installed in it, to each participant. The participants had four one-hour meetings (10 days before the performance, 7 days before, 4 days before and one day before). We asked them to use the application as much as possible both during the meetings and at other times. After a performance, we had them answer in five levels from 1 to 5 in regard to the following functions.

Table 1. Overview of participants

	Age	Sex	Experience	Role
Participant 1	20s	Female	6 years	Actress
Participant 2	20s	Female	6 years	Director & lighting
Participant 3	20s	Female	4 years	Sound
Participant 4	20s	Male	4 years	Actor
Participant 5	20s	Male	4 years	Actor

Table 2. Experimental results

	Q1				Q2				Q3			
	Light	Snd	StgSet	Act	Light	Snd	StgSet	Act	Light	Snd	StgSet	Act
Participant 1	4	3	4	4	3	4	3	3	2	3	4	5
Participant 2	4	4	1	3	4	5	1	1	3	3	1	1
Participant 3	5	4	3	3	4	4	3	3	4	4	3	3
Participant 4	5	5	4	2	5	5	4	4	2	2	1	2
Participant 5	4	4	2	2	3	3	3	3	1	1	3	2
Average	4.4	4.0	2.8	2.8	3.8	4.2	2.8	2.8	2.4	2.6	2.4	2.6

- Subject functions:
  - Lighting
  - Sound
  - Stage set
  - Actors
- Question:
  Q1. Did it become easier to picture your performance with the function?
  Q2. Did the function help you in your performance plan?
  Q3. Was the function easy to use?

3.2 Experimental Results

The experimental results are listed in Table 2. For the *actors* function, they had a low rating (average of 2.8) for both Q1 and Q2. As a result, it was thought that the solution for **Difficulty 1** was inadequate. The reasons given for this were that the movement of actors could not be recorded and their specific movements could not be fixed. Other parts, especially *lighting* and *sound*, had high ratings in Q1 and Q2 (although the *stage set* had a low score). From the open-ended questions, there were views that the application was useful, with people saying that they could easily check the lighting and sound. This implies that **Difficulty 2** has been partly resolved. Q3 had a low rating overall. It was found that there was no problem with the application concept and function design itself but there was a need to review the usability of the packaging. From the participants, we obtained an opinion that the simulation of lighting and sound was useful to share the idea during the meeting. This implies that **Difficulty 3** has also been partly resolved. However, the function of information sharing through the network sometimes did not work. We have to improve the implementation of this function.

4 Conclusions

An Android application was proposed in which the user can enter, check and share the lighting, sound and stage performance to support amateur theatre. It was confirmed from the experiment that the functions of the lighting and sound were effective but we realized that there was a particular problem with the user-friendliness of the function in entering the movement of the actors. We would like to do a much bigger-scaled experiment along to improve the user-friendliness in the future.

References

1. Kato, S., Onisawa, T.: The support system for story creation using pictures. In: 22nd Fuzzy System Symposium, pp. 6–8 (2006)
2. Lewis, M.: Bowen virtual theatre. In: ACM SIGGRAPH 2003 Conference on Web Graphics (2003)
3. Slater, M., Howell, J., Steed, A., Pertaub, D.-P., Gaurau, M.: Acting in virtual reality. In: Proceedings of the Third International Conference on Collaborative Virtual Environments, pp. 103–110 (2000)
4. Horiuchi, Y., Inoue, T., Okada, K.: Virtual theatrical space linked with a physical miniature stage for multiple users' easy image share. Trans. Virtual Reality Soc. Jpn. **16**(4), 567–576 (2011)

The Space Design of Hackerspace in the "Internet Plus" Era

Haozhou Yuan[✉] and Minggang Yang

School of Art, Design and Media, East China University of Science and Technology,
M. Box 286, No. 130, Meilong Road, Xuhui District, Shanghai 200237, China
dfyhz@vip.qq.com, yangminggang@163.com

Abstract. China's "Internet +" era has come, and the Hackerspace, as an emerging business service platform which meets the public demand innovative undertaking under the new era and has a strong professional service ability, has a long-term and important meaning for stimulating the innovation ability of ordinary people and creating new economic growth point. Under this background, the harmony, efficient and orderly office space design shall play a significant role for the makers to improve work efficiency and working attitude, so as to achieve the more convenient and comfortable communication among people. This paper explored the area environment design of the Hackerspace under the background of China's co-make era. Based on the analysis and comparison on the space construction of Shanghai New Workshop, Shenzhen Firewood Hackerspace and Tsinghua i.center, analyze the space division and design elements of the future Hackerspace starting from their features. The research of this paper is based on the exploration of the design key of Hackerspace office environment, so as to promote the ecological construction of the Hackerspace, and create a shared platform to communicate, cooperate, and relax for the entrepreneurs.

Keywords: Hackerspace · Space design · Area construction

1 Introduction

Hackerspace is a new sharing platform, which is a kind of learning and production space for the makers who have the same interests and the ability of doing-by-oneself to exchange and share knowledge, as well as work together to create a new thing. A typical Hackerspace shall be usually equipped with the laser cutting machine, CNC machine, 3D printers, open-source hardware platform and a series of tools, as well as the services space arrangement such as the learning exhibition area, discussion area, and the production area.

In 2015, China's general office of the state council issued the guidance on the development of the Hackerspace and the promotion of the innovation in the public business, whose purpose was to deepen the Internet reform of the traditional enterprise, serve the innovation and entrepreneurial zeal of the general public, actively contribute to the establishment of the Hackerspace and incubator in the campus and society, which marked that China has gradually entered the co-make era of "public entrepreneurship

© Springer International Publishing Switzerland 2016
C. Stephanidis (Ed.): HCII 2016 Posters, Part II, CCIS 618, pp. 564–569, 2016.
DOI: 10.1007/978-3-319-40542-1_92

innovation". At present, the ministry of science and technology announced two batches of the Hackerspace list, which showed that there are 498 Hackerspaces being concluded into the national management service system.

This paper's research is based on the case study of the engineering training center of Shanghai Now Workshop, Shenzhen Firewood Hackerspace and Tsinghua i.center. Analyze the three Hackerspaces' function orientation and operation mode, based on which to explore its theory, practice and experience of the space construction art, which can provide reference for the physical space planning and design of the domestic Hackerspace by comparing with each other and integrating their function areas.

2   Literature Review

The literature for the Hackerspace at home and abroad was concentrated in the analysis on its operation mode, policy support and academic research, while the related literature about space design relatively lacks. Tao (2013) analyzed the Hackerspace of the library of DelaMare science and engineering and public libraries in Allen County, in which she divided the future libraries into a multifunctional space composition such as learning, discussion, creativity, and implementation. After the research and analysis on university laboratory and social space in the USA, Yang Jianxin and Sun Hongbing found that the open physical space and extensible information space are important to the Hackerspace. Liu (2015) argued that the ratio of the function areas in the Hackerspace should dynamically adjust to the elasticity of the function, which may make the space functional flexibility and expansibility. Ma (2015) pointed out that the color performance of the Hackerspace shall be more emotional than itself on the basis of studying on the Hackerspace of the USA library.

3   Method

One is the literature research method. This paper studied and compiled the literature and books on the space design and function layout of the Hackerspace, on which designed and analyzed the status of Hackerspace in the campus and society; At the same time, through the comparison and analysis on the space color, space utilization, lighting, and decoration material in the literature material, this paper initially sorted the space design strategy taking maker as the design center.

The other one is the method of case analysis. The author takes the engineering training center of Shanghai New Workshop, Shenzhen Firewood Hackerspace and Tsinghua i.center as examples, compare them on their division and interior design, so as to conclude the highlights of the above Hackerspace, thus to screen and summarize the design mode that can give reference to the internal structure of the Hackerspace.

4   The Study on the Area Construction and Space Design of Hackerspace

In China, Hackerspace is mainly divided into social Hackerspace leaded by individuals and groups and campus Hackerspace leaded by government and universities.

Social Hackerspace such as Shanghai new workshop and Shenzhen firewood Hackerspace are both non-profit organizations, supported mainly by the membership fee and corporate sponsorship to pay for daily consumption, and open for social workers and students who share this same interest hobby. Usually such a Hackerspace covers a small area, the utility rate of space is relatively high, for space layout and structure are restricted by site and funds, it's usually a kind of compact Composite space.

Campus maker room like Tsinghua "I. Center" is a student collaborative innovation area whose original model is "students' basic engineering training Center" in Tsinghua university. It's mainly used to provide services for university students, and it's where they have innovation training, the popular science lectures and daily game. Compared to social Hackerspace, it's more spacious and multivariate, laser cutting machine, fixed 3 d printer and other heavy machinery equipments are also more abundant.

Through our inspect into social Hackerspace and campus Hackerspace, as well as our functional study and integration of its interior zone, the primary region of maker room is divided as follows:

The Entrance Area. Entrance area is the comprehensive service area of the whole Hackerspace, decorated with service counter, passageway, storage room or storage shelves, and so on. Its essential functions include consulting service, membership service, storing and picking parcels, the staff here will provide basic services to guests. Interior design is in line with the internal, at the joint between workplace and entrance area partition can be installed. On the one hand, it can improve the area layering, on the other hand, it can reduce the mutual influence between different area, while enough space shall be left for undertake transfer of personnel (Fig. 1).

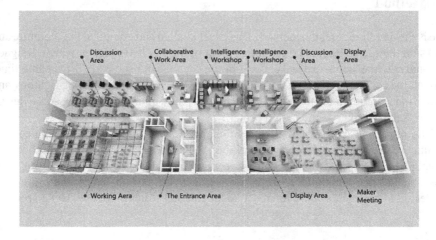

Fig. 1.   Tsinghua I. Center, the model of maker room prototype

Collaborative Work Area. Collaborative work area is the main part of Hackerspace. Facility is equipped with small tools and materials (In the center workspace area in Shanghai new workshop, they place a part of small tools and equipments in the toolkit, then hang the toolkit on the wall, and the other part just goes to the nearby shelves), the main workbench and chairs and tables that go along with. On the choice of indoor color, we generally choose low purity and high lightness pastel color as metope color, it can help you from having the feelings of fatigue. Floor color has the function of foiling environment and matching metope color at the same time, low chroma or gray tone color (Ma 2015) shall be adopted. About the lighting issue in the main working area, the ceiling can use more scattering light source of light fusion to meet the needs of providing overall lighting for working area. On the other hand, the droplight design of concentrated light can be stalled right above the workbench (as shown in Fig. 2), so it can make up for the shortage of the scattering light from the ceiling when people are operating tools in the need of strong light.

Fig. 2. The droplight design in firewood Hackerspace

Fig. 3. The display and study area in Tsinghua university Hackerspace

The Display and Study Area. The display and study area is the area to provide learning and results display for makers. Infrastructure has the support of computer and network, there is projection screen on metope or interactive whiteboard and combined type desks and chairs (as shown in Fig. 3). At the same time there are liquid display stands for makers to show their ideas and results. Hackerspace is also a learning space, people can DIY various entities device here and learn a lot of skills related to computer, campus maker room is equipped with their own computer center, compared to the social Hackerspace, its hardware facility is better. As for social Hackerspace, more consideration should be put into the diversity and compound type of its spatial layout, and so it can be convenient for conducting different practice in learning area. For example, removable light source and the layout of the outlet are worth considering.

Workshop. Work-shop is specially equipped with heavy machinery or professional workshop, it's a closed enclosed space. The Artisan's Asylum Hackerspace in Boston is equipped with carpentry workshop, welding workshop, painting workshop, precision metal processing workshop, electronic products production studio, computer aided design studio, sewing studio, robots studio and many other stuff. When designing the space, Sound insulation and safety problems should be paid attention to, think twice about the use of sound absorption and insulation fireproof materials when constructing the wall and floor. Pay attention to natural ventilation, keep indoor air flow freely, at the same time, the atelier area shall be connected to the fire fighting escape.

Social and Recreational Area. Social and recreational area is a platform of offline activities and gathering together for makers, here everyone can freely exchange ideas and share originality. The garage coffee maker room in Beijing is a Hackerspace whose prototype is a coffee shop, makers can work here for one whole day after ordering a cup of coffee, there is more casual and open space design atmosphere here, which can give makers the freer and more casual communication experience.

5   Conclusion

From the perspective of practicability and function, Hackerspace's spatial construction should take the use of economic and durable, safe and stable materials and equipments into consideration when decorating. And about the dimensional layout, diversity of space activities should be considered, so the flexible compound type space can be created. On the choice of furniture, better choose economic and durable furniture with moving tables and chairs that are easily cleaned and maintained. The interior design of Hackerspace is never invariable, it changes constantly according to makers' activities, but always with the ultimate goal to create an indoor environment that is comfortable and beautiful, convenient and flexible, and with rational layout.

References

Guiding idea from General Office of the State Council on the developing public Hackerspace to promote the innovation and entrepreneurship among the masses. http://www.gov.cn/zhengce/content/2015-03/11/content_9519.html

Tao, L.: Study on library maker room construction. Libr. Inf. Work **57**(14), 54–56 (2013)

Liu, X.F.: Discussion based on the function and layout of library physical space in Hackerspace. Jiangsu Sci. Technol. Inf. **2015**(26), 16–18 (2015)

Yang, J.X., Sun, H.B., Li, S.S.: The US university innovative education laboratory and social Hackerspace study. Mod. Educ. Technol. **25**(5), 27–32 (2015)

Ma, J.: Study on structure art in campus library Hackerspace. Libr. Theory Pract. **2015**(8), 68–71 (2015)

okinesio – Evaluation and Development of an Open Hardware Activity Tracker

Michael Zöllner[✉], Andreas Zapf, and Nhân Duc Truong

Hof University, Kulmbacher Strasse 76, 95213 Münchberg, Germany
{michael.zoellner,andreas.zapf,duc.nhan.truong2}@hof-university.de
http://mediendesign.hof-university.de

Abstract. The main concern about commercial activity trackers from companies like Fitbit, Sony, Polar, Garmin and others is that users don't own their data and they don't have control about how their data is used by the companies. That's why we started developing an open hardware and open source alternative: okinesio. In our paper we are presenting the results and lessons learned from our first year of developing of open hardware. We are describing the methods and results of our evaluation of a range of top-selling activity trackers regarding accuracy, underlying hardware sensors, user experience and data accessibility.

Keywords: Data mining and decision making · Motion prediction and motion capture · Quality and safety in healthcare · Smart service system design · Open Hardware · Arduino

1 Introduction

In 2014 we began searching for a commercial activity tracker with an accessible data interface. We have tested devices by Fitbit, Misfit and Nike and learned that accessing your own data from the device or the corresponding web service is hard or impossible. Moreover your privacy is at risk when you don't know what is happening with your activity data once uploaded to a web service.

Thus we have learned that users of current commercial activity trackers do not own their data and they do not have control about how their data is used by the companies. All recorded activity, motion of the users and the resulting data are stored directly to cloud servers in the USA. This data consists of motion, steps and sleeping data and tells a lot about sensitive topics like daily routines and health issues.

Therefore our goal was to develop an open hardware and open software activity tracker with focus on user experience and privacy: okinesio [5]. In the first year of the project we focused on the evaluation of existing products and hardware and later the hardware development.

2 Related Work

The following part describes a partial overview of related work (hardware and software) regarding quantified self, open hardware development and inertial

© Springer International Publishing Switzerland 2016
C. Stephanidis (Ed.): HCII 2016 Posters, Part II, CCIS 618, pp. 570–574, 2016.
DOI: 10.1007/978-3-319-40542-1_93

measurement. There are several open hardware projects in the area of motion analysis and quantified self in development. We are building on top of the Arduino [6] platform for hardware development. Thanks to the Arduino project there is a vast number of microcontroller boards for different purposes, different PCB sizes featuring different Atmel [18] microchips. We are building on Leah Buechley's Arduino Lilypad [7] open hardware design. MbientLab's Metawear [9] is a wireless sensing platform providing temperature, accelerometer, gyroscope, barometer, light and temperature sensors plus a Bluetooth LE interface and API for rapid development. Angel Sensor [10] provides an open protocol wristband for mobile health tracking heart rate, skin temperature, steps, sleep quality, calories, acceleration and orientation. Hardware and algorithms for counting steps from accelerometers (pedometer) were proposed by Neil Zhao [1], UkJae Ryu et al. [2] and Jim Scarlett [3]. Bosch Sensortec's BMI160 [4] integrated similar algorithms in a small and low power inertial measurement unit that provides accurate acceleration and angular rate (gyroscopic) measurement from a triaxial accelerometer and a triaxial gyroscope. Until 2013 OpenYou [11] was a community platform for reverse engineering and developing inofficial APIs to activity trackers and motion platforms like Fitbit and Nike Fuelband.

3   Project Overview

3.1   Evaluation of Current Hardware and Components

In order to evaluate current activity trackers we chose a set of the most popular and best selling devices from 2015: Fitbit Flex [12], Misfit Shine [13], Jawbone UP24 [14], Withings Activite Pop [15], Sony SWR10 [16], Garmin vivosmart [17]. For every tracker we had to access the step data in a different way as they each provided different APIs and also different resolution and detail. Some of them provided minute-by-minute step data, some only half hour or even only a daily summary of data sets. Jawbone and Fitbit provided the best access to detailed step data. In contrast Misfit's and Sony's API provided the worst access to detailed step data (at least when dealing with less like 100 steps).

We designed two different test scenarios for the evaluation of the activity trackers in order to compare our own hardware regarding accuracy. First we tested the trackers' with a runner on an indoor race track. She took several runs wearing one tracker at a time and also ran wearing all trackers simultaneously on one arm. We always let the same person running in order to avoid errors resulting from different body height and weight. We tested walking 100 steps, walking 600 steps and running 100 steps (jogging). In order to avoid human inaccuracy we also created a simulation with a simple self designed step generator robot. This simple robot consisted of an arm moved by a servo motor (Fig. 1).

The table and graph with results (Table 1) of the runs with each 100 steps are showing the number of counted steps by the different trackers. Fitbit Flex proved to be the most reliable tracker in this series, but it also experienced weak phases in some tests. Misfit Shine only provided very poor data for analysis because the API provided no access to detailed step data for a run of 100 steps.

Fig. 1. Testing setup wearing all trackers on one arm. Simulation robot arm.

Therefore it is not suitable for this kind of test. Jawbone UP24 seems to be an excellent tracking device in our test setup. It is accurate and provides access to step data grouped by moves (like one activity). Withings Activite Pop proved to be a good tracker but during the tests it sometimes generated unreliable results, that maybe seemed to be a matter of unstable measurement due to outer circumstances. Garmin vivosmart is also a good tracker regarding accuracy but sadly it does not provide detailed step data (only step summary every 15 min). Luckily it features a small display where you can read the current step count after each run. Sony SWR10 claims to detect activities automatically, but it often did not catch short activities (like 100 steps) or missed steps when it detected activities. Our own okinesio prototype hardware did well in the tests. Small inaccuracies while counting steps resulted from a lack of calibration. Unlike commercial trackers we didn't implement the runner's height, weight and step length into the measurement, yet.

Table 1. 100 steps (jogging) simultaneously

Fitbit	Jawbone	Withings	Garmin	okinesio
98	99	100	97	96
84	99	99	107	99
97	100	95	103	98
96	101	97	101	101
72	101	97	109	101
91	100	98	101	99

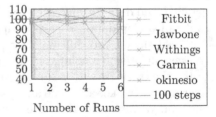

3.2 Hardware Development

Our first prototype simply consisted of a Sparkfun Arduino Micro and Analog Devices ADXL362 accelerometer. We were calculating steps according to Neil Zhao's [1] pedometer algorithm from the ADXL362 accelerometer's x, y and z values. We were not happy about the accuracy, the CPU load and the battery drainage of this approach. With Bosch Sensortec's BMI160 [4] we found a small and low power inertial measurement chip with integrated algorithms for counting steps and access to raw accelerometer and gyroscope data. In order to evaluate this chip we designed and produced a breakout board. Hence the second prototype was built again with the Sparkfun Arduino Micro and our new BMI160 breakout board. The testing results (Table 1) from the evaluation of several commercial activity trackers and our prototype were good. The performance of our prototype was nearly par with the commercial ones.

Fig. 2. From prototype to assembled board

Consequently we decided to merge our prototype's components into an own custom designed PCB. We build on top of Leah Buechley's Arduino Lilypad USB [7] open hardware design featuring Atmel's ATMEGA32U4 microcontroller since it fit our idea regarding size and performance and voltage base (3.3v). We modified the board layout from a round outline (Lilypad) to a rectangular one. The size of our board fits around a CR2032 coin cell battery that drives the okinesio board. Coin cells are also used in Misfit's and Withings' activity trackers. The resulting PCB was produced by Fritzing Fab [8]. In our lab we assembled the components (processor, inertial sensor, clock, ...) in a re-flow oven. Therefore we designed and laser-cut a masking stencil from Mylar foil for applying solder paste on the PCB. Finally we flashed the okinesio board with the Arduino Lilypad firmware (Fig. 2).

4 Lessons Learned

First and all we've learned that for designers in times of open hardware it's possible to develop professional quality hardware for activity tracking. With open hardware the design and production process of electronic devices is a remix. On the software side we recognized that currently there is no standard interface to commercial activity trackers data. Even if the data is accessible it may be of different resolution and quality. During our evaluation we have learned that some trackers may might lack accuracy when they are not placed directly at the wrist but slightly above. During the production of the PCB there are some obstacles to avoid. Cutting stencils with a vinyl plotter might work for larger pads.

But due to the size of the blade it does not really work well for smaller pads like for QFN packages with a pitch of 0.5 mm or less. Applying too much or too little solder paste may have negative results, the height of our Mylar foil with 0,125 mm seemed quite fitting, if the stencil was well made.

5   Conclusion and Future Work

During the second year of our project we will finish our hardware design, design our case and develop the software for iOS and Android. Currently we are transmitting data from the board to the phones via audio jack and USB. Later we will work on a prototype with Bluetooth LE, too. The final hardware design and specification and the software will be open sourced, soon. During the next month we will enhance our testing robot and test different industrial robots for the simulation task.

References

1. Zhao, N.: Full-featured pedometer design realized with 3-Axis digital accelerometer. Analog Dialogue 44.06 (2010)
2. Ryu, U., et al.: Adaptive step detection algorithm for wireless smart step counter. In: 2013 International Conference on Information Science and Applications (ICISA). IEEE (2013)
3. Scarlett, J.: Enhancing the performance of pedometers using a single accelerometer. Application Note, Analog Devices (2007)
4. BOSCH Sensortec, Data sheet BMI160 (2015). https://ae-bst.resource.bosch.com/media/_tech/media/datasheets/BST-BMI160-DS000-07.pdf
5. okinesio. http://okinesio.org
6. Arduino. https://arduino.cc
7. Arduino Lilypad. http://lilypadarduino.org
8. Fritzing Fab. http://fab.fritzing.org
9. MbientLab Metawear. https://mbientlab.com
10. Angel Sensor. http://angelsensor.com
11. OpenYou. http://www.openyou.org
12. Fitbit Flex (2015). https://www.fitbit.com/flex
13. Misfit Shine (2015). http://misfit.com/products/shine
14. Jawbone UP24 (2015). https://jawbone.com/support/up24
15. Withings Activite Pop (2015). https://www.withings.com/eu/en/products/activite-pop
16. Sony SWR10 (2015). http://www.sonymobile.com/gb/products/smartwear/smartband-swr10
17. Garmin vivosmart. http://explore.garmin.com/vivo-fitness
18. Atmel Corporation. http://www.atmel.com

Author Index

Printed in the United States
By Bookmasters